Canadian Youth & the Criminal Law

ONE HUNDRED YEARS
OF YOUTH JUSTICE LEGISLATION IN CANADA

Sherri Davis-Barron

LexisNexis

Canadian Youth and the Criminal Law: One Hundred Years of Youth Justice
Legislation in Canada
© LexisNexis Canada Inc. 2009
September 2009

Members of the LexisNexis Group worldwide

Canada	LexisNexis Canada Inc, 123 Commerce Valley Dr. E. Suite 700, MARKHAM, Ontario
Australia	Butterworths, a Division of Reed International Books Australia Pty Ltd, CHATSWOOD, New South Wales
Austria	ARD Betriebsdienst and Verlag Orac, VIENNA
Czech Republic	Orac, sro, PRAGUE
France	Éditions du Juris-Classeur SA, PARIS
Hong Kong	Butterworths Asia (Hong Kong), HONG KONG
Hungary	Hvg Orac, BUDAPEST
India	Butterworths India, NEW DELHI
Ireland	Butterworths (Ireland) Ltd, DUBLIN
Italy	Giuffré, MILAN
Malaysia	Malayan Law Journal Sdn Bhd, KUALA LUMPUR
New Zealand	Butterworths of New Zealand, WELLINGTON
Poland	Wydawnictwa Prawnicze PWN, WARSAW
Singapore	Butterworths Asia, SINGAPORE
South Africa	Butterworth Publishers (Pty) Ltd, DURBAN
Switzerland	Stämpfli Verlag AG, BERNE
United Kingdom	Butterworths Tolley, a Division of Reed Elsevier (UK), LONDON, WC2A
USA	LexisNexis, DAYTON, Ohio

Library and Archives Canada Cataloguing in Publication

Davis-Barron, Sherri, 1958-
    Canadian youth and the criminal law: one hundred years of youth justice legislation in
Canada / Sherri Davis-Barron.

Includes bibliographical references and index.
ISBN 978-0-433-45200-3

    1. Canada. Youth Criminal Justice Act. 2. Juvenile justice, Administration of—Canada—
History. 3. Juvenile delinquents—Legal status, laws, etc.—Canada. I. Title.

KE9445.D39 2009   345.71'08   C2009-903666-5
KF9780 ZA2 D39 2009

Printed and bound in Canada.

This book is dedicated to my father, Reginald Roy Barron, and
to Lee Horner, with love, respect and gratitude, and heartfelt thanks for
their steadfast support and encouragement.

ABOUT THE AUTHOR

Sherri Davis-Barron was a full-time journalist for many years, largely for *The Ottawa Citizen*, before she left journalism to pursue a second career in law. She graduated from the University of Ottawa, *magna cum laude*, in 1997, and was called to the Ontario Bar in 1999. Ms. Davis-Barron joined the federal government in 1999, and now works as an advisory Crown counsel with the Public Prosecution Service of Canada (PPSC). Among her duties since she joined the Federal Prosecution Service of Canada, now the PPSC, in 2002, is to routinely advise federal prosecutors on the criminal prosecution of cases involving young persons. Ms. Davis-Barron has taught youth justice at Carleton University on an intermittent basis since 1999. She also has an honours degree in journalism from Carleton University and a Master of Arts in international affairs from the prestigious Norman Paterson School of International Affairs in Ottawa.

PREFACE

Canada has just celebrated the centenary of comprehensive federal youth justice legislation in this country; the *Juvenile Delinquents Act* became the law on July 20, 1908. One hundred years later, in 2008, the federal government launched a review of the current youth justice law, the *Youth Criminal Justice Act* (*YCJA*), which has been in force since April 1, 2003. It was, in part, in anticipation or acknowledgement of these milestones in our legal history that I undertook to write a contemporary legal textbook on youth justice law in Canada to serve as a benchmark document.

When I began this project, I had three main goals: Firstly, I wanted to chart the origins and evolution of Canada's youth criminal justice system through the centuries. I wanted to delve extensively into that history, to chronicle in a basic textbook the roots and development of our thinking about the need for a separate youth criminal justice system in Canada. Secondly, I wanted to examine how the case law has developed since the *YCJA* came into force in 2003. While a number of excellent texts had examined the *Young Offenders Act* and/or discussed how the *YCJA* was expected to be different, no textbook had actually considered in detail how the jurisprudence had developed under the *YCJA*. Since I was teaching youth justice law at Carleton University in Ottawa at the time and also held the *YCJA* file for what was then the Federal Prosecution Service of the Department of Justice, the project was of particular professional interest to me. I believed it would be useful to have in one textbook a detailed historical account and record of how Canada's youth justice system had evolved over the centuries, as well as an examination of how the *YCJA* has altered the jurisprudential landscape. Finally, I wanted to document, in an objective fashion, the perceived shortcomings of the *YCJA* that have been identified in the public discourse since its implementation.

Thus, this basic text on Canadian youth criminal justice law is designed to increase awareness and knowledge about the philosophy, purpose and substance of the *YCJA*, to serve as a useful and timely addition to the public record in relation to the evolution of the criminal law as it applies to young persons, and to identify weaknesses in the *YCJA* that may justify reform.

While researching this book, I relied exclusively on information in the public domain, from the earliest legal codes, to the writings of Glanvill, Bracton, Bacon, Coke and Blackstone, through the many scholarly academic articles, books and studies, parliamentary debates, and findings of commissions, to the contemporary examination of youth justice law by the judiciary across this country. While many books and collections of essays on youth justice law in Canada have been written over the years and were of great assistance during this extensive literature review, the two classic Canadian texts on youth justice law, in my view, at the time were Nicholas Bala's 2003 textbook, *Youth Criminal Justice Law*, and Priscilla Platt's 1995 book, *Young Offenders Law in Canada* (second edition). These books are both excellent, and, as a university lecturer of youth justice law since 1999, I have relied on them as teaching texts.

That said, a lot has changed in youth justice law since 2003. Some would argue that the *YCJA* constitutes an entirely new legal direction and era for youth justice law in this country. It was thus important, in my view, to examine closely the development of the jurisprudence since 2003, which my book does.

The breadth of this project was deliberately circumscribed. This book concerns the criminal law as it applies to young persons in Canada who are suspected or charged with crimes. It is about what the law is, not what the law ought to be. It is about youth justice law, not about youth justice policy. I do not delve into the "why" of youth crime, or seek to navigate the terrain of the criminologist, the sociologist, or the psychologist. Neither do I attempt to identify the most effective youth crime prevention strategies. I also leave it to the statisticians to categorically determine whether youth crime is increasing in Canada. Rather, save for the historical survey chapter and a discussion of the evolution of thinking and policy in relation to the age of criminal responsibility in Canada in the second part of Chapter 2, I generally keep to my discipline and training as a lawyer, and focus on examining the jurisprudence under the *YCJA*.

This book is thus designed for those who require a sound understanding and knowledge of the purpose, content, and meaning of the *YCJA*. It is intended to assist those who must work with the Act every day, and make decisions in relation to the Act. Thus, this text will be highly useful to law students, lawyers, judges, prosecutors, defence counsel, police officers, probation officers, teachers, academics, and others who work with young persons in conflict with the law and/or need to understand well the philosophy and substance of our contemporary youth justice law.

The first part of the book provides a detailed historical overview that explains how we arrived at the introduction of a new youth Act in 2003. This chapter is a very useful survey chapter, outlining as it does the evolution of youth justice law in Canada. The remainder of the book is devoted to considering and discussing how the *YCJA* has been judicially interpreted during the first six years of its life.

Nevertheless, I hope the curious layperson will find it helpful and accessible. Canadians who merely have an interest in knowing more about the current criminal justice legal regime that governs young persons between ages 12 and 17 might wish to pick up this book to better inform themselves about the philosophy, the powers, and the penalties in the *YCJA*. It is also my fervent hope that the information in this timely textbook will assist politicians and policy-makers if and when further reforms to the Act are contemplated or undertaken by the federal government.

Finally, it must be said that, while I am a Crown advisory counsel with the federal government who works on legal issues relating to the *YCJA*, the views expressed in this book are entirely my own. I am solely responsible for this book, with all of its strengths and weaknesses.

SDB
Wakefield, Quebec
July 2009

[*Editor's Note*: Just before this book went to press, the Supreme Court of Canada released its decisions in *R. v. Grant*, [2009] S.C.J. No. 32, 2009 SCC 32 (S.C.C.), and *R. v. Suberu*, [2009] S.C.J. No. 33, 2009 SCC 33 (S.C.C.), respectively varying and affirming the Ontario Court of Appeal decisions, which are discussed in Chapter 6 of this book.]

ACKNOWLEDGEMENTS

I would like to thank my family as well as my friends and colleagues who have provided assistance and encouragement throughout the life of this project. Their words of support bolstered my morale, often at critical junctures, and their questions, comments and insights have made this a better book by inspiring me to revisit issues or to address issues I may not otherwise have addressed. After considerable thought, I have chosen not to identify these many individuals by name at risk of inadvertently overlooking someone. I am deeply grateful to all of you for your support. However, I must identify and express my sincere thanks and gratitude to André A. Morin, Justice Peter Wright, Justice Andrea Tuck-Jackson, Julian V. Roberts and Jean-Pierre Baribeau for giving up precious time to read chapters of this text and for their invaluable comments and observations. Their grace and generosity in doing so was greatly appreciated. I also wish to thank George Dolhai, my immediate supervisor, who made it possible for me to take a leave in order to work on this project.

I would also like to acknowledge and thank the many compassionate, dedicated and hard-working federal prosecutors in Yukon, Northwest Territories and Nunavut with whom I have had the pleasure and the privilege of working over the years, and from whom I have learned a great deal. Your questions, comments and experience working with the *YCJA* have been of immeasurable assistance.

I must also thank the exceptional library staff at the federal Department of Justice, who have provided superb and steadfast legal research assistance to me in relation to youth cases since I joined the federal government 10 years ago and soon began working with federal prosecutors on youth cases.

At LexisNexis Canada, I must thank Janet Kim and Sheila Nemet-Brown for their help, kindness, and enthusiasm in the early stages of this project; however, I would like to especially thank Rose Knecht for her impressive grace, diligence, and hard work during the painstaking editing process.

Finally, to my future students, I offer a cautionary note:

> [N]o one should profess to understand any part of a statute or of any other document before he has read the whole of it.[1]

In other words, there is no getting around it; the only way to know the *YCJA* is to read it.

---

[1]   *A.G. v. Prince Ernest Augustus of Hanover*, [1957] A.C. 436, at 463 (H.L).

DISCLAIMER

The views and opinions expressed in this book are solely those of the author and do not necessarily reflect the views or position of the Public Prosecution Service of Canada, the federal Department of Justice or the federal government.

TABLE OF CONTENTS

TABLE OF CASES

(All references are to page numbers)

TABLE OF LEGISLATION

(All references are to page numbers)

NUNAVUT

Justices of the Peace Act (Nunavut), S.N.W.T. 1998, c. 34

ONTARIO

Provincial Offences Act, R.S.O. 1990, c. P.33

Chapter 1

FROM THE EARLY LEGAL CODES TO THE YOUTH CRIMINAL JUSTICE ACT: THE DEVELOPMENT OF A SEPARATE CRIMINAL JUSTICE SYSTEM FOR YOUTH

Let us now peruse our ancient authors, for out of the old fields must come the new corn.

Yet law-abiding scholars write:
Law is neither wrong nor right,
Law is only crimes
Punished by places and by times ...

W. H. Auden

The life of the law has not been logic: it has been experience. The felt necessities of the time, the prevalent moral and political theories, intuitions of public policy, avowed or unconscious, even the prejudices which judges share with their fellow-men, have had a good deal more to do than the syllogism in determining the rules by which men should be governed. The law embodies the story of a nation's development through many centuries, and it cannot be dealt with as if it contained only the axioms and corollaries of a book of mathematics. In order to know what it is, we must know what it has been, and what it tends to become.

Oliver Wendell Holmes Jr., *The Common Law*[1]

---

[1]   The first passage is from Sir Edward Coke, as quoted and referenced in Catherine Drinker Bowen, *The Lion and the Throne, The Life and Times of Sir Edward Coke* (Toronto: Little,

I.   INTRODUCTION

From the ancient legal codes of past millennia to the modern *Youth Criminal Justice Act*,[2] legal thinkers through the ages have reasoned that children and young persons should be treated differently than adults for criminal conduct by virtue of their lesser maturity and lesser capacity to appreciate the nature and consequences of their acts and to distinguish between right and wrong.

"As far back as written records go children who have broken the law have been treated on the whole more leniently than have adult offenders."[3]

The hallowed roots of this legal principle in our Western legal tradition burrow backward through many centuries, to some of the earliest legal codes, such as the Twelve Tables of the Roman Republic, or the codes of some of the earliest Christian kings, when rulers distinguished between youthful and adult perpetrators. Many centuries would pass, however, before the Canadian state codified this distinction in the first *Criminal Code* of 1892,[4] and by implementing the *Juvenile Delinquents*

Brown and Company, 1956), at 520. The Auden stanza is from the poem "Law Like Love" by W.H. Auden. A copy of this poem appears in Ephraim London, ed., *The World of Law: The Law as Literature*, Vol. 2 (New York: Simon and Schuster, 1960), at 778-79. The third passage is from Oliver Wendell Holmes, Jr., *The Common Law* (Boston: Little, Brown and Company, 1881), at 1.

[2]   S.C. 2002, c. 1, in force from April 1, 2003 [hereafter "*YCJA*"].

[3]   Wiley B. Sanders, ed., *Juvenile Offenders for a Thousand Years: Selected Readings from Anglo-Saxon Times to 1900* (Chapel Hill: University of North Carolina Press, 1970), at xviii. Today, see s. 3(1) of the *YCJA*, which states: "(b) the criminal justice system for young persons must be separate from that of adults and emphasize the following: ...(ii) fair and proportionate accountability that is consistent with the greater dependency of young persons and their reduced level of maturity ... ."

[4]   See for example the explanation in Nicholas C. Bala and Kenneth L. Clarke, *The Child and the Law* (Toronto: McGraw-Hill Ryerson Ltd., 1981), at 163. In Canada's first *Criminal Code* (*The Criminal Code, 1892*, S.C. 1892, c. 29.), which was proclaimed in force in 1893, s. 9 stated that no person under seven could be convicted of an offence. Section 10 stated that a person aged 7 or more, but under 14, could be convicted if the offender was competent to know the nature and consequences of his conduct and to appreciate that it was wrong. The burden of proof was on the Crown. When the *Young Offenders Act* was proclaimed in force in 1984, the age of criminal responsibility was raised to 12. It remains so today. See *Young Offenders Act*, R.S.C. 1985, c. Y-1, enacted as S.C. 1980-81-82-83, c. 110, proclaimed in force 2 April 1984 [hereafter "*YOA*"]. Section 13 of the modern *Criminal Code* also states that no person can be convicted of an act or omission on his part while under the age of 12. Any person under 12 years old who has committed a criminal offence can be dealt with by other means and through other legislation, such as provincial child welfare or mental health legislation. For further discussion of the Age of Criminal Responsibility in Canada, as well as the age of criminal responsibility in other countries, such as the United States, Britain and Australia, see Chapter 2, Jurisdiction and the Age of Criminal Responsibility.

Act in July 1908,[5] the first comprehensive federal legislation in Canada concerning young persons who commit crimes.

In our contemporary legal lexicon, this concept of reduced criminal responsibility for young persons is often referred to as diminished (criminal) responsibility or limited accountability. "This was and is an important principle, for without it there would be no need for a separate system for youthful offenders. If we were to hold youth as accountable for their offences as adults, we could simply process all young people through the adult system."[6] Chief Justice Lamer made that clear in the 1991 case *Reference re Young Offenders Act (P.E.I.)*: "The essence of the young offenders legislation is a distinction based on age and on the diminished responsibility associated with this distinction."[7]

While the recognition of the limited accountability of young persons as a critical aspect of a separate youth criminal justice system has been a legal principle of Canada's formal youth criminal justice system since 1908,[8] precisely one century later, the Supreme Court of Canada affirmed that the presumption of the diminished moral blameworthiness or culpability of young persons by virtue of their age is a principle of fundamental justice[9] recognized in s. 7 of the *Canadian Charter of Rights and Freedoms*.[10]

The U.S. Supreme Court also endorsed the concept in *Roper v. Simmons*,[11] when Kennedy J., for the majority, acknowledged the diminished

---

[5] S.C. 1908, c. 40, assented to 20 July 1908 [hereafter "*JDA*"]; subject to minor amendments over the years, finally as *JDA*, R.S.C. 1970, c. J-3. The *JDA* did not come into force in all parts of Canada simultaneously; indeed, s. 42 of the *JDA* provided that provinces had to proclaim it in force in part or all of the province after passing legislation establishing or designating courts as juvenile courts and establishing detention homes. As a result, when considering the prosecution of an adult today for a crime committed many years ago when the adult was a young person, such as an historical sexual assault, it may be necessary to verify whether the *JDA* was in force in the region at the time. Such cases must also be considered in light of the transitional provisions in the *YCJA*.

[6] Sandra J. Bell, *Young Offenders and Juvenile Justice: A Century After the Fact*, 2d ed. (Scarborough: Nelson, a division of Thomson Canada Ltd., 2003), at 52.

[7] *Reference re Young Offenders Act P.E.I.*, [1990] S.C.J. No. 60, [1991] 1 S.C.R. 252, at para. 23 (S.C.C.).

[8] Indeed, Abella J., writing for the majority in *R. v. D.B.*, [2008] S.C.J. No. 25, 2008 SCC 25, at paras. 48 and 59, respectively (S.C.C.) held that Canada has consistently acknowledged the diminished responsibility and distinctive vulnerability of young persons in all of the *YCJA*'s statutory predecessors, and that the recognition of a presumption of diminished moral culpability for young persons is a long-standing legal principle.

[9] *R. v. D.B.*, [2008] S.C.J. No. 25, 2008 SCC 25, at paras. 41 to 70 (S.C.C.). Although this was a 5-4 split decision, all members of the court agreed that young persons are entitled, based on their reduced maturity and judgement, to a presumption of diminished moral blameworthiness and that this presumption is a principle of fundamental justice.

[10] Part I of the *Constitution Act, 1982*, being Schedule B to the *Canada Act 1982* (U.K.), 1982, c. 11.

[11] 543 U.S. 551 (2005).

culpability of juveniles as a general principle, and held that it is unconstitutional to subject any young person under 18 to the death penalty.[12]

The acceptance of the principle of diminished accountability of young persons is also reflected in various international instruments, such as the *U.N. Convention on the Rights of the Child*.[13]

Nevertheless, not all countries in the world today have youth criminal justice laws or youth criminal justice systems operating separately from their adult criminal justice systems.[14] Yet every legal system at least recognizes that young persons are different from adults and should be held accountable for crimes in a manner different from that of adults.[15] Western nations in particular tend to have specific laws and/or policies regarding the differential treatment of young persons who commit crimes.[16] In doing so, nations acknowledge and pay heed to centuries-old legal principles.

II. EARLY LEGAL CODES AND THE ORIGIN OF LIMITED ACCOUNTABILITY

A.   The Twelve Tables

The publication of the Twelve Tables has been described as the birthday of modern law. While the Twelve Tables is part of early Roman law, the Tables has nevertheless been characterized as having laid the foundation for the law of the Western world.[17] In the middle of the 5th century B.C.,

---

[12]   The minority concluded that one should not generalize about all young persons and that, in fact, a particular 17-year-old could well be as mature and responsible as any adult and eminently capable of fully appreciating the nature and consequences of his or her actions. Cases should be examined on a case-by-case basis rather than adhering to an arbitrary marker, the minority (which includes Scalia J., Thomas J. and Rehnquist C.J.) concluded in a strongly worded dissent.

[13]   U.N. Doc. A/44/736, adopted November 20, 1989. Para. 1 of Article 40 of the Convention states that the age of a child is to be taken into account where a child is alleged as, accused of, or recognized as, having infringed the penal law. See also Articles 37(c) and 40.3 on this point. Canada made a reservation to Article 37, which states in part that children deprived of liberty shall be separated from adults unless this is not in their best interests. The Convention is available online at: <http://www.unicef.org/crc/>.

[14]   Hans-Jurgen Kerner, President of the European Society of Criminology, Foreword in *International Handbook of Juvenile Justice*, Josine Junger-Tas and Scott Decker, eds. (The Netherlands: Springer, 2006), at xi.

[15]   Nicholas Bala, *Youth Criminal Justice Law* (Toronto: Irwin Law Inc., 2003), at 1.

[16]   Anthony N. Doob and Michael Tonry, "Varieties of Youth Justice" in Michael Tonry and Anthony N. Doob, eds., *Youth Crime and Youth Justice: Comparative and Cross-National Perspectives*, Crime and Justice: A Review of Research, Vol. 31 (Chicago: University of Chicago Press, 2004), at 1.

[17]   See T.R. Glover, *The Ancient World* (Middlesex: Penguin Books, 1935), at 181-83.

around 451-450 B.C., 10 magistrates called Decemvirs were chosen to codify the existing Roman law and to engrave it onto Twelve Tables, which were then displayed in the most noticeable area of the Roman forum.[18] The Tables were a comprehensive collection of rules consisting largely of ancient Latin custom.[19] Indeed, children, including Cicero, learned them by heart "as required songs".[20]

Only remnants of the Twelve Tables remain, but those isolated fragments contain evidence that the Romans turned their minds to the criminal liability of *young persons*. Certain sections of the Twelve Tables recognize young persons as distinct from adults, and suggest that young persons be held less accountable than adults in certain circumstances for conduct considered criminal. For example, in Table II of the Twelve

---

Ancient Babylonia's *Code of Hammurabi*, which was written about 1700 B.C., is actually the oldest complete legal code discovered to date, but it does not appear to distinguish between crimes or wrongs committed by children and those committed by adults in terms of determining the penalty. There is no indication in the Code that children were to be treated more leniently than adults for infractions by virtue of their tender years, lesser maturity, or lesser capacity to appreciate or understand the nature of right and wrong. The Code predates the Hebrew Ten Commandments by about 500 years, establishes penalties for all kinds of acts, from robbery to adultery, but there is no express distinction between crimes committed by young persons and those committed by adults. Rather, the Code, as translated, generally outlines in its 282 laws the punishment for "any one" who wrongs another. The focus is on the conduct, the nature of the wrong committed, not the characteristics of the offender. Each item or law of the Code describes the unacceptable conduct and the punishment (which is often described as being put to death). Whether the perpetrator is a child or an adult does not appear relevant. Some of the rules refer to wrongs committed by a man or a woman (the terms, man and woman, are not defined), while others identify penalties for wrongs committed by people from different walks of life: shepherds, herdsmen, physicians, barbers, merchants, tavern keepers, etc. Perpetrators are identified by occupation and by the wrong committed in the course of those duties, such as the physician who could have his hands cut off for making an error during an operation or the builder who could be executed for a poorly constructed house.

It appears from the wording of the written Code that young persons could be brutally punished for wrongs. Item 195 of the Code states: "If a son strike his father, his hands shall be hewn off." Item 157 states: "If any one be guilty of incest with his mother after his father, both shall be burned." (The age is not specified, but presumably a teenage boy would be burned for committing incest with his mother.) There are other references to sons and daughters in the context of the family. For example, a son who denies his adoptive parents was to have his tongue cut off. If he deserted his adoptive family, his eye was to be put out. Of course, these observations are gleaned from the written word and do not necessarily capture societal views, customs or assumptions that may have seemed too obvious or widely understood to require commitment to a written record.

Information on Ancient Babylonia's *Code of Hammurabi* can be found on the Constitution Society's Liberty Library at: <http://www.constitution.org/liberlib.htm>.

[18] Lord Thomas MacKenzie, *Studies in Roman Law*, 3d ed. (Edinburgh: William Blackwood and Sons, 1870), at 5-6.

[19] W.W. Buckland, *A Text-Book of Roman Law from Augustus to Justinian* (Cambridge: University Press, 1921), at 1-2.

[20] Montesquieu, quoting Cicero's *De legibus*, bk. 2[2:23:59], reminds us of this in his *The Spirit of the Laws* (Cambridge: Cambridge University Press, 1989), at 612.

Tables, which concerns judgments and thefts, Law V states that anyone caught in the act of theft during the day shall be scourged (whipped) and given up as a slave to the person against whom the theft was committed. If the perpetrator were a slave, he was to be beaten with rods and hurled from a rock. If he were under the age of puberty, however, the Praetor (an annually elected magistrate who had the power to issue proclamations of the principles he intended to follow)[21] could choose to whip him instead and surrender him in reparation for the injury.[22] The judge was clearly afforded some flexibility in certain circumstances to decide how to punish the pre-pubescent thief. (The onset of puberty as a sign that an individual was sufficiently mature to understand the nature and consequences of his or her acts, and therefore that puberty was a logical starting point for criminal liability, was to remain an underlying theme in the criminal law for many centuries.)

Further, Law VI of Table II indicates that when any person committed a theft during the day, whether they were freemen or slaves, of full age or minors, and defended themselves with weapons, the party against whom the violence was directed was legally entitled to kill them in defence of his person or property.[23] The legal thinkers of Ancient Rome were at least considering the age of the perpetrator. Age was a factor worthy of note, even if it resulted in no penal discount.

The meaning of leniency, however, like the definition of crime itself,[24] is a relative concept. Such definitions change over time. Punishments meted out several centuries after the inscription of the Twelve Tables illustrate the enduring harshness of Roman penal laws during that period. Punishments for crimes, such as arson or murder, were brutal and included being burned alive or fed to ravenous beasts.[25] No punishment was more macabre than the punishment for parricide — killing your parent. A person who killed a parent was to be beaten with rods until he or she bled, and then drowned in

---

[21]   W.W. Buckland and Arnold D. McNair, *Roman Law and Common Law*, 2d ed. revised by F.H. Lawson (Cambridge: University Press, 1965), at 3.

[22]   *The Laws of the Twelve Tables*, Table II, Law V, as found on the Constitution Society's Liberty Library: <http://www. constitution.org/liberlib.htm>.

[23]   *The Laws of the Twelve Tables*, Table II, Law VI.

[24]   The term "crime" is derived from the Latin, *crimen-minis*, meaning judgment or offence. While young persons have always committed "crimes" or perceived wrongs against society, the notion of criminality is a protean concept that is in a constant state of flux and re-formulation within intellectually robust societies. As Canadian academic Barry Wright notes in "Overview: Historical Perspectives on Criminal Law, Legal Historical Research Methods, and Early Developments in English Criminal Law" in Barry Wright, *Coursepack: Crime and State in History* (Department of Law, Carleton University, Fall 2004), at 4: "History, first of all, underlines the relativity of what is defined as crime."

[25]   Sadakat Kadri, *The Trial: A History, from Socrates to O.J. Simpson* (New York: Random House, 2005), at 14.

a sack with a dog, a cock, a monkey and a snake or some equally reprehen-
sible mélange of squirming varmints.[26] While some young persons may
have been spared, presumably at least some young persons would have
suffered this horrific fate.

B.   The First Christian Kings

The first known record of a written English legal code is attributed
to the first Christian King, Ethelbert of Kent, who committed the local
customs to writing in about 600 A.D. based on the Roman model. Ethelbert's laws were called dooms, or, as we say today, judgments. They are
the oldest surviving writings in the English language.[27] Ethelbert's
successors in Kent also issued legal codes; so did Ine of Wessex (688-
726) and King Alfred, among others.[28]

None of these early English codes specifically discusses the criminal
liability of children, but some of them contain isolated references suggesting
that the age of the perpetrator was relevant.[29] In the laws of Ine, who
recorded the earliest laws of the Kingdom of Wessex some time between
688 and 694 A.D., a sub-clause to Law 7 states: "A ten year old child can be
[regarded as] accessory to a theft."[30] A later ordinance drawn up by the
bishops and reeves who held jurisdiction in London under King Aethelstan,
circa 925-939, stipulated: "No thief shall be spared [who has stolen goods
worth] more than twelve pence, and who is over twelve years old."[31]
Relative leniency toward the young criminal clearly existed prior to the
Norman conquest in some circumstances. The age of the perpetrator was
relevant, even then, in determining accountability and punishment: A child
under 12 could be spared or pardoned for theft, while a child over 12 would
be held accountable.[32] In fact, Aethelstan was apparently so horrified at the

---

[26] Sadakat Kadri, *The Trial: A History, from Socrates to O.J. Simpson* (New York: Random
House, 2005), at 14.

[27] W.J.V. Windeyer, *Lectures on Legal History*, 2d ed., revised (Sydney, Australia: Law Book
Company, 1957), at 1-5.

[28] Dorothy Whitelock, *The Beginnings of English Society* (Middlesex, England: Penguin
Books, 1968), at 134-35.

[29] F.L. Attenborough, M.A., *The Laws of the Earliest English Kings* (Cambridge: University
Press, 1922).

[30] F.L. Attenborough, M.A., *The Laws of the Earliest English Kings* (Cambridge: University
Press, 1922), at 39.

[31] F.L. Attenborough, M.A., *The Laws of the Earliest English Kings* (Cambridge: University
Press, 1922), at 157.

[32] A.W.G. Kean, "The History of the Criminal Liability of Children" (1937) 53 L.Q. Rev. 364,
at 364-65. Kean derives the same conclusions from these references in Aethelstan. In fact,
Kean goes further and argues that later evidence confirms that in early times, infancy was no
defence, but that it was usual for the child to receive a pardon.

execution of young thieves for petty theft that he allowed the death penalty to be applied only if the thief were over 15, instead of 12.[33]

Nevertheless, it would be unwise to conclude that because we do not find in the earliest legal codes an express and comprehensive rationale for the differential treatment of youthful offenders, that there was no common understanding within particular societies on this point. We cannot assume that the entire law, customs and understanding of ancient societies were committed to writing. Certain customs may simply have been understood and accepted so widely that there was no need to commit them to writing. These early legal codes do not necessarily capture the law of the period in its entirety. It is possible that the dooms, for example, recorded only matters of customary law that were unclear or in doubt. "There would be no need for a King to publish dooms dealing with the law which every freeman learnt by oral tradition. Sometimes the dooms made rules for matters which were not the subject of the customary law."[34]

Despite suggestions in some of the early legal codes that the age of the perpetrator could have a bearing on the degree to which he or she would be held accountable, common law legal scholars generally contend that children and adults were largely treated similarly under the criminal law in the Western legal tradition until about the 13th century. The rationale for the similar treatment of all offenders was that the criminal law "was grounded in vengeance: harm is harm and should be paid for".[35] The focus was on the nature of the offence, the harm done, rather than on the characteristics of the offender. The offender was obliged to make amends for that harm. This is certainly the general tenor of the *Code of Hammurabi*, the oldest complete legal code discovered to date. The focus in that Code is on the magnitude of the wrong done, and the compensation or reparation considered "just" to rectify that wrong, not on the intention or characteristics of the wrongdoer.[36]

---

[33] Dorothy Whitelock, *The Beginnings of English Society* (Middlesex, England: Penguin Books, 1968), at 146.

[34] W.J.V. Windeyer, *Lectures on Legal History*, 2d ed., revised (Sydney, Australia: Law Book Company, 1957), at 6. See also Dorothy Whitelock, *The Beginnings of English Society* (Middlesex, England: Penguin Books, 1968), at 135.

[35] See Sanjeev Anand, "Catalyst for Change: The History of Canadian Juvenile Justice Reform" (Spring 1999) Vol. 24, No. 2, Queen's L.J. 515, at 517. See also A.W.G. Kean, "The History of the Criminal Liability of Children" (1937) 53 L.Q. Rev. 364, at 364-65. For an elaborate discussion of the place of vengeance in the development of early forms of liability and in the criminal law, see Oliver Wendell Holmes, Jr., *The Common Law* (Boston: Little, Brown and Company, 1881), particularly Lecture I.

[36] Information on Ancient Babylonia's Code of Hammurabi can be found on the Constitution Society's Liberty Library at: <http://www.constitution.org/liberlib.htm>. See also Sadakat Kadri, *The Trial: A History, from Socrates to O.J. Simpson* (New York: Random House, 2005), at 3. This Code is discussed extensively at footnote 17.

To some extent, we are left to speculate regarding the degree to which children and young persons were held accountable for wrongs against society in the Western legal tradition prior to the first relevant written records of the early common law.

C. Limited Accountability

In the 1200s, the age of full criminal responsibility varied from region to region across Western Europe, and according to the crime, as did sentences, but children often received more lenient sentences than adults for the same crimes, including that of murder. Pardons were not uncommon.[37] St. Thomas Aquinas, the 13th century Italian medieval philosopher theologian, recorded in his writings that "the law for children and adults was not the same and that many acts permitted by children were punishable offences for adults. In Volume 28 of his *Summa Theologiae*, Law and Political Theory, Aquinas recognizes that "the same course of action is not possible ... for a grown-up and a child: this is why the same laws do not apply, for many things are allowed in the young for which older people are punished, or at least blamed".[38] Within a century, the concept of diminished responsibility and its rationale was expressly evident in the English common law.[39] Two 14th century cases illustrate the point.

The first case is dated 1302 and involves an 11-year-old boy. The young boy had come to his brother's defence by trying to stop a thief who had stolen some wheat. The boy struck the thief on the head; the thief died. Justice Spigurnel opined: "If he had done the deed before his age of seven years, he should not suffer judgment; but if before his age of twelve years he had done any other deed not involving the loss of life or limb, and against the peace, he should not answer, because before that age he is not with the peace."[40] In a later case, Spigurnel J. recognized that if there were evidence indicating that the young person could discern between good and evil and had acted with malice in committing a crime, then that young person should be held accountable. In that latter case, Spigurnel J. was dealing with an 11-year-old who was condemned to hang because it

---

[37] Shulamith Shahar, *Childhood in the Middle Ages* (London: Routledge, 1990), at 25.

[38] St. Thomas Aquinas, *Summa Theologiae* (Latin text and English translation, Introductions, Notes, Appendices, and Glossaries) (London: Blackfriars, in conjunction with Eyre and Spottiswoode, and New York: McGraw-Hill, 1966), at 123. The quote is from the Prima Secundae, vol. 28, Law and Political Theory, Question 96 (the power of human law), Article 2.

[39] Sanjeev Anand, "Catalyst for Change: The History of Canadian Juvenile Justice Reform" (Spring 1999) Vol. 24, No. 2, Queen's L.J. 515, at 518.

[40] *Year Books of the Reign of King Edward the First*, edited and translated by Alfred J. Horwood (London: Longman, Green, Longman, Roberts and Green, 1868), at 510-12.

was found that he had killed his companion and then hid. The act of hiding was evidence that the young person knew the difference between good and evil.[41]

A.W.G. Kean, who recounts the 1302 case in a 1937 legal article in The Law Quarterley Review,[42] also refers to a 1488 case where a nine-year-old killed another nine-year-old and then confessed. In that case, it was found that the child had hidden the body after the killing and concocted a story to explain the blood on him. Since the young person's conduct revealed evidence of cunning, he was condemned to hang.[43] Kean cites later cases in the 1500s and 1600s that confirmed the principle that an infant of tender age could be held criminally liable only if the judge concluded that the infant understood the nature of the act and that it was wrong. The judge had to be satisfied that the accused had a criminal intent and understood the nature of good and evil.[44]

Generally, however, the case law of this period did not specify a standard age, below which a young person could not be held criminally liable. It was left to the judge to determine this on a case-by-case basis. In practice, from the 1300s to the 1600s, children tended to be found criminally liable if they had entered puberty, which was determined by a physical examination. If they had not reached puberty, they would be punished only if malice could be proven.[45] In the 1600s jurists tried to fix specific age limits at which point a child could be held criminally responsible. A consensus was reached that children under seven would not be held criminally responsible.[46] This age may have been based on the *infantia* rule that had developed in Ancient Rome by about 407 A.D. prohibiting the criminal prosecution of children under seven. Some scholars have posited that the English may have learned of this rule during the Renaissance when knowledge of ancient civilizations became more accessible.[47]

---

[41]   A.W.G. Kean, "The History of the Criminal Liability of Children" (1937) 53 L.Q. Rev. 364, at 367.

[42]   A.W.G. Kean, "The History of the Criminal Liability of Children" (1937) 53 L.Q. Rev. 364.

[43]   A.W.G. Kean, "The History of the Criminal Liability of Children" (1937) 53 L.Q. Rev. 364, at 367, and Sanjeev Anand, "Catalyst for Change: The History of Canadian Juvenile Justice Reform" (Spring 1999) Vol. 24, No. 2, Queen's L.J. 515, at 518.

[44]   A.W.G. Kean, "The History of the Criminal Liability of Children" (1937) 53 L.Q. Rev. 364, at 369.

[45]   Sanjeev Anand, "Catalyst for Change: The History of Canadian Juvenile Justice Reform" (Spring 1999) Vol. 24, No. 2, Queen's L.J. 515, at 518.

[46]   Sanjeev Anand, "Catalyst for Change: The History of Canadian Juvenile Justice Reform" (Spring 1999) Vol. 24, No. 2, Queen's L.J. 515, at 519.

[47]   Sanjeev Anand, "Catalyst for Change: The History of Canadian Juvenile Justice Reform" (Spring 1999) Vol. 24, No. 2, Queen's L.J. 515, at 519. See also Lord Thomas MacKenzie, *Studies in Roman Law*, 3d ed. (Edinburgh: William Blackwood and Sons, 1870), at 78. See

Oxford professor and jurist, Sir William Blackstone, writing on the Criminal Responsibility of Children under the Criminal Law, 1769, in his *Commentaries on the Laws of England: In Four Books*, explained that under the civil law, the age of minors (those under 25) was divided into categories. *Infantia* covered the period of birth to age seven, *pueritia* covered the period from age 7 to 14, while *pubertas* extended from the age of 14 upwards. The stage of *pueritia*, or childhood, was subdivided into early and late childhood, the first half running from 7 to 10.5 years. According to Blackstone, from infancy up to the end of the first half of *pueritia*, children were not punishable for any crime. During the latter half of *pueritia*, from 10.5 to 14 years, they were punishable only if found to be *doli capaces*, or capable of mischief, "but with many mitigations, and not with the utmoft [utmost] rigor of the law".[48] At the age of *pubertas* (from 14 upwards), minors were liable to be punished.[49]

Under ancient Saxon law, Blackstone explained, 12 years was established as the age of possible discretion:[50] between this age and 14, the offender could be found guilty of the crime depending on his natural capacity or incapacity. Under 12, according to Blackstone, he could not be guilty "in will". As far back as the reign of Edward the Third (1327-1377), Blackstone noted, culpability had been measured not in days or years, but by the strength of the delinquent's understanding and judgement. Under 7 years of age, Blackstone said, an infant could not be guilty of a crime for, at this age, crime was almost impossible by nature.[51] While an infant under 14

---

some further discussion of this in Thomas Collett Sandars, M.A., *The Institutes of Justinian* (New York: Longmans, Green and Co., 1917), at 69-70 and 347. As some scholars have observed, it is difficult to locate information concerning the meaning and application of the *infantia* rule because historians of Roman law pay little attention to it. For example, Edward Gibbon's *The Decline and Fall of the Roman Empire* (New York: Random House, reprinted, 2003), Vol. II, at 322, contains a thorough chapter XLIV concerning Roman jurisprudence, but there is no discussion of the *infantia* rule.

[48] Blackstone's *Commentaries on the Laws of England, Book the Fourth — Chapter the Second: Of the Persons Capable of Committing Crimes.* Blackstone's Commentaries on the Laws of England are available on the Internet, through websites such as the Yale Law School's Avalon Project at: <http://avalon.law.yale.edu/subject_menus/blackstone.asp>. See also "Blackstone on the Criminal Responsibility of Children under the Common Law, 1769" in Sir William Blackstone, *Commentaries on the Laws of England: In Four Books* (London: J. Murray, 1857), Vol. IV, Of Public Wrongs, Chapter II, Of the Persons Capable of Committing Crimes.

[49] Blackstone's *Commentaries on the Laws of England, Book the Fourth — Chapter the Second: Of the Persons Capable of Committing Crimes.*

[50] Blackstone's footnotes suggest that he is referring to the reign of Aethelstan.

[51] Blackstone's *Commentaries on the Laws of England, Book the Fourth — Chapter the Second: Of the Persons Capable of Committing Crimes.* Blackstone's Commentaries on the Laws of England are available on the Internet, through websites such as the Yale Law School's Avalon Project at: <http://avalon.law.yale.edu/subject_menus/blackstone.asp>. See also "Blackstone on the Criminal Responsibility of Children under the Common Law, 1769" in Sir William Blackstone, *Commentaries on the Laws of England: In Four Books* (London:

shall be *prima facie* adjudged to be *doli incapax*, if it appeared to the court and jury that he was *doli capax* and could discern between good and evil, he could be convicted and put to death.[52] Blackstone cited cases of young persons ranging in age from 8 to 13 who had been executed in various ways because there was evidence that they knew what they were doing. But, in all such cases, said Blackstone, evidence of malice "ought to be ftrong [strong] and clear beyond all doubt or contradiction".[53]

Doli incapax literally means incapable of an unlawful act.[54]

By the 17th century, the concept of *doli incapax* had crystallized into a common law defence. A child under seven could not be held criminally liable under any circumstances; this was known as the age of absolute immunity. Children under seven were considered incapable of committing crimes because they lacked the capacity to form the intent; they were not sufficiently intellectually developed to appreciate the wrongfulness of their act. The period between 7 and 14 was considered the period of conditional responsibility: it was presumed that a person in this age bracket was incapable of committing a crime, but this presumption could be rebutted if the prosecution could demonstrate that the child or young person appreciated the wrongfulness of his or her conduct and could discern between good and evil.[55]

The doctrine of *doli incapax* was imported to the colonies, and eventually incorporated into Canada's first *Criminal Code* in 1892, which came into force in 1893. As a result, until the *doli incapax* defence was repealed in 1984 when the *Young Offenders Act* came into force, a child between 7 and 14 could be held criminally responsible if the Crown could

---

Murray, 1857), Vol. IV, Of Public Wrongs, Chapter II, Of the Persons Capable of Committing Crimes.

[52] Blackstone's *Commentaries on the Laws of England, Book the Fourth — Chapter the Second: Of the Persons Capable of Committing Crimes.*

[53] Blackstone's *Commentaries on the Laws of England, Book the Fourth — Chapter the Second: Of the Persons Capable of Committing Crimes.* Some contemporary youth justice experts suggest it is a mistake to assume that young persons do not understand that certain acts are morally wrong. Anthony Doob and Carla Cesaroni suggest that the reason we should have a separate justice system for youths has more to do with the fact that youths do not reason and consider consequences in the same manner as adults. See Anthony N. Doob and Carla Cesaroni, *Responding to Youth Crime in Canada* (Toronto: University of Toronto Press, 2004), at 34 and 50.

[54] James Morwood, *A Dictionary of Latin Words and Phrases* (Oxford: Oxford University Press, 1998), at 48. See a discussion of *doli incapax* in Sanjeev Anand, "Catalyst for Change: The History of Canadian Juvenile Justice Reform" (Spring 1999) Vol. 24, No. 2, Queen's L.J. 515, at 520, as well as in Jeffrey Wilson, *Children and the Law* (Toronto: Butterworths, 1978), at 180-81.

[55] Nicholas C. Bala and Kenneth L. Clarke, *The Child and the Law* (Toronto: McGraw-Hill Ryerson Ltd., 1981), at 163. See also Sanjeev Anand, "Catalyst for Change: The History of Canadian Juvenile Justice Reform" (Spring 1999) Vol. 24, No. 2, Queen's L.J. 515, at 520.

prove that the youthful offender was competent to know the nature and consequences of his or her conduct and to appreciate that it was wrong.[56] The defence of *doli incapax* was the only formal special legal consideration afforded children accused of crimes in Canada under the criminal law until the mid-1800s. However, this legal principle was not uniformly applied.[57] When the doctrine *was* applied, children who were found not to fall within its umbrella were convicted, were generally subject to the same penalties as adults, housed in the same jails, in the same cells, and subject to the same rules.[58] In other words, if the young person was found to understand and appreciate the nature and consequences of his or her actions, such young persons were generally treated as if they were adults.

And herein lies an enduring paradox within the youth criminal justice law of Western nations, such as the United States, Canada and Britain: On the one hand, common law countries such as Canada have enshrined in common law and/or statute law the principle that youthful offenders should be treated differently, and, in essence, more leniently, than adults, because, they are, after all, young persons and not adults. On the other hand, Western nations have historically retained the power to treat youthful offenders as if they were adults when they see fit. As discussed in Chapter 8, countries such as the U.S. and Britain retain the power to try a young person as an adult in certain circumstances. Canada, likewise, has retained the power to impose an adult sentence on a young person in certain circumstances following a youth justice court trial, typically when the young person is found guilty of committing a particularly serious or heinous crime. While the common law tradition has long recognized that young persons should

[56] This is the wording of s. 13 of the 1983 *Criminal Code*. Section 13 was repealed when the *Young Offenders Act* came into force in April 1984. As previously noted, since 1984, the age of criminal responsibility has been 12. The age of criminal responsibility remains an occasionally controversial subject in Canada. Indeed, in August 2006, former federal Justice Minister Vic Toews proposed lowering it to 10. For a full discussion of this topic, see Chapter 2.

[57] "Juvenile Justice Before 1908" in *The Evolution of Juvenile Justice in Canada*, a paper prepared by the International Cooperation Group of the Department of Justice, based on the work of historian Owen Carrigan, at 4. The paper is available online at: <http://www.justice. gc.ca/eng/pi/icg-gci/jj2-jm2/sec01.html>. For a more fulsome, contemporary discussion of the inconsistent application of the *doli incapax* doctrine and related issues, see L. Micucci, "Responsibility and the Young Person" (1998) 11 Can. J.L. & Juris. 277-309, at paras. 21 and 22.

[58] Nicholas C. Bala and Kenneth L. Clarke, *The Child and the Law* (Toronto: McGraw-Hill Ryerson Ltd., 1981), at 163. Sanjeev Anand, "Catalyst for Change: The History of Canadian Juvenile Justice Reform" (Spring 1999) Vol. 24, No. 2, Queen's L.J. 515, indicates in footnote 17 that in 1846 at the Kingston Penitentiary, men, women and children "were all caged together". Anand further indicates that the records show that 16 children were imprisoned along with 11 adult murderers and 10 adult rapists. An excellent description of the treatment of young persons in pioneer Canada can be found in D. Owen Carrigan, "The Treatment of Juvenile Delinquents before 1900" in *Juvenile Delinquency in Canada: A History* (Toronto: Irwin Publishing, 1998), at 31.

generally be held less accountable than adults for their crimes in part because they are less able to appreciate the consequences of their acts, this principle has never been consistently applied. Within the common law tradition today, a young person is a young person, unless the state wants to treat him or her as an adult.[59]

III. CHILDREN IN PIONEER CANADA: MINIATURE ADULTS ... MINIATURE CRIMINALS

Youthful offenders in colonial Canada who were found to be criminally responsible (when the *doli incapax* defence either was ignored or failed) were usually treated just like adults and incarcerated right alongside of them. Subjecting child criminals to the same harsh penalties and warehousing as adults reflected the dominant attitudes toward children in France and Britain, attitudes that crossed the Atlantic with the boatloads of immigrants. From the early days of pioneer Canada until the mid-19th century, in many respects, children were considered miniature adults.[60] They were perceived as adults from a young age and generally held to adult standards of conduct in their daily lives. According to social historian D. Owen Carrigan, they were generally expected to behave like adults. Consequently, when young persons committed crimes, they were often considered miniature criminals who should suffer the same penalties.[61] "Since children were subject to the rules and expectations of adults, it is not surprising that they also faced adult penalties if they failed to conform."[62] In pioneer Canada, this meant that child convicts of both sexes were generally

---

[59] Under the *YCJA*, a young person who is at least 14 at the time of the alleged offence can receive an adult sentence in the *Criminal Code* in certain circumstances. In the U.S., in the 1980s and 1990s, most states implemented laws that expanded the number of young persons who could be transferred from the juvenile court to the adult criminal court for trial and expedited this transfer process. See Donna Bishop and Scott Decker, "Punishment and Control: Juvenile Justice Reform in the USA" in Josine Junger-Tas and Scott Decker, eds., *International Handbook of Juvenile Justice* (The Netherlands: Springer, 2006), at 18-19.

[60] This is the predominant view of historians regarding attitudes toward children as far back as the Middle Ages. Historian Barbara Tuchman, writing about childhood in the 1300s in her book *A Distant Mirror* (New York: Ballantine Books, 1978), at 52, states: "If children survived to age 7, their recognized life began, more or less as miniature adults. Childhood was already over."

French demographic historian Philippe Ariès, in *Centuries of Childhood: A Social History of Family Life* (New York: Vintage Books, 1962), also makes this argument. See, for example, Chapter II, the Discovery of Childhood, at 33-49, as well as the Conclusion at 411-15.

[61] D. Owen Carrigan, *Juvenile Delinquency in Canada: A History* (Toronto: Irwin Publishing, 1998), at 31.

[62] D. Owen Carrigan, *Juvenile Delinquency in Canada: A History* (Toronto: Irwin Publishing, 1998), at 32.

subject to the same harsh penalties that were being imposed on children in their mother countries, primarily France and England.

In 1649, a young girl aged 15 or 16 was hanged in Quebec for theft.[63] Penalties changed little during the next two centuries. In 1813, a 13-year-old boy was hanged in Montreal for stealing a cow.[64] In the 1840s, at the Kingston Penitentiary, a 10-year-old boy was whipped 57 times over an eight-month period for staring and laughing, and an 11-year-old French Canadian boy was given 12 lashes on Christmas Eve for speaking his native tongue.[65] In one of the most illuminating late 19th century examples of the enduring severity of criminal sanctions imposed on young persons, in 1880, a young girl was convicted of stealing a gooseberry from a garden. She was jailed for two weeks and *then* sentenced to six months in an Ontario reformatory.[66]

In New France, severe penalties were imposed for major and minor crimes alike, ranging from hanging, breaking on the wheel and branding, to flogging, the iron collar, pillory (a wooden framework with holes for the head and hands, which permitted the public to assault or ridicule the confined person),[67] mutilation and jail. Accused persons could be put to the *question extraordinaire*, in other words, tortured, if they refused to admit the crime. This could involve strapping boards to the shins, inserting wedges, and then hitting the boards to crush the bones. Mercy was sometimes extended, to both adults and children, in New France. According to Carrigan, it became customary to whip children instead of executing them for crimes that were normally punishable by death.[68] There is also some evidence that sentences were sometimes reduced to reflect the young age of the accused.[69]

Jail conditions were foul and sometimes horrendous: the jails were humid and damp during the summer, and very cold in winter because they were unheated. On one occasion, in 1686, a governor reported having to

---

[63] D. Owen Carrigan, *Juvenile Delinquency in Canada: A History* (Toronto: Irwin Publishing, 1998), at 34.

[64] D. Owen Carrigan, *Juvenile Delinquency in Canada: A History* (Toronto: Irwin Publishing, 1998), at 38.

[65] D. Owen Carrigan, *Juvenile Delinquency in Canada: A History* (Toronto: Irwin Publishing, 1998), at 38-39.

[66] D. Owen Carrigan, *Juvenile Delinquency in Canada: A History* (Toronto: Irwin Publishing, 1998), at 61.

[67] As defined in the Concise Oxford Dictionary, 9th ed., Della Thompson, ed. (Oxford: Clarendon Press, 1995), at 1035.

[68] D. Owen Carrigan, *Juvenile Delinquency in Canada: A History* (Toronto: Irwin Publishing, 1998), at 35.

[69] D. Owen Carrigan, *Juvenile Delinquency in Canada: A History* (Toronto: Irwin Publishing, 1998), at 35-36. The description in this paragraph generally is found in Carrigan, at 33-36.

excise the feet of certain prisoners who had developed gangrene from the cold. Prisoners were fed a diet of bread and water, and sometimes kept in ankle irons.[70]

Similar to New France, English Canada imported the laws and severe penalties from its mother country: in February 1814, five children between the ages of 8 and 12 were sentenced to death in the Old Bailey for burglary and stealing shoes.[71] Whipping was common in English Canada, especially as a convenient and less costly alternative in communities without jails. Females were not spared flogging.[72]

If incarcerated, children could be thrown in with adult murderers, rapists and other seasoned criminals, from whom they could learn new tricks. When Upper Canada opened its first prison in Kingston in 1835, many young boys were sent there. Young girls were housed there as well, in the female quarters with adult women.

Jails proliferated to match population growth. More and more children were warehoused in them, where they were lumped into cells, alongside adults, enduring the same horrid conditions.[73]

IV. THE DEVELOPMENT OF THE CONCEPT OF CHILDHOOD

As the 19th century progressed, there was an increasing tendency to treat young persons differently from adults when they were convicted of criminal acts. This shifting inclination may have, in part, reflected evolving perceptions about the concept of childhood itself. French demographic historian Philippe Ariès, in his book *Centuries of Childhood: A Social History of Family Life*, researched the perception and place of children in Western European culture from the Middle Ages to the 19th century. Prior to the 17th century, he argues, few distinctions were made on the basis of age. During the Middle Ages, a child was absorbed into the

---

[70] This information is taken from the work of D. Owen Carrigan, *Juvenile Delinquency in Canada: A History* (Toronto: Irwin Publishing, 1998), at 34. Regarding conditions in French prisons in pioneer Canada, Carrigan relies in part on the work of André Lachance, "Les Prisons au Canada sous le Régime français" Revue d'histoire de l'Amerique francaise 19 (1966): 563.

[71] D. Owen Carrigan, *Juvenile Delinquency in Canada: A History* (Toronto: Irwin Publishing, 1998), at 31.

[72] D. Owen Carrigan, *Juvenile Delinquency in Canada: A History* (Toronto: Irwin Publishing, 1998), at 39.

[73] D. Owen Carrigan, *Juvenile Delinquency in Canada: A History* (Toronto: Irwin Publishing, 1998), at 39.

adult world once he or she was aged five to seven.[74] "They immediately went straight into the great community of men, sharing in the work and play of their companions, old and young alike."[75] Young persons were fully integrated into the larger society. They looked and acted like adults and generally were treated like adults from a young age.

In large part, children in medieval times were treated like adults because of their importance to the economic health of the family.[76] Every pair of hands was crucial. Children were a critical part of the family unit and were expected to work the land, alongside their parents.[77] Children were basically considered possessions or chattels of the father. Historians often describe the lives of children during this period as arduous (although this depended to some degree on the class of the child). Wars, famine and plague abounded; consequently there was little time for nurturing. Working the land and basic survival were preoccupations.[78]

Ariès argues that this non-recognition of childhood as a particular phase of life is clearly visible in the art of the Middle Ages. Until the 1600s, children were portrayed as miniature adults. Only in the 17th century does it become customary to preserve in art the appearance of childhood, only then is there a notable awareness and consciousness of children.[79] Ariès contends that the recognition of the distinct phase of development known as childhood, was, in essence, "discovered" in Western Europe in the 17th century.

Ariès's work later inspired criminologists to draw links between the "discovery" or recognition of childhood as a distinct phase of life and the identification of the need for a separate system of youth justice.[80] Based on Ariès's work, some scholars posited that the progression toward a separate youth criminal justice system in the Western world (certainly in Canada and the U.S.) coincided with increasing societal recognition of childhood as a distinct stage of human development. The increased focus

---

[74] Philippe Ariès, *Centuries of Childhood: A Social History of Family Life* (New York: Vintage Books, 1962), at 329.

[75] Philippe Ariès, *Centuries of Childhood: A Social History of Family Life* (New York: Vintage Books, 1962), at 411.

[76] J. Thomas Dalby, "Criminal Liability in Children" (1985) 27 Can. J. Crim. 137, at 138.

[77] D. Owen Carrigan, *Juvenile Delinquency in Canada: A History* (Toronto: Irwin Publishing, 1998), at 31-32.

[78] Nicholas C. Bala and Kenneth L. Clarke, *The Child and the Law* (Toronto: McGraw-Hill Ryerson Ltd., 1981), at 4.

[79] Philippe Ariès, in *Centuries of Childhood: A Social History of Family Life* (New York: Vintage Books, 1962), at 42-43.

[80] Russell C. Smandych, "Accounting for Changes in Canadian Youth Justice: From the Invention to the Disappearance of Childhood" in Russell C. Smandych, ed., *Youth Justice, History, Legislation and Reform* (Toronto: Harcourt Canada Ltd., 2001), 4 at 10.

and attention on childhood as a specific stage in life influenced scholarly discourse concerning the treatment of children and young persons who violated the law and gave rise to the related question of whether the answer lay in a separate criminal justice system for youth. Some scholars note that LaMar Empey, who wrote *American Delinquency: Its Meaning and Construction*, was greatly influenced by Ariès in developing his analysis about the origins of a separate youth justice system in the U.S.[81]

Empey traces the thinking about childhood and delinquency from the "indifference" of childhood in the Middle Ages, to the discovery of childhood in the 16th and 17th centuries, to the "preoccupation" with childhood that some would argue characterizes Western society today.

Empey wrote:

> It was not until Europe began to awaken from the intellectual hibernation and social stagnation of the Middle Ages that a handful of moral philosophers began to question the customary treatment of children. Over a period of the next two or three centuries, age-old tendencies either to ignore or to exploit them were replaced with an ardent concern for their moral welfare: parental care for children became a sacred duty; the school gradually replaced the apprenticeship system as the second most important child-raising institution; and childhood became a transitional period in which protection from, rather than indulgence in, adult activities became the rule. Out of this process grew the modern concept of childhood — a concept stressing the idea that children have value in their own right and that because of their sweetness and simplicity they require a careful preparation for the harshness and sinfulness of an adult world. Furthermore, it was only after childhood became a special status in the life cycle that the concept of a special court for juveniles began to develop. Along with the changing image of childhood, there was an increasing tendency to be less harsh with children charged with crimes.[82]

According to some scholars, some criminologists have placed undue emphasis on Ariès's thesis, which has resulted in an over-reliance on the link between the discovery of the concept of childhood and the development of a separate youth justice system to the extent that other significant influences on the development of a separate youth criminal justice system

---

[81]   Russell C. Smandych, "Accounting for Changes in Canadian Youth Justice: From the Invention to the Disappearance of Childhood" in Russell C. Smandych, ed., *Youth Justice, History, Legislation and Reform* (Toronto: Harcourt Canada Ltd., 2001), 4 at 10.

[82]   LaMar T. Empey, *American Delinquency: Its Meaning and Construction* (Illinois: The Dorsey Press, 1978), at 8. For a more recent discussion of Ariès's work, see Robert Epstein, Ph.D., *The Case Against Adolescence: Rediscovering the Adult in Every Teen* (Sanger, California: Quill Driver Books/Word Dancer Press, 2007), at 27-30.

have been ignored or underemphasized.[83] These critics tend to associate changing ideas about the treatment of children in Western society with underlying social and economic changes in the late 19th century.[84] Children in the 1800s shifted from producers to pupils, as they were increasingly excluded from the labour force.[85] "Canadian farms began to replace child labour with adult wage-labour and children increased their formal education. Children moved from economic and social parity with adults to a state of dependency. This shift was accompanied by changes in the attitudes towards their misdeeds."[86]

Despite competing theories about the origin and evolution of societal perceptions of children, by the 1800s, and certainly as the century progressed, more public attention was being paid to the most impoverished and vulnerable children and their perceived needs were increasingly the subject of public discourse. Changes aimed at improving living conditions and otherwise assisting poor, neglected and delinquent children formed part of a growing reform movement. The push for a separate criminal justice system for youth in Canada was part of this larger social welfare reform agenda.

V. THE REFORM IMPULSE AND THE ESTABLISHMENT OF A YOUTH CRIMINAL JUSTICE SYSTEM IN CANADA

Canadian historians credit the ideas of the 18th century's Age of Enlightenment for inspiring a widespread penal reform movement that would eventually prompt child advocates to press for a separate youth criminal justice system in Canada.

In England and in continental Europe, in the 1700s and on into the next century, the intelligentsia challenged conventional thinking regarding many facets of life, including the harsh treatment and punishment of

---

[83] Russell C. Smandych, "Accounting for Changes in Canadian Youth Justice: From the Invention to the Disappearance of Childhood" in Russell C. Smandych, ed., *Youth Justice, History, Legislation and Reform* (Toronto: Harcourt Canada Ltd., 2001), at 10.

[84] Russell C. Smandych, "Accounting for Changes in Canadian Youth Justice: From the Invention to the Disappearance of Childhood" in Russell C. Smandych, ed., *Youth Justice, History, Legislation and Reform* (Toronto: Harcourt Canada Ltd., 2001), at 17.

[85] Russell C. Smandych, "Accounting for Changes in Canadian Youth Justice: From the Invention to the Disappearance of Childhood" in Russell C. Smandych, ed., *Youth Justice, History, Legislation and Reform* (Toronto: Harcourt Canada Ltd., 2001), at 17-18.

[86] J. Thomas Dalby, "Criminal Liability in Children" (1985) 27 Can. J. Crim. 137, at 138.

criminals.[87] "The natural was substituted for the supernatural, science challenged theology, natural law replaced divine law, human reason was exalted, a belief in progress and the ultimate perfectibility of the human race was posited, and a concept of individual rights and the advantages of humanitarianism were put forward."[88] The writers, philosophers, politicians and penal reformers within this group over this extended period included Cesare Beccaria of Italy, as well as Jeremy Bentham, Elizabeth Fry, Samuel Romilly, John Howard, Mary Wollstonecraft, and William Wilberforce in Great Britain, Jean Jacques Rousseau of Switzerland, and François-Marie Arouet de Voltaire and Montesquieu in France. While they were not an intellectually homogenous group, they tended to be progressive thinkers who sought change, and were passionate about their vision of justice, equality, fairness and humanity, and the belief that society could be improved. They fought ardently for greater humanity, for equality, for social justice reform. They engaged in political activism on many fronts: some pushed for the abolition of slavery, others pressed for widespread education while others devoted their considerable passion and energy to advocating for penal reform.[89] "The repressive laws and severe punishments that characterized the judicial system in all countries were not compatible with the humanitarian view of mankind.... Liberals who believed in individual worth and dignity recoiled at the sight of human beings being whipped, mutilated, or hung for minor transgressions. They called for a system that would help, improve, and reform rather than simply punish."[90]

Despite varying strains of philosophic thought within the larger penal reform movement (some reformers were inspired by religious or humanitarian convictions and drew on the work of John Howard and Beccaria while others were drawn to Benthamite philosophy),[91] they were generally united in seeking the causes of crime in environmental factors, in emphasizing reform of the individual offender, and in urging leniency in the treatment of offenders.[92] As Canadian historian D.O. Carrigan has observed, the Age of Enlightenment spawned a penal reform movement

---

[87]   D. Owen Carrigan, *Crime and Punishment in Canada* (Toronto: McClelland and Stewart, 1991), at 317-23.

[88]   D. Owen Carrigan, *Crime and Punishment in Canada* (Toronto: McClelland and Stewart, 1991), at 317-18.

[89]   D. Owen Carrigan, *Crime and Punishment in Canada* (Toronto: McClelland and Stewart, 1991), at 318.

[90]   D. Owen Carrigan, *Crime and Punishment in Canada* (Toronto: McClelland and Stewart, 1991), at 318-19.

[91]   J. Jerald Bellomo, "Upper Canadian Attitudes Towards Crime and Punishment (1832-1851)" (1972) 64 Ontario History 11, at 21.

[92]   J. Jerald Bellomo, "Upper Canadian Attitudes Towards Crime and Punishment (1832-1851)" (1972) 64 Ontario History 11, at 22.

that would inspire profound and fundamental change in the treatment of criminals in the Western world.[93]

The writing of Italian law professor and economist Cesare Beccaria was particularly influential. His 1764 essay on criminal law, *Of Crimes and Punishments*,[94] was immediately acclaimed by the international community and eventually translated into at least 20 languages. It was highly influential in Europe, Asia and the United States regarding individual rights generally, but particularly germane to the penal reform movement of the 1800s. In his text, Beccaria denounced torture and capital punishment, advocated for more humane treatment in prisons and punishment proportionate to the crime, and recommended that more focus be placed on crime prevention than on punishment. Beccaria saw education as the surest way to prevent crime.[95]

Beccaria's work had a major impact on penal reform and has been described as one of the "first systemic and concise expressions of a blueprint for reform".[96] In fact, fundamental criminal law concepts such as proportionality in sentencing, which Beccaria outlined in his 1764 essay, remain key principles of criminal law in the Western legal tradition today.

Other reformers of the era, such as Bentham, Fry, Romilly and Howard, used their unique talents to push for penal reform in their chosen professional venues: Bentham through his writing, Romilly by entering Parliament where, in the early 1800s, he was able to get several bills passed to reduce penalties for minor crimes, and Howard and Fry by writing about and/or otherwise advocating for improvements to the abysmal prison conditions in Britain.[97]

In a book published in 1777, Howard drew attention to the particular plight of child prisoners. In his book, which was the first detailed examination of prison conditions in England, he lambasted the state for lumping together in "seminaries" of crime, males and females of all ages and experience:

[93]   D. Owen Carrigan, *Crime and Punishment in Canada* (Toronto: McClelland and Stewart, 1991), at 318.

[94]   The original Italian title is *Dei delitti e delle pene*. This English translation is by Jane Grigson, reprinted by arrangements with Oxford University Press, 1964.

[95]   Cesare Beccaria, *Of Crimes and Punishments*. English translation by Jane Grigson, reprinted by arrangements with Oxford University Press, 1964, 112-18.

[96]   D. Owen Carrigan, *Crime and Punishment in Canada* (Toronto: McClelland and Stewart, 1991), at 319.

[97]   D. Owen Carrigan, *Crime and Punishment in Canada* (Toronto: McClelland and Stewart, 1991), at 320-21. Among women advocates, Elizabeth Fry fought hard to improve conditions for female prisoners, and established an association to that end in 1817.

In some Gaols you see (and who can see it without pain?) boys of twelve or fourteen eagerly listening to the stories told by practised and experienced criminals, of their adventures, successes, stratagems, and escapes.... Multitudes of young creatures, committed for some trifling offence, are totally ruined there ... if it were the wish and aim of Magistrates to effect the destruction present and future of young delinquents, they could not devise a more effectual method, than to confine them so long in our prisons, those seats and seminaries (as they have been very properly called) of idleness and every vice.[98]

A century later, the dreadful circumstances of child prisoners remained the subject of public condemnation. Irish writer Oscar Wilde wrote in the London daily press of children housed in various prisons who subsisted largely on bread and water and were confined to cells for 23 hours out of every 24.[99] Indeed, the general living and working conditions of destitute and orphaned children in Britain, as well as the experience of children in British prisons during the 1800s, were documented, discussed, and reported in the British press, in the country's literature[100] and in other British documents and materials with growing frequency, thus fuelling the ire of a nation that was becoming increasingly humane in its thinking as to how young delinquents should be treated while incarcerated. Some of the punishments documented included an 11-year-old (who had not even been convicted) receiving two hours in a dark cell for trying to communicate with another person while a 14-year-old unconvicted child received nine hours in a dark cell on bread and water for talking in chapel.[101]

By the 1820s and 1830s, the underlying humanitarianism of the British and European penal reform movements was having a significant influence in North America. Among the first and most visible signs on this side of the Atlantic was a reduction in the severity of punishments. "Floggings, mutilations, and branding were being replaced with fines,

---

[98]   John Howard, "The State of the Prisons in England and Wales (Warrington 1777)", at 15-16, 21 (editor's lib.), as cited in Wiley B. Sanders, ed., *Juvenile Offenders for a Thousand Years, Selected Readings from Anglo-Saxon Times to 1900* (Chapel Hill: University of North Carolina Press, 1970), at 63. Prison conditions in Britain in the later 1700s are also described well in Thomas Keneally, *A Commonwealth of Thieves: The Improbable Birth of Australia* (New York: Anchor Books, 2007), at 10-11.

[99]   Oscar Wilde, "The Case of Warder Martin: Some Cruelties of Prison Life", Letter to the Editor, *Daily Chronicle* (May 28, 1897) (Brit. Mus.) as cited in Wiley B. Sanders, ed., *Juvenile Offenders for a Thousand Years, Selected Readings from Anglo-Saxon Times to 1900* (Chapel Hill: University of North Carolina Press, 1970), at 311-13.

[100]   No fiction writer detailed the plight and poverty of children in industrial England in the 1800s more consistently, or wrote with greater understanding about what it meant to be an impoverished child of that period, than Charles Dickens. See, for example, *Oliver Twist*, *David Copperfield*, and *Little Dorrit*.

[101]   *Tenth Report of the Inspectors of Prisons for the Home District*, as cited in Wiley B. Sanders, ed., *Juvenile Offenders for a Thousand Years, Selected Readings from Anglo-Saxon Times to 1900* (Chapel Hill: University of North Carolina Press, 1970), at 177-79.

incarceration, and hard labour."[102] In 1832 the death penalty was abolished for cattle stealing and larceny. By 1841, only murder, rape and treason carried the death penalty in Upper Canada. Punishments, such as pillory and banishment, also fell by the wayside in the 1840s.[103]

A. Lone Voices

In pre-Confederation Canada of the 1830s and 1840s, the mantra among penal reformers was reformation of the criminal.[104] Among the most prominent advocates in Upper Canada were Dr. Charles Duncombe, a physician and politician, and Scottish-born journalist turned politician George Brown, founder and editor of the *Toronto Globe*, which is now *The Globe and Mail*. They preached moral, spiritual and intellectual reformation of the criminal as the only solution to the perceived crime problems in colonial Canada. Initially, the public was not receptive to their sermons.

The 19th century generally was a period of industrialization, urbanization and rapid population growth. Law and order were among the most pressing social issues in Upper Canada at the time. Violent crime, which was being attributed to the influx of criminal elements from outside the country, was of considerable concern.[105] The arrival of destitute and landless immigrants, including many orphaned children, in part as a result of Irish immigrants fleeing the Potato Famine, had raised fears that they would be the source of increasing crime.[106] Since adult immigrants did not always survive the voyage across the Atlantic, or died of sickness shortly after arrival, a significant number of children arrived as orphans, or were orphaned soon afterward,[107] which exacerbated concerns about juvenile crime. (Children were also among the boatloads of convicts who were shipped from Britain to the colonies throughout the 17th and 18th

---

[102] D. Owen Carrigan, *Crime and Punishment in Canada* (Toronto: McClelland and Stewart, 1991), at 322. As Cory and Iacobucci JJ. observe in *R. v. Gladue*, [1999] S.C.J. No. 19, [1999] 1 S.C.R. 688, at para. 53 (S.C.C.), penitentiaries were originally conceived as alternatives to the harsher sanctions of death, flogging or imprisonment in local jails. Penitentiary imprisonment was initially considered to contain a strong rehabilitative component with long hours spent in contemplation and hard work.

[103] D. Owen Carrigan, *Crime and Punishment in Canada* (Toronto: McClelland and Stewart, 1991), at 322-23.

[104] J. Jerald Bellomo, "Upper Canadian Attitudes Towards Crime and Punishment (1832-1851)" (1972) 64 Ontario History 11, at 23.

[105] J. Jerald Bellomo, "Upper Canadian Attitudes Towards Crime and Punishment (1832-1851)" (1972) 64 Ontario History 11, at 11.

[106] Sanjeev Anand, "Catalyst for Change: The History of Canadian Juvenile Justice Reform" (Spring 1999) Vol. 24, No. 2, Queen's L.J. 515, at 522.

[107] D. Owen Carrigan, *Juvenile Delinquency in Canada: A History* (Toronto: Irwin Publishing, 1998), at 3.

centuries; sometimes they had committed only petty crimes such as theft[108] or were simply poor vagrants or escaping from houses of correction.)[109]

For a multitude of reasons, poor, orphaned, neglected or abandoned children were sometimes on the streets and living in situations that put them at risk of joining the ranks of youthful criminals. They were cause for growing concern.

Duncombe was one of the first Canadian reformers to suggest that the roots of juvenile delinquency were to be found in social and environmental factors and that it was up to society to identify solutions.[110] He rejected the thinking of classical criminologists, who saw crime as a deliberate choice by a rational decision-maker and focused instead on the circumstances in which young persons found themselves for the answers to their criminality. Elected to the legislature of Upper Canada in 1834, Duncombe chaired a commission established to report on prisons and penitentiaries. In his 1835 Report on Prisons, he outlined his views on penal reform and advocated rehabilitation rather than vengeance as the principle sentencing objective.[111] Prisons and punishment should be aimed at reforming the criminal as well as achieving general and specific deterrence, he said.[112]

Duncombe's report reflected the humanitarian approach to reform that was sweeping across the U.S. and Canada, where treatment was to be just and consistent, and as lenient as possible.[113] He advocated radical change in the treatment of youthful offenders, many of whom he believed had ended up on the streets as a result of, poverty and neglect.[114] Duncombe encouraged the separation of youthful offenders from older and more seasoned criminals, an idea that would gain momentum in the ensuing decades.

---

[108] The plight of two adolescent convicts who ended up being transported from Britain to the colonies is detailed in Thomas Keneally, *A Commonwealth of Thieves: The Improbable Birth of Australia* (New York: Anchor Books, 2007), at 22-29.

[109] There is an interesting discussion of the transportation phenomenon in Thomas Keneally, *A Commonwealth of Thieves: The Improbable Birth of Australia* (New York: Anchor Books, 2007), at 5-6. Prison conditions in Britain were so notoriously horrible at the time that some convicts and vagrants may have preferred transportation to the colonies as welcome relief from the squalor. Transportation was considered an alternative to the death penalty in some cases.

[110] D. Owen Carrigan, *Juvenile Delinquency in Canada: A History* (Toronto: Irwin Publishing, 1998), at 41.

[111] J. Jerald Bellomo, "Upper Canadian Attitudes Towards Crime and Punishment (1832-1851)" (1972) 64 Ontario History 11, at 19-20.

[112] J. Jerald Bellomo, "Upper Canadian Attitudes Towards Crime and Punishment (1832-1851)" (1972) 64 Ontario History 11, at 20.

[113] J. Jerald Bellomo, "Upper Canadian Attitudes Towards Crime and Punishment (1832-1851)" (1972) 64 Ontario History 11, at 20.

[114] D. Owen Carrigan, *Juvenile Delinquency in Canada: A History* (Toronto: Irwin Publishing, 1998), at 40.

Among the greatest impediments to the reform of young persons, Duncombe argued, was the indiscriminate housing together of people of all ages so that the prisons had become "schools and colleges of crime".[115] Youthful offenders should not be treated like adult criminals. Their rehabilitation would not be found in jails, he said, but in the creation of reformatories for youthful offenders, where they "would be protected from both the degrading influences of parental dissipation and the demoralizing influences of experienced criminals while at the same time being instructed in more respectable values under the paternal care of the government".[116]

Duncombe's ideas gained widespread acceptance in the 1840s.[117] Canadian leaders had been paying attention to the more robust penal reform movements in Britain and the U.S. In 1839, British researchers concluded that adult criminality was rooted in youthful delinquency. This research was coupled with a longstanding concern in Britain that housing youthful offenders with adult prisoners created an atmosphere of moral contagion.[118] The U.S. was moving in the same philosophical direction. Both countries were taking steps to establish separate facilities for youthful offenders to spare them from the corrupting influence of adult offenders.[119]

Inspired by the reform movements abroad, Brown of the *Globe* led the crusade for change to the penal system in Upper Canada. Brown would later become a Reform party politician of note and a Father of Confederation, but in the 1840s, he was preoccupied with penal reform and the abolition of slavery.

The Canadian penal reform movement of the 1840s focused on prison conditions generally but some advocates targeted the plight of young prisoners. Persistent and increasing calls for prison reform soon led to the establishment of a commission of investigation in 1848. Brown, as *Globe* publisher, spearheaded the Royal Commission on the Penitentiary.

In the second volume of the report, Brown set out his penological philosophy. The chief aim of prisons, he said, was the moral reform of the convict, which could best be achieved through moral, religious and secular instruction. Brown relied on statistics to support his argument that

---

[115] As cited in J. Jerald Bellomo, "Upper Canadian Attitudes Towards Crime and Punishment (1832-1851)" (1972) 64 Ontario History 11, at 20.

[116] J. Jerald Bellomo, "Upper Canadian Attitudes Towards Crime and Punishment (1832-1851)" (1972) 64 Ontario History 11, at 21.

[117] J. Jerald Bellomo, "Upper Canadian Attitudes Towards Crime and Punishment (1832-1851)" (1972) 64 Ontario History 11, at 21.

[118] Sanjeev Anand, "Catalyst for Change: The History of Canadian Juvenile Justice Reform" (Spring 1999) Vol. 24, No. 2, Queen's L.J. 515, at 522-23.

[119] Sanjeev Anand, "Catalyst for Change: The History of Canadian Juvenile Justice Reform" (Spring 1999) Vol. 24, No. 2, Queen's L.J. 515, at 522-24.

many criminals were victims of circumstance. Like Duncombe, Brown believed punishments should be few and mild. Discipline should be maintained largely through moral suasion.[120]

In the report, Brown exposed the extreme abuse and cruelty at Kingston Penitentiary as part of a wider examination of conditions inside Upper Canada's prisons and penitentiary. It was Brown who publicized the case of the 10-year-old boy who was whipped 57 times over an eight-month period for staring and laughing, and the case of the 11-year-old French Canadian boy who was given 12 lashes on Christmas Eve for speaking French.[121] As Duncombe had a decade earlier, the Commission criticized the practice of housing youthful offenders with adults at Kingston Penitentiary:

> It is distressing to think that no distinction is now made between the child who has strayed for the first time from the path of honesty, or who perhaps has never been taught the meaning of sin, and the hardened offender of mature years. All are consigned together to the unutterable contamination of the common gaol; and by the lessons there learnt, soon become inmates of the Penitentiary (Brown Commission 1849:73).[122]

The commissioners concluded that reform of the young offender was the unquestionable goal. "There is no department so satisfactory, so encouraging, as the rescue and reformation of the young; and there it is the battle should be fought with utmost warmth."[123] Harsh treatment of juvenile offenders was not the answer. The commissioners recommended the immediate establishment of Houses of Refuge.

The Brown report was a defining moment, a turning point in Canadian penal history. Graphic and public accounts of young children imprisoned in Kingston Penitentiary, alongside adult career criminals, compelled Upper Canadians to consider how youthful offenders should be treated, what course of action would best achieve their rehabilitation, and whether they deserved greater care and consideration by virtue of their age.

---

[120] J. Jerald Bellomo, "Upper Canadian Attitudes Towards Crime and Punishment (1832-1851)" (1972) 64 Ontario History 11, at 23.

[121] D. Owen Carrigan, *Juvenile Delinquency in Canada: A History* (Toronto: Irwin Publishing, 1998), at 39. See also "First Report of the Commissioners Appointed to Investigate into the Conduct, Discipline, and Management of the Provincial Pen" Journal of the Legislative Assembly, 12 Victoria 1849. Appendix B.B.B.B.B., 10, 190, 192.

[122] As cited in Bryan Hogeveen, "'Winning Deviant Youth Over by Friendly Helpfulness': Transformations in the Legal Governance of Deviant Children in Canada, 1857-1908" in Russell Smandych, ed., *Youth Justice: History, Legislation, and Reform* (Toronto: Harcourt Canada, 2001), at 49.

[123] D. Owen Carrigan, *Juvenile Delinquency in Canada: A History* (Toronto: Irwin Publishing, 1998), at 42. See also the *Second Report of the Commissioners Appointed to Inquire into the Condition and Management of the Provincial Penitentiary in Journal of the Legislative Assembly* (1849) App. B.B.B.B.B. at 71.

The findings of the Brown report initiated a new way of thinking about the detention and incarceration of deviant young persons that would soon broaden to a reconsideration of their legal governance generally. Contemporary scholars characterize the report as the key and final impetus toward establishing separate correctional institutions for juvenile offenders in Canada.[124] But the report's significance extended far beyond that. By acknowledging the value and importance of separating young persons from adults within the criminal justice system, the Brown report foreshadowed the development of a formal and separate youth criminal justice system in Canada.

Using Brown's work as crucial ammunition, prison reformers, including prison inspectors and religious officials, lobbied for youth facilities modelled on the reformatories that were envisioned or had already opened in the United States and Europe, which they argued would have a constructive influence on youths.[125] Britain passed legislation in 1854 establishing separate reformatory schools for juvenile offenders.[126]

In 1857, the government in Canada followed suit by enacting *An Act for establishing Prisons for Young Offenders — for the better government of Public Asylums, Hospitals and Prisons, and for the better construction of Common Gaols.*[127] This Act enabled the building of reformatories in Upper and Lower Canada. It also permitted courts to sentence any person 21 years or younger to a reformatory on certain conditions, and to remove anyone who appeared to be under 21 from the penitentiary and to place him or her in a reformatory for the rest of the sentence.

The Canadian reformatories for young persons did not meet expectations. There were various problems: The age range of the institutions meant that 10-year-olds and 20-year-olds were being housed together, thus, younger children were still subject to the negative influences of older teenagers and young adults. There were also allegations of sexual misconduct among the staff, education was lacking, and punishment remained severe — including bread and water and lashes with the birch.[128] In essence,

---

[124] Sanjeev Anand, "Catalyst for Change: The History of Canadian Juvenile Justice Reform" (Spring 1999) Vol. 24, No. 2, Queen's L.J. 515, at 524.

[125] Bryan Hogeveen, "History, Development, and Transformations in Canadian Juvenile Justice, 1800-1984" in Kathryn Campbell, ed., *Understanding Youth Justice in Canada* (Toronto: Pearson Education Canada Inc., 2005), 24 at 27.

[126] *An Act for the better Care and Reformation of Youthful Offenders in Great Britain, 1854* (U.K.), 17 & 18 Vict., c. 86, as cited in Sanjeev Anand, "Catalyst for Change: The History of Canadian Juvenile Justice Reform" (Spring 1999) Vol. 24, No. 2, Queen's L.J. 515, at 523.

[127] 1857 (3d Sess., 5th Parl.), c. 28.

[128] Sanjeev Anand, "Catalyst for Change: The History of Canadian Juvenile Justice Reform" (Spring 1999) Vol. 24, No. 2, Queen's L.J. 515, at 527.

the reformatories failed to emphasize education or, curiously, reform, and remained largely institutions of work and punishment rather than rehabilitation.[129] Later inquiries into the nature of prisons and reformatories concluded that, for all intents and purposes, reformatories were not a whole lot different from prisons.[130] What was needed, said the critics, were industrial schools — places of refuge under the care of matrons and guards who would act as quasi-parents.[131]

These industrial schools were to be stricter than public schools, but less severe than reformatories,[132] and would accept not only youths who had been convicted of crimes but those who were at high risk of engaging in criminal behaviour,[133] such as poor and neglected children.[134] By expanding the profile of youths who could be housed in industrial schools, more attention was paid to their backgrounds and circumstances. These wards began to be seen as victims who needed love, guidance and support.[135] The focus of penal reform shifted from punishment to child rescue.

It wasn't long before the industrial schools, too, came under scrutiny. By the late 1880s, the quandary of how best to assist poor, neglected and delinquent youth remained very much a live issue. Research was revealing a significant correlation between child and adult illiteracy, and criminality,[136] yet industrial schools were being criticized for failing to focus adequately on formal education. Concerns were no doubt exacerbated by the arrival of increasing numbers of orphaned or otherwise bereft children from England, an influx that began in the latter part of the 19th century. Between 80,000 and 100,000 children were shipped to homes in Canada; some were orphans, but all were destitute. They came in part from the streets of London and were sent to temporary homes here before being distributed out as farm workers, where they worked for their room and board and some-

---

[129] D. Owen Carrigan, *Juvenile Delinquency in Canada: A History* (Toronto: Irwin Publishing, 1998), at 45.

[130] Sanjeev Anand, "Catalyst for Change: The History of Canadian Juvenile Justice Reform" (Spring 1999), Vol. 24, No. 2, Queen's L.J. 515, at 528.

[131] Sanjeev Anand, "Catalyst for Change: The History of Canadian Juvenile Justice Reform" (Spring 1999), Vol. 24, No. 2, Queen's L.J. 515, at 528.

[132] Jeffrey S. Leon, "The Development of Canadian Juvenile Justice: A Background for Reform" (1977) Osgoode Hall L.J. Vol. 15, No. 1, 71 at 80.

[133] D. Owen Carrigan, *Juvenile Delinquency in Canada: A History* (Toronto: Irwin Publishing, 1998), at 48.

[134] D. Owen Carrigan, *Juvenile Delinquency in Canada: A History* (Toronto: Irwin Publishing, 1998), at 51.

[135] D. Owen Carrigan, *Juvenile Delinquency in Canada: A History* (Toronto: Irwin Publishing, 1998), at 50.

[136] D. Owen Carrigan, *Juvenile Delinquency in Canada: A History* (Toronto: Irwin Publishing, 1998), at 49.

times small wages. Some thrived. Others suffered terrible abuse and neglect.[137] Many ended up on the streets, where they fell into crime.

Social reformers continued to press for effective solutions to juvenile crime. A group of influential citizens who called themselves the Prisoners' Aid Association were among those pushing for significant change. The PAA firmly believed that housing youths with adults had a corrupting influence on the youth, and that reformatories and industrial schools should be places of true reform. The PAA called for special courts for young persons and restrictions on detention for young persons under 14.[138] In 1889, the PAA lobbied the Ontario government to appoint a commission to investigate the causes of crime, particularly among juveniles. Premier Oliver Mowat appointed J.W. Langmuir, the province's former Inspector of Prisons, Asylums and Public Charities, to head the commission. After a six-month investigation, the commission published its report.[139]

The 1891 Report of the Commissioners Appointed to Enquire into the Prison and Reformatory System of Ontario, promoted industrial schools over reformatories, effectively precipitating the closing of reformatories and the expansion of the industrial schools.[140] But it was the report's other recommendations that were most influential in terms of youth criminal justice. Several of the report's recommendations established the skeletal framework for the *Juvenile Delinquents Act* of 1908. The report recommended, among other things, the separate trial and detention of all children, special courts for children, greater use of suspended sentences, and perhaps most significantly, the development of a probation system.[141]

These recommendations corresponded with a significant shift in criminological discourse regarding the causes of delinquency. Until the 1880s, the criminal law relating to the treatment of both juvenile and adult offenders had been based on the classical school of criminology. Crime was understood as a deliberate choice of a rational individual who

---

[137]   *The Ottawa Citizen* (11 August 2006), at F1 and F8.

[138]   D. Owen Carrigan, *Juvenile Delinquency in Canada: A History* (Toronto: Irwin Publishing, 1998), at 62.

[139]   John Bullen, "J.J. Kelso and the 'New' Child-savers: The Genesis of the Children's Aid Movement in Ontario" in Russell Smandych, Gordon Dodds and Alvin Esau, eds., *Dimensions of Childhood: Essays on the History of Children and Youth in Canada* (Winnipeg: Legal Research Institute of the University of Manitoba, 1991), 135 at 140.

[140]   Sanjeev Anand, "Catalyst for Change: The History of Canadian Juvenile Justice Reform" (Spring 1999) Vol. 24, No. 2, Queen's L.J. 515, at 528-29.

[141]   Sanjeev Anand, "Catalyst for Change: The History of Canadian Juvenile Justice Reform" (Spring 1999) Vol. 24, No. 2, Queen's L.J. 515, at 528-29. See also D. Owen Carrigan, *Juvenile Delinquency in Canada: A History* (Toronto: Irwin Publishing, 1998), at 62-63.

conducted a cost-benefit analysis.[142] In the 1880s, however, positivism became a prominent theory in mainstream criminology.[143] Positivists rejected the classicist explanation that crime was the result of a deliberate choice by a responsible offender, and argued instead that one had to look to external forces over which the offender had no control for the real cause of deviance.[144]

B.   The Final Push to the *Juvenile Delinquents Act*

The Child Savers movement arose simultaneously with the advent of positivism,[145] in the last quarter of the 19th century in the U.S., Britain and Canada, when juvenile crime and vagrancy were perceived to be increasing, and there was continual and growing concern about the harsh treatment of children in jails and prisons.[146] Child Savers adopted the thinking of the positivists, who saw crime and delinquency as a disease. Juvenile offenders were not criminals, but rather sick children in need of care and guidance either because of the evil influence of society or parental neglect.[147]

> ... a system which provided the proper treatment for deviants at a young age would "cure" delinquents and, at the same time, serve to protect society. Accordingly, it became popular to state that juvenile offenders should never, as a report at the time cautioned, "be treated or spoken of as criminals, but should be studied and dealt with in exactly the same way that a sick or defective child is handled.... If the children were wayward, argued the reformers, it was as a result of the evil influence of society or the neglect of parents.... In the opinion of the reformers, then, there was little distinction between the neglected and delinquent child as

---

[142] Sanjeev Anand, "Catalyst for Change: The History of Canadian Juvenile Justice Reform" (Spring 1999) Vol. 24, No. 2, Queen's L.J. 515, at 529-30.

[143] Sanjeev Anand, "Catalyst for Change: The History of Canadian Juvenile Justice Reform" (Spring 1999) Vol. 24, No. 2, Queen's L.J. 515, at 529.

[144] Sanjeev Anand, "Catalyst for Change: The History of Canadian Juvenile Justice Reform" (Spring 1999) Vol. 24, No. 2, Queen's L.J. 515. See also J. Bolton *et al.*, "The *Young Offenders Act*: Principles and Policy — The First Decade in Review" (1993) 38 McGill L.J. 939, at 945-46.

[145] Sanjeev Anand, "Catalyst for Change: The History of Canadian Juvenile Justice Reform" (Spring 1999) Vol. 24, No. 2, Queen's L.J. 515, at 530.

[146] Sanjeev Anand, "Catalyst for Change: The History of Canadian Juvenile Justice Reform" (Spring 1999) Vol. 24, No. 2, Queen's L.J. 515, at 530. See also a discussion of the Canadian Child Savers' Movement in D. Owen Carrigan, *Juvenile Delinquency in Canada: A History* (Toronto: Irwin Publishing, 1998), at 63-70, in Jeffrey S. Leon, "The Development of Canadian Juvenile Justice: A Background for Reform" (1977) Osgoode Hall L.J. Vol. 15, No. 1, 71 at 81, and in J. Bolton *et al.*, "The *Young Offenders Act*: Principles and Policy — The First Decade in Review" (1993) 38 McGill L.J. 939, at 944-945.

[147] Sanjeev Anand, "Catalyst for Change: The History of Canadian Juvenile Justice Reform" (Spring 1999) Vol. 24, No. 2, Queen's L.J. 515, at 530. But see also J. Bolton *et al.*, "The *Young Offenders Act*: Principles and Policy — The First Decade in Review" (1993) 38 McGill L.J. 939, at 946.

this distinction related only to whether the child was potentially or actually criminal.... Ultimately, positivist principles proved highly influential in the drafting of the JDA. The combination of concerns about the welfare of children and the need for treatment formed the cornerstone for the philosophy of the legislation.[148]

The Child Savers were motivated by the visible cadre of poor and neglected children on the streets: "What the reformers wanted was a more adequate social and legal system for 'the protection and reclaiming of destitute youths, exposed either by death or neglect of their parents to evil influences and the acquisition of evil habits, which in too many cases, lead to the commission of crime'."[149] These late 19th century reformers were arguably progressive thinkers for their time, whose prime aim was to change the behaviour of young persons by providing adequate guidance and support.

Some contemporary criminologists and youth justice experts would no doubt suggest that these 19th century reformers had it right, at least to some degree, by focusing on treatment and support for young persons, and that the seminal question judges and other criminal justice players should routinely pose today when dealing with young persons who come into conflict with the criminal law is this: What criminal justice system response, or series of responses, is most likely to change the behaviour of this young person? What response is most likely to prevent this young person from committing further crimes?[150]

Despite a broad measure of common purpose, the Child Savers movement was beset with conflict. While some supported industrial schools and reformatories, others considered these institutions overly punitive, and favoured an approach that focused on keeping youths out of jails, reformatories and the like.

A young, passionate and crusading Toronto newspaper reporter, J.J. Kelso, was among the most outspoken and dedicated proponents of de-institutionalization for young people. As a journalist, Kelso observed

---

[148] J. Bolton *et al.*, "The *Young Offenders Act*: Principles and Policy — The First Decade in Review" (1993) 38 McGill L.J. 939, at 946.

[149] J. Bolton *et al.*, "The Young Offenders Act: Principles and Policy — The First Decade in Review" (1993) 38 McGill L.J. 939, at 945.

[150] The approach of the therapeutic and problem-solving courts, which seek to address the underlying issues that may be driving, or contributing to, criminal behaviour, is not unlike the underlying philosophy of the Child Savers, whose work was premised on the question: What does this young person need? Nevertheless, the Child Savers were not without their critics. See for example Sanjeev Anand, "Catalyst for Change: The History of Canadian Juvenile Justice Reform" (Spring 1999) Vol. 24, No. 2, Queen's L.J. 515, at 537-38, where it is suggested that elements of the developing youth criminal justice regime preserved and enhanced economic opportunities for the middle and upper classes.

first-hand the plight of poor and neglected children — on the streets of Toronto, at the police stations, and in the courtrooms.[151] And there were many of them. The nearly 100,000 orphans, paupers and delinquent children who came from Britain in the late 1800s and early 20th century swelled the ranks of young persons at risk.[152] Kelso used his pen to document their needs, which, in his view, often included safe refuge from the abuse and neglect they were experiencing in their own homes. While earlier Child Savers had addressed the needs of orphans and deserted children by arranging guardianships and apprenticeships, and later, orphans' homes, Kelso pressed for foster homes.[153] He favoured keeping all but the most serious offenders out of institutions and encouraged the extension of probation and greater supervision in the home environment.[154]

The Canadian Child Savers movement had gained momentum after the release of the 1891 report. Reformers drew satisfaction from the fact that Canada's first *Criminal Code* of 1892 contained s. 9, which said that no one under seven years old could be convicted of an offence. Section 10 incorporated the *doli incapax* defence. But Kelso knew that far more changes were required. Kelso and Langmuir, who had chaired the 1891 commission, were determined to get the federal government to implement the report's reforms. On the top of their list was a provision providing for the separate trials of young persons.[155] After some targeted lobbying of federal Justice Minister Sir John Thompson, Kelso and his disciples persuaded Thompson to pass legislation so that the *Criminal Code* also provided that, where expedient and practicable, trials of persons under 16 be held separate and apart from those of adult offenders, and without publicity.[156] The problem was, judges virtually *never* found it expedient and practicable to grant separate trials, so Kelso pressed for legislation

---

[151] John Bullen, "J.J. Kelso and the 'New' Child-savers: The Genesis of the Children's Aid Movement in Ontario" in Russell Smandych, Gordon Dodds and Alvin Esau, eds., *Dimensions of Childhood: Essays on the History of Children and Youth in Canada* (Winnipeg: Legal Research Institute of the University of Manitoba, 1991), 135 at 138.

[152] D. Owen Carrigan, *Juvenile Delinquency in Canada: A History* (Toronto: Irwin Publishing, 1998), at 82.

[153] John Bullen, "J.J. Kelso and the 'New' Child-savers: The Genesis of the Children's Aid Movement in Ontario" in Russell Smandych, Gordon Dodds and Alvin Esau, eds., *Dimensions of Childhood: Essays on the History of Children and Youth in Canada* (Winnipeg: Legal Research Institute of the University of Manitoba, 1991), 135 at 135-36.

[154] Jeffrey S. Leon, "The Development of Canadian Juvenile Justice: A Background for Reform" (1977) Osgoode Hall L.J. Vol. 15, No. 1, 71 at 81.

[155] Sanjeev Anand, "Catalyst for Change: The History of Canadian Juvenile Justice Reform" (Spring 1999) Vol. 24, No. 2, Queen's L.J. 515, at 530.

[156] D. Owen Carrigan, *Juvenile Delinquency in Canada: A History* (Toronto: Irwin Publishing, 1998), at 67. Sanjeev Anand, "Catalyst for Change: The History of Canadian Juvenile Justice Reform" (Spring 1999) Vol. 24, No. 2, Queen's L.J. 515, at 531.

that would make it compulsory for juveniles to be tried separately and without publicity.[157]

In 1894, Parliament responded by passing *An Act Respecting Arrest, Trial, and Imprisonment of Youthful Offenders*, which achieved Kelso's goal of providing for *in camera* and mandatory separate trials for young persons under 16. The 1894 Act also provided for the separation of youthful offenders from older offenders and habitual criminals during arrest and trial, and for their placement in places other than jails, where they could be reformed and trained. As a general principle, young persons were to be kept in custody separate and apart from older persons facing criminal charges or under sentence, and were not to be housed at police stations or lock-ups with older persons charged with crimes or with ordinary criminals.[158] In essence, the 1894 Act enshrined in statute the principle that young persons were to be dealt with separate and apart from older offenders during the trial process, and were also to be housed separate and apart from older and habitual prisoners while in custody, thereby prescribing in legislation the general and fundamental principle of a separate youth criminal justice system, which is expressly provided for today in various sections of the *Youth Criminal Justice Act* and which has now been affirmed by the Supreme Court of Canada.[159] Reformers not only feared the moral contagion of adult criminals and their negative impact on youthful rehabilitation, but they believed that youth were more amenable to reform than adults.[160]

> The 1894 act encompassed many of the changes that reformers had sought since at least the early part of the century. Children would now be kept away from the contaminating influence of adult criminals, afforded more privacy, and processed separately by the courts. The essence of the legislation was that delinquents would be treated not as criminals in need of punishment but as young people requiring help and understanding.[161]

---

[157] Jeffrey S. Leon, "The Development of Canadian Juvenile Justice: A Background for Reform" (1977) Osgoode Hall L.J. Vol. 15, No. 1, 71 at 88. See also D. Owen Carrigan, *Juvenile Delinquency in Canada: A History* (Toronto: Irwin Publishing, 1998), at 66-67.

[158] D. Owen Carrigan, *Juvenile Delinquency in Canada: A History* (Toronto: Irwin Publishing, 1998), at 66-67.

[159] See, for example, s. 3(1)(b) and s. 84 of the *Youth Criminal Justice Act*. See also *R. v. S.J.L.*, [2009] S.C.J. No. 14, 2009 SCC 14 (S.C.C.), where Deschamps J. held for the majority (in fact, the court was unanimous on this point) that a criminal justice system for young persons separate from the adult system is a governing principle of the *YCJA*, based on a recognition of the presumption of diminished moral blameworthiness of young persons; thus, young persons and adults cannot be tried together.

[160] Bryan Hogeveen, "History, Development, and Transformations in Canadian Juvenile Justice, 1800-1984" in Kathryn Campbell, ed., *Understanding Youth Justice in Canada* (Toronto: Pearson Education Canada Inc., 2005), 24 at 24.

[161] D. Owen Carrigan, *Juvenile Delinquency in Canada: A History* (Toronto: Irwin Publishing, 1998), at 68.

The framework was now in place for a separate youth criminal justice system in Canada. It would be more than a decade, however, before the introduction of the *Juvenile Delinquents Act* of 1908, which was to implement the remainder of the 1891 report's recommendations, including the key concept of probation and separate courts for young persons charged with offences. It would take another strong and passionate social welfare advocate — W.L. Scott, Ottawa master of the Supreme Court of Ontario and president of the Ottawa Children's Aid Society — to bring the *JDA* to fruition.[162]

In May 1906, Scott attended a national conference in Philadelphia, a time when the new juvenile court and probation system that had been inaugurated in Chicago in 1900 was spreading to other U.S. cities. He was apparently greatly inspired by what he saw and heard. During the conference, Scott was exposed to the thinking of various youth justice advocates. Julian Mack, one of the first juvenile court judges in Chicago, said at the time that the goal of juvenile courts was "not so much to punish as to reform, not to degrade but to uplift, not to crush but to develop, to make him not a criminal but a worthy citizen".[163] During the conference, Scott, who was well versed in criminology and penology,[164] attended a seminar by a well-known court reformer Hannah Kent Schoff. Scott returned to Canada "filled with great enthusiasm",[165] having conceived the idea for the *JDA* and the attendant probation system. He committed to reform the Canadian youth justice system based on the American model. In a June 4, 1906 letter from Scott to Kelso about the conference, Scott remarked that he was particularly taken with the system of juvenile probation.[166] Probation officers were to figure prominently in the new Canadian legislation; it would be their job to delve into the child's life to ascertain the root cause of the criminality in order to share this information with the court, and to supervise the young person in the

---

[162] D. Owen Carrigan, *Juvenile Delinquency in Canada: A History* (Toronto: Irwin Publishing, 1998), at 66-67.

[163] This comment is referred to in Greg Berman and John Feinblatt, *Good Courts* (New York: The New Press, 2005), at 53.

[164] Bryan Hogeveen, "'Winning Deviant Youth Over by Friendly Helpfulness': Transformations in the Legal Governance of Deviant Children in Canada, 1857-1908" in Russell Smandych, ed., *Youth Justice: History, Legislation, and Reform* (Toronto: Harcourt Canada, 2001), 43 at 54.

[165] Bryan Hogeveen, "'Winning Deviant Youth Over by Friendly Helpfulness': Transformations in the Legal Governance of Deviant Children in Canada, 1857-1908" in Russell Smandych, ed., *Youth Justice: History, Legislation, and Reform* (Toronto: Harcourt Canada, 2001), 43 at 54.

[166] Sanjeev Anand, "Catalyst for Change: The History of Canadian Juvenile Justice Reform" (Spring 1999) Vol. 24, No. 2, Queen's L.J. 515, at 531.

community.[167] Canada was unquestionably following the lead of the United States. Probation was crucial to the new U.S. juvenile court system: Judge Richard Tuthill, Chicago's first juvenile court judge, described it this way: Probation is "the cord upon which all the pearls of the juvenile court are strung.... Without it the juvenile court would not exist".[168]

Scott drafted the preliminary version of the *Juvenile Delinquents Act* of 1908 based on Acts in Colorado, Illinois, Pennsylvania and New York.[169] In what some scholars later described as an act of bad judgement, however, Scott subsequently sought the aid of his father, R.W. Scott, who was federal Secretary of State at the time, to assist him in getting the new Act passed. The senior Scott mentioned the possibility of such a bill in a 1906 speech from the throne without consulting Liberal Justice Minister A.B. Aylesworth. Aylesworth was apparently not amused.[170] Nevertheless, under pressure from Governor General Lord Grey, Aylesworth permitted the introduction of the bill in the Senate. The bill was received favourably although some critics feared the new Act did not adequately respect the due process rights of young persons. Detractors complained that both judges and probation officers were granted broad discretionary powers under the proposed *JDA*. Victorian reformers reputedly dismissed this opposition. "Most were not the least concerned about children's rights because they were convinced that what they were doing was protecting children. Since this was their motive, they believed that decisions and actions of those working in the justice system would similarly always be in the 'best interest' of children."[171] Police officials, by contrast, criticized the bill for being too lenient.[172] Toronto police Staff Inspector David Archibald's comments reveal the sentiments of some:

> [The reformers] work upon the sympathies of philanthropic men and women for the purpose of introducing a jelly-fish and abortive system

---

[167] For an excellent description of how the juvenile court and probation system was designed to work in the United States in the early 1900s, see David Rothman, "The Invention of the Juvenile Court in Progressive America, 1898-1920" in Russell C. Smandych, ed., *Youth Justice: History, Legislation, and Reform* (Toronto: Harcourt Canada, 2001), 24.

[168] David J. Rothman, *Conscience and Convenience: The Asylum and Its Alternatives in Progressive America* (Addison-Wesley Educational Publishers, 1980), at 215, as cited in Greg Berman and John Feinblatt, *Good Courts* (New York: The New Press, 2005), at 56.

[169] Sanjeev Anand, "Catalyst for Change: The History of Canadian Juvenile Justice Reform" (Spring 1999) Vol. 24, No. 2, Queen's L.J. 515, at 531.

[170] Sanjeev Anand, "Catalyst for Change: The History of Canadian Juvenile Justice Reform" (Spring 1999) Vol. 24, No. 2, Queen's L.J. 515, at 532.

[171] Sandra J. Bell, *Young Offenders and Juvenile Justice: A Century After the Fact*, 2d ed. (Scarborough: Nelson, a division of Thomson Canada Ltd., 2003), at 49.

[172] Jeffrey S. Leon, "The Development of Canadian Juvenile Justice: A Background for Reform" (1977) Osgoode Hall L.J. Vol. 15, No. 1, 71 at 95.

of law enforcement, whereby the judge or magistrate is expected to come down to the level of the incorrigible street arab and assume an attitude absolutely repulsive to British Subjects. The idea seems to be that by profuse use of slang phraseology he should place himself in a position to kiss and coddle a class of perverts and delinquents who require the most rigid disciplinary and corrective measures to ensure the possibility of their reformation.[173]

In the face of such vitriolic opposition, Scott, Kelso and others campaigned vigorously to garner support for the bill: They published the bill in various public fora, they went on speaking tours, they met their detractors and tried to mollify them. Scott even invited both Mrs. Schoff from Philadelphia and prominent American juvenile court proponent Judge Ben B. Lindsay of Denver, Colorado, to address Senators and Members of the House of Commons regarding the benefits of a juvenile justice system for Canada.[174]

Canadian criminologist Jean Trépanier, who has analyzed the parliamentary debates that led to the passage of the *JDA*, contends that the federal government showed no leadership whatsoever in the preparation and adoption of the bill, and that the initiative came from groups and persons outside of Parliament.[175] Indeed, it was in response to intensive and persistent lobbying that Aylesworth eventually sponsored the bill.

Whatever lack of enthusiasm Aylesworth may have initially harboured toward the bill, he deftly defended it in the House of Commons on July 8, 1908, after it was read a second time. (The bill had actually been introduced in the Senate and extensively debated there.)[176] Aylesworth told the House that the main purpose of the bill was to provide for the establishment of juvenile courts for young persons charged with criminal offences under the age of 16, and to spare them incarceration:

---

[173] Jeffrey S. Leon, "'The Development of Canadian Juvenile Justice': A Background for Reform" (1977) Osgoode Hall L.J. Vol. 15, No. 1, 71 at 96.

[174] Bryan Hogeveen, "'Winning Deviant Youth Over by Friendly Helpfulness': Transformations in the Legal Governance of Deviant Children in Canada, 1857-1908" in Russell Smandych, ed., *Youth Justice: History, Legislation, and Reform* (Toronto: Harcourt Canada, 2001), 43 at 54.

[175] J. Trépanier, "The Origins of the Juvenile Delinquents Act of 1908: Controlling Delinquency through Seeking Its Causes and through Youth Protection" in R. Smandych, G. Dodds and A. Esau, eds., *Dimensions of Childhood: Essays on the History of Children and Youth in Canada* (Winnipeg: Legal Research Institute of the University of Manitoba, 1991), 205 at 207.

[176] Bryan Hogeveen, "'Winning Deviant Youth Over by Friendly Helpfulness': Transformations in the Legal Governance of Deviant Children in Canada, 1857-1908" in Russell Smandych, ed., *Youth Justice: History, Legislation, and Reform* (Toronto: Harcourt Canada, 2001), 43 at 55.

> The general effect of this Bill I think I may summarize by saying that it is intended to obviate the necessity for children, when accused of crime, being tried before the ordinary tribunals ... Instead of the juvenile court imposing sentence of imprisonment, as of necessity under the existing criminal law, the child may be released on probation. Under no circumstances is it to be sent to jail, but if not released on probation, or a home found for it, either in some public institution or with some private family, provision is made with regard to the disposition that the court can make of the child ... I want to prevent the possibility of children who might be reclaimed if treated otherwise than as criminals, being sent to the ordinary prisons of the country with the older and possibly hardened offenders.[177]

Despite the exceedingly long lead-up, the bill drew only a 10-minute debate in the House of Commons. One member expressed strong reservations. Ontario lawyer Edward Arthur Lancaster, a Conservative MP, in a spirited and impassioned critique of the bill, sharply criticized its lack of due process rights, its failure to provide defence counsel for young persons, as well as the lack of an inherent right to trial by jury for young persons.

> I do not see one word in it, for instance, in the hurried glance which I have been able to give to it, providing for the protection of the child or as to how he is to be defended. He seems to be entirely at the mercy of a person called a probation officer. There should be some provision for the child being able to say he is not guilty if he is not guilty.[178]

Lancaster's concerns received little support or attention at the time. The bill passed on July 8, 1908, apparently not long past midnight, after Lancaster's short harangue, and amid his complaints that the Justice Minister was rushing it through in the "dying hours of the session ... and after midnight we are asked to pass, but not consider it".[179] It received Royal Assent less than two weeks later, on July 20, 1908. To what degree Lancaster's comments were heartfelt and not mere politicking by an articulate lawyer may never be known. Nevertheless, his comments about the lack of due process rights in the *JDA* were remarkably prophetic. The very shortcomings he highlighted in 1908 played a pivotal role in the ultimate demise of the *JDA* many decades later.

---

[177] *Official Report of the Debates of the House of Commons of the Dominion of Canada*, Fourth Session, Tenth Parliament, 7-8 Edward VII, 1907-8, Vol. LXXXVIII 12399-400.

[178] *Official Report of the Debates of the House of Commons of the Dominion of Canada*, Fourth Session, Tenth Parliament, 7-8 Edward VII, 1907-8, Vol. LXXXVIII at 12402.

[179] *Official Report of the Debates of the House of Commons of the Dominion of Canada*, Fourth Session, Tenth Parliament, 7-8 Edward VII, 1907-8, Vol. LXXXVIII at 12400-401.

C.   The *Juvenile Delinquents Act* of 1908: Its Philosophy and Substance

For the next 76 years, the pithy *JDA* (which contained only 36 sections when it was assented to on July 20, 1908) was the primary piece of federal youth criminal justice legislation in Canada. The concept of a separate youth criminal justice system in Canada had at last been enshrined in a comprehensive federal bill. The preamble stated:

> WHEREAS it is inexpedient that youthful offenders should be classed or dealt with as ordinary criminals, the welfare of the community demanding that they should on the contrary be guarded against association with crime and criminals, and should be subjected to such wise care, treatment and control as will tend to check their evil tendencies and to strengthen their better instincts … .[180]

Among other things, the *JDA* established separate juvenile courts, informal, private trials to spare the child publicity, separate detention and custodial facilities, and probation programs and services.

The *JDA* based its philosophy and approach on the *parens patriae* jurisdiction of the English Chancery Court. *Parens patriae* means "parent of the country". The court steps into the shoes of the parent and, in essence, becomes a surrogate parent, guardian or protector of those who cannot protect themselves, intervening for the welfare of the child when other institutions fail to properly care for him or her. "The drafters of the Act intended the juvenile court to adopt the role of a "wise and kind, though firm and stern, father … [asking] not, 'What has the child done?' but 'How can this child be saved?'"[181]

The doctrine of *parens patriae* originated in medieval England where it related to the King's right to control the property of orphaned heirs for the purpose of protection.[182] By the 18th century, *parens patriae* had evolved to include the "best interest" principle, whereby the court was to act in the best interest of the child.[183] The doctrine was explained in the 1722 case of *Eyre v. Shaftsbury*:[184]

---

[180]   S.C. 1908, c. 40.

[181]   J. Bolton *et al.*, "The *Young Offenders Act*: Principles and Policy — The First Decade in Review" (1993) 38 McGill L.J. 939, at 947. (The Bolton article is citing the words of W.L. Scott.)

[182]   Sandra J. Bell, *Young Offenders and Juvenile Justice: A Century After the Fact*, 2d ed. (Scarborough: Nelson, a division of Thomson Canada Ltd., 2003), at 43.

[183]   Sandra J. Bell, *Young Offenders and Juvenile Justice: A Century After the Fact*, 2d ed. (Scarborough: Nelson, a division of Thomson Canada Ltd., 2003), at 43.

[184]   (1722), 24 E.R. 659.

the care of all infants is lodged in the King as *pater patriae*, and by the King this care is delegated to the Court of Chancery ... there is not any one act that has taken away the original jurisdiction of this Court with respect to this care and superintendency in the case of infants ... the King is protector of all his subjects; that in virtue of his high trust, he is more particularly to take care of those who are not able to take care of themselves, consequently of infants, who by reason of their nonage are under incapacities ...[185]

By the 1800s, the principle had broadened to encompass not only the monarchy but the state as well, and applied to children without property who were either without parents or guardians or neglected by them. Various piecemeal Acts passed in the 19th century in Canada relating to children and juveniles reflected this principle, thus, the doctrine was enshrined in common and statutory law.[186] The concept of state intervention in children's lives when it was deemed to be in their best interests had become part of the underlying philosophy of youth justice legislation and practice.[187]

The courts elaborated on the principle in later cases, including *R. v. Gyngall*,[188] where Lord Esher held that the Court of Chancery has exercised a paternal jurisdiction over infants since time immemorial to act in the place of a parent:

The court is placed in a position by reason of the prerogative of the Crown to act as a supreme parent of children, and must exercise that jurisdiction in the manner in which a wise, affectionate, and careful parent would act for the welfare of the child. The natural parent in the particular case may be affectionate, and may be intending to act for the child's good, but may be unwise, and may not be doing what a wise, affectionate, and careful parent would do. The Court may say in such a case that, although they can find no misconduct on the part of the parent, they will not permit that to be done with the child which a wise, affectionate and careful parent would not do.[189]

Section 31 of the *JDA* enshrined the concept of *parens patriae*:

This Act shall be liberally construed to the end that its purpose may be carried out, to wit: That the care and custody and discipline of a juvenile delinquent shall approximate as nearly as may be that which should be given by its parents, and that as far as practicable every juvenile delinquent shall

---

[185] (1722), 24 E.R. 659, at 664 and 666.

[186] Sandra J. Bell, *Young Offenders and Juvenile Justice: A Century After the Fact*, 2d ed. (Scarborough: Nelson, a division of Thomson Canada Ltd., 2003), at 43.

[187] Bryan Hogeveen, "History, Development, and Transformations in Canadian Juvenile Justice, 1800-1984" in Kathryn Campbell, ed., *Understanding Youth Justice in Canada* (Toronto: Pearson Education Canada Inc., 2005), 24 at 35-36.

[188] [1893] 2 Q.B. 232.

[189] [1893] 2 Q.B. 232, at 241-42.

be treated, not as a criminal, but as a misdirected and misguided child, and one needing aid, encouragement, help and assistance.[190]

The *JDA* codified a paternalistic, welfare-oriented approach toward delinquent young persons. The focus was on curing the delinquent, healing the illness as opposed to punishing them. It was designed to assist the child, who should not be treated as an offender but as one in a condition of delinquency who required help, guidance and supervision.[191] In order to achieve these laudable goals as quickly as possible, however, the *JDA* contained little in the way of procedural formality and protections common to the ordinary adversarial system within which adults were tried. In fact, under the *JDA*, the concept of due process was virtually non-existent;[192] there was no express mention in the *JDA* of the rights of the child.[193] Conversely, what was enshrined was informality.[194]

The juvenile court adopted a non-adversarial approach where the parties within the criminal justice system — judges, lawyers, probation officers — were thought to share the common goal of acting in the child's best interests. The goal was rehabilitation, not punishment.[195]

Despite the *JDA*'s benevolent intentions, the result was that children — among the most vulnerable members of society — had less legal protection against the state than adults when charged with an offence that could result in the loss of their liberty. Under the *JDA*, children were generally represented by probation officers instead of lawyers, whose main responsibility was to the court. Unlike the traditional adversarial system, where the defence lawyer's foremost duty is to his client, in juvenile court, the judge and probation officer were expected to co-operate. "This lack of representation violated the most basic of due process guarantees because representation by a lawyer is necessary for the enforcement of all other rights."[196] In fact, at least 95 per cent of young persons charged under the *JDA* ended up pleading guilty in youth court. A later review of many of these cases revealed that, had they had counsel, a

---

[190]   S.C. 1908, c. 40, s. 31.

[191]   S.C. 1908, c. 40, s. 3(2).

[192]   J. Bolton *et al.*, "The *Young Offenders Act*: Principles and Policy — The First Decade in Review" (1993) 38 McGill L.J. 939, at 959.

[193]   J. Bolton *et al.*, "The *Young Offenders Act*: Principles and Policy — The First Decade in Review" (1993) 38 McGill L.J. 939, at 947.

[194]   S.C. 1908, c. 40, s. 17(1).

[195]   Sandra J. Bell, *Young Offenders and Juvenile Justice: A Century After the Fact*, 2d ed. (Scarborough: Nelson, a division of Thomson Canada Ltd., 2003), at 49.

[196]   J. Bolton *et al.*, "The Young Offenders Act: Principles and Policy — The First Decade in Review" (1993) 38 McGill L.J. 939, at 960.

large majority would have been advised not to plead guilty.[197] The *JDA* gave judges and probation officers immense power to make or influence decisions about a child's life, including detaining the young person in an institution until the age of 21 for conduct that could be very minor.

Under the *JDA*, a juvenile delinquent was defined broadly as "any child who violates any provision of *The Criminal Code* ..., or of any Dominion or provincial statute, or of any by-law or ordinance of any municipality, for which violation punishment by fine or imprisonment may be awarded; or, who is liable by reason of any other act to be committed to an industrial school or juvenile reformatory under the provisions of any Dominion or provincial statute".[198] The Act was amended in 1924 to include an even broader definition of delinquency. Under s. 2(1) of the revised *JDA*, a delinquent was "any child who violates any provision of the *Criminal Code* ... or of any Dominion or provincial statute, or of any bylaw or ordinance of any municipality, for which violation punishment by fine or imprisonment may be awarded, or who is guilty of sexual immorality or any similar form of vice, or who is liable by reason of any other act to be committed to an industrial school or juvenile reformatory under the provisions of any Dominion or provincial statute".[199]

From the outset, the breadth of offences captured by the Act went far beyond *Criminal Code* offences, to include provincial offences and violations of municipal bylaws. That scope increased with the revised wording of the 1924 Act, which included as an offence, *sexual immorality or any similar form of vice*. The *JDA* effectively introduced the concept of status offences: An act of perceived sexual immorality or conduct equated with it was an offence only because of the offender's age. The same offence committed by an adult would not constitute an offence. The ambiguity of the wording of s. 2 gave judges enormous discretion to determine what conduct warranted a finding that the young person was a juvenile delinquent. What was to constitute sexual immorality or any similar form of vice? In effect, the definition of delinquent under the *JDA* captured the child murderer, as well as the seven-year-old who rode a bicycle in the park or threw a tennis ball in violation of local park rules or other municipal bylaws.[200]

---

[197] Susan Reid and Marvin Zuker, "Conceptual Frameworks for Understanding Youth Justice in Canada: From the *Juvenile Delinquents Act* to the *Youth Criminal Justice Act*" in Kathryn Campbell, ed., *Understanding Youth Justice in Canada* (Toronto: Pearson Education Canada Inc., 2005), 89 at 99.

[198] S.C. 1908, c. 40, s. 2(c).

[199] *Juvenile Delinquents Act*, R.S.C. 1924, c. 53.

[200] Anthony Doob and Jane Sprott, "Sentencing under the *Youth Criminal Justice Act*: An Historical Perspective" in Kathryn Campbell, ed., *Understanding Youth Justice in Canada* (Toronto: Pearson Education Canada Inc., 2005), 221 at 222-23.

Once the judge determined that the young person was a juvenile delinquent, the sentences that could be imposed ranged from fines, to committing the child to the care or custody of a probation officer, allowing the child to remain in the home under the supervision of a probation officer, placing the child in a foster home subject to the supervision of a probation officer, committing the child to the care of the Children's Aid Society or placing the child in an industrial school. Under the *JDA*, a child under 16 could generally no longer be housed in penitentiaries, jails, prisons or police stations, or any other place where adults were imprisoned.[201] Even in regions where there was no detention home, children were not to be incarcerated in jails unless it was necessary to guarantee their attendance in court.[202] However, if a child was 14, and was charged with committing an indictable offence, s. 7 of the original *JDA* permitted the judge to order the young person to be tried in the ordinary courts as an adult if the court determined that "the good of the child and the interest of the community demand it", in which case the young person would be subject to the penalties in the *Criminal Code* available to adults upon conviction.[203]

By contemporary standards, the powers under the Act were enormous. On the one hand, the Act empowered officials to act as a parent would, and to treat delinquents as misguided children rather than criminals; on the other hand, judges had the power to commit "delinquents" to institutions until they were 21 for a wide range of conduct, not all of which was criminal. The institutions were not *called* jails but, for all intents and purposes, they were, arguably, because they involved a non-voluntary confinement to an institution.

Philosophy and perception aside, in practice, the *JDA* was *not* lenient. A child could conceivably receive a sentence of an unknown length for a minor theft.[204] At the time of sentencing, it was unclear how long that child would be detained in the institution. Once determined to be a delinquent, the young person would remain a ward of the court until the

---

[201] S.C. 1908, c. 40, ss. 11, 20 and 22. Under s. 11, the *JDA* made clear that this requirement to house young persons separate and apart from adults did not apply to young persons who were ordered by the judge to be tried in the adult system. In addition, under s. 11, it was not necessary to detain young persons separate and apart from adults pending a hearing under the *JDA* if the child were over 14 and could not safely be confined in any place other than a jail or lock-up. Under s. 22, no juvenile delinquent, upon or after conviction, was to be sentenced or incarcerated in any penitentiary, or county or other jail, or police station, or any other place in which adults are or may be imprisoned.

[202] S.C. 1908, c. 40, s. 12.

[203] S.C. 1908, c. 40, s. 7.

[204] Bryan Hogeveen, "History, Development, and Transformations in Canadian Juvenile Justice, 1800-1984" in Kathryn Campbell, ed., *Understanding Youth Justice in Canada* (Toronto: Pearson Education Canada Inc., 2005), 24 at 34-35.

court released them, or until they reached the age of 21.[205] Under the *JDA*, the youth could be returned to the court for a review of sentence any time up until the age of 21.

That said, the aim of the *JDA* was to keep youthful offenders out of institutions to the extent feasible, and to focus instead on rehabilitating young persons within their communities, which, interestingly, is the focus of the *YCJA*, at least in relation to non-violent young persons. As envisioned by its drafters, the *JDA* was to feature probation prominently. W.L. Scott said at the time that probation was the most important element in Canada's new youth justice system, "the keystone of the arch".[206] Contemporary youth justice scholars characterize the formal introduction of the concept of probation into the *JDA* as "the most important innovation in juvenile justice in the twentieth century".[207]

Under the *JDA*, it was incumbent on the probation officer to investigate cases as required by the court, to seek the input and advice of trained professionals where necessary, such as psychologists and psychiatrists, to represent the interests of the child when the case was heard, to provide information and assistance to the judge, as required, and to take charge of any child, before or after trial, as directed by the court. With the introduction of the probation system under the *JDA*, the juvenile court became concerned with "learning what led the child to do wrong and how it can be taught to do better... The erring child was considered a product of the home, school and social environment. It became the task of the probation officer to understand the situation and pass on to a juvenile judge the administrative knowledge accumulated through interviews and personal visits with those close to the child".[208]

---

[205] Sandra J. Bell, *Young Offenders and Juvenile Justice: A Century After the Fact*, 2d ed. (Scarborough: Nelson, a division of Thomson Canada Ltd., 2003), at 45. See s. 16(3) of the original *JDA*, S.C. 1908, c. 40.

[206] Sandra J. Bell, *Young Offenders and Juvenile Justice: A Century After the Fact*, 2d ed. (Scarborough: Nelson, a division of Thomson Canada Ltd., 2003), at 44.

[207] Bryan Hogeveen, "'Winning Deviant Youth Over by Friendly Helpfulness': Transformations in the Legal Governance of Deviant Children in Canada, 1857-1908" in Russell Smandych, ed., *Youth Justice: History, Legislation, and Reform* (Toronto: Harcourt Canada, 2001), 43 at 58.

[208] Bryan Hogeveen, "'Winning Deviant Youth Over by Friendly Helpfulness': Transformations in the Legal Governance of Deviant Children in Canada, 1857-1908" in Russell Smandych, ed., *Youth Justice: History, Legislation, and Reform* (Toronto: Harcourt Canada, 2001), 43 at 56-57. Ironically, today, 100 years later, we are seeing a veritable explosion of problem-solving courts in the U.S. and Canada, including the establishment of drug treatment courts and mental health courts in various Canadian cities that, much like the juvenile court of 100 years ago, seek to address the underlying causes of crime. Greg Berman and John Feinblatt, *Good Courts* (New York: The New Press, 2005), at 52-58.

The second aspect of the probation officer's job was to monitor the young person in the community, including routinely visiting the home to assist in addressing problems. The advent of probation transferred supervision and discipline back into the community and was expected to be cheaper, more humane, and more successful at rehabilitation. In practice, large caseloads coupled with staff shortages and lack of qualified staff resulted in probation officers not having the time to do the job that reformers such as Scott and Kelso had so enthusiastically envisioned.[209]

D.   From the *Juvenile Delinquents Act* to the *Young Offenders Act*

(i)   Overview

For the first 50 years of its life, the *JDA* was scarcely questioned or challenged. There were amendments, but they were minor and did not alter the fundamental philosophy and approach. Only in the 1960s did the *JDA* fall under intense scrutiny.[210] Over the course of the next two decades, it would be death by 1,000 criticisms but death *would* come. The *Young Offenders Act* was passed in 1982 and proclaimed in force in April 1984.

Was it because the *JDA* was so perfect in its wisdom that it reigned blissfully for 50 odd years before it fell under the critic's scythe? The pedestrian answer is that it wasn't on the radar screen for most of that time. As some scholars suggest, the *JDA* remained largely untouched until the 1960s because it operated in a "critical vacuum".[211]

Positivism flourished in the early decades of the 20th century. By mid-century, the field of corrections was replete with professionals who believed in treatment and rehabilitation. It was all about curing pathologies through treatment. Thus, *parens patriae*, which focused on helping the juvenile delinquent, "went unchallenged as the prevailing correctional

---

[209]   Bryan Hogeveen, "'Winning Deviant Youth Over by Friendly Helpfulness': Transformations in the Legal Governance of Deviant Children in Canada, 1857-1908" in Russell Smandych, ed., *Youth Justice: History, Legislation, and Reform* (Toronto: Harcourt Canada, 2001), 43 at 58.

[210]   Sanjeev Anand, "Catalyst for Change: The History of Canadian Juvenile Justice Reform" (Spring 1999) Vol. 24, No. 2, Queen's L.J. 515, at 539. See also Sandra J. Bell, *Young Offenders and Juvenile Justice: A Century After the Fact*, 2d ed. (Scarborough: Nelson, a division of Thomson Canada Ltd., 2003), at 49.

[211]   J. Bolton *et al.*, "The *Young Offenders Act*: Principles and Policy — The First Decade in Review" (1993) 38 McGill L.J. 939, at 948.

ideology"[212] until the 1960s. In addition, prior to the 1960s, there was little empirical research regarding the effectiveness of rehabilitation programs, therefore, there was no basis upon which to challenge *parens patriae*.[213]

Criminal lawyers, for their part, largely ignored the *JDA* during the early decades of its existence. They did not consider it criminal law but viewed it instead as social welfare legislation that was more properly the domain of other professionals,[214] such as social workers, whose main occupation was to discern how to help troubled youth.

The beginning of the end of the *JDA* began in 1962, when it fell under the glare of the political headlights. The federal government was to undertake a major review of the *JDA* for the first time in the history of the Act, and appointed a Committee of the Department of Justice to study the problem of juvenile delinquency.[215]

The study appeared to have been prompted in part by a perceived and worrisome increase in youth crime as well as fears that it would worsen if the federal government did not take steps to address the issue. The report's advisory committee notes in the study's introduction that the Correctional Planning Committee of the Department of Justice had established a plan in 1960 for the development of federal correctional services because Canada needed an organized and integrated approach to juvenile delinquency to identify at an early age those children in danger of becoming delinquent, and to correct their problems. "Unless this is done there is no real hope of stopping the flow of an ever increasing number of young adult offenders through the criminal courts and into Canadian prisons."[216] The committee explains in the report that the percentage of Canada's population that was 19 years of age or younger had grown from 38 per cent of the total population in 1956 to 42 per cent in 1961. After noting the significant increase in the number of juveniles brought before the court and found delinquent between 1957 and 1961, the committee predicted a marked increase in juvenile delinquency in the years ahead and concluded that it

---

[212] J. Bolton *et al.*, "The *Young Offenders Act*: Principles and Policy — The First Decade in Review" (1993) 38 McGill L.J. 939, at 948.

[213] J. Bolton *et al.*, "The *Young Offenders Act*: Principles and Policy — The First Decade in Review" (1993) 38 McGill L.J. 939, at 948, n. 34.

[214] J. Bolton *et al.*, "The *Young Offenders Act*: Principles and Policy — The First Decade in Review" (1993) 38 McGill L.J. 939, at 957.

[215] J. Bolton *et al.*, "The *Young Offenders Act*: Principles and Policy — The First Decade in Review" (1993) 38 McGill L.J. 939, at 948.

[216] *Juvenile Delinquency in Canada: The Report of the Department of Justice Committee on Juvenile Delinquency* (Ottawa: Queen's Printer, 1965), at 1.

was necessary to study the problem and seek solutions.[217] Canada was probably also motivated to study juvenile delinquency at this juncture because both the United Kingdom and the U.S. had established similar committees.

Canada's five-person committee was mandated to make recommendations concerning steps that should be taken to address the problem of juvenile delinquency. The committee engaged in broad consultation and released its report in 1965. Among the report's 100 recommendations were the following, which, in retrospect, foretold the direction and substance of juvenile reform for the next 20 years:

- the minimum age of criminal responsibility should be raised to 10 years, or at most 12;

- where a juvenile is subject to a finding that he is a child offender or a young offender, the maximum period of institutional commitment should not exceed three years;

- there should be a Crown Attorney or similar officer in attendance in proceedings in the juvenile court;

- the notice to a parent informing the parent of the child's appearance in court should contain a statement that the child is entitled to be represented by counsel;

- a finding that a young person is a child offender or a juvenile offender should only be made for the commission of a *Criminal Code* offence (the young person could not be committed to a training school or removed from the parental home for the commission of a lesser offence);

- conduct now variously described as incorrigibility, unmanageability, being beyond the control of a parent or guardian, or being in moral danger, should not be included with the offence provisions of the federal Act but should be dealt with under provincial legislation;

- where a child is to be questioned by the police — and particularly if the child is invited to make a statement that may be used against the child — a responsible adult who is concerned with protecting the child's interest should be present;

- every effort should be made to experiment with new approaches to the treatment of the juvenile offender, and in particular with measures that are community-based; and

---

[217] *Juvenile Delinquency in Canada: The Report of the Department of Justice Committee on Juvenile Delinquency* (Ottawa: Queen's Printer, 1965), at 1-8.

- there should be a systematic and studied attempt to devise programs in Canada designed to meet the need for a more intensive and organized concentration on measures designed to prevent delinquency.[218]

The report and its recommendations prompted widespread debate concerning the future direction of juvenile justice reform in Canada. While many criticisms were levelled against the *JDA* during the ensuing years, the major concerns included the *JDA*'s lack of due process rights, its broad definition of delinquency, and the Act's philosophical focus on treatment and rehabilitation in the face of growing empirical consensus that rehabilitation programs were not effective in reducing recidivism. "More and more people began to question *parens patriae* as a foundation for juvenile justice, as well as the ability of the *JDA* to ensure due process for young people."[219]

(ii)   Due Process

The rights movement of the 1960s was among the most important influences on the nature and substance of the debate over juvenile justice reform and the actual content of the *Young Offenders Act* 20 years later. Although the rights discourse increased rapidly within academic, legal and political circles during the post-World War II era, it reached a crescendo in the 1960s.[220] The children's rights movement coincided with the broader North American civil and human rights movement of the 1960s,[221] where various disenfranchised groups in the U.S., such as women and African Americans, demanded legal and constitutional recognition. Such developments beyond Canada's borders, including a proliferation of American scholarship and jurisprudence, pervaded the Canadian socio-political context and challenged some of the fundamental assumptions of the *JDA*.[222] This was also the decade when Canada introduced its Bill of Rights.[223] The 1960s and 1970s, of course, were also years filled with

---

[218] *Juvenile Delinquency in Canada: The Report of the Department of Justice Committee on Juvenile Delinquency* (Ottawa: Queen's Printer, 1965), at 283-99.

[219] Sandra J. Bell, *Young Offenders and Juvenile Justice: A Century After the Fact*, 2d ed. (Scarborough: Nelson, a division of Thomson Canada Ltd., 2003), at 49.

[220] J. Bolton *et al.*, "The *Young Offenders Act*: Principles and Policy — The First Decade in Review" (1993) 38 McGill L.J. 939, at 957 (see n. 77 in particular).

[221] J. Bolton *et al.*, "The *Young Offenders Act*: Principles and Policy — The First Decade in Review" (1993) 38 McGill L.J. 939, at 957 (see n. 77 in particular).

[222] "Bryan Hogeveen, "History, Development, and Transformations in Canadian Juvenile Justice, 1800-1984" in Kathryn Campbell, ed., *Understanding Youth Justice in Canada* (Toronto: Pearson Education Canada Inc., 2005), 24 at 37.

[223] *Canadian Bill of Rights*, S.C. 1960, c. 44, assented to August 10, 1960.

debate and scholarship within Canada, leading up to the enactment of the *Canadian Charter of Rights and Freedoms* in 1982.

It is not surprising that some of the key features of the *JDA*, such as its indeterminate sentences, and the fact that accused young persons had no express right to counsel under the *JDA*, became untenable. An increasing number of lawyers, academics, social workers and other professionals pressed for juveniles to be given the same due process rights as adults.[224] The concerns were common sense: A juvenile should not have less procedural protection against the state than a similarly situated adult merely because the *JDA* was considered social welfare legislation rather than criminal legislation. Despite its benevolent intentions, the *JDA* enabled the state to detain a young person in an institution for years without that young person having had the benefit of legal representation or other fundamental rights available to adults. A child's increased vulnerability, lack of sophistication, and immaturity should, in fact, result in greater protections against the powers of the state, not less.

Canadian juvenile justice reform advocates were encouraged by a trilogy of significant American decisions in the late 1960s, which resonated in Canada. These cases served as a catalyst in Canada regarding the legal rights of young persons charged with a wide range of acts that could result in determinations of delinquency.

In 1966, the U.S. Supreme Court decided *Kent v. United States*.[225] *Kent* involved a 16-year-old boy who was accused of entering a woman's apartment on a September day in 1961, stealing her wallet and raping her. Morris Kent, who had a record for break and enters and attempted theft, was taken into custody a few days later and interrogated by the police at the police station for seven hours, during which time he admitted his involvement in the incident as well as his involvement in similar incidents. He was interrogated further the next day.

The juvenile court judge waived jurisdiction and ordered Kent to be tried in adult court, without first holding a hearing or giving Kent, his parents or his counsel an opportunity to be heard. Kent was eventually sentenced to serve a total of 30 to 90 years in prison. Although Kent's counsel argued on appeal before the United States Supreme Court that Kent had been denied certain basic rights that would have been provided had he been an adult, such as his right to have counsel present during his interrogation, his right to remain silent and to receive advice as to his

---

[224] J. Bolton *et al.*, "The *Young Offenders Act*: Principles and Policy — The First Decade in Review" (1993) 38 McGill L.J. 939, at 957.

[225] 383 U.S. 541 (1966).

right to counsel, the U.S. Supreme Court confined the bulk of its analysis to the validity of the juvenile court waiving its jurisdiction.

Justice Fortras, writing for the court, concluded that even though proceedings under the District of Columbia's *Juvenile Court Act* were "civil" rather than "criminal", where the court is engaged in a "parental relationship" rather than acting as prosecuting attorney and judge deciding a criminal matter, this *parens patriae* philosophy was not an invitation to procedural arbitrariness:[226]

> ... there is no place in our system of law for reaching a result of such tremendous consequences without ceremony—without hearing, without effective assistance of counsel, without a statement of reasons. It is inconceivable that a court of justice dealing with adults, with respect to a similar issue, would proceed in this manner. ...[227]

The Supreme Court explained in *Kent* that the right to representation by counsel is not a formality but the "essence of justice".[228]

A year later, in *In Re Gault*,[229] the U.S. Supreme Court extended the due process principles decided in *Kent*. *Gault* concerned a 15-year-old boy who was committed as a juvenile delinquent to the Arizona State Industrial School for up to six years for making an obscene telephone call. During the 1964 incident, Gerald Francis Gault was taken into custody without notice to his parents after a neighbour complained that she had received a telephone call during which lewd and indecent comments were made. The next day, Gerald Gault, his mother and older brother, as well as two probation officers, appeared before the Juvenile Judge in chambers for a hearing. The complainant was not there. No one was sworn at the hearing. No transcript or recording was made. Neither the boy nor his parents were advised of the boy's right to be represented by counsel and of the right to have counsel appointed if they could not afford a lawyer.

Later, there was disagreement as to what was said at that hearing. Both the officer and the judge recalled that Gerald admitted making all, or some, of the lewd remarks. However, Gerald's mother recalled that Gerald said he only dialled the telephone number and then passed the telephone receiver to his friend. At a second hearing a week later, there were again differences about what was said. The officer agreed that Gerald denied making the lewd remarks while the judge recalled that there was some admission. The complainant was not present at this hearing either, the judge having concluded that it was not necessary. At the

---

[226]   383 U.S. 541, at 555 (1966).
[227]   383 U.S. 541, at 554 (1966).
[228]   383 U.S. 541, at 561 (1966).
[229]   387 U.S. 1 (1967).

conclusion of the second hearing, Gerald was ordered committed to an industrial school until he was 21 unless discharged sooner according to law "after a full hearing".[230] The penalty for an adult for the same conduct was a fine of $5 to $50 or imprisonment for up to two months.[231] Had Gerald Gault committed the same offence as an adult he would have been entitled to substantial rights under the American Constitution, as well as under Arizona's laws and constitution.

The U.S. Supreme Court held that Gault and his parents were denied the right of notice, the right to counsel, the right against self-incrimination and the right to confront the witnesses against young Gault.[232] Delinquency proceedings, which may lead to commitment in a state institution, must comply with the essentials of due process and fair treatment, including: written notice of the specific or factual allegations, notice to the child and his parents of the child's right to be represented by counsel retained by them, or, if they are unable to afford counsel, the appointment of counsel, the privilege against self-incrimination, and, absent a valid confession, a determination of delinquency based only on sworn testimony that includes an opportunity for cross-examination. Throughout the judgment, the court made numerous strong statements about the importance of due process for all accused persons, including juveniles.

> ... it would be a plain denial of equal protection of the laws — an invidious discrimination — to hold that others subject to heavier punishments could, because they are children, be denied these same constitutional safeguards.[233]

Expanding on *Kent* and *Gault*, in 1970, the U.S. Supreme Court decided *Re Winship*,[234] in which it held that proof beyond a reasonable doubt was required in juvenile cases just as it is in adult cases. *Winship* involved a 12-year-old boy who was alleged to have stolen some money. A New York Family Court judge held that pursuant to a New York statute, he could base his determination of guilt upon a preponderance of the evidence. The judgment resulted in the youth being placed in a training school for up to six years. On appeal, the Supreme Court of the United States in a majority decision written by Brennan J. held that the due process clause of the American Constitution requires that juveniles, like adults, have a right to the essentials of due process and fair treatment when charged with a crime, including the constitutional right to be found

---

[230]   387 U.S. 1, at 8 (1967).
[231]   387 U.S. 1, at 8-9 (1967).
[232]   387 U.S. 1, at 61 (1967), as per Black J. in concurring reasons.
[233]   387 U.S. 1, at 61 (1967), as per Black J. in concurring reasons.
[234]   397 U.S. 358 (1970).

guilty based on proof beyond a reasonable doubt.[235] "The same considerations that demand extreme caution in fact finding to protect the innocent adult apply as well to the innocent child."[236]

This trilogy of cases had forced the highest court in the United States in the late 1960s and early 1970s to review and re-consider the logic and fairness of affording young persons fewer constitutional protections than adults when facing allegations of crime. The cases compelled the U.S. Supreme Court to review the underlying philosophy of its juvenile justice system (which was strikingly similar to ours since Scott modelled our law on theirs). The cases also obliged governments and the legal community in both the U.S. and Canada to address a disturbing contradiction: Legislation that was designed to be rehabilitative rather than punitive was in fact proving highly punitive and unjust. Youths were being treated more harshly than adults for similar offences. For decades, juvenile legislation had been considered social welfare legislation, not criminal legislation. It was characterized as civil rather than criminal legislation although it could operate in a highly punitive fashion.

Based on the philosophy of the American juvenile court movement, Fortas J. had explained in *Gault* that children were to feel they were the object of the state's care and solicitude, not that they were under arrest or trial. The rules of criminal procedure were not relevant. The technicalities and harshness of both the substantive and procedural criminal law were to be discarded. The idea of crime and punishment was to be abandoned in favour of treatment and rehabilitation. The procedures, from apprehension through to institutionalization, were to be clinical and not punitive.[237] In accordance with the philosophy of *parens patriae*, being placed in custody was considered a *right* for a young person, not a punishment. In other words, when a child was ordered detained in an institution under the Act, this was interpreted as the state benevolently providing them with shelter or custody, rather than the state depriving them of liberty.[238] Custody was a good thing, a benefit, unlike incarceration. However, the court in *Gault* concluded that the highest motives and most enlightened impulses had actually led to a very peculiar system of justice for young persons.[239] Whether one labelled it criminal law or social welfare legislation, the juvenile justice legislation gave the state tremendous power over young persons' lives, yet denied them the fundamental rights and freedoms afforded adults in similar circumstances.

---

[235] 397 U.S. 358, at 366-67 (1970).
[236] 397 U.S. 358, at 365 (1970).
[237] *In Re Gault*, 387 U.S. 1, at 15-16 (1967).
[238] 387 U.S. 1, at 17 (1967).
[239] 387 U.S. 1, at 17 (1967).

Justice Fortas described it aptly in *Gault*:

> A boy is charged with misconduct. The boy is committed to an institution where he may be restrained of liberty for years. It is of no constitutional consequence — and of limited practical meaning — that the institution to which he is committed is called an Industrial School. ... however euphemistic the title, a "receiving home" or an "industrial school" for juveniles is an institution of confinement in which the child is incarcerated for a greater or lesser time. ...

> ... In view of this, it would be extraordinary if our Constitution did not require the procedural regularity and the exercise of care implied in the phrase "due process." Under our Constitution, the condition of being a boy does not justify a kangaroo court.[240]

Canada, in the late 1960s, had no comparable decisions from its Supreme Court. The Canadian jurisprudence at the lower court level was inconsistent and, consequently, unhelpful. The American jurisprudence, as well as the American legal commentary that flowed from it, influenced Canadian academics and advocates.[241] The Canadian critique of the *JDA* broadened and deepened.

Linked to concerns over the lack of due process rights was the issue of status offences. Status offences under the *JDA* were a major source of tension and controversy since these were not offences if committed by adults. The Canadian Corrections Association had argued as early as 1963 that by grouping together youths who had committed serious crimes with those who had committed only minor violations, the *JDA* cast a wide and indiscriminate net over all forms of deviant youthful behaviour, and that solutions had to be found to reduce the *JDA*'s broad stigmatizing effect.[242]

Members of the Department of Justice Committee agreed and concluded in the 1965 report that:

> The definition [of a juvenile delinquent] thus fails to differentiate between a violation such as truancy or a breach of a provincial liquor statute, on the one hand, and an act such as assault or theft, on the other. Every child inevitably violates some ordinance or law while growing up. All certainly do not fall within the popular conception of "juvenile delinquent".[243]

---

[240] 387 U.S. 1, at 27-28 (1967).

[241] J. Bolton *et al.*, "The *Young Offenders Act*: Principles and Policy — The First Decade in Review" (1993) 38 McGill L.J. 939, at 959. In the *In Re Gault* decision, the judiciary cited a number of legal articles demonstrating the prevalence of the discussion and debate in U.S. legal journals in the 1960s regarding the scope and breadth of due process rights for juveniles.

[242] J. Bolton *et al.*, "The *Young Offenders Act*: Principles and Policy — The First Decade in Review" (1993) 38 McGill L.J. 939, at 955.

[243] *Juvenile Delinquency in Canada: The Report of the Department of Justice Committee on Juvenile Delinquency* (Ottawa: Queen's Printer, 1965), at 6.

Furthermore, offences of sexual immorality or any similar form of vice were highly ambiguous and gave judges great power in terms of determining what conduct fell within the definition. "In this way, a young female convicted of sexual immorality for being out late with her boyfriend could be handed an indeterminate reformatory sentence (as often happened)."[244] This vague definition of delinquency gave judges (who for much of the life of the *JDA* did not have legal training)[245] immense power over the lives of young persons that they could not exercise over adults, a power that could no longer be reconciled with the purpose of the *JDA*. As set out in s. 38 of the 1952 version, the *JDA* stated that "the care and custody and discipline of a juvenile delinquent shall approximate as nearly as may be that which should be given by its parents, and that as far as practicable every juvenile delinquent shall be treated, not as a criminal, but as a misdirected and misguided child, and one needing aid, encouragement, help and assistance".[246] It had become alarmingly clear to critics that the powers available under the Act were undermining its purpose. A wide range of conduct by young persons was being criminalized under the Act. Generations of young persons were being caught within its web. Many young lives were being irrevocably altered by the reach of this benevolent legislation that labelled them criminals.

By the 1960s, Canada's first piece of comprehensive youth justice legislation was viewed increasingly as a model of philosophical paradox. The intent of the legislation was that young persons charged under the *JDA* were to be treated not as criminals but as misdirected and misguided children in need of assistance.[247] Yet under this social welfare legislation, young persons had virtually no due process rights, lawyers were largely invisible, judges and probation officers had extremely broad powers, and a young person could be institutionalized for years for conduct in which an adult could, in some cases, engage with impunity. While the facilities in which young persons were being housed were not jails in the classic sense, the youths were still being detained against their will by the state in institutions. They *were* in custody.

---

[244] Bryan Hogeveen, "History, Development, and Transformations in Canadian Juvenile Justice, 1800-1984" in Kathryn Campbell, ed., *Understanding Youth Justice in Canada* (Toronto: Pearson Education Canada Inc., 2005), 24 at 36.

[245] Nicholas Bala and Julian V. Roberts, "Canada's Juvenile Justice System: Promoting Community-Based Responses to Youth Crime" in J. Junger-Tas and S.H. Decker, eds., *International Handbook of Juvenile Justice* (The Netherlands: Springer, 2006), 37 at 38.

[246] *Juvenile Delinquents Act*, R.S.C. 1952, c. 160, s. 38.

[247] *Juvenile Delinquents Act*, R.S.C. 1952, c. 160, s. 38.

Developments in the social sciences in the 1960s would dovetail with these concerns and play an instrumental role in the ultimate substance of the new *Young Offenders Act*. Two concepts in particular figured significantly in shaping the content of new youth justice legislation: labelling theory and diversion.

Labelling theorists contended that merely exposing a youth to the court system could have a damaging effect on his or her psyche and future behaviour. By labelling conduct as delinquent or criminal, and the offender as a juvenile delinquent, the community's perception of the young person would change. That perception would, in turn, affect the child's self image. The young person becomes bad because he or she is perceived as bad.[248] The very act of exposing young persons to the court system and compelling them to appear in courtrooms could have a damaging effect on their self-image to the point that they might be more likely to commit further criminal acts; they perceive themselves as criminals and believe that society also perceives them that way.

Labelling theory was even more disturbing in the context of the *JDA* because such a wide range of conduct could bring a young person under the aegis of the *JDA*. "Society's wide definition of 'juvenile delinquency' has the effect of 'stigmatizing' non-conforming young persons, who, under a different societal definition of 'delinquency', might otherwise be considered normal."[249] (The Department of Justice Committee members who wrote the 1965 report on juvenile delinquency were aware of labelling theory and referred to it in their report.)[250]

The critique of the *JDA* and the ultimate content of the *YOA* were also influenced in the 1960s and 1970s by research suggesting that rehabilitation programs were not working, that they were not effective in reducing recidivism. The work of R. Martinson was particularly influential.[251] In 1974, he published an article outlining his views regarding the ineffectiveness of rehabilitation after examining 231 studies from

---

[248] J. Bolton *et al.*, "The *Young Offenders Act*: Principles and Policy — The First Decade in Review" (1993) 38 McGill L.J. 939, at 953.

[249] J. Bolton *et al.*, "The *Young Offenders Act*: Principles and Policy — The First Decade in Review" (1993) 38 McGill L.J. 939, at 953-54.

[250] *Juvenile Delinquency in Canada: The Report of the Department of Justice Committee on Juvenile Delinquency* (Ottawa: Queen's Printer, 1965), at 36-40. Contemporary Canadian youth justice experts such as Nicholas Bala suggest that there is no clear empirical evidence to categorically support or refute labelling theory. The research is at best equivocal as to whether merely identifying a young person as an offender increases the likelihood that he or she will reoffend. Nicholas Bala, *Youth Criminal Justice Law* (Toronto: Irwin Law, 2003), at 273.

[251] J. Bolton *et al.*, "The *Young Offenders Act*: Principles and Policy — The First Decade in Review" (1993) 38 McGill L.J. 939, at 967-69.

various countries over a 22-year period, from 1945 to 1967. The data "give us very little reason to hope that we have in fact found a sure way of reducing recidivism through rehabilitation", Martinson concluded.[252] His succinct but disturbing summary that "nothing works" in rehabilitative programming struck a cord among criminologists. Although other professionals reached similar conclusions, Martinson later retracted his conclusions.[253] This perceived failure of rehabilitation programs caused some officials working within the juvenile justice system to re-examine the underlying philosophy of the *JDA*.[254]

The concept of labelling theory, as well as Martinson's findings and that of others, led some professionals to question the need for institutional programming and the value of incarceration in reducing recidivism. They began to explore alternatives to prosecution and jail, which became known as diversion, the act of diverting young persons from the mainstream criminal justice court system into the community.[255] Those who favoured diversion shared common ground with labelling theorists, and shared the view that the court process is stigmatizing and that non-judicial community-based programming would be better for young persons[256] and, at least, no less effective.[257] The concept of diversion was developing simultaneously in England, Scotland and the United States. The novel concept would figure prominently in the *YOA* of 1984, and indeed, diversion plays an even greater role in the *YCJA*.[258]

Other criticisms of the *JDA* included the age range over which the *JDA* had jurisdiction. The maximum age of persons who fell under the *JDA* varied among provinces. (Section 2(2)(a) of the *JDA* permitted provinces some flexibility in establishing the maximum age of young

---

[252] R. Martinson, "What Works? Questions and Answers About Prison Reform" (1974) 35 The Public Interest 22, at 49.

[253] Bryan Hogeveen, "History, Development, and Transformations in Canadian Juvenile Justice, 1800-1984" in Kathryn Campbell, ed., *Understanding Youth Justice in Canada* (Toronto: Pearson Education Canada Inc., 2005), 24 at 37.

[254] Bryan Hogeveen, "History, Development, and Transformations in Canadian Juvenile Justice, 1800-1984" in Kathryn Campbell, ed., *Understanding Youth Justice in Canada* (Toronto: Pearson Education Canada Inc., 2005), 24 at 37.

[255] J. Bolton *et al.*, "The *Young Offenders Act*: Principles and Policy — The First Decade in Review" (1993) 38 McGill L.J. 939, at 970.

[256] J. Bolton *et al.*, "The *Young Offenders Act*: Principles and Policy — The First Decade in Review" (1993) 38 McGill L.J. 939, at 970.

[257] Youth justice expert Nicholas Bala contends that it has not been proven that programs that divert the young person from the youth court system rather than charging the youth and allowing him to be dealt with in the conventional youth court system reduce recidivism. Nevertheless Bala suggests that, at very least, diversion generally does not increase the likelihood of recidivism. Nicholas Bala, *Youth Criminal Justice Law* (Toronto: Irwin Law, 2003), at 273-74.

[258] Diversion, which was called alternative measures under the *YOA*, and is known as extrajudicial measures in the *YCJA*, is discussed in Chapter 5.

persons caught by the *JDA*; they could set the upper age limit between 16 and 18. As a result, Manitoba set the upper age limit at 18, while Ontario established 16 as the upper age limit. This meant that a young person in Manitoba of 17 would be dealt with under the *JDA* while the same young person in Ontario would be dealt with as an adult.)[259] Many of these issues were identified as far back as the 1965 report.

The first attempts at new legislation began as early as 1967. Bill C-192 was introduced in the House of Commons in 1970.[260] Its main goals were to introduce due process protections, narrow the definition of delinquency, and modify the age range over which the juvenile court had jurisdiction.[261] However, the federal government abandoned the bill in response to opposition from interest groups, parliamentarians and the media, who characterized it as, among other things, overly legalistic, punitive and retrogressive.[262] There were also concerns that there had been inadequate consultation, that the cost of raising the maximum age would create financial burdens for the affected provinces, and finally, that it was premature to abandon the *parens patriae* philosophy.[263]

After that bill died on the Order Paper, a special committee was established to reconsider reform. A report was issued four years later, which set out the framework for draft legislation in the late 1970s that ultimately resulted in the *YOA* of 1984.[264] This time, the reception was different.

Various ideological changes had occurred by the late 1970s that created fertile ground for a new Act. The work of Martinson and that of others had led to considerable disillusionment within academia regarding the effectiveness of rehabilitation and the whole notion of treatment, which threw into doubt the continued legitimacy of *parens patriae* as the guiding philosophy underlying the youth criminal justice system. The academic community had shifted its focus from the external causes of crime back to the individual, and resurrected the classicist philosophy of deliberate choice,

---

[259] Bryan Hogeveen, "History, Development, and Transformations in Canadian Juvenile Justice, 1800-1984" in Kathryn Campbell, ed., *Understanding Youth Justice in Canada* (Toronto: Pearson Education Canada Inc., 2005), 24 at 36.

[260] Bill C-192, *An Act Respecting Young Offenders and to Repeal the Juvenile Delinquents Act*, 3d Sess., 28th Parl., 1970.

[261] J. Bolton *et al.*, "The *Young Offenders Act*: Principles and Policy — The First Decade in Review" (1993) 38 McGill L.J. 939, at 961.

[262] J. Bolton *et al.*, "The *Young Offenders Act*: Principles and Policy — The First Decade in Review" (1993) 38 McGill L.J. 939, at 963-64.

[263] J. Bolton *et al.*, "The *Young Offenders Act*: Principles and Policy — The First Decade in Review" (1993) 38 McGill L.J. 939, at 965.

[264] J. Bolton *et al.*, "The *Young Offenders Act*: Principles and Policy — The First Decade in Review" (1993) 38 McGill L.J. 939, at 967. The report was produced by the Ministry of the Solicitor General and was entitled *Young Persons in Conflict with the Law* (Ottawa: Communication Division, 1975).

responsibility and accountability. The discussion had come full circle: The classicist view of criminology had re-emerged to replace the positivist school, which had formed the original philosophical backdrop for the *JDA*.[265] While labelling theorists feared the impact of placing an increasing number of youthful offenders in institutions, and the attendant risk of more young persons being labelled deviant, others had lost confidence that rehabilitation programs worked better than incarceration, and sought greater emphasis on punishment and accountability.[266] By the late 1970s, Canadians had also become more concerned about juvenile crime.[267] New legislation could play a role in convincing Canadians that the federal government was taking concrete steps to address youth crime.

From 1975 to 1982, three successive federal governments tried to draft legislation based on the many recommendations for reform that arose from the multi-faceted and detailed critique of the *JDA*. The *YOA* was finally passed in 1982 with widespread support, including that of all federal political parties.[268] Having passed the same year as the *Canadian Charter of Rights and Freedoms*, the *YOA* was obviously drafted to comply with the *Charter*. As youth justice expert Nicholas Bala has observed, the informal procedures and lack of due process in the *JDA* were inconsistent with the legal protections afforded by the *Charter*, while differences among provinces permitted under the *JDA* (such as the demarcation line for adulthood in criminal law) were inconsistent with s. 15 of the *Charter*, which guarantees equal protection under the law.[269] The *YOA* came into force in April 1984.

Paradoxically, the broad political acceptance of the *YOA* also explains, in part, its short honeymoon, and the series of amendments that occurred over the next decade. The *YOA* was compromise legislation. Rather than reflecting a clear and consistent philosophy, with ranked priorities, the *YOA* attempted to address wide-ranging concerns that were sometimes inconsistent. Consequently, its provisions would prove a challenge to

---

[265] J. Bolton *et al.*, "*The Young Offenders Act*: Principles and Policy — The First Decade in Review" (1993) 38 McGill L.J. 939, at 972.

[266] Priscilla Platt, *Young Offenders Law in Canada*, 2d ed. (Markham: Butterworths Canada Ltd., 1995), at 2. See also J. Bolton *et al.*, "The *Young Offenders Act*: Principles and Policy — The First Decade in Review" (1993) 38 McGill L.J. 939, at 973.

[267] J. Bolton *et al.*, "The *Young Offenders Act*: Principles and Policy — The First Decade in Review" (1993) 38 McGill L.J. 939, at 971-72.

[268] Nicholas Bala, "The Development of Canada's Youth Justice Law" in Kathryn Campbell, ed., *Understanding Youth Justice in Canada* (Toronto: Pearson Education Canada Inc., 2005), 41 at 44.

[269] Nicholas Bala, "Youth as Victims and Offenders in the Criminal Justice System: A Charter Analysis — Recognizing Vulnerability" in James Stribopoulos and Jamie Cameron, eds., *The Charter and Criminal Justice: Twenty-Five Years Later* (Toronto: LexisNexis, 2008), 595 at 597.

interpret. The *YOA* contained some elements that reflected the welfare-oriented *parens patriae* philosophy of its predecessor, other features that captured long-standing legalistic and due process concerns, as well as aspects that focused on the accountability and responsibility of the offender and the protection of the public. While the *YOA* retained the principle that young persons were to be held less accountable than adults for their crimes by virtue of their youth and lesser maturity, the *YOA* stated expressly that young persons were to be held responsible for their crimes.[270]

Accountability for one's criminal transgressions was an express principle in the *YOA*, as it had not been in the *JDA*. The *YOA* retained elements of the paternalistic, welfare-oriented *JDA*, but it was criminal law in a way the *JDA* was not. Nevertheless, its focus was unclear and its priorities were not ranked in order of importance. Was the prime thrust of the new legislation that young persons were to be held accountable for their actions, that punishment was key, and that there was a viable and significant place for incarceration within that equation? Was the underlying message that incarceration could be effective in reducing criminal behaviour? How important a principle was rehabilitation in the *YOA*?

The *YOA* contained a Declaration of Principle in s. 3, which, for the first time, provided a detailed philosophical roadmap that was designed to aid in the interpretation of the legislation. However, the principles in s. 3 were competing and inconsistent.[271] Nowhere did s. 3 of the *YOA* state that a particular principle, such as rehabilitation or protection of the public (which some interpreted as a code phrase for incarceration), was the fundamental principle of the youth criminal justice system. Section 3 of the *YOA* was amended in 1995 so that the protection of society was identified as a *primary objective* of the criminal law applicable to youth but this objective was described as being best served by rehabilitation, which clouded its meaning.[272]

The priorities of the *YOA* were ambiguous. The *YOA* had something for everyone.[273] It was left to judges to decide in any particular

---

[270]   *YOA*, see in particular s. 3(1)(a.1) and (c).

[271]   See the discussion of this point in Susan A. Reid and Marvin A. Zuker, "Conceptual Frameworks for Understanding Youth Justice in Canada: From the *Juvenile Delinquents Act* to the *Youth Criminal Justice Act*" in Kathryn Campbell, ed., *Understanding Youth Justice in Canada* (Toronto: Pearson Education Canada Inc., 2005), 89 at 91. See also Priscilla Platt, *Young Offenders Law in Canada*, 2d ed. (Markham: Butterworths Canada Ltd., 1995), at 17, and more recently, Nicholas Bala, *Youth Criminal Justice Law* (Toronto: Irwin Law, 2003), at 68. The Declarations of Principle in the *YOA* and the *YCJA* are examined in Chapter 3.

[272]   Nicholas Bala, *Youth Criminal Justice Law* (Toronto: Irwin Law, 2003), at 67.

[273]   Susan A. Reid and Marvin A. Zuker, "Conceptual Frameworks for Understanding Youth Justice in Canada: From the *Juvenile Delinquents Act* to the *Youth Criminal Justice Act*" in

case which principle was most important. As a result, court decisions across the country were inconsistent, and often dependent on the interpretation of a particular judge in a certain region.[274] What was clear was that the *YOA* incorporated a strong due process element that was not present in the *JDA*. This largely explains why the *YOA* was a longer, more complex and more legalistic piece of legislation, which resembled criminal law far more than its predecessor, given its entrenchment of rights and its greater focus on the accountability of the offender and the protection of society.

The *YOA* nevertheless included significant changes that provided for more individualized and arguably more lenient treatment of young persons, such as determinate sentences, and diversion, which encouraged non-judicial responses to offending behaviour to the extent feasible (although there was no detailed guidance, direction or principles regarding the criteria for diversion). The *YOA* also circumscribed the term "offence" so that only criminal offences, such as offences under the *Criminal Code* or offences under other federal Acts such as the *Controlled Drugs and Substances Act* were captured. As a result, far less deviant conduct by young persons was captured and criminalized under the *YOA* as compared to the *JDA*. It was expected that fewer young persons would be brought into contact with the criminal justice system. The *YOA* also established a national age jurisdiction so that the age of young persons captured by the *YOA* would be standard nation-wide. The *YOA* would apply to young persons who were at least 12 years old at the time of the alleged incident but under 18.

Some Canadian academics suggest that young persons ceased to be considered reformable subjects under the *YOA*, and that rehabilitation was no longer the focus of youth criminal justice legislation.[275] This view is not uniformly shared. As Chapter 3 demonstrates, the purpose and principles of the *YOA* were more nuanced in this regard.[276] It would be left largely to the judiciary to assess the priority to be given to rehabilitating the young person in a given case since s. 3 provided no clear guidance.

Kathryn Campbell, ed., *Understanding Youth Justice in Canada* (Toronto: Pearson Education Canada Inc., 2005), 89 at 102.

[274] Susan A. Reid and Marvin A. Zuker, "Conceptual Frameworks for Understanding Youth Justice in Canada: From the *Juvenile Delinquents Act* to the *Youth Criminal Justice Act*" in Kathryn Campbell, ed., *Understanding Youth Justice in Canada* (Toronto: Pearson Education Canada Inc., 2005), 89 at 91.

[275] Bryan Hogeveen, "History, Development, and Transformations in Canadian Juvenile Justice, 1800-1984" in Kathryn Campbell, ed., *Understanding Youth Justice in Canada* (Toronto: Pearson Education Canada Inc., 2005), 24 at 37.

[276] See Priscilla Platt's thoughtful discussion of s. 3, the Declaration of Principle, in Priscilla Platt, *Young Offenders Law in Canada*, 2d ed. (Markham: Butterworths Canada Ltd., 1995), at 17-34.

The failure to create a hierarchy of principles in s. 3 would ultimately result in a significant lack of uniformity in sentencing practices and outcomes across the country over the next 20 years. The disparity in the sentencing of youthful offenders for similar offences committed in similar circumstances across the country[277] would be only one of the issues that would contribute to the demise of the *YOA*.

E.   The 1990s — Reform of the *YOA* and the Road to the *Youth Criminal Justice Act*

The *YOA* was the subject of debate and criticism from its inception; calls for reform began almost immediately. No less than three sets of amendments occurred between 1984 and 1995. Minor amendments were made in 1986 in response to concerns from the police and the provinces, which, as a result, made it easier to charge young persons with breach of probation and to permit the publication of information concerning dangerous young persons at large in the community.[278]

By the late 1980s, the substance and pervasiveness of the criticism had deepened. Police reports of youth crime in Canada had increased (although this was believed to be, at least in part, a reflection of increased reporting of incidents as well as increases in charging by police due to raised awareness and zero tolerance policies within school systems).[279] The media is also perceived to have played a role: Reports about youth crime and the youth criminal justice system were common in the late 1980s, and political concerns mounted.[280] The focus of the criticism was on the perceived leniency of the *YOA*, both the leniency of sentences for the most serious crimes as well as the perceived difficulty in transferring young persons to adult court for trial, where they would be liable to harsher penalties.[281]

---

[277] Julian V. Roberts and Nicholas Bala, "Understanding Sentencing Under the *Youth Criminal Justice Act*" (2003) 41 Alta. L. Rev. 395, at para. 19 (QL).

[278] As discussed in Nicholas Bala, "The Development of Canada's Youth Justice Law" in Kathryn Campbell, ed., *Understanding Youth Justice in Canada* (Toronto: Pearson Education Canada Inc., 2005), 41 at 43.

[279] Nicholas Bala, "The Development of Canada's Youth Justice Law" in Kathryn Campbell, ed., *Understanding Youth Justice in Canada* (Toronto: Pearson Education Canada Inc., 2005), 41 at 44-45.

[280] Sanjeev Anand, "Catalyst for Change: The History of Canadian Juvenile Justice Reform" (Spring 1999) Vol. 24, No. 2, Queen's L.J. 515, at 552.

[281] Nicholas Bala, "The Development of Canada's Youth Justice Law" in Kathryn Campbell, ed., *Understanding Youth Justice in Canada* (Toronto: Pearson Education Canada Inc., 2005), 41 at 43.

In 1992, the Progressive Conservative government implemented further amendments, which included raising the maximum sentence in youth court for murder from three years to five years less a day and amending the transfer provisions so that the paramount consideration for transferring a young person to adult court was "protection of the public".[282]

Youth justice was part of the federal election campaign of 1993, for the first time in Canadian history.[283] Reported youth crime had peaked in the early 1990s,[284] and all federal parties spoke out against the *YOA*, advocating a get-tough approach.[285] Only the Bloc Québécois supported the Act.[286]

Amendments were tabled in June of 1994, which resulted in a final round of reforms in 1995. These 1995 amendments implemented various changes, including increasing to 10 years in custody the maximum sentence for first degree murder. The 1995 changes also created a presumption that 16- and 17-year-old young persons charged with the most serious violent offences (murder, attempted murder, manslaughter and aggravated sexual assault) would be tried in adult court.[287]

Despite three sets of amendments during the first 11 years of its existence, the *YOA* remained the subject of continued and often intense controversy. Calls for further reform continued. Critics charged that the *YOA* was too lenient, that victims of crime did not have a voice, and that the *YOA* did not adequately protect the public from violent young offend-

---

[282] Nicholas Bala, "The Development of Canada's Youth Justice Law" in Kathryn Campbell, ed., *Understanding Youth Justice in Canada* (Toronto: Pearson Education Canada Inc., 2005), 41 at 43.

[283] Sanjeev Anand, "Catalyst for Change: The History of Canadian Juvenile Justice Reform" (Spring 1999) Vol. 24, No. 2, Queen's L.J. 515, at 552.

[284] Nicholas Bala, "The Development of Canada's Youth Justice Law" in Kathryn Campbell, ed., *Understanding Youth Justice in Canada* (Toronto: Pearson Education Canada Inc., 2005), 41 at 44.

[285] Nicholas Bala, "The Development of Canada's Youth Justice Law" in Kathryn Campbell, ed., *Understanding Youth Justice in Canada* (Toronto: Pearson Education Canada Inc., 2005), 41 at 44 and Sanjeev Anand, "Catalyst for Change: The History of Canadian Juvenile Justice Reform" (Spring 1999) Vol. 24, No. 2, Queen's L.J. 515, at 552.

[286] Nicholas Bala, "The Development of Canada's Youth Justice Law" in Kathryn Campbell, ed., *Understanding Youth Justice in Canada* (Toronto: Pearson Education Canada Inc., 2005), 41 at 44 and 48.

[287] See Department of Justice, *A Strategy for the Renewal of Youth Justice* (Ottawa: Ministry of Supply and Services, 1998) (section regarding Concerns about the Current Youth Justice System). This document was the federal government's response to *Renewing Youth Justice: Thirteenth Report of the Standing Committee on Justice and Legal Affairs*, released in April 1997. At the time of writing, this 1998 document could be readily accessed through the Department of Justice website at: <http://www.justice.gc.ca/eng/pi/yj-jj/about-apropos/toc-tdm.html>. In this document, the federal government reviews the shortcomings of the *YOA* and outlines its rationale for introducing the *Youth Criminal Justice Act*.

ers.[288] There was a public "misperception" that the *YOA* was associated with a substantial increase in youth crime.[289] While the Act was perceived to be soft on crime, in fact, the *YOA* resulted in much higher rates of incarceration for young persons.[290] The public perception that the *YOA* was too lenient would be among the main issues the federal government would seek to address in the new *Youth Criminal Justice Act*.[291]

In fact, as the final set of amendments to the *YOA* was being tabled on June 2, 1994, federal Justice Minister Allan Rock wrote to the Chair of the Standing Committee on Justice and Legal Affairs, proposing a fundamental review of the *YOA*. Rock acknowledged that the *YOA* was controversial, and that questions remained as to whether it was the best juvenile justice model for Canada. A Task Force on Youth Justice was established by the federal, provincial and territorial Ministers responsible for justice (excepting Quebec, which had just completed its own review of the *YOA*)[292] to review the Act. The task force released its report in 1996, which prompted further study and consultations by the Standing Committee on Justice and Legal Affairs. The Liberal-dominated Standing Committee then released its watershed report on the youth justice system in Canada, *Renewing Youth Justice*, in April 1997.[293]

This report included 14 recommendations.[294] Initial federal government plans in 1997 had called for amendments to the *YOA* rather than enacting an entirely new statute. During consultations with the provinces, however, it became clear that the changes that were required were more extensive than originally envisioned, and that the solution lay in a new

---

[288] Bryan Hogeveen, "History, Development, and Transformations in Canadian Juvenile Justice, 1800-1984" in Kathryn Campbell, ed., *Understanding Youth Justice in Canada* (Toronto: Pearson Education Canada Inc., 2005), 24 at 38.

[289] Nicholas Bala, "The Development of Canada's Youth Justice Law" in Kathryn Campbell, ed., *Understanding Youth Justice in Canada* (Toronto: Pearson Education Canada Inc., 2005), 41 at 45.

[290] Nicholas Bala, "The Development of Canada's Youth Justice Law" in Kathryn Campbell, ed., *Understanding Youth Justice in Canada* (Toronto: Pearson Education Canada Inc., 2005), 41 at 45.

[291] In *A Strategy for the Renewal of Youth Justice*, in various sections, the federal government discusses its concerns about the incarceration rates of young persons in Canada, which were reported to be four times the rate of incarceration of adults in Canada and also greater than the incarceration rates for young persons in most other Western countries, including the U.S. Department of Justice, *A Strategy for the Renewal of Youth Justice* (Ottawa: Ministry of Supply and Services, 1998), online at: <http://www.justice.gc.ca/eng/pi/yj-jj/about-apropos/toc-tdm.html>.

[292] *Reference re: Bill C-7 respecting the criminal justice system for young persons*, [2003] Q.J. No. 2850, at para. 7 (Que. C.A.).

[293] Canada, House of Commons, *Renewing Youth Justice: Thirteenth Report of the Standing Committee on Justice and Legal Affairs*, April 1997.

[294] Canada, House of Commons, *Renewing Youth Justice: Thirteenth Report of the Standing Committee on Justice and Legal Affairs*, April 1997.

Act, which would be simpler and easier to understand than one with many amendments.[295] A new Act was also perceived to be more politically palatable since the federal government could claim that it had introduced an entirely new youth justice regime, signalling to the public and to criminal justice participants that significant change was afoot.[296] As the federal government proceeded with plans to draft and implement new legislation, and to effectively design a new youth criminal justice regime, youth justice was again an election issue in the June 1997 federal election campaign.[297]

The federal government issued its response to the Committee report, *Renewing Youth Justice*, in May 1998. In its response, *A Strategy for the Renewal of Youth Justice*,[298] the federal government announced that it would replace the *YOA* with a new youth justice statute. The strategy outlined the reasoning and philosophical foundation for what would eventually be introduced as the *Youth Criminal Justice Act*. The introduction of a brand new Act, with a number of significant new features, including a Preamble, a revamped Declaration of Principle (which included an express recognition of the role of victims), a significantly expanded section on diversion, new sentences and sentencing principles (which had never before existed in youth criminal justice legislation), and a provision that included a presumption of an adult sentence for offenders as young as 14 charged with the most serious violent offences, would send a clear message to the public that the federal government was introducing an entirely new youth justice regime. When it was introduced, the *YCJA* was certainly a much bigger and ostensibly more complex Act, with its nearly 200 sections, in sharp contrast to the succinct and compact 70 sections of the *YOA*.

In terms of discerning the federal government's rationale for a new Act, *A Strategy for the Renewal of Youth Justice* is a key document.[299] The

---

[295] Nicholas Bala, "The Development of Canada's Youth Justice Law" in Kathryn Campbell, ed., *Understanding Youth Justice in Canada* (Toronto: Pearson Education Canada Inc., 2005), 41 at 49.

[296] Nicholas Bala, "The Development of Canada's Youth Justice Law" in Kathryn Campbell, ed., *Understanding Youth Justice in Canada* (Toronto: Pearson Education Canada Inc., 2005), 41 at 49-50.

[297] Nicholas Bala, "The Development of Canada's Youth Justice Law" in Kathryn Campbell, ed., *Understanding Youth Justice in Canada* (Toronto: Pearson Education Canada Inc., 2005), 41 at 44.

[298] Department of Justice (Ottawa: Ministry of Supply and Services, 1998), online at: <http://www.justice.gc.ca/eng/pi/yj-jj/about-apropos/toc-tdm.html>.

[299] See Department of Justice, *A Strategy for the Renewal of Youth Justice* (Ottawa: Ministry of Supply and Services, 1998). This document was the federal government's response to *Renewing Youth Justice: Thirteenth Report of the Standing Committee on Justice and Legal Affairs*, released in April 1997. At the time of writing, *A Strategy for the Renewal of Youth*

1998 document acknowledged that the Canadian public generally perceived the *Young Offenders Act* and youth court judges to be too lenient,
and that the public was sceptical about the capacity of the youth justice
system to provide meaningful penalties proportionate to the seriousness of
the crime. The objective of the strategy, it said, is the protection of society
by reducing youth crime, and that this requires a concerted effort by
various parties to address the root causes of crime. The strategy outlined
three fundamental weaknesses of the youth justice system as it then was:
not enough was being done to prevent young persons from committing
crimes, the system needed to improve the way it dealt with the most
serious violent youth, and the system relied too strongly on custody in
response to the vast majority of non-violent youth when alternative
community-based responses could do a better job. The document noted
that the incarceration rate for youths in Canada was four times higher than
the adult incarceration rate, and that the youth incarceration rate in Canada
was also much higher than that of many other Western countries, including the U.S., Australia and New Zealand. This observation was particularly poignant because a substantial majority of youths were being
committed to custody for non-violent offences. The federal government
stated in the document that "the belief in the rehabilitative capacity of
young people is a fundamental principle of the youth justice system", that
the best way to address youth crime is to prevent it through community
programs and by addressing the social factors linked to the underlying
causes of delinquency, that alternatives to the formal justice system can
address the majority of non-violent offenders but that "firm measures" are
required to protect the public from violent and repeat young offenders.[300]

These themes were repeated when the bill finally made it into the
House of Commons. The Liberal government introduced the *Youth
Criminal Justice Act* as Bill C-68 on March 11, 1999, but it died on the
Order Paper. It was reintroduced as Bill C-3 on October 14, 2000. The
bill was the subject of extensive consultation and exhaustive review
before the Standing Committee on Justice and Human Rights. When a
federal election intervened, youth justice was once more an election
platform issue during the November 27, 2000 election.[301] Justice Minister

Justice could be accessed through the Department of Justice website at:
<http://www.justice.gc.ca/eng/pi/yj-jj/about-apropos/toc-tdm.html>. In this document, the
federal government reviews the short-comings of the *YOA* and outlines its rationale for
introducing the *Youth Criminal Justice Act*. This document is the evidentiary and philosophical foundation for the *YCJA*; it is the policy paper.

[300] Department of Justice, *A Strategy for the Renewal of Youth Justice* (Ottawa: Ministry of
Supply and Services, 1998) (section on Concerns about the Current Youth Justice System).

[301] Nicholas Bala, "The Development of Canada's Youth Justice Law" in Kathryn Campbell,
ed., *Understanding Youth Justice in Canada* (Toronto: Pearson Education Canada Inc.,
2005), 41 at 44.

Anne McLellan reintroduced the bill in the House of Commons on February 5, 2001 as Bill C-7. The re-introduced bill retained the overall direction and key elements of the original bill but included amendments brought forward in the fall of 2000 during the parliamentary hearings.

The intent of the Liberal government's bill is readily apparent in the parliamentary record. The key messages had not changed from those contained in *A Strategy for the Renewal of Youth Justice*. Among the seminal points that Anne McLellan made on February 14, 2001 regarding the intent of the new *YCJA* when she moved in the House of Commons that Bill C-7 be read a second time and referred to committee was that Canada had been incarcerating too many young persons under the *YOA*, and had failed to adequately distinguish between serious violent offences and less serious offences. Under the *YCJA*, she said, custody was to be reserved primarily for violent offenders and serious repeat offenders. "[A] basic policy direction of the new legislation is that serious violent offences are to be treated seriously and less serious offences are to be dealt with through less intrusive yet still meaningful consequences."[302]

McLellan explained:

> ... the existing *YOA* has resulted in the highest youth incarceration rate in the western world, including our neighbors to the south, the United States. Young persons in Canada often receive harsher custodial sentences than adults receive for the same type of offence. Almost 80 per cent of custodial sentences are for non-violent offences. Many non-violent offenders found guilty of less serious offences such as minor theft are sentenced to custody.
>
> The proposed youth criminal justice act is intended to reduce the unacceptably high level of youth incarceration that has occurred under the *Young Offenders Act*. ...
>
> In contrast to the *YOA*, the new legislation provides that custody is to be reserved primarily for violent offenders and serious repeat offenders. The new youth justice legislation recognizes that non-custodial sentences can often provide more meaningful consequences and be more effective in rehabilitating young persons.[303]

McLellan further stated that the *YOA* had resulted in the overuse of court for minor cases that could be better dealt with outside the court. Experience in Canada and in other countries had demonstrated that measures outside of the court process could provide effective and timely responses to less serious youth crime. Although the *YOA* had permitted alternative measures, it had not provided enough legislative direction

---

[302] *House of Commons Debates* (14 February 2001), at 1535.
[303] *House of Commons Debates* (14 February 2001), at 1530.

regarding their use, she said. "The proposed youth criminal justice act is intended to enable the courts to focus on serious youth crimes by increasing the use of effective and timely non-court responses to less serious offences."[304]

Opposition MPs criticized the bill. Vic Toews,[305] who would eventually become the federal Justice Minister, spoke on behalf of the now defunct Canadian Alliance party in saying that the Canadian Alliance still had "grave concerns about the bill".[306] Not only had there been a lack of consultation with the provinces and a failure by the Liberal government to provide adequate funding, the federal government had stubbornly refused to consider suggestions for further amendments.[307] Toews criticized the *YCJA* for being costly, complex and cumbersome, and for attempting to be all things to all people.[308] In particular, he lamented the fact that the restrictive disclosure provisions that generally prohibit publication of the names of youthful offenders often serve the interests of youthful criminal predators living in communities while preventing communities from being notified of their presence, thus favouring the rights of dangerous criminals over the rights of victims and potential victims. Toews complained about the extensive extrajudicial measures (formerly called alternative measures) that permitted violent offenders to have access to alternative measures. "The real question that needs to be answered is not whether the legislation is too soft or too tough. The real question is whether the legislation will be effective in meeting goals of rehabilitation, deterrence and denunciation of crime."[309]

Meanwhile, the Bloc Québécois maintained its position that the new *YCJA* was not needed and that the *YOA* was working in Quebec. The problem, if one existed, was not with the legislation but with the manner in which it was being enforced in some provinces,[310] the Bloc claimed. Quebec had both the lowest crime rate and the lowest recidivism rates in Canada, the Bloc asserted.[311]

---

[304] *House of Commons Debates* (14 February 2001), at 1530.
[305] Mr. Toews became federal Justice Minister in February 2006, after the Conservatives formed a minority government under Prime Minister Stephen Harper. Robert Nicholson replaced Mr. Toews as Justice Minister following a cabinet shuffle in January 2007.
[306] *House of Commons Debates* (14 February 2001), at 1605.
[307] *House of Commons Debates* (14 February 2001), at 1605.
[308] *House of Commons Debates* (14 February 2001), at 1600.
[309] *House of Commons Debates* (14 February 2001), at 1605.
[310] *House of Commons Debates* (14 February 2001), at 1610. Comments are from Michel Bellehumeur, the BQ member from Berthier-Montcalm.
[311] *House of Commons Debates* (14 February 2001), at 1615. Recent statistics on youth crime are included in Chapter 10.

Despite opposition, the bill received Royal Assent on February 19, 2002 under the Liberal government when Martin Cauchon was federal Justice Minister. In order to give provinces time to prepare for new programs and policies that were part of the new *YCJA*, the federal government delayed the bill's coming into force until April 1, 2003.[312]

VI. CONCLUSION

Canada's formal youth criminal justice system has now been in operation for more than a century. The remainder of this book considers fundamental questions about the youth criminal justice system in Canada at a pivotal time in our legal history:

- What should Canadians expect youth criminal justice legislation to achieve?

- What is the role and impact of youth justice legislation in addressing youth crime?

- Does the *YCJA* contain a principled and evidence-based youth justice philosophy for the 21st century, with clear goals and priorities?

- What does the jurisprudence reveal about the purpose and meaning of the *YCJA*?

- Is the *YCJA* achieving its purpose and objectives? If not, how and where has it failed?

- Does the *YCJA* provide adequate guidance and direction to the judiciary and other criminal justice system players, who must interpret its provisions?

- What changes, if any, are required to the *YCJA*?

- Is Canada headed in the proper direction regarding proposed reform of the *YCJA*?

- Are we taking the correct steps in order to achieve the common goal of preventing youth crime in Canada?

Following the centenary of the establishment of a formal youth criminal justice system in Canada, it is appropriate to reflect upon the origin and the evolution of that system, the nature of the system today,

---

[312] Nicholas Bala, "The Development of Canada's Youth Justice Law" in Kathryn Campbell, ed., *Understanding Youth Justice in Canada* (Toronto: Pearson Education Canada Inc., 2005), 41 at 48-49.

and what changes are needed to improve it. We must understand the path we have travelled in order to navigate the decades of the 21st century with wisdom.

> The law embodies the story of a nation's development through many centuries, and it cannot be dealt with as if it contained only the axioms and corollaries of a book of mathematics. In order to know what it is, we must know what it has been, and what it tends to become.[313]

---

[313] Oliver Wendell Holmes, Jr., *The Common Law* (Boston: Little, Brown and Company, 1881), at 1.

Chapter 2

JURISDICTION AND THE AGE OF CRIMINAL RESPONSIBILITY

In order to determine the meaning of an undefined term in a statute, it is now well established that a court is to read the words making up the term "in their entire context and in their grammatical and ordinary sense harmoniously with the scheme of the Act, the object of the Act, and the intention of Parliament".

R. v. C.D.; R. v. C.D.K., [2005] S.C.J. No. 79, at para. 27 (S.C.C.). (Justice Bastarache is quoting E.A. Driedger, *Construction of Statutes*, 2d ed. (Markham: Butterworths Canada Ltd., 1983), at 87.

I.   INTRODUCTION

The *YCJA* has been in force since only 2003;[1] thus, many of its provisions have yet to be judicially considered by the higher courts in Canada. The jurisprudence to date is largely from the lower courts and is often inconsistent across jurisdictions. Jurisdictional questions are a case in point: It will be some years before many of the emerging jurisdictional issues are clarified by the higher courts. Where there is no case law under the *YCJA* regarding a particular jurisdictional issue, the decisions under the *YOA*[2] often provide useful guidance since the wording of at least some of the *YCJA* jurisdictional provisions are identical, or at least highly similar, to the wording of provisions under the *YOA*.

Similar to the *YOA*, the *YCJA* grants the youth justice court exclusive jurisdiction *in respect of any offence* alleged to have been committed by a person while he or she was a young person, and that person is to be dealt with as provided in the *YCJA*,[3] despite any other Act

---

[1]   *Youth Criminal Justice Act*, S.C. 2002, c. 1 [hereafter "*YCJA*"].
[2]   *Young Offenders Act*, R.S.C. 1985, c. Y-1 [hereafter "*YOA*"], enacted as S.C. 1980-81-82-83, c. 110, s. 1.
[3]   *YCJA*, s. 14. The wording of s. 14 of the *YCJA* is arguably clear on its face and Department of Justice documents support an interpretation that the intent of the legislation was to ensure

of Parliament and subject to only the *Contraventions Act*[4] and the *National Defence Act.*[5] (These two jurisdictional exceptions are discussed later in this chapter.) As this chapter illustrates, the focus of the jurisprudence in this area to date relates to the meaning to be attached to expressions such as *in respect of any offence* and how broadly or narrowly that term should be interpreted. For example, was that phrase intended to capture all criminal proceedings involving the young person or only those proceedings relating strictly to an offence alleged to have been committed by the young person?

Unlike the *YOA*, the clear intent of the *YCJA* is to ensure that the trial of a young person charged with a federal offence (which largely means offences under the *Criminal Code*[6] and the *Controlled Drugs and Substances Act*[7]) will always be conducted by a youth justice court judge[8] in youth justice court, even though this means, in certain circumstances, that the superior court of criminal jurisdiction and a superior court judge will be deemed to be the youth justice court and a youth justice court judge, respectively, for the purpose of the proceedings. For example, when a young person is facing a serious charge, such as murder, he or she has the right to elect the mode of trial.[9] If he or she elects trial by judge alone in relation to a s. 469 offence such as murder, the *YCJA* stipulates that a superior court judge shall hear the matter but that he or she is

---

that all criminal proceedings involving young persons charged with federal offences would occur in youth justice court, subject to only the *Contraventions Act* and the *National Defence Act*. See for example the Department of Justice document *Why Did the Government Introduce New Youth Justice Legislation?*, point 4, on pp. 2-3. At the time of writing, this document was available from the Department of Justice website at: <http://www.justice. gc.ca/eng/pi/yj-jj/ycja-lsjpa/why-pourq.html>. Nevertheless, as this chapter illustrates, some courts are interpreting the jurisdictional provisions to permit some proceedings involving young persons, such as applications and bail hearings, to occur in ordinary (adult) court in various circumstances based, in part, on the argument that the youth justice court has exclusive jurisdiction in relation to only the offence but does not necessarily have exclusive jurisdiction over other proceedings in relation to the young person, such as prohibition orders.

The key federal government document, *A Strategy for the Renewal of Youth Justice*, released in 1998, is also important in terms of the government's intent regarding the *YCJA*. The section concerning the intent of the legislation is entitled Legislative and Supporting Program Components. At the time of writing, the website address was: <http://www.justice.gc.ca/eng/pi/yj-jj/about-apropos/toc-tdm.html>.

4   S.C. 1992, c. 47.
5   R.S.C. 1985, c. N-5.
6   R.S.C. 1985, c. C-46.
7   S.C. 1996, c. 19, ss. 1 to 60.
8   Youth justice court judge is defined in s. 14(6) of the *YCJA* to include a Justice of the Peace, but see also s. 20, which circumscribes the powers of a Justice of the Peace in relation to young persons.
9   *YCJA*, s. 67(1) and (2).

deemed to be a youth justice court judge and the court is deemed to be a youth justice court for the purpose of the proceeding.[10]

This procedural change guarantees that the young person retains the enhanced procedural protections of the *YCJA* throughout his or her trial because he or she remains under the umbrella of the youth justice court. Upon a finding of guilt in youth justice court, the young person can be found eligible for an adult sentence in certain circumstances. Under the *YCJA*, the eligibility hearing for the adult sentence occurs in youth justice court, not in adult court.

Under the *YOA*, the young person could be transferred to adult court *for trial.* This transfer hearing to adult court has been eliminated under the *YCJA*. Thus, the trial and the sentencing of the young person will always occur, technically, in youth justice court, or in a court deemed to be a youth justice court for purposes of the proceeding, subject to only the *Contraventions Act* or the *National Defence Act.*[11] As Goudge J.A. of the Ontario Court of Appeal explains: "The *YCJA* provides that all proceedings are conducted before the youth justice court. As in this case, where the charge is sufficiently serious that the young person is entitled to elect trial in the superior court of criminal jurisdiction, that court is then deemed to be a youth justice court for the proceedings, although retaining the jurisdiction and powers of a superior court."[12]

The Quebec Court of Appeal[13] further indicates that: "Section 13 of the *YCJA* enshrines the priority given to the specialized court for young persons and subjects justices of the Superior Court of criminal jurisdiction to all the provisions of the *YCJA* by imposing on them the same obligations in regard to the young person as those of judges of the specialized court."[14]

The prime aim of such jurisdictional provisions, is to ensure that young persons, including those facing the most serious charges and longest sentences, will retain the additional protections afforded young

---

[10] *YCJA* s. 13(2) and (3). As this chapter explains, members of the judiciary are interpreting these provisions differently. Some are finding that "proceeding" refers to only the trial, while others take the position that "proceeding" refers to all matters in relation to the prosecution of the offence, not just the trial.

[11] The key *YCJA* sections here are ss. 13 and 14.

[12] *R. v. D.B.*, [2006] O.J. No. 1112 (Ont. C.A.), affd [2008] S.C.J. No. 25, 2008 SCC 25 (S.C.C.).

[13] *Reference re: Bill C-7 respecting the criminal justice system for young persons*, [2003] Q.J. No. 2850 (Que. C.A.).

[14] *Reference re: Bill C-7 respecting the criminal justice system for young persons*, [2003] Q.J. No. 2850, at para. 154 (Que. C.A.).

persons under the *YCJA* throughout the court proceedings.[15] Federal
government documents demonstrate that this was the intention.[16] In cases
where the youth justice court imposes an adult sentence, the young person
generally loses the additional protections afforded young persons under
the *YCJA* as of this point. For example, upon receiving an adult sentence,
the name of a young person can be published,[17] and the record of the
young person in relation to the offence for which he or she received an
adult sentence is treated as an adult record and, thus, the record in relation
to the adult sentence is not protected to the same degree as a youth
record.[18]

These jurisdictional provisions are also designed to ensure that, to
the extent feasible, the judges who traditionally have the greatest expertise
and knowledge regarding youth cases (generally the provincial court
judges who traditionally dealt with youth cases under the *YOA*) will
continue to handle most of the youth cases.[19] Some youth justice experts
have expressed concern that superior court judges do not always have the
necessary knowledge of the youth justice legislation to deal with youth
cases since provincial court judges have generally dealt with these cases.[20]
This criticism has not gone unchallenged. Justice Gage of the Ontario
Court of Justice has suggested that the assumption that provincial court
judges have a superior ability to understand and apply the values and
scheme of the *YCJA* is not established or well founded.[21]

---

[15] See A. Doob and J. Sprott, "Sentencing under the *Youth Criminal Justice Act*: An Historical Perspective" in Kathryn Campbell, ed., *Understanding Youth Justice in Canada* (Toronto: Pearson Education Canada Inc., 2005) 221, at 237. See also Nicholas Bala's discussion of the same point in *Youth Criminal Justice Law* (Toronto: Irwin Law, 2003), at 356.

[16] As mentioned, on this point, see in particular the discussion in the Department of Justice document *Why Did the Government Introduce New Youth Justice Legislation?*, point 4, on pp. 2-3. At the time of writing, this document was available from the Department of Justice website at: <http://www.justice.gc.ca/eng/pi/yj-jj/ycja-lsjpa/why-pourq.html>.

[17] *YCJA*, s. 110(2)(a) permits the automatic publication of a young person's name upon his or her receiving an adult sentence under the *YCJA*.

[18] *YCJA*, s. 117. The guilty finding is also considered a conviction for purposes of the *Criminal Records Act*, R.S.C. 1985, c. C-47.

[19] The courts are structured differently in some provinces and territories. For example, the Nunavut Court of Justice is a Unified Court, Canada's first and only single-level court. Under this unified court, the powers of the territorial court and the superior court have been melded so that this one court can handle any type of case. More information is available by accessing the website of the Nunavut Court of Justice at: <http://www.nucj.ca/unifiedcourt.htm>.

[20] Nicholas Bala, *Youth Criminal Justice Law* (Toronto: Irwin Law, 2003), at 513.

[21] *R. v. M.F.*, [2006] O.J. No. 1805, at paras. 47 and 48 (Ont. C.J.).

II. JURISDICTION UNDER THE YOUTH CRIMINAL JUSTICE ACT

Under s. 13(1) of the *YCJA*, the provinces and territories can establish or designate certain courts as youth justice courts for the purpose of the *YCJA*. A youth justice court judge is defined as a person who may be appointed or designated as a judge of the youth justice court or a judge sitting in a court established or designated as a youth justice court. The *YOA* had similar wording in its definition section.[22] In most provinces and territories, provincial or territorial court judges who generally deal with adult criminal cases have been given jurisdiction to deal with youth criminal cases. In Ontario, for example, judges of the Ontario Court of Justice (the provincial court) generally deal with youth cases rather than judges of the Superior Court.

The Supreme Court of Canada settled this issue in 1990 in relation to the *Young Offenders Act* when the court was asked to decide, among other things, whether the *YOA* was unconstitutional to the extent that it did not specifically require the youth court to be presided over by a judge appointed pursuant to s. 96 of the *Constitution Act, 1867, i.e.*, a superior court judge.[23] The majority held that the *YOA* did not offend s. 96 of the *Constitution Act, 1867*. Jurisdiction over young persons charged with criminal offences was not significantly exercised by any judicial body at Confederation, the court found. These adjudicative powers were created after Confederation and could therefore be constitutionally entrusted to inferior courts. The kinds of offences governed by the *YOA* would have been within the jurisdiction of inferior courts in any event had a separate scheme similar to that in the *YOA* existed in 1867.[24] Since new powers of jurisdiction are not part of the core jurisdiction of superior courts protected by s. 96, permitting inferior courts to exercise jurisdiction in relation to a scheme designed to respond to a novel concern in society does not offend s. 96 of the *Constitution Act*.[25] "Parliament's power over criminal law and procedure enables it not only to create the substantive

---

[22]   *YOA*, s. 2(1).

[23]   *Constitution Act, 1867* (U.K.), 30 & 31 Vict., c. 3. See *Reference Re Young Offenders Act (P.E.I.)*, [1990] S.C.J. No. 60, at para. 11, [1991] 1 S.C.R. 252 (S.C.C.).

[24]   *Reference Re Young Offenders Act (P.E.I.)*, [1990] S.C.J. No. 60, at para. 11, [1991] 1 S.C.R. 252 (S.C.C.). See also *Reference Re Residential Tenancies Act 1979 (Ontario)*, [1981] S.C.J. No. 57, [1981] 1 S.C.R. 714 (S.C.C.).

[25]   *Reference Re Young Offenders Act (P.E.I.)*, [1990] S.C.J. No. 60, at para. 13, [1991] 1 S.C.R. 252 (S.C.C.).

law relating to crimes but also to grant jurisdiction over the offences it creates to specific courts."[26]

The jurisprudence also suggests that provincial court judges do not require an express, specific or individual appointment to the youth justice court in order to preside as youth justice court judges. In Yukon, for example, the Court of Appeal held in relation to the *YOA* that no specific individual appointment by Order-in-Council was required to designate a judge as a youth court judge.[27] A B.C. Supreme Court case held similarly: The province of B.C. had designated the Provincial Court of B.C. as the youth court but did not expressly appoint all Provincial Court judges as also judges of the youth court. The court held that once the Provincial Court is designated as a youth court, all duly appointed Provincial Court judges are indirectly appointed youth court judges. No individual appointment is necessary. Such appointments can be made indirectly and collectively.[28]

Further, s. 165(2) of the *YCJA* indicates that any person who was appointed (the term "appointed" is not defined in s. 165(2) or in the definition section of the *YCJA*) to be a youth court judge under the *YOA* is deemed to be a youth justice court judge under the *YCJA*, upon the coming into force of the *YCJA*.

A.   Powers of the Justice of the Peace

For the purpose of carrying out the provisions of the *YCJA*, a youth justice court judge means a justice (which includes a Justice of the Peace)[29] and a provincial court judge, who has the jurisdiction and powers of a summary conviction court under the *Criminal Code*.[30] In addition, as previously mentioned, in certain circumstances, a superior court judge can

---

[26]   *Reference Re Young Offenders Act (P.E.I.)*, [1990] S.C.J. No. 60, at para 11, [1991] 1 S.C.R. 252 (S.C.C.).

[27]   *R. v. G. (A.P.)*, [1990] Y.J. No. 127, 57 C.C.C. (3d) 496 (Y.T.C.A.).

[28]   *R. v. J.H.L.*, [1984] B.C.J. No. 2942, 13 C.C.C. (3d) 148 (B.C.S.C.). See also *R. v. N.*, [1984] O.J. No. 340, 12 C.C.C. (3d) 350 (Ont. S.C.).

[29]   *YCJA*, s. 2. While the term "justice" is not defined in the *YCJA*, s. 2(2) of the *YCJA* indicates that, unless otherwise provided, words and expressions used in the *YCJA* have the same meaning as in the *Criminal Code*. The definition section of the *Criminal Code*, also s. 2, indicates that a justice means a Justice of the Peace or a provincial court judge.

[30]   *YCJA*, s. 14(6). The wording of s. 14(6) is virtually identical to the wording of s. 5(4) of the *YOA*. The reference to the fact that the youth justice court judge has the jurisdiction and powers of a summary conviction court under the *Criminal Code* generally means that youth justice courts are courts of summary procedure that sit without a jury. The summary procedure process in youth justice court is discussed in greater depth in Chapter 4.

be deemed a youth justice court judge for the purpose of the proceeding upon the election of the young person.[31]

Under the *Criminal Code*, Justices of the Peace can deal with a range of procedural issues, such as adjournments, first appearances, bail hearings,[32] the receiving of an information, the signing of search warrants, issuing summonses to witnesses, as well as initiating proceedings by issuing summonses or warrants for the accused. In ordinary "adult" court, Justices of the Peace tend to routinely conduct bail hearings, preside over first appearance court, which often involves the granting of adjournments, and conduct trials in relation to provincial offences, such as offences under provincial highway traffic legislation (although the practice varies among jurisdictions).

By contrast, the *YCJA* restricts the powers of Justices of the Peace ("JPs") in relation to cases involving young persons. Under the *YCJA*, a JP can oversee any proceeding or issue any process that he or she is authorized to oversee or issue in relation to an adult under the *Criminal Code*. The *YCJA* also expressly gives JPs jurisdiction to order young persons to enter into peace bonds under s. 810 of the *Criminal Code* provided the young person consents to the order. If the young person fails or refuses to enter into the recognizance, the justice must refer the matter to the youth justice court.[33] However, s. 20 of the *YCJA* expressly prohibits a Justice of the Peace from taking pleas, conducting trials or adjudicating (such as imposing sentence) regarding young persons charged with criminal offences.[34]

Despite the express wording of s. 20 of the *YCJA*, JPs in some jurisdictions preside over a wider range of youth matters. This practice relates largely to statutory powers granted by provincial or territorial legislation, as well as the interpretation some courts ascribe to s. 13 of the *YCJA*. Section 13 defines a youth justice court judge as a person who may be appointed or designated as a judge of the youth justice court or a judge sitting in a court established or designated as a youth justice court judge.[35] In some jurisdictions, the courts have found that JPs have been appointed or designated as youth justice court judges.

Under the Yukon *Territorial Court Act*,[36] JPs can be appointed to exercise administrative and presiding functions in relation to criminal

---

[31] *YCJA*, s. 13(2) and (3).
[32] A Justice of the Peace cannot preside over a bail hearing in relation to a murder charge. See s. 515(1) and (11) and s. 522 of the *Criminal Code*.
[33] *YCJA*, s. 20(2).
[34] *YCJA*, s. 20.
[35] *YCJA*, s. 13.
[36] R.S.Y. 2002, c. 217, ss. 53-56.

matters involving young persons, provided that neither the custodial sentence to be imposed exceeds 90 days, nor the conditional sentence exceeds 180 days. The Act states that if the JP becomes aware during the course of hearing the criminal matter that the sentence being sought may require the JP to exceed his or her jurisdiction, the justice must adjourn the matter so that it can be heard by a judge.[37] In practice, JPs in Whitehorse, Yukon, accept pleas and impose sentence in less serious matters, but they do not conduct criminal trials or impose sentences in matters involving technical legal issues. In most communities outside of Whitehorse, the youth matters are generally dealt with by a judge. In a few Yukon communities outside of Whitehorse, the JPs deal with appearances by young persons and with minor sentencings.[38]

In Yukon, the Court of Appeal held in the 1990 case of *R. v. G. (A.P.)*[39] that s. 6 of the *YOA* (the virtual equivalent of s. 20 of the *YCJA*), which restricts the powers of JPs in youth criminal cases, applied only to situations where a JP had not been designated as a member of the youth court, whereas, in Yukon, Justices of the Peace had been designated judges of the youth court under the *Territorial Court Act*.[40] *R. v. G. (A.P.)* was decided under the *YOA*, but since the wording of s. 6 of the *YOA* regarding the powers of JPs is virtually identical to the wording of s. 20(1) under the *YCJA*, it provides useful guidance.

Likewise, in Nunavut, under the *Justices of the Peace Act*,[41] JPs can be appointed youth court judges and assigned powers and duties in relation to youth criminal justice matters, including the power to preside over the criminal trials of young persons. In Nunavut, Justices of the Peace are permitted to sit with the judge in the courtroom and are given the opportunity to speak with the accused following sentencing submissions and prior to the passing of sentence.[42]

Permitting JPs greater powers enables criminal matters to be dealt with more speedily in isolated Northern communities, where delay may be a concern, since the court party visits most communities in the three territories on circuit a limited number of times per year.

---

[37] R.S.Y. 2002, c. 217, s. 56.

[38] This was the practice in Yukon as of December 2006.

[39] [1990] Y.J. No. 127, 57 C.C.C. (3d) 496 (Y.T.C.A.), leave to appeal refused (1991), 61 C.C.C. (3d) vi (note) (S.C.C.).

[40] R.S.Y. 1986, c. 169. *R. v. G. (A.P.)*, [1990] Y.J. No. 127, 57 C.C.C. (3d) 496 (Y.T.C.A.), leave to appeal refused (1991), 61 C.C.C. (3d) vi (note) (S.C.C.).

[41] Consolidation of *Justices of the Peace Act (Nunavut)*, S.N.W.T. 1998, c. 34, s. 2.

[42] This information comes from the website for the Nunavut Court of Justice, which can be accessed at: <http://www.nucj.ca/unifiedcourt.htm>.

Nevertheless, some youth justice experts question the powers being exercised by JPs in some jurisdictions, since these powers appear to be in direct contrast to the intent of Parliament to restrict the powers of a Justice of the Peace in youth matters, as outlined in s. 20 of the *YCJA*. They suggest that jurisdiction can be conferred upon inferior courts only by express legislation, and that only the federal Parliament pursuant to its criminal law power can confer such jurisdiction. "Even if a provincial or territorial government chose to designate a 'justice of the peace court' as a youth court, one would not envisage that it could explicitly derrogate [*sic*] from Parliament's intention and expand the jurisdiction of a justice of the peace, a role which traditionally does not require formal legal training."[43]

In addition, the s. 20 restrictions on JPs recognize that youth matters are more delicate than those involving adults and require more qualified judicial officers.[44] JPs are lay persons who, generally speaking, are not lawyers and have limited knowledge of the criminal law and of the *Canadian Charter of Rights and Freedoms*[45] (although JPs receive training). Given the greater vulnerability of young persons *vis-à-vis* the state, s. 20 attempts to ensure that those with the most expertise and knowledge regarding young persons in conflict with the law are generally dealing with young persons, particularly in relation to the most serious charges.

If expanded powers for JPs are proving to be in the best interests of Northerners by allowing matters to be dealt with more speedily, however, the practice may go unchallenged unless there is evidence that the JPs are not adequately presiding over criminal matters involving young persons.

B.   Youth Justice Court

A prime purpose of the *YCJA* is to create a criminal justice system for young persons that is separate from adults[46] so that criminal matters involving young persons will be addressed within the four corners of the youth justice court unless the Act expressly states otherwise. Significantly, the Supreme Court of Canada affirmed the existence of a separate legal system for young persons in 2008 in *R. v. D.B.*,[47] when Abella J. acknowledged for the majority that the *YCJA* confirms in s. 3(1)(b) that

---

[43]   Priscilla Platt, *Young Offenders Law in Canada*, 2d ed. (Markham: Butterworths Canada Ltd., 1995), at 188.

[44]   Nicholas Bala, *Youth Criminal Justice Law* (Toronto: Irwin Law Inc., 2003), at 152.

[45]   Part I of the *Constitution Act, 1982*, being Schedule B to the *Canada Act 1982* (U.K.), 1982, c. 11.

[46]   This intent is clearly evident in the plain wording of s. 3(1)(b) of the *YCJA*. Justice Charron of the Supreme Court of Canada acknowledges this point in *R. v. B.W.P.*; *R. v. B.V.N.*, [2006] S.C.J. No. 27, 2006 SCC 27, at para. 22 (S.C.C.).

[47]   [2008] S.C.J. No. 25, 2008 SCC 25 (S.C.C.).

there is a separate legal system for young persons because young persons, due to age, have heightened vulnerability, less maturity and a reduced capacity for moral judgement.[48] The high court reiterated this basic premise a year later in *R. v. S.J.L.*[49] Justice Deschamps held that a separate criminal justice system for young persons is a governing principle of the *YCJA*, and, thus, young persons and adults cannot be tried together.[50] The *YCJA* also recognizes that the youth criminal justice system is aimed at providing young persons with enhanced procedural protection in relation to criminal proceedings in light of their greater dependency and lesser maturity.[51]

As previously mentioned, under s. 14(1) of the *YCJA*, the youth justice court has exclusive jurisdiction *in respect of any offence* alleged to have been committed by a person while he or she was a young person, and that person shall be dealt with as provided in the *YCJA*, subject only to the *Contraventions Act* and the *National Defence Act*. On the face of it, this provision,[52] when read within the context and overall scheme of the *YCJA*, appears to grant to the youth justice court exclusive jurisdiction in relation to any federal offence alleged to have been committed by a young person,[53] which would presumably encompass all proceedings in relation to the prosecution of that offence, such as applications for bail and youth records, and prohibition orders, unless the *YCJA* expressly says otherwise. From a statutory interpretation perspective, this is common sense. It is now well established, that, in order to determine the meaning of an undefined term in a statute, "a court is to read the words making up the term in their entire context and in their grammatical and ordinary sense harmoniously with the scheme of the Act, the object of the Act, and the intention of Parliament".[54] Section 14(1) should also be interpreted in keeping with the doctrine of liberal construction outlined in s. 3(2) of the *YCJA*, which states: "This Act shall be liberally construed so as to ensure that young persons are dealt with in accordance with the principles set out in subsection (1) (of the Declaration of Principle)." Among those express

---

[48]   *R. v. D.B.*, [2008] S.C.J. No. 25, at paras. 40 and 41, 2008 SCC 25 (S.C.C.).

[49]   [2009] S.C.J. No. 14, 2009 SCC 14 (S.C.C.).

[50]   [2009] S.C.J. No. 14, at para. 56, 2009 SCC 14 (S.C.C.).

[51]   *YCJA*, s. 3(1)(b)(iii). See also Sandra J. Bell, *Young Offenders and Juvenile Justice: A Century After the Fact*, 2d ed. (Scarborough: Nelson, a division of Thomson Canada Ltd., 2003), at 52, as well as Nicholas Bala, *Youth Criminal Justice Law* (Toronto: Irwin Law Inc., 2003), at 79.

[52]   A virtually identical provision appeared in the *YOA*, s. 5(1).

[53]   "Offence" in s. 2(1) of the *YCJA* means an offence created by an Act of Parliament; therefore, similar to the *YOA*, provincial and municipal offences are excluded. For example, offences under provincial highway traffic laws are not captured by this definition.

[54]   *R. v. C.D.; R. v. C.D.K.*, [2005] S.C.J. No. 79, at para. 27 (S.C.C.). Justice Bastarache is quoting E.A. Driedger, *Construction of Statutes*, 2d ed. (Markham: Butterworths Canada Ltd., 1983), at 87.

principles in s. 3(1) of the Declaration of Principle of the *YCJA* is that the criminal justice system for young persons must be separate from that of adults.[55]

In *L. (S.) v. B. (N.)*,[56] the Ontario Court of Appeal considered the jurisdiction of the youth justice court under the *YCJA* in relation to the powers of the superior court. Justice Doherty interpreted the provisions in keeping with the overall intent of the *YCJA*. In that case, the Ontario Court of Appeal was considering which court, the superior court or the youth justice court, had jurisdiction to compel the production of youth records. In his decision, Doherty J.A. considered the limited jurisdiction of the superior court in relation to youth matters under the *YCJA*. Justice Doherty observed that the superior court is deemed to be a youth justice court only for the purpose of proceedings as described in s. 13(2) and (3) of the *YCJA*, which flow from a young person's election or deemed election of trial by judge alone or by judge and jury. Therefore, in the case before him, since the request for access to the records had come long after the proceeding had ended, the superior court could not be deemed to be the youth justice court for purposes of the application for access to the documents. "Parliament can create a discrete criminal justice system for young offenders and vest exclusive jurisdiction over that system in a court other than a superior court of general jurisdiction ... In this case, as in the vast majority of cases, the Ontario Court of Justice [the provincial court] will be the youth justice court for the purposes of the *YCJA*."[57]

Nevertheless, at least some courts are interpreting ss. 13 and 14 of the *YCJA*, so that both the provincial court that hears adult matters and the superior court (rather than the youth justice court) are being granted jurisdiction to hear youth matters more widely than may have been intended. Some lower courts have held that the exclusive jurisdiction of the youth justice court applies to only the offence. Where an application is made regarding a young person and no offence is involved, the courts have found that a provincial court judge sitting in adult court and not a youth justice court judge has jurisdiction to hear the matter. In *R. v. R.A.M.*,[58] which was decided in 2004 in relation to the virtually identical jurisdictional provision under the *YOA*,[59] Durno J. of Ontario's superior court held that

---

[55] *YCJA*, s. 3(1)(b) and (2).

[56] [2005] O.J. No. 1411, 195 C.C.C. (3d) 481 (Ont. C.A.).

[57] *L. (S.) v. B. (N.)*, [2005] O.J. No. 1411, at paras. 60 and 38, respectively, 195 C.C.C. (3d) 481 (Ont. C.A.).

[58] [2004] O.J. No. 489, 182 C.C.C. (3d) 14 (Ont. S.C.).

[59] Section 5(1) of the *YOA* is the predecessor section to s. 14(1) of the *YCJA*. The only difference in wording is that s. 5(1) does not refer to the *Contraventions Act*, which had not yet come into force. It also refers to s. 16 transfer hearings, which were eliminated under the *YCJA*. But for purposes of this discussion, the wording referred to is identical.

the provincial court judge in adult court had jurisdiction to hear a Crown's s. 111 application for a prohibition order in relation to a young person because an application is not an offence. The *YOA* was found to be a complete code for young persons charged with federal offences, but was *not* a complete code for all criminal law matters concerning young persons. "Had Parliament wanted to make the legislation a complete code in regards to all aspects of criminal law it would have said so."[60] The exclusive jurisdiction of the youth court relates only to federal offences, the court found.

R. v. R.A.M. concerned a s. 111 application under the *Criminal Code* for a prohibition order against a young person after police found firearms at his home following the execution of a search warrant. The young person had not been charged with any offence. In his analogous reasoning, Durno J. noted that the majority of judgments that had considered whether the youth court had jurisdiction to hear a peace bond application had concluded that the youth court did not have such jurisdiction under s. 810 of the *Criminal Code* because the section did not create an offence.[61] Justice Durno agreed with those authorities because the youth justice court's exclusive jurisdiction relates to offences, not applications, and also because the youth court has exclusive jurisdiction over young persons charged under federal legislation and a young person facing a s. 111 application is not charged under any such legislation. Although Durno J. held that peace bond applications and s. 111 applications are not identical, he concluded that for the same reasons that a youth court has no jurisdiction to hear a peace bond application, it has no jurisdiction to hear a s. 111 application. (The *YCJA* now expressly gives the youth justice court jurisdiction to make orders against a young person in certain circumstances that are spelled out in s. 14(2): orders under ss. 810, 810.01 and 810.2).[62] This provision is arguably a response to decisions similar to *R. v. R.A.M.*, which considered the

---

[60]   *R. v. R.A.M.*, [2004] O.J. No. 489, at para. 39, 182 C.C.C. (3d) 14 (Ont. S.C.).

[61]   *R. v. R.A.M.*, [2004] O.J. No. 489, at para. 26, 182 C.C.C. (3d) 14 (Ont. S.C.). But see *R. v. P.R.*, [1996] N.S.J. No. 581 (N.S. Youth Ct.), where Gibson J. concluded that the youth court should have jurisdiction because s. 52 of the *YOA* made it clear that Parliament intended youth courts to have jurisdiction over matters involving young persons other than offences. Justice Gibson found that s. 52 of the *YOA* focuses on the application of Part XXVII of the *Criminal Code* regarding summary conviction proceedings (s. 810 is found within Part XXVII) to proceedings under the *YOA*. Justice Gibson concluded that it would be inconsistent to have s. 810 proceedings brought against young persons in adult court. Such persons would be denied the benefit of the right to counsel and parental notice provisions found in the *YOA*.

[62]   *YCJA*, s. 14(2).

jurisdiction of the youth court to hear applications for peace bonds under s. 810 of the *Criminal Code*.[63]

Justice Durno acknowledged that the most problematic aspect of his ruling that applications concerning young persons can be brought in adult court is that the procedural safeguards in the youth justice legislation do not apply in adult court. He nevertheless concluded that whether such an application raises *Charter* issues would have to be determined in another proceeding and agreed with the trial judge that Parliament should address this issue notwithstanding his conclusion. "The potential Charter issues referred to in the consideration of the procedural safeguards, if nothing else, would seem to indicate the applications would be better dealt with in youth court."[64]

In fact, Durno J. gets to the crux of the matter in *R. v. R.A.M.*: The purpose of creating a separate criminal justice regime for young persons is to afford them greater protection when they come into conflict with the criminal justice system. Permitting applications and other matters relating to young persons who come into conflict with the criminal law to be dealt with outside of the youth justice system defeats the purpose of a separate youth criminal justice regime for young persons in Canada and cannot have been intended. Justice Durno appeared to conclude in *R. v. R.A.M.* that he was making the decision he considered correct, in law, but that the law itself needed to be re-examined to ensure that all criminal matters involving young persons would be addressed in youth justice court, to the extent feasible.[65]

In another case, the Ontario Superior Court concluded that it was proper to bring a *habeas corpus* application concerning a young person before the superior court.[66] The judge held that there had been a s. 7 breach when the youth was placed in custody and that s. 24 of the *Charter*, as well as the inherent power of a superior court judge, which was clearly retained by s. 14(7) of the *YCJA*, allowed him to provide a proper remedy.

C. Bail Applications: A Jurisdictional Battleground

Bail applications are proving to be the early battleground for much of the jurisdictional wrangling under the *YCJA*. Before examining the jurisprudence, the relevant provisions must be reviewed: s. 28 of the *YCJA*

---

[63] *R. v. R.A.M.*, [2004] O.J. No. 489, at para. 26, 182 C.C.C. (3d) 14 (Ont. S.C.).

[64] *R. v. R.A.M.*, [2004] O.J. No. 489, at para. 62, 182 C.C.C. (3d) 14 (Ont. S.C.).

[65] *R. v. R.A.M.*, [2004] O.J. No. 489, at para. 62, 182 C.C.C. (3d) 14 (Ont. S.C.). The intent of the *YCJA* is discussed at length in Chapter 3, which concerns the Preamble and the Declaration of Principle in s. 3 of the *YCJA*.

[66] *R. v. M.C.*, [2003] O.J. No. 5727 (Ont. S.C.).

states that the bail provisions of the *Criminal Code* apply to young persons *except to the extent that they are inconsistent with, or excluded, by the YCJA*. Sections 29 through 33 of the *YCJA* are the key provisions concerning bail, which modify the general bail scheme that applies to adults in the *Criminal Code*.

The *YCJA* bail scheme generally contemplates that if a JP does the first bail hearing, a review of his or her order may be sought before a youth justice court judge pursuant to s. 33(1) of the *YCJA*. The *YCJA* appears to prohibit a superior court judge from reviewing a bail order by a JP.[67] In other words the scheme is arranged hierarchically so that the youth justice court judge reviews the JP's order and the superior court judge reviews the youth justice court judge's order. This interpretation of the bail scheme is supported by various sections of the *YCJA*.[68]

The provisions clearly contemplate that, in most instances, a justice or a youth justice court judge will address the bail matter. For example, s. 33(8) of the *YCJA* states that if a young person is charged with an offence listed in s. 522 of the *Criminal Code* (which includes murder) only a youth justice court judge may release the young person from custody. Section 33(8) conflicts with s. 522 of the *Criminal Code* because s. 522 states that only a superior court judge can preside in these circumstances. Although it would appear clear that s. 33(8) of the *YCJA* trumps s. 522 of the *Criminal Code* due to the obvious inconsistency between these two provisions, courts are reaching different conclusions. In large part, in the course of this debate, the judiciary are focusing on the two key jurisdictional sections, and are at odds over the meaning and intent of ss. 13 and 14 of the *YCJA*.

The crux of the disagreement concerns the interpretation of the word "proceeding" in s. 13(2) and (3). Section 13(2) states that:

> When a young person elects to be tried by a judge without a jury, the judge shall be a judge as defined in section 552 of the Criminal Code, or if it is an offence set out in section 469 of that Act, the judge shall be a judge of the superior court of criminal jurisdiction in the province in which the election is made. In either case, the judge is deemed to be a youth justice court judge and the court is deemed to be a youth justice court for the purpose of the proceeding.

The question that arises from this wording is this: Does the word "proceeding" in this subsection mean that the superior court acquires jurisdiction only in relation to the trial of the matter, upon an election, or

---

[67]   *YCJA*, s. 33(7).
[68]   *YCJA*, s. 33(5) and (7).

does it mean that the superior court acquires jurisdiction in relation to all matters that arise in the course of, and in relation to, the trial, upon election, such as bail applications? In other words, once the young person elects under s. 13(2) or (3), does the superior court[69] assume jurisdiction for only the trial while all other matters in relation to the offence, such as bail applications, remain within the jurisdiction of the youth justice court?

In *R. v. W. (E.E.)*,[70] Sherstobitoff J.A. of the Saskatchewan Court of Appeal sought to reconcile the provisions of the *Criminal Code* and the *YCJA* that relate to the issue of which court, the youth justice court or the superior court, has jurisdiction over bail hearings regarding young persons charged with s. 469 offences. While he observed that s. 33(8) of the *YCJA* conflicts with s. 522 of the *Criminal Code*, which prohibits the release of s. 469 offenders by anyone other than a superior court judge, he concluded that s. 33(8) prevails because s. 28 of the *YCJA* states clearly that the bail provisions of the *Criminal Code* apply to the *YCJA only* to the extent that they are not inconsistent with the *YCJA*. However, reading these sections in light of s. 13(2) of the *YCJA*, which states that a superior court judge shall oversee the proceeding when it is a s. 469 offence, Sherstobitoff J.A. concluded that s. 13(2) applies to s. 469 offenders from the time of election of mode of trial. Once the young person elects, all proceedings related to the matter, and not just the trial, fall within the jurisdiction of the superior court judge. Up until that time, s. 13(1) judges (youth justice court judges) have exclusive jurisdiction over all proceedings in respect of s. 469 offenders.[71]

The Provincial Court of Manitoba reached a different conclusion just a year later. In *R. v. H. (B.W.)*,[72] Devine J. held that s. 13(2) and (3) relates only to the *trial* of the young person and identifies the judge before whom the trial is to be heard, but does not mean that all matters relating to the trial are to be dealt with by the superior court judge. On the facts of the case before him, the young person had been charged with second degree murder, had elected to be tried by a judge and jury, and his preliminary inquiry date had been set. The defence counsel sought to have the provincial court conduct the bail hearing. The Crown maintained that the provincial court did not have jurisdiction to hear the application. Justice Devine concluded that the provincial court had jurisdiction to conduct bail hearings in these matters pursuant to s. 33(8) of the *YCJA*, and that

---

[69] Note that in relation to s. 13(2), it is a judge of the Court of Quebec or a judge of the Nunavut Court of Justice who will have jurisdiction in relation to non-s. 469 offences upon election.

[70] [2004] S.J. No. 538, 188 C.C.C. (3d) 467 (Sask. C.A.).

[71] *R. v. W. (E.E.)*, [2004] S.J. No. 538, at para. 19, 188 C.C.C. (3d) 467 (Sask. C.A.).

[72] [2005] M.J. No. 398, 202 C.C.C. (3d) 566 (Man. Prov. Ct.).

s. 13(2) and (3) of the *YCJA* indicates only that the *trial* of the young person must occur before a superior court judge in those circumstances. Section 13(2) and (3) indicates that a superior court judge is to be the judge for the purpose of the proceeding, but the reference to "the proceeding" is a reference to only the trial, rather than to the entirety of the prosecution. Justice Devine concluded that this interpretation is consistent with the scheme and object of the *YCJA* as it reflects the intention of Parliament.

The Declaration of Principle in s. 3 of the *YCJA* indicates clearly that Parliament intended to create a separate youth criminal justice system. In recognition of the differences between youths and adults, enhanced procedural protections for youth are also created by the legislation, Devine J. observed. "In my view then the operative presumption in interpreting the *YCJA* must be that the jurisdiction under the *YCJA* rests with the youth justice court, the provincial court, except where expressly ousted by the statutory language of a given section. This interpretation of s. 13(2) and (3) is consistent with the scheme of the *YCJA* legislation which as much as possible seeks to maintain a separate and specialized system for dealing with young persons, having regard to the ways in which relative maturity and different needs may require safeguards and treatment that is distinct from that afforded to adult offenders."[73] Justice Devine further observed that under s. 33(8) of the *YCJA* and similar *YOA* provisions, the provincial court in its capacity as a youth court has always had original bail jurisdiction for youths charged with murder until the youths were transferred to adult court on the murder charge. Therefore, it makes sense that the provincial court's jurisdiction over bail should not be transferred to the superior court unless and until there is a committal for trial following a preliminary inquiry and/or arraignment in Superior Court. This procedure also mirrors that for adults in the *Criminal Code* regarding which court has jurisdiction for bail hearings and when.[74]

The Ontario Court of Justice held similarly in *R. v. K. (T.)*,[75] where Robertson J. found that while a young person may elect to be tried on certain offences in the superior court, the proper forum for bail for a youth charged with murder in Ontario is the youth justice court. Section 33(8) of the *YCJA* expressly gives jurisdiction to the youth justice court in those situations where the young person is charged with offences referred to in s. 522, including murder.

---

[73]   *R. v. H. (B.W.)*, [2005] M.J. No. 398, at para. 30, 202 C.C.C. (3d) 566 (Man. Prov. Ct.).

[74]   *R. v. H. (B.W.)*, [2005] M.J. No. 398, at paras. 36, 37, 202 C.C.C. (3d) 566 (Man. Prov. Ct.).

[75]   [2004] O.J. No. 5744, at para. 20, 192 C.C.C. (3d) 279 (Ont. C.J.).

If s. 33(8) were meant to exclude the provincial court for murder bails, the section would have said that the judge shall be a superior court judge for a s. 522 case. It says, however that a youth justice court judge, and no other court has jurisdiction. It would have to take clear language to oust the jurisdiction of the provincial court from that of the youth court. I find no such language.[76]

The *YOA* had a provision virtually identical to s. 33(8) of the *YOA*; under s. 8(8), the courts reached similar conclusions that the youth court and not the superior court had jurisdiction for murder bails.[77]

In his May 2006 ruling in *R. v. M.F.*,[78] Gage J. considered earlier rulings on this subject, including the Saskatchewan Court of Appeal ruling in *R. v. W. (E.E.)*,[79] and held that once the young person elects trial by judge and jury on a charge of second degree murder, the jurisdiction to conduct the bail hearing vests exclusively with a youth justice court judge as defined in s. 13(3) of the *YCJA*, *i.e.*, a superior court judge sitting as a youth justice court judge. His analysis and conclusion turned, in part, on the interpretation of the word "proceeding". In both s. 13(2) and (3), when the young person elects or is deemed to have elected, a superior court judge will be the judge *for the purpose of the proceeding*. Justice Gage concluded that the meaning of "proceeding" need not be restricted to the trial. "Whether used in its singular or plural form the term 'proceeding' in civil, matrimonial and criminal litigation context is usually and ordinarily understood to encompass the entirety of the processes within an action, application or prosecution," Gage J. held "It would seem to me that the objectives of the *YCJA* might very well be undermined if the jurisdiction of section 13(2) and 13(3) judges were unnecessarily circumscribed to presiding over the trial."[80] In relation to the s. 469 offence, Gage J. concluded that after the young person had elected trial by judge and jury, the jurisdiction to conduct the bail hearing vested exclusively with the superior court judge under s. 13(3).

In *R. v. O. (A.J.)*,[81] McLean J. considered whether a s. 525 *Criminal Code* inquiry in relation to a young person's continued detention when the trial is delayed must be held before a superior court judge. (In Ontario, superior court judges conduct these bail inquiries in relation to adults.) These s. 525 hearings are essentially inquiries into the reason for the

---

[76]   *R. v. K. (T.)*, [2004] O.J. No. 5744, at para. 20, 192 C.C.C. (3d) 279 (Ont. C.J.).
[77]   *R. v. M.R.*, [2001] O.J. No. 2598, 155 C.C.C. (3d) 93 (Ont. S.C.).
[78]   [2006] O.J. No. 1805 (Ont. C.J.).
[79]   [2004] S.J. No. 538, 188 C.C.C. (3d) 467 (Sask. C.A.).
[80]   *R. v. M.F.*, [2006] O.J. No. 1805, at paras. 44 and 48 (Ont. C.J.).
[81]   [2004] O.J. No. 1220, 185 C.C.C. (3d) 120 (Ont. S.C.).

continued detention of the accused. In *R. v. A.O.*,[82] Payne J. of the Ontario Court of Justice had held that he did not have jurisdiction to hear it. However, McLean J. of the Ontario Superior Court reached the opposite conclusion. He held that a s. 525 hearing is not a review of a court order but merely an inquiry into the reason for the continued incarceration of the accused. He further held that, as a general rule, the Ontario Court is the Youth Court and the Superior Court is considered part of the Youth Court only in special circumstances.[83] Justice McLean concluded that there is nothing in the wording of s. 14 of the *YCJA* that would require s. 525 applications to be brought only before a superior court.[84]

Justice McLean stopped short of saying that the youth justice court had exclusive jurisdiction to conduct these hearings. "Notwithstanding that s. 14 does not specifically exclude the jurisdiction of the Superior Court, it is to be noted that it does not specifically require a hearing under s. 525 to be held before a Superior Court judge only."[85]

Other judges have since held that s. 14 is not a bar to a superior court judge hearing a bail review under s. 520, which is an inquiry similar to a s. 525 hearing except that the latter occurs when the trial has been delayed. There is a difference between having exclusive jurisdiction over an offence, for which s. 14 of the *YCJA* provides, and having jurisdiction to hear a bail review, the courts have held. "The latter is not an interference with the exclusive jurisdiction of a youth justice court over the offence."[86]

The *YCJA* clearly contemplates that the superior court will conduct bail hearings in some instances. For example, s. 33(5) states that: "An application under section 520 or 521 of the *Criminal Code* for a review of an order made in respect of a young person by a youth justice court judge who is a judge of a superior court shall be made to a judge of the court of appeal." One can expect this to occur when the superior court is sitting as a youth justice court upon the election of the accused under s. 13(2) or (3).

While the common law in relation to which court has jurisdiction to conduct bail hearings and s. 525 bail inquiries involving young persons may be unsettled, the *YCJA* is fairly clear that the superior court can conduct s. 520 or s. 521 bail reviews involving young persons, as they do in relation to adult accused. The wording of s. 33(7) of the *YCJA* states that an application for a review of a detention order under s. 520 or 521 of the

---

[82]   [2003] O.J. No. 5219 (Ont. C.J.).

[83]   *R. v. O. (A.J.)*, [2004] O.J. No. 1220, at para. 21, 185 C.C.C. (3d) 120 (Ont. S.C.). See s. 13(2) of the *YCJA* for example.

[84]   *R. v. O. (A.J.)*, [2004] O.J. No. 1220, at para. 22, 185 C.C.C. (3d) 120 (Ont. S.C.).

[85]   *R. v. O. (A.J.)*, [2004] O.J. No. 1220, at para. 23, 185 C.C.C. (3d) 120 (Ont. S.C.).

[86]   *R. v. I.M.*, [2008] O.J. No. 3953, at para. 18 (Ont. S.C.).

Criminal Code cannot be made in relation to an order by a justice who is not a youth justice court judge. These sections have prompted some judges to conclude that "the inference might be drawn that the Act contemplates that if the order is made by a youth court judge, then a review under s. 520 would be by a superior court judge".[87] In fact, the weight of authority, at least in Ontario, favours the view that a s. 520 review of an order by a youth court judge should be heard by the superior court.[88]

As mentioned, youth justice court judges have also been given express jurisdiction to conduct hearings and order young persons to enter into recognizances (peace bonds) under ss. 810, 810.01 and 810.2. If the young person fails or refuses to enter into a recognizance in relation to any of those sections, the court may impose a youth sentence under s. 42, except that a custody and supervision order under s. 42(2)(n) cannot exceed 30 days.[89] There was no provision in the *YOA* permitting the youth court to hold such hearings.

D.   Offence Jurisdiction Under the *YCJA*

As discussed in Chapter 1, the definition of the offence of delinquency under the *Juvenile Delinquents Act* was extremely broad. It captured not only federal, provincial and municipal offences, but also acts of "sexual immorality or any similar form of vice".[90] The *YOA* narrowed the definition significantly when it came into force in 1984 so that the new Act captured only federal offences. In practice, this meant primarily criminal offences under the *Criminal Code* and the *Controlled Drugs and Substances Act*. Provincial and municipal offences were no longer included in the definition of an offence; nor was the broad and ambiguous status offence of "sexual immorality or any similar form of vice".

The *YCJA* maintains this focus on criminal offences. Subject to two exceptions outlined below, the *YCJA* gives the youth justice court exclusive jurisdiction over any (federal) offence[91] alleged to have been committed by a young person and provides that the young person shall be dealt with as provided in the *YCJA*.[92]

---

[87]   *R. v. I.M.*, [2008] O.J. No. 3953 (Ont. S.C.).

[88]   *R. v. I.M.*, [2008] O.J. No. 3953, at para. 9 (Ont. S.C.).

[89]   *YCJA*, s. 14(2).

[90]   *Juvenile Delinquents Act*, R.S.C. 1924, c. 53, s. 2 [hereafter "*JDA*"].

[91]   A federal offence is defined in s. 2 of the *YCJA* as any offence under a federal Act.

[92]   This would appear to suggest, for example, that in relation to the sentencing of a young person for a federal offence under an Act such as the *Excise Act, 2001*, the young person would receive a youth sentence in accordance with the penalties provided in the *YCJA*

Similar to the *YOA*, the definition of an offence under the *YCJA* does not include status offences, or offences under provincial or territorial statutes such as highway traffic Acts, or violations of municipal bylaws, such as those relating to the regulation of noise. Most provinces and territories have specific legislation outlining the procedure and sentencing for young persons charged with violations of provincial and municipal bylaws.[93] These statutes generally give the youth justice court jurisdiction to deal with these less serious offences although the proceedings may differ. In Ontario, under the *Provincial Offences Act*,[94] where an offence is alleged to have been committed by a person 12 years of age or more and under 17, special provisions apply. These young persons charged with provincial or municipal offences generally receive some, but not all, of the protections that they receive under the *YCJA* when charged with federal offences. Most jurisdictions require that parents be notified when a young person is charged with a provincial or municipal offence.[95] But young persons facing less serious violations under provincial or municipal laws will generally not have the same access to counsel under s. 25 of the *YCJA* as they would if charged with a criminal offence.[96] For young persons aged 16 and 17, provincial offences are dealt with in "adult" Provincial Offences Court in some jurisdictions.

Although most of the offences that are prosecuted under the *YCJA* are contained in other federal Acts, primarily the *Criminal Code* and the *Controlled Drugs and Substances Act*, the *YCJA* creates some offences. These offences generally relate to the administration of the Act, such as the offence under s. 137 of the *YCJA* concerning failing to comply with a community-based youth sentence. Other provisions, such as ss. 138 and 139, create offences directed at police, journalists, parents and other adults in relation to the unauthorized disclosure or publication of

---

despite the fact that the *Excise Act, 2001* has its own penalty scheme. In the event of a conflict in this regard between two federal statutes, the *YCJA*'s specific sentencing scheme trumps the penalty scheme in any other federal Act. The only exception to this is where a young person is found to be eligible for an adult sentence, in which case the sentencing scheme in the *Criminal Code* would apply. This is in keeping with the basic paramountcy rule of statutory interpretation expressed by the Latin maxim *specialia generalibus non derogant*, which stands for the proposition that in the event of a conflict between a specific provision concerning a particular matter and a more general provision dealing with the specific matter as well as other matters, the specific provision prevails. On this point, see Ruth Sullivan, *Statutory Interpretation* (Concord: Irwin Law, 1997), at 226.

[93] For example, in Newfoundland and Labrador, the *Young Persons Offences Act* sets out a detailed scheme and procedure for dealing with young persons charged with provincial offences. Many of the procedures are similar to those found in the *YCJA* in relation to young persons charged with federal offences. See *R. v. M.A.*, [2008] N.J. No. 34 (N.L. Prov. Ct.) for a discussion of the *Young Persons Offences Act*.

[94] R.S.O. 1990, c. P.33, Part VI.

[95] Nicholas Bala, *Youth Criminal Justice Law* (Toronto: Irwin Law Inc., 2003), at 155.

[96] Nicholas Bala, *Youth Criminal Justice Law* (Toronto: Irwin Law Inc., 2003), at 155.

information about young persons dealt with under the *YCJA*, or wilfully failing to comply with an undertaking to supervise a youth released pending trial. A parent can be found guilty of contempt of court under the *YCJA* for disobeying a judge's order to attend youth justice court "without reasonable excuse".[97] Adults can also be charged with various offences under s. 136 in relation to interfering with a young person's compliance with his or her sentence, for example, by inducing or assisting the young person to leave unlawfully a place of custody, or wilfully inducing or assisting a young person to breach or disobey a term or condition of a youth sentence or other order of the youth justice court.

E.   Contempt of Court

The power to punish for contempt derives from the common law,[98] however, it is expressly provided for in the *YCJA*, as it was in the *YOA*. Section 15 of the *YCJA* describes the youth justice court's jurisdiction over conduct constituting contempt of court by young persons in the criminal context in various circumstances, as well as contempt of court by adults in the face of the youth justice court. Generally speaking, criminal contempt is meant to capture words or conduct that are considered likely to obstruct, or interfere with, the administration of justice or to bring discredit upon the justice system. Criminal contempt in the face of the court *(in facie)* covers a range of conduct such as behaviour that disrupts the courtroom proceedings, the refusal of a witness to be sworn or to answer questions, or failure of counsel to attend court as required. Contempt of court outside the face of the court *(ex facie)* in the criminal context generally involves conduct such as the publication of material likely to interfere with the fair trial of the case, obstruction of justice, by

---

[97]   *YCJA*, s. 27(4).

[98]   *R. v. Vaillancourt*, [1981] S.C.J. No. 8, [1981] 1 S.C.R. 69 (S.C.C.). The Supreme Court of Canada held that the superior court had jurisdiction to sentence a 15-year-old young person to two months' detention for contempt committed in the face of the court for refusing to testify, although the young person was not charged with any offence in relation to his conduct. The superior court judge acted in accordance with his inherent power to impose penalties for contempt committed in the face of the court. It was admitted that if the refusal of the child to testify had constituted an offence, the youth court would have had sole jurisdiction. Justice Chouinard referred to a number of cases that affirmed the power of every court of justice to punish for contempt committed in the face of the court. Section 9 of the *Criminal Code* preserves the common law power of judges to punish for contempt of court. Section 484 of the *Criminal Code* further clarifies that every judge or provincial court judge has the same power and authority to preserve order in a court over which he or she presides as may be exercised by the superior court of criminal jurisdiction of the province during the sittings thereof.

interfering with a witness or a juror, or scandalizing the court by criticizing a court or judge.[99]

Every youth justice court has the same power, jurisdiction and authority to deal with contempt of court against the court as the superior court of criminal jurisdiction of the province in which the court is situated.[100]

The youth justice court has jurisdiction (but note that the subsection does not say *exclusive* jurisdiction) regarding contempt of court committed by a young person against the youth justice court whether or not the act that constitutes contempt is committed in the face of the court, and every contempt of court committed by a young person against any other court otherwise than in the face of that court.[101] (As suggested above, contempt occurs outside the face of the court, for example, when a court order is disobeyed.) Section 47(2) of the *YOA* had a provision similar to s. 15(2) of the *YCJA*, except that it gave the youth justice court *exclusive* jurisdiction over contempt of court by a young person outside the face of the court *for all courts*. The Supreme Court of Canada subsequently held that s. 47(2) violated s. 96 of the *Constitution Act, 1867* because it gave exclusive jurisdiction over contempt of a superior court order to an inferior court, *i.e.*, the youth court. Although Lamer C.J.C. observed that the inherent jurisdiction of the superior court is difficult to define, he concluded that the power to control its process and enforce its orders, in part, by punishing for contempt, was clearly within its jurisdiction. "While it will in most instances be preferable for the youth court to try and punish a youth in ex facie contempt of a superior court, the provincial superior court's jurisdiction cannot be ousted. It will always be for the superior court to elect whether to hold contempt proceedings against a youth in order to exert control over its process, or to defer to the youth court."[102] In other words, in a situation where a youth contravenes a superior court order (*ex facie* contempt), the Supreme Court of Canada held that there was concurrent

---

[99]   Regarding criminal contempt in the face of the court, see *R. v. K. (B.)*, [1995] S.C.J. No. 96, [1995] 4 S.C.R. 186 (S.C.C.). This case concerned s. 47(3) of the *YOA*; however the wording of s. 47(3) and s. 15(3) is virtually identical. *R. v. Radio OB Ltd.*, [1976] M.J. No. 245, 70 D.L.R. (3d) 311 (Man. Q.B.) is an excellent example of criminal contempt *ex facie*. In that case, the court held that a radio journalist committed contempt of court by interviewing the mother of an accused juvenile on radio and by discussing on the radio many facts about the case, which was likely to prejudice the fair trial of the accused. This case also provides a good definition of criminal contempt at 5-6 (QL).

[100]   *YCJA*, s. 15(1).

[101]   *YCJA*, s. 15(2).

[102]   *MacMillan Bloedel Ltd. v. Simpson*, [1995] S.C.J. No. 101, at paras. 33, 42, 43, [1995] 4 S.C.R. 725 (S.C.C.).

jurisdiction, and that the superior court could exercise its jurisdiction or refer the matter to the youth court.[103]

Section 15(3) of the *YCJA* states that a youth justice court also has jurisdiction regarding every contempt of court by a young person against any other court in the face of the court,[104] as well as jurisdiction over every contempt of court by an adult against the youth justice court in the face of the youth justice court. The powers given to the youth justice court in s. 15(3) do not affect the power, jurisdiction or authority of any other court to deal with or impose punishment for contempt of court,[105] which basically means that the youth justice court does not have exclusive jurisdiction to deal with contempt of court committed by a young person against another court in the face of that court. Practically speaking, this means that a contempt charge in the face of another court (generally creating some disruption in the courtroom) by a young person can be dealt with by the court in which it occurs, or the presiding judge can refer the matter to a youth justice court judge.[106]

Similar to an argument made in relation to s. 47(3) of the *YOA*, the wording of s. 15(3) of the *YCJA* appears to conflict with s. 14 of the *YCJA*, which says that the youth justice court has exclusive jurisdiction over offences alleged to have been committed by young persons, subject to only the *Contraventions Act* or the *National Defence Act*. This apparent conflict can be resolved when one considers the definition of "offence" in s. 2(1) of the *YCJA*. An "offence" means an offence created by an Act of Parliament (or by any regulation, rule, order, bylaw or ordinance made under an Act of Parliament other than an ordinance of the Northwest Territories or a law of the Legislature of Yukon or the Legislature for Nunavut). The Supreme Court of Canada ruled in *Vaillancourt*[107] that the power to punish for contempt does not derive from an Act of Parliament, but rather from the inherent power of a superior court to control its own process. A juvenile could therefore be punished for contempt other than before a juvenile court.[108] Section 14 is not in conflict with s. 15(3) because contempt is not an offence created by an Act of Parliament.[109]

---

[103] *MacMillan Bloedel Ltd. v. Simpson*, [1995] S.C.J. No. 101, at paras. 33, 42, 43, [1995] 4 S.C.R. 725 (S.C.C.).

[104] *YCJA*, s. 15(3).

[105] *YCJA*, s. 15(3).

[106] Nicholas Bala, *Youth Criminal Justice Law* (Toronto: Irwin Law Inc., 2003), at 158-59.

[107] *R. v. Vaillancourt*, [1981] S.C.J. No. 8, [1981] 1 S.C.R. 69 (S.C.C.).

[108] *R. v. Vaillancourt*, [1981] S.C.J. No. 8, [1981] 1 S.C.R. 69 (S.C.C.).

[109] Priscilla Platt, *Young Offenders Law in Canada*, 2d ed. (Markham: Butterworths Canada Ltd., 1995), at 389-90. Platt sets out this argument in relation to s. 47(3) of the *YOA*. Section 47(3) of the *YOA* and s. 15(3) of the *YCJA* are, for all intents and purposes, identical; therefore, Platt's point remains relevant.

In summary, a judge citing a youth for contempt in the face of the court can generally decide whether to have the contempt dealt with in the court where it occurred or have it referred to the youth justice court. Contempt out of the face of the court generally involves superior court orders, such as injunctions. The court that made the order and the youth justice court have concurrent jurisdiction in these cases. Some scholars suggest that the benefit of this concurrent jurisdiction is that contempt matters can be referred to youth justice court judges. This may be desirable, because youth justice court judges have greater expertise in dealing with young persons and may have a more sophisticated understanding of the extenuating circumstances influencing the behaviour of young accused persons, and may thus be more discriminating in their exercise of the contempt power.[110]

When a young person is found guilty of contempt of court, whether in youth justice court or in any other court, the sentencing provisions of the *YCJA* apply.[111] The basic rules of natural justice also generally require that witnesses be given notice that they must show cause why they should not be found in contempt and given an opportunity to consult counsel and to be represented by counsel. In the event that they are found in contempt, they should be permitted to make submissions regarding sentence.[112] Some youth justice experts contend that a judge should ensure that notice is provided to the young person's parents before dealing with the issue.[113]

A parent can be found guilty of contempt of court under the *YCJA* for disobeying a judge's order to attend youth justice court "without reasonable excuse".[114] Section 708 of the *Criminal Code* applies to adults,[115] in relation to contempt proceedings involving adults in youth justice court.[116] A finding of guilt under s. 15 for contempt of court or a sentence imposed regarding the finding can be appealed as if the finding were a conviction, or the sentence were a sentence in relation to a prosecution by indictment.[117] This means that the appeal is to the Court of Appeal.[118]

---

[110] Nicholas Bala, *Youth Criminal Justice Law* (Toronto: Irwin Law Inc., 2003), at 161.

[111] *YCJA*, s. 15(4).

[112] See *R. v. K. (B.)*, [1995] S.C.J. No. 96, at para. 15, [1995] 4 S.C.R. 186 (S.C.C.), and *R. v. M. (S.)*, [1987] N.S.J. No. 610, 40 C.C.C. (3d) 242 (N.S.C.A.). See also Priscilla Platt, *Young Offenders Law in Canada*, 2d ed. (Markham: Butterworths Canada Ltd., 1995), at 390.

[113] Priscilla Platt, *Young Offenders Law in Canada*, 2d ed. (Markham: Butterworths Canada Ltd., 1995), at 390. Platt makes this point in relation to the *YOA*, but it remains relevant under the *YCJA*.

[114] *YCJA*, s. 27(4).

[115] *YCJA*, s. 15(4).

[116] *YCJA*, s. 15(5).

[117] *YCJA*, s. 37(2).

[118] *Criminal Code*, s. 675.

F.   The Definition of a Young Person

In order to fall within the jurisdiction of the youth justice court, the accused must have been a *young person* as defined in s. 2(1) of the *YCJA* *at the time of the alleged offence.* "Young person" means "a person who is or, in the absence of evidence to the contrary, appears to be twelve years old or older, but less than eighteen years old and, if the context requires, includes any person who is charged under this Act with having committed an offence while he or she was a young person or who is found guilty of an offence under this Act".[119] For purposes of determining if a person is a "young person" as defined by the *YCJA*, the date of the arrest or the date that the charge is laid is irrelevant. The *YCJA* emphasizes this point by stating that the Act applies to persons 18 years old or older who are alleged to have committed an offence *while a young person.*[120]

It is also important to bear in mind that it is a person's chronological age and not his or her mental age at the time of the alleged offence that determines whether he or she is a young person for purposes of the *YCJA*. In *R. v. Sawchuk*,[121] the appellant's counsel argued that the accused should be immune from prosecution because, although he was 23, his mental age was that of a child under 12.[122] In *Sawchuk*, an expert witness testified that the accused had a mental age of between 7 and 11. The Court of Appeal dismissed the appeal on the grounds that, for purposes of determining whether one is a child or a young person under the *YOA*, it is chronological age rather than intellectual capacity that decides the matter.[123]

While determining the jurisdiction of the youth justice court is generally straightforward in relation to the age of the accused, some scenarios cause confusion. The following example is a case in point: A young person is placed on probation in accordance with s. 42(2)(k) of the *YCJA* after being found guilty of an offence. The young person then turns 18 and breaches a condition of the probation order. If the police charge this offender with the offence of breach of probation, the offender will be charged with breach of probation under the *Criminal Code* and dealt with in adult court, as an adult, because he was 18 at the time of the alleged breach. This scenario highlights the salient fact that for purposes of determining which court has jurisdiction over the individual, it is the age

---

[119]   *YCJA*, s. 2(1).
[120]   *YCJA*, s. 14(5).
[121]   [1991] M.J. No. 362 (Man. C.A.).
[122]   Similar arguments can also arise in cases where the individual is alleged to suffer from Fetal Alcohol Spectrum Disorder, where the level of cognitive functioning can be much lower than the chronological age.
[123]   [1991] M.J. No. 362 (Man. C.A.).

of the accused at the time of the alleged offence — in this case, the breach — that is determinative. Since the alleged breach is a new offence, and he was 18 at the time he is alleged to have committed it, the individual will be charged under the *Criminal Code* as an adult rather than as a young person under the *YCJA*. Although the breach of probation is related to the original offence committed by the offender when he or she was a young person, the breach is a new offence committed by the offender after he turned 18. The youth justice court loses jurisdiction. The charge will be laid under the breach of probation provisions of the *Criminal Code*[124] rather than the *YCJA*, and the accused will be dealt with within the adult system rather than the youth system.[125]

The wording and definition of "young person" in the *YCJA* also provides for the prosecution of adults for crimes they committed while young persons. Provided there are no legal impediments to prosecution, an adult can be charged years later for a crime committed while a young person.[126]

Even if the young person is not charged with the crime until after becoming an adult, he will have the benefit of at least some of the enhanced protections under the *YCJA* during the court process because he was a young person at the time of the alleged incident. As Lamer C.J.C. suggested in *R. v. Z. (D.A.)*,[127] an adult who is charged with having committed a crime as a young person is generally entitled to the additional protections under youth legislation for the mistakes of youth that would have been available to him had he been charged while he was under 18.

---

[124] *Criminal Code*, s. 733.1.

[125] The preponderance of the case law supports this interpretation. See, for example, under the *YCJA*, *R. v. Simmard*, [2003] B.C.J. No. 2172 (B.C. Prov. Ct.). See under the *YOA*, *R. v. Mather*, [1988] B.C.J. No. 2543, 46 C.C.C. (3d) 315 (B.C.S.C.); *R. v. Ellsworth*, [1991] N.J. No. 310, 68 C.C.C. (3d) 246 (Nfld. T.D.) and *R. v. Merrick*, [1987] M.J. No. 667, 37 C.C.C. (3d) 285 (Man. Q.B.). *Contra*: *R. v. Scott*, [1989] O.J. No. 1874 (Ont. Prov. Ct.). Nicholas Bala and Priscilla Platt, foremost Canadian experts on youth justice law, adopt this interpretation (that the adult court has jurisdiction to prosecute the breach charge in these circumstances). See Nicholas Bala, *Youth Criminal Justice Law* (Toronto: Irwin Law Inc., 2003), at 161 and Priscilla Platt, *Young Offenders Law in Canada*, 2d ed. (Markham: Butterworths Canada Ltd., 1995), at 107. Platt explains *Scott* on the basis that the Ontario Provincial Court in *Scott* appeared not to have had the benefit of earlier Supreme Court decisions in B.C. and Ontario, both of which took a position consistent with *Ellsworth*: *R. v. Schuller*, unreported, May 12, 1987 (Ont. S.C.) and *Mather*, [1989] W.D.F.L. 308 (B.C.S.C.).

[126] *YCJA*, s. 14(5). See cases such as *R. v. Daniels*, [1995] S.J. No 577 (Sask. Q.B.) under the *YOA*, where the complainant waited 10 years to report the sexual abuse, by which time the accused was 26. See also more recent historical cases such as *R. v. E.J.A.*, [2004] Y.J. No. 98 (Y.T. Terr. Ct.) and *R. v. Michel*, [2004] N.W.T.J. No. 47 (N.W.T.S.C.), which are cited later in this chapter for different reasons.

[127] [1992] S.C.J. No. 80, at para. 38, [1992] 2 S.C.R. 1025 (S.C.C.).

However, a person who is charged as an adult for a crime he or she committed while a young person will not necessarily have the benefit of *all* of the protections afforded young persons under youth justice legislation.[128] For example, s. 56 of the *YOA* (the precursor to s. 146 of the *YCJA*), stipulated that a statement from a young person on arrest or detention, or in circumstances where the person in authority had reasonable grounds to believe that the young person had committed an offence, was inadmissible against the young person unless the person in authority (most often a police officer) had complied with a number of conditions prior to the taking of the statement. But Lamer C.J.C. held for the majority that the protections of s. 56 of the *YOA* did not apply to a young person who was 18 or older at the time he or she gave a statement to police because:

> It is the age of an accused at the time of the offence which must determine the appropriate measure of accountability and not his or her age at the time of being charged or tried.
>
> ...
>
> Persons over the age of 18 have long been deemed to possess sufficient maturity and control over the situation they may find themselves in to no long [*sic*] require the watchful eye of a parent or adult relative to ensure any statement made is voluntary and made with full knowledge of their legal rights. It would be absurd to say that a statement made by a 25-year-old accused, for example, cannot be deemed to be made by a person having sufficient maturity because it was in regard to an offence he or she allegedly committed at a time when the law deemed him or her not to possess such maturity.[129]

The intent of s. 56 was to protect young persons who might not be able to fully appreciate the consequences and implications of giving a statement to police. It was not designed to protect people over the age of 18, who have reached the age of majority and are expected to be fully able to appreciate the consequences of their actions.

---

[128] [1992] S.C.J. No. 80, at para. 38, [1992] 2 S.C.R. 1025 (S.C.C.). Chief Justice Lamer observed that in enacting certain special provisions in the *YOA*, Parliament sought to address concerns specific to the fact that the accused being brought through the judicial system is a youth rather than an adult. While making the point that the applicability of the various special protections in the *YOA* to an adult accused would have to be considered over time on an individual basis, Lamer C.J.C. noted that some protections in youth justice legislation do not make sense when the accused is over 18 at the time the charge is laid, such as the requirement that a young person be detained separate and apart from any adult. "It would be absurd to hold that this requirement applies to a 35-year-old accused who absconded while a youth. It is clear that the concerns underlying some of the special protections and rules within the Act no longer arise once an accused reaches adulthood."

[129] *R. v. Z. (D.A.)*, [1992] S.C.J. No. 80, at paras. 37, 46, [1992] 2 S.C.R. 1025 (S.C.C.).

The wording of s. 146(2) of the *YCJA* codifies Lamer C.J.C.'s findings in *R. v. Z. (D.A.)*. The police are required to comply with the many conditions outlined in s. 146(2) of the *YCJA* before taking a statement from a young person only if the young person is under 18 at the time he or she gives the statement. In other words, if a young person is 17 at the time of the alleged offence, but turns 18 before providing a statement, the police are no longer obliged to comply with all of the requirements in s. 146(2) before taking that statement. The wording of s. 146(2) is clear on this point: *"No oral or written statement made by a young person who is less than eighteen years old ... is admissible against the young person unless...."*[130]

Although *R. v. Z. (D.A.)* was decided in relation to the *YOA*, in *R. v. T.S.K.L.*,[131] the B.C. Provincial Court relied on *R. v. Z. (D.A.)* to reach the same conclusion in relation to s. 146(2) of the *YCJA*. (The wording in s. 146(2) of the *YCJA* is virtually identical to the wording in s. 56(2) in any event.) In *R. v. T.S.K.L.*, the young person was 17 at the time he was charged but did not give a statement until two years later. Since he was over 18 at the time he gave the statement, the police were not obligated to comply with the requirements in s. 146(2) of the *YCJA*.

An analogous decision was reached in the case of *R. v. R.K.*,[132] where an Alberta Provincial Court judge held that even though the young person was under 18 at the time he was charged, he was over 18 when the DNA warrant was issued and therefore he was not entitled to the rights provided to a young person under s. 487.07(l)(e)(ii) and (4) of the *Criminal Code*. In addition to any other right arising from his or her detention under the warrant, a young person against whom a warrant is issued under these sections has (a) the right to a reasonable opportunity to consult with, and (b) the right to have the warrant executed in the presence of, counsel and a parent or, in the absence of a parent, an adult relative or, in the absence of a parent and an adult relative, any other appropriate adult chosen by the young person.[133] In *R. v. R.K.*, Franklin J. held that while s. 487.07 provides additional protections for young persons against whom warrants are executed, in this case, the young man was not a young person at the time the warrant was issued. Justice Franklin relied on *R. v. Z. (D.A.)*,[134] and noted that the Supreme Court of Canada stated that the definition of a young person in s. 2 of the *YOA* (which is essentially the same wording as the definition of a young person in s. 2 of the *YCJA*)

---

[130] Section 146 of the *YCJA* is discussed in greater detail in Chapter 7 of this text.
[131] [2004] B.C.J. No. 1279 (B.C. Prov. Ct.).
[132] [2001] A.J. No. 444 (Alta. Prov. Ct.).
[133] *Criminal Code*, s. 487.07(4).
[134] [1992] S.C.J. No. 80, [1992] 2 S.C.R. 1025 (S.C.C.).

makes it clear that the procedural matters and special protections do not apply regardless of the age of the accused at the time he is charged with having committed an offence while he or she was under the age of 18. The special protections under review must be considered on an individual basis.[135] Justice Franklin interpreted this as a direction to the court to consider the context of the particular provision and its relevance to persons who are over 18 but charged as described in s. 2.[136]

G.   Establishing the Age of a Young Person

Under the *JDA*, proof of age was an essential element of the offence. If the Crown failed to prove the age of the accused, the accused was entitled to an acquittal.[137] Under the *YCJA*, similar to the *YOA*, the Crown is not required to prove the age of a young person as part of its case or to establish that the youth justice court has jurisdiction in relation to the age of the accused. Similar to ordinary (adult court), where it is unnecessary to prove that an accused is an adult, the age of the accused need only be addressed in youth justice court if the judge or the accused raises it.[138] If the matter is raised, s. 148 of the *YCJA* provides that age can be established through various means, such as through a birth or baptismal certificate, the testimony of a parent, or any other information the court considers reliable. The court can also draw inferences regarding the accused's age from his or her appearance, as well as from statements made by the accused during examination-in-chief or cross-examination.[139] Section 148 does not state that age must be proven.[140]

Jurisdictional questions have sometimes arisen in cases where the young person was on the cusp of his 18th birthday at the time of the incident. For example, under the *YOA*, in *R. v. A. (E.A.)*,[141] the accused was convicted in youth court of sexually assaulting the child he was babysitting. It was established that the offence occurred between 9 p.m.

---

[135] *R. v. R.K.*, [2001] A.J. No. 444, at para. 21 (Alta. Prov. Ct.).

[136] *R. v. R.K.*, [2001] A.J. No. 444, at para. 22 (Alta. Prov. Ct.).

[137] *R. v. Crossley*, [1950] B.C.J. No. 34, 10 C.R. 348 (B.C.S.C.).

[138] The Nova Scotia Court of Appeal held in *R. v. J. (C.K.)*, unreported, February 17, 1995 (N.S.C.A.) that proof of age was not an element of the offence. See also *R. v. H. (D.W.)*, [1986] N.J. No. 97, 62 Nfld. & P.E.I.R. 55 (Nfld. T.D.), where the Newfoundland Trial Division held that the youth court could presume jurisdiction unless and until evidence to the contrary is placed before the court.

[139] *YCJA*, s. 148. Section 148 is similar to s. 57 of the *YOA*. See *R. v. L. (T.A.)*, [1986] A.J. No. 87, 75 A.R. 147 (Alta. Prov. Ct.).

[140] There is a good discussion of proof of age in Priscilla Platt, *Young Offenders Law in Canada*, 2d ed. (Markham: Butterworths Canada Ltd., 1995), at 107-10.

[141] [1987] O.J. No. 674 (Ont. C.A.).

and 1 a.m.; the young victim could not say precisely when the assault occurred. The accused turned 18 at midnight. Since it was not clear whether the accused was under or over 18 at the time of the offence, the Ontario Court of Appeal upheld the jurisdiction of the youth court in relation to the case to permit the accused the benefit of the more lenient Act in light of the uncertainty. "It would be most favourable to the appellant to conclude that the time of the commission of the offence was when he was a young person since the disposition and the alternative remedies available under the *Young Offenders Act* are more favourable to the appellant than if he were tried in an adult court."[142] The *YCJA* has attempted to clarify this matter by stating that where a person is alleged to have committed an offence during a period that includes his or her birthday, the youth justice court has jurisdiction to try the matter.[143] However, in terms of sentencing, s. 16 of the *YCJA* states that if it is subsequently proven that the offence was committed before the person turned 18, the youth justice court can impose a youth sentence. Conversely, if it is proven that the offence occurred after the person turned 18, the youth justice court can impose a sentence under the *Criminal Code* or under any other Act of Parliament that could be imposed on an adult. If it is not proven that the offence was committed after the person turned 18, the youth justice court must impose a sentence under the *YCJA*.[144]

H.   Transitional Provisions

Police officers, counsel, and judges must be mindful of the transitional provisions in the *YCJA* when addressing youth justice matters. As of the coming into force of the *YCJA* on April 1, 2003, no proceedings can be commenced under either the *YOA* or the *JDA*.[145] However, if proceedings were already commenced under the *YOA* prior to the coming into force of the *YCJA*, those proceedings and all related matters are to be dealt with under the *YOA*, except that the young person, upon a finding of guilt, will be sentenced under the provisions of the *YCJA*, with certain exceptions, presumably unless he or she has already been sentenced under the *YOA*.[146]

---

[142] *R. v. A. (E.A.)*, [1987] O.J. No. 674, at para. 3 (Ont. C.A.). See also *R. v. J.F.*, [2002] O.J. No. 4434 (Ont. C.A.).

[143] *YCJA*, s. 16. The meaning of s. 16 is a matter of some contention. See for example *R. v. A.M.*, [2004] A.J. No. 67 (Alta. Prov. Ct.) and *R. c. X*, [2008] J.Q. no 9341 (Que. S.C.). See also T. Cohen, "Driver ordered to stand trial as adult" *The Globe and Mail* (25 April 2009).

[144] *YCJA*, s. 16(c).

[145] *YCJA*, s. 158.

[146] *YCJA*, ss. 159 and 161. *R. v. I.L.B.*, [2004] S.J. No. 367 (Sask. Prov. Ct.). But see *R. v. J.J.C.*, [2003] P.E.I.J. No. 99 (P.E.I. S.C.A.D.), where a young person was sentenced under

In contrast, if proceedings were commenced under the *JDA* prior to the coming into force of the *YCJA*, the proceedings and all related matters are to be dealt with under the *YCJA* as if the delinquency were an offence that had occurred after the coming into force of the transitional provisions.[147] Upon a finding of guilt, the offender will be subject to the sentencing provisions of the *YCJA*, with certain exceptions spelled out in s. 161.[148]

If a young person is alleged to have committed an offence before the coming into force of the *YCJA* but no proceedings were commenced, the young person shall be dealt with under the *YCJA*, subject to certain exceptions spelled out in s. 160.

The recent case of *R. v. E.J.A.*[149] illustrates the application of s. 160 of the *YCJA*, and demonstrates the challenges of applying the transitional provisions. E.J.A. was charged with assault on a male. The offence was alleged to have occurred between July 5, 1971 and September 30, 1974. The *JDA* was in force at the time. Had E.J.A. been tried then, he would have been tried as an adult. He was 16 at the time and considered an adult under the legislation. However, the proceeding was not commenced until November 20, 2003, at which time the *YCJA* was in force. Justice Lilles, as he then was, concluded that the wording of s. 160 was plain and unambiguous and obliged the court to apply the *YCJA* to a young person in his situation: he had committed an offence before the coming into force of the *YCJA* but no proceedings had been commenced until after the coming into force of the *YCJA*. Justice Lilles found that the *YCJA* overrides the principle that a young person must be tried in accordance with his status at the time of the commission of the offence.[150]

---

the *YOA* for property offences. The *YCJA* came into force after his sentencing; the *YCJA* prohibited custodial sentences except in certain circumstances, none of which fit the accused. The court held that the new provisions of the *YCJA* applied to the sentencing appeal of the accused largely on the basis of *R. v. Dunn*, [1995] S.C.J. No. 5, [1995] 1 S.C.R. 226 (S.C.C.), which stands for the proposition that pursuant to s. 44(e) of the *Interpretation Act*, R.S.C. 1985, c. I-21, the appellant is entitled to receive the benefit of the sentencing provisions of the *YCJA*. J.J.C. was therefore placed on 24 months' probation. He had originally been sentenced to a custodial period plus 21 months' probation. See also *R. v. M.D.B.*, [2003] N.W.T.J. No. 41 (N.W.T.C.A.), where the court came to a different conclusion about the applicability of the *YCJA* to a sentence appeal where the sentence was handed down while the *YOA* was law.

[147]   *YCJA*, s. 159(2).

[148]   *R. v. M.N.*, [2005] Nu.J. No. 4, at para. 5 (Nu. C.J.).

[149]   [2004] Y.J. No. 98 (Y.T. Terr. Ct.).

[150]   *R. v. E.J.A.*, [2004] Y.J. No. 98 (Y.T. Terr. Ct.). But see, *contra, R. v. Michel*, [2004] N.W.T.J. No. 47 (N.W.T.S.C.), which was decided just two months earlier. In *Michel*, the court held that the accused was an adult under the criminal law in 1975 where and when the offence occurred and should be dealt with in accordance with his status at the time of the commission of the offence and, thus, should be tried as an adult in 2004, even though he was only 15 at the time of the alleged offence. However, notably, s. 160 of the *YCJA* was not

Proceedings are commenced by the laying of an information or an indictment.[151]

One of the transitional issues that has arisen concerns which Act, the *YOA* or the *YCJA*, governs sentence reviews in cases where the original finding of guilt occurred under the *YOA* but the review of sentence occurs after the coming into force of the *YCJA* in April 2003. To date, the case law is inconclusive. In *R. v. B. (R.)*, a 2003 case of the Ontario Court of Justice, the court did not have to decide the issue but nevertheless suggested that it favoured s. 94 of the *YCJA* as the applicable review provision when dealing with a sentence under the *YOA*. The Ontario Court of Justice reasoned that the Supreme Court of Canada clarified in *R. v. M. (J.J.)*[152] that sentence reviews are an integral part of the sentencing process, that s. 161(3) of the *YCJA* suggests on its face that s. 94 of he *YCJA* is the applicable review provision even when dealing with a *YOA* sentence and that, as a matter of statutory interpretation, a young person should receive the benefit of the more lenient sentencing options under the *YCJA*.[153] Conversely, in *R. v. Z. (J.)*,[154] a later decision of the Ontario Court of Justice, the court considered whether the sentence review sought after the *YCJA* came into force in relation to a *YOA* sentence should occur under s. 28 of the *YOA* or under s. 161 of the *YCJA*, and concluded that the sentence review mechanism under s. 94 of the *YCJA* applied only to a sentence under the *YCJA*, which has been blended with a *YOA* sentence. Since this case concerned a sentence only under the *YOA*, s. 159 of the *YCJA* governs; that is to say, when proceedings are commenced under the *YOA* before the coming into force of the *YCJA* transitional provisions, the proceedings and all related matters are to be dealt with in all respects as if the *YCJA* had not come into force.[155]

Similar uncertainty exists regarding sentence appeals in youth matters. The common law is inconsistent across jurisdictions. In *R. v.*

---

considered in the course of that decision. It is the submission of this author that s. 160 should have been considered and, as *per* Lilles J. in *E.J.A.*, s. 160 of the *YCJA* is a complete answer to the question, given the clear wording of s. 160 of the *YCJA*. (Interestingly, the *Michel* decision also reveals that the *JDA*, which came into force in 1908, was not in force in all parts of Canada in the 1970s and, in particular, was not in force in all parts of the Northwest Territories in 1975.)

[151] *YCJA*, s. 162.
[152] [1993] S.C.J. No. 14, [1993] 2 S.C.R. 421 (S.C.C.).
[153] [2003] O.J. No. 1856, 57 W.C.B. (2d) 420 (Ont. C.J.).
[154] [2003] O.J. No. 3735, 59 W.C.B. (2d) 197 (Ont. C.J.).
[155] See also *R. v. B. (I.L.)*, [2004] S.J. No. 367, 188 C.C.C. (3d) 110 (Sask. Prov. Ct.); *R. v. M.D.B.*, [2003] N.W.T.J. No. 41 (N.W.T.C.A.); and *R. v. G.T.P.*, [2003] B.C.J. No. 2517 (B.C. Youth Ct.).

M.D.B.,[156] among the issues before the Northwest Territories Court of Appeal was whether the one-year custodial sentence for robbery could or should be reduced because the *YCJA* sentencing provisions came in after the sentence but prior to the appeal. The court held that the *YCJA* did not apply because all of the proceedings relating to M.D.B. except for the Crown's appeal were completed prior to the *YCJA* coming into force. For purposes of this discussion it is necessary to reiterate that s. 159(1) states that, subject to s. 161, where, before the coming into force of the *YCJA*'s transitional provisions, proceedings are commenced under the *YOA* in relation to a young person alleged to have committed an offence while a young person, the proceedings and all related matters shall be dealt with in all respects as if the *YCJA* had not come into force. Section 161 qualifies the application of the *YOA* to the extent that it says that a young person found guilty under the *YOA* shall be sentenced under the *YCJA*. The practical effect of s. 161 must be that the young person will be sentenced under the *YCJA* only if they have not already been sentenced under the *YOA*. Otherwise, the result would be absurd: individuals who had already been sentenced under the *YOA* would have to be re-sentenced under the *YCJA*. Such an interpretation would be contrary to the basic rule of statutory interpretation that consequences that are judged to be absurd are presumed not to have been intended.[157] By way of illustration, the court in *M.D.B.* concluded that:

> In our opinion, s. 161 is directed at findings of guilt and related sentences imposed after April 1, 2003, the effective date of the new Act. There is no language in this provision to suggest that s. 161 is meant to apply to findings of guilt and related sentences imposed prior to that date. This Young Person's situation is not, therefore, covered by s. 161, since all his proceedings were completed before the new Act came into effect. The fact that his appeal was argued after April 1, 2003 does not alter the outcome.[158]

To find otherwise, the court reasoned, any sentences imposed before April 1, 2003 but argued in an appeal after that date would have to be returned to the sentencing judge so that all of the provisions in the new *YCJA* could be taken into account in crafting a sentence. "We do not believe

---

[156] [2003] N.W.T.J. No. 41 (N.W.T.C.A.). But see, *contra*, *R. v. N.A.J.*, [2003] P.E.I.J. No. 83 (P.E.I.T.D.)

[157] Ruth Sullivan, *Statutory Interpretation* (Concord: Irwin Law, 1997), at 149. As some commentators have noted, if a young person sentenced under the *YOA* could have the benefit of the *YCJA* simply by appealing, in theory every young person in custody should appeal to get the benefit of the community supervision portion of sentences under the *YCJA*, as well as the benefit of the sentencing provisions under the *YCJA*.

[158] [2003] N.W.T.J. No. 41, at para. 7 (N.W.T.C.A.).

this was Parliament's intention, as it could result in great administrative uncertainty and complexity."[159]

In *R. v. C. (J.J.)*,[160] the Prince Edward Island Court of Appeal reached the opposite conclusion regarding a matter where a young person was sentenced under the *YOA* but the sentence appeal was heard after the coming into force of the *YCJA*. The sentencing provisions of the *YCJA* were found to apply on appeal. The court relied on *R. v. Dunn*[161] to find that s. 44(e) of the *Interpretation Act* applies to appeals and that, as a result, appellants are to get the benefit of any mitigated punishments. Section 44(e) states that:

> Where an enactment, in this section called the "former enactment", is repealed and another enactment, in this section called the "new enactment", is substituted therefor,
>
> ...
>
> (e) when any punishment, penalty or forfeiture is reduced or mitigated by the new enactment, the punishment, penalty or forfeiture if imposed or adjudged after the repeal shall be reduced or mitigated accordingly ... .[162]

In *R. v. C. (J.J.)*, the court held that based on the Supreme Court of Canada ruling in *Dunn*, the meaning of the word *adjudged* in s. 44(e) of the *Interpretation Act* applies to an appeal as well as to a trial. In *R. v. C. (J.J.)*, therefore, this meant that the appellant was entitled to the benefit of the restrictions against custody under s. 39 of the *YCJA* at the appeal stage. The appellant, who had been sentenced to three months secure custody, was found to be ineligible for custody under the *YCJA*.[163] (In *R. v. M.D.B.*,[164] the court had held that s. 44(e) of the *Interpretation Act* was not meant to govern the situation where an entirely new Act is replacing a previous one.)

A year after *R. v. C. (J.J.)*, the Saskatchewan Provincial Court adopted its reasoning to conclude that the sentencing provisions of the *YCJA* applied to the sentence review.[165]

---

[159] *R. v. M.D.B.*, [2003] N.W.T.J. No. 41, at para. 8 (N.W.T.C.A.). In *R. v. G.T.P.*, [2003] B.C.J. No. 2517 (B.C. Youth Ct.), Phillips J. followed *R. v. M.D.B.*

[160] [2003] P.E.I.J. No. 99, 180 C.C.C. (3d) 137 (P.E.I.C.A.).

[161] [1995] S.C.J. No. 5, [1995] 1 S.C.R. 226 (S.C.C.).

[162] See *R. v. Dunn*, [1995] S.C.J. No. 5, at para. 11, [1995] S.C.R. 226 (S.C.C.)

[163] *R. v. C. (J.J.)*, [2003] P.E.I.J. No. 99, 180 C.C.C. (3d) 137 (P.E.I.C.A.).

[164] [2003] N.W.T.J. No. 41 (N.W.T.C.A.).

[165] *R. v. B. (I.L.)*, [2004] S.J. No. 367 (Sask. Prov. Ct.). In this case, Whelan Prov. Ct. J. conducts a comprehensive review of the relevant cases.

The application of the transitional provisions in the *YCJA* can be complicated, depending on the facts of a given case. It will take some time for the jurisprudence in this area to be clarified.

I.   Jurisdictional Exceptions

The youth justice court retains jurisdiction over any federal offence alleged to have been committed by a young person subject to two exceptions: in cases where a federal offence has been designated a contravention under the *Contraventions Act*[166] and in cases where the Department of National Defence has jurisdiction under the *National Defence Act.*[167] (As previously discussed, when a superior court or other court presides over a matter under s. 13(2) or (3) of the *YCJA*, upon election or deemed election by the young person, the superior court (or other court in the case of Nunavut or Quebec in relation to s. 13(2)) is *deemed* to be a youth justice court for the purpose of the proceeding and thus the youth justice court retains jurisdiction.)

(i)   The Contraventions Act

The *Contraventions Act* was enacted in 1992 to establish a simplified procedure for the prosecution of certain designated federal offences. It permits the federal government to designate less serious federal offences, such as speeding on federal roads or boating without the proper safety equipment on board, as contraventions, and, as a result of later amendments, now enables these offences to be dealt with by way of provincial or territorial ticketing schemes rather than by way of the *Criminal Code.*[168] However, the Act is not yet operational in all provinces.

To date, more than 1,800 offences under federal laws and regulations have been designated as contraventions.[169] Designating an offence as a contravention removes the criminal stigma for people who plead guilty or who are found guilty of committing contraventions (unless they are prosecuted by indictment). In such cases, there is no criminal conviction or record,[170] no requirement to be fingerprinted, and no liability

---

[166] S.C. 1992, c. 47; as am. by S.C. 1996, c. 7; S.C. 2002, c. 1.

[167] R.S.C. 1985, c. N-5.

[168] Department of Justice, *Contraventions Act Digest*, May 2006.

[169] Department of Justice, *Contraventions Act Digest*, May 2006, at 2.

[170] *Contraventions Act*, s. 63. At the time of writing, the *Contraventions Act* was available online at: <http://laws.justice.gc.ca/en/C-38.7/index.html?noCookie>.

to be sentenced to jail.[171] The maximum fine for a young person under the *Contraventions Act*, other than a contravention relating to parking a vehicle, cannot exceed $100.[172]

The *Contraventions Act* works by making it possible to prosecute contraventions using the same means that already exist in the provinces or territories to prosecute provincial and municipal offences.[173] The *Contraventions Act* provides for the possibility of implementing it progressively through regulations (the *Application of Provincial Laws Regulations*). These regulations are the mechanism by which provincial regimes are incorporated and make it possible for enforcement agencies to enforce federal contraventions committed in those provinces. As previously mentioned, in Ontario, for example, the *Provincial Offences Act*[174] provides for the prosecution of provincial and municipal offences. The *Contraventions Act* now makes it possible to prosecute contraventions as well under the *Provincial Offences Act*.

Sections 93-108 of the *Provincial Offences Act* describe how young persons are to be dealt with when they commit a provincial or municipal offence. These sections now also apply to a young person who commits a contravention under the *Contraventions Act* in Ontario. Section 5 of the *Contraventions Act* concerns the application of the *YCJA* if not provided for in the Act (or incorporation).

Legislation similar to Ontario's *Provincial Offences Act* exists in other jurisdictions.

The *Contraventions Act* excludes in each of the applicable pieces of provincial legislation any provision that conflicts with the principles in the *Contraventions Act*. For example, any provision in provincial legislation that provides that an offender prosecuted by means of a ticket could receive a jail term as a penalty has been excluded. Under the *Contraventions Act*, an offender who is found guilty of a contravention can receive only a fine.[175]

---

[171] *Contraventions Act*, s. 42(2). See also ss. 65.1 and 65.2 of the *Contraventions Act*, which clarify how the *Contraventions Act* and its regulations are intended to function in relation to provincial or territorial legislation.

[172] *Contraventions Act*, s. 8(4). See also the Department of Justice, *Contraventions Act Digest*, May 2006, at 2.

[173] *Contraventions Act*, s. 65.1.

[174] R.S.O. 1990, c. P.33; S.O. 2006, c. 19, Sched. D, s. 18.

[175] Department of Justice, *Contraventions Act Digest*, May 2006, at 3. See also s. 42 of the *Contraventions Act*.

(ii)   The National Defence Act

Similar to the *YOA*, under the *YCJA*, the jurisdiction of the youth justice court is also subject to the *National Defence Act* (hereafter "*NDA*"), which generally means that the youth justice court does not have jurisdiction over a young person who is a member of the armed forces in relation to discipline or court martials under the *NDA*.

Under s. 60 of the *NDA*'s Code of Service Discipline, a member of the force is subject to the Code. An offence under the Code of Service Discipline captures offences under the *NDA*, the *Criminal Code* or any other Act of Parliament, committed by a person while subject to the Code of Service Discipline.[176] Subject to certain exceptions, the *NDA* also indicates that nothing in the Code of Service Discipline affects the jurisdiction of any civil court to try a person for any offence triable by that court.[177] Consequently, except for certain crimes spelled out in s. 70 of the *NDA* over which the service tribunal is prohibited from exercising jurisdiction — murder, manslaughter, or offences under ss. 280 to 283 of the *Criminal Code* relating to abduction — it is not clear in legislation when the military as opposed to the civil court will have jurisdiction over an offence committed by a member of the military who is under 18 and technically a young person. There appears to be no clear or formal procedure for determining this.[178] Historically, violations of military law are generally tried by the service tribunal. Other violations of federal law that are sufficiently connected to the military, such as if the alleged offence occurred on military premises, will generally be tried by the service tribunal. Federal offences that have no reasonable connection to the military are generally tried by the civil court.[179]

Cadets under 18, as well as young persons who are not members of the forces (such as the children of members) but commit offences on military premises, can be charged with offences under the *NDA* but will be tried in youth justice court.[180]

Pursuant to s. 20(3) of the *NDA*, a youth under 18 can join the military with the consent of one parent or a guardian.[181] Some scholars suggest the rationale for this is that if one is mature enough to be accepted

---

[176] *NDA*, s. 2.
[177] *NDA*, s. 71. But see the exceptions in s. 66.
[178] Priscilla Platt, *Young Offenders Law in Canada*, 2d ed. (Markham: Butterworths Canada Ltd., 1995), at 92.
[179] Priscilla Platt, *Young Offenders Law in Canada*, 2d ed. (Markham: Butterworths Canada Ltd., 1995), at 91 and 92.
[180] Nicholas Bala, *Youth Criminal Justice Law* (Toronto: Irwin Law Inc., 2003), at 157-58.
[181] *NDA*, s. 20.

into the armed forces, one is mature enough to undergo its discipline, and that the military would be reluctant to have members who are not subject to its discipline code and procedures.[182]

J.   Jurisdiction of Youth Court to Hear Constitutional Matters

The youth justice court (a provincial court) is a court of competent jurisdiction, capable of hearing *Charter* matters and granting remedies under s. 24(1) of the *Charter*.[183] In addition, the Supreme Court of Canada has held that provincial courts have jurisdiction to declare legislation invalid in criminal cases under s. 52 of the *Constitution Act, 1982*.[184]

III. THE AGE OF CRIMINAL RESPONSIBILITY

When does the age of reason begin? Every country has its own answer, its own baseline … . The mad arbitrariness.[185]

Before the age of reason we do good and bad without knowing it, and there is no morality in our actions. A child wants to upset everything he sees; he smashes, breaks everything he can reach. He grabs a bird as he would grab a stone, and he strangles it without knowing what he does.[186]

A.   Canada

The age of criminal responsibility has been discussed, debated and deliberated upon in the common law since at least the 14th century.[187] In Canada, the age of criminal responsibility is currently fixed at 12. Children who are alleged to have committed crimes while under the age of 12 cannot be dealt with under the criminal law in Canada. They can be dealt with

---

[182]   Nicholas Bala, *Youth Criminal Justice Law* (Toronto: Irwin Law Inc., 2003), at 157.

[183]   *R. v. R. (D.P.)*, [1987] O.J. No. 1958 (Ont. Prov. Ct. (Youth Div.)).

[184]   *R. v. Big M Drug Mart Ltd.*, [1985] S.C.J. No. 17, at paras. 35, 44-47 (S.C.C.). In *R. v. E.F.*, [2007] O.J. No. 1000 (Ont. C.J.), MacLean J. considered the constitutionality of s. 42(5)(a) and (2)(p) of the *YCJA*. While he concluded that the sections were constitutional, he acknowledged his powers to declare the sections invalid and to impose a remedy, such as severance with a reading down of the legislation.

[185]   Blake Morrison, *As If: A Crime, a Trial, a Question of Childhood* (New York: Picador, 1997), at 78.

[186]   Jean-Jacques Rousseau, *Emile or On Education* (U.S.: Basic Books, 1979), Book I, at 67.

[187]   Early deliberations in the common law concerning the age of criminal responsibility, including the development of the *doli incapax* defence, are discussed in detail in Chapter 1.

through provincial welfare or mental health legislation or through other means, but they cannot be subject to criminal proceedings.[188]

Young persons in Canada who are alleged to have committed a criminal act while between the ages of 12 and 17 can be held criminally liable, but will be tried in youth justice court under the *YCJA* rather than being subject to the procedures and more severe penalties of the *Criminal Code* that apply to adults (although they can receive adult sentences under the *Criminal Code* in certain circumstances). Once they reach 18, young persons are considered adults for purposes of the criminal law and are charged and dealt with under the adult system if they are alleged to have committed criminal offences.

The federal Liberal government raised the age of criminal responsibility in Canada from 7 to 12 in April 1984, when most aspects of the *YOA* came into force. Suddenly, children between the ages of 7 and 11 could no longer be held accountable under criminal law in Canada for criminal conduct in any circumstances, even if that conduct involved murder and there was evidence that the child appreciated the nature and consequences of his or her conduct and knew that it was wrong.

This dramatic change was controversial. The age of criminal responsibility in Canada has been the subject of periodic, and often heated, debate ever since. Media reports of serious crimes committed by young persons under 12, in Canada or abroad, routinely imbue the public discourse on this topic with renewed energy and emotion. In fact, in August 2006, federal Conservative Justice Minister Vic Toews suggested publicly that the age of criminal responsibility should be lowered so that 10- and 11-year-olds who commit criminal offences could be dealt with by the courts. Opposition parties, defence lawyers and journalists immediately accused him of wanting to incarcerate 10- and 11-year-olds.[189] The public response to his comments was so immediate and intense that Toews clarified his concerns in a letter to the editor of *The Ottawa Citizen* just days after making his remarks to the annual meeting of the Canadian Bar Association:

> Young people who engage in criminal behaviour before the age of 12 need effective intervention and treatment to ensure that this pattern of behaviour is not continued. They do not need incarceration, nor have I

---

[188] This point was highlighted in a now notorious Canadian murder case, where a 12-year-old girl, known as J.R., stabbed to death her entire family in Medicine Hat, Alberta, in April 2006, with the aid of a much older accomplice. J.R. was 12½ at the time of the murders. Had she been six months younger, she could not have been charged in Canada. As it was, she was charged and eventually convicted of three counts of first degree murder. In November 2007, she was sentenced to the maximum 10 years under the *YCJA*.

[189] Janice Tibbetts, "Take 10-year-olds to court: Toews" *The Ottawa Citizen* (15 August 2006) A1 and A2.

suggested they do. In some cases, young people have had extensive police and social service interaction before age 12. For these youths, the justice system has no mechanism to ensure that they get the treatment they need. To preserve them from falling through the cracks, we need to discuss whether the courts should have some legal recourse to intervene in a positive fashion. I am open to having the discussion about a treatment-based approach with all the stakeholders in the youth justice system. When it comes to young people of that age, we cannot afford to wait for them to turn 12 and then be dealt with by the courts.[190]

Several months later, in October 2006, Minister Toews ate humble pie and told the media that there was little appetite among his provincial counterparts for lowering the age of criminal responsibility, and that he had no plans to change the law in that regard.[191] Minister Toews's remarks occurred amid renewed debate in Canada regarding how the criminal justice system should handle deviant children, after two Winnipeg boys, aged eight and nine, locked a disabled 14-year-old boy in a shed in a public housing complex in Winnipeg's north end and set it ablaze. The teenager was rescued from the burning building.[192]

As discussed in Chapter 1, prior to 1984, and indeed as far back as Canada's first *Criminal Code* of 1892, children under 7 were formally exempted from criminal liability, while children between 7 and 14 were presumed under the common law doctrine of *doli incapax* to be incapable of committing criminal offences. The Crown could rebut this presumption of incapacity by proving that the young person appreciated the nature and consequences of his or her conduct and knew that it was wrong. Where the Crown was successful, the young person could be held criminal liable. Once 14, the young person was considered capable of forming criminal intent and could no longer rely on the *doli incapax* defence. In such cases, the young person would be dealt with under the *JDA* rather than under the *Criminal Code* for at least a few years. The upper age limit for remaining under the jurisdiction of the *JDA* varied among the provinces and territories; in most jurisdictions, young persons would remain under the jurisdiction of the *JDA* until they turned 16, at which point they would be considered adults for purposes of the criminal law.[193]

[190] Vic Toews, "Correcting the record on youth crime" *The Ottawa Citizen* (17 August 2006).
[191] "Toews backs off prosecuting 10-year-olds" *The Ottawa Citizen* (18 October 2006) A8.
[192] "Do it, push him in there or I'll beat you up" *The Globe and Mail* (21 October 2006) A1 and A6.
[193] Sandra J. Bell, *Young Offenders and Juvenile Justice*, 2d ed. (Scarborough: Nelson, a Division of Thomson Canada Limited, 2003), at 45. See also the *Report of the Department of Justice Committee on Juvenile Delinquency* (Ottawa: Queen's Printer, reprinted 1967), at 54.

The modern phase of the debate regarding the appropriate age of criminal responsibility in Canada began with the 1965 report on Juvenile Delinquency. The report specifically addressed and discussed this topic. Committee members noted that virtually all interested organizations with whom they consulted during their work recommended that the minimum age of criminal responsibility be raised, although there was wide disagreement as to what the appropriate age should be.[194] Although committee members acknowledged that there was no "right" age of criminal responsibility, they ultimately recommended that the age of criminal responsibility in Canada be raised to 10 years or at most, 12, and that the youth court retain jurisdiction over young persons until their 17th birthday, at which point they would be treated like any other adult charged with a crime.[195]

Members suggested that it was preferable to establish a uniform minimum age across the country, and that the federal government and the provinces should discuss the matter before a final decision was made. In concluding that the age should be raised to at least 10 years, committee members stated that they could not see how very young children captured by the *JDA* could be held responsible at all "on any reasonable conception of the purpose and function of the criminal law ... we do not think it proper for Parliament to impose community condemnation, in however attenuated a form, on a very young child. Furthermore, the inevitable community condemnation inherent in an adjudication of delinquency makes it unfair to allow such a child to be found delinquent in a proceeding in which he is unable to participate effectively".[196]

The committee concluded that the age of criminal responsibility had to meet two basic requirements: it had to be an age at which serious offences occurred frequently enough that criminal type proceedings were required and it also had to be an age at which one could expect that adversarial proceedings would be effective.[197] The committee also concluded that the maximum age for dealing with young persons who committed criminal acts under youth justice legislation should be standardized across the country and set at 17. In other words, the committee recommended that the juvenile court have exclusive original jurisdiction over all offenders aged

---

[194] *The Report of the Department of Justice Committee on Juvenile Delinquency* (Ottawa: Queen's Printer, reprinted 1967), at 41.

[195] *The Report of the Department of Justice Committee on Juvenile Delinquency* (Ottawa: Queen's Printer, reprinted 1967), at 284.

[196] *The Report of the Department of Justice Committee on Juvenile Delinquency* (Ottawa: Queen's Printer, reprinted 1967), at 49 and 50.

[197] *The Report of the Department of Justice Committee on Juvenile Delinquency* (Ottawa: Queen's Printer, reprinted 1967), at 51.

16 and under.[198] (At the time of the committee's report, the *JDA* permitted provinces to establish the maximum age limit for young persons in the juvenile court anywhere between 16 and 18, which meant that in Ontario, for example, a 16-year-old was considered an adult and not covered by the *JDA*, while in Manitoba, the *JDA*, covered youths until they turned 18.)[199]

Committee members reasoned that it took longer for modern teenagers to reach full maturity socially and economically since it was more common for them to depend on their families while pursuing higher education. They further concluded that one court should generally be responsible for teenagers as an identifiable group, and that young people should be protected as long as possible from the corrupting influence of adult jails.[200]

The committee also recommended the abolition of the *doli incapax* rule because it was difficult to apply and interpret, and also because they believed it would no longer be needed once the minimum age was raised since its main value was in protecting very young children.[201] The committee observed that the rule had been created at a time when there were no juvenile courts and when penalties for criminal conduct were much more severe.[202] Several decades would pass before these recommendations regarding the age of criminal responsibility would be reflected in new youth justice legislation, the *YOA*.

In making their recommendations, the drafters of the report were influenced by the work of developmental psychologists. Experts argued that very young children lacked the moral and cognitive skills to appreciate the wrongfulness of their conduct and therefore should not be held criminally responsible. They also argued that adolescence (from 14 to 18) was a distinct phase in moral and cognitive development and that these teenagers should be protected from the adult system.[203]

The Committee's recommendations regarding the age of criminal responsibility as well as the upper age limit for keeping youths under the jurisdiction of the youth court reflected an international trend. A U.K.

---

[198]   *The Report of the Department of Justice Committee on Juvenile Delinquency* (Ottawa: Queen's Printer, reprinted 1967), at 60.

[199]   *The Report of the Department of Justice Committee on Juvenile Delinquency* (Ottawa: Queen's Printer, reprinted 1967), at 51.

[200]   *The Report of the Department of Justice Committee on Juvenile Delinquency* (Ottawa: Queen's Printer, reprinted 1967), at 57.

[201]   *The Report of the Department of Justice Committee on Juvenile Delinquency* (Ottawa: Queen's Printer, reprinted 1967), at 53 and 54.

[202]   *The Report of the Department of Justice Committee on Juvenile Delinquency* (Ottawa: Queen's Printer, reprinted 1967), at 54.

[203]   J. Bolton *et al.*, "The *Young Offenders Act*: Principles and Policy — the First Decade in Review" (1993) 38 McGill L.J. 939, at 956.

report (the Ingleby Report of 1960) had recommended raising the age in Britain from 10 to 12. At the time of the report, the age of criminal responsibility was already higher in various European countries than it was in Canada: in England, it was 10 (and remains 10 today); in France it was 13; in Germany, Austria and Norway, it was 14; and in Denmark and Sweden, it was 15.[204]

The report's recommendations regarding the age of criminal responsibility (which drew on the work of behavioural psychologists and labelling theorists) significantly influenced the content of the Canadian youth justice legislation that followed. In Bill C-192, which was introduced in the House of Commons on November 16, 1970,[205] the federal government proposed raising the age from 7 to 10 years. The government also proposed raising the upper age limit of youth justice legislation from 16 to 17 with an option for the provinces to raise it to 18.[206] However, the federal government eventually left Bill C-192 to die on the Order Paper in response to major opposition from interest groups, Parliamentarians and the media.[207] Among the main reasons for the opposition was that some provinces were concerned about the cost implications of raising the maximum age of young persons. Extra custodial facilities would be required for those young persons who would now fall under the aegis of the new youth legislation and remain within the youth criminal justice system as a result of the maximum age being raised.[208]

A new round of youth justice reform followed the demise of Bill C-192, including the establishment of a special committee by Solicitor General Warren Allmand. In July 1975, the committee released its report, *Young Persons in Conflict with the Law*, which included 108 recommendations for proposed legislation to replace the *JDA* as well as an actual draft Act. The report proved to be highly influential and, in fact, provided the philosophical framework for the draft legislation in 1977 and 1979 that would eventually result in the *YOA*.[209] Interestingly, that 1975 report recommended 14 as a minimum age of criminal responsibility, meaning

---

[204] J. Bolton *et al.*, "The *Young Offenders Act*: Principles and Policy — the First Decade in Review" (1993) 38 McGill L.J. 939, at 956.

[205] J. Bolton *et al.*, "The *Young Offenders Act*: Principles and Policy — the First Decade in Review" (1993) 38 McGill L.J. 939, at 961 and 962. Bill C-192, *An Act Respecting Young Offenders and to Repeal the Juvenile Delinquents Act*, 3d Sess., 28th Parl., 1970.

[206] J. Bolton *et al.*, "The *Young Offenders Act*: Principles and Policy — the First Decade in Review" (1993) 38 McGill L.J. 939, at 962.

[207] J. Bolton *et al.*, "The *Young Offenders Act*: Principles and Policy — the First Decade in Review" (1993) 38 McGill L.J. 939, at 963.

[208] J. Bolton *et al.*, "The *Young Offenders Act*: Principles and Policy — the First Decade in Review" (1993) 38 McGill L.J. 939, at 963 and 964.

[209] J. Bolton *et al.*, "The *Young Offenders Act*: Principles and Policy — the First Decade in Review" (1993) 38 McGill L.J. 939, at 967.

that any young person under 14 could not be dealt with under criminal legislation but would have to be dealt with under provincial child welfare, youth protection or juvenile correctional legislation.[210] Quebec supported this proposal, but there was considerable opposition from other provinces about such a high minimum age. Finally, in 1977, the federal department of the Solicitor General recommended 12 as the minimum age of criminal responsibility.[211]

Between 1975 and 1982, three separate governments attempted to draft successful legislation based on suggested reforms; ultimately Bill C-61 was introduced in 1982 under a Liberal government and passed with general approval as the *YOA*.[212] Most of its provisions were proclaimed in force in 1984. Ironically, as scholars who have studied the period observe, many of the proposals in Bill C-192 that were so passionately rejected in the 70s were incorporated with a large measure of consensus into the *YOA* in 1982.[213]

When the provisions of the *YOA* came into force, the age of 12 was the age of criminal responsibility.[214] As previously discussed, this was a significant change in the criminal law as it applied to young persons. Provinces would now have to identify programs and resources to deal with the needs of young persons between 7 and 11 who had committed acts previously defined as criminal. Under the *YOA*, the Liberal government also established 17 as the upper age limit across the country for dealing with young persons who committed criminal offences within the more lenient youth criminal justice system.[215]

---

[210]   Nicholas Bala, *Youth Criminal Justice Law* (Toronto: Irwin Law Inc., 2003), at 168.

[211]   Nicholas Bala, *Youth Criminal Justice Law* (Toronto: Irwin Law Inc., 2003), at 168 and 169.

[212]   J. Bolton *et al.*, "The *Young Offenders Act*: Principles and Policy — the First Decade in Review" (1993) 38 McGill L.J. 939, at 973.

[213]   J. Bolton *et al.*, "The *Young Offenders Act*: Principles and Policy — the First Decade in Review" (1993) 38 McGill L.J. 939, at 967 and 973.

[214]   Nicholas Bala, *Youth Criminal Justice Law* (Toronto: Irwin Law Inc., 2003), at 169. Bala, who has written on youth justice issues for many years, suggests that in the end, the choice of 12 was at least, in part, a political compromise, although he acknowledges that the period between 12 and 17 corresponds roughly with the period of adolescence, with the age of 12 signifying the approximate beginning of puberty and also the time at which one prepares to enter intermediate or senior elementary school.

[215]   Chief Justice Lilles of the Yukon Territorial Court, as he then was, who is also co-author with N. Bala of *The Young Offenders Act: Annotated S.C. 1980-81-82, c. 110*, notes in *R. v. E.J.A.*, [2004] Y.J. No. 98 (Y.T. Terr. Ct.) that, at the time the *YOA* was introduced, society was becoming increasingly knowledgeable about child and adolescent development. Two pioneers in child development, Jean Piaget and Lawrence Kohlberg, had developed theories, which had become widely accepted, that children develop their cognitive and moral capacities in stages. As Lilles C.J. noted, according to Kohlberg, a child's moral development may not be fully completed until late adolescence, and sometimes not until early adulthood. By increasing the maximum age to 18, Lilles C.J. argued, Parliament

At the time the *YOA* was enacted, there was little vocal opposition to the minimum age; only B.C. was advocating a lower minimum age.[216] The issue of whether 12 was an appropriate age for the onset of criminal responsibility in Canada re-emerged as a matter of public debate after the implementation of the *YOA*. The February 1993 slaying of 2-year-old British toddler James Bulger by two 10-year-old boys brought the issue surging to the fore in Canada. "Seldom has a trial aroused such passions and public feelings of hate towards the defendants."[217]

In the *Bulger* case, the two 10-year-olds, Robert Thompson and Jon Venables, were caught on a grainy video camera luring the toddler by the hand from a shopping centre in the Liverpool suburb of Bootle. The disturbing footage from the security video was broadcast across Canada. The two children led the child on a long walk along nearby streets to the railroad tracks where they splashed him with blue paint, battered him with bricks and an iron bar, and placed him, still alive, on the railway tracks, encircling his head with bricks. A train later severed James Bulger's body.[218]

---

recognized that in general, a 16- or 17-year-old would not have the maturity and developmental capacity that a normal adult would have. It was therefore unjust to hold a 16- or 17-year-old to the moral standard of an adult. The youth criminal justice system was thus extended to encompass these older adolescents.

[216]   Nicholas Bala, *Youth Criminal Justice Law* (Toronto: Irwin Law Inc., 2003), at 169.

[217]   Blake Morrison, "Robert Thompson and John Venables" in R. Wilkes, ed., *The Mammoth Book of Famous Trials* (New York: Carroll and Graf, 2006), at 447.

[218]   Blake Morrison, "Robert Thompson and John Venables" in R. Wilkes, ed., *The Mammoth Book of Famous Trials* (New York: Carroll and Graf, 2006), at 447. See also R. Boswell, "The horror of 'baby-faced killers'" *The Ottawa Citizen* (27 November 2000) A4. The accused, Thompson and Venables, were tried in Britain as adults in November 1993. At the time of their trial, a child between 10 and 14 was subject to a presumption that he did not know what he was doing was wrong (*doli incapax*). The prosecution had to rebut this presumption by proving beyond a reasonable doubt that, at the time of the offence, the children knew that the act was wrong, as distinct from being merely naughty or childish mischief. The *doli incapax* presumption was abolished in Britain as of September 30, 1998. During the Bulger trial, psychiatrists testified that both Thompson and Venables knew the severity of their crime. The two boys were convicted. Under the applicable British procedure, the trial judge recommended the boys serve 8 years; the Lord Chief Justice recommended 10 years, but the British Home Secretary increased that to a minimum of 15 years. The House of Lords later quashed that decision. In December 1999, the European Court of Human Rights condemned their conviction and sentence for various reasons, including that they were denied a fair hearing because they were so immature and emotionally vulnerable that they were unable to participate effectively in the criminal proceedings. The court also concluded that the formality and ritual of the court must, at times, have seemed incomprehensible and intimidating to the boys. The court further found a violation of Article 6.1 of the *U.N. Convention on the Rights of the Child* because the Home Secretary, who pronounced sentence, was not independent of the executive; therefore, the children were denied a fair hearing by an independent and impartial tribunal. The two boys were released in June 2001 after serving eight years of their sentences. Both were promised anonymity and, to that end, were given new identities. A comprehensive summary

Former British Home Secretary Michael Howard, who was reported to have supported the aggressive prosecution of Thompson and Venables, wrote some years after the incident that "the murder of James Bulger was an event of such horror that the facts remain indelibly impressed on the minds of people all over the world.... The horror was magnified by the fact that those who were alleged to be responsible were themselves only 10 years old".[219] Many Canadians were acutely aware that, had the killing occurred here, the two young boys could not have been held criminally responsible.[220]

The *Bulger* case was followed a few years later by a highly publicized Toronto sexual assault of a 13-year-old girl by an 11-year-old boy. The accused was reported to have taunted the police for not being able to charge him. "You got me. So what are you going to do?"[221]

In September 1993, the then Canadian federal Justice Minister Pierre Blais issued a public consultation paper entitled *Toward Safer Communities: Violent and Repeat Offending by Young People*. The paper acknowledged that youths who commit violent or repeat offences had become a subject of particular public concern, and that there was a need to explore ways to better deal with these youths.[222] In that document, the federal government again specifically examined the minimum age of criminal responsibility, as well as the most appropriate age for young persons to be dealt with under the adult criminal justice system rather than within the youth justice system. The federal government canvassed the arguments both for and against retaining 12 as the minimum age, as well as the arguments for lowering the upper age limit of the youth justice system so that more young persons would be treated like adults upon the alleged commission of a crime.

Regarding the minimum age, the government observed that some Canadians wanted to see the minimum age of criminal responsibility lowered, and that the age most commonly suggested was 10. The paper then explained that the government was retaining 12 as the minimum age because most children under 12 lack the necessary knowledge and experience to understand the consequences of their actions and that children under 12 would not be able to fully participate in proceedings against them. The

---

of the facts and legal history of the *Bulger* case can be found in the decision of the European Court of Human Rights: *V. v. The United Kingdom* (24888/94) [1999] ECHR 171 (16 December 1999).

[219] R. Boswell, "The horror of 'baby-faced killers'" *The Ottawa Citizen* (27 November 2000) A4.

[220] Priscilla Platt, *Young Offenders Law in Canada*, 2d ed. (Markham: Butterworths Canada Ltd., 1995), at 99.

[221] Nicholas Bala, *Youth Criminal Justice Law* (Toronto: Irwin Law Inc., 2003), at 170.

[222] Department of Justice, *Toward Safer Communities: Violent and Repeat Offending by Young People* (September 3, 1993), at 1.

federal government acknowledged that some Canadians favoured lowering the age of criminal responsibility because they believed excluding children from the criminal justice system contributed to their lack of respect for the law, that children could get support from the criminal justice system that they could not get otherwise because child protection systems were either overburdened or lacked the facilities that some children needed (such as secure custody), and that the public would be better protected from the serious anti-social behaviour of some children if these children were captured by the *YOA*.

Conversely, the paper noted that those who wished to retain the age of 12 argued that research suggested that younger children did not understand legal concepts such as their right to instruct counsel, that children were referred to the youth justice system because child protection agencies lacked the resources to deal with them and that this problem would worsen if the age were lowered when what was needed was a strengthening of the child protection systems. Finally, the federal government concluded, it was too costly to include more children in the youth justice system and that, in addition, a federal-provincial-territorial committee had studied the minimum age issue in 1990 and recommended keeping it at 12 while bolstering provincial legislation where necessary.[223]

The report explained that the upper age limit of the *YOA* was set at 17 because many adult rights and responsibilities begin at 18.

Some Canadians wanted to see the maximum age lowered to 15, arguing that older youths are more mature and are better dealt with in the adult system, where they may receive longer sentences, and that youths would commit fewer crimes if they knew they would be tried in adult court. The youth court caseload would consequently be reduced, allowing the youth justice system's resources to be used for younger offenders.

Canadians who wanted to retain 17 as the upper limit of the youth justice system had argued that youth court sentences for some crimes were actually longer than adult sentences for the same crimes due in part to the remission and parole processes available in the adult system, that older youths were not committing more violent crimes than their younger counterparts, that young offenders were more likely to be rehabilitated in the youth system than in the adult system and that the Act allowed for transfers to the adult system in serious cases, such as murder.[224]

---

[223] Department of Justice, *Toward Safer Communities: Violent and Repeat Offending by Young People* (September 3, 1993), at 10 and 11.

[224] Department of Justice, *Toward Safer Communities: Violent and Repeat Offending by Young People* (September 3, 1993), at 12.

Liberal Justice Minister Allan Rock wrote to the Chair of the Standing Committee on Justice and Legal Affairs in June 1994, proposing a fundamental review of the *YOA*. Rock acknowledged that the *YOA* was controversial, and that questions remained as to whether it was the best juvenile justice model for Canada. A Task Force on Youth Justice was established by the federal, provincial and territorial Ministers responsible for justice (except for Quebec, which had just completed its own review of the *YOA*)[225] to review the Act.

The task force released its report in 1996, which prompted further study and consultation by the Standing Committee on Justice and Legal Affairs. The standing committee issued its report, *Renewing Youth Justice*, in April 1997. This report included 14 recommendations.[226] Among them was the recommendation that both the *YOA* and s. 13 of the *Criminal Code* be amended to give the youth court jurisdiction to deal with 10- and 11-year-olds alleged to have committed criminal offences causing death or serious harm. The recommendation also suggested that the Attorney General be required to personally consent to the prosecution, and that the youth court judge review the seriousness and circumstances of the alleged offence, the character and background of the young person and the availability of appropriate child protection/child welfare, mental health, education or other services or programs before deciding if the young person should be dealt with in the youth justice system. According to this recommendation, if the youth court judge decided to refer the young person to services and programs outside of the youth justice system, the criminal charges would be held in abeyance while the young person was dealt with by these other services and programs. If these services and programs dealt effectively with the young person's offending behaviour, the youth court judge could dismiss the criminal charges. (The Committee did not recommend changes to the maximum age of young persons who could be dealt with under the *YOA*.)[227]

The federal Reform Party also issued a report in 1997 concerning reform of the *YOA* in which it rejected the majority of the recommendations of the Standing Committee on Justice and Legal Affairs. Among its 17 recommendations, the Reform Party suggested that

---

[225] *Reference re: Bill C-7 respecting the criminal justice system for young persons*, [2003] Q.J. No. 2850, at para. 13 (Que. C.A.).

[226] Canada, House of Commons, *Renewing Youth Justice: Thirteenth Report of the Standing Committee on Justice and Legal Affairs* (Ottawa: Ministry of Supply and Services, 1997), at 61.

[227] Canada, House of Commons, *Renewing Youth Justice: Thirteenth Report of the Standing Committee on Justice and Legal Affairs* (Ottawa: Ministry of Supply and Services, 1997), at 63.

the age range of youth justice legislation should be between 10 and 15. The Reform Party argued that a 1992 Statistics Canada survey indicated that children under 12 commit about 1.2 per cent of all crime but cannot be held criminally liable. Lowering the age to 10 would not mean that a large influx of 10- and 11-year-olds would be drawn into the system, the report argued, but only that children under 12 who commit violent offences could be held criminally accountable and provided with the rehabilitation they required. Once they turn 16, however, young persons who commit crimes should be in the adult system, its report stated. "For all intents and purposes, 16 and 17-year-olds are adults and should be treated as such under the criminal law.... 16-year-olds are legally allowed to drive cars, get married and live on their own. They have the knowledge and capacity to know right from wrong. They also have the physical strength equal to most adults, and in many cases, greater strength."[228]

(Regarding the percentage of crime committed by persons under 12, the figures have changed little during the last decade. Figures from the Uniform Crime Survey for 2004 indicate that young persons under 12 were involved in 1 per cent of all incidents involving criminal offences; they were involved in 1.1 per cent of all incidents involving crimes against persons.)[229]

The federal government responded to the committee and to its various detractors a year later when it issued *A Strategy for the Renewal of Youth Justice*, a document that became the philosophical framework for the new *YCJA*.[230] In it, the federal government rejected recommendations that it lower the age of criminal responsibility in order to hold at least some 10- and 11-year-olds criminally accountable. Any discussion of lowering the age of criminal responsibility must consider various factors, including concern for public safety, the capacity of young persons to form criminal intent, the ability of the child to instruct counsel and participate in criminal proceedings and the possibility that the child could be handled more effectively through the child welfare or mental health system, the

---

[228] *The Reform Party Report on Amending the Young Offenders Act*, submitted by Jack Ramsay, M.P. Reform Party Justice Critic, April 22, 1997, at 19 to 27.

[229] Uniform Crime Reporting Survey. These figures are taken from a table provided by Justice Canada's Research and Statistics Division containing the most recent available data (2004) concerning the age of the accused by offence type.

[230] Department of Justice, *A Strategy for the Renewal of Youth Justice* (Ottawa: Ministry of Supply and Services, 1998). This document can be accessed through the Department of Justice website at: <http://www.justice.gc.ca/eng/pi/yj-jj/about-apropos/toc-tdm.html>. In this document, the federal government examines the shortcomings of the *YOA* and outlines its rationale for introducing the *YCJA*.

federal government said.[231] The federal government stated that very few offenders under the age of 12 are involved in serious, violent offences in any event. The government concluded that most of these children could be dealt with more effectively by parents and the community without involving the state. "When a more formal approach is required, child welfare or mental health systems are usually the preferred approach. These systems have access to a wider array of services that are more age-appropriate, family-oriented and therapeutic than those available through the criminal justice system."[232]

The federal government explained that it preferred to work with the provinces to identify and respond to the child welfare and mental health needs of the small number of children in this category. "The commission of serious violence by very young children indicates significant developmental, emotional or psychiatric issues that can best be addressed through provincial child welfare and mental health programs."[233]

Regarding the maximum age of young persons who are dealt with within the youth criminal justice system, the federal government said that the *YCJA* would retain the age of 17. Eighteen is the age at which young people in Canada acquire full adult civil rights and responsibilities, the government noted. This upper age limit is also consistent with international standards and the practices of most Western industrialized countries as well as with the views and recommendations of the vast majority of stakeholders.[234]

The Progressive Conservative party and the Canadian Alliance continued to call for the age range of the new bill to capture young persons between the ages of 10 and 15 when the bill was being debated in the House of Commons in September 2000.[235] The Liberal government did not budge. When the *YCJA* came into force in April 2003, the age of criminal responsibility remained 12. Some academics suggest that the Liberal government retained 12, in part, in order to gain support for the *YCJA* from Quebec, which opposed the *YCJA* in general and objected strongly to lowering the age of criminal responsibility.[236]

---

[231] Department of Justice, *A Strategy for the Renewal of Youth Justice* (Ottawa: Ministry of Supply and Services, 1998) (section on Legislative and Supporting Program Components).

[232] Department of Justice, *A Strategy for the Renewal of Youth Justice* (Ottawa: Ministry of Supply and Services, 1998) (section on Legislative and Supporting Program Components).

[233] Department of Justice, *A Strategy for the Renewal of Youth Justice* (Ottawa: Ministry of Supply and Services, 1998) (section on Legislative and Supporting Program Components).

[234] Department of Justice, *A Strategy for the Renewal of Youth Justice* (Ottawa: Ministry of Supply and Services, 1998) (section on Legislative and Supporting Program Components).

[235] *House of Commons Debates*, No. 121 (25 September 2000), at 1155.

[236] Nicholas Bala, *Youth Criminal Justice Law* (Toronto: Irwin Law Inc., 2003), at 181.

At the heart of this difficult issue is the fact that reasonable people, including experts in developmental psychology, disagree over the age at which young persons should be held accountable under the criminal law.[237] As many scholars have aptly noted over the years, if choosing the age of criminal responsibility were merely a matter of applying developmental psychology, why is there such disparity internationally in the ages adopted? It is because youth justice experts and related professionals disagree as to precisely how age affects the capacity to understand crime and/or the court process, and that insufficient empirical research has been done to assist policymakers in determining an appropriate minimum age for youth court jurisdiction.[238] A recent study of Canadian young offenders concluded that a child's understanding of legal rights and procedures may be more illusion than reality. Rather than awareness and insight into the legal process, confusion and misunderstanding may be the norm.[239]

Psychologists have suggested that one of the unstudied areas of developmental psychology involves the cognitive capacities and development of children as this relates to public policy. Some have identified the need for a systematic examination of the relevance of the age established in juvenile legislation to developmental issues studied by

---

[237]   See Bala's discussion in *Youth Criminal Justice Law* (Toronto: Irwin Law Inc., 2003), at 171-72, where he argues little empirical research has been done in this area. See also J. Thomas Dalby, "Criminal Liability in Children" (1985) 27 Can. J. Crim. 137, at 140-43, where Dalby argues that children at about the age of seven not only possess the cognitive capacity for a "guilty mind" but are able to make judgements about this intent in others. Dalby argues that most children at about the age of seven meet at least the minimum criteria for criminal responsibility. He suggests the focus should be on decreased consequences for their acts because of their social status rather than on their having reduced legal responsibility. Conversely, see Michele Peterson "Children's Understanding of the Juvenile Justice System: A Cognitive-Developmental Perspective" (1988) 30 Can. J. Crim. 381, at 394, in which she concludes that, to the extent that understanding that an act is illegal constitutes the criterion by which criminal intent and responsibility are assessed, then 12 appears to be a reasonable minimum for the application of formal criminal sanctions. However, in a later study she co-authored with R. Abramovitch, "Grade Related Changes in Young People's Reasoning about Plea Decisions" (1993) 17 Law and Human Behaviour 537, at 548, she concluded that most of the 10-year-olds could understand the legal domain and distinguish it from the moral realm.

[238]   Nicholas Bala, *Youth Criminal Justice Law* (Toronto: Irwin Law Inc., 2003), at 171.

[239]   M. Dufresne, R. Maclure, and K. Campbell, *The Rights of Young Offenders* (2003) [unpublished manuscript], referred to in M.S. Denov, "Children's Rights, Juvenile Justice, and the *UN Convention on the Rights of the Child*", c. 4, in Kathryn M. Campbell, ed., *Understanding Youth Justice in Canada* (Toronto: Pearson Education Canada Inc., 2005), 83. A more recent study of Irish school children found that young people between the ages of 12 and 15 who are old enough to be held criminally responsible have a very poor understanding of common legal terminology that lawyers appear to assume is well understood. See E. Crawford and R. Bull, "Teenagers' Difficulties with Key Words Regarding the Criminal Court Process" (2006) 12(6) Psychology, Crime & Law 653.

psychologists.[240] Psychologist Michele Peterson-Badali has contended that 12 years appears to be a reasonable minimum for criminal responsibility, but in a later study concerning competency to make plea decisions[241] she found that a majority of even 10-year-old subjects used legal rather than moral criteria in making their plea decisions.

Other scholars and legal practitioners suggest it is worthwhile considering an inverted version of the *doli incapax* defence, where young persons between 7 and 12 could be held accountable for criminal conduct unless the young person (and not the Crown) could prove he or she was not sufficiently cognizant to appreciate the nature, consequences and wrongfulness of his or her conduct.[242] While the *doli incapax* defence has been criticized for being ambiguous, difficult to apply, and often easier for judges to ignore than understand,[243] its use avoids the arbitrary choosing of a particular age at which one suddenly becomes criminally responsible, and it also recognizes that young persons mature at different rates. One 10-year-old may be eminently capable of appreciating and understanding the consequences of his or her own conduct while another may not. That said, the resurrection of an approach similar to the *doli incapax* defence, where there is no fixed age of criminal responsibility for young persons, also opens the door to greater judicial discretion with all the inherent risks that would entail.

Still other scholars suggest that the state should shift its focus from the fruitless task of trying to determine a precise age at which a young person has the capacity to commit a crime and focus instead on the best process and forum for addressing criminal conduct in young persons.[244] They argue that the focus of the attention and discourse should shift to

---

[240] M. Peterson-Badali, "Children's Understanding of the Juvenile Justice System: A Cognitive-Development Perspective" (1988) 30 Can. J. Crim. 381, at 382-83.

[241] M. Peterson-Badali and R. Abramovitch, "Grade Related Changes in Young People's Reasoning about Plea Decisions" (1993) 17 Law & Human Behaviour 537, at 548. See also Anthony N. Doob and and Carla Cesaroni, "The Youth Justice System and Very Young Children" in *Responding to Youth Crime in Canada* (Toronto: University of Toronto Press, 2004) and also J. Thomas Dalby, "Criminal Liability in Children" (1985) 27 Can. J. Crim. 137.

[242] Lisa Micucci, "Responsibility and the Young Person" (1998) 11 Can. J.L. & Jur. 277, at paras. 90 and 96 (QL). This article by Lisa Micucci is a thoughtful and comprehensive discussion of when young persons should be held criminally accountable for their conduct.

[243] Lisa Micucci, "Responsibility and the Young Person" (1998) 11 Can. J.L. & Jur. 277, at paras. 20-22 (QL). See also Nicholas Bala, *Youth Criminal Justice Law* (Toronto: Irwin Law Inc., 2003), at 167-68.

[244] Gerry Maher, "Age and Criminal Responsibility" (2005) Vol. 2, Ohio State Journal of Criminal Law 493. Mr. Maher is identified in the article as a Queen's Counsel (Scotland) and a Professor of Criminal Law at Edinburgh University in Scotland. In this article, he examines a project on the age of criminal responsibility conducted by the Scottish Law Commission, the official law reform body in Scotland.

trying to determine how best and most effectively the state can address the deviant conduct of young persons and which process, criminal or otherwise, or some combination, would be most effective. In other words, the focus should be on substance and not forum.

The common goal of those who work within the youth criminal justice system is to reduce and to prevent youth crime. So long as the state takes the position that a specific age of criminal responsibility must be identified, the age chosen will ultimately be, to some degree, arbitrary and political,[245] and a decision that may not be firmly rooted in the empirical evidence about cognitive development.[246] So long as an age *is* chosen, that age will never suitably address all possible situations, or satisfy all Canadians. Invariably, there will be some 10- or 11-year-olds (and sometimes even younger persons) who are thought to be adequately intelligent, sophisticated and mature to justify their being held criminally responsible. Likewise, there will always be some 12-year-olds who are less mature and intellectually developed than other 12-year-olds.

In addition, youth justice experts and representatives from provincial social agencies and similar organizations across the country have long suggested that, despite the change in legislation in 1984, provincial agencies have never received the necessary resources and funding to provide the services needed to assist children under 12 who commit serious acts, and that current social and legal approaches are not adequate to address offending behaviour by young persons under 12.[247] Research and creative programs for the under-12 group should be a priority for both juvenile justice and child welfare personnel, some suggest.[248] They contend that the federal government and the provinces, and perhaps non-governmental organizations as well, have not paid enough attention to high risk children in the under-12 age category. Some experts advocate the enactment of special provincial legislation focusing on children under 12 who commit offences, and advise the establishment of special community committees or agencies to address the problems of these child offenders.[249]

---

[245] Anthony N. Doob and Carla Cesaroni, *Responding to Youth Crime in Canada* (Toronto: University of Toronto Press, 2004), at 53. See also Nicholas Bala, *Youth Criminal Justice Law* (Toronto: Irwin Law Inc., 2003), at 181.

[246] Thomas Dalby, "Criminal Liability in Children" (1985) 27 Can. J. Crim. 137, at 139.

[247] For a discussion of how the provinces address offending behaviour by children under 12, see, for example, Nicholas Bala, *Youth Criminal Justice Law* (Toronto: Irwin Law Inc., 2003), at 172-83.

[248] See Leschied, Alan D.W. and Susan K. Wilson, "Criminal Liability of Children Under Twelve: A Problem for Child Welfare, Juvenile Justice, or Both?" (1988) 30 Can. J. Crim. 17.

[249] Nicholas Bala, *Youth Criminal Justice Law* (Toronto: Irwin Law Inc., 2003), at 182.

The age of criminal responsibility is likely to remain the subject of public debate and discourse in Canada during the years ahead. It tends to resurge every time a crime by a person under 12 raises the ire of the public. For the short-term, at least, it appears that the minimum age of criminal responsibility in Canada will remain at 12. Regarding the upper age limit for dealing with children under the *YCJA*, the federal government is likely to remain mindful of the *United Nations Convention on the Rights of the Child* (hereafter "*UNCRC*"), which it ratified in 1992. Children are defined in that document as those under 18.[250]

B.   Other Countries

The Age of Criminal Responsibility varies throughout the Western world. In England and Wales, the minimum age at which a child can face criminal proceedings is 10, which is among the lowest age thresholds in Europe.[251] Scotland has established 8 as the age of criminal responsibility but it has a unique, welfare-oriented Children's Hearing System,[252] which results in its minimum age being somewhat misleading. The United Nations has criticized the United Kingdom for its low age of criminal responsibility for being out of step with norms elsewhere in Europe.[253]

In the United States, criminal law is largely a matter of state responsibility; the minimum age for being brought before the courts is set by state law and varies among states. In North Carolina, a person as young as six can be brought to juvenile court; however, most states (33 to be precise) have no minimum age enshrined in statute.[254] The states generally

---

[250]   Sandra J. Bell, *Young Offenders and Juvenile Justice: A Century After the Fact*, 2d ed. (Scarborough: Nelson, a division of Thomson Canada Ltd., 2003), at 65.

[251]   J. Graham and C. Moore, "Beyond Welfare Versus Justice: Juvenile Justice in England and Wales" in J. Junger-Tas and S.H. Decker, eds., *International Handbook of Juvenile Justice* (The Netherlands: Springer, 2006), 65 at 72. Charts and related information concerning the age of criminal responsibility in various countries can be found on the UNICEF website at: <http://www.unicef.org/pon97>. The Wikipedia online encyclopedia also publishes a chart on the age of criminal responsibility in various countries that, at the time of writing in June 2007, could be accessed at: <http://en.wikipedia.org/wiki/defense_of_infancy>.

[252]   Michele Burman *et al.*, "The End of an Era? — Youth Justice in Scotland" in J. Junger-Tas and S. Decker, eds., *International Handbook of Juvenile Justice* (The Netherlands: Springer, 2006), 439 at 441.

[253]   J. Graham and C. Moore, "Beyond Welfare Versus Justice: Juvenile Justice in England and Wales" in J. Junger-Tas and S.H. Decker, eds., *International Handbook of Juvenile Justice* (The Netherlands: Springer, 2006), 65 at 73.

[254]   D. Bishop and S. Decker, "Punishment and Control: Juvenile Justice Reform in the USA" in J. Junger-Tas and S.H. Decker, eds., *International Handbook of Juvenile Justice* (The Netherlands: Springer, 2006), 3 at 13-14. The National Criminal Justice Reference Service, which is administered by the Office of Justice Programs for the U.S. Department of Justice,

rely on the common law, which holds that a person as young as seven can be found to be criminally responsible.[255] In the states that have established a minimum age by statute, one state has set the minimum age at 6, three at 7, eleven at 10 and one at 12.[256] The trend across the U.S. has been to lower the minimum age at which a young person can be brought before the court.[257]

The age at which a young person can be tried in adult court also varies throughout the United States. In some states, children as young as seven can be tried as adults.[258]

In Australia, the statutory minimum age of criminal responsibility is uniformly set at 10.[259] Scandinavian countries, such as Sweden, Finland, Denmark and Norway, have established 15 as the minimum age.[260] However, in youth criminal justice systems around the world, the demarcation lines that connote the onset of criminal responsibility are not always definitive. In Sweden, for example, the responsibility for addressing criminal conduct by young persons is shared by the social services and the justice system: For those under 15, social services has the main responsibility. For young persons between 15 and 17 and sometimes up to

---

is a good source of current information on justice issues in the U.S. It can be accessed at: <http://www.ncjrs.gov>.

[255] Nicholas Bala, *Youth Criminal Justice Law* (Toronto: Irwin Law Inc., 2003), at 136-38. See also discussion in Priscilla Platt, *Young Offenders Law in Canada*, 2d ed. (Markham: Butterworths Canada Ltd., 1995), at 567.

[256] D. Bishop and S. Decker, "Punishment and Control: Juvenile Justice Reform in the USA" in J. Junger-Tas and S.H. Decker, eds., *International Handbook of Juvenile Justice* (The Netherlands: Springer, 2006), at 13.

[257] D. Bishop and S. Decker, "Punishment and Control: Juvenile Justice Reform in the USA" in J. Junger-Tas & S.H. Decker, eds., *International Handbook of Juvenile Justice* (The Netherlands: Springer, 2006), at 13.

[258] Nicholas Bala, *Youth Criminal Justice Law* (Toronto: Irwin Law Inc., 2003), at 136-38. This subject is discussed further in Chapter 8 concerning sentencing.

[259] The Age of Criminal Responsibility, Crime Facts Info No. 106, Australian Institute of Criminology (13 September 2005). See also Gregor Urbas, No. 181, The Age of Criminal Responsibility, Australian Institute of Criminology, November 2000. For information concerning the age of criminal responsibility in various states across the United States, see the Office of Juvenile Justice and Delinquency Prevention of the U.S. Department of Justice, which can be accessed at: <http://www.ojjdp.ncjrs.gov/>. See also a chart on the age of criminal responsibility at: <http://www.ojjdp.ncjrs.org/pubs/tryingjuvasadult/table8.html>.

[260] Priscilla Platt, *Young Offenders Law in Canada*, 2d ed. (Markham: Butterworths Canada Ltd., 1995), at 567. On the Swedish youth justice system, see more recently J. Sarnecki and Felipe Estrada, "Keeping the Balance between Humanism and Penal Punitivism: Recent Trends in Juvenile Delinquency and Juvenile Justice in Sweden" in J. Junger-Tas and S.H. Decker, eds., *International Handbook of Juvenile Justice* (The Netherlands: Springer, 2006), at 473.

the age of 20, the responsibility is shared between social services and the justice system.[261]

C.   *United Nations Convention on the Rights of the Child*

The *UNCRC* is an international treaty that recognizes the need for special protections and rights for young persons under 18. The Convention establishes the civil, political, economic, social and cultural rights of children; its 41 articles establish minimum standards for the protection of children. Article 1 states: For the purposes of the present Convention, a child means every human being below the age of 18 years unless, under the law applicable to the child, majority is attained earlier.[262]

Article 40 of the *UNCRC* requires signatory states to seek to promote the establishment of laws, procedures, authorities and institutions specifically applicable to children, in particular: "(a) The establishment of a minimum age below which children shall be presumed not to have the capacity to infringe the penal law." The *UNCRC* does not specify a minimum age, but the United Nations committee responsible for monitoring compliance with it has criticized jurisdictions where the minimum age is 12 or less.[263] Canada ratified this treaty in 1991, promising to respect internationally accepted minimum standards regarding state treatment of young persons in various areas, including health, education and juvenile justice.[264] The U.S. and Somalia are the only countries that have not ratified the Convention.[265]

While the United Nations does not set a minimum age of criminal responsibility, it recommends in Rule 4 of the Standard Minimum Rules for the Administration of Juvenile Justice (the Beijing Rules) that "in

---

[261]   J. Sarnecki and Felipe Estrada, "Keeping the Balance between Humanism and Penal Punitivism: Recent Trends in Juvenile Delinquency and Juvenile Justice in Sweden" in J. Junger-Tas and S.H. Decker, eds., *International Handbook of Juvenile Justice* (The Netherlands: Springer, 2006), at 487.

[262]   U.N. Doc. A/44/736 (1989), adopted November 20, 1989, by the General Assembly of the United Nations.

[263]   Gregor Urbas, No. 181, The Age of Criminal Responsibility, Australian Institute of Criminology, November 2000, at 2.

[264]   Nicholas Bala, *Youth Criminal Justice Law* (Toronto: Irwin Law Inc., 2003), at 130. As the Quebec Court of Appeal observed in *Reference re: Bill C-7 respecting the criminal justice system for young persons*, [2003] Q.J. No. 2850, at para. 89 (Que. C.A.), mere ratification of an international law does not give the treaty force of law or any coercive effect in domestic law unless it is subsequently incorporated into domestic law through the legislation of Parliament. Nevertheless, in the event of ambiguity between the *YCJA* and international law, it can be presumed that Parliament legislates in a manner that respects Canada's international commitments, the Quebec Court of Appeal said, at para. 93.

[265]   This was based on information accessed on the following site: <http://en.wikipedia.org/wiki/Convention_on_the_Rights_of_the_Child>.

those legal systems recognizing the concept of the age of criminal responsibility for juveniles, the beginning of that age shall not be fixed at too low an age level, bearing in mind the facts of emotional, mental and intellectual maturity".[266]

The commentary to the Beijing Rules explains that: "The minimum age of criminal responsibility differs widely owing to history and culture. The modern approach would be to consider whether a child can live up to the moral and psychological components of criminal responsibility; that is, whether a child, by virtue of her or his individual discernment and understanding, can be held responsible for essentially antisocial behaviour. If the age of criminal responsibility is fixed too low or if there is no lower age limit at all, the notion of responsibility would become meaningless."[267]

---

[266] *United Nations Standard Minimum Rules for the Administration of Juvenile Justice (Beijing Rules)* (New York: Department of Public Information, 1986), Part 1, General Principles, Rule 4.1. All of the international instruments that are relevant to the juvenile justice issues can be accessed through the website for the Office of the United Nations High Commissioner for Human Rights at: <http://www.ohchr.org/english/law/index.htm>.

[267] *United Nations Standard Minimum Rules for the Administration of Juvenile Justice (Beijing Rules)* (New York: Department of Public Information, 1986), Part 1, General Principles, Rule 4.1. All of the international instruments that are relevant to the juvenile justice issues can be accessed through the website for the Office of the United Nations High Commissioner for Human Rights at: <http://www.ohchr.org/EN/Pages/WelcomePage.aspx>.

Chapter 3

THE PREAMBLE AND THE DECLARATION OF PRINCIPLE: THE PHILOSOPHICAL ROADMAP TO THE YOUTH CRIMINAL JUSTICE ACT

Just as a "free" doctor explains the patient's illness to him, and tries to make him understand the reasons for the measures to be prescribed, in order to gain his co-operation, so the legislator must explain and justify his laws. Hence, every law must be headed by a preamble justifying its provisions; further, the preamble must be rhetorical in character: it must not only instruct, but persuade.[1]

Plato, *The Laws*

From preambles, the lawyers of this realm were wont always to take light. Our preambles are annexed for exposition, and this gives aim to the body of the statute. For the preamble sets up the mark, and the body of the law levels at it.[2]

Francis Bacon

I.   INTRODUCTION

The Preamble and the Declaration of Principle in the *Youth Criminal Justice Act*[3] provide the philosophical framework for Canada's modern youth justice system generally, and also act as the interpretive guide to the substantive provisions of the *YCJA*. How influential are these two

---

[1]   Plato, *The Laws* (Harmondsworth, Middlesex, England: Penguin Books Ltd., 1980), at 178.
[2]   Sir Francis Bacon, Lord Chancellor of England, as quoted in Catherine Drinker Bowen, *Francis Bacon: The Temper of a Man* (Boston: Little, Brown and Company, 1963), at 147-48.
[3]   S.C. 2002, c. 1, in force April 1, 2003 [hereafter "*YCJA*"].

elements of the *YCJA*? How do they differ from similar elements in the *Juvenile Delinquents Act*[4] and the *Young Offenders Act*[5]? To what degree, if at all, have they influenced the development of the jurisprudence since the *YCJA* came into force in 2003?

II. KEY PHILOSOPHICAL DIFFERENCES BETWEEN THE JDA, THE YOA AND THE YCJA: LEGISLATIVE PROVISIONS

The *JDA* had a Preamble, but no Declaration of Principle. The *YOA* had a Declaration of Principle, but no Preamble. Parliament chose to include both elements in the *YCJA* of 2003. The differing themes that can be gleaned from these three Acts by contrasting these key aspects in all of them reveal their striking philosophical differences.

The Preamble of the *JDA* is reproduced below:

> Whereas it is inexpedient that youthful offenders should be classed or dealt with as ordinary criminals, the welfare of the community demanding that they should on the contrary be guarded against association with crime and criminals, and should be subjected to such wise care, treatment and control as will tend to check their evil tendencies and to strengthen their better instincts: Therefore His Majesty, by and with the advice and consent of the Senate and House of Commons of Canada, enacts as follows:[6]

Section 31 of the *JDA* is a further illustration of the spirit of that legislation, which was the first comprehensive piece of youth criminal justice legislation in Canada:

> This Act shall be liberally construed to the end that its purpose may be carried out, to wit: That the care and custody and discipline of a juvenile delinquent shall approximate as nearly as may be that which should be given by its parents, and that as far as practicable every juvenile delinquent shall be treated, not as a criminal, but as a misdirected and misguided child, and one needing aid, encouragement, help and assistance.[7]

Although the *JDA* did not contain a policy statement similar to the Declaration of Principle in the *YOA* or the *YJCA*, its provisions were infused with paternalism toward the treatment of young persons who were alleged to have committed crimes. They were not to be treated as criminals, but rather were to be shielded from the corrupting influence of adult

---

[4]   S.C. 1908, c. 40 [hereafter "*JDA*"].
[5]   R.S.C. 1985, c. Y-1 [hereafter "*YOA*"].
[6]   *JDA*, S.C. 1908, c. 40; subject to minor amendments over the years, finally as the *JDA*, R.S.C. 1970, c. J-3.
[7]   R.S.C. 1970, c. J-3, s. 31.

criminals and to be supported and controlled by the state in their own "best interests". It was the meaning of best interests that would come to be questioned in the ensuing decades.

The *JDA* was unquestionably a welfare-oriented piece of legislation that was guided by the principle of *parens patriae*,[8] where the state effectively stepped into the shoes of the parent to provide the kind of support the juvenile was perceived to require. While its purpose and objectives may have been laudable, the *JDA* enabled the state to exercise great power over the lives of young persons in Canada for more than 75 years.[9] Young persons could be brought within its broad swath for a wide range of offences, many of which would not be considered offences today. As a result of conduct that fell within the broad definition of *delinquency*, children and teenagers could be detained in institutions by the state until they reached the age of 21.

By the time the *YOA* came into force in 1984, there had been a clear philosophical shift from the benevolent welfare model of the *JDA* to a modified justice model[10] that was much closer to pure criminal law and also clearly indicative of the new rights focus of criminal legislation. The *YOA* was the product of a different era; it was drafted during the rights-oriented age of the *Canadian Charter of Rights and Freedoms*[11] and solidly reflects the consciousness and spirit of the times.

While the Declarations of Principle in the *YOA* and the *YCJA* bear far closer resemblance to each other than either does to similar provisions in the *JDA*, there are distinct differences between them, differences that reflect new societal preoccupations and concerns, and to some degree the learning that permeated Canadian legal culture during the 1990s. The addition of the Preamble in the *YCJA* plus distinct additions to its Declaration of Principle in s. 3 illustrate new concerns that Parliament was attempting to address.

The YOA Declaration of Principle

Policy for Canada with respect to young offenders

   3. (1) It is hereby recognized and declared that

---

8   As discussed in Chapter 1.

9   The *YOA* was enacted in 1982 and came into force in 1984.

10 Priscilla Platt, *Young Offenders Law in Canada*, 2d ed. (Markham, Ontario: Butterworths Canada Ltd., 1995), at 17.

11 Part I of the *Constitution Act, 1982* being Schedule B to the *Canada Act 1982* (U.K.), 1982, c. 11 [hereafter "*Charter*"].

(a)   crime prevention is essential to the long-term protection of society and requires addressing the underlying causes of crime by young persons and developing multi-disciplinary approaches to identifying and effectively responding to children and young persons at risk of committing offending behaviour in the future; (a.1) while young persons should not in all instances be held accountable in the same manner or suffer the same consequences for their behaviour as adults, young persons who commit offences should nonetheless bear responsibility for their contraventions;

(b)   society must, although it has the responsibility to take reasonable measures to prevent crime conduct by young persons, be afforded the necessary protection from illegal behaviour;

(c)   young persons who commit offences require supervision, discipline and control, but, because of their state of dependency and level of development and maturity, they also have special needs and require guidance and assistance;

(c.1) the protection of society, which is a primary objective of the criminal law applicable to youth, is best served by rehabilitation, wherever possible, of young persons who commit offences, and rehabilitation is best achieved by addressing the needs and circumstances of a young person that are relevant to the young person's offending behaviour;

(d)   where it is not inconsistent with the protection of society, taking no measures or taking measures other than judicial proceedings under this Act should be considered for dealing with young persons who have committed offences;

(e)   young persons have rights and freedoms in their own right, including those stated in the Canadian Charter of Rights and Freedoms or in the Canadian Bill of Rights, and in particular a right to be heard in the course of, and to participate in, the processes that lead to decisions that affect them, and young persons should have special guarantees of their rights and freedoms;

(f)   in the application of this Act, the rights and freedoms of young persons include a right to the least possible interference with freedom that is consistent with the protection of society, having regard to the needs of young persons and the interests of their families;

(g)   young persons have the right, in every instance where they have rights or freedoms that may be affected by this Act, to be informed as to what those rights and freedoms are; and

(h)   parents have responsibility for the care and supervision of their children, and, for that reason, young persons should be removed from parental supervision either partly or entirely only when measures that provide for continuing parental supervision are inappropriate.

Act to be liberally construed

(2) This Act shall be liberally construed to the end that young persons will be dealt with in accordance with the principles set out in subsection (1).

The YCJA Preamble

WHEREAS members of society share a responsibility to address the developmental challenges and the needs of young persons and to guide them into adulthood;

WHEREAS communities, families, parents and others concerned with the development of young persons should, through multi-disciplinary approaches, take reasonable steps to prevent youth crime by addressing its underlying causes, to respond to the needs of young persons, and to provide guidance and support to those at risk of committing crimes;

WHEREAS information about youth justice, youth crime and the effectiveness of measures taken to address youth crime should be publicly available;

WHEREAS Canada is a party to the United Nations Convention on the Rights of the Child and recognizes that young persons have rights and freedoms, including those stated in the Canadian Charter of Rights and Freedoms and the Canadian Bill of Rights, and have special guarantees of their rights and freedoms;

AND WHEREAS Canadian society should have a youth criminal justice system that commands respect, takes into account the interests of victims, fosters responsibility and ensures accountability through meaningful consequences and effective rehabilitation and reintegration, and that reserves its most serious intervention for the most serious crimes and reduces the over-reliance on incarceration for non-violent young persons;

NOW, THEREFORE, Her Majesty, by and with the advice and consent of the Senate and House of Commons of Canada, enacts as follows:

The YCJA Declaration of Principle

Policy for Canada with respect to young persons

    3. (1) The following principles apply in this Act:

    (a)   the youth criminal justice system is intended to

        (i) prevent crime by addressing the circumstances underlying a young person's offending behaviour,

        (ii) rehabilitate young persons who commit offences and reintegrate them into society, and

        (iii) ensure that a young person is subject to meaningful consequences for his or her offence

        in order to promote the long-term protection of the public;

    (b)   the criminal justice system for young persons must be separate from that of adults and emphasize the following:

        (i) rehabilitation and reintegration,

        (ii) fair and proportionate accountability that is consistent with the greater dependency of young persons and their reduced level of maturity,

        (iii) enhanced procedural protection to ensure that young persons are treated fairly and that their rights, including their right to privacy, are protected,

        (iv) timely intervention that reinforces the link between the offending behaviour and its consequences, and

        (v) the promptness and speed with which persons responsible for enforcing this Act must act, given young persons' perception of time;

    (c)   within the limits of fair and proportionate accountability, the measures taken against young persons who commit offences should

        (i) reinforce respect for societal values,

        (ii) encourage the repair of harm done to victims and the community,

        (iii) be meaningful for the individual young person given his or her needs and level of development and, where appropriate, involve the parents, the extended family, the community and social or other agencies in the young person's rehabilitation and reintegration, and

(iv) respect gender, ethnic, cultural and linguistic differences and respond to the needs of aboriginal young persons and of young persons with special requirements; and

(d) special considerations apply in respect of proceedings against young persons and, in particular,

(i) young persons have rights and freedoms in their own right, such as a right to be heard in the course of and to participate in the processes, other than the decision to prosecute, that lead to decisions that affect them, and young persons have special guarantees of their rights and freedoms,

(ii) victims should be treated with courtesy, compassion and respect for their dignity and privacy and should suffer the minimum degree of inconvenience as a result of their involvement with the youth criminal justice system,

(iii) victims should be provided with information about the proceedings and given an opportunity to participate and be heard, and

(iv) parents should be informed of measures or proceedings involving their children and encouraged to support them in addressing their offending behaviour.

Act to be liberally construed

(2) This Act shall be liberally construed so as to ensure that young persons are dealt with in accordance with the principles set out in subsection (1).

The philosophical shift in the *YCJA vis-à-vis* the *YOA* is reflected first and most obviously in changes to its legal lexicon, beginning with its title, which emphasizes that the *YCJA* is criminal legislation. The substantive provisions of the new Act also remove references to the term "young offender", which was contained in the *YOA*. In the *YCJA*, the term "young offender" has been replaced throughout by the more neutral reference to a young person. This change arguably operates to reduce the premature labelling of young persons who are dealt with under the *YCJA* as offenders, and highlights the fact that not all young persons who are dealt with under the *YCJA* will be found guilty of offences. A young person may be dealt with under the *YCJA* but is not an offender in law until a court determines him or her to be so. The title of the *YOA*, the *Young Offenders Act*, was sweeping in its categorization of young persons who could conceivably be dealt with under the *YOA*. The title of the Act did not appear to account for the fact that many young persons would be diverted from the youth criminal justice system and would never be found to be young offenders.

Other key changes to the legal lexicon under the *YCJA* include references to "sentences" under the *YCJA* rather than to "dispositions" under the *YOA*, another reminder that the *YCJA* is fundamentally criminal law. But these are cosmetic changes to language that only imply philosophical shift. It is the content of the Preamble and s. 3 of the Declaration of Principle in the *YCJA* that clearly demarcate its philosophical departure points from the *YOA*.

The Preamble in the *YCJA* establishes the basic tenets of the modern Canadian youth justice system, such as outlining society's responsibility to assist young persons and to prevent youth crime, the necessity of making information about the youth justice system publicly available, and the recognition of the rights and freedoms of young persons. The Preamble in the *YCJA* also identifies one fundamental goal of the youth criminal justice system. The last portion of the final clause of the Preamble states in clear language that one of the goals of the modern Canadian youth justice system is to reserve the most serious intervention (*i.e.*, prison) for the most serious crimes and to reduce the over-reliance on incarceration for non-violent young persons.

The *YCJA* also contains several new principles in its Declaration of Principle. The *YCJA* acknowledges the needs of victims as the *YOA* had not. The *YOA* came to fruition in the late 1970s and early 1980s in tandem with the *Charter* "at a time when the emphasis in criminal justice was on the accused and the state. The *YOA*'s themes of rights and responsibilities reflected that bipolar focus". By contrast, the *YCJA* was being developed in the 1990s when increasing attention was being paid to victims.[12]

The Declaration of Principle in the *YCJA* also includes significant new direction to criminal justice system participants in s. 3(1)(c)(iv) by directing that, within the limits of fair and proportionate accountability, the measures taken against young persons should respect gender, ethnic, cultural and linguistic differences and respond to the needs of aboriginal young persons and young persons with special requirements.

Various sections of the Declaration of Principle refer to restorative justice principles as well. Finally, there is express instruction to decision-makers in s. 3 of the Declaration of Principle regarding their obligation to

---

[12]   Kent Roach, "The Role of Crime Victims Under the *Youth Criminal Justice Act*" (2003) 40 Alta. L. Rev. 965, at para. 1 (QL).

respond to the offending behaviour of young persons in a timely fashion. While this was recognized in the jurisprudence under the *YOA*, the Declaration of Principle in the *YOA* contained no express provision on this point.

Notably absent from the Declaration of Principle in the *YCJA* is the key principle in s. 3(1)(c.1) of the *YOA* (which was added by way of amendment in 1995)[13] that states that the protection of society "is a primary objective of the criminal law applicable to youth". The phrase in the *YOA* went on to say that the protection of society is best served by rehabilitation of young persons, wherever possible. In other words, rehabilitating young persons so that they are no longer likely to commit criminal offences is the best way to guarantee our protection. One can also interpret s. 3(1)(c.1) to mean that rehabilitative programs rather than incarceration are the best way to guarantee our protection.

III. THE PREAMBLE AND THE DECLARATION OF PRINCIPLE IN THE YCJA

A.   An Overview

When read together, the Preamble and the Declaration of Principle in the *YCJA* identify the fundamental purpose, goals and principles of Canada's youth justice system, which are expected to guide criminal justice participants who must act in accordance with the *YCJA*: judges, Crown prosecutors, defence counsel, police, youth workers, and others. As this chapter illustrates, despite long-standing academic debate as to the weight that should be given to these components of the legislation, particularly the Preamble, eminent Canadian jurists routinely look to both the Preamble and the Declaration of Principle to divine parliamentary intent when seeking to interpret specific and substantive provisions of the *YCJA*.

B.   The Preamble

(i)   *The Preamble in the YCJA: A Detailed Examination*

Preambles, as components of legislation, have existed for millennia, but their popularity and ascribed importance has ebbed and flowed with the

---

[13]   Nicholas Bala, *Youth Criminal Justice Law* (Toronto: Irwin Law Inc., 2003), at 66-67.

centuries. Plato, more than 2,000 years ago, lauded the legal construct as a wise and artful means of communicating directly to the citizens by speaking to their hearts and minds through language, thereby persuading them why a certain law mattered and should be respected.[14] Francis Bacon was equally enamoured of them, much to the chagrin of Queen Elizabeth I. While she apparently thought them unnecessary unless she wrote them herself, Bacon (who eventually served as both her Attorney General and Lord Chancellor), considered them an essential component of legislation, a tool of persuasion to convince Parliament to pass new laws and to satisfy the people.[15] In Bacon's day, every significant bill had a preamble, which was read aloud or posted by the Justices of the Peace.[16]

Modern preambles are ostensibly intended to identify the goals of legislation and the societal concerns they are meant to address.[17] Contemporary scholars are inclined to view them with a healthy measure of scepticism, sometimes dismissing them as little more than political advertising with no legal heft.[18] They suggest that some drafters consider them too vague to be useful, or too political.[19] Some contend that governments are apt to include preambles in "politically charged" legislation,[20] which may largely explain why the *YCJA* has a Preamble, given that the years leading up to its enactment were mired in controversy. Public opinion surveys, media reports and anecdotal evidence in the 1990s demonstrated widespread discontent and disillusionment with the *YOA*. The public tended to perceive youth court judges as lenient and saw harsher penalties in the form of longer sentences as the panacea. There was also a widespread public perception that violent youth crime was increasing.[21] Presumably to address these concerns, the federal government chose to make some general statements in the Preamble to the *YCJA* about the youth justice system in Canada. Professor Ruth Sullivan, a Canadian scholar of statutory interpretation, has

---

[14]   Kent Roach, "The Uses and Audiences of Preambles in Legislation" (2001) 47 McGill L.J. 129, at 129.

[15]   Catherine Drinker Bowen, *Francis Bacon: The Temper of a Man* (Boston: Little, Brown and Company, 1963), at 147.

[16]   Catherine Drinker Bowen, *Francis Bacon: The Temper of a Man* (Boston: Little, Brown and Company, 1963), at 147.

[17]   Section 13 of the *Interpretation Act*, R.S.C. 1985, c. I-21 states: "The preamble of an enactment shall be read as a part of the enactment intended to assist in explaining its purport and object."

[18]   Kent Roach, "The Uses and Audiences of Preambles in Legislation" (2001) 47 McGill L.J. 129, at 132. See also Ruth Sullivan, *Statutory Interpretation* (Concord, Ontario: Irwin Law, 1997), at 116-17.

[19]   Ruth Sullivan, *Statutory Interpretation* (Concord, Ontario: Irwin Law, 1997), at 116.

[20]   Nicholas Bala, *Youth Criminal Justice Law* (Toronto: Irwin Law Inc., 2003), at 76.

[21]   Canada, House of Commons, *Renewing Youth Justice: Thirteenth Report of the Standing Committee on Justice and Legal Affairs* (Ottawa: Public Works and Government Services, 1997), c. 3 at 1.

prophesied that "the free-ranging and overtly political character of preambles often serves political needs, and for this reason preambles may not soon disappear".[22]

In terms of their value as interpretive tools, their influence may have grown over time. Traditionally, according to the plain meaning rule of statutory interpretation, jurists were not to refer to preambles unless the meaning of the provision was unclear and there was a need to resolve an ambiguity.[23] Even when a Preamble was considered, it was given little weight by the courts.[24]

As components of modern legislation, their importance and influence remains the subject of considerable scholarly debate. While some scholars concede that preambles can sometimes be helpful as a source of legislative values and principles upon which the judiciary draw,[25] they are not a required element of modern legislation and many statutes do not have them. Some experts observe they are not technically part of the Act because they are positioned before the enacting clause and are therefore not enacted as part of the Act.[26] Commercial *Criminal Codes* often omit them.[27]

In addition, Interpretation Acts across the country ascribe to preambles varying degrees of influence *vis-à-vis* the interpretation of a statute. The relevant Interpretation Act must be consulted. For example, the federal *Interpretation Act*,[28] which applies to federal legislation such as the *YCJA*, indicates that preambles are to be read as part of the Act, and are designed to assist in explaining an Act's purport and object.

Nevertheless modern academics contend that preambles are ascribed more weight than they once were, and that, in fact, a modern preamble can be given whatever weight the court considers appropriate in the circumstances.[29] They suggest that modern Canadian jurists tend to consider all

---

[22]   Ruth Sullivan, *Statutory Interpretation* (Concord, Ontario: Irwin Law, 1997), at 117.

[23]   *Sussex Peerage Case* (1844), 8 E.R. 1034, at 1057. But see Ruth Sullivan's discussion and critique of this rule in Ruth Sullivan, *Statutory Interpretation* (Concord, Ontario: Irwin Law, 1997), at 49.

[24]   Nicholas Bala, *Youth Criminal Justice Law* (Toronto: Irwin Law Inc., 2003), at 76.

[25]   Ruth Sullivan, *Statutory Interpretation* (Concord, Ontario: Irwin Law, 1997). See also Kent Roach, "The Uses and Audiences of Preambles in Legislation" (2001) 47 McGill L.J. 129, at 159. Roach clearly recognizes some value in well-written preambles.

[26]   Ruth Sullivan, *Statutory Interpretation* (Concord, Ontario: Irwin Law, 1997), at 116.

[27]   Kent Roach, "The Uses and Audiences of Preambles in Legislation" (2001) 47 McGill L.J. 129, at 133-34. While Roach found this to be true in 2001, the Preamble to the *Youth Criminal Justice Act* has been included in recent editions of Martin's Annual *Criminal Code*, such as the 2008 edition.

[28]   R.S.C. 1985, c. I-21, s. 13.

[29]   Nicholas Bala, *Youth Criminal Justice Law* (Toronto: Irwin Law Inc., 2003), at 76.

components of legislation as part of the legislative context when seeking to determine the purpose and meaning of a text.[30] In other words, jurists today no longer look to a preamble only in the event that a specific provision is unclear.

Esoteric debate aside, the judiciary at all levels in Canada, including the Supreme Court of Canada, is very much aware of the Preamble in the *YCJA*, they refer to it in their decisions,[31] and consider it when attempting to discern the meaning, purpose and intent of the *YCJA*. It forms part of the philosophical backdrop to their deliberations about the meaning and purpose of the *YCJA*. The content of the *YCJA* Preamble is unquestionably part of the jurisprudential discourse in youth justice law. This may well be in part because the *YCJA* is relatively new. Members of the judiciary often find themselves in the position of considering a certain provision of the *YCJA* for the first time and routinely look to sections of the Preamble for insight and guidance.

Scholars did not predict such influence. In the early days of the *YCJA*, most clauses of the Preamble were expected to be of limited legal significance, not only because the Preamble appears before the actual enactment but also because of the very general nature of most of its clauses. While youth justice experts opined that the general policy statements in the Preamble would perhaps be helpful to the courts in establishing the general purpose of the legislation, the Preamble was expected to have little impact on key areas such as sentencing.[32] Most of the clauses were characterized as simply not specific or clear enough to be considered of much utility or legal significance.[33] In fact, in *R. v. D.L.C.*,[34] one of the first decisions to consider the Preamble and the Declaration of Principle in the *YCJA*, Gorman J. of the Newfoundland and Labrador Provincial Court suggested that interpreting the provisions of the new Act was not easy, due to some curious language. "It almost appears that its drafters have been purposely obtuse."[35]

The first two clauses in the Preamble essentially call on members of Canadian society to provide support to young persons as they move toward adulthood and to help prevent youth crime by assisting young

[30] Ruth Sullivan, *Statutory Interpretation* (Concord, Ontario: Irwin Law, 1997), at 115.
[31] See for example recent Supreme Court of Canada cases such as *R. v. C.D.; R. v. C.D.K.*, [2005] S.C.J. No. 79 (S.C.C.) and *R. v. B.W.P.; R. v. B.V.N.*, [2006] S.C.J. No. 27, 2006 SCC 27 (S.C.C.).
[32] J.V. Roberts and N. Bala, "Understanding Sentencing Under the *Youth Criminal Justice Act*" (2003) 41 Alta. L. Rev. 395, at para. 7 (QL).
[33] Nicholas Bala, *Youth Criminal Justice Law* (Toronto: Irwin Law Inc., 2003), at 77-78.
[34] [2003] N.J. No. 94 (N.L. Prov. Ct.).
[35] *R. v. D.L.C.*, [2003] N.J. No. 94, at para. 18 (N.L. Prov. Ct.).

persons with underlying problems that may be driving their youthful criminality. Canadians are not told that they must assist young persons or that they are legally obliged to, only that we share a responsibility to assist young persons and that we "should" help them. Many Canadians could facetiously reply that we should do a lot of things. The first two clauses identify a moral obligation, with which Canadians may or may not agree. They impose no specific legal obligations.

The third clause is also devoid of practical impact. It simply says that information about youth justice, youth crime and the effectiveness of measures taken to address youth crime should be publicly available. Most Canadians would not find it difficult to agree with that. Such compliance is buoyed by the fact that the precise nature of the information is not specified nor does the clause indicate whose responsibility it is to supply this information. No particular criminal justice system participant, such as the Attorney General or the police, is tasked with the duty of ensuring that information about the youth justice system, youth crime and the effectiveness of measures to address youth crime, finds its way into the public domain. Individual criminal justice players in a vast system can choose to ignore this or to effectively argue that it is not directed at them.

Nor is it clear what type of information, in particular, is envisioned by this clause. A plain reading of the clause suggests that it means that general information about the youth justice system, statistics regarding the prevalence of youth crime, as well as information about the types of programs and criminal justice responses that are effective in reducing youth crime, should be readily available to the public. This interpretation is supported by the findings of the House of Commons Standing Committee on Justice and Legal Affairs. In its report, released in April 1997, the Committee discussed public understanding of youth crime[36] and noted the discrepancy between public perception of youth crime and the youth justice system, and the reality. Its research revealed that opinion polls consistently showed public overestimation of the incidence of violent crime in Canada, public underestimation of the prevalence of jail sentences, as well as a widespread belief, unsupported by empirical research, that harsher penalties would deter young people from offending. The committee's research also revealed widespread public misunderstanding and lack of knowledge of the provisions and effects of the *YOA*. Generally, the public believed that youth court judges were too lenient, that youth crime, particularly violent crime, was on the increase and that

---

[36] Canada, House of Commons, *Renewing Youth Justice: Thirteenth Report of the Standing Committee on Justice and Legal Affairs* (Ottawa: Public Works and Government Services, 1997), c. 3.

longer sentences were necessary, the Committee found.[37] Witnesses who testified before the committee lobbied for a national educational campaign to provide accurate information about youth crime and the youth justice system. Consequently, the Committee recommended that the federal Department of Justice begin discussions with the provinces and territories and other parties to develop an educational campaign on youth crime, the *YOA* and the youth justice system, to be directed at the general public, those who work in the system and those who come into contact with it.[38]

In its response to that report, the federal government acknowledged in *A Strategy for the Renewal of Youth Justice* the need to improve the public's access to information about youth crime and the youth justice system. "Steps need to be taken by all partners in the youth justice system to provide Canadians with better and more complete information about youth crime in their communities."[39]

Thus, this clause in the Preamble was apparently a response to concerns and comments in both the Report of the Standing Committee and the federal government's response in its Strategy document the following year. There was a recognized need to provide the public (including victims) with accurate information about the youth justice system and the *YCJA* generally, as well as information about the extent of youth crime in Canada and the effectiveness of various measures and programs in reducing it.

Some courts have since suggested that this clause is intended to re-fer to the principle of general deterrence. Justice Davis held in *R. v. D.G.* that:

> This must mean that people in general, and perhaps young persons in par-ticular ought to be aware of what will happen to them if they do not comply with the law. In other words, Parliament must have intended that sentences will come to the attention of other young persons and hopefully prevent those others from doing the same thing. That is, the "effectiveness of meas-ures taken" must mean that the sentences imposed, "to address youth

---

[37] Canada, House of Commons, *Renewing Youth Justice: Thirteenth Report of the Standing Committee on Justice and Legal Affairs* (Ottawa: Public Works and Government Services, 1997), c. 3.

[38] Canada, House of Commons, *Renewing Youth Justice: Thirteenth Report of the Standing Committee on Justice and Legal Affairs* (Ottawa: Public Works and Government Services, 1997), c. 3 at 1.

[39] Department of Justice, *A Strategy for the Renewal of Youth Justice* (Ottawa: Ministry of Supply and Services, 1998) (section on Concerns about the Current Youth Justice System). At the time of writing, this 1998 document could still be readily accessed through the De-partment of Justice website at: <http://www.justice.gc.ca/eng/pi/yj-jj/about-apropos/toc-tdm.html>. In this document, the federal government reviews the shortcomings of the *YOA* and outlines its rationale for introducing the *YCJA*.

crime," to deal with young persons, "should be publicly available" i.e. someone other than the young person must be aware of what will happen if one commits an offence. This must mean, given its everyday meaning, the public must be aware that there are effective measures being taken against young persons who commit offences. This must mean that deterrence is something that was meant to be taken into account and these words provide the assistance in explaining its purport and objective.[40]

The Supreme Court of Canada has given short shrift to this argument. Justice Charron in *R. v. B.W.P.; R. v. B.V.N.*[41] refuted the Crown's argument that the clause in the Preamble referring to the need to make information about the youth justice system and youth crime publicly available suggests that Parliament intended by those words to include general deterrence as part of the new regime. This clause in the Preamble cannot reasonably support that interpretation, Charron J. held.[42]

Conversely, the latter two clauses in the Preamble are specific and clear in their wording and have been cited in the jurisprudence to a marked degree. From a jurisprudential standpoint, they are proving to be the most significant clauses in the Preamble.

The fourth clause not only reminds Canadians that Canada is a party to the *United Nations Convention on the Rights of the Child* but is also a clear message early in the *YCJA* that young persons have rights and freedoms, including rights under both the *Canadian Bill of Rights*[43] (yes, it is still technically in effect), as well as under the *Charter* and that, in addition, young persons have special guarantees of their rights and freedoms. In other words, young persons have the same rights as adults in Canada when charged with a crime and *then some*.[44] This fundamental message is an underlying theme throughout the *YCJA* but it is introduced in the Preamble.

The Preamble is the only place in the *YCJA* that expressly mentions that Canada is a party to the *U.N. Convention on the Rights of the Child*. The Convention is an international treaty that sets out minimum standards regarding the treatment of young persons under 18. It has specific provisions regarding the treatment of young persons who are alleged to have violated the criminal law.[45] All states that have ratified the treaty are

---

[40]   [2004] B.C.J. No. 2330, at para. 23 (B.C. Prov. Ct.).
[41]   [2006] S.C.J. No. 27, 2006 SCC 27 (S.C.C.).
[42]   *R. v. B.W.P.; R. v. B.V.N.*, [2006] S.C.J. No. 27, at para. 36, 2006 SCC 27 (S.C.C.).
[43]   S.C. 1960, c. 44 (assented to August 10, 1960).
[44]   Chapter 7 outlines the special protections that young persons have under the *YCJA* in addition to their rights under the *Canadian Bill of Rights* and the *Charter*.
[45]   The *United Nations Convention on the Rights of the Child* (*UNCRC*) is binding on countries that have ratified it. It came into force on September 2, 1990. All countries that are members of the United Nations have ratified the Convention, at least in part, except the United States

expected to adhere to it, subject to any reservations they have made. The U.N. has established a committee that monitors state compliance. While the Convention does not have the same legal status in Canada as a Canadian statute or the *Charter*,[46] negative publicity attaches to nations who do not honour their international commitments.

The final clause describes the ideal Canadian youth justice system although the first portion of the clause contains a number of ambiguous terms. Canadian society should have a youth criminal justice system that "ensures accountability through meaningful consequences and effective rehabilitation and reintegration", the final clause of the Preamble states in part. The terms "accountability" and "meaningful consequences", are introduced in the Preamble but reappear throughout the Act in relation to the use of extrajudicial measures, for example, as well as in relation to formal judicial responses such as youth sentences and adult sentences. Jurists, academics, practitioners and others who work routinely with the *YCJA* have spent, and continue to spend, considerable time discerning the practical meaning of such terms.

While neither "accountability" nor "meaningful consequences" is defined in the Preamble or elsewhere in the Act, the distinct phraseology at least enables one to conclude that the two terms are not equivalent in meaning.

In *R. v. A.O.*,[47] the Ontario Court of Appeal defined accountability. The court equated the concept to the adult sentencing principle of retribution as defined by Lamer C.J.C. in the 1996 Supreme Court of Canada case *R. v. C.A.M.*[48] The court accepted Lamer C.J.C.'s definition that retribution is "an objective, reasoned and measured determination of an appropriate punishment which properly reflects the *moral culpability* of

---

and Somalia. The full text of the Convention and related information can be accessed by clicking onto the website of the Office of the High Commissioner for Human Rights at: <http://www.unhchr.ch/html/menu3/b/k2crc.htm>. Regarding juvenile justice, see Article 40 in particular.

[46] The Convention is generally regarded as an interpretive guide rather than another source of legal rights; the Convention is helpful when legislation is silent or unclear. For more on this point, see Nicholas Bala, *Youth Criminal Justice Law* (Toronto: Irwin Law Inc., 2003), at 130-35. See also M.S. Denov, "Children's Rights, Juvenile Justice, and the UN Convention on the Rights of the Child", chapter 4, in Kathryn M. Campbell, ed., *Understanding Youth Justice in Canada* (Toronto: Pearson Education Canada, Inc., 2005), at 65. That said, Canada's top courts have paid notable attention to such international conventions in youth cases. In *Khadr v. Canada (Prime Minister)*, [2009] F.C.J. No. 462, 2009 FC 405 (F.C.) (albeit an exceptional case by all accounts), at para. 55, O'Reilly J. stated not only that the principles of fundamental justice in s. 7 of the *Charter* are informed by Canada's international obligations but that the court must take into account Canada's international obligations. This case was under appeal at the time of writing.

[47] [2007] O.J. No. 800, 218 C.C.C. (3d) 409 (Ont. C.A.).

[48] [1996] S.C.J. No. 28, [1996] 1 S.C.R. 500 (S.C.C.).

the offender, having regard to the intentional risk-taking of the offender, the consequential harm caused by the offender, and the normative character of the offender's conduct".[49] The court noted that, as Lamer C.J.C. explained, unlike vengeance, retribution incorporates the principle of restraint. It requires the imposition of a just and appropriate punishment, nothing more. Further, as Lamer C.J.C. held, retribution should be distinguished from denunciation because retribution requires that the sentence reflect the moral blameworthiness of the particular offender whereas denunciation mandates that the sentence should communicate society's condemnation of the particular offender's conduct.[50]

After considering Lamer C.J.C.'s definition of retribution, the Ontario Court of Appeal concluded in *R. v. A.O.* that this was the only rational way to measure accountability.[51] While the Court of Appeal ultimately held that the need to consider the normative character of an offender's behaviour requires the court to consider societal values, this is not the same thing as adding to a youth sentence an element of general deterrence or denunciation.[52] In other words, in holding a young person accountable, the court is free to consider how society perceives the crime in terms of its degree of seriousness.[53] Several months later, building on this definition of accountability established by the Ontario Court of Appeal, Wong J. in *R. v. M.J.*[54] sought to more clearly define the meaning of the ambiguous phrase "normative character". The term "normative", Wong J. held, refers to society's values and acceptable standards regarding a particular offence. For example, "the basic code of values our society holds is that handguns are unacceptable".[55]

The term "meaningful consequences", also first appears in the Preamble. Discerning the meaning of the term is complicated by the fact that it is linked to numerous other concepts. The Preamble states that Canadian society should have a youth justice system that fosters responsibility and ensures accountability through meaningful consequences *and* effective rehabilitation and reintegration. Meaningful consequences are intended to foster responsibility *and* to ensure accountability but so too are rehabilitation and reintegration.

---

[49]   *R. v. C.A.M.*, [1996] S.C.J. No. 28, at para. 80, [1996] 1 S.C.R. 500 (S.C.C.), as referred to in *R. v. A.O.*, [2007] O.J. No. 800, at para. 46, 218 C.C.C. (3d) 409 (Ont. C.A.).

[50]   *R. v. C.A.M.*, [1996] S.C.J. No. 28, [1996] 1 S.C.R. 500 (S.C.C.).

[51]   *R. v. A.O.*, [2007] O.J. No. 800, at para. 47, 218 C.C.C. (3d) 409 (Ont. C.A.).

[52]   *R. v. A.O.*, [2007] O.J. No. 800, at para. 48, 218 C.C.C. (3d) 409 (Ont. C.A.).

[53]   *R. v. A.O.*, [2007] O.J. No. 800, at para. 52, 218 C.C.C. (3d) 409 (Ont. C.A.).

[54]   *R. v. M.J.*, [2007] O.J. No. 2696 (Ont. C.J.).

[55]   *R. v. M.J.*, [2007] O.J. No. 2696, at para. 62 (Ont. C.J.).

The federal government shed some light on the term prior to the coming into force of the *YCJA*. In *A Strategy for the Renewal of Youth Justice*, the federal government explained that consequences will be meaningful when they instruct the offender about the impact of the crime and focus on repairing the damage or paying back society in a constructive fashion, thus reinforcing underlying social values such as responsibility, accountability and respect for people and their property.[56] The Ontario Court of Appeal defined the concept in reference to its appearance in s. 38 of the *YCJA* by saying that it is not synonymous with rehabilitation and reintegration because Parliament used different terms and must be presumed to have intended different meanings here as well.[57] The term is arguably broad enough to include an array of responses to criminal behaviour; it does not necessarily mean a formal court response or a prison sentence. A meaningful consequence can conceivably run the gamut from a stern lecture for speeding from a police officer to a custodial term. As Roscoe J.A. held for the Nova Scotia Court of Appeal in *R. v. J.R.L.*, a sentence does not necessarily require an imprisonment component to be meaningful.[58] An extrajudicial measure can be a meaningful consequence for some young persons in some circumstances. The meaning of this term is discussed further during the ensuing discussion of the Declaration of Principle.

Other aspects of the final substantive clause in the Preamble are clear, and send new and strong messages about the youth justice system. For example, the Preamble contains the first reference in the Act to the notion that the Canadian youth justice system should take into account the *interests of victims*, which is significant since neither the *YOA* nor the *JDA* expressly mentioned victims. The interests of victims is a recurring theme in the *YCJA*, which reflects the increased attention that was being paid to the concerns of crime victims in the late 1990s, when the *YCJA* was being contemplated and drafted.[59] Some commentators understand this reference to the interests of victims as an allusion to victims' interests in tougher sentences.[60]

The linked concepts of rehabilitation and reintegration as two integral parts of a whole, which are prominent themes throughout the *YCJA*, also appear for the first time in the Preamble.

---

[56]   Department of Justice, *A Strategy for the Renewal of Youth Justice* (Ottawa: Ministry of Supply and Services, 1998) (section on Concerns about the Current Youth Justice System).

[57]   *R. v. A.O.*, [2007] O.J. No. 800, at para. 45, 218 C.C.C. (3d) 409 (Ont. C.A.).

[58]   *R. v. J.R.L.*, [2007] N.S.J. No. 214, at para. 50 (N.S.C.A.).

[59]   Kent Roach, "The Role of Crime Victims Under the *Youth Criminal Justice Act*" (2003) 40 Alta. L. Rev. 965, at paras. 1-5 (QL). As Roach notes, victims were not included in earlier versions of the *YCJA* Preamble.

[60]   Kent Roach, "The Role of Crime Victims Under the *Youth Criminal Justice Act*" (2003) 40 Alta. L. Rev. 965, at para. 15 (QL).

It is the latter portion of the final substantive clause of the Preamble, however, that is arguably the most significant in terms of its jurisprudential implications. Canadian society should have a youth criminal justice system "that reserves its most serious intervention for the most serious crimes and reduces the over-reliance on incarceration for non-violent young persons".[61] This portion of the clause introduces the concept of proportionality in a broad sense and clarifies that the youth criminal justice system is intended to reduce the use of prison for non-violent young persons. This principle of restraint[62] and the discouraging of jail for non-violent young persons is a dominant theme throughout the YCJA.

The latter two substantive clauses of the Preamble have been cited and considered often by all levels of court, including the Supreme Court of Canada, which had rendered just slightly more than half a dozen decisions specifically concerning the YCJA by mid-2009, six years after the YCJA came into force.[63] Conversely, the first three clauses have been the subject of considerably less judicial discussion.

In *R. v. C.D.; R. v. C.D.K.*,[64] Bastarache J. relied on these clauses in the Preamble in part to reach his conclusion that a prime goal of the YCJA is to restrict custody.

R. v. C.D.; R. v. C.D.K. concerns the meaning of the term "violent offence" in s. 39(1)(a) of the YCJA for the purpose of imposing a sentence under that paragraph. (As discussed in Chapter 8, a young person can receive a youth custodial sentence under the YCJA only if they commit an offence that falls into one of the categories described in s. 39, one of which is that the young person has committed a violent offence.)

During his ruling, Bastarache J., who wrote the 8-1 majority ruling, obviously considered the Preamble relevant. The specific goal of restricting the use of custody for young persons is evidenced in the Preamble in the final two clauses, Bastarache J. held.[65] For example, the aspect of the Preamble that states that Canada is a party to the *U.N. Convention on the*

---

[61]   YCJA, Preamble, unnumbered Clause 5.
[62]   Richard Barnhorst, "The *Youth Criminal Justice Act*: New Directions and Implementation Issues" (April 2004) Vol. 46, No. 3, Can. J. Crim. & Crim. Jus. 231, at 233-34.
[63]   As of the end of May 2009, the Supreme Court had ruled on the following cases involving aspects of the YCJA: *R. v. C.D.; R. v. C.D.K.*, [2005] S.C.J. No. 79, [2005] 3 S.C.R. 668 (S.C.C.); *R. v. B.W.P.; R. v. B.V.N.*, [2006] S.C.J. No. 27, 2006 SCC 27 (S.C.C.); *R. v. R.C.*, [2005] S.C.J. No. 62, [2005] 3 S.C.R. 99 (S.C.C.); *R. v. D.B.*, [2008] S.C.J. No. 25 (S.C.C.); *R. v. S.A.C.*, [2008] S.C.J. No. 48, 2008 SCC 47 (S.C.C.); *R. v. L.T.H.*, [2008] S.C.J. No. 50, 2008 SCC 49 (S.C.C.); and *R. v. S.J.L.*, [2009] S.C.J. No. 14, 2009 SCC 14 (S.C.C.).
[64]   [2005] S.C.J. No. 79 (S.C.C.). This decision is dealt with at length in Chapter 8 concerning sentencing under the YCJA.
[65]   *R. v. C.D.; R. v. C.D.K.*, [2005] S.C.J. No. 79, at para. 35 (S.C.C.).

Rights of the Child is important, Bastarache J. opined, because Article 37 of the Convention makes the point that arrest, detention or imprisonment of a child shall be in conformity with the law and shall be used only as a measure of last resort and for the shortest period of time. Justice Basta-rache then pointed to the wording of the final clause of the Preamble as clear evidence that the Act is aimed at restricting custody.[66]

The result in *R. v. C.D.; R. v. C.D.K.* is a clear example of the impact and weight that the Preamble can have on individual sentencing outcomes. In *R. v. C.D.; R. v. C.D.K.*, as a result of Bastarache J.'s narrow interpreta-tion of a violent offence, which was based in part on his consideration of the Preamble, the custodial sentences of both young persons were quashed. The matters were ordered returned to the youth court sentencing judges so that the young persons' eligibility for custody could be decided in accordance with Bastarache J.'s decision. The outcome rested on Bastarache J.'s conclusion early in the ruling that his reading of the Preamble and s. 38, as well as his review of the history of the evolution of youth justice law in Canada, led him to the clear conclusion that the *YCJA* was unquestionably aimed, philosophically and practically, at restricting the use of custody for young persons.

A year later, in *R. v. B.W.P.; R. v. B.V.N.*,[67] the Supreme Court of Canada again cited and considered the Preamble, this time to reinforce the court's support for the conclusion in *R. v. C.D.; R. v. C.D.K.* that Parlia-ment's goal in enacting the youth sentencing regime was to restrict the use of custody and thereby reduce the over-reliance on incarceration. More recently in *R. v. D.B.*,[68] Abella J. for the majority referred to Bastarache J.'s conclusion that the *YCJA* was designed in part to reduce over-reliance on custodial sentences for young persons.[69]

At the appellate level, the courts have also given considerable atten-tion to the Preamble, particularly in the early days of the *YCJA*, in their effort to discern the underlying guiding principles of the new regime. The day before the new *YCJA* came into force, on March 31, 2003, the Quebec Court of Appeal released its decision in relation to a reference case on the *YCJA*.[70] This was a highly significant decision at the time, as it was obviously the first appellate level decision concerning the *YCJA*. It remains the most thorough decision to date at any court level regarding

---

[66]   *R. v. C.D.; R. v. C.D.K.*, [2005] S.C.J. No. 79, at paras. 35-36 (S.C.C.).

[67]   [2006] S.C.J. No. 27, at para. 35, 2006 SCC 27 (S.C.C.).

[68]   [2008] S.C.J. No. 25, 2008 SCC 25 (S.C.C.).

[69]   *R. v. D.B.*, [2008] S.C.J. No. 25, at para. 44, 2008 SCC 25 (S.C.C.).

[70]   *Quebec (Minister of Justice) v. Canada (Minister of Justice)* (*sub nom. Reference re: Bill C-7 respecting the criminal justice system for young persons*), [2003] Q.J. No. 2850, 175 C.C.C. (3d) 321 (Que. C.A.).

many provisions and aspects of the *YCJA*, including the constitutionality of the expanded alternative measures in the *YCJA* (now known as extrajudicial measures) as well as Canada's obligations to young persons under international law.[71]

The five-member panel noted that the provisions at issue in the *YCJA* could not be considered in a vacuum but had to be read in the context of the *YCJA* as a whole, including its Preamble.[72] The panel observed that s. 39(1) of the *YCJA*, which limits the court's power to impose a custodial sentence, is "designed to apply"[73] the fifth clause of the Preamble.

The court also devotes considerable time to discussing the fourth substantive clause of the Preamble. While the court recognizes that the simple reference in clause four to the fact that Canada is a party to the *International Convention on the Rights of the Child* is not sufficient to give the treaty the force of law in Canada unless the treaty is subsequently incorporated into domestic law through legislation, the court nevertheless recognizes that the fact that the Preamble mentions the Convention creates a "relative interdependence" between the *YCJA* and the Convention. The interrelationship may be of limited impact but it nevertheless guides the courts in interpreting domestic legislation. In the event of doubt or ambiguity between the *YCJA* and international law, it can be presumed that Parliament legislates in a manner that respects Canada's international commitments, the court held.[74] Nevertheless, the specific reference to the Convention in the Preamble forces decision-makers to consider its provisions, at the administrative or judicial stage in every decision they must make in relation to the young person.[75] Article 3 of the Convention[76]

---

[71]   But see *Khadr v. Canada (Prime Minister)*, [2009] F.C.J. No. 462, 2009 FC 405 (F.C.).

[72]   *Quebec (Minister of Justice) v. Canada (Minister of Justice)* (*sub nom. Reference re: Bill C-7 respecting the criminal justice system for young persons*), [2003] Q.J. No. 2850, at para. 131, 175 C.C.C. (3d) 321 (Que. C.A.).

[73]   *Quebec (Minister of Justice) v. Canada (Minister of Justice)* (*sub nom. Reference re: Bill C-7 respecting the criminal justice system for young persons*), [2003] Q.J. No. 2850, at para. 31, 175 C.C.C. (3d) 321 (Que. C.A.).

[74]   *Quebec (Minister of Justice) v. Canada (Minister of Justice)* (*sub nom. Reference re: Bill C-7 respecting the criminal justice system for young persons*), [2003] Q.J. No. 2850, at paras. 89-93, 175 C.C.C. (3d) 321 (Que. C.A.).

[75]   *Quebec (Minister of Justice) v. Canada (Minister of Justice)* (*sub nom. Reference re: Bill C-7 respecting the criminal justice system for young persons*), [2003] Q.J. No. 2850, at paras. 135-136, 175 C.C.C. (3d) 321 (Que. C.A.).

[76]   Article 3 of the *U.N. Convention on the Rights of the Child* states: "In all actions concerning children, whether undertaken by public or private social welfare institutions, courts of law, administrative authorities or legislative bodies, the best interests of the child shall be a primary consideration." <http://www2.ohchr.org/english/law/index.htm#core>.

provides insight into the manner in which the powers conferred on decision-makers under the *YCJA* should be interpreted, the court held.[77]

In summary, the final two substantive clauses of the Preamble in the *YCJA* have been given careful consideration by Canada's eminent jurists and figure prominently in the reasoning of even our highest court. Thus, the Preamble in the *YCJA*, at least in part, has had considerable impact on youth justice jurisprudence since 2003.

C.   The Declaration of Principle — Section 3 of the *YCJA*

The Declaration of Principle in the *YCJA* can be characterized as a purpose statement,[78] an interpretive provision that functions as a guide to interpreting the substantive provisions of the *YCJA*. It is a series of clauses and sentences that, together, reveal the purpose of the *YCJA* and outline the general policy and principles that should guide its interpretation. Other principles are included in other sections of the *YCJA* but s. 3 provides the overarching philosophical framework.

While the Declaration of Principle is a section of the *YCJA*, whereas the Preamble is not, these two elements of the legislation serve similar purposes and, in terms of statutory interpretation, these elements are often considered simultaneously.[79] However, the Declaration of Principle includes more detailed and specific principles regarding the youth justice system and has consequently been discussed in the jurisprudence more than the Preamble, whether it be in relation to extrajudicial measures, sentencing, or the appropriateness of custody. The principles in the Declaration of Principle are routinely considered in conjunction with other sections of the Act as well when decision-makers are making decisions under the *YCJA*, such as deciding whether to use an extrajudicial measure under ss. 4 to 12 or imposing a youth sentence based on the specific sentencing principles in s. 38 of the *YCJA*. In fact, the Act expressly directs decision-makers to consider the principles in s. 3 when imposing a youth sentence under the *YCJA*,[80] or when deciding whether to use an extrajudicial measure under ss. 4 to 12.[81]

---

[77]   *Quebec (Minister of Justice) v. Canada (Minister of Justice) (sub nom. Reference re: Bill C-7 respecting the criminal justice system for young persons)*, [2003] Q.J. No. 2850, at para. 135, 175 C.C.C. (3d) 321 (Que. C.A.).

[78]   Ruth Sullivan, *Statutory Interpretation* (Concord, Ontario: Irwin Law, 1997), at 118.

[79]   Ruth Sullivan, *Statutory Interpretation* (Concord, Ontario: Irwin Law, 1997), at 118.

[80]   *YCJA*, s. 38(2).

[81]   *YCJA*, s. 4.

Under the former *YOA*, L'Heureux-Dubé J. considered the influence of the Declaration of Principle as an element of legislation in *R. v. T. (V.)*.[82] The central issue in the case was prosecutorial discretion but it provided cause for L'Heureux-Dubé J. to consider the import of s. 3. Justice L'Heureux-Dubé held that the Declaration of Principle in s. 3 is more than a Preamble and therefore carries the same force one would normally attribute to substantive provisions, especially since Parliament chose to include the section in the body of the Act[83] contrary to the Preamble, which appears prior to the actual enactment. Her analysis is equally applicable to the Declaration of Principle in s. 3 of the *YCJA*, given that the Declarations are highly similar in substance and purpose, and identical in place in the legislation.

The fact that the Declaration of Principle, as a legal construct, is to be given the same weight as the substantive provisions in the body of the Act is of limited significance, however, because the provisions in the *YCJA*'s Declaration of Principle are ambiguous and not ranked in order of importance. Judges and other decision-makers under the Act have been given no clear direction as to which s. 3 principles matter most. In this regard, it is not significantly clearer than the *YOA* although it was advertised as such.

Following the last major review of youth justice legislation in Canada in 1996 by the Standing Committee on Justice and Legal Affairs, the committee urged the federal government in its report to replace the Declaration of Principle in the *YOA* with a statement of purpose establishing that the protection of society is the main goal of the criminal law, followed by a hierarchy of additional ranked principles.[84]

In fact, when former federal Liberal Justice Minister Anne McLellan outlined the intent of the new *YCJA* in the House of Commons in the spring of 2001, she explained that new youth justice legislation was necessary because the *YOA* lacked a coherent youth justice philosophy and that the *YCJA* had cured that shortcoming.

She said of the *YOA* at the time: "Its principles are unclear and conflicting and do not effectively guide decision makers in the youth justice

---

[82] [1992] S.C.J. No. 29, 71 C.C.C. (3d) 32 (S.C.C.).

[83] *R. v. T. (V.)*, [1992] S.C.J. No. 29, at para. 26, 71 C.C.C. (3d) 32 (S.C.C).

[84] Canada, House of Commons, *Renewing Youth Justice: Thirteenth Report of the Standing Committee on Justice and Legal Affairs* (Ottawa: Public Works and Government Services, 1997), c. 2.

system. Unlike the *YOA*, the proposed youth criminal justice act provides guidance on the priority that should be given to key principles."[85]

Former Minister McLellan was certainly correct that the principles in s. 3 of the *YOA* were generally considered unclear and conflicting. During the many years leading up to the coming into force of the *YCJA*, the *YOA* was widely and routinely criticized by academics and the judiciary, among others, on this point. In the 1990s, youth justice experts lambasted the principles in the Declaration of Principle in the *YOA* as "positively inconsistent",[86] and reflecting the disparate goals of the various interest groups who sought juvenile justice reform in the decades before the passage of the *YOA*.[87] For example, under s. 3 of the *YOA*, protection of society was described as a primary objective of the criminal law applicable to youth,[88] society was entitled to necessary protection,[89] and young persons were to bear responsibility for their contraventions.[90] On the other hand, young persons were not necessarily to be held as accountable as adults, and had special needs, required guidance and assistance, and had special guarantees of their rights and freedoms.[91] In practice, such ambiguity in priority and purpose due to contradictory principles, coupled with broad and vague language, prevented uniform interpretation.[92] Criminal justice system participants, such as police, defence counsel, Crowns, and judges, could justify virtually any decision under one or more of the s. 3 principles.[93] There was something for everyone.

---

[85]   *House of Commons Debates* (February 14, 2001), at 1525 and 1530.

[86]   P. Platt, *Young Offenders Law in Canada* (Toronto: Butterworths, 1989), at 2.18. In the second edition of the book in 1995, she softened this criticism. See also Nicholas Bala and Mary-Anne Kirvan, "The Statute: Its Principles and Provisions and their Interpretation by the Courts" in Alan W. Leschied, Peter G. Jaffe and Wayne Willis, eds., *The Young Offenders Act: A Revolution in Canadian Juvenile Justice* (Toronto: University of Toronto Press, 1991), at 80-81. This critique is noted by L'Heureux-Dubé J. in *R. v. T. (V.)*, [1992] S.C.J. No. 29, at para. 28, 71 C.C.C. (3d) 32 (S.C.C.), where she acknowledges that these apparent inconsistencies stem from societal ambivalence in Canada about the appropriate response to young offenders. Ongoing societal ambivalence continues to explain the inconsistencies and ambiguity in the Declaration of Principle under the *YCJA* today.

[87]   Priscilla Platt, *Young Offenders Law in Canada*, 2d ed. (Markham, Ontario: Butterworths Canada Ltd., 1995), at 17.

[88]   *YOA*, s. 3(1)(c.1).

[89]   *YOA*, s. 3(1)(b).

[90]   *YOA*, s. 3(1)(a.1).

[91]   *YOA*, s. 3(1)(a.1), (c) and (e).

[92]   Janet Bolton *et al.*, "The *Young Offenders Act*: Principles and Policy — The First Decade in Review" (1993) 38 McGill L.J. 939, at 973-75.

[93]   Richard Barnhorst, "The *Youth Criminal Justice Act*: New Directions and Implementation Issues" (April 2004) Vol. 46, No. 3, Can. J. Crim. & Crim. Jus. 231, at 233.

In one of the most often cited sentencing decisions under the *YOA*, Cory J. of the Supreme Court of Canada opined that the Declaration of Principle in s. 3 of the *YOA* revealed a marked ambivalence, but that such ambivalence should not be surprising given that the *YOA* "reflects a courageous attempt to balance concepts and interests that are frequently conflicting".[94] Justice L'Heureux-Dubé, in *R. v. T. (V.)*, had earlier described the former Declaration of Principle as an honest attempt to achieve an appropriate balance for dealing with a very complex social problem. She appeared to justify its apparent contradictions: "The *YOA* does not have a single, simple underlying philosophy, for there is no single, simple philosophy that can deal with all situations in which young persons violate the criminal law. ... The underlying philosophical tensions in the *YOA* reflect the very complex nature of youthful criminality. ... Judges and the other professionals who work with young persons who violate the criminal law require a complex and balanced set of principles like those found in the *YOA*."[95] Parliament was attempting to achieve disparate goals in its Declaration of Principle; thus, the Declaration of Principle lacks a clear, singular intention,[96] L'Heureux-Dubé J. held.

Years later, on the eve of the *YCJA*, prominent jurists had not changed their view of the Declaration of Principle in the *YOA*. In *Re F.N.*,[97] which is largely a case about the disclosure of a *YOA* record, Binnie J. noted and affirmed the ambivalence created by the disparate goals (or competing objectives) inherent in the scheme of the *YOA*.[98]

Unfortunately, s. 3 of the *YCJA* fails to resolve these concerns, or to provide the clear, coherent and consistent youth justice philosophy that its predecessor lacked and that the federal government promised. The guiding principles in s. 3 of the *YCJA*, which are described as the Policy for Canada With Respect to Young Persons, are listed and grouped into four paragraphs but, similar to its predecessor Declaration of Principle in the *YOA*, the principles are not ranked in order of importance. There is no hierarchy of principles. Unlike s. 718.1 of the *Criminal Code*, which identifies proportionality as the fundamental principle of sentencing for adults, for example, the Declaration of Principle does not identify the fundamental principle of the *YCJA*, or expressly identify through the use of clear, unequivocal language which principle should be considered the

---

[94]   *R. v. M. (J.J.)*, [1993] S.C.J. No. 14, at para. 9 (S.C.C.).
[95]   *R. v. T. (V.)*, [1992] S.C.J. No. 29, at paras. 28, 71 C.C.C. (3d) 32 (S.C.C.).
[96]   *R. v. T. (V.)*, [1992] S.C.J. No. 29, at para. 29, 71 C.C.C. (3d) 32 (S.C.C.).
[97]   *Re F.N.*, [2000] S.C.J. No. 34, at para. 10, [2000] 1 S.C.R. 880 (S.C.C.).
[98]   *Re F.N.*, [2000] S.C.J. No. 34, at para. 10, [2000] 1 S.C.R. 880 (S.C.C.).

most important in the youth justice system in Canada.[99] There remains no clear direction to decision-makers as to which principle matters most.

Like its predecessor, the Declaration of Principle in the *YCJA* fails to "take a stand" in strong, clear and plain language. Rather, it captures all relevant concerns and interests, and illustrates the ongoing lack of consensus among federal political parties in Canada, as representatives of Canadians, as to how best to respond to young persons who commit crimes, including the divisive issue of the role and value of prison sentences for young persons. Once again, judges are left to interpret an array of sometimes conflicting principles. This general lack of clarity regarding the order and rank of the s. 3 principles is arguably even more evident in s. 38 of the Act, which concerns the sentencing principles.

One judge observed early in the life of the new *YCJA* that, like the *YOA*, youth workers, counsellors, lawyers and judges are continuing to balance principles and interests that are frequently conflicting.[100] While some youth justice experts suggest that the *YCJA* provides clearer philosophical direction to decision-makers than the *YOA* did,[101] this may be in large part because other sections of the *YCJA* now contain principles as well. If s. 3 is read in combination with other sections of the *YCJA*, the skeleton of the philosophical framework created by s. 3 assumes greater flesh and substance. Nevertheless, the Declaration of Principle, as the flag-bearer for the *YCJA*, when read in isolation, compels decision-makers to continue the challenging task of discerning for themselves its priorities and fundamental philosophical message.

(i)   Section 3(1)(a) — Goals of the Youth Justice System

Section 3(1)(a) of the Declaration of Principle, in its entirety, refers to the general goals of the youth justice system. This paragraph points to the need for the youth criminal justice system to do what it can to address the underlying causes of the young person's criminality in order to prevent further crime. Since s. 3(1)(a) states that the youth justice system is intended to prevent crime by addressing the underlying causes of youthful criminality, this paragraph is arguably suggesting that the "youth

---

[99]   For example, Nova Scotia's Nunn Commission recommended in its 2006 report that the Nova Scotia government should advocate for an amendment to the Declaration of Principle in s. 3 of the *YCJA*, stating that the protection of the public is a primary goal of the Act.

[100]   *R. v. N.A.C.*, [2004] B.C.J. No. 165, at para. 25 (B.C. Prov. Ct.), *per* Tweedale J.

[101]   Nicholas Bala, *Youth Criminal Justice Law* (Toronto: Irwin Law Inc., 2003), at 74. See also Ian Carter, "Playing the Youth Card: The Impact of the Declaration of Principle in the *Youth Criminal Justice Act*" (2006) 32 C.R. (6th) 232, at 241.

criminal justice system" should provide the necessary supports to address any apparent problems, ranging from substance abuse, to poverty, homelessness or Fetal Alcohol Spectrum Disorder,[102] that are driving or contributing to the criminality. This first paragraph has little practical significance.

The *youth criminal justice system* is not defined in s. 3(1)(a). The system includes both the federal and provincial or territorial governments, as well as many other non-governmental players. Such terms invariably raise questions concerning the division of responsibilities between the federal and provincial/territorial governments in relation to preventing youth crime and rehabilitating young persons. Through its Preamble and s. 3, the Act generally places the responsibility for preventing crime and rehabilitating young persons at the feet of all of us. The federal, provincial and territorial governments have a long-standing partnership in relation to youth criminal justice as a result of their shared jurisdiction, but the parameters of that shared responsibility have been characterized by nebulous borders. The federal government has jurisdiction to enact legislation under the criminal law power while the provinces, by virtue of s. 92(14) of the *Constitution Act*, have jurisdiction over the administration of justice in the province.[103]

In light of the statutorily mandated intention of the youth criminal justice system to prevent crime and rehabilitate young persons, the judiciary has sometimes attempted to order the province or territory to pay for treatment programs for young persons where these are lacking. The issue arose under the *YOA*. A number of appeal courts held that judges do not have the statutory power to order governments to provide and pay for treatment or rehabilitative programs. In *R. v. L.E.K.*,[104] the court held that the jurisdiction of the youth court judge was limited not only by the terms of the statute but by the constitutional principles that delineate between the roles of the judiciary and the executive. In *R. v. R.J.H.*,[105] the court reasoned that even if judges were granted the power to order provinces to provide and pay for certain treatment programs, the granting of such power would be held to be unconstitutional because the provinces have exclusive jurisdiction over the administration of justice in the province. In

---

[102] This is a complex cognitive disorder that relates to the consumption of alcohol by the mother during pregnancy. A conference concerning this disorder was held in Whitehorse, Yukon, on September 17-19, 2008. Among the materials provided to participants was a review of reported judicial decisions in Canada by Andrea Bailey where this disorder was mentioned or considered.

[103] *Constitution Act, 1867* (U.K.), 30 & 31 Vict., c. 3, s. 92(14).

[104] [2000] S.J. No. 844, at para. 20 (Sask. C.A.).

[105] See *R. v. R.J.H.*, [2000] A.J. No 396, at paras. 35-36 (Alta. C.A.).

short, s. 3(1)(a) identifies the prevention of youth crime as a goal of Canada's youth criminal justice system but it does not indicate how those responsibilities are to be shared between levels of government nor does it provide statutory authority for judges to order treatment programs into existence where they are absent, to achieve the objectives in s. 3(1)(a).[106]

a.   Section 3(1)(a)(i)

This subparagraph recognizes the limits of the *YCJA*. It clarifies that the youth criminal justice system is designed to respond to young persons who have *already* come into contact with the criminal justice system when causes that lead a young person into conflict with the criminal law generally originate earlier in his or her life. Effective intervention and support at an earlier stage might well have prevented the young person from becoming involved in criminal activity.

b.   Section 3(1)(a)(ii)

The rehabilitation and reintegration into society of young persons who commit crimes is a major goal of Canada's modern youth criminal justice system. The root of the controversy within Canada concerns how best to achieve such rehabilitation and the extent to which incarceration is effective in that regard. The *YCJA* merely identifies the goal of rehabilitation but does not definitively state how best rehabilitation can be achieved. An underlying premise of Canada's youth justice system is that young persons are more amenable to reform than adults and that, as a result, there should be more emphasis on rehabilitation in the youth justice system than in the adult system.[107] The word "rehabilitation" is mentioned three times in the Declaration of Principle in the *YCJA* and many of the other principles relate to it such as the timeliness of responses to youth crime. By contrast, in the sentencing principles for adults under the *Criminal Code*, the objective of rehabilitation is mentioned once. It is significant that the *YCJA* states clearly that the youth criminal justice system must emphasize rehabilitation and reintegration whereas, in the *Criminal Code*, s. 718 states only that assisting in rehabilitation is one of the objectives of sentencing. It is not mandated or

---

[106]   See some discussion of this matter in Nicholas Bala, *Youth Criminal Justice Law* (Toronto: Irwin Law Inc., 2003), at 105-109.

[107]   Department of Justice, *A Strategy for the Renewal of Youth Justice* (Ottawa: Ministry of Supply and Services, 1998) (section on Legislative and Supporting Program Components). At the time of writing, this 1998 document could still be readily accessed through the Department of Justice website at: <http://www.justice.gc.ca/eng/pi/yj-jj/about-apropos/toc-tdm.html>. See also Nicholas Bala, *Youth Criminal Justice Law* (Toronto: Irwin Law Inc., 2003), at 101.

required that rehabilitation be a consideration in any particular sentence for an adult.[108] Section 718 of the *Criminal Code* states that every sentence must have one or more of the following objectives: denunciation, specific and general deterrence, separation of the offender from society where necessary, assist in rehabilitation, provide reparation for harm done to victims or the community and promote a sense of responsibility in the offender and acknowledgment of harm done to victims and to the community.[109] It is questionable if this is enlightened sentencing policy for Canada in the 21st century, given that, arguably, the best way to ensure our long-term protection is to focus on rehabilitating all persons who commit crimes, recognizing that, in some cases, it may not be possible. A consideration of rehabilitation should be routinely canvassed during all sentencing hearings because only a small percentage of offenders will remain in prison for the rest of their lives. Developing and implementing programming that has proven effective in reducing criminality is unquestionably in Canada's long-term public interest.

The principle of rehabilitation has been an underlying principle of comprehensive youth justice legislation in Canada since its inception. The *JDA* was aimed at reforming the juvenile, although at the time it was perhaps understood as rescuing the young person from environmental factors and removing him or her from evil influences and the moral contagion of corrupt adult influences. Juveniles under the *JDA* were not to be treated as criminals but as misguided children who needed help, support, encouragement, guidance and supervision.[110] The thinking had changed by the 1960s. The compassion and sympathy with which the *JDA* was imbued would not be found in the *YOA* in equal measure. The goal of rehabilitation was not an express principle in the *YOA* when it came into force in 1984. This reorientation in the *YOA* away from the benevolent welfare model of youth justice conveyed by the *JDA* was influenced in part by research in the 1960s and 1970s that suggested rehabilitation programs were not working and that they were not effective in reducing recidivism. The 1974 publication of an article by American R. Martinson, in which he analyzed 231 studies concerning the effectiveness of rehabilitation programs in different countries from 1945 through 1967, was significant. The data "give us very little reason to hope that we have in fact found a sure way of reducing recidivism through rehabilitation", Martinson concluded.[111] His pithy but disturbing summary that "nothing

---

[108]   *Criminal Code*, s. 718.
[109]   *Criminal Code*, s. 718.
[110]   *Juvenile Delinquents Act, 1929*, S.C. 1929, c. 46, ss. 3(2) and 38.
[111]   R. Martinson, "What Works? Questions and Answers About Prison Reform" (1974) 35 The Public Interest 22, at 49.

works" in rehabilitative programming struck a cord among criminologists. This perceived failure of rehabilitation programs caused some officials working within the juvenile justice system to re-examine the underlying philosophy of the *JDA*.[112] Notably, while other researchers reached conclusions similar to those of Martinson, he later retracted his.[113]

In the early 1990s, the work of researchers such as Dr. Don Andrews *et al.* and Lipsey challenged Martinson's "nothing works" conclusion regarding youth rehabilitation.[114] Some researchers concluded that certain types of youth rehabilitation programs work to some degree, at least some of the time. The work of Andrews suggested that community-based interventions were more effective than institution-based treatment, and that effective correctional treatment is more cost-effective and successful than deterrence strategies such as increasing the severity of the sentence.[115]

Some suggest that such findings may have been partly responsible for the 1995 amendment to the *YOA* that expressly recognized rehabilitation as a guiding youth justice principle.[116] While the *YOA* was certainly more focused on rehabilitation than punishment in contrast to the *Criminal Code*,[117] the principle of rehabilitation did not have the place and prominence in the *YOA* that it has today under the *YCJA*.

---

[112] Bryan R. Hogeveen, "History, Development, and Transformations in Canadian Juvenile Justice, 1800-1984" in Kathyrn Campbell, ed., *Understanding Youth Justice in Canada* (Toronto: Pearson Education Canada, Inc., 2005), 24 at 37.

[113] Bryan R. Hogeveen, "History, Development, and Transformations in Canadian Juvenile Justice, 1800-1984" in Kathyrn Campbell, ed., *Understanding Youth Justice in Canada* (Toronto: Pearson Education Canada, Inc., 2005), 24 at 37.

[114] See for example D.A. Andrews *et al.*, "Does Correctional Treatment Work? A Clinically Relevant and Psychologically Informed Meta-Analysis" (1990) Vol. 28, No. 3, Criminology 369, at 370; P. Gendreau and D.A. Andrews, "Tertiary Prevention: What the Meta-analyses of the Offender Treatment Literature Tell Us About 'What works'", Can. J. Crim., January 1990 and M.W. Lipsey, "Juvenile Delinquency Treatment: A Meta-Analytic Inquiry into the Variability of Effects" in T.D. Cook *et al.*, *Meta-Analysis for Explanation: A Casebook* (New York: Russell Sage Foundation, 1992), at 83.

[115] See for example D.A. Andrews *et al.*, "Does Correctional Treatment Work? A Clinically Relevant and Psychologically Informed Meta-Analysis" (1990) Vol. 28, No. 3, Criminology 369, at 370; P. Gendreau and D.A. Andrews, "Tertiary Prevention: What the Meta-analyses of the Offender Treatment Literature Tell Us About 'What works'" (1990) 32 Can. J. Crim. 173; and M.W. Lipsey, "Juvenile Delinquency Treatment: A Meta-Analytic Inquiry into the Variability of Effects" in T.D. Cook *et al.*, *Meta-Analysis for Explanation: A Casebook* (New York: Russell Sage Foundation, 1992), at 83.

[116] Sanjeev Anand, "Catalyst for Change: The History of Canadian Juvenile Justice Reform" (Spring 1999) Vol. 24, No. 2, Queen's L.J. 515, at 555. In 1995, s. 3(1)(c.1) was added to the Declaration of Principle in the *YOA*.

[117] *Reference Re Young Offenders Act (P.E.I.)*, [1990] S.C.J. No. 60, [1991] 1 S.C.R. 252 (S.C.C.).

c.   Section 3(1)(a)(iii) — Meaningful Consequences

Section 3(1)(a)(iii) of Canada's policy concerning its youth justice system informs readers that Canada's youth justice system is intended to ensure that young persons are subject to *meaningful consequences* in order to promote the *long-term* protection of the public.

The nebulous term "meaningful consequences", which was discussed earlier in this chapter in reference to its appearance in the Preamble, is among the most discussed aspects of s. 3(1)(a). Meaningful to whom? On a plain reading of this subparagraph, it is unclear whether the concept of "meaningful" is to be viewed from the perspective of the young person, from the perspective of society, or from the perspective of both. Even if one presumes that the concept of "meaningful" is to be viewed from the perspective of the young person, what is a meaningful consequence to a young person? This depends to some degree on the psychological make-up of the young person. What is meaningful to one young person is not meaningful to another. A stern lecture can impact one young person and have no effect on another. By one definition, a response to the offending behaviour will be meaningful to the young person if it deters him or her from committing further crimes.[118] A consequence can also be perceived as meaningful (to other young persons and to society) if knowledge of it deters other young persons from committing similar crimes, or because it brings with it what society considers to be an appropriate measure of public condemnation. However, a sentence could also be meaningful to the young person without deterring him or her from committing further crimes. A sentence that involves participation in a victim-offender reconciliation program for example could be meaningful to the young person as it could provide some insight into his or her conduct, but it may not result in deterring him or her from further crime.

As suggested above, some criminal justice experts contend that the term "meaningful consequences" can be construed as a reference to responses adequate to deter the offender and others. "If not to serve as a deterrent, why should wrongful conduct be accompanied by 'meaningful consequences'. In everyday discourse, when someone is informed that certain actions on their part will have 'meaningful consequences', this information is imparted in an attempt to inhibit the conduct in question — deterrence in other words."[119]

---

[118]   Julian V. Roberts and Nicholas Bala, "Understanding Sentencing Under the *Youth Criminal Justice Act*" (2003) 41 Alta. L. Rev. 395, at paras. 12-13 (QL), suggest that meaningful consequences can be seen to include some elements of deterrence.

[119]   Julian V. Roberts and Nicholas Bala, "Understanding Sentencing Under the *Youth Criminal Justice Act*" (2003) 41 Alta. L. Rev. 395, at para. 13 (QL).

While at its simplest, a meaningful consequence may mean no more than punishment, a truly meaningful consequence must have been intended to mean a response that causes, or results in, the young person gaining insight into the reasons for the criminality, and as a result of that learning, altering his or her behaviour so as to no longer engage in criminal conduct. A meaningful consequence, then, taken to its natural end, must, at least, mean specific deterrence.

In *R. v. D.L.C.*,[120] Gorman J. held that the term "meaningful consequences" mandates a very individualized judicial approach to sentencing. The circumstances of the young person must be the primary focus and the sentence must be fashioned with the personal circumstances of the specific young person in mind. Meaningful consequences must be construed from the vantage point of the particular young person. Justice Gorman held that a very meaningful consequence for a specific young person could involve prohibiting him or her from participating in particular activities that the young person enjoys.[121] By way of further illustration, a period of probation could be meaningful for one young person but not for another, Gorman J. held.

This offender-centric approach to interpreting the meaning of meaningful consequences was later endorsed by the Supreme Court of Canada in *R. v. B.W.P.; R. v. B.V.N.*[122] The main issue before the court was whether general deterrence is a factor to be considered when sentencing a person to a youth sentence under the *YCJA*. In reaching the conclusion that it is not, Charron J. discussed the meaning of s. 3(1)(a) of the Declaration of Principle. She held for the majority that s. 3(1)(a) described an individualized sentencing process by focusing on underlying causes, rehabilitation, reintegration and meaningful consequences *for the offender*.[123] Justice Charron concluded that the concept of meaningful consequences and related concepts in s. 3(1)(a) were to be viewed from the perspective of the young person rather than from society at large.[124] Likewise, the references to meaningful consequences in s. 3(1)(a)(iii), accountability in s. 3(1)(b)(ii) and meaningful in s. 3(1)(c)(iii) are expressly targeting the young person; Parliament has made it clear that these principles are offender-centric and not aimed at the general public, Charron J. held.[125]

---

[120] [2003] N.J. No. 94, at para. 30 (N.L. Prov. Ct.).
[121] *R. v. D.L.C.*, [2003] N.J. No. 94, at para. 31 (N.L. Prov. Ct.).
[122] [2006] S.C.J. No. 27, 2006 SCC 27 (S.C.C.).
[123] *R. v. B.W.P.; R. v. B.V.N.*, [2006] S.C.J. No. 27, 2006 SCC 27 (S.C.C.).
[124] *R. v. B.W.P.; R. v. B.V.N.*, [2006] S.C.J. No. 27, at paras. 31-33, 2006 SCC 27 (S.C.C.).
[125] *R. v. B.W.P.; R. v. B.V.N.*, [2006] S.C.J. No. 27, at paras. 32-34, 2006 SCC 27 (S.C.C.).

d.   Section 3(1)(a) — Long-Term Protection of the Public

The wording of s. 3(1)(a) also suggests that the best way to promote the long-term protection of society is to address the underlying causes of young persons' offending behaviour, to rehabilitate them and re-integrate them into society, and to ensure they are subject to meaningful consequences for their offending behaviour. The use of the phrase "*long-term* protection" rather than simply "protection" implies that the best way to guarantee the protection of the public in the long term is to focus on rehabilitating young persons rather than simply incapacitating them for a period of time through a jail sentence. The unstated assumption may well be that most young persons who are jailed will eventually be released and a focus on rehabilitation is the best means to help ensure societal protection upon their release. "Custody has typically been used as a way of incapacitating the offender, at least in the short term. The phrase 'long-term protection' — particularly when accompanied by specific strategies — suggests the use of remedies that change the young offender and his or her relations with the community, rather than those that simply isolate him or her from society for a period of time."[126] Thus, measures aimed only at incapacitation, such as a jail sentence that exposes one to the criminal subculture but has no effective rehabilitative component, protects society during the period of the offender's incapacitation but may provide no guarantee of protection from that young person upon his or her release. This interpretation is consistent with the interpretation of the Supreme Court of Canada.

When Charron J. discussed the term in *R. v. B.W.P.; R. v. B.V.N.*,[127] she observed that the meaning of "long-term protection of the public", which is also used in s. 38(1) of the *YCJA*, is expressed not as an immediate objective of sentencing but rather as the long-term effect of a successful youth sentence. Noting that the phrase is also to be found in s. 3(1) of the *YCJA*, Charron J. observed that the means of promoting the long-term protection of the public describe an individualized process by focusing on underlying causes, rehabilitation, reintegration and meaningful consequences for the offender.[128]

The meaning that members of the judiciary attach to this term may be influenced to some degree by their views of the rehabilitative potential

---

[126] Julian V. Roberts and Nicholas Bala, "Understanding Sentencing Under the *Youth Criminal Justice Act*" (2003) 41 Alta. L. Rev. 395, at para. 10 (QL).

[127] [2006] S.C.J. No. 27, 2006 SCC 27 (S.C.C.).

[128] *R. v. B.W.P.; R. v. B.V.N.*, [2006] S.C.J. No. 27, at paras. 31 and 32, 2006 SCC 27 (S.C.C.).

of incarceration.[129] In a particular case, based on evidence of particular programs available to the offender while incarcerated, the judge may well conclude that a prison sentence combined with those programs will promote the long-term protection of the public. Unlike the *YOA* as amended in 1995,[130] the *YCJA* does not identify the protection of the public (which is interpreted by some as "code" for a prison sentence) as a primary objective of the criminal law applicable to youth.

The Nunn Commission of inquiry[131] recommended in 2006 that the Nova Scotia government lobby the federal government to amend the Declaration of Principle to state that the protection of the public is one of the primary goals of the Act.[132] Commissioner Nunn stated in strong language in the report that highlighting public safety as one of the goals or principles of the Act is a must.[133] In fact, an earlier version of the *YCJA*, Bill C-3, which was introduced in 1999, stated that the "principal goal of the youth criminal justice system is to protect the public" by preventing crime, imposing meaningful consequences for offences and rehabilitating

---

[129]   *Unlocking America*, a November 2007 report by the JFA Institute on the U.S. prison system concluded that the growing literature on "what works" in correctional programming has found that many programs have no impact on recidivism rates. It reported that a recent meta-analysis of treatment programs reviewed 291 evaluations of adult offender treatment programs, both in-prison and in-community, conducted in the United States and other English-speaking nations. The meta-analysis led to the conclusion that 42 per cent of the evaluated programs had no impact on recidivism. Of the 167 effective programs, only one-fourth were prison-based treatment programs. Even under the most optimistic assumptions, the effect of in-prison rehabilitative programs reduced failure rates by about 10 per cent, the authors of *Unlocking America* concluded. The JFA Institute is a non-profit agency that works with various levels of government and philanthropic organizations to evaluate criminal justice policies and to design research-based policy solutions. It is headed by Dr. James Austin, former director of the Institute on Crime, Justice and Corrections at George Washington University in Washington D.C. See James Austin *et al.*, *Unlocking America* (Washington, D.C: The JFA Institute, 2007). At the time of writing, the report could be accessed at the following website: <http://www.jfa-associates.com>.

[130]   *An Act to amend the Young Offenders Act and the Criminal Code*, S.C. 1995, c. 19, s. 1 added s. 3(1)(a) and (c.1).

[131]   The Nunn Commission was an inquiry by D. Merlin Nunn, former justice of the Supreme Court of Nova Scotia, into the October 2004 death of 52-year-old Theresa McEvoy. She was killed instantly in a car crash after a 16-year-old boy joyriding in a stolen car in Halifax went through a red light at high speed and crashed into her car. The report (*Spiralling out of Control: Lessons Learned from a Boy in Trouble: Report of the Nunn Commission of Inquiry* (Halifax, NS: Nunn Commission of Inquiry, 2006)) can be accessed online at: <http://www.gov.ns.ca/just/nunn_commission/_docs/Report_Nunn_Final.pdf>.

[132]   Nova Scotia Nunn Commission of Inquiry, *Spiralling out of Control: Lessons Learned from a Boy in Trouble: Report of the Nunn Commission of Inquiry* (Halifax, NS: Nunn Commission of Inquiry, 2006), at 234-36, available online at: <http://www.gov.ns.ca/just/nunn_commission/_docs/Report_Nunn_Final.pdf>.

[133]   Nova Scotia Nunn Commission of Inquiry, *Spiralling out of Control: Lessons Learned from a Boy in Trouble: Report of the Nunn Commission of Inquiry* (Halifax, NS: Nunn Commission of Inquiry, 2006), at 235, available online at: <http://www.gov.ns.ca/just/nunn_commission/_docs/Report_Nunn_Final.pdf>.

offenders.[134] The final version of the Act, which was enacted in 2002 and became law the following year, did not identify a primary or fundamental goal of the *YCJA*. The reference to protection of the public as the main goal had been removed.

It is also interesting that the long-term protection of the public is not characterized as a goal of the youth justice system under the *YCJA* but, rather, as a consequence, outcome or result, of efforts taken to address the underlying causes of the young person's behaviour, to rehabilitate him or her, and to ensure the offender is subject to meaningful consequences. In other words, it is not the judge's direct responsibility under the *YCJA* to protect the public but rather to impose sentences based in part on s. 3 principles that are designed to promote the long-term protection of the public.[135]

(ii)   Section 3(1)(b) — A Separate Youth Justice System

The long-standing reality of a separate youth criminal justice system for young persons is now codified in s. 3(1)(b) of the Declaration of Principle. This is highly significant. While a formal and comprehensive separate youth criminal justice system has existed in Canada since 1908, the *YCJA* marks the first time this fact has been expressly codified in comprehensive youth justice legislation in Canada, in keeping with the *U.N. Convention on the Rights of the Child*.[136] While it can be argued that the concept of a separate youth justice system was codified in certain provisions of both the *JDA* and the *YOA*, neither Act used language as clear and express as the wording in s. 3(1)(b) of the Declaration of Principle in the *YCJA*.

Significantly, the Supreme Court of Canada affirmed the existence of a separate legal system for young persons in *R. v. D.B.*,[137] when Abella J. acknowledged for the majority that the *YCJA* confirms in s. 3 (1)(b) that

---

[134] Bill C-3, Second Session, Thirty-Sixth Parliament, First Reading, October 14, 1999: not enacted.

[135] A. Doob and J. Sprott, "Sentencing under the *Youth Criminal Justice Act*: An Historical Perspective" in K. Campbell, ed., *Understanding Youth Justice in Canada* (Toronto: Pearson Education Canada Inc., 2005), 221 at 232-33.

[136] See the Preamble, as well as Articles 37(c) and 40 3. on this point. Canada made a reservation to Article 37, which states that children deprived of their liberty shall be separated from adults unless it is considered in their best interests not to do so. Article 40.3 obliges state parties to promote the establishment of laws, procedures, authorities and institutions specifically applicable to children alleged or found to have infringed the penal law. The Convention is available online at: <http://www.unhchr.ch/html/menu3/b/k2crc.htm>.

[137] [2008] S.C.J. No. 25, 2008 SCC 25 (S.C.C.).

there is a separate legal system for young persons because young persons, due to age, have heightened vulnerability, less maturity and a reduced capacity for moral judgement.[138] The Supreme Court of Canada reinforced this fact in *R. v. S.J.L.*, which identifies a separate youth criminal justice system in Canada as a governing principle of the *YCJA*.[139]

a.   Section 3(1)(b)(i) — Rehabilitation and Reintegration

This subparagraph says in clear language that the criminal justice system for young persons must emphasize rehabilitation and reintegration, a theme that first appears in the Preamble where *effective rehabilitation and reintegration* is identified along with meaningful consequences as the means to ensure accountability within Canada's youth criminal justice system. While the goal of rehabilitation was eventually included in the Declaration of Principle in the *YOA* during the final round of amendments in 1995, what is significant in the *YCJA* is that the concept is linked to the young person's reintegration into society. The underlying premise is that the majority of young persons who are imprisoned will eventually be released into society and their reintegration must therefore be carefully considered and planned. Under the *YCJA*, as Chapter 8 discusses, every custodial sentence must now be accompanied by a period of supervision in the community.[140]

b.   Section 3(1)(b)(ii) — Fair and Proportionate Accountability

The concept of rehabilitation and reintegration is only one of five factors that the youth criminal justice system must emphasize. Four other factors must also be emphasized, including fair and proportionate accountability that is consistent with the greater dependency of young persons and their reduced level of maturity. Practically speaking, to what extent can a decision-maker under the *YCJA*, such as a Crown prosecutor or a judge, emphasize both fair and proportionate accountability and rehabilitation in one sentence? To some degree this may depend on the decision-maker's understanding of the concepts, and whether he or she holds the view, for example, that a prison sentence can emphasize both. A decision-maker may well conclude that it is practically impossible to emphasize both rehabilitation and fair and proportionate accountability in one sentence. In other cases, there may

---

[138]   *R. v. D.B.*, [2008] S.C.J. No. 25, at paras. 40-41, 2008 SCC 25 (S.C.C.).
[139]   *R. v. S.J.L.*, [2009] S.C.J. No. 14, at para. 56, 2009 SCC 14 (S.C.C.).
[140]   Section 90 of the *YCJA* requires that a reintegration plan be developed for the young person while he or she is in custody that identifies the most effective programs to assist the young person in reintegrating into society.

be evidence that a particular detention centre has certain treatment programs with a demonstrated success rate, and that both rehabilitation and accountability can be emphasized. However, s. 3(1)(b) does not state that any one sentence must emphasize both of these factors; it says only that the *youth criminal justice system* must emphasize both. In fact, the Standing Committee on Justice and Legal Affairs, which conducted the last full-scale review of Canada's youth justice system in 1996, concluded that concepts such as protection of the public and rehabilitation are not mutually exclusive and that the public discourse often sets up a false dichotomy between rehabilitation and public safety.[141] The committee quoted Cory J.'s comments in *R. v. M. (J.J.)*[142] as well as the remarks of various witnesses to make the point that the best way to protect society in the long run is to reform and rehabilitate the young person.[143]

Fair and proportionate accountability in s. 3(1)(b)(ii) is a clear reference to the diminished responsibility of young persons. Young persons are to be held accountable for their criminal conduct in accordance with their greater dependency and reduced level of maturity *vis-à-vis* adult criminals. A young person, as a general rule, is to be held less accountable than an adult would be for the same crime. This is essentially a codification of the long-standing concept of diminished responsibility or the limited accountability of a young person, which has long been recognized in the common law.[144] This principle appeared in slightly different wording in the *YOA* Declaration of Principle.[145]

The U.S. Supreme Court endorsed the concept in its 2005 decision *Roper v. Simmons*. In concluding that it was unconstitutional to subject anyone younger than 18 to the death penalty, Kennedy J. held for the majority in a 5-4 decision that young persons were less morally culpable than adults by virtue of their youth. After reviewing relevant scientific and sociological literature, Kennedy J. found for the majority, *inter alia*, that

---

[141] Canada, House of Commons, *Renewing Youth Justice: Thirteenth Report of the Standing Committee on Justice and Legal Affairs* (Ottawa: Public Works and Government Services, 1997), c. 2 at 5.

[142] [1993] S.C.J. No. 14, [1993] 2 S.C.R. 421 (S.C.C.).

[143] *R. v. J.J.M.*, [1993] S.C.J. No. 14, [1993] 2 S.C.R. 421 (S.C.C.).

[144] The *Juvenile Delinquents Act* epitomizes the concept that young persons are to be held less accountable than adults for criminal conduct. But see more recently Lamer J.'s comments in *Reference re Young Offenders Act (P.E.I.)*, [1990] S.C.J. No. 60, [1991] 1 S.C.R. 252 (S.C.C.), and more recently, the pronouncement of the Supreme Court of Canada in *R. v. D.B.*, [2008] S.C.J. No. 25, 2008 SCC 25 (S.C.C.), where Abella J. says at para. 41 that young persons are entitled to a presumption of diminished moral blameworthiness or culpability because their younger age renders them more vulnerable, less mature and less capable of moral judgement.

[145] *YOA*, s. 3(1)(a.1) and (c).

young persons under 18 lack maturity and have an underdeveloped sense of responsibility that can result in impetuous and ill-considered actions and decisions.[146]

The phrase "fair and proportionate accountability" in the *YCJA* is a concept unique to young persons who are being dealt with under the *YCJA*. The terms "greater dependency" and "reduced level of maturity" that are integrally linked to it have been characterized as "classic justifications for imposing mitigated punishments on juvenile offenders; [footnote omitted] as such, they represent the first direction to judges that the severity of sentences in youth justice court should be less than that of sentences imposed in adult criminal courts".[147] This principle is also reflected in the lesser sentences that can be imposed on young persons under the *YCJA* as compared to the *Criminal Code*. A young person can receive a maximum 10-year sentence upon a finding of guilt for first degree murder under the *YCJA*,[148] compared with a life sentence if convicted under the adult sentencing regime in the *Criminal Code*. Even when a young person is sentenced as an adult for first degree murder, they are eligible for parole earlier than an adult.[149]

The principle of proportionate accountability in s. 3 of the *YCJA* is not equivalent to the fundamental principle of proportionality for adults under s. 718.1 of the *Criminal Code*, which states that the sentence must be proportionate to the gravity of the offence and the degree of responsibility of the offender. The *Criminal Code* notion of proportionality is present in the *YCJA*, but it is found in the Purpose and Principles of Sentencing under s. 38 of the Act, in s. 38(2)(c), which states that a youth sentence must be proportionate to the seriousness of the offence and the degree of responsibility of the young person for that offence.

Proportionality of this kind was not an express principle under s. 3 of the *YOA*. The Supreme Court of Canada eventually held that it was a principle in the sentencing of young persons under the *YOA* but it was of lesser significance than in the sentencing of an adult.[150]

---

[146]   *Roper v. Simmons*, 543 U.S. 551 (2005).

[147]   Julian V. Roberts and Nicholas Bala, "Understanding Sentencing Under the *Youth Criminal Justice Act*" (2003) 41 Alta. L. Rev. 395, at para. 16 (QL). But see also Andrew von Hirsch, "Proportionate Sentences for Juveniles: How Different Than for Adults?" (2001) 3 Punishment and Society 221.

[148]   *YCJA*, s. 42(2)(q). See also *Criminal Code*, s. 745.

[149]   *Criminal Code*, ss. 745 and 745.1.

[150]   [1993] S.C.J. No. 14, [1993] 2 S.C.R. 421 (S.C.C.).

c.   Section 3(1)(b)(iii) — Enhanced Procedural Protection

The third factor that Canada's youth criminal justice system must emphasize is enhanced procedural protection. While due process and the rights of young persons was a focus of the *YOA*, the express characterization of those rights as *enhanced procedural protection* is another new and significant aspect of the *YCJA*. Young persons are entitled to all of the rights and protections afforded to adults under the *Canadian Bill of Rights* and the *Charter* but, in recognition of their greater vulnerability *vis-à-vis* the state by virtue of their youth and vulnerability, the *YCJA* includes additional protections. In some cases, a young person has greater rights than an adult would have in similar circumstances due to additional protections in the *YCJA*, such as the right to have legal counsel paid for by the state if the young person cannot obtain counsel. An adult can have counsel paid for by the state but in a narrower range of circumstances.[151] The enhanced procedural rights of young persons are emphasized throughout the *YCJA*.

The Supreme Court of Canada has given the concept of enhanced procedural protection in the *YCJA* a liberal interpretation. In *R. v. C. (R.W.)*,[152] Fish J. for the 5-4 majority, restored the decision of a Nova Scotia trial judge, who had refused to grant a DNA order in relation to a 13-year-old boy. The boy had stabbed his mother in the foot with a pen after she dumped a pile of dirty laundry on him as he lay in bed. This decision is significant because of the breadth and scope that Fish J. ascribes to the principles of the *YCJA*, particularly the principles of the diminished accountability of young persons and their enhanced procedural protections. Justice Fish held that the principles of the *YCJA* (and the *YOA* as well) apply to a consideration of whether a DNA order for a young person should issue under s. 487.051 of the *Criminal Code*[153] because Parliament intended that youth justice principles should be respected whenever young persons are brought within the Canadian system of justice. "In creating a separate criminal justice system for young persons, Parliament has recognized the heightened vulnerability and reduced maturity of young persons. In keeping with its international obligations, Parliament has sought as well to extend to young offenders enhanced procedural protections, and to interfere with their personal freedom and privacy as little as possible."[154]

---

[151] See some discussion of this in Nicholas Bala, *Youth Criminal Justice Law* (Toronto: Irwin Law Inc., 2003), at 113-17.

[152] [2005] S.C.J. No. 62, 259 D.L.R. (4th) 1 (S.C.C.).

[153] Amendments to the DNA provisions came into force in 2008, and are discussed in Chapter 6.

[154] *R. v. C. (R.W.)*, [2005] S.C.J. No. 62, at para. 41, 259 D.L.R. (4th) 1 (S.C.C.).

d.   Section 3(1)(b)(iv) and (v)

These two subparagraphs are new in the *YCJA* and reflect beliefs in the mid to late 1990s that responses to offending behaviour have the greatest impact on young persons if there is a short time period between the criminal conduct and the justice system response to that behaviour. In part, this is related to the fact that the research suggests that young persons have shorter memories and a different perception of time.[155] In its report, *Renewing Youth Justice*, the Standing Committee on Justice and Legal Affairs concluded, after hearing from many experts, that responses to youthful offending behaviour did not necessarily have to involve the criminal justice system but the response had to be timely.[156] The federal government adopted this observation in its response to the report when it concluded that long delays between the time an offence is committed and the time formal sentences are imposed can reduce the meaningfulness of the sentence for the offender, the victims and the community.[157] The concern found its way into the *YCJA*.

In interpreting this new provision, in *R. v. S. (L.)*,[158] Gage J. noted that the *YOA* contained no provisions similar to s. 3(1)(b)(iv) and (v). Considering this distinction between the two Declarations of Principle, Gage J. held that the new provisions in the *YCJA* constitute a clear direction from Parliament that the meaning of a (right to) trial within a reasonable time within the context of the youth justice system will be subject to a new paradigm "in which the swift and efficient processing and resolution of criminal charges is a vital, important and statutorily endorsed principle".[159] At the very least, police and officers of the court should

---

[155] Nicholas Bala, *Youth Criminal Justice Law* (Toronto: Irwin Law Inc., 2003), at 110. See also comments on this point in Department of Justice, *A Strategy for the Renewal of Youth Justice* (Ottawa: Ministry of Supply and Services, 1998) (section on Concerns about the Current Youth Justice System). At the time of writing, this 1998 document could still be readily accessed through the Department of Justice website at: <http://www.justice.gc.ca/eng/pi/yj-jj/about-apropos/toc-tdm.html>.

　　Justice Gage accepts the proposition that young persons have a different perception of time in *R. v. S. (L.)*, [2005] O.J. No. 1324, at para. 60 (Ont. C.J.).

[156] Canada, House of Commons, *Renewing Youth Justice: Thirteenth Report of the Standing Committee on Justice and Legal Affairs* (Ottawa: Public Works and Government Services, 1997(2005), c. 2.

[157] Department of Justice, *A Strategy for the Renewal of Youth Justice* (Ottawa: Ministry of Supply and Services, 1998) (section on Concerns about the Current Youth Justice System). At the time of writing, this 1998 document could still be readily accessed through the Department of Justice website at: <http://www.justice.gc.ca/eng/pi/yj-jj/about-apropos/toc-tdm.html>.

[158] *R. v. S. (L.)*, [2005] O.J. No. 1324 (Ont. C.J.).

[159] *R. v. S. (L.)*, [2005] O.J. No. 1324, at para. 29 (Ont. C.J.).

handle the processing of criminal complaints against young persons with a greater sense of urgency than in the adult context.[160]

This analysis was soon to be revisited by the appellate courts, which generally rejected its conclusion. In *R. v. T.R.*,[161] MacPherson J.A., writing for the panel, which also consisted of McMurtry C.J.O., and Laskin J.A., overturned the decision of a youth court judge who held that the new provisions of the *YCJA* imposed an enhanced responsibility on the Crown and police to reduce delay in youth cases. The *YCJA* was merely a codification of the jurisprudence under the *YOA* rather than the harbinger of a new regime, MacPherson J.A. ruled. Although delay that may be reasonable in the adult system may not be reasonable in the youth system, young persons are not entitled to a special constitutional guarantee to trial within a reasonable time. A pronounced judicial focus on ensuring the prompt resolution of youth justice proceedings was a prominent component of the *YOA* and the *YCJA* introduces no change in that regard, MacPherson J.A. held. The new provisions in the *YCJA* do not import a new and special constitutional guarantee for young persons to a trial within a reasonable time that differs in substance from that available to adults.[162]

Following the Ontario Court of Appeal ruling in May 2005, Gage J. again considered the matter in September 2005. While noting that the Ontario Court of Appeal had rejected his reasoning that s. 3 of the Declaration of Principle had fundamentally changed the landscape insofar as the calculus of acceptable delay in youth matters was concerned, Gage J. reiterated his view that s. 3(1)(b)(iv) and (v) constitutes a specific statutory direction that the processing of criminal complaints against young persons should be carried out by police officers and officers of the court with all due dispatch and with a greater sense of urgency than in the adult context.[163] Justice Gage nevertheless accepts the recommended time guidelines of five to six months for youth cases to reach the trial stage in Ontario from the time the charge is laid (minus the intake period), which are spelled out in *R. v. M. (G.C.)* and *R. v. T.R.* In *R. v. T.F.*, Gage J. stops short of expressly saying that the new provisions of the *YCJA* provide young persons with a special constitutional guarantee of the right to be

---

[160] *R. v. S. (L.)*, [2005] O.J. No. 1324, at para. 31 (Ont. C.J.). *R. v. S. (L.)* and related cases are discussed further in Chapter 6 concerning the *Charter* in terms of their impact on the meaning of s. 11(b) for young persons.

[161] [2005] O.J. No. 2150 (Ont. C.A.).

[162] *R. v. T.R.*, [2005] O.J. No. 2150, at para. 31 (Ont. C.A.), where MacPherson J.A. accepts the reasoning of Osborne J.A. in *R. v. M. (G.C.)*, [1991] O.J. No. 885, 3 O.R. (3d) 223 (Ont. C.A.).

[163] *R. v. T.F.*, [2005] O.J. No. 4168, at paras. 24-26 (Ont. C.J.).

tried within a reasonable time. In fact, his comments in *R. v. T.F.* can be read as consistent with those of Osborne J.A. in *R. v. M. (G.C.)* because, although Osborne J.A. denies a special constitutional guarantee for young persons, he makes the point that, as a general proposition, youth court proceedings should proceed to a conclusion more quickly than those in the adult criminal justice system.[164]

This is the essential point made by Gage J. in *R. v. S. (L.)* and *R. v. T.F.*: the *YCJA* provides clear statutory direction that matters involving young persons should proceed though the system with a greater sense of urgency than cases in the adult court. However, as some commentators point out, unless one recognizes this proposition as a new constitutional guarantee, it is nothing more than a theoretical nicety. "If the principle that those responsible for enforcing the Act must act with promptness and speed is to have any relevance in the youth criminal justice system, it surely must be in the context of an accused person's constitutional right to a trial within a reasonable time. Absent such relevance, the principle will have no real meaning and become unenforceable in practice."[165]

In *R. v. R.C.D.*,[166] the British Columbia Court of Appeal upheld the finding of the Ontario Court of Appeal that subparagraphs (iv) and (v) in s. 3(1)(b) merely codify the jurisprudence as it was under the *YOA*. In fact, Hall J.A. suggests that the *YCJA* drafters may have based their wording for these subparagraphs on comments made by Osborne J.A. in *R. v. M. (G.C.)*.

(iii)   Section 3(1)(c) — Measures Taken Within the Limits of Fair and Proportionate Accountability

a.   Section 3(1)(c)(i) — Reinforce Respect for Societal Values

Within the limits of fair and proportionate accountability, the measures taken against young persons who commit offences should reinforce respect for societal values. The use of the phrase "who commit offences" suggests that this subparagraph is intended to apply to young persons who have been found guilty of committing offences, and is thus aimed at the sentencing stage. That said, provided the response recognizes the concept of proportionate accountability, it should reinforce respect for societal

---

[164]   *R. v. M. (G.C.)*, [1991] O.J. No. 885, 3 O.R. (3d) 223 (Ont. C.A.).

[165]   Ian Carter, "Playing the Youth Card: The Impact of the Declaration of Principle in the *Youth Criminal Justice Act*" (2006) 32 C.R. (6th) 232, at 241.

[166]   [2006] B.C.J. No. 947 (B.C.C.A.).

values. This is another principle introduced in the *YCJA* which was not found in the *YOA*.

For purposes of this subparagraph, how are societal values to be determined and defined? In part, one must look to key documents, such as the *Charter*, to identify societal values in Canada. In terms of the criminal law, the *Criminal Code* and other federal statutes are also key sources for the purpose of identifying these values. Societal values in relation to youth crime and how to address it are also to be found in the *YCJA* and the other federal government documents that provide its philosophical foundation, such as *A Strategy for the Renewal of Youth Justice*.[167] Societal values are defined in that document to include responsibility, accountability and respect for people and their property.[168]

While some academics suggest that the judiciary can look to the *Criminal Code* as a key source of societal values,[169] that may prove to be problematic in youth cases because key aspects of the *Criminal Code*, such as the sentencing regime, have been expressly excluded from the *YCJA*. For example, it has been suggested that the Crown could point to aggravating factors in the *Criminal Code* that can be raised when an adult is being sentenced as a source of societal values, such as evidence that the offence was motivated by bias, prejudice or hate based on race, national or ethnic origin, language, colour, religion, sex, age, mental or physical disability, sexual orientation or any other similar factor. The Crown could arguably point to such facts at sentencing in order to argue for a more severe sentence on the basis of s. 3(1)(c)(i).[170] Youth justice expert Nicholas Bala suggests that certain provisions in the *Criminal Code* can be regarded as a source of societal values when dealing with young persons under the *YCJA* to the extent that the provisions are not inconsistent with the *YCJA*.[171] Section 140 of the *YCJA* supports this approach since it says that the provisions of the *Criminal Code* apply to the *YCJA* to the extent that they are not inconsistent

---

[167] Department of Justice, *A Strategy for the Renewal of Youth Justice* (Ottawa: Ministry of Supply and Services, 1998). At the time of writing, this 1998 document could still be readily accessed through the Department of Justice website at: <http://www.justice.gc.ca/eng/pi/yj-jj/about-apropos/toc-tdm.html>.

[168] Department of Justice, *A Strategy for the Renewal of Youth Justice* (Ottawa: Ministry of Supply and Services, 1998) (section on Legislative and Supporting Program Components). At the time of writing, this 1998 document could still be readily accessed through the Department of Justice website at: <http://www.justice.gc.ca/eng/pi/yj-jj/about-apropos/toc-tdm.html>.

[169] Nicholas Bala, *Youth Criminal Justice Law* (Toronto: Irwin Law Inc., 2003), at 95-96.

[170] Nicholas Bala, *Youth Criminal Justice Law* (Toronto: Irwin Law Inc., 2003), at 95-96. See also s. 718.2(a)(i) of the *Criminal Code*.

[171] Nicholas Bala, *Youth Criminal Justice Law* (Toronto: Irwin Law Inc., 2003), at 95-96.

with it. However, s. 50 of the *YCJA*, which is the more specific provision on point, expressly excludes the sentencing regime in the *Criminal Code* with certain exceptions. The aggravating factors in the *Criminal Code* are not among the exceptions. A preferred approach may be to focus on documents such as the *Charter* and the *YCJA*, as well as the youth justice jurisprudence to define societal values in relation to youth crime.

The jurisprudence under the *YCJA* often refers to societal values without defining them. In many cases, the values are patently obvious. For example, one judge imposed a significant custodial sentence in relation to a guilty finding for the sexual assault of a 15-year-old girl while she was unconscious[172] to reinforce respect for societal values without identifying those values. In *R. v. C.M.P.*,[173] however, one of the early sentencing decisions under the *YCJA*, Gorman J. of the Newfoundland and Labrador Provincial Court considered the meaning of societal values. He appeared to agree with earlier decisions of the Supreme Court of Canada that our criminal law is a system of values, that society's basic code of values are enshrined within our substantive criminal law, and that the basic set of communal values shared by all Canadians can be found in the *Criminal Code*.[174] He did not define those values or suggest if they differ in relation to a young person, at least to some degree. In other words, as suggested above, not all of the values expressed in the *Criminal Code* apply to the sentencing of young persons. Denunciation and deterrence are two obvious examples. To some degree, we are left with vague notions of what these societal values are in relation to a youthful offender.

b.   Section 3(1)(c)(ii) — Encourage Repair of Harm to Victims and the Community

The language used in this paragraph is a clear attempt to incorporate principles of restorative justice into the *YCJA*. It is linked to other statements in the Declaration of Principle, which are discussed below.[175]

---

[172] *R. v. K.G.B.*, [2005] N.B.J. No. 433 (N.B.C.A.)
[173] [2003] N.J. No. 277, at paras. 22-26 (N.L. Prov. Ct.).
[174] *R. v. C.M.P.*, [2003] N.J. No. 277, at paras. 22-26 (N.L. Prov. Ct.).
[175] *YCJA*, s. 3(1)(c)(iii) and (d)(ii) and (iii). Repairing harm, victim inclusion and the involvement of families and communities, which are captured by these sections of the *YCJA*, are recognized aspects of restorative justice. See some discussion of this in L. Elliott, "Restorative Justice in Canadian Approaches to Youth Crime: Origins, Practices, and Retributive Frameworks" in K. Campbell, ed., *Understanding Youth Justice in Canada* (Toronto: Pearson Education Canada Inc., 2005), at 252.

c.   Section 3(1)(c)(iii) — Meaningful Measures Involving Family, Community and Others

This is a very general statement aimed at the importance of identifying a response to the criminal conduct that is specifically tailored to the needs of the particular young person, that involves his or her family and the community, and that draws on social supports to the extent feasible to aid in the young person's rehabilitation and reintegration.

d.   Section 3(1)(c)(iv) — Respectful of Gender, Ethnic and Other Differences

Within the limits of fair and proportionate accountability, the measures taken against young persons who commit offences should also respect gender, ethnic, cultural and linguistic differences and respond to the needs of aboriginal young persons and of young persons with special requirements. Again, this section refers to young persons *who commit offences*, which suggests it is aimed at the stage of proceedings *after* a finding of guilt has been imposed. This subparagraph is further qualified by the use of permissive language: the measures contemplated *should*, not *must*, respect gender, ethnic, cultural and linguistic differences and respond to the needs of aboriginal young persons and of young persons with special requirements. This permissive language could be seen to significantly limit the ambit of the subparagraph were it not for the fact that this subparagraph is bolstered by related sections in the sentencing section of the *YCJA*. Repeated references to the needs of aboriginal young persons in particular in both s. 3 and s. 38 are highly significant, as these references were not contained in the *YOA*. At the very least, this subparagraph is designed to raise the consciousness, sensitivity and awareness of decision-makers under the *YCJA* to the potential relevance in youth cases of gender, ethnicity, culture, language, disability or the young person's aboriginal (including Inuit or Métis) heritage. For example, this subparagraph encourages an aboriginal young person to be dealt with by the justice system in accordance with his or her aboriginal values and beliefs, although clearly such values, traditions and beliefs are not homogenous across First Nations and Inuit cultures.

Sections such as this have been controversial for appearing to sanction the special treatment of aboriginal persons.[176] In its report, the

---

[176] See the discussion in Philip Stenning and Julian V. Roberts, "Empty Promises: Parliament, the Supreme Court and the Sentencing of Aboriginal Offenders" (2001) 64 Sask. L. Rev. 137. This subject is discussed at greater length in Chapter 8 concerning sentencing in relation to a similar provision in s. 38(2)(d) of the *YCJA*.

Standing Committee on Justice and Legal Affairs did not generally explore the issues except to acknowledge that one's ancestry, gender, or race may be important in one's contact with the youth justice system.[177]

In its response to that report, the federal government recognized the need to deal fairly and effectively with all young people. In particular, the report noted the disproportionately high level of aboriginal youth in the justice system, especially in custody, and that this overrepresentation highlighted the need for measures that address the root causes of crime, as well as procedures that hold youth accountable in "culturally appropriate" and "meaningful" ways in their communities. The government response also expressed concern about the lack of programs for female offenders.[178]

A related provision specifically targeting aboriginal young persons appears in the sentencing principles of the *YCJA*, where the sentencing judge is directed to consider all available sanctions other than custody that are reasonable in the circumstances, with particular attention to the circumstances of aboriginal young persons.[179] This provision is virtually identical to the sentencing provision in the *Criminal Code* concerning adult aboriginal persons.[180] Youth justice experts contend that these references in s. 3 and in s. 38 reflected the federal government's intention to lower the number of aboriginal youth in custody. At the time the *YCJA* was being finalized, aboriginal Canadians represented about 3 per cent of the general population, but accounted for 17 per cent of provincial admissions to custody. Aboriginal youth accounted for about 5 per cent of the juvenile population while under the *YOA* they accounted for about 25 per cent of sentenced custodial admissions.[181]

In *R. v. Pratt*,[182] which largely concerned whether the sentencing principles in s. 3 of the *YCJA* had any application to a young person who was to receive an adult sentence for manslaughter, Saunders J.A. considered the meaning of s. 3(1)(c)(iv). The court held that this subparagraph provides specific direction regarding the attention that must be given to

---

[177] House of Commons, *Renewing Youth Justice: Thirteenth Report of the Standing Committee on Justice and Legal Affairs* (Ottawa: Public Works and Government Services, 1997), c. 1 at 2.

[178] Department of Justice, *A Strategy for the Renewal of Youth Justice* (Ottawa: Ministry of Supply and Services, 1998) (section on Concerns about the Current Youth Justice System). At the time of writing, this 1998 document could still be readily accessed through the Department of Justice website at: <http://www.justice.gc.ca/eng/pi/yj-jj/about-apropos/toc-tdm.html>.

[179] *YCJA*, s. 38(2)(d).

[180] *Criminal Code*, s. 718.2(e).

[181] J.V. Roberts and N. Bala, "Understanding Sentencing Under the *Youth Criminal Justice Act*" (2003) 41 Alta. L. Rev. 395, at para. 47 (QL).

[182] [2007] B.C.J. No. 670 (B.C.C.A.).

the aboriginal background of a young person. "Parliament has said to the courts that they must respond to the needs of aboriginal young persons that come before them, while maintaining a standard of fair and proportionate accountability. It is a consideration that, if it has any consequence, can only lead to mitigation of sentence, either in duration or as to its terms."[183] Justice Saunders acknowledged that the instruction in s. 3 along with similar instruction in s. 718 of the *Criminal Code* were among the factors considered in reducing the sentence of the 17-year-old aboriginal young person from nine to seven years.

R. v. E.F.[184] also considered the meaning and implications of s. 3(1)(c)(iv). Although the case largely concerned whether the court should designate a certain offence a serious violent offence, the case involved an African Canadian young person, which gave MacLean J. cause to consider the meaning of s. 3(1)(c)(iv). In holding that the *YCJA*, as a whole, is designed to combat systemic racism, he cited s. 3(1)(c)(iv) and related sentencing provisions. "An examination of these provisions leads the Court to conclude that in all sentencing situations, a judge must recognize and consider the race of a young person in the context of the inherent dangers of systemic racism."[185]

The meaning and implications of this subparagraph is discussed further in Chapter 8 in relation to the sentencing principles under the *YCJA*.

(iv) Section 3(1)(d) — Special Considerations in Respect of Young Persons

a. Section 3(1)(d)(i) — Procedural Protections

To further emphasize the rights of young persons under the *YCJA*, s. 3(1)(d)(i) states that special considerations apply in respect of proceedings against young persons and that young persons have rights and freedoms in their own right, such as a right to be heard in the course of and to participate in the processes, *other than the decision to prosecute*, that lead to decisions that affect them, and young persons have special guarantees of their rights and freedoms. This section existed in the *YOA*, with one significant difference. The *YCJA* includes the phrase "other than the decision to prosecute" to emphasize the point that a young person has no right to be heard on the core issue of whether he or she should be prosecuted. The decision to prosecute remains a decision for the Crown. While in practice,

---

[183] *R. v. Pratt*, [2007] B.C.J. No. 670, at para. 81 (B.C.C.A.).
[184] [2007] O.J. No. 1000 (Ont. C.J.).
[185] *R. v. E.F.*, [2007] O.J. No. 1000, at para. 122 (Ont. C.J.).

defence counsel may well have discussions with the Crown regarding whether, from defence counsel perspective, the matter can, or should be, diverted from the court process, this subparagraph clarifies that the young person has no legally enforceable right to a hearing on this point.[186]

This interpretation has been affirmed by the trial court of the Northwest Territories. In a January 2008 decision, Gorin J. accepted the Crown argument that the wording of s. 3(1)(d)(i) of the *YCJA* makes it clear that a young person does not have a right to be heard in relation to the decision to prosecute or, alternatively, with respect to whether the Crown should divert the young person. Whether to proceed with a prosecution remains exclusively a matter of prosecutorial discretion, Gorin J. held. "In my view the wording now contained in subsection 3(1)(d)(i) of the *Youth Criminal Justice Act* is dispositive. I agree with the Crown that it is abundantly clear that in enacting the subsection Parliament intended to provide that a young person does not have a right to be heard in relation to the Crown's decision on whether or not to prosecute. The decision on whether or not to prosecute covers a decision on whether or not to attempt alternative measures either before or after the initial charge has been laid. Consequently, the Crown need not consult with the young person or his counsel when deciding whether or not to offer alternative measures."[187]

That said, the young person certainly retains the right to retain and instruct counsel before deciding whether to participate in an extrajudicial sanction (which is one form of extrajudicial measure) if such a measure is offered,[188] and his or her counsel is free to make submissions to the Crown as to why extrajudicial measures should be used in a given case. But under the *YCJA*, a young person does not have a right to a formal hearing regarding whether the Crown should proceed with the prosecution or divert the young person instead.

Defence counsel had argued that s. 25(1) of the *YCJA* permits a young person or his counsel the right to be involved in the Crown's determination of whether the Crown should attempt to deal with the matter through extrajudicial measures. The Crown successfully argued that the most persuasive jurisprudence under s. 11(1) of the *YOA*, the virtually identical predecessor section to s. 25(1) of the *YCJA*, had held that this section did not entitle the young person to a hearing regarding the

---

[186] *R. v. T. (V.)*, [1992] S.C.J. No. 29, 71 C.C.C. (3d) 32 (S.C.C.) was decided under the *YOA*, but remains good authority for this point. See also *R. v. W. (T.)*, [1986] S.J. No. 182, 25 C.C.C. (3d) 89 (Sask. Q.B.). But see *R. v. B. (J.)*, [1985] B.C.J. No. 9, 20 C.C.C. (3d) 67 (B.C. Prov. Ct.).
[187] *R. v. P.L.N.B.*, [2008] N.W.T.J. No. 1, at para. 29 (N.W.T.T.C.).
[188] *YCJA*, s. 10(2)(d).

decision to divert,[189] and further, that s. 3(1)(d)(i) of the *YCJA* now provides a complete and clear answer to the question.

b. Section 3(1)(d)(ii) and (iii) — Rights of Victims

These subparagraphs, together with s. 12[190] of the *YCJA* and the allusion to the interests of victims in the Preamble, are significant. These principles in the Declaration of Principle in the *YCJA* were not included in the *YOA*, and demonstrate the greater attention and respect that victims are expected to be paid under the modern youth criminal justice system. Within the limits of fair and proportionate accountability, as discussed above, measures taken against young persons who commit offences should encourage the repair of harm done to victims and the community. This phraseology is a clear allusion to restorative justice approaches, which generally mean approaches aimed at healing and restoring the relationship between the offender and the victim as well as restoring the relationship between the offender and the broader community.[191] The new subparagraphs, s. 3(1)(d)(ii) and (iii), are strong reminders to criminal justice system participants within the youth criminal justice system that victims should be treated with courtesy, compassion and respect for their dignity and privacy, and that they are to be inconvenienced as little as possible as a result of having to be involved in the criminal proceeding. These sections also entrench an obligation on the youth criminal justice "system" to provide information about the proceedings to the victim and to also ensure that victims have an opportunity to participate and be heard.[192] Yet, s. 3(1)(d)(iii) does not identify which youth criminal justice system participants are expected to supply such information to victims or to ensure that the victims participate in the proceeding and are heard. Obviously the parties who deal most with alleged victims during criminal proceedings are the police and the Crown prosecutors, although in some jurisdictions, including the three Northern territories, victim witness co-ordinators play a key support role to victims and supply a great deal of information to them concerning how the criminal process works.

---

[189] *R. v. W. (T.)*, [1986] S.J. No. 182, 25 C.C.C. (3d) 89 (Sask. Q.B.).

[190] Section 12 of the *YCJA* relates to the victim's right to be given information, upon request, concerning a young person who has been dealt with by an extrajudicial sanction. It is discussed in Chapter 5, which concerns extrajudicial measures under the *YCJA*.

[191] Nicholas Bala, *Youth Criminal Justice Law* (Toronto: Irwin Law Inc., 2003), at 121.

[192] Amendments to the *YOA* in 1995 provided for the admissibility of Victim Impact Statements in youth court proceedings. Section 50 of the *YCJA* clarifies that such statements are admissible in youth court proceedings based on the same rules regarding their admission in adult proceedings pursuant to s. 722 of the *Criminal Code*.

Generally speaking, these subparagraphs emphasize the respect that should be shown alleged victims during criminal proceedings but, in fact, these subparagraphs have little practical or legal significance. They do not place specific legal obligations on particular criminal justice system participants such as the Crown, for example, to keep victims informed of the status of proceedings, although this will generally be a matter of best practice.

These principles concerning victims that are now entrenched in the *YCJA* arguably transcend the youth criminal justice system and should apply to the criminal justice system generally. That valid observation aside, they are unquestionably now express principles in the *YCJA*. Academics reason that the *YOA* was developed at a time when the emphasis in criminal justice was on the accused and the state. By contrast, the *YCJA* was developed in the late 1990s when there was increasing recognition of the concerns of victims and potential victims of crime.[193] These references to victims in the Declaration of Principle in the *YCJA* have been described as an "important addition" that "affirms that crime victims have assumed a significant role in youth justice".[194]

c.   Section 3(1)(d)(iv) — Involvement of Persons

The basic premise of this subparagraph, when considered in combination with s. 3(1)(c)(iii), which is discussed briefly above, is that it is expected that young persons will have a better chance of resolving the underlying problems that have led to their criminality if they have the support and involvement of their parents or other supportive individuals or agencies during their rehabilitation, where appropriate.[195] "Parent" is defined in s. 2 of the *YCJA* to include any person who is under a legal duty to provide for the young person or any person who has, in law or in fact, the custody or control of the young person but does not include a person who has the custody or control of the young person by reason only of proceedings under the *YCJA*.

---

[193]   Kent Roach, "The Role of Crime Victims Under the *Youth Criminal Justice Act*" (2003) 40 Alta. L. Rev. 965, at para. 1 (QL).

[194]   Kent Roach, "The Role of Crime Victims Under the *Youth Criminal Justice Act*" (2003) 40 Alta. L. Rev. 965, at para. 1 (QL).

[195]   Nicholas Bala, *Youth Criminal Justice Law* (Toronto: Irwin Law Inc., 2003), at 123-30.

(v)   Section 3(2) — The Doctrine of Liberal Construction

The wording of this subsection is virtually identical to the wording under the *YOA*. The jurisprudence under the *YOA* is therefore instructive. In *R. v. S. (S.)*,[196] Dickson C.J.C. acknowledged that s. 3(2) dictates that a liberal interpretation be given to the Act but that such an interpretation does not require the abandonment of the basic principles of statutory interpretation nor does it preclude resort to the ordinary meaning of words in interpreting a statute. In other words, s. 3(2) should not be permitted to allow a more liberal interpretation of sections of the Act, including s. 3(1), than would be permissible under the normal and accepted rules of statutory interpretation. Chief Justice Dickson's approach to s. 3(2) was adopted in *R. v. T. (V.)*.[197]

In interpreting the *YCJA*, the judiciary often cite and refer to s. 3(2) when they wish to emphasize the broad and liberal interpretation that is to be given to various sections of the Act. In *R. v. Pratt*,[198] Saunders J.A. of the British Court of Appeal relied on s. 3(2) in part to conclude that the principles in s. 3 of the *YCJA* apply to a young person who is being sentenced as an adult pursuant to s. 74 of the *YCJA*.

Section 3(2) has also been cited to emphasize the need to interpret broadly the enhanced procedural protections provided for in the *YCJA*, such as protections relating to the taking of a statement from a young person under s. 146 of the *YCJA*[199] or the privacy rights of a young person.[200]

Section 12 of the federal *Interpretation Act* makes the related point that every federal Act is deemed remedial, and shall be given such fair, large and liberal construction and interpretation as best ensures the attainment of its objects.[201] The challenge in applying s. 12 of the *Inter-pretation Act* to key sections of the *YCJA*, such as the pivotal s. 3(1), is that some of the objectives described in s. 3(1) conflict with one another. When the objectives of an Act are unclear or contradictory, how does a judge practically apply s. 12 of the *Interpretation Act*?

---

[196]   [1990] S.C.J. No. 66, [1990] 2 S.C.R. 254 (S.C.C.).
[197]   [1992] S.C.J. No. 29, 71 C.C.C. (3d) 32 (S.C.C.). See also *R. v. Z. (D.A.)*, [1992] S.C.J. No. 80, at para. 47, [1992] 2 S.C.R. 1025 (S.C.C.).
[198]   [2007] B.C.J. No. 670, at para. 51 (B.C.C.A.).
[199]   *R. v. S.S.*, [2007] O.J. No. 2552, at paras. 27-31 (Ont. C.A.).
[200]   *R. v. Sheik-Qasim*, [2007] O.J. No. 4799 (Ont. S.C.).
[201]   R.S.C. 1985, c. I-21, s. 12.

IV. CONCLUSION

Despite significant substantive additions to the Declaration of Principle in the *YCJA* that distinguish it from its counterpart in the *YOA*, the overarching philosophy of the *YCJA*, as demonstrated largely by the Preamble and the Declaration of Principle, lacks clarity, coherence and cohesiveness. It remains largely a series of often conflicting values and principles that are not prioritized. No principle is identified as the fundamental or most important principle of the youth criminal justice system, with the exception that the principle of proportionality in the sentencing of young persons under s. 38 of the *YCJA* is given more importance than certain other principles in that section.

The other key exception to the general absence of a hierarchy of principles in s. 3 of the *YCJA* is that the *YCJA* generally is imbued with the overarching philosophical premise that incarceration and judicial responses generally are to be used with restraint, particularly in relation to non-violent and first-time offenders and certainly in relation to young persons who commit minor offences. This premise was present in the *YOA* but it has assumed greater importance in the *YCJA*.

That said, only a hierarchy of principles, where the principles of the youth criminal justice system are ranked and prioritized in order of importance, will provide decision-makers with clear direction from Parliament.

Chapter 4

PROCEDURES AND PROCESS UNDER THE YOUTH CRIMINAL JUSTICE ACT

I. OVERVIEW

The *Youth Criminal Justice Act* is largely a procedural Act. It establishes a specific procedural scheme to guide the prosecution of young persons who commit offences[1] under other federal Acts, such as the *Criminal Code* and the *Controlled Drugs and Substances Act*. As a general rule, the *YCJA* does not contain offences.[2] By contrast, when adults are charged with offences under the *Criminal Code*, both the substantive offences and the procedures are found in the *Criminal Code*.

The establishment of a specific procedural code in the *YCJA* achieves two fundamental objectives: it enables the state to provide young persons with enhanced procedural protections throughout the criminal process in recognition of their youth, and it creates more informal and expeditious proceedings, both of which are considered to be in the best interests of young persons.

Regarding the first objective, the *YCJA* adopts the procedures in the *Criminal Code* as a general rule and then modifies these procedures to provide enhanced procedural protections to young persons throughout the

---

[1] An offence is defined in s. 2 of the *Youth Criminal Justice* Act, S.C. 2002, c. 1 [hereafter "*YCJA*"] as an offence under an Act of Parliament, in other words, a federal offence. In practice, this generally means criminal offences that are set out in either the *Criminal Code*, R.S.C. 1985, c. C-46 or the *Controlled Drugs and Substances Act*, S.C. 1996, c. 19. In addition to the procedures spelled out in the *YCJA*, s. 17 of the *YCJA* empowers the youth justice court in a province (which includes a territory by virtue of the *Interpretation Act*, R.S.C. 1985, c. I-21, s. 35) to regulate the practice and procedure within the jurisdiction of the youth justice court. See also s. 155 of the *YCJA* re the powers of the Governor in Council to make regulations to establish uniform rules of court that apply to youth justice courts across Canada.

[2] But see ss. 136-139 of the *YCJA* regarding the offences that are created under the *YCJA*, such as failing to comply with a youth sentence or the offences of wrongly publishing the identity of a young person or wrongly disclosing information about a young person.

criminal process.[3] Section 140 of the *YCJA* stipulates that the provisions of the *Criminal Code* apply in relation to offences alleged to have been committed by young persons, with any modifications that the circumstances require, *except to the extent that these provisions are inconsistent with or excluded by the YCJA.* The following examples illustrate the point: the *YCJA* expressly says that, subject to certain exceptions that are identified in the *YCJA*,[4] Part XXIII of the *Criminal Code* (the sentencing regime) does not apply to *YCJA* proceedings.[5] The sentencing provisions and principles of the *Criminal Code* generally do not apply to youth sentences imposed under the *YCJA* because the *YCJA* has its own specific sentencing principles in ss. 38 and 39 that govern these sentences. By contrast, the *YCJA* is clear that the bail provisions of the *Criminal Code* apply to young persons who are being dealt with in youth justice court[6] subject to specific provisions in the *YCJA* that circumscribe the general bail procedure under the *Criminal Code*.[7] As this chapter demonstrates, however, it is not always clear when a provision of the *Criminal Code* is inconsistent with or excluded by the *YCJA*.

The second major purpose of this specific procedural code in the *YCJA* is that it generally provides for expeditious proceedings in youth cases. Regardless of whether the young person is charged with a summary or indictable offence, the proceedings in youth justice court follow the procedural rules that apply to summary conviction offences under Part XXVII of the *Criminal Code*.[8] As a result, youth justice court proceedings are generally shorter, more informal and less complex than the proceedings that apply to indictable offences in adult court. This ensures that youth justice court proceedings proceed as expeditiously as possible, and are not unacceptably intimidating for young persons, in light of their reduced age, maturity and sophistication, and their general lack of familiarity with criminal law, their constitutional rights, and criminal justice proceedings generally.[9]

Although the procedures that apply to summary conviction matters in adult court generally apply to all criminal offences dealt with in youth

---

[3]   These enhanced protections in the *YCJA* are discussed in Chapter 7 of this text.

[4]   One of the key exceptions outlined in s. 50 is that the sentencing regime in the *Criminal Code* applies to young persons who receive adult sentences. See also s. 74 of the *YCJA*. The dangerous and long-term offender regimes in the *Criminal Code* also apply to young persons who receive adult sentences.

[5]   *YCJA*, s. 50.

[6]   *YCJA*, s. 28.

[7]   *YCJA*, ss. 29-33. These sections are discussed in detail later in this chapter.

[8]   *YCJA*, s. 142.

[9]   See some discussion of this in Nicholas Bala, *Youth Criminal Justice Law* (Toronto: Irwin Law Inc., 2003), at 353-54.

justice court, regardless of whether the offence itself is summary, indictable, or hybrid, the offence retains its fundamental characteristics. For example, if the young person is charged with an indictable offence, the young person will be subject to stiffer penalties, a record of the offence can be retained for a longer period of time than the record of a summary offence, the young person can be subject to an adult sentence in certain circumstances, and there is generally no limitation period on the prosecution of the offence. Conversely, a summary offence involves less severe penalties, a record of the offence can be retained for a shorter period of time, the young person is not at risk of receiving an adult sentence, and the limitation period for the prosecution of a summary offence is generally six months from the date that the subject matter of the offence arose.[10]

Preliminary inquiries and jury trials are generally not part of procedures in youth justice court although a young person can choose to have a preliminary inquiry in certain circumstances[11] and also has a constitutional right to a jury trial in the same circumstances as an adult.[12] A young person charged with murder, for example, which has a maximum youth sentence of 10 years, can choose to have a preliminary inquiry and a jury trial. A young person facing certain other serious charges that could result in an adult sentence also has the right to choose to have a preliminary inquiry and a jury trial.[13] When a young person elects a jury trial, the superior court will be deemed to be a youth justice court for the purpose of the proceeding so that the young person retains the procedural protections of the *YCJA* during that trial.[14] If the young person has requested a preliminary inquiry, the preliminary inquiry will generally be conducted in youth justice court by a youth justice court judge and the trial will occur in superior court.[15]

---

[10] *Criminal Code*, s. 786(2).

[11] This point is discussed later in this chapter in relation to procedures regarding adult sentences.

[12] The *Canadian Charter of Rights and Freedoms*, Part I of the *Constitution Act, 1982*, being Schedule B to the *Canada Act 1982* (U.K.), 1982, c. 11, s. 11(f) [hereafter "*Charter*"] provides that any person charged with an offence has the right to the benefit of a jury trial, where the maximum penalty for the offence is five years in prison or a more severe penalty (except in the case of an offence under military law, tried before a military tribunal).

[13] *YCJA*, ss. 66 and 67.

[14] *YCJA*, s. 13(3).

[15] While a Justice of the Peace can technically conduct a preliminary inquiry, as a matter or practice, preliminary inquiries are routinely conducted by provincial court judges.

II.   COMMENCING PROCEEDINGS UNDER THE YCJA

During any interaction between the police and a young person who is alleged to have committed an offence, a police officer can exercise his or her discretion[16] and choose not to charge the young person. In fact, the *YCJA* now obliges police officers to consider in every case, prior to initiating court proceedings, whether it would be sufficient instead to take no further action, to give the young person a warning, to caution the young person, or, with the young person's consent, to refer the young person to a community program or agency.[17] Nevertheless, the failure of the police officer to consider any of these options does not invalidate any charges flowing from the interaction. Assuming the police have reasonable grounds to believe that the young person has committed an offence, the police may decide to charge the young person rather than diverting him or her from the formal court process by exercising any of the options available to a peace officer under s. 6 or 7 of the *YCJA*. The formal court process begins by the swearing of an information before a justice.[18]

Although the police may be more likely to divert young persons as compared to adults, the police can arrest young persons in the same circumstances and on the same grounds that permit the arrest of adults under the criminal law.[19] That said, upon the arrest of a young person, there are immediate obligations on the police to comply with the enhanced procedural protections to which young persons are entitled under the *YCJA*. For example, any time the police initiate formal proceedings against a young person, even if the police are not detaining the young person in custody and are merely issuing to the young person a summons or appearance notice, or are releasing the young person on a promise to appear, an undertaking or recognizance, the parents of the young person must be notified.[20] Young persons who are arrested for less serious offences are generally released on an appearance notice or a recognizance or undertaking, but the police may decide to detain a young person pending a bail hearing, also known as a show-cause hearing, if he or she is

---

[16]   The classic case on police discretion is *R. v. Metropolitan Police Commissioner, Ex Parte Blackburn*, [1968] 1 All E.R. 763, at 769.

[17]   *YCJA*, s. 6. Section 6 is contained in Part 1 of the *YCJA*, which concerns extrajudicial measures (ss. 4-12). Extrajudicial measures are discussed in Chapter 5.

[18]   See s. 788 of the *Criminal Code* in relation to summary conviction matters and ss. 504 and 505 in relation to indictable offences. Pursuant to s. 162 of the *YCJA*, the *YCJA* can be taken to define the commencement of proceedings as the laying of an information or an indictment.

[19]   See Part XV of the *Criminal Code*, ss. 494 to 514. See also *R. v. Storrey*, [1990] S.C.J. No. 12, [1990] 1 S.C.R. 241 (S.C.C.), which defines reasonable and probable grounds for arrest.

[20]   *YCJA*, s. 26.

facing a serious charge or has a record, or if there are concerns the young person would not appear in court if released.[21]

The enhanced procedural protections afforded young persons become evident at the point of detention or arrest. These enhanced protections reinforce, and, in some cases, augment, protections provided under the *Canadian Charter of Rights and Freedoms*. From the point of detention, the arresting officer or the officer in charge must advise the young person without delay of the right to retain and instruct counsel and give the young person an opportunity to obtain counsel.[22] The form that the young person receives upon release also advises the young person in writing of his or her right to counsel.[23]

During any ensuing bail hearing, the young person not only has a right to be represented by counsel but has a right to have such counsel appointed and paid for by the state if the young person cannot get a lawyer paid for through legal aid.[24] If a Justice of the Peace (JP) is presiding at the bail hearing, which is often the case, the JP must refer the matter to a youth justice court judge for the appointment of counsel in situations where a legal aid program does not exist or the young person is unable to obtain legal representation through the program and wishes to obtain counsel.[25]

III. BAIL UNDER THE YCJA

A. Bail

The *Charter* guarantees to any person charged with an offence the right not to be denied reasonable bail without just cause.[26] Pursuant to s. 28 of the *YCJA*, the bail provisions in Part XVI of the *Criminal Code*, which apply to adult accused, apply to young persons who are being dealt with under the *YCJA*, except to the extent that these provisions are

---

[21] Samples of the forms used to release young persons can be found on the Department of Justice website at: <http://www.justice.gc.ca/eng/pi/yj-jj/repos-depot/Forms/form.html>. Implicit in the wording of these various release forms are the differences among these various forms of release. A recognizance generally involves the young person agreeing to forfeit money if he or she fails to show up in court as required, whereas an undertaking requires the young person to agree to certain specific conditions.

[22] *YCJA*, s. 25(2).

[23] Samples of the forms used to release young persons can be found on the Department of Justice website at: <http://www.justice.gc.ca/eng/pi/yj-jj/repos-depot/Forms/form.html>.

[24] These s. 25 right to counsel protections are discussed in detail in Chapter 7.

[25] *YCJA*, s. 25(6)(b) and (4)(b).

[26] *Charter*, s. 11(e).

inconsistent or excluded by the *YCJA*. In other words, the bail scheme set out in s. 515 of the *Criminal Code* applies to young persons, except to the extent that the *YCJA* circumscribes its application. Thus, in cases where the police decide to detain the young person, that young person, similar to an adult, must be brought before a judge or Justice of the Peace within 24 hours of his or her arrest, if such a person is available. If such a person is not available, the young person must be brought before the court as soon as possible.[27]

Under the bail provisions in s. 515 of the *Criminal Code*, if the Crown wants to detain an individual in custody, the onus is generally on the Crown[28] to justify to the court or to "show cause" as to why it wishes to do so. The detention of an accused can be justified only on one or more of the following grounds in s. 515(10): An individual can be detained on the primary ground, (a) where the detention is necessary to ensure his or her attendance in court in order to be dealt with according to law, (b) on the secondary ground, where the detention is necessary for the protection or safety of the public, including any victim of or witness to the offence, having regard to all of the circumstances, including any substantial likelihood that the accused will, if released from custody, commit a criminal offence or interfere with the administration of justice and (c) on the tertiary ground, if the detention is necessary to maintain confidence in the administration of justice, having regard to all of the circumstances, including the apparent strength of the Crown's case, the gravity of the offence, the circumstances surrounding the commission of the offence, including whether a firearm was used, and the fact that the accused is liable, on conviction, to a potentially lengthy jail term, or in the case of an offence that involves, or whose subject matter is a firearm, a minimum punishment of imprisonment for a term of three years or more.

That said, the *YCJA* limits significantly the application of the bail provisions in the *Criminal Code* to young persons. Sections 29 to 31 of the *YCJA* make it more difficult to detain a young person in custody at the pre-trial stage compared to an adult accused. Under s. 29(1) of the *YCJA*, a young person cannot be denied bail and kept in custody at the pre-trial stage (or at the sentencing stage for that matter)[29] as a substitute for appropriate child protection, mental health or other social measures.[30] By way of example, this means that a youth justice court judge or a Justice of the Peace cannot deny a young person bail because the young person is

---

[27]   *Criminal Code*, s. 503.

[28]   The onus switches to the accused in certain cases when he or she is charged with certain very serious offences. See *Criminal Code*, ss. 515(6) and 522(2).

[29]   *YCJA*, s. 39(5).

[30]   *YCJA*, s. 29(1).

homeless and has nowhere else to go, or even in a case where the young person has indicated that he or she wishes to be detained in order to have a roof over his or her head or a hot meal. It also follows that a justice or judge cannot deny a young person bail under the *YCJA* even if there is evidence that the young person is suicidal and may pose significant harm to himself or herself if released and there is nowhere in the community to send the young person.

Section 29(1) of the *YCJA* is believed to have been a reaction to the Supreme Court of Canada ruling in *R. v. J.J.M.*,[31] in which Cory J. upheld the decision of the lower courts that a two-year open custody sentence was an appropriate and fit sentence for a young person in relation to guilty findings for three property offences and one breach of probation, in part because the young person's home life was intolerable and the young person needed guidance and assistance. Although the majority of the Manitoba Court of Appeal agreed with the trial judge, the dissenting judge would have reduced the open custody period to one year. Justice Helper, in dissent, expressed concern that the sentence was attempting to provide welfare assistance for the young person rather than assessing the appropriate sentence.[32] Justice Helper's concerns appear to have been subsequently codified in s. 29(1), which clarifies that a young person cannot be denied bail to address social or child welfare concerns. A similar provision is contained in s. 39(5) of the *YCJA* to clarify that a young person cannot be sentenced to custody as a substitute for appropriate child protection, mental health or other social measures.

Alternatively, the *YCJA* permits the youth justice court to refer a young person to a child welfare agency at any stage of the proceedings for assessment to determine if the young person is in need of child welfare services.[33] A youth justice court judge also has the power to order a medical, psychological or psychiatric assessment of the young person for the purposes of considering a bail application if the court has reasonable grounds to believe that the young person may be suffering from a physical or mental illness or disorder, a psychological disorder, an emotional disturbance, or a learning or mental disability.[34] The young person can be remanded for up to 30 days for this purpose.[35]

Although presumably drafted in the best interests of young persons, in practice, s. 29(1) can create significant ethical, moral and legal quanda-

---

[31]   [1993] S.C.J. No. 14 (S.C.C.).
[32]   *R. v. M. (J.J.)*, [1993] S.C.J. No. 14 (S.C.C.), as per Cory J.
[33]   *YCJA*, s. 35.
[34]   *YCJA*, ss. 33 and 34.
[35]   *YCJA*, s. 34(3).

ries for prosecutors and judges in some communities where social supports are sorely lacking and there is simply no place in the community for a young person to go. Prosecutors and judges working in small and isolated northern communities in the provinces and in the territories may sometimes find themselves unable to detain young persons due to s. 29(1) in cases where the young person has no safe or appropriate place in the community to go, and there is no child welfare agency in the community to which to refer the young person. Sections 34 and 35 of the *YCJA* are of little practical value to judges when there are no child welfare agencies or qualified persons to whom to refer young persons under these sections.

Provisions such as ss. 29(1), 34 and 35 do not reflect the realities of prosecuting young persons in small, impoverished and isolated northern communities in the three territories or in the northern parts of some provinces, where community social services readily available in the "South" simply do not always exist.

A compelling argument can be made that the *YCJA* should permit the temporary detention of young persons in custody at the pre-trial stage in their best interests, or in the public interest, in various situations, including where they need food and shelter during the harsh Arctic winter or appear to pose a safety risk to themselves and there is nowhere in the community for them to go.

Section 29(2) of the *YCJA* also significantly differentiates the bail regime for young persons from that of adults. Section 29(2) stipulates that the youth justice court judge or justice shall presume that detention of the young person is not necessary on the secondary ground (protection or safety of the public) unless the young person could be committed to custody under s. 39(1)(a) to (c) upon a finding of guilt for the offence. In other words, during the bail hearing, the bail judge must consider s. 39(1)(a) to (c) of the *YCJA* and *presume* that denial of bail is not an option on the secondary ground unless the young person has committed a violent offence, has failed to comply with non-custodial sentences or has committed an indictable offence for which an adult would be liable to more than two years in prison and also has a history that indicates a pattern of findings of guilt under either the *Young Offenders Act* or the *YCJA*.[36]

Key to understanding this presumption, however, is the fact that it is only a *presumption* against custody on the secondary ground unless the young person has committed an offence that could result in a custodial sentence under s. 39(1)(a) to (c) upon a guilty finding. *Presumptions are distinguishable from prohibitions and are rebuttable.* When attempting to

---

[36]   The meaning of the terms in s. 39(1)(a) to (c) is discussed in detail in Chapter 8.

show cause in a given case, the Crown must identify this distinction. The presumption *can* be rebutted and a young person can be ordered detained on the secondary ground even if they have committed an offence that does not fit into any of the categories in s. 39(1)(a) to (c). It is possible, legal, and sometimes appropriate for a justice or judge to deny a young person bail on the secondary ground even if the young person could not be sentenced to custody under s. 39(1)(a) to (c) upon a guilty finding for the offence.[37]

On the other hand, the presumption does not apply if the facts are such that the young person fits into any of the categories in s. 39(1)(a) to (c), and the young person can be denied bail.[38]

Regarding the meaning of s. 39(1)(a), the Supreme Court of Canada has now defined a violent offence to mean an offence in which the young person causes, attempts to cause or threatens to cause bodily harm.[39]

In relation to s. 39(1)(b), a young person who repeatedly fails to comply with the conditions of one sentence retains the benefit of the presumption against custody in relation to this paragraph. Rather, the Crown must be able to show that the young person has failed to comply with at least two separate non-custodial sentences, such as violating two separate probation orders.[40] Multiple breaches of a single sentence are not adequate to engage the section. For example, two breaches under s. 137 of the *YCJA* that relate to the same probation order will not qualify.[41] This requires the prosecutor to lead evidence that the young person has failed

---

[37]   The following cases are examples of situations where the circumstances were such that the judge or justice found that the presumption had been rebutted, and ordered the young person detained. In *R. v. T.S.*, [2003] B.C.J. No. 1066 (B.C. Prov. Ct.), the court found that continuous breaches and the alleged commission of further offences were sufficient to rebut the presumption. In *R. v. A.S.D.*, [2003] B.C.J. No. 1831 (B.C. Prov. Ct.), the young person continued to breach his releases but had not yet been convicted of a breach. The court concluded that the young person was spiralling out of control and that the presumption against custody had been rebutted. Finally, in *R. v. H.E.*, [2003] N.J. No. 299 (N.L. Prov. Ct.), the court concluded that, relative to the secondary ground, at a certain point the Crown cannot continue to consent to the young person's release when the young person continues to commit offences after being released, regardless of how minor those offences may be. The judge held that releasing the young person on another undertaking was tantamount to inviting him to breach. See also *R. v. D.W.*, [2006] S.J. No. 683, at paras. 9-10 (Sask. Q.B.), and *R. v. W.S.C.*, [2003] S.J. No. 18, at para. 23, 240 Sask. R. 117 (Sask. Prov. Ct.).

[38]   Section 39(1)(a) to (c) is discussed at length in Chapter 8.

[39]   *R. v. C.D.; R. v. C.D.K.*, [2005] S.C.J. No. 79 (S.C.C.). Bodily harm includes physical or psychological harm.

[40]   *R. v. A.M.*, [2007] N.J. No. 76, at paras. 31 and 33 (N.L. Prov. Ct.); *R. v. J.S.*, [2004] O.J. No. 754 (Ont. C.J.).

[41]   *R. v. A.M.*, [2007] N.J. No. 76, at paras. 28 and 29 (N.L. Prov. Ct.).

to comply[42] with at least two separate non-custodial sentences. Repeatedly breaching bail conditions or undertakings does not bring one within s. 39(1)(b).[43] Breaches of release orders under s. 145 of the *Criminal Code* are not caught by the section. A complicating factor in relation to s. 39(1)(b) is that a number of offences are sometimes lumped together and dealt with simultaneously so that a young person receives one sentence in relation to a number of offences.[44]

In order for a young person to be denied bail on the secondary ground on the basis that he or she could get sentenced to custody upon a guilty finding for the offence under s. 39(1)(c), the prosecutor must be able to show that the young person is alleged to have committed an indictable offence for which an adult would be liable to imprisonment for more than two years *and* the young person has a *history* that indicates a *pattern* of findings of guilt under the *YCJA* or under the *Young Offenders Act*. Varying judicial interpretations of terms such as "history", and "pattern of findings of guilt" have created confusion and a lack of uniformity across the country regarding the meaning of this phrase. The Supreme Court of Canada clarified the meaning of the phrase "a history that indicates a pattern of findings of guilt" in 2008 when it held in *R. v. S.A.C.*[45] that the only guilty findings to be considered for the purposes of the provision are the ones that were entered prior to the commission of the offence for which the young person is being sentenced. Further, to show a pattern of findings of guilt, the Crown is required, as a general rule, to adduce evidence of a minimum of three prior guilty findings, unless the court finds that the offences are so similar that a pattern can be found in only two prior guilty findings. Therefore in order to rebut the presumption on the grounds that the facts of the case bring the young person within s. 39(1)(c), the Crown must consider whether the young person he or she is trying to detain is charged with an indictable offence for which an adult would be liable to more than two years in custody *and* whether three guilty findings (or possibly two, depending on the facts) had been entered against the young person prior to the commission of the offence for which the Crown now wishes to detain the young person at the pre-trial stage.

---

[42]   The jurisprudence suggests that failing to comply does not require a guilty finding, only evidence of failing to comply. See *R. v. J.E.C.*, [2004] B.C.J. No 2244 (B.C.S.C.).

[43]   *R. v. O.J.R.*, [2008] B.C.J. No. 1110 (B.C. Prov. Ct.).

[44]   Among the amendments contained in Bill C-25, which died on the Order Paper in the fall of 2008, was an amendment to s. 39(1)(b), which would have allowed for a young person to be detained in custody for breaches of non-custodial sentences *or release orders*. The plural wording of the terms suggests this to mean that at least two breaches are required.

[45]   [2008] S.C.J. No. 48, 2008 SCC 47 (S.C.C.).

This provision has proven problematic when superimposed on the daily workings of the court. In practice, a young person may be facing multiple charges but these charges are sometimes lumped together and dealt with all at once at the time of sentencing. It is sometimes the case that findings of guilt are not entered until the time of sentencing in relation to these charges, leading to arguments that the young person has *no history* that indicates a pattern of findings of guilt at this stage (unless there is a previous record). The current wording also fails to capture a situation where the young person is charged with a slew of offences in a short span of time and is arguably spiralling out of control but has not yet received any findings of guilt or has not received enough findings of guilt to constitute a pattern.[46] Thus, a young person who gets picked up for several trafficking and related drug charges within a couple of weeks but has no record other than pending matters has the presumption in his or her favour.

A young person can also be detained on the tertiary ground. While detention on these grounds is less common, it does happen.[47]

The *YCJA* also provides that a young person who would otherwise be denied bail can be placed in the care of a responsible person, provided both parties are willing. In fact, if the justice or judge has decided to detain the young person, he or she is obligated to inquire as to the availability of a responsible person in the community willing and able to take care of and exercise control over the young person and the young person's willingness to be placed in that person's care.[48] This provision is another illustration of the underlying objective of the *YCJA* to restrict the use of custody for young persons, a principle that has been clearly and repeatedly recognized by the Supreme Court of Canada[49] since the *YCJA* came into force in 2003.

Generally, a Justice of the Peace will preside at the bail hearing, since the *YCJA* permits JPs to perform most functions that a JP can

---

[46]   As previously mentioned, the Nunn Commission has recommended (Recommendation 17) that the Public Prosecution Service of Nova Scotia continue its practice of requesting that a presiding judge make a finding of guilt as required under s. 36 of the *YCJA* at the time a young person pleads guilty to a charge, not at the time of sentencing.

[47]   See *R. v. M. (E.W.)*, [2006] O.J. No. 3654 (Ont. C.A.); *R. v. C.P.*, [2006] O.J. No. 3709 (Ont. S.C.) and, in particular, *R. v. A.M.*, [2007] N.J. No. 65 (N.L. Prov. Ct.), where a 14-year-old girl without a record or any outstanding charges was charged with 61 breaches of curfew conditions in release orders. The court found that she displayed a total disregard for court orders and that her detention was required to maintain confidence in the administration of justice.

[48]   *YCJA*, s. 31(1) and (2).

[49]   See for example comments from Bastarache J. in *R. v. C.D.; R. v. C.D.K.*, [2005] S.C.J. No. 79, at para. 35 (S.C.C.).

perform in adult court.[50] However, the *YCJA* provides that, following the order of the JP, an application can be made at any time to the youth justice court for the release from or detention of the young person and the youth justice court shall hear the matter as an original "*de novo*" application.[51] The party that is seeking the bail hearing before the youth justice court must give the other party two days clear notice[52] unless the parties waive this requirement.

The young person also has the right to have the decision of the youth justice court judge in relation to the bail application reviewed by a higher court.[53] The *YCJA* sets out very specific rules in that regard. The young person cannot apply under s. 520 for a review of a bail order made by a Justice of the Peace. The young person must first have the JP order reviewed by a youth justice court judge. The young person can then apply to have the order of the youth justice court judge reviewed under s. 520, if appropriate. An application under s. 520 or 521 of the *Criminal Code* for a review of an order by a youth justice court judge who is a superior court judge must be made to the Court of Appeal.[54] If a young person is charged with an offence listed in s. 522 of the *Criminal Code*, which generally means s. 469 offences, such as murder, the *YCJA* stipulates that a youth justice court judge, but no other court, judge or justice, may release the young person from custody.[55] A decision made by a youth justice court judge in these circumstances can be reviewed by the Court of Appeal pursuant to s. 680 of the *Criminal Code*.[56]

---

[50]   A JP cannot conduct the bail hearing of a young person in relation to murder. See *YCJA*, s. 33(8). It is the submission of this author that s. 33(8) is clear that only a youth justice court judge can preside over such bail hearings. However, see the case law discussion of this matter in Chapter 2.

[51]   *YCJA*, s. 33.

[52]   *YCJA*, s. 33(2) and (3).

[53]   Section 33 of the *YCJA* spells out specific rules in this regard: see s. 33(5) to (9). It is submitted that these provisions prevail in the event of a conflict between s. 33 and the bail provisions of the *Criminal Code*, such as ss. 520-522 of the *Criminal Code*. The relationship between the bail sections in the *YCJA* and those in the *Criminal Code*, and, in particular, which court has jurisdiction over bail applications involving young persons, is discussed in Chapter 2 concerning jurisdiction.

[54]   *YCJA*, s. 33(5).

[55]   *YCJA*, s. 33(8). Presumably, this means that a youth justice court judge is only a person who has been appointed or designated as a judge of the youth justice court or a judge sitting in a court established or designated as a youth justice court as defined by s. 13. It therefore appears that the intent of this section was to exclude superior court judges from presiding over bail hearings in relation to s. 469 offences involving young persons, since s. 13 appears to permit superior court judges to act as youth justice court judges only in relation to the trial proper once the young person has elected trial by a judge without a jury or elects or is deemed to have elected to be tried by judge and jury.

[56]   *YCJA*, s. 33(9).

If a young person is refused bail in relation to any offence except for murder, that decision must be reviewed every 30 days for a summary offence and every 90 days for a hybrid or pure indictable offence.[57]

The *YCJA* bail regime is excessively complex for busy practitioners, and has been the subject of considerable criticism for this reason as well as for the limits it imposes on the detention of young persons at the pre-trial stage. Among the most prominent critics of the current bail regime under the *YCJA* is D. Merlin Nunn, the former Nova Scotia Supreme Court judge who chaired the commission of inquiry into the 2004 death of 52-year-old Theresa McEvoy.[58] The teacher's assistant was killed by a 16-year-old young person who was released on bail while facing many outstanding charges. The young person was joyriding in a stolen car when he went through a red light on a Halifax street and crashed into her vehicle.

In his report, Nunn made 34 recommendations for changes to the youth justice system in Nova Scotia. Several of them relate to the bail regime under the *YCJA*. He suggested that the province of Nova Scotia advocate for changes to the definition of a violent offence, so that the definition also captures conduct that endangers or is likely to endanger the life or safety of another person, and that s. 39(1)(c) be amended so that both a young person's prior findings of guilt as well as pending charges can be considered when determining if denial of bail is appropriate.

Perhaps most important for practitioners, Nunn recommended that the province of Nova Scotia press the federal government to simplify the bail regime so that s. 29 stands alone, without Crowns and defence counsel having to read it in conjunction with s. 39 of the *YCJA*.[59]

It may also make sense to include an "exceptional cases" category or residual clause in the *YCJA* bail regime, which would allow for the detention of a young person where the circumstances are such that releasing the young person would not be in the public interest, similar to the residual clause that is currently contained in s. 39(1)(d) of the *YCJA*.[60]

---

[57] *Criminal Code*, s. 525. As per s. 522(4), a bail review in relation to a murder charge is not subject to review except in accordance with s. 680 of the *Criminal Code*.

[58] Nova Scotia Nunn Commission of Inquiry, *Spiralling out of Control: Lessons Learned from a Boy in Trouble: Report of the Nunn Commission of Inquiry* (Halifax, NS: Nunn Commission of Inquiry, 2006), available online at: <http://www.gov.ns.ca/just/nunn_commission/_docs/Report_Nunn_Final.pdf>.

[59] Nova Scotia Nunn Commission of Inquiry, *Spiralling out of Control: Lessons Learned from a Boy in Trouble: Report of the Nunn Commission of Inquiry* (Halifax, NS: Nunn Commission of Inquiry, 2006), available online at: <http://www.gov.ns.ca/just/nunn_commission/_docs/Report_Nunn_Final.pdf>, but see Recommendations 21, 22 and 23 in particular.

[60] Bill C-25, which died on the Order Paper when the October 14, 2008 election was called, attempted to address some of these concerns. It is likely that similar amendments will be re-introduced.

As it stands, the exceptional cases category outlined in s. 39(1)(d) does not apply at the bail stage.[61] It applies only at the sentencing stage.

Another question that has arisen among practitioners is whether the reverse onus provisions of the bail regime in the *Criminal Code* are inconsistent with the bail provisions in the *YCJA* and thus, in accordance with s. 28 of the *YCJA*, do not apply to bail hearings involving young persons to the extent of that inconsistency. At this stage, there is no definitive case law on point, although the trend of the courts appears to be that the reverse onus provisions of the bail regime in the *Criminal Code* are not inconsistent with the *YCJA*.[62]

B.   Place of Temporary Detention

In keeping with the general principle in the *YCJA* that the criminal justice system for young persons must be separate from that of adults,[63] s. 30 of the *YCJA* provides that, as a general rule, young persons who are denied bail are to be housed separate and apart from adults unless the judge or justice is satisfied that the young person, due to safety concerns, cannot be detained in a place of detention for young persons or no place of detention for young persons is available within a reasonable distance,[64] which may often be the case in small and isolated communities across the three Northern territories. It is also important to keep in mind that a young person can be transferred to an adult provincial correctional facility during the temporary detention stage once the young person reaches the age of 18. In addition, if the young person is at least 20 at the time his or her temporary detention begins (in a situation, for example, where the person is arrested as an adult for an offence alleged to have occurred when he or she was a young person), the individual is to be detained in a provincial correctional facility for adults.[65]

IV. PREPARING FOR TRIAL

Whether the young person is detained in custody pending trial, the matter will nevertheless be moving forward toward resolution in one

---

[61] *YCJA*, s. 29(2).
[62] *R. v. N.W.*, [2008] N.J. No. 293 (N.L. Prov. Ct.); *R. v. M.K.*, [2006] B.C.J. No. 3576 (B.C. Prov. Ct.); *R. v. J.D.*, [2005] O.J. No. 5729 (Ont. C.J.) and *R. v. T.S.*, [2003] B.C.J. No. 1066 (B.C. Prov. Ct.).
[63] *YCJA*, s. 3(1)(b).
[64] *YCJA*, s. 30(3) and (7).
[65] *YCJA*, s. 30(4) and (5).

form or another, assuming the Crown has decided not to divert the young person from the formal court process after reviewing the file provided by the police.[66] Unless the young person pleads guilty immediately, which would be unusual, the matter will generally involve a number of court appearances and adjournments to provide time for the young person to obtain counsel and for counsel to have a chance to receive and review the Crown disclosure,[67] to consult his or her client, to do legal research if necessary, and to determine the best way to proceed given the facts of the case.

During the first appearance of the young person before a JP or a youth justice court judge, the JP or judge is obliged to have the information or the indictment (the document that sets out the formal charge against the young person) read to the young person unless the young person's lawyer waives this aspect of the process, which is formally known as the arraignment. At this stage, the justice or judge must also advise the young person of the right to retain and instruct counsel if the young person does not yet have a lawyer, and must also advise the young person that he or she could be liable to an adult sentence if such a warning is appropriate.[68]

A. Crown Election

While some offences are purely summary or purely indictable, other offences are hybrid, which means the Crown must elect to proceed either summarily or by indictment and must inform the court and the accused of that decision. Proceeding by indictment means that the Crown considers the matter more serious and that the accused will face a stiffer penalty upon a guilty finding. In youth justice court, when the young person is charged with a hybrid offence, the Crown should advise the judge and the young person, prior to the young person entering a plea, how the Crown has chosen to proceed.[69] Under the *YCJA*, when the Crown has not elected which way to proceed in relation to a hybrid offence, for purposes of appeals, as well as for access to records, the

---

[66] Extrajudicial measures under the *YCJA* are discussed in Chapter 5.

[67] The right of all accused persons, including young persons, to disclosure of the case against them, is discussed in detail in Chapter 6. The seminal case in this area remains *R. v. Stinchcombe*, [1991] S.C.J. No. 83, [1991] 3 S.C.R. 326 (S.C.C.). But see more recently *R. v. McNeil*, [2009] S.C.J. No. 3, 2009 SCC 3 (S.C.C.).

[68] *YCJA*, s. 32(1).

[69] Provided the Crown had no reasonable opportunity to elect prior to plea, an election following the plea may be permitted: *R. v. J. (H.W.)*, [1992] B.C.J. No. 809, 71 C.C.C. (3d) 516 (B.C.C.A.).

Crown is deemed to have elected to have proceeded summarily.[70] Otherwise, based on the jurisprudence, the Crown is generally deemed to have elected to proceed summarily in cases where the Crown has failed to elect, but these cases tend to depend very much on the specific facts of the case.[71]

In the case of hybrid offences, the Crown election should generally be clear prior to the plea being made by the young person. This election is obviously important because it will impact the young person's future decision-making, including in some cases the nature of the plea.

B.   Guilty Pleas

Prior to accepting a guilty plea from a young person, the *YCJA* imposes a host of obligations on criminal justice officials, including the youth justice court judge, to ensure the young person understands the implications of pleading guilty.[72] For example, if a young person is unrepresented, the youth justice court judge, before permitting the young person to plea, must be satisfied that the young person understands the charge, and, if the young person is charged with an offence for which an adult sentence could be imposed, the young person must be advised of the rights that arise from this, including the young person's right to elect his or her mode of trial.[73] If the youth justice court is not satisfied that an unrepresented young person understands the matters that have been explained to him or her under s. 32(3) during the first appearance, the judge must direct that the young person be represented by counsel.[74] When the youth justice court is not satisfied that the young person understands the charge, unless the young person must be put to his or her election, the court must enter a plea of not guilty and proceed with the trial.[75]

---

[70]   *YCJA*, ss. 37 and 121.

[71]   *R. v. M. (F.H.)*, [1984] M.J. No. 458, 14 C.C.C. (3d) 227 (Man. Q.B.). But see *R. v. B. (I.)*, [1994] O.J. No. 2100, 20 O.R. (3d) 341 (Ont. C.A.), where the Ontario Court of Appeal held that the failure of the Crown to elect did not result in the deemed summary procedure in circumstances where the Crown had no opportunity to elect because the arraignment was waived and the indictable procedure could be inferred, since the matter would be statute-barred had the Crown elected to proceed summarily. See more recently *R. v. D.H.*, [2005] M.J. No. 538 (Man. Prov. Ct.), which reviews some of the nuances in the case law, and refers to cases at para. 18, which stand for the principle that in cases where the Crown fails to elect prior to plea the proceedings are deemed to be summary. See *R. v. S.D.*, [1997] N.J. No. 202 (Nfld. C.A.) and *R. v. J. (H.W.)*, [1992] B.C.J. No. 809, 71 C.C.C. (3d) 516 (B.C.C.A.).

[72]   These protections are discussed in Chapter 7.

[73]   *YCJA*, s. 32(3).

[74]   *YCJA*, s. 32(5).

[75]   *YCJA*, ss. 32(4) and 36(2).

While duty counsel are generally available at the courthouse and can provide some legal assistance to young persons, a young person facing a serious charge should have the benefit of legal representation and the *YCJA* goes to considerable lengths to ensure that such representation is provided.[76]

If the young person nevertheless decides to plead guilty after having the opportunity to consult counsel, a hearing will be held during which the Crown will read into the record the facts and evidence that support the charge. The defence counsel or the young person must indicate agreement with the facts as alleged by the Crown. Any disagreement as to the relevant facts that form the basis of the offence must be resolved by way of an amendment to the statement of facts in order for the matter to be resolved without a trial.

Before accepting the guilty plea, the youth justice court judge must be satisfied that the facts support the charge. If the judge is not satisfied that the facts support the charge, the court shall proceed with a trial of the matter.[77]

As discussed in Chapter 7, the protections built into the *YCJA* through sections such as 32 and 36 illustrate the greater protections afforded young persons under the *YCJA* to ensure that they understand their rights and the implications of pleading guilty to a charge.[78] The judge hearing adult matters may not be required to engage in the same level of inquiry but must still nevertheless be satisfied that the adult accused understands the nature and consequences of a guilty plea before the court accepts it.[79]

C.   The Trial

When a youth matter proceeds to trial, the same fundamental rules of criminal law and evidence that apply to adult accused generally apply to young persons. The onus and standard of proof remain the same: The burden is on the Crown to prove the case beyond a reasonable doubt.[80] And the *Canadian Charter of Rights and Freedoms* is no less relevant.

---

[76]   *YCJA*, s. 25. The right to counsel is discussed in Chapter 7.

[77]   *YCJA*, s. 36.

[78]   The issues and concerns that arise in relation to guilty pleas taken from young persons is discussed in *R. v. T.W.B.*, [1998] B.C.J. No. 1044 (B.C.C.A.).

[79]   *Criminal Code*, s. 606.

[80]   *R. v. Lifchus*, [1997] S.C.J. No. 77, [1997] 3 S.C.R. 320 (S.C.C.) provides a contemporary definition of this fundamental concept in criminal law. See also *R. v. M.B.*, [1997] B.C.J. No. 2184 (B.C.C.A.).

However, the *YCJA* provides additional protections to young persons and thus operates to vary the rules to some degree. The rules regarding the admissibility of the statements of young persons is a classic example. Section 146 clarifies that the common law rules of evidence regarding the voluntariness of statements apply to young persons no less than they do to adult accused;[81] however, s. 146 establishes additional rules that must be observed, generally by peace officers who are taking these statements, before a statement from a young person will be admissible in evidence against the young person.[82]

D.   Preliminary Inquiries and Election Re Mode of Trial

Proceedings involving young persons are generally conducted in accordance with the summary procedures outlined in Part XXVII of the *Criminal Code*, which means that generally, a provincial or territorial court judge (and sometimes a Justice of the Peace) presides, there is usually no preliminary inquiry and trials are conducted by a judge alone without a jury. However, a young person has the right to elect his or her mode of trial if facing certain serious charges, which means that, in certain situations, the young person can request a preliminary inquiry and elect trial by jury. The *Charter* guarantees all persons the right to a jury trial if facing a maximum penalty of five years or more, save for trials before military tribunals.[83] In addition, the *YCJA* stipulates that the Attorney General can require a young person to have a jury trial even if the young person requests to be tried without a jury.[84] In practice, however, the courts are finding that they have the discretion to overrule the Attorney General in this regard.[85] Further, the Alberta Queen's Bench has held that, in order to lawfully invoke s. 67(6) of the *YCJA*, the Attorney General must provide a convincing reason to use this unusual discretionary power.[86]

While Justices of the Peace or provincial court judges can conduct preliminary inquiries in relation to most indictable offences,[87] s. 96 of the *Constitution Act, 1867*[88] stipulates that only a superior court judge can conduct a jury trial. Thus, in practice, the provincial court judge

---

[81]   *YCJA*, s. 146(1).
[82]   Section 146 is discussed in detail in Chapter 7.
[83]   *Charter*, s. 11(f).
[84]   *YCJA*, s. 67(6).
[85]   *R. v. K.P.H.*, [2007] A.J. No. 1467, at paras. 35-36 (Alta. Q.B.).
[86]   *R. v. K.P.H.*, [2007] A.J. No. 1467, at paras. 42-45 (Alta. Q.B.).
[87]   *Criminal Code*, s. 535.
[88]   (U.K.) 30 & 31 Vict., c. 3 (formerly the *British North America Act, 1867*).

generally conducts the preliminary inquiry, and the superior court judge conducts the trial in these cases (but is deemed to be a youth justice court judge for the purpose).[89]

An accused person has the right to re-elect the mode of trial at various stages in the process.[90] For example, after the preliminary inquiry, an accused person who has elected trial by judge and jury in superior court may re-elect to be tried by a provincial court judge, with the consent of the prosecutor.[91] It is noteworthy that the courts have said that young persons have broader re-election rights than adults as to the mode of trial,[92] and in fact are entitled to the broadest right to decide upon the mode of trial that the young person prefers.[93] The courts tend to apply and interpret these election and re-election provisions with maximum flexibility when dealing with young persons; in other words the courts can be expected to invariably accede to the young person's request.

If the young person is committed to trial as a result of the preliminary inquiry, in most provinces, the trial will be conducted by a superior court judge,[94] sitting as a youth justice court judge. It is important to emphasize that the trial is still a youth justice court trial.[95] The young person remains under the umbrella of the *YCJA* and retains the benefits of the protections afforded by the Act. The superior court judge is deemed to be a youth justice court judge and the court is deemed to be a youth justice court for purposes of the proceeding.

Under the *YCJA*, if the youth justice court has made an order that the young person is not liable to an adult sentence before the young person is required to elect his or her mode of trial, the young person is not to be put to his or her election unless he or she is facing a murder charge.[96] Other-

---

[89] *YCJA*, s. 13(3).
[90] *Criminal Code*, s. 561.
[91] *Criminal Code*, s. 561(1)(a).
[92] *R. v. F. (M.)*, [2007] O.J. No. 3370, 223 C.C.C. (3d) 209, at para. 14 (Ont. S.C).
[93] *R. v. K.P.H.*, [2007] A.J. No. 1467 (Alta. Q.B.).
[94] For example, as per s. 13(2) of the *YCJA*, a young person in Quebec who elects trial by judge alone after a preliminary inquiry will be tried by a judge of the Court of Quebec, except for murder which must be tried by a superior court judge. Section 13(2) must be read in combination with s. 552 of the *Criminal Code*, as well as the definitions of superior court of criminal jurisdiction and court of criminal jurisdiction in s. 2 of the *Criminal Code*. The *YCJA* makes clear in s. 2(2) that, unless otherwise provided, words and expressions in the *YCJA* have the same meaning as in the *Criminal Code*. The practice is different in Nunavut, as well; the Nunavut Court of Justice is a unified court, Canada's first and only single level court. In this new court, which came into existence on April 1, 1999, the powers of the provincial and superior courts have been melded into one so that this court can hear any type of case.
[95] *YCJA*, s. 13.
[96] *YCJA*, s. 66.

wise, a young person has a right to elect his or her mode of trial prior to plea in the following circumstances:[97]

- if the young person is charged with murder, attempt to commit murder, manslaughter or aggravated sexual assault and was at least 14 at the time of the alleged offence;

- the Crown has given notice under s. 64(2) that it intends to seek an adult sentence for an offence not listed directly above committed by the young person after the age of 14 (this captures other indictable offences for which an adult could receive more than two years in jail or a third serious violent offence);

- the young person is charged with having committed murder while under the age of 14; or

- the person whose age at the time of the commission of the offence is uncertain (s. 16 of the *YCJA*) is charged with having committed an offence after attaining the age of 14 for which an adult would be entitled to an election under s. 536 or 536.1 of the *Criminal Code* (indictable offences except for s. 469 offences or those over which the provincial court has absolute jurisdiction), or over which the superior court has exclusive jurisdiction under s. 469 of the *Criminal Code*, such as murder or accessory after the fact to murder.[98]

V.   ADULT SENTENCES — PROCEDURES AND NOTICE REQUIREMENTS

Sections 61 to 81 concern adult sentences for young persons. These sections describe the eligibility criteria for an adult sentence, as well as the important procedures and processes, including the notice provisions, which apply in relation to adult sentences.[99] However, a number of the procedures in relation to adult sentences have been altered by the 2008 ruling in *R. v.*

---

[97]   *YCJA*, s. 67.

[98]   The wording of the election in s. 67 indicates that a young person charged with murder can elect to be tried by a youth justice court judge despite s. 469 of the *Criminal Code*, which suggests that only a superior court can try a murder charge. Section 13(2) of the *YCJA* resolves this apparent conflict by clarifying that when a young person elects to be tried by a judge without a jury in relation to a s. 469 offence, the judge shall be a superior court judge who is deemed to be a youth justice court judge for the purpose of the proceeding. Likewise, when the young person elects a jury trial, the superior court is deemed to be the youth justice court for the purpose of the proceeding.

[99]   The Department of Justice website provides excellent material regarding the notice requirements and related procedural requirements in this regard and is a useful resource for practitioners. At the time of writing, it could be accessed at the following link: <http://www.justice.gc.ca/eng/pi/yj-jj/repos-depot/3modules/09notic-avis/3090301e.html>.

D.B.,[100] which ruled unconstitutional the provisions that placed the onus on a young person to justify a youth sentence rather than placing the onus on the Crown to justify the more severe adult sentence. Given this ruling, certain procedures in the adult sentencing regime in the *YCJA* no longer make sense, since they were based on the young person having the burden of justifying a youth sentence in certain circumstances. The *YCJA* had not been amended to reflect this decision at the time of writing. Practitioners should read the provisions of the *YCJA* regarding adult sentences through the lens of *R. v. D.B.*

Adult sentences are addressed in Chapter 8; however, the essential points are these:

- a young person must, in all cases, have been at least 14 at the time of the commission of the offence before he or she is eligible for an adult sentence;[101]

- a young person is eligible for an adult sentence only if he or she is alleged to have committed an indictable offence for which an adult could receive more than two years in jail;

- a young person who is found guilty of committing an offence before the age of 14, including murder, is not eligible for an adult sentence; and[102]

- the Crown must apply for an order for an adult sentence, and give notice of its intention to seek an adult sentence, to the young person and the youth justice court, in every case where it wishes to seek this higher penalty[103] before the young person enters a plea, or, with leave of the court, before the commencement of the trial.

Justice Abella in *R. v. D.B.*[104] does not explain how the ruling would affect procedures in relation to adult sentences under the *YCJA*. The decision focuses on its finding that the reverse onus provisions in relation to presumptive offences are unconstitutional. In light of the overall

---

[100] [2008] S.C.J. No. 25, 2008 SCC 25 (S.C.C.).

[101] *YCJA*, s. 62, when read in combination with the s. 2 definition of presumptive offences in the *YCJA*.

[102] *YCJA*, ss. 2 and 62. Thus, a young person found guilty of first or second degree murder committed at the age of 12 or 13 can receive only the maximum sentences for these offences under the *YCJA*. A young person who commits murder under the age of 12, as previously discussed, is below the age of criminal responsibility in Canada and cannot be held criminally responsible for the crime.

[103] *YCJA*, ss. 63 to 81. It is submitted that, as a result of *R. v. D.B.*, [2008] S.C.J. No. 25, 2008 SCC 25 (S.C.C.), this procedure naturally follows. On this point, see *R. v. M.T.*, [2009] O.J. No. 1351, at para. 9 (Ont. S.C.).

[104] [2008] S.C.J. No. 25, 2008 SCC 25 (S.C.C.).

scheme of the Act, including its explicit recognition of the enhanced procedural protection of young persons, however, the decision has arguably modified the application and notice procedures in relation to adult sentences. As a result of *R. v. D.B.*, it is submitted that the Crown should now apply and provide notice of its intention to seek an adult sentence in all cases where it intends to seek an adult sentence. This practice naturally follows from the ruling.[105]

Prior to *R. v. D.B.*, the Crown was not required to give notice of its intention to seek an adult sentence in cases of murder, manslaughter, attempt to commit murder or aggravated sexual assault because an adult sentence was presumed if a young person were found guilty of one of these offences unless the young person could convince the court to impose a youth sentence instead. Since the presumptive offences in the *YCJA* have now been found unconstitutional to the extent that they impose an onus on the young person to justify a youth sentence rather than on the state to justify the more severe adult sentence, and the majority of the Supreme Court of Canada found that the onus must be on the Crown to justify the more severe adult sentence, the Crown should now apply and give notice in every case where it intends to seek an adult sentence.

The obligation on various parties in the youth criminal justice system to notify a young person in certain circumstances that he or she may be liable to an adult sentence is a theme throughout the *YCJA*. As Chapter 8 explains, the notice requirements in relation to the possibility of an adult sentence for a young person arise at the earliest stages of youth justice court proceedings, from the time of the young person's first appearance in court.[106] The Crown is only one of various parties who is obliged to ensure the young person is put on notice early in the youth justice court proceeding when there is a possibility of an adult sentence.[107]

In cases where a young person gives notice that he or she does not oppose the Crown's application for an adult sentence, the youth justice court must impose the adult sentence upon a finding of guilt for an offence for which an adult is liable to imprisonment for more than two years.[108] Likewise, if the Crown has given notice to the young person that an adult sentence will not be sought in relation to the offences of murder, attempt to commit murder, manslaughter or aggravated sexual assault, the

---

[105]   The courts are beginning to recognize this implication. See *R. v. M.T.*, [2009] O.J. No. 1351, at para. 9 (Ont. S.C.).

[106]   *YCJA*, s. 32.

[107]   *YCJA*, s. 32.

[108]   *YCJA*, s. 64(5).

court is obliged to order that the young person is not liable to an adult sentence and to also order a publication ban.[109]

Applications and notices to the court under s. 63, 64, 65 or 76 must be made or given orally, in the presence of the other party, or in writing with a copy served personally on the other party.[110]

The youth justice court judge is also obliged to inquire of the young person before evidence is called and submissions made regarding sentence whether the young person wishes to apply for a youth sentence, and, if so, whether the Crown objects, in cases where:

- the young person has been found guilty of a presumptive offence;[111]

- the young person has not already applied for a youth sentence under s. 63; and

- the judge has not already made an order under s. 65 that the young person is not liable to an adult sentence.[112]

If the young person indicates that he or she does not wish to apply for a youth sentence or fails to indicate a preference, the court is obliged to order that an adult sentence be imposed.[113]

VI. THE (PROCEDURAL) MEANING OF A SEPARATE YOUTH JUSTICE SYSTEM

Enshrined in the *YCJA* is the principle that the criminal justice system for young persons must be separate from that of adults.[114] The existence of a separate criminal justice system for young persons has been acknowledged and affirmed by the Supreme Court of Canada in several

---

[109] *YCJA*, s. 65.

[110] *YCJA*, s. 81.

[111] While this remains the wording of the *YCJA*, as a result of *R. v. D.B.*, when a young person is found guilty of a presumptive offence, the onus is now on the Crown to justify the more severe sentence. The presumption is no longer that of an adult sentence; thus, the young person no longer has to apply for a youth sentence in these circumstances.

[112] See s. 70 of the *YCJA*, but, as mentioned, it is submitted that the operation of these sections has been altered by *R. v. D.B.*, [2008] S.C.J. No. 25, 2008 SCC 25 (S.C.C.). The presumptive offences have been ruled unconstitutional to the extent that they impose an onus on the young person to justify a youth sentence and, thus, a young person should no longer have to apply for a youth sentence when found guilty of a presumptive offence. Rather the Crown should have to apply for an adult sentence.

[113] *YCJA*, s. 70. Again, it is argued that this provision is subject to *R. v. D.B.*, [2008] S.C.J. No. 25, 2008 SCC 25 (S.C.C.).

[114] *YCJA*, s. 3(1)(b).

cases, including *R. v. D.B.*,[115] where the court held that a separate criminal justice system for young persons is necessary because, due to their age, young persons have heightened vulnerability, less maturity and a reduced capacity for moral judgement, and are thus entitled to a presumption of diminished moral blameworthiness. Justice Fish made similar comments concerning Parliament's decision to create a separate criminal justice system for young persons in *R. v. C. (R.W.)*.[116]

The Supreme Court of Canada is now beginning to elaborate on what a separate youth justice system in Canada actually means, in terms of procedure. The top court affirmed in *R. v. S.J.L.*[117] that young persons and adults cannot be tried together. "[S]uch a proceeding would be inconsistent with the governing principle of the *YCJA*, which maintains a justice *system* for young people that is separate from the system for adults."[118] In the course of her reasoning for the majority, Deschamps J. noted that the main purpose of the *YCJA* is to lay down special rules for young persons.[119] Justice Deschamps observed that since the introduction of the *Juvenile Delinquents Act* in 1908, young persons have been dealt with within a separate justice system with its own principles, based on the recognition of the presumption of diminished moral blameworthiness of young persons. The abolition of the transfer of young persons to adult court for trial in certain cases under the *YCJA*, which was still possible under the *Young Offenders Act*, is illustrative of the breadth of that separateness, Deschamps J. held.[120] Under the *YCJA*, "... Parliament intended to establish a youth criminal justice system that is hermetic, and completely separate from the system for adults, and thus to make it impossible to hold joint trials of adults and young persons."[121]

Yet, in practice, Canada, even now, does not have an *entirely* separate criminal justice system for young persons. As noted in *R. v. S.J.L.*, Canada's criminal justice system for young persons, up until 2003, permitted young persons to be tried as adults in adult court in certain circumstances. This procedure was modified under the *YCJA* so that young persons are now always tried in youth justice court regardless of the seriousness of the offence. However, the *YCJA* provides that, upon a finding of guilt in youth justice court, a young person who was at least 14 at the time of the commission of the offence, can be found eligible for an

---

[115]   [2008] S.C.J. No. 25, at paras. 40-41, 2008 SCC 25 (S.C.C.), *per* Abella J.
[116]   [2005] S.C.J. No. 62, at para. 41, 259 D.L.R. (4th) 1 (S.C.C.).
[117]   [2009] S.C.J. No. 14, 2009 SCC 14 (S.C.C.).
[118]   [2009] S.C.J. No. 14, at para. 56, 2009 SCC 14 (S.C.C.) (emphasis in original).
[119]   [2009] S.C.J. No. 14, at para. 6, 2009 SCC 14 (S.C.C.).
[120]   [2009] S.C.J. No. 14, at paras. 72 and 76, 2009 SCC 14 (S.C.C.).
[121]   [2009] S.C.J. No. 14, at para. 74, 2009 SCC 14 (S.C.C.).

adult sentence for certain serious crimes. This means that, contrary to public perception, under the *YCJA*, a young person of 14 can receive a life sentence for murder.[122] In some cases, a young person can receive a sentence as severe as the sentence an adult would receive. A young person can also be required to serve his or her sentence in an adult institution.[123] Thus, the youth justice system, in effect, is not totally separate from the adult system.

That said, through three pieces of legislation over the last century, the youth criminal justice system has provided for separate juvenile or youth courts for young persons with special rules and procedures that reflect the fact that the accused is a young person. In fact, the provision of separate trials and courts for juveniles was among the central aims of the *Juvenile Delinquents Act*.[124]

R. v. S.J.L. raised fundamental questions about the meaning and breadth of a separate youth criminal justice system in Canada as well as the intent of s. 3(1)(b) of the Declaration of Principle, which says explicitly that the criminal justice system for young persons must be separate from that of adults. No similar provision was contained in the *Young Offenders Act*, which indicates that Parliament clearly turned its mind to the concept of a separate criminal justice system for young persons and considered it necessary to include an express reference to it in the *YCJA*. Of even greater significance, the *YCJA*, unlike the *Juvenile Delinquents Act* and the *Young Offenders Act*, makes it impossible to try a young person in adult court in any circumstances. Rather, the *YCJA* merely permits the imposition of an adult sentence in certain cases.

These new and fundamental aspects of the *YCJA* suggest that it was Parliament's intention that the concept of a separate youth criminal justice system was to be interpreted broadly.

---

[122] However, parole eligibility differs in the case of young persons who receive life sentences. See *Criminal Code*, s. 745.1.

[123] *YCJA*, s. 76 re placement when subject to an adult sentence.

[124] There is considerable discussion of this in Chapter 1 of this text.

Chapter 5

THE EXPANSION OF DIVERSION UNDER THE YOUTH CRIMINAL JUSTICE ACT

I. OVERVIEW

The practice of police exercising their discretion and choosing not to charge individuals with criminal offences despite having the grounds to do so is as old as Canada's first police forces.[1] Police have been informally diverting individuals from the court process since the inception of formal law enforcement. Although the concept of diversion or alternative measures was not expressly identified in the *Juvenile Delinquents Act*[2] of 1908, the practice was prevalent in relation to young persons dealt with under the Act. It was not only common for the police to apprehend young persons for minor offences and to release them after warning them (and sometimes their parents as well) that they could be charged and taken to court if the offending continued,[3] but school officials and probation officers also routinely used courts as a last resort under the *JDA*.[4] Nevertheless, it was not until the 1970s that formal diversion programs began to be established in Canada by community agencies, which enabled the police and prosecutors to refer persons to specific programs rather than charging them and processing them

---

[1] Peter Harris, Brian Weagant and David Cole, "Working 'In the Trenches' with the YCJA" (April 2004) 46(3) Canadian Journal of Criminology and Criminal Justice 367, at 376. See also various articles detailing the establishment and development of Canada's first police forces, such as R.C. Macleod, "Canadianizing the West: The North-West Mounted Police as Agents of the National Policy, 1873-1905" in L.M. Thomas, ed., *Essays on Western History* (Edmonton: University of Alberta Press, 1976), 101 at 103 and C. Schuh, "Justice on the Northern Frontier: Early Murder Trials of Native Accused" (1979) 22 Crim. L.Q. (Can.) 74, at 101.

[2] S.C. 1908, c. 40 [hereafter "*JDA*"]. Nicholas Bala, "Community-Based Responses to Youth Crime: Cautioning, Conferencing and Extrajudicial Measures" in Kathryn Campbell, ed., *Understanding Youth Justice in Canada* (Toronto: Pearson Education Canada Inc., 2005), at 177.

[3] Nicholas Bala, "Community-Based Responses to Youth Crime: Cautioning, Conferencing and Extrajudicial Measures" in Kathryn Campbell, ed., *Understanding Youth Justice in Canada* (Toronto: Pearson Education Canada Inc., 2005), at 177.

[4] Nicholas Bala, "Diversion, Conferencing and Extrajudicial Measures for Adolescent Offenders" (2003) 40 Alta. L. Rev. 991, at para. 5 (QL).

through the court system. Part of the impetus for the movement toward diversion for young persons related to concerns that exposing young persons to the criminal justice system, involving them in it, and essentially labelling them as delinquents, would increase the likelihood that they would see themselves as criminals and that such self-identification would increase their criminal behaviour.[5] While the empirical evidence is equivocal regarding whether identifying young persons as offenders actually increases their propensity to reoffend, and Canadian research suggests there is no significant difference in recidivism rates when a young person is processed through the court system versus being diverted, youth justice experts suggest that young persons who are diverted are no more likely to reoffend.[6] Diversion offers other benefits as well, such as resolving minor matters more expeditiously and thus leaving valuable court resources for the more serious cases. Diversion programs can also have restorative aspects that can result in a higher level of satisfaction for both victims and accused persons. Finally, diversion programs, depending on their design and structure, can enable greater community involvement in the resolution of the case, which is a feature that may be of great interest to small communities, including communities with a significant proportion of First Nations and Inuit people.[7]

By the time the drafting of the *YOA* was under way in the late 1970s, proponents of diversion had succeeded in attracting the attention of the federal government. The concept of alternative measures was formally and expressly included in the *YOA* of 1984.[8] The principle was stated simply in the Declaration of Principle: "... where it is not inconsistent with the protection of society, taking no measures or taking measures other than judicial proceedings under this Act should be considered for dealing with young persons who have committed offences".[9] The Declara-

---

[5]   Nicholas Bala, "Community-Based Responses to Youth Crime: Cautioning, Conferencing and Extrajudicial Measures" in Kathryn Campbell, ed., *Understanding Youth Justice in Canada* (Toronto: Pearson Education Canada Inc., 2005), at 177-78. See also J. Bolton *et al.*, "The *Young Offenders Act*: Principles and Policy — The first Decade in Review" (1993) 38 McGill L.J. 939, at 953. The concept of labelling theory and its influence on the substance of the *Young Offenders Act*, R.S.C. 1985, c. Y-1 [hereafter "*YOA*"] is discussed in Chapter 1. A good discussion of labelling theory can also be found in Kathryn Campbell, "Introduction: Theoretical Overview" in Kathryn Campbell, ed., *Understanding Youth Justice in Canada* (Toronto: Pearson Education Canada Inc., 2005), 1 at 12.

[6]   Nicholas Bala, "Community-Based Responses to Youth Crime: Cautioning, Conferencing and Extrajudicial Measures" in Kathryn Campbell, ed., *Understanding Youth Justice in Canada* (Toronto: Pearson Education Canada Inc., 2005), 176 at 177-78.

[7]   Nicholas Bala, "Community-Based Responses to Youth Crime: Cautioning, Conferencing and Extrajudicial Measures" in Kathryn Campbell, ed., *Understanding Youth Justice in Canada* (Toronto: Pearson Education Canada Inc., 2005), 176 at 177-78.

[8]   *YOA*, ss. 3(1)(d) and 4.

[9]   *YOA*, s. 3(1)(d).

tion of Principle in the *YOA* also acknowledged that young persons have a right to the least possible interference with freedom that is consistent with the protection of society,[10] which can also be interpreted as an allusion to the use of alternative measures.

Section 4 of the *YOA* officially permitted the use of alternative measures for young persons provided certain conditions were met but s. 4 provided no principles to guide decision-makers in the use of alternative measures. The value of alternative measures continued to be heralded throughout the 1990s, not only by academics, but by prominent criminal justice officials, such as G. Arthur Martin, author of Ontario's *Report of the Attorney General's Advisory Committee on Charge Screening, Disclosure, and Resolution Discussions:*

> The criminal law is a blunt instrument of social policy that ought to be used with restraint. The criminal law aims to achieve rehabilitation, specific deterrence, general deterrence and the protection of society. However, there is no reason to think that the criminal law is the only method of achieving these socially desirable goals. Accordingly, it is clearly in the public interest to consider the existing alternatives to any given prosecution and their efficacy, remembering that these alternatives may be able to deal more sensitively and comprehensively with the particular problem at hand, while at the same time meeting the goals of the criminal justice system.[11]

Despite the express acknowledgment in the *YOA* of the clear place for alternative measures as part of the youth criminal justice system, there was a dramatic and documented increase in the use of formal court responses as opposed to alternative measures in most parts of Canada[12] (Quebec is the notable exception) during the approximate 20-year life of the *YOA*.[13] Some youth justice experts suggest that the introduction of the *YOA* was accompanied by the phenomenon of net widening in most parts of Canada. In other words, young persons who committed minor offences and would have been dealt with informally under the *JDA* were now being brought into the criminal justice system and charge rates remained stable or increased. Restrictive provincial policies regarding the use of alternative measures as well as the increased pressure on the police to get tough on youth crime by charging young persons more frequently are cited as explanations for the

---

[10]   *YOA*, s. 3(1)(f).

[11]   Queen's Printer for Ontario, 1993.

[12]   Nicholas Bala, "Community-Based Responses to Youth Crime: Cautioning, Conferencing and Extrajudicial Measures" in Kathryn Campbell, ed., *Understanding Youth Justice in Canada* (Toronto: Pearson Education Canada Inc., 2005), 176 at 178.

[13]   Nicholas Bala, "Diversion, Conferencing and Extrajudicial Measures for Adolescent Offenders" (2003) 40 Alta. L. Rev. 991, at para. 5 (QL).

increased use of formal court responses under the *YOA*.[14] In fact, the province of Ontario was so resistant initially to alternative measures that it refused to establish an alternative measures program for various reasons, including its view that research into the effectiveness of alternative measures was ambiguous.[15] Its refusal to do so was challenged as a violation of the right to the equal benefit of the law established under s. 15 of the *Canadian Charter of Rights and Freedoms*.[16] The argument, in part, was that young persons in every province should have access to alternative measures programs. If Ontario did not establish such programs, young persons in Ontario would be denied a benefit available to other young persons across the country. However, the Supreme Court of Canada held in *R. v. S. (S.)*[17] that provinces and territories are not obliged to establish alternative measures programs.

In a separate but related decision, the Supreme Court of Canada held that if provinces or territories chose to establish alternative measures programs, they could establish their own criteria, which meant that some provinces or territories could have more restrictive criteria than others, which is exactly what transpired.[18]

During the 1990s, all provinces and territories, including Ontario, established alternative measures programs but their eligibility criteria and general admission policies varied, and continue to vary today.

It soon became clear that the express approval of alternative measures in the *YOA* did not result in their increased use by key criminal justice players, such as the police and prosecution services. Research relied upon by the federal government demonstrated that, under the *YOA*, Canada was diverting only about 25 per cent of young persons, while countries such as the United States, Britain and New Zealand were

---

[14]   See various studies on this point by Peter Carrington and Sharon Moyer, which are cited in the bibliography of the study by Peter J. Carrington and Jennifer L. Schulenberg, *The Impact of the Youth Criminal Justice Act on Police Charging Practices with Young Persons: A Preliminary Statistical Assessment: Report to the Department of Justice Canada* (2005). See also comments by Nicholas Bala, "Community-Based Responses to Youth Crime: Cautioning, Conferencing and Extrajudicial Measures" in Kathryn Campbell, ed., *Understanding Youth Justice in Canada* (Toronto: Pearson Education Canada Inc., 2005), 176 at 178.

[15]   Nicholas Bala, "Community-Based Responses to Youth Crime: Cautioning, Conferencing and Extrajudicial Measures" in Kathryn Campbell, ed., *Understanding Youth Justice in Canada* (Toronto: Pearson Education Canada Inc., 2005), 176 at 179.

[16]   Part I of the *Constitution Act, 1982*, being Schedule B to the *Canada Act 1982* (U.K.), 1982, c. 11 [hereafter "*Charter*"].

[17]   [1990] S.C.J. No. 66, [1990] 2 S.C.R. 254 (S.C.C.).

[18]   *R. v. S. (G.)*, [1990] S.C.J. No. 68, 57 C.C.C. (3d) 92 (S.C.C.). See Nicholas Bala, "Community-Based Responses to Youth Crime: Cautioning, Conferencing and Extrajudicial Measures" in Kathryn Campbell, ed., *Understanding Youth Justice in Canada* (Toronto: Pearson Education Canada Inc., 2005), 176 at 178-80.

diverting more than half of all young persons who were coming into contact with the police.[19] The U.S. was diverting from the formal court process about half of its young persons (53 per cent), England was diverting 57 per cent and New Zealand was diverting 61 per cent of its young persons who came into contact with the police.[20] Canada was also significantly overusing courts and custody, and often for non-violent young persons. Canada's youth incarceration rates were much higher than those of many other Western nations, including the U.S., Australia and New Zealand.[21] Canada's youth incarceration rate also varied widely among provinces, being as much as three to four times higher in some provinces than in others, with no comparable variation in crime rates.[22] A substantial majority of young persons were being committed to custody for non-violent offences[23] and Canada's youth incarceration rate at sentencing was four times higher than the adult incarceration rate.[24]

This statistical reality was acknowledged by the federal government in 1998 in a major federal government policy document, *A Strategy for the Renewal of Youth Justice*. This document provided the philosophical framework and foundation for the new *Youth Criminal Justice Act*, which was to come into force five years later, after much drafting, re-drafting, dissection and debate. Among its findings, the document concluded that alternatives to the formal justice system can often be employed effectively to deal with the majority of non-violent young offenders, including measures such as family group conferencing, circle sentencing, diversion programs and police cautioning, and that community-based penalties are

---

[19] Nicholas Bala, *Youth Criminal Justice Law* (Toronto: Irwin Law Inc., 2003), at 135. See also Youth Justice Statistics, Department of Justice News Communique, March 29, 1999, Ottawa.

[20] Nicholas Bala, *Youth Criminal Justice Law* (Toronto: Irwin Law Inc., 2003), at 135. See also Youth Justice Statistics, Department of Justice News Communique, March 29, 1999, Ottawa.

[21] See Department of Justice, *A Strategy for the Renewal of Youth Justice* (Ottawa: Ministry of Supply and Services, 1998) (section on Concerns about the Current Youth Justice System). This document was the federal government's response to *Renewing Youth Justice: Thirteenth Report of the Standing Committee on Justice and Legal Affairs*, released in April 1997. At the time of writing, *A Strategy for the Renewal of Youth Justice* could be accessed through the Department of Justice website at: <http://www.justice.gc.ca/eng/pi/yj-jj/about-apropos/toc-tdm.html>. In this document, the federal government reviews the shortcomings of the *YOA* and outlines its rationale for introducing the *Youth Criminal Justice Act*, S.C. 2002, c. 1 [hereafter "*YCJA*"]. This document is the evidentiary and philosophical foundation for the *YCJA*; it is the policy paper.

[22] Department of Justice, *A Strategy for the Renewal of Youth Justice* (Ottawa: Ministry of Supply and Services, 1998) (section on Concerns about the Current Youth Justice System).

[23] Department of Justice, *A Strategy for the Renewal of Youth Justice* (Ottawa: Ministry of Supply and Services, 1998) (section on Legislative and Supporting Program Components).

[24] Department of Justice, *A Strategy for the Renewal of Youth Justice* (Ottawa: Ministry of Supply and Services, 1998) (section on Children, Youth and Youth Crime).

often more effective than custody and should be encouraged for lower-risk, non-violent offenders. In essence, the document affirmed that the new legislation that was to replace the *YOA* would focus on non-court and non-custody responses for non-violent offenders to the extent feasible. Citing the success of New Zealand, Australia, the U.S. and Britain, the document concluded that "alternatives to the formal youth justice system are an important component of the youth justice strategy for the less-serious and temporary behaviour that accounts for the majority of youth crime".[25]

The federal government noted that programs involving formal police warnings and cautions had worked well in other jurisdictions. The report cited the greater use of police cautioning as among the factors that enabled countries such as Great Britain, New Zealand and a number of European countries to substantially reduce the number of young persons in custody in the 1980s.[26] Thus, despite an outright acknowledgment in *A Strategy for the Renewal of Youth Justice* that the general public was concerned about youth crime and believed that youth laws were too lenient,[27] the federal government prepared to introduce new legislation that unquestionably encouraged non-court responses for non-violent young persons, expanded the range of diversionary options, and provided significant and specific guidance and direction regarding the use of diversion. In other words, the federal government moved toward what could be perceived as more lenient dispositions for many youthful offenders at a time when the public was demanding the opposite.

Alternative measures under the *YOA* were renamed extrajudicial measures under the *YCJA*. The expanded extrajudicial measures regime is clearly directed at reducing the use of custody and court responses. From its Preamble onward, the *YCJA* emphasizes a graduated approach to the treatment and punishment of young persons. As noted during the discussion of the Preamble in Chapter 3, a fundamental goal of the youth criminal justice system is to reduce the over-reliance on incarceration for non-violent young persons and to reserve the most serious intervention

---

[25] Department of Justice, *A Strategy for the Renewal of Youth Justice* (Ottawa: Ministry of Supply and Services, 1998) (section on Legislative and Supporting Program Components).

[26] Department of Justice, *A Strategy for the Renewal of Youth Justice* (Ottawa: Ministry of Supply and Services, 1998) (section on Legislative and Supporting Program Components). Canadian professor and scholar Kent Roach has observed that Britain has considerable experience with police cautions including police cautions that are designed to be restorative. Such cautions are administered in the presence of family or other supporters of the offenders and, where possible, in the presence of crime victims and their supporters. However, this attempt at restorative police cautions is apparently proving problematic. See Kent Roach, "The Role of Crime Victims Under the *Youth Criminal Justice Act*" (2003) 40 Alta. L. Rev. 965, at para. 30 (QL).

[27] Department of Justice, *A Strategy for the Renewal of Youth Justice* (Ottawa: Ministry of Supply and Services, 1998) (section on Concerns about the Current Youth Justice System).

(*i.e.*, jail) for the most serious crimes. While this clause in the Preamble is not a direct reference to extrajudicial measures, it follows that responses to the less serious crimes are more likely to be non-judicial responses, such as extrajudicial measures, which, under the new regime, now clearly and formally include the option of taking no action at all.

II. EXTRAJUDICIAL MEASURES UNDER THE YCJA

Extrajudicial measures, known generally as diversion, are defined in s. 2 of the *YCJA* as measures other than judicial proceedings under the *YCJA* used to deal with a young person alleged to have committed an offence. These measures include extrajudicial sanctions. An extrajudicial sanction is only one type of extrajudicial measure available under the *YCJA* and is defined in s. 10 of the *YCJA*. An extrajudicial measure therefore can be any measure designed to address the alleged criminal conduct of a young person but it is clearly a measure that does not involve the formal court process or a conventional prosecution.

In addition to various sections of the Declaration of Principle that refer to extrajudicial measures,[28] the *YCJA* directly addresses extrajudicial measures in ss. 4 to 12, and in ss. 18, 19 and 157 as well. Not only does the *YCJA* now provide clear guidance and direction on the use of extrajudicial measures in ss. 4 and 5, it provides an expanded range of extrajudicial measures that can be employed by the police and prosecutors.[29]

A. Diversion Principles Under the *YCJA*

While s. 4 of the *YCJA* clarifies that decision-makers should also consider s. 3 principles in the *YCJA* when deciding whether to divert a young person from the formal court system, s. 4 contains four principles that are specifically intended to guide the parties in their use of extrajudicial measures. Section 4 states that (a) extrajudicial measures are often the most appropriate and effective way to address youth crime, (b) extrajudicial measures allow for effective and timely interventions focused on correcting offending behaviour, (c) extrajudicial measures are presumed to be adequate to hold a young person accountable for his or her offending behaviour if the young person has committed a non-violent offence and has not previously been found guilty of an offence, and (d) extrajudicial

---

[28] *YCJA*, s. 3(1)(c)(ii).

[29] A lot of excellent background on extrajudicial measures under the *YCJA* can be found by accessing the Department of Justice website at: <http://www.justice.gc.ca/eng/pi/yj-jj/repos-depot/3modules/01extjud/3010301d.html>.

measures should be used if they are adequate to hold a young person accountable for his or her offending behaviour and, if the use of extrajudicial measures is consistent with the principles set out in s. 4, nothing in the *YCJA* precludes their use in respect of a young person who (i) has previously been dealt with by the use of extrajudicial measures, or (ii) has previously been found guilty of an offence.

Among the most significant principles above are the presumption that an extrajudicial measure is adequate to hold a first-time offender accountable for a non-violent offence and the fact that nothing precludes the use of an extrajudicial measure even in a case where the young person has already been dealt with through extrajudicial measures or has previously been found guilty of an offence, provided the measure is adequate to hold the young person accountable and its use is consistent with the principles in s. 4. While this section directs that one must presume that an extrajudicial measure is adequate to hold a first-time offender accountable for a non-violent offence, there may well be situations where the presumption can be effectively rebutted. For example, a young person with no record who is alleged to have trafficked in heroin or cocaine at or near a school has arguably not committed a violent offence but the facts of this offence are so aggravating that there is a strong argument to be made that this individual should not receive an extrajudicial measure and should be charged and dealt with by the courts. On the other hand, there may be available in a given community a specific extrajudicial sanction that the Crown believes could be effective in assisting the young person not to re-offend so that the Crown may decide that an extrajudicial sanction is the most appropriate response for the first-time offender. If there is evidence that the young person has a drug addiction, for example, and is trafficking to support this addiction, a specific extrajudicial sanction program that addresses the addiction may be the most appropriate response.

Provincial and federal prosecution services in Canada have policies to guide prosecutors in the use of extrajudicial measures; these policies generally clarify the kind of offences and circumstances that preclude a young person from eligibility for extrajudicial measures. These prosecution policies are generally available to the public.[30]

Police, Crowns, probation officers and youth workers should also be mindful of the additional factors in s. 5 of the *YCJA*, which state that extrajudicial measures are intended to achieve five objectives: (a) provide an effective and timely response to offending behaviour outside the

---

[30] For example, the extrajudicial measures policy of the Public Prosecution Service of Canada can be found in the policy deskbook, which can be accessed at: <http://www.ppsc-sppc.gc.ca/eng/fps-sfp/fpd/index.html>.

bounds of judicial measures; (b) encourage young persons to acknowledge and repair the harm caused to the victim and the community; (c) encourage families of young persons — including extended families where appropriate — and the community to become involved in the design and implementation of those measures; (d) provide an opportunity for victims to participate in decisions related to the measures selected and to receive reparation; and (e) respect the rights and freedoms of young persons and be proportionate to the seriousness of the offence.

Several of these objectives emphasize the restorative impact that extrajudicial measures can have, and the importance of victims, the offender's family and the community playing a role in the choice of extrajudicial measure. The *YCJA* arguably provides for a greater role for victims to participate in, and to benefit from, extrajudicial measures, since the *YCJA* contemplates that crime victims can be informed about the extrajudicial measures, participate in them, and receive reparation and acknowledgement of the harm suffered. Nevertheless, it has been suggested that the *YCJA* may not go far enough in endorsing a restorative justice and conference-based approach to youth crime.[31]

B.   Diversionary Options for Police

Section 6 of the *YCJA* effectively codifies long-standing police discretion not to lay a charge so that a police officer now is specifically directed to consider other options before choosing to charge the young person with an offence. Section 6 states that a police officer shall, before starting judicial proceedings or taking any other measures under the *YCJA* against a young person alleged to have committed an offence, consider whether it would be sufficient, having regard to the principles set out in s. 4, "to take no further action, warn the young person, administer a caution, if a program has been established under section 7, or, with the consent of the young person, refer the young person to a program or agency in the community that may assist the young person not to commit offences". Clearly, the *YCJA* is directing the police officer to specifically and actively turn his or her mind to the question of whether it is necessary in the case at hand to charge the young person. The failure of the police officer to consider these options does not invalidate any subsequent charges against the young person for the offence.[32] Given this caveat, s. 6 must be understood as a section that primarily aims to strongly encourage

---

[31]   Kent Roach, "The Role of Crime Victims Under the *Youth Criminal Justice Act*" (2003) 40 Alta. L. Rev. 965, at para. 29 (QL).

[32]   *YCJA*, s. 6(2).

police officers in every case to consider all possible options before deciding to lay the charge and thus expose the young person to the criminal process.

What do these various police options under s. 6 look like, in practice? Taking no action is obvious: the police officer basically decides that it is not necessary to do anything further, perhaps because the officer has discovered that the parents, school officials or even the victim have taken measures to hold the young person sufficiently accountable.

Since the other police options are not defined in the Act, they can take various forms, but generally the distinctions are the following: A police warning is designed to be an informal warning, generally involving a face-to-face lecture by the officer during which the police officer warns the young person that if he or she is observed repeating the behaviour, the young person could be charged. (Experience under the *YOA* had led to concerns that the police had decreased their use of this type of response and replaced it with charges or referrals to programs that in some cases may have amounted to disproportionate responses.)[33]

A police caution is a more formal warning, generally in writing in the form of a letter.[34] The officer may choose to issue it in person, in the presence of the parents, so that the parents are aware that their child has received a caution from the police. The caution letter generally advises the young person that the police have grounds to believe the young person has committed a crime and that the young person is not going to be charged this time, but if the young person is observed by the police engaging in similar conduct in the future, the young person could be charged. Police cautioning has been widely used in England and Wales, and in New Zealand and in parts of Australia. Both New Zealand and Australia have reported that high percentages of young persons who were cautioned were not convicted of subsequent offences within two years in the case of New Zealand, and did not come to the attention of the police again in the case of Australia.[35]

A police referral to a community program or agency is another type of pre-charge, police-based diversion that the police can use, provided the

---

[33]   See Department of Justice website at: <http://www.justice.gc.ca/eng/pi/yj-jj/repos-depot/3modules/01extjud/3010301d.html#warning>.

[34]   The Department of Justice has a lot of excellent information and background materials and reports on its website concerning the youth justice system in Canada. For example, sample forms for police cautions can be found at the attached website: <http://www.justice.gc.ca/eng/pi/yj-jj/repos-depot/Forms/form.html>.

[35]   See the Department of Justice's website at: <http://www.justice.gc.ca/eng/pi/yj-jj/repos-depot/3modules/01extjud/3010301d.html#warning>.

young person consents without any pressure or coercion to participate in the program. A referral can work like this: The police officer sees a young person vandalizing the exterior walls of a school, stops the young person and soon realizes that the young person appears to have some obvious problems, such as an addiction issue. After interviewing the young person and doing some further investigation about his or her background, school performance, etc., the officer could decide to refer the young person to a program that could assist the young person with the addiction issue.

C.   Crown Cautions

The new extrajudicial measures regime under the *YCJA* also introduces the concept of a formal Crown caution, which a prosecutor can use instead of proceeding with a prosecution against the young person. Provided the Attorney General[36] has established a Crown caution program, the Crowns can deal with a young person by way of a caution rather than starting or continuing judicial proceedings. In other words, once the police refer the case/file to the Crown, after reviewing the file, the Crown may choose to resolve the matter by cautioning the young person instead of proceeding with the charge.

Crown cautions are a formal warning from the Crown to the young person generally in the form of a written letter through which the young person is warned that future criminal conduct could result in criminal charges. Since the police also have the right to issue police cautions, Crown cautions are presumably intended to be perceived as more serious. A young person who receives a police caution and then receives a Crown caution as a result of a subsequent incident could expect that the next incident could lead to a formal charge depending on the nature of the conduct. Unlike a police caution, a Crown caution will generally occur post-charge.

While the *YCJA* does not define a Crown caution or specify whether it must be delivered orally or in written form, a Crown caution is most likely to be considered a more formal response than a warning and thus is most likely to be delivered in writing in the form of a caution letter, in which the Crown indicates that the Crown has sufficient evidence to

---

[36] The *YCJA* indicates in s. 2 that the definition of Attorney General as defined in s. 2 of the *Criminal Code* is the applicable definition. In general terms, the Attorney General of the province prosecutes most matters under the *Criminal Code* in the provinces, while the Attorney General of Canada prosecutes matters in the provinces under other federal statutes such as the *Controlled Drugs and Substances Act*, S.C. 1996, c. 19. In the three territories, however, the Attorney General of Canada prosecutes all matters under the *Criminal Code* and the *Controlled Drugs and Substances Act*.

believe that the young person has committed a crime. The letter will then indicate that the Crown has decided not to proceed with the matter but should the young person engage in further criminal conduct, the Crown may well decide to proceed with a prosecution.[37]

Anecdotal evidence[38] from prosecutors suggests that Crown caution letters are not used extensively across the country largely because, if the matter has found its way to the Crown, it is usually because the police have chosen not to divert the young person because the matter is perceived as sufficiently serious to warrant a prosecution. Thus, most of the files that reach the Crown's office are generally found, upon review, to be sufficiently serious that a Crown caution is generally considered inappropriate.

Another reason that the new police and Crown cautions under the *YCJA* may not be widely used in Canada to date is that these new options are permissive.[39] The Attorney General has discretion as to whether to establish Crown caution programs.[40]

D. Restriction on Future Use of Extrajudicial Measures

The *YCJA* restricts the future use that can be made of evidence indicating that a young person has been dealt with by a warning, police or Crown caution, or police referral, or that the police took no further action, in respect of an offence, as outlined in ss. 6, 7 and 8. In accordance with s. 9 of the *YCJA*, such evidence is inadmissible in any youth justice court proceeding to prove prior offending behaviour by the young person. In other words, evidence in relation to matters that could have led to charges but were instead resolved through any of these informal measures cannot be used against the young person in subsequent proceedings as evidence of prior offences. In essence, the young person is not to be prejudiced during the course of a youth justice court proceeding by the fact that he or she had some previous relatively minor contact with the authorities that was resolved very informally.

---

[37] Samples of Crown caution letters can be found on the Department of Justice website at: <http://www.justice.gc.ca/eng/pi/yj-jj/repos-depot/Forms/form.html>.

[38] The reference to anecdotal evidence means that the author has not engaged in empirical research and bases this observation on interviews and informal polling of federal and provincial Crowns across the country.

[39] Nicholas Bala, "Community-Based Responses to Youth Crime: Cautioning, Conferencing and Extrajudicial Measures" in Kathryn Campbell, ed., *Understanding Youth Justice in Canada* (Toronto: Pearson Education Canada Inc., 2005), 176 at 180.

[40] *YCJA*, ss. 7 and 8.

III. EXTRAJUDICIAL SANCTIONS: SECTIONS 10-12

Most provinces and territories in Canada do not have pre-charge screening in place, whereby the Crown approves the charges that the police want to lay. Thus, in most jurisdictions, the Crown receives the file from the police after charges have been laid. However, once the Crown receives the file from the police after charges have been laid, the prosecutor can still choose to divert the young person. Even if the Crown does not consider a Crown caution appropriate in the circumstances, the prosecutor can consider whether the case is appropriate for an extrajudicial sanction under s. 10. If the Crown determines that the case is appropriate for a sanction, the matter will be diverted and will not proceed through the formal court system.

Extrajudicial sanctions are defined and described in s. 10 of the *YCJA*. Extrajudicial sanctions are the most severe form of extrajudicial measure within the new extrajudicial measures regime. These sanctions under s. 10 of the *YCJA* are identical to alternative measures under the *YOA*. If one characterizes the panoply of extrajudicial measures under the *YCJA* as a spectrum of options, a police officer taking no action in a case where the young person is alleged to have committed an offence is at the far left of the spectrum whereas the imposition of an extrajudicial sanction is at the far right. It is the most severe extrajudicial measure the state can consider imposing instead of proceeding with a formal prosecution.

Extrajudicial sanctions under s. 10 are to be used to deal with a young person alleged to have committed an offence only if the young person cannot be adequately dealt with by a police warning, a police or Crown caution or a police referral, as described in ss. 6, 7 and 8, because of the seriousness of the offence, the nature and number of previous offences committed by the young person or any other aggravating circumstances. The wording of the preceding phrase is important. Given the use of the disjunctive "or", it appears that only one of the conditions is required. In other words, a sanction can be used if none of the other options in s. 6, 7 or 8 is adequate because of the seriousness of the offence, because of the nature and number of previous offences committed by the young person *or* because of any other aggravating circumstances. For example, arguably, it is not mandatory that the young person have committed other offences before the Crown can resolve the matter by way of a sanction. The young person may be a first-time offender but may have committed an offence sufficiently serious that a sanction is the only extrajudicial measure that would be considered appropriate in the circumstances.

Provided the person who is considering using the sanction is satisfied that a less severe extrajudicial measure would not be adequate, the sanction can be used only if the seven conditions described in s. 10(2) are satisfied:

- the extrajudicial sanction must be part of a program of sanctions authorized by the Attorney General[41] or authorized by a person, or a member of a class of persons, designated by the lieutenant governor in council of the province (or territory);[42]

- the person considering whether to use the sanction must be satisfied that it would be appropriate, having regard to the needs of the young person and the interests of society;

- the young person, having been informed of the sanction, fully and freely consents to it;

- the young person, before consenting to the sanction, has been advised of the right to be represented by counsel and been given a reasonable opportunity to consult counsel;

- the young person accepts responsibility for the act or omission that forms the basis of the offence that he or she is alleged to have committed;

- there is, in the opinion of the Attorney General, sufficient evidence to proceed with the prosecution of the offence; and

- the prosecution is not in any way barred at law.

All of these conditions must be satisfied before a sanction can be used. In addition, a sanction may not be used if the young person denies participation or involvement in the commission of the offence or expresses the desire to have the matter dealt with by the youth justice court.[43]

Several of the conditions deserve particular attention. The second condition states only that the person who is considering the sanction must be satisfied that it would be appropriate. This phrase, which was the same under the *YOA*, does not stipulate that the person who makes this decision must be the prosecutor. Some youth justice experts have taken the position that it is within the discretion of the Attorney General in each jurisdiction as to whether the prosecutor or others can make this decision.[44] Under the *YOA*, it was held that the youth justice court judge has the authority to change or make the decision if the diversion program gives him or her the

---

[41]   *YCJA*, s. 2.

[42]   A province includes a territory by virtue of s. 35 of the *Interpretation Act*, R.S.C. 1985, c. I-21. The same section also clarifies the meaning of lieutenant governor in council.

[43]   *YCJA*, s. 10(3).

[44]   Priscilla Platt, *Young Offenders Law in Canada* (Markham: Butterworths Canada Ltd., 1995), at 151-52.

power to do so.[45] But where the prosecutor makes the decision as to whether the person can be diverted, the court cannot intervene. The Supreme Court of Canada has clarified that, absent circumstances that would amount to abuse of process, the exercise of prosecutorial discretion in relation to whether or not charges should proceed against a young person is for the prosecutorial authorities and not for the court.[46] The decision to divert a young person is essentially the "flipside" of the decision to prosecute.

In effect, the prosecutor is the person who decides whether a sanction would be appropriate under s. 10(2)(b) because it is the prosecutor who has the ultimate discretion to decide whether the matter should proceed through the formal court process. In the course of considering whether to prosecute the young person, the Crown will often have to consider whether the matter could be appropriately dealt with by way of a sanction.

In addition, under the YCJA, it is now clear that a young person does not have a right to a hearing in relation to whether he or she should be diverted.[47]

The young person must also validly consent to the sanction and must have a chance to consult counsel prior to consenting. It is necessary that a young person consult counsel prior to consenting to the sanction in order to be apprised of the implications of consenting. For example, the record of a sanction can be accessed for two years from the date that the young person consents to it,[48] and the record of the sanction can also be included in a pre-sentence report,[49] whereas information about other extrajudicial measures is not as readily accessible.[50] Since the young person is required to accept responsibility for the conduct that forms the basis of the offence, it is also important that counsel advise young persons that they should not admit responsibility unless they are, in fact, responsible. Some young persons may be inclined to admit responsibility, some under pressure from their parents, so that the matter can be resolved quickly, even if they are not responsible. The young person must therefore be aware that a record of this sanction will remain accessible for two years. While the admission

---

[45]   *R. v. J.L.*, [1992] Y.J. No. 64 (Y.T. Terr. Ct.).

[46]   *R. v. T. (V.)*, [1992] S.C.J. No. 29, 71 C.C.C. (3d) 32 (S.C.C.).

[47]   While this point was unsettled under the YOA and the case law was inconsistent, the wording of s. 3(1)(d)(i) specifically addresses and settles this point: a young person does not have a right to a hearing in relation to whether he or she should be diverted. That said, clearly, his or her counsel remains free to make submission to the Crown in this regard. See the recent case of *R. v. P.L.N.B.*, [2008] N.W.T.J. No. 1 (N.W.T.T.C.).

[48]   YCJA, s. 119(2)(a).

[49]   YCJA, s. 40(2)(d)(iv).

[50]   YCJA, s. 119(4).

of responsibility itself in the form of an admission, confession or statement from the young person is inadmissible in evidence in criminal or civil proceedings[51] against the young person, it will be apparent that the young person has admitted responsibility for the act or omission at issue in relation to the sanction imposed because the admission of responsibility is a condition precedent for a sanction.

The Crown must also be aware that a matter cannot be resolved by way of a sanction if the Crown could not otherwise proceed with a prosecution. The prosecutor cannot choose to use a sanction because there is insufficient evidence to proceed with the prosecution. Nor can the Crown proceed by way of sanction if the offence is barred at law, for example, if the offence is a summary offence for which the limitation period for prosecution has passed.

If a young person has been charged with an offence and it is decided that it will be resolved through the use of an extrajudicial sanction, the court is obliged to eventually dismiss the charge if it is satisfied on a balance of probabilities that the young person has totally complied with the terms and conditions of the sanction. Even if the young person has only partially complied with the terms and conditions of the sanction, the judge has the discretion to dismiss the charge. In this latter case, the court can dismiss the charge if it is satisfied on a balance of probabilities that the young person has partially complied with the terms and conditions of the sanction and if, in the opinion of the court, prosecution of the matter would be unfair, having regard to the circumstances and the young person's performance in relation to the sanctions.[52]

In keeping with one of the objectives of the *YCJA*, which is for communities, families and parents to play a role in providing guidance and support to young persons at risk of committing crimes,[53] the *YCJA* also obliges those who administer sanction programs to inform a young person's parent when a young person is dealt with by a sanction,[54] presumably when the sanction is imposed so that the parent[55] can support the young person in successfully completing it.

Victims also have a right to know the identity of a young person who has been dealt with by way of a sanction in relation to an offence involving them, as well as the precise nature of the sanction imposed. It is up to the police officer, the Crown, the provincial director, or any organi-

---

[51]   *YCJA*, s. 10(4).

[52]   *YCJA*, s. 10(5).

[53]   *YCJA*, Preamble, Clause 2 in particular.

[54]   *YCJA*, s. 11.

[55]   "Parent" is defined in s. 2 of the *YCJA*.

zation established by the province (or territory) to assist victims, to provide this information to the victim, upon request from the victim.[56] Similar to comments about the interests of victims found in the Preamble and in ss. 3 and 5, the right of a victim to know how the offence was dealt with, especially in a case where the Crown chose not to proceed with a prosecution, illustrates the greater attention paid to the needs and concerns of victims under the *YCJA*.

A wide range of programs can qualify as sanctions for purposes of s. 10, provided the program is authorized by the Attorney General or otherwise by the province or territory. Sanction programs vary widely, from requiring young persons to apologize to the victims of their crimes, to requirements that they volunteer at local boys and girls clubs, to going to schools to share their stories as lessons to others, to working for the proprietors of the establishments, whose properties they have damaged. A sanction program can even involve meeting with the victim of the crime to give the victim a chance to tell the young person how the crime affected him or her. Victim-offender reconciliation programs are among the types of programs mentioned in the *YCJA* as an alternative to judicial proceedings. Other examples of programs cited are mediation and restitution.[57] There are an increasing range of sanction programs in communities across Canada, including programs that specifically target First Nations and Inuit peoples, such as on-the-land programs and programs linking First Nations and Inuit young persons with community elders. Such programs are often aimed at encouraging First Nations and Inuit young persons to reconnect with their traditional teachings and culture.

It must be clearly understood, however, that an extrajudicial sanction is an alternative to the formal court process, which means that it is not part of a sentence. It is a program to which a young person is referred instead of being prosecuted and sentenced through the formal court process. It is possible that a young person's sentence, upon a finding of guilt, could also involve participation in a similar program, such as a requirement to perform a certain number of hours of community service at a local organization[58] or to attend a program as part of his or her sentence.[59] But participating in a program as part of an extrajudicial sanction is different from being ordered to attend a program as part of a sentence. An extrajudicial sanction is a non-judicial, non-court response, whereas being

---

[56] *YCJA*, s. 12.
[57] *YCJA*, s. 157.
[58] An order to perform community service is among the sentences that a young person can receive under s. 42(2)(i).
[59] An order to attend a non-residential program for up to 240 hours over six months can be made under s. 42(2)(m).

ordered to attend a program following a guilty finding for an offence is part of the young person's sentence.

IV. YOUTH JUSTICE COMMITTEES AND CONFERENCES UNDER THE YCJA

Youth justice committees and conferences tend to operate differently in communities across the country. Sometimes there appears to be little distinction between them, especially because one of the functions of a youth justice committee is to sit as a conference. The main difference between the two entities is that a youth justice committee has a broader mandate under the legislation, which includes addressing issues that affect young persons generally while a conference is generally called to seek advice and direction in relation to addressing the criminal behaviour of a specific young person. That said, as suggested, these two entities vary in their structure and operation in communities across the country, and sometimes perform the same functions. Information regarding the intent and purpose of each entity is available through the Department of Justice website.[60]

A.   Youth Justice Committees — Section 18

The existence of youth justice committees pre-dates the *YCJA* of 2003. The *YOA* permitted the establishment of youth justice committees,[61] which were described as unpaid committees of citizens who could assist with any aspect of the administration of the Act or with any programs or services for young offenders. The Attorney General of Canada or of the province or territory, or other minister such as the lieutenant governor in council of the province[62] could specify the method of appointment and the functions of the committee. The *YCJA* now expressly describes the functions of each entity, and has removed the requirement that the members serve without remuneration.[63]

Under the *YCJA*, the functions of a youth justice committee can include, but are not limited to, the following roles in relation to a young person alleged to have committed an offence: giving advice on the appropriate extrajudicial measure, supporting the victim of the alleged offence by soliciting his or her concerns and facilitating the reconciliation

---

[60]   See <http://www.justice.gc.ca/eng/pi/yj-jj/repos-depot/3modules/01extjud/3010301a.html>.

[61]   *YOA*, s. 69.

[62]   The federal *Interpretation Act* defines the lieutenant governor in council of the province in s. 35 as essentially the executive council (the cabinet) of the province.

[63]   *YCJA*, s. 18.

of the victim and the young person, ensuring that community support is available to the young person by arranging for the use of services within the community and enlisting community members to provide mentoring and supervision, and co-ordinating the interaction of social welfare agencies and the criminal justice system in cases where the young person is also being assisted by a child protection agency or a community group. In addition to these specific functions in relation to particular young persons, these committees can also advise the federal, provincial and territorial governments whether certain provisions of the *YCJA* are being complied with, advise the federal and provincial/territorial governments on policies and procedures related to the youth criminal justice system, provide information to the public in relation to the *YCJA* and the youth criminal justice system and act as a conference, as well as any other functions assigned by the person who established the committee.

Youth justice committees have an open-ended mandate, since they can be assigned additional functions. They tend to operate differently in communities across Canada, and, to some extent, the breadth of their mandate and the variety of cases they handle may be related to how much confidence other criminal justice players have in them.

Since one of the functions of a youth justice committee is to act as a conference, sometimes there will appear to be little difference, in practice, between a youth justice committee and a conference.

B.   Conferences — Section 19[64]

While conferences occurred under the *YOA*, often by other names, such as sentencing circles, collaborative justice, or victim-offender reconciliation, the concept of conferences was formally introduced into the *YCJA* in 2003. Like youth justice committees, conferences draw on restorative justice concepts and principles,[65] and can take many forms but most often involve a group of professionals gathering together to exchange views about

---

[64]   General information re the intent of conferences under the *YCJA* can be found on the Department of Justice website at: <http://www.justice.gc.ca/eng/pi/yj-jj/repos-depot/over-aper/2010001e.html>.

[65]   Some academics suggest that the concept of the conference in the *YCJA* has been inspired in part by the family conferences common in New Zealand, and that conferences that take the form of victim-offender reconciliation may be particularly effective with young persons. See Kent Roach, "The Role of Crime Victims Under the *Youth Criminal Justice Act*" (2003) 40 Alta. L. Rev. 965, at para. 11 (QL). But see a more focused article on restorative justice in relation to youth crime that includes a critical analysis of conferencing in Liz Elliott, "Restorative Justice in Canadian Approaches to Youth Crime: Origins, Practices, and Retributive Frameworks" in Kathryn Campbell, ed., *Understanding Youth Justice in Canada* (Toronto: Pearson Education Canada Inc., 2005), at 242.

how to deal with a particular young person, or the offender and the victim being brought together with other parties such as family members to try to achieve some measure of reconciliation as an act of restorative justice, an attempt to repair the harm done. Conferences can be convened throughout the youth criminal justice process, from the bail stage to the sentencing stage, to provide advice on how to deal with a specific case and, thus, are not used solely in relation to extrajudicial measures.

A youth justice court judge, the provincial director (a probation officer), a police officer, a Justice of the Peace (JP), the prosecutor or a youth worker may convene a conference for the purpose of making a decision that must be made under the *YCJA* (although the Act does not state that these are the only parties who can convene a conference). The mandate of a conference may be, among other things, to give advice on appropriate extrajudicial measures, bail conditions, sentences, sentence reviews and reintegration plans. The Act does not restrict the conference to these functions.

A conference, therefore, has a more circumscribed role than a youth justice committee since a conference is generally established to seek a resolution in a particular case. The participants are identified based on the type of case and the kind of advice and input required. Thus the participants required at a conference vary from case to case.

Under s. 41 of the *YCJA*, a youth justice court judge can convene a conference after a guilty finding against a young person to receive advice on the appropriate sentence. Recommendations from the conference participants are recommendations only. The judge is not obliged to follow them. The conference mechanism merely provides an avenue for the youth justice court judge to receive advice from various parties, including professionals, which may assist him or her in imposing sentence.[66] As some judges have noted, a conference can bring valuable information to light that may not otherwise have been available.

Nevertheless, there appears to be some reticence on the part of judges to convene judicial conferences under s. 41. This can be explained partially by the lack of rules and infrastructure in relation to judicial

---

[66]   *R. v. T.D.P.*, [2004] S.J. No. 254, 250 Sask. R. 3 (Sask. Prov. Ct.) is an excellent example of the use of a conference in the case of an aboriginal young person. The *Gladue* factors (*R. v. Gladue*, [1999] S.C.J. No. 19 (S.C.C.)) were also considered and applied in this case. See, in addition, a case comment by Charmaine Panko, "*R. v. T.D.P.*: A Young Offender, His Sentencing Circle, and the YCJA" (2005) 68 Sask. L. Rev. 455. See also *R. v. M. (B.)*, [2003] S.J. Nos. 377 and 602 (Sask. Prov. Ct.), reversed on appeal in *R. v. B.L.M.*, [2003] S.J. No. 870 (Sask. C.A.), where Turpel-Lafond Prov. Ct. J. uses the conferencing process to explore the underlying causes of the young person's criminality.

conferences. The *YCJA* provides that the Attorney General or another designated official of the province can establish rules to guide the functioning of conferences *unless* the youth justice court judge or the JP convenes the conference. It is unclear why these parties cannot establish rules if a youth justice court judge or JP convenes the conference. The practical effect of the lack of rules in cases where a JP or a youth court judge convenes the conference is that these parties must develop rules themselves for the functioning of the conference, which may serve as a disincentive for these parties to convene the conference. In fact, some judges suggest that there have been few judicial conferences other than those known as sentencing circles or family conferences mainly because the infrastructure necessary to support such restorative justice conferences has not been adequately developed.[67]

V. IMPACT OF THE EXPANDED REGIME

One of the questions that inevitably arises in relation to the expanded extrajudicial measures regime is whether it has achieved its goal of reducing the number of young persons who are formally charged and processed through the court system. A 2005 report by Peter J. Carrington and Jennifer L. Schulenberg for the Department of Justice provides insight into that question. The study found that there was, in 2003, a substantial reduction at the national level and in most provinces and territories, in the number of young persons charged or recommended by police to be charged and a corresponding increase in the use of extrajudicial measures with apprehended young persons.[68] The study found a 28 per cent drop in the charge rate for criminal offences involving young persons in 2003 from the average annual rate during the 1986-2002 period, when the *YOA* was in force, or a drop of 16 per cent from the charge rate in 2002. As the study notes, put another way, in 2003, about one out of six young persons apprehended in Canada were not charged who would have been charged had police continued to use 2002 charging practices.[69] Charging levels were reduced in 2003 by more than one-third for minor offences such as theft-under and drug-related offences, while charge rates for serious

---

[67]   Miriam Bloomenfeld and David Cole, "The Roles of Legal Professionals in Youth Court" in Kathryn Campbell, ed., *Understanding Youth Justice in Canada* (Toronto: Pearson Education Canada Inc., 2005), 198 at 207. Both authors are now Ontario judges.

[68]   Peter J. Carrington and Jennifer L. Schulenberg, *The Impact of the Youth Criminal Justice Act on Police Charging Practices with Young Persons: A Preliminary Statistical Assessment: Report to the Department of Justice Canada* (2005), at 44.

[69]   Peter J. Carrington and Jennifer L. Schulenberg, *The Impact of the Youth Criminal Justice Act on Police Charging Practices with Young Persons: A Preliminary Statistical Assessment: Report to the Department of Justice Canada* (2005), at 14.

property and violent offences (other than common assault) decreased only slightly.[70]

That said, among the expectations not borne out by the research is that there was no substantial decrease in the case of young persons charged with administration of justice offences, such as violations of bail and probation, and failure to appear for court. Researchers had expected a substantial decrease in 2003 in the use of these charges and a corresponding increase in extrajudicial measures for these non-violent, "victimless" offences; however the data revealed little change from previous years in the way in which police respond to young persons accused of these offences.[71]

---

[70]   Peter J. Carrington and Jennifer L. Schulenberg, *The Impact of the Youth Criminal Justice Act on Police Charging Practices with Young Persons: A Preliminary Statistical Assessment: Report to the Department of Justice Canada* (2005), at 44.

[71]   Peter J. Carrington and Jennifer L. Schulenberg, *The Impact of the Youth Criminal Justice Act on Police Charging Practices with Young Persons: A Preliminary Statistical Assessment: Report to the Department of Justice Canada* (2005), at 44-45.

Chapter 6

YOUNG PERSONS AND THE CHARTER

I.   PRELUDE: LESSONS FROM STEVEN TRUSCOTT

The Steven Truscott story is among the most famous criminal cases in Canadian history. During the past five decades, his story has seeped into Canadian culture and become part of our collective psyche.[1] Regardless of one's opinion of the factual innocence of Steven Truscott, who was eventually acquitted in 2007, the 1959 prosecution of 14-year-old Truscott for the rape and murder of a 12-year-old classmate can be studied as a purely academic exercise: The case serves as a significant benchmark in Canadian legal history from which to examine how much has changed in youth criminal justice law in Canada in the past 50 years. That is the purpose of its inclusion here. The goal is not to consider the guilt or innocence of Steven Truscott but rather how the youth criminal justice system has evolved since he was dealt with under the *Juvenile Delinquents Act.*

Truscott was investigated, charged, prosecuted, convicted, and ordered sent to the gallows in approximately three months for the rape and murder of Lynne Harper. His death sentence was commuted in 1960 to life in prison. Truscott spent the next 10 years incarcerated, first at the Ontario Training School for Boys in Guelph, Ontario, and then at Collins Bay Penitentiary, to where he was transferred at the age of 18. Truscott maintained his innocence throughout,[2] but the courts, including the

---

[1]   In addition to the numerous books, articles and television programs over the years concerning the murder of 12-year-old Lynne Harper, Canadian writer Ann-Marie MacDonald drew on the facts of the case as part of the backdrop for her fictional work *The Way the Crow Flies* (Toronto: Vintage Canada Edition, 2004). The details of the Truscott case have also been outlined extensively in various court decisions, including the 2007 ruling of the Ontario Court of Appeal. The case is also thoroughly examined in Julian Sher, *Until You Are Dead* (Toronto: Alfred A. Knopf Canada, 2001). However, the book that was instrumental in first bringing this case to the attention of the Canadian public was written by Isabel LeBourdais, *The Trial of Steven Truscott* (Toronto: McClelland and Stewart Ltd., 1966).

[2]   In his book about the Truscott case, journalist Julian Sher reports that Truscott admitted to the parole board in a 1964 application to having made "one dreadful mistake" but later explained that he was speaking generally about the lessons of jail rather than admitting to a specific crime. See Julian Sher, *Until You Are Dead* (Toronto: Alfred A. Knopf Canada, 2001), at 372.

Supreme Court of Canada,[3] upheld his conviction. Upon his release from prison in 1969, at the age of 24, Truscott assumed a different surname, married, raised a family and worked as a millwright in small-town Ontario, with few knowing his true identity.

In 2001, he emerged from a lifetime of obscurity to launch a public fight for vindication by applying to the federal Justice Minister under a special provision of the *Criminal Code* for a review of his conviction.[4] Truscott, in his 60s, won that absolution in 2007, 48 years after his conviction, when the Ontario Court of Appeal acquitted him of the crime.[5]

To some Canadians, his story symbolizes the frailties of the Canadian criminal justice system: a young teenager is convicted of a crime he did not commit and forfeits his reputation and an irreplaceable part of his life and liberty. In the eyes of some, the case highlights factors that have since been identified as common to wrongful convictions, including tunnel vision, flawed police investigations and interrogations, eyewitness misidentification, the unreliability of expert evidence and incomplete disclosure.[6]

To others who remain unconvinced of Steven Truscott's factual innocence despite his 2007 acquittal,[7] the case nevertheless serves as a classic case study of Canada's youth criminal justice system at a critical juncture in our legal history, a period that pre-dates the *Canadian Bill of Rights*,[8] the *Canadian Charter of Rights and Freedoms*,[9] and modern youth criminal justice legislation that emphasizes the due process rights of young Canadians. It is reasonable to consider, for example, how differently the police would have handled the detention and questioning of Steven Truscott had Truscott had the benefit of the constitutional rights now entrenched in the *Charter*, such as the right to silence, the right to

---

3   *Reference re: Truscott*, [1967] S.C.J. No. 26, [1967] S.C.R. 309 (S.C.C.). Justice Hall dissented on the grounds that Truscott had not received a fair trial.

4   His application was made under s. 690 of the *Criminal Code*, R.S.C. 1985, c. C-46, which is now s. 696.1 (am., S.C. 2002, c. 13, s. 71).

5   *R. v. Truscott*, [2007] O.J. No. 3221 (Ont. C.A.). The following year, Truscott was awarded $6.5 million in compensation.

6   A great deal has been written over the decades regarding the factors that have contributed to wrongful convictions in Canada and elsewhere. See, for example, Bruce MacFarlane, "Convicting the Innocent: A Triple Failure of the Justice System" (2006) 31 Man. L.J. 403. See also the 2005 Canadian FPT Heads of Prosecutions Committee Working Group *Report on the Prevention of Miscarriages of Justice*. This report is available online at: <http://www.justice.gc.ca/eng/dept-min/pub/pmj-pej/toc-tdm.html>.

7   The five-member panel of the Ontario Court of Appeal that acquitted Truscott did not go so far as to declare him factually innocent.

8   S.C. 1960, c. 44.

9   Part I of the *Constitution Act, 1982*, being Schedule B to the *Canada Act 1982* (U.K.), 1982, c. 11; proclaimed in force April 17, 1982 [hereafter "*Charter*"].

counsel and the right to be secure against unreasonable search or seizure, as well as the benefit of the many additional protections in the *Youth Criminal Justice Act*,[10] including those governing the taking of statements from young persons.

As it was, Truscott was dealt with under the *Juvenile Delinquents Act* decades before the *Charter* and the *YCJA* became law in this country, before young persons had all of the procedural protections they have today. In fact, the *JDA* provided for his transfer to adult court for trial, which was ordered in his case.[11] Truscott was convicted and sentenced as an adult, at the age of 14. Had his sentence not been commuted, he would have been executed.

A young person cannot be tried in adult court today under the *YCJA*.[12] Under the *YCJA*, a young person will always be tried in youth justice court although in some circumstances the youth justice court judge can impose an adult sentence. (A superior court can be deemed to be a youth justice court in certain cases.)[13]

As discussed in Chapter 1, the *JDA* was a vastly different piece of legislation than either the *Young Offenders Act*[14] or the *YCJA*. Unlike these Acts, due process was not a significant theme in the *JDA*, indeed it was not a theme at all. The *JDA* was not considered criminal law in the classic sense. It was far closer to social welfare legislation than to criminal law; concepts of due process and rights were largely irrelevant. The *JDA* was about helping misguided youths. All appeared fair when the legislation was perceived to be benevolent. Parties were considered to be acting in the best interests of the misguided youth. Conversely, both the *YOA* and the *YCJA* are products of the *Charter* era. Had Truscott been tried under either piece of legislation, with extensive due process protections, his journey through the criminal justice system, not to mention his journey through life, may have been dramatically different.

II.   SPECIFIC CHARTER PROVISIONS

Young persons in Canada enjoy the rights and protections of the *Charter* just as adults do, as well as additional protections afforded them

---

[10]   S.C. 2002, c. 1 [hereafter "*YCJA*"].
[11]   *Juvenile Delinquents Act*, R.S.C. 1952, c. 160, s. 9 [hereafter "*JDA*"]. See also *Re S.M.T.*, [1959] O.J. No. 737, 125 C.C.C. 100 (Ont. H.C.), in which Schatz J. refused Truscott's leave to appeal application in relation to the transfer order.
[12]   *R. v. S.J.L.*, [2009] S.C.J. No. 14, 2009 SCC 14 (S.C.C.).
[13]   *YCJA*, s. 13.
[14]   R.S.C. 1985, c. Y-1 [hereafter "*YOA*"].

under the *YCJA*.[15] The applicability of the *Charter* to young persons is highlighted throughout the *YCJA*. The Preamble of the *YCJA* states that Canada recognizes that young persons have rights and freedoms, including those stated in the *Charter* and in the *Canadian Bill of Rights*, and that they have special guarantees of their rights and freedoms. In fact, the *YCJA* imposes obligations on various criminal justice system players, including the police, judges and justices of the peace, to ensure they remind young persons of their *Charter* rights, such as the right to counsel, throughout the criminal justice process.

This chapter does not examine the vast body of *Charter* jurisprudence. Nor does it discuss every section of the *Charter*. Rather, the central purpose of this chapter is to explore the manner in which the Canadian judiciary has interpreted and applied various *Charter* rights in relation to criminal cases involving young persons. As a result, young persons will find in this chapter basic information regarding their rights upon being stopped by the police. Young persons, and indeed, many adults, lack understanding of the *Charter* rights that may be engaged during interactions with state authorities. The right to silence, the right to be secure against unreasonable search or seizure, the right not to be arbitrarily detained, the right to counsel, and the right to be tried within a reasonable time, are among the specific *Charter* rights considered in this chapter in relation to interactions between young persons and state actors, such as the police.

The cases considered tend to suggest that greater judicial scrutiny is exercised when the courts are assessing alleged *Charter* violations in relation to incidents involving young persons. The courts generally recognize that young persons are more vulnerable than a similarly situated adult *vis-à-vis* the powers of the state and are less likely to understand their rights during interactions with the police. The cases examined in this chapter also suggest that young persons may sometimes be subject to "age profiling". In other words, some cases suggest that young persons may be more apt to be stopped and questioned by the police merely because they are young persons, even if there is no reason to suspect them of wrongdoing. While the police may simply be reacting to research that suggests criminality peaks in late adolescence and early adulthood, age profiling can result in the harassment of innocent young persons and may also lead to unconstitutional questioning and searches by the police.[16] These are among the issues this chapter addresses.

---

[15]   The additional protections afforded young persons in the *YCJA* are discussed in Chapter 7.

[16]   See Nicholas Bala, "Youth as Victims and Offenders in the Criminal Justice System: A Charter Analysis — Recognizing Vulnerability" in Jamie Cameron and James Stribopoulos,

A.   Section 7

Life, liberty and security of person

7. Everyone has the right to life, liberty and security of the person and the right not to be deprived thereof except in accordance with the principles of fundamental justice.

Section 7 of the *Charter* is traditionally regarded as the umbrella provision for the other specific legal rights under the *Charter* (ss. 8 to 14). Among the key rights that it guarantees for individuals charged with crimes in Canada, including, of course, young persons, are the right to silence, and the right of the accused to disclosure of the Crown's case as a component of the constitutional right to make full answer and defence.[17]

(i)   *Right to Silence*

Section 7 of the *Charter* guarantees to everyone in Canada, adults and young persons alike,[18] a right to silence during the police investigative stage as well as at trial. "In the context of police questioning or interrogation, it means the subject has the choice as to whether to speak to the police or not."[19] The right to silence, like the presumption of innocence, is among the most important rights that Canadians have in relation to the state upon being charged with a crime. Law-abiding Canadians, young persons in particular, often do not understand the meaning and breadth of the right to silence, particularly if they have had little or no previous contact with the police. That is why it is so important for young persons to exercise their right to counsel upon detention or arrest so that counsel can advise that they are not obligated to provide information to the police.

The right to silence, as an aspect of the principle against self-incrimination, has long been a feature of the common law: simply put, under the common law, an individual in Canada is not obliged to give information to the police or to answer their questions, absent statutory or

---

eds., *The Charter and Criminal Justice: Twenty-five Years Later* (Markham, Ont.: LeisNexis, 2008), 595 at 608.

[17] *R. v. Stinchcombe*, [1991] S.C.J. No. 83, at paras. 17 and 26 (S.C.C.). See also *R. v. McNeil*, [2009] S.C.J. No. 3, 2009 SCC 3 (S.C.C.).

[18] *R. v. C.K.*, [2005] O.J. No. 4853 (Ont. C.J.).

[19] *R. v. C.K.*, [2005] O.J. No. 4853, at para. 13 (Ont. C.J.).

other legal compulsion.[20] The right to silence became constitutionally entrenched under s. 7 when the Supreme Court of Canada recognized that the right to silence forms part of the basic tenets of Canada's legal system.[21] The residual protection afforded the right to silence under s. 7 of the *Charter* is triggered only upon detention.[22]

Standard police cautions given to a person who has been charged with a criminal offence normally advise the person that he or she is not obligated to give a statement, effectively informing him or her of the right to silence.[23] The *Charter* does not expressly mandate that the police advise individuals of their right to silence, in those exact words, upon detention. The *Charter* says only that the police must promptly advise everyone upon detention or arrest of the reasons for the detention or arrest, and must also advise them of their right to retain and instruct counsel without delay. (If and when the individual exercises the right to counsel, presumably the lawyer will advise the individual that there is no obligation to talk with the police; it is expected that the lawyers will also impress upon the suspect or the accused the possible implications of providing information to the police.) The right to counsel and the right to silence are thus inextricably linked. Young persons in particular may not fully appreciate the meaning and importance of the right to silence until they have spoken with counsel.

To ensure that young persons are aware of their *Charter* rights, the *YCJA* creates an explicit statutory obligation on the police under s. 146 to clearly explain to a young person "in language appropriate to his or her age and understanding", upon the arrest or detention of the young person or in circumstances where the peace officer or other person has reasonable grounds to believe that the young person has committed an offence, that the young person is under no obligation to make a statement to the police.[24] This express inclusion in s. 146 illustrates the nature of the additional procedural protections that are afforded young persons who are suspected or charged with crimes in Canada. Youth criminal justice law requires that greater efforts be made by the state to ensure a young person understands such important constitutional rights.

---

[20] *R. v. Singh*, [2007] S.C.J. No. 48, at para. 27 (S.C.C.). But see *R. v. Moore*, [1978] S.C.J. No. 82, [1979] 1 S.C.R. 195 (S.C.C.), where the court held that an individual had an obligation to identify himself after the police observed him committing an offence.

[21] *R. v. Singh*, [2007] S.C.J. No. 48, at para. 34 (S.C.C.). But note that Charron J. in *R. v. Singh* cites *R. v. Hebert*, [1990] S.C.J. No. 64, [1990] 2 S.C.R. 151 (S.C.C.) on this point.

[22] *R. v. Singh*, [2007] S.C.J. No. 48, at paras. 32 and 46 (S.C.C.).

[23] *R. v. Singh*, [2007] S.C.J. No. 48, at para. 31 (S.C.C.).

[24] *YCJA*, s. 146(2)(b)(i). In *R. v. L.T.H.*, [2008] S.C.J. No. 50, 2008 SCC 49 (S.C.C.), the Supreme Court of Canada elaborated on the meaning of s. 146(2)(b). This case is discussed further in Chapter 7.

The Supreme Court of Canada reconsidered the nature and meaning of the right to silence in the 2007 case of *R. v. Singh*.[25] While the case concerned an adult accused, its overarching legal principles apply to young persons as well. In *Singh*, the accused, who had been arrested for murder, asserted his right to silence repeatedly during police questioning, after having consulted with counsel. The police persisted in questioning him and he eventually made incriminating statements. The Supreme Court of Canada upheld the lower courts in concluding that the admissions were admissible because the statements were made voluntarily and Singh freely chose to speak to the authorities after consulting counsel.

Speaking for the majority, Charron J. observed that the burden is on the Crown to prove the case against the accused beyond a reasonable doubt; the accused is not required to assist the prosecution,[26] including by providing incriminating information.[27] The purpose of the right to silence is to limit the use of the coercive power of the state to force detained persons to incriminate themselves, Charron J. explained.[28] In these circumstances, detainees have the right to choose whether to speak with the authorities. Nevertheless, the Supreme Court of Canada affirmed in *Singh* that the right to silence is not equivalent to saying that the police have no right to speak to individuals or to ask questions.[29]

The Supreme Court of Canada rejected Mr. Singh's argument that the police should refrain from questioning a detainee once he or she has asserted the right to silence. Rather, the court held that, in deference to the importance of police interrogation in the investigation of crime,[30] the police can continue to try to persuade suspects to talk with them and to provide information, but such police persuasion cannot exceed certain boundaries.[31] The police can use only legitimate means of persuasion to get suspects to talk.[32] Police tactics cannot effectively deny the individual the right to

---

[25] [2007] S.C.J. No. 48 (S.C.C.).

[26] *R. v. Stinchcombe*, [1991] S.C.J. No. 83, at para. 12 (S.C.C.).

[27] Justice Iacobucci describes well the principle against self-incrimination in *R. v. White*, [1999] S.C.J. No. 28, at para. 44, [1999] 2 S.C.R. 417 (S.C.C.).

[28] *R. v. Broyles*, [1991] S.C.J. No. 95, at para. 22, [1991] 3 S.C.R. 595 (S.C.C.). See also ss. 11(c) and 13 of the *Charter*.

[29] *R. v. Singh*, [2007] S.C.J. No. 48, at para. 28 (S.C.C.).

[30] *R. v. Singh*, [2007] S.C.J. No. 48, at para. 28 (S.C.C.).

[31] *R. v. Singh*, [2007] S.C.J. No. 48, at paras. 46 and 47 (S.C.C.). In a strongly worded dissent, Fish J. found that Singh's right to silence had been violated in that he asserted his right to silence 18 times and yet the police continued to question him relentlessly until he eventually capitulated and made several incriminating statements. During his dissent, Fish J. noted at para. 89 that the law in the United States for more than 40 years has been that, where a suspect indicates in any manner at any time prior to, or during, questioning that he wishes to remain silent, the interrogation must cease. (See *R. v. Singh*, [2007] S.C.J. No. 48, at paras. 55-100 (S.C.C.).)

[32] *R. v. Singh*, [2007] S.C.J. No. 48, at para. 47 (S.C.C.).

choose, or deprive him or her of an operating mind.[33] It must be clear on the facts that the individual understood that he or she had a right to silence and was not obliged to speak with the police, but knowingly and freely chose to do so anyway. "The ultimate question is whether the accused exercised free will by choosing to make a statement."[34] During any assessment of whether the right to silence of the accused has been breached, the focus will necessarily be on the conduct of the police during the questioning and the effect of the police conduct on the suspect's capacity to exercise free will as to whether to speak with the police.[35]

It is noteworthy that *Singh* concerned an adult accused. The judiciary may well assess such situations with greater scrutiny when the accused is a young person. *R. v. C.K.*[36] is illustrative of this point, where the court held that "young persons are particularly vulnerable to the coercive effects of detention and police questioning".[37] *R. v. C.K.* was a murder case with certain facts similar to *Singh*. It was decided prior to *Singh*. The court in *R. v. C.K.* reached the opposite conclusion from *Singh* and found that the young person's right to silence had been violated. It is unlikely the conclusion in *R. v. C.K.* would have been different had it been decided after *Singh* because *Singh* essentially affirmed the existing law regarding the meaning of the right to silence in any event.[38]

In *R. v. C.K.*, Duncan J. of the Ontario Court of Justice held that a teenager's right to silence was violated when police repeatedly questioned her following her clear assertions that she wished to invoke her right to silence and did not want to speak to the police. She was arrested at 7 a.m., taken to the police station, and confessed to the murder under investigation at around 1 p.m. Prior to her confession, she was advised of her rights under the *Charter* and the *YCJA*, and had been given an opportunity to consult legal counsel, which she did. An experienced police officer then questioned her for several hours, during which time she asserted her right to silence an estimated 17 times.[39] The police questioning continued until C.K. began making admissions of guilt around 12:30 p.m. Justice Duncan ruled that C.K.'s right to silence was violated in the circumstances in light of "the gross power imbalance between this young offender and the police".

---

[33] This reasoning is essentially from *R. v. Hebert*, [1990] S.C.J. No. 64, [1990] 2 S.C.R. 151 (S.C.C.) and is adopted in *R. v. Singh*, [2007] S.C.J. No. 48, at paras. 46 and 47 (S.C.C.).

[34] *R. v. Singh*, [2007] S.C.J. No. 48, at para. 53 (S.C.C.).

[35] *R. v. Singh*, [2007] S.C.J. No. 48, at para. 36 (S.C.C.).

[36] [2005] O.J. No. 4853 (Ont. C.J.).

[37] *R. v. C.K.*, [2005] O.J. No. 4853, at para. 12 (Ont. C.J.).

[38] The critical reasoning in *Singh* is from *R. v. Hebert*, [1990] S.C.J. No. 64, [1990] 2 S.C.R. 151 (S.C.C.).

[39] *R. v. C.K.*, [2005] O.J. No. 4853, at para. 6 (Ont. C.J.).

Her 17 assertions of her right to silence do not stand alone—they occur within the context of her prolonged detention and after hours of denials that are ignored, or dismissed as being lies or unacceptable. I have no doubt at all but that her will and freedom of choice were over-ridden by the superior power of the police.[40]

Her confession was excluded from evidence.

The court in *C.K.* applied the same legal principles regarding the right to silence but arrived at a different result from *Singh* after balancing the power of the state *vis-à-vis* a young person. As the comments of Duncan J. suggest, the fact that the suspect was a young person was a significant aspect of the assessment. In *C.K.*, Duncan J. held that, in all of the circumstances, the suspect did not freely choose to speak with the police.

(ii)   The Right to Make Full Answer and Defence and the Duty of Disclosure

Section 7 of the *Charter* also guarantees to an accused person the right to make full answer and defence, which is not only a principle of fundamental justice but one of the pillars of criminal justice, to ensure that the innocent are not convicted.[41] Failure by the Crown to disclose relevant information in its possession[42] can impede the ability of the accused to make full answer and defence,[43] and the accused is thus deprived of knowing the case he or she must meet. A young person has the constitutional right to make full answer and defence no less than an adult. Thus, receiving disclosure of the Crown's case is equally important to a young accused person. For these reasons, some basic discussion of this fundamentally important duty is included in this chapter.

R. v. Stinchcombe[44] recognizes the Crown's duty to disclose to the defence all relevant information in its possession.[45] The Crown has a

---

[40]   *R. v. C.K.*, [2005] O.J. No. 4853, at para. 20 (Ont. C.J.).

[41]   *R. v. Stinchcombe*, [1991] S.C.J. No. 83, at para. 17 (S.C.C.). *R. v. McNeil*, [2009] S.C.J. No. 3, 2009 SCC 3 (S.C.C.) further clarified the law in this area.

[42]   The police have a corollary duty to disclose to the prosecuting Crown all relevant information in their possession pertaining to the investigation of the accused. See *R. v. McNeil*, [2009] S.C.J. No. 3, at paras. 23-24, 2009 SCC 3 (S.C.C.).

[43]   *R. v. Stinchcombe*, [1991] S.C.J. No. 83, at para. 17 (S.C.C.). See also *R. v. McNeil*, [2009] S.C.J. No. 3, 2009 SCC 3 (S.C.C.), which summarizes the *Stinchcombe* principles well at paras. 17 and 18.

[44]   [1991] S.C.J. No. 83 (S.C.C.).

[45]   *R. v. Stinchcombe*, [1991] S.C.J. No. 83, at paras. 23, 26 and 29 (S.C.C.). *Stinchcombe* suggests at para. 26 that the content of the right to make full answer and defence may be circumscribed in the case of summary offences.

general duty to disclose to the defence all material it proposes to use at trial, including all evidence that may assist the accused, even if the Crown does not propose to adduce it, subject to privilege.[46] The Crown must disclose relevant material, whether it is inculpatory or exculpatory.[47] However, this duty is not absolute. It is subject to the Crown's discretion regarding the timing and manner of disclosure, as well as the withholding of information, such as information that is privileged. Nor does the Crown have to produce information that is clearly irrelevant.[48]

The Crown's discretion in this regard is reviewable by the trial judge, who is to be guided by the general principle "that information ought not to be withheld if there is a reasonable possibility that the withholding of information will impair the right of the accused to make full answer and defence, unless the non-disclosure is justified by the law of privilege".[49]

(iii)   Constitutional Challenges to Reverse Onus Provisions in the YCJA

Constitutional challenges have arisen under s. 7 of the *Charter* in relation to sections of the *YCJA* that place the onus on a young person in certain circumstances to persuade the court that he or she should not receive an adult sentence or that his or her name should not be published.[50] Until the 2008 Supreme Court of Canada ruling in *R. v. D.B.*,[51] the *YCJA* provided that a young person would receive an adult sentence if he or she were found guilty of certain serious crimes, such as murder, attempt to commit murder, manslaughter, aggravated sexual assault or a third serious violent offence,[52] unless the young person could satisfy the court that a youth sentence should be imposed instead.[53] Prior to the 2008 ruling, the lower courts, including the appellate courts, were divided on

---

[46]   *R. v. Stinchcombe*, [1991] S.C.J. No. 83, at paras. 19 and 20 (S.C.C.).

[47]   *R. v. Stinchcombe*, [1991] S.C.J. No. 83, at para. 29 (S.C.C.).

[48]   *R. v. Stinchcombe*, [1991] S.C.J. No. 83, at para. 20 (S.C.C.).

[49]   *R. v. Stinchcombe*, [1991] S.C.J. No. 83, at paras. 19-22 (S.C.C.).

[50]   *YCJA*, ss. 62, 63, 64(1), 64(5), 70, 72(1), 72(2), 73(1), 75 and 110(2)(b).

[51]   [2008] S.C.J. No. 25, 2008 SCC 25 (S.C.C.).

[52]   These are characterized in s. 2 of the *YCJA* as presumptive offences. But now, by virtue of *R. v. D.B.*, in these cases, if the Crown wishes an adult sentence to be imposed, the onus is on the Crown to convince the court of this upon a young person being found guilty of any of these s. 2 offences.

[53]   The Crown can also give notice that it does not oppose the young person's application for a youth sentence (s. 64(2)), or that it is not seeking an adult sentence in relation to the presumptive offence. In either case, a youth sentence will be imposed for the presumptive offence upon a guilty finding.

the constitutionality of such reverse onus provisions.[54] (Similar provisions that presumed a young person of at least 16 charged with certain serious offences would be *tried* in adult court unless the court could be convinced otherwise were incorporated into the *YOA* in 1995, but their constitutionality had never been considered by the Supreme Court of Canada.)[55]

The Supreme Court of Canada settled the matter in 2008 by ruling unconstitutional the sections of the Act that created a presumption of an adult sentence in certain circumstances, and a presumption that the name of the young person would be published in certain circumstances.

In *R. v. D.B.*, the accused was at a shopping mall with two friends on December 13, 2003. They met the victim, aged 18, accompanied by his sister and two friends. There was an altercation. The victim and a friend left the mall with the accused and his friends in order to fight. While two males wrestled each other to the ground, the accused asked the victim if he wanted to fight. The victim declined and continued to observe the fight in progress. The accused then "sucker punched" the victim to the neck and face. The victim fell to the ground. The accused continued the assault, landing four more punches on the victim's face and neck. The victim was knocked unconscious and died just past midnight the following day. A post-mortem revealed that his death was a direct result of the assault. At the time of the assault, the accused was bound by two probation orders.

The accused was arrested and eventually pled guilty to manslaughter, which is a presumptive offence. Under the *YCJA*, as it was prior to the Supreme Court of Canada ruling in *R. v. D.B.*, it was presumed that D.B. would receive an adult sentence unless he could convince the court to impose a youth sentence instead. D.B. challenged the constitutionality of this reverse onus provision.

Both the trial court and the Ontario Court of Appeal[56] agreed that this provision was unconstitutional. In fact, prior to the Supreme Court of Canada ruling in *R. v. D.B.*, the Quebec Court of Appeal[57] had also held that the *YCJA* provisions that place the onus on the young person to justify a

---

[54] *Quebec (Minister of Justice) v. Canada (Minister of Justice) (sub nom. Reference re: Bill C-7 respecting the criminal justice system for young persons)*, [2003] J.Q. no 2850, 175 C.C.C. (3d) 321 (Que. C.A.); *R. v. D.B.*, [2006] O.J. No. 1112 (Ont. C.A.) and *R. v. S.R.B.*, [2008] A.J. No. 56 (Alta. Q.B.) but see *R. v. K.D.T.*, [2006] B.C.J. No. 253 (B.C.C.A.) and *R. v. G.D.S.*, [2007] N.S.J. No. 232 (N.S. Youth Ct.).

[55] *YOA*, s. 16. As noted by Abella J. in *R. v. D.B.*, [2008] S.C.J. No. 25, at para. 56, 2008 SCC 25 (S.C.C.). See also *S.R.B.*, [2008] A.J. No. 56 (Alta. Q.B.) on this point at para. 12.

[56] *R. v. D.B.*, [2006] O.J. No. 1112 (Ont. C.A.).

[57] *Quebec (Minister of Justice) v. Canada (Minister of Justice) (sub nom. Reference re: Bill C-7 respecting the criminal justice system for young persons)*, [2003] J.Q. no 2850, 175 C.C.C. (3d) 321 (Que. C.A.).

youth sentence in certain circumstances violate the liberty and security interests of the young person because they compel the young person to convince the court that the young person should not be liable to the harsher sentencing regime of the *Criminal Code* rather than placing the onus on the state to persuade the court that the young person should be liable to the stricter sentencing regime. The B.C. Court of Appeal took the opposite view.[58]

In *R. v. D.B.*, the Supreme Court of Canada agreed with the Ontario and Quebec appellate courts regarding their conclusions on the constitutionality of these provisions. Justice Abella, writing for the 5-4 majority, held that young persons are entitled to a legal presumption of diminished moral blameworthiness because of their heightened vulnerability, lesser maturity and reduced capacity for moral judgement.[59] This presumption of diminished moral culpability of young persons is not only a long-standing legal principle[60] but a principle of fundamental justice,[61] the court held. It was thus an unjustifiable violation of s. 7 of the *Charter* and therefore unconstitutional to place the onus on the young person to justify why he or she should receive a youth sentence. Rather, the burden should be on the Crown to justify why a more severe adult sentence is appropriate in the circumstances.[62]

Justice Abella applied the same rationale to reverse onus provisions under the *YCJA* that permit the publication of an accused young person's name in certain circumstances[63] unless the young person convinces the court that his or her name should not be published. Again, Abella J. held, the onus must be on the Crown to convince the court why the young person's name should be published.

While it may be years before the legal implications of *R. v. D.B.* are fully clear, in the short term, the practical procedural effect appears to be that, in all cases where the Crown is seeking an adult sentence, and the young person opposes the application, the onus is on the Crown to satisfy the court that the presumption of diminished moral culpability has been rebutted and the more severe adult sentence is justified.[64] Likewise with the

---

[58]   *R. v. K.D.T.*, [2006] B.C.J. No. 253 (B.C.C.A.).

[59]   *R. v. D.B.*, [2008] S.C.J. No. 25, at para. 41, 2008 SCC 25 (S.C.C.).

[60]   *R. v. D.B.*, [2008] S.C.J. No. 25, at para. 59, 2008 SCC 25 (S.C.C.).

[61]   *R. v. D.B.*, [2008] S.C.J. No. 25, at para. 70, 2008 SCC 25 (S.C.C.).

[62]   *R. v. D.B.*, [2008] S.C.J. No. 25, at para. 95, 2008 SCC 25 (S.C.C.).

[63]   *YCJA*, s. 75. Under this section, prior to *R. v. D.B.*, if a young person received a youth sentence for a presumptive offence, the name of the young person would be published unless the young person applied for a publication ban and the court agreed that it was appropriate.

[64]   *R. v. D.B.*, [2008] S.C.J. No. 25, at para. 93, 2008 SCC 25 (S.C.C.). Adult sentences are discussed in Chapter 8.

provisions of the *YCJA* that require a young person who is found guilty of a presumptive offence but receives a youth sentence to apply for a publication ban, the court in *R. v. D.B.* has held that the onus or burden is now on the Crown to justify the lifting of the publication ban in these circumstances.[65]

(iv) Duty to Protect

Finally, it is notable that the Federal Court of Canada, in an April 2009 decision, recognized the duty to protect as a principle of fundamental justice within s. 7 of the *Charter*, which extends to persons in circumstances like those of Omar Khadr.[66] Khadr, at the time of writing, had been held in a U.S. prison for seven years, awaiting trial. Khadr was arrested in Afghanistan in July 2002 when he was 15 years old and imprisoned at Guantanamo Bay on charges of murder, conspiracy and support of terrorism. He is accused of having thrown a grenade that caused the death of an American soldier.[67] His detention and treatment have been the subject of ongoing media attention.

In the course of his ruling, O'Reilly J. reviewed aspects of international human rights law that pertain to the treatment of young persons who come into conflict with the criminal law, and Canada's international obligations in that regard.[68] He noted, among other points, that Khadr, upon detention, was given no special status as a minor, had virtually no communication with anyone outside Guantanamo Bay until he met with legal counsel in November 2004 and was subjected to sleep deprivation and other practices later recognized as violations of international law, including the Convention Against Torture.[69]

Justice O'Reilly found that Canada had "a duty to protect Mr. Khadr from being subjected to any torture or other cruel, inhuman or degrading treatment or punishment, from being unlawfully detained, and from being locked up for a duration exceeding the shortest appropriate period of time. ... Canada had a duty to take all appropriate measures to promote Mr.

---

[65] *R. v. D.B.*, [2008] S.C.J. No. 25, at para. 87, 2008 SCC 25 (S.C.C.). Sections 75 and 110(2)(b) of the *YCJA*. The constitutionality of the publication provisions and the implications that flow from *R. v. D.B.* are discussed further in Chapter 9.

[66] *Khadr v. Canada (Prime Minister)*, [2009] F.C.J. No. 462, at para. 71, 2009 FC 405 (F.C.). This case was under appeal at the time of writing.

[67] *Khadr v. Canada (Prime Minister)*, [2009] F.C.J. No. 462, at para. 1, 2009 FC 405 (F.C.).

[68] *Khadr v. Canada (Prime Minister)*, [2009] F.C.J. No. 462, at paras. 55-75, 2009 FC 405 (F.C.).

[69] *Khadr v. Canada (Prime Minister)*, [2009] F.C.J. No. 462, at paras. 9, 10, 11, 17, 34 and 51, 2009 FC 405 (F.C.).

Khadr's physical, psychological and social recovery".[70] The principles of fundamental justice obliged Canada to protect Mr. Khadr by taking appropriate steps to ensure that his treatment was in line with international norms, O'Reilly J. held.[71]

Citing Khadr's youth at the time of apprehension as among the additional factors relevant to his decision,[72] O'Reilly J. ordered the federal government to seek his repatriation as the only practical remedy. "I find that the Government of Canada is required by s. 7 of the *Charter* to request Mr. Khadr's repatriation to Canada in order to comply with a principle of fundamental justice, namely, the duty to protect persons in Mr. Khadr's circumstances by taking steps to ensure that their fundamental rights, recognized in widely-accepted international instruments such as the *Convention on the Rights of the Child*, are respected."[73]

Although the mistreatment of Khadr was carried out by non-Canadians, Canada was implicated because Canadian officials interrogated Mr. Khadr, knowing that he had been subjected to treatment that offended international human rights norms to which Canada was a signatory, O'Reilly J. explained.[74]

At the time of writing, this decision was under appeal.

B.   Sections 8, 9 and 10 of the *Charter*

Search or seizure

8. Everyone has the right to be secure against unreasonable search or seizure.

Detention or imprisonment

9. Everyone has the right not to be arbitrarily detained or imprisoned.

Arrest or detention

10. Everyone has the right on arrest or detention

---

[70]   *Khadr v. Canada (Prime Minister)*, [2009] F.C.J. No. 462, at paras. 64 and 65, 2009 FC 405 (F.C.).
[71]   *Khadr v. Canada (Prime Minister)*, [2009] F.C.J. No. 462, at para. 75, 2009 FC 405 (F.C.).
[72]   *Khadr v. Canada (Prime Minister)*, [2009] F.C.J. No. 462, at para. 70, 2009 FC 405 (F.C.).
[73]   *Khadr v. Canada (Prime Minister)*, [2009] F.C.J. No. 462, at para. 91, 2009 FC 405 (F.C.).
[74]   *Khadr v. Canada (Prime Minister)*, [2009] F.C.J. No. 462, at para. 83, 2009 FC 405 (F.C.).

> *(a) to be informed promptly of the reasons therefor;*
>
> *(b) to retain and instruct counsel without delay and to be in-
>   formed of that right; and ... .*

Sections 8, 9 and 10 of the *Charter* have given rise to extensive litigation in the last quarter century. It is not uncommon for one case to
involve allegations relating to all three sections. In relation to young
persons, allegations involving breaches of these sections of the *Charter*
often arise as a result of incidents that begin as street encounters between
young persons and the police. The litigation often revolves around the fact
that it is not clear, in law, at what point, if at all, the young person was
being detained by the police. The young person may argue that the
conduct of the police led the young person to reasonably believe that he or
she was being detained and had no choice but to respond to the police
officers' questions whereas the police may take the position that they were
simply engaged in a conversation with the young person during a voluntary encounter and that the young person was free to leave at any point.

If the court finds that the young person was detained in law during
such an encounter, the court must then examine the constitutional implications: for example, under the *Charter*, a detention cannot be arbitrary (*i.e.*,
police must have the requisite grounds), and, upon detention or arrest, a
young person has the right to be informed promptly of the reasons for that
detention or arrest and also has the right to retain and instruct counsel
without delay and to be informed of that right. An alleged unreasonable
search is also often an aspect of many of these encounters; therefore, the
courts will also often have to consider whether there was a search in law,
and if so, whether it was unreasonable.

Additional legal questions are often canvassed in these cases, such
as: What are the constitutional parameters regarding the nature and
substance of the police questions that can be properly posed during
various encounters? In what circumstances can police questioning lead to
the conclusion that the young person was detained in law or amount to a
search in law? When can the police lawfully search a young person, or his
or her belongings, locker, bedroom or apartment? Other cases involving
young persons relate to searches on school premises, some of which
involve the use of drug detector dogs.

The remainder of this chapter explores such issues through a consideration of various criminal cases involving young persons or youthful
accused. As a prelude to that case law examination, it is necessary to
identify certain fundamental criminal law concepts that often arise in
these cases, such as the meaning of detention in law, the concept of an

investigative detention, the meaning and breadth of the right to counsel and basic search law concepts.

(i)   The Meaning of Detention

The Supreme Court of Canada defined the legal concept of detention in *R. v. Therens*,[75] and refined it in *R. v. Mann*[76] about 20 years later. In *Therens*, Le Dain J. defined detention for purposes of s. 10 of the *Charter* in relation to an impaired driving case where the police demanded the accused provide a breath sample. Justice Le Dain's definition of detention has become the classic articulation of the concept, and is traditionally cited during any significant legal discussion of detention.

Justice Le Dain held that detention includes a restraint of liberty other than arrest that can occur as a result of physical constraint or psychological compulsion. "The issue is whether a person who is the subject of a demand or direction by a police officer or other agent of the state may reasonably regard himself or herself as free to refuse to comply."[77] Justice Le Dain recognized that most citizens are unaware of the limits of police authority and may not know if the police are acting lawfully and, thus, are likely to err on the side of caution and comply with a police demand. He therefore concluded that a reasonable perception by the person that he or she is no longer free to leave the scene, to refuse to answer the police officer's questions, *etc.* is enough to make the restraint of liberty involuntary.[78]

> Detention may be effected without the application or threat of application of physical restraint if the person concerned submits or acquiesces in the deprivation of liberty and reasonably believes that the choice to do otherwise does not exist.[79]

Nearly two decades later, the Supreme Court of Canada refined the definition of detention. While the focus of *R. v. Mann* concerns the scope of police powers during an investigative detention (a brief detention where the police have reasonable suspicion that the individual is involved or was recently involved in criminal activity),[80] the court commented on the

---

75   [1985] S.C.J. No. 30, [1985] 1 S.C.R. 613 (S.C.C.).

76   [2004] S.C.J. No. 49 (S.C.C.).

77   *R. v. Therens*, [1985] S.C.J. No. 30, at para. 50, [1985] 1 S.C.R. 613 (S.C.C.).

78   *R. v. Therens*, [1985] S.C.J. No. 30, at para. 53, [1985] 1 S.C.R. 613 (S.C.C.).

79   *R. v. Therens*, [1985] S.C.J. No. 30, at para. 53, [1985] 1 S.C.R. 613 (S.C.C.).

80   *R. v. Mann*, [2004] S.C.J. No. 49, at paras. 34 and 45 (S.C.C.). Despite the ambiguity in terminology regarding the grounds for an investigative detention in *Mann*, based on the subsequent jurisprudence, it is fair to say that the grounds for an investigative detention remain that of reasonable suspicion, as defined in *R. v. Simpson*, [1993] O.J. No. 308, 12 O.R. (3d) 182

concept of detention as it is to be understood for purposes of the *Charter*. The court held that not every suspect who is stopped by the police for purposes of identification or interview can be held to be detained in law. While such persons are clearly delayed or kept waiting, the delay must involve *significant physical or psychological restraint*[81] before the person will be found to be detained in law for purposes of s. 9 or 10 of the *Charter*.[82]

In considering whether a young person has been detained in a particular case, at which point the police are obligated to provide certain *Charter* rights, the courts must determine based on the facts whether the young person and the police were engaged in a voluntary encounter or whether the young person was detained, as the law has defined the term. As the following cases demonstrate, determining the point at which a person can be said to be detained in law when physical restraint has not been used can be a challenging exercise when assessing fluid and dynamic street encounters between the police and citizens. The determination is highly dependent on the facts and context of the particular case.

Factors that are key to determining whether a legal detention has occurred include the age of the person,[83] the conduct, demeanour, and words spoken by the police during the incident, as well as the responses, perception and conduct of the young person.[84] A 12-year-old can be expected to be less sophisticated in terms of legal knowledge and understanding of his or her rights, and is thus likely to be more vulnerable to police intimidation, than a 17-year-old young person who has had previous dealings with the police. In these cases, the courts will invariably

---

(Ont. C.A.). *R. v. Kang-Brown*, [2008] S.C.J. No. 18, 2008 SCC 18 (S.C.C.) is authority for that proposition.

[81] *R. v. Mann*, [2004] S.C.J. No. 49, at para. 19 (S.C.C.).

[82] Random vehicle stops by the police for road safety purposes along public highways are a unique situation. While the courts have held that these are arbitrary detentions under s. 9, they are justifiable under s. 1 due to the importance of maintaining road safety. However, the only questions that can be asked during such stops must relate to road safety or driving-related offences, unless the police develop at least reasonable suspicion during the stop that the driver is involved in criminal activity. See a line of case law, including: *R. v. Hufsky*, [1988] S.C.J. No. 30, [1988] 1 S.C.R. 621 (S.C.C.); *R. v. Ladouceur*, [1990] S.C.J. No. 53, [1990] 1 S.C.R. 1257 (S.C.C.); and *R. v. Mellenthin*, [1992] S.C.J. No. 100, [1992] 3 S.C.R. 615 (S.C.C.).

[83] See *R. v. R.T.B.*, [2009] B.C.J. No. 886, at para. 39 (B.C.S.C.); *R. v. K.W.*, [2004] O.J. No. 5327, at para. 29 (Ont. C.J.). See also *R. v. Grafe*, [1987] O.J. No. 796 (Ont. C.A.)

[84] See for instance the analysis of Laskin J.A. in *R. v. Grant*, [2006] O.J. No. 2179, at paras. 29-30 (Ont. C.A.), in concluding that 18-year-old Grant had been detained prior to arrest during a street encounter with the police that involved pointed police questioning. (*Grant* was appealed to the Supreme Court of Canada; the Supreme Court of Canada had yet to release its decision as of July 6, 2009.) See also *R. v. Moran*, [1987] O.J. No. 794, 36 C.C.C. (3d) 225 (Ont. C.A.) regarding the factors that are considered most salient to the determination of detention.

focus on the evidence regarding what the officers said and did, such as the nature of the questions asked, and whether the officers told the young person that he or she was free to go and did not have to remain in discussion with the police, as well as the young person's response to any questions posed.[85]

Since various *Charter* rights arise upon detention, when the court finds that the young person was detained in a given case, the court will then have to assess the conduct of the police as of the point of detention to determine whether *Charter* violations ensued, and if so, what proper remedy should result.

(ii)   Section 10

a.   Section 10(a) — Right to Prompt Information Respecting Reasons for Arrest and Detention

Generally, where it is fairly obvious why the person has been detained and the facts indicate that the young person is aware of his jeopardy, the courts have found that s. 10(a) has been complied with, even if the person has not been advised of the specific reason for the detention. For example, if the facts are such that it would be obvious to a young person that the police were checking on the Canadian Police Information Centre (C.P.I.C.) to see if he or she were in breach of any court orders, the reasons for the detention would be obvious.[86]

b.   Section 10(b) — Right to Retain and Instruct Counsel Without Delay and to Be Informed of that Right

The principle against self-incrimination is embodied in various procedural protections in the *Charter*, including the right to counsel in s. 10(b).[87] As previously suggested, the most important purpose of exercising one's right to counsel under s. 10(b) upon detention is to ensure that an accused person understands his rights, including the right to silence.[88]

The right to counsel under s. 10(b) imposes several obligations on the police: upon arrest or detention, individuals must be informed of their right to retain and instruct counsel without delay (the informational component) and individuals must also be given a reasonable opportunity to consult counsel once they indicate to the police that they wish to do so

[85]   *R. v. Grant*, [2006] O.J. No. 2179 (Ont. C.A.).
[86]   *R. v. J.D.*, [2007] O.J. No. 1365 (Ont. C.J.).
[87]   *R. v. White*, [1999] S.C.J. No. 28, at para. 44, [1999] 2 S.C.R. 417 (S.C.C.).
[88]   *R. v. Hebert*, [1990] S.C.J. No. 64, [1990] 2 S.C.R. 151, at 176 (S.C.C.).

(the implementational component). The Supreme Court of Canada has explained fully in a line of decisions, including *R. v. Prosper*[89] and *R. v. Bartle*,[90] what steps the police must take in order to comply with s. 10(b).

Regarding the informational component of s. 10(b), the Supreme Court of Canada has held that it is not enough for the police to merely repeat the words of the *Charter* and advise detainees of the right to retain and instruct counsel without delay. Information about the existence and availability of duty counsel and Legal Aid Plans should be part of the standard s. 10(b) caution upon detention or arrest.[91] A person under detention is entitled to be advised of whatever system of free preliminary legal advice exists in the jurisdiction and how to access such advice, for example, by dialling a 1-800 toll free number. Where no such duty counsel exists, a detainee must still be advised upon detention of his or her right to apply for legal aid.[92] Section 10(b) does not, however, impose a constitutional obligation on governments to ensure that duty counsel is available, or to provide individuals under detention with a guaranteed right to free and immediate preliminary legal advice upon request.[93]

Concerning the implementational component, once a detained person has expressed a desire to consult counsel, the police must provide him or her with a reasonable opportunity to do so.[94] What constitutes a reasonable opportunity will depend on the circumstances.[95] In addition, absent urgent and compelling circumstances, the authorities are obliged to hold off on eliciting incriminatory evidence from a detainee until he or she has had a reasonable opportunity to reach counsel.[96]

c.   The Scope of s. 10(b) During Investigative Detentions

An encounter between a young person and the police sometimes occurs in the context of what the courts may later characterize as an investigative detention. *R. v. Mann* defines the general concept of detention in law, as well as the concept of an investigative detention, which, by common law definition, is a brief detention for purposes of criminal investigation. But *R. v. Mann* fails to clarify the duties of the police in relation to the scope of s. 10(b) during an investigative detention. In

---

[89]   [1994] S.C.J. No. 72, [1994] 3 S.C.R. 236 (S.C.C.).
[90]   [1994] S.C.J. No. 74, [1994] 3 S.C.R. 173 (S.C.C.).
[91]   *R. v. Prosper*, [1994] S.C.J. No. 72, at para. 18, [1994] 3 S.C.R. 236 (S.C.C.).
[92]   *R. v. Prosper*, [1994] S.C.J. No. 72, at para. 51, [1994] 3 S.C.R. 236 (S.C.C.).
[93]   *R. v. Prosper*, [1994] S.C.J. No. 72, at para. 49, [1994] 3 S.C.R. 236 (S.C.C.).
[94]   *R. v. Prosper*, [1994] S.C.J. No. 72, at para. 34, [1994] 3 S.C.R. 236 (S.C.C.).
[95]   *R. v. Prosper*, [1994] S.C.J. No. 72, at para. 35, [1994] 3 S.C.R. 236 (S.C.C.).
[96]   *R. v. Prosper*, [1994] S.C.J. No. 72, at paras. 34 and 35, [1994] 3 S.C.R. 236 (S.C.C.).

Mann, the court held that, at a minimum, individuals who are detained for investigative purposes prior to an arrest must be advised in clear and simple language of the reasons for the detention.[97] Regarding the s. 10(b) right, however, the court said only that the right to counsel must be interpreted in light of its purpose but that an investigative detention short of arrest must be brief and cannot be artificially prolonged to enable the police to comply with s. 10(b).[98] Thus, *R. v. Mann* did not clarify the extent to which the police must comply with s. 10(b) of the *Charter* during an investigative detention; the court chose to await full consideration of the issue in the lower courts.

Since the 2004 decision in *Mann*, the appellate courts have begun to consider how far the police must go in complying with s. 10(b) during investigative detentions. The Ontario Court of Appeal held in the 2007 case of *R. v. Suberu*[99] that the police do not have to advise a suspect immediately of his or her right to counsel during an investigative detention. In *Suberu*, the adult accused was detained and questioned by police in a store parking lot before being advised of his right to counsel. The accused made incriminating statements and was then arrested and advised of his right to counsel. The accused contended that the police were obliged to advise him immediately upon detention and before asking him any questions of his right to counsel. However, Doherty J.A. held for the court that the term "without delay" in s. 10(b) of the *Charter* should be interpreted more broadly in the context of detentions other than arrests. The term has been construed to mean immediately in the context of detentions *following* arrest,[100] but this is justifiable, Doherty J.A. held, because detentions following arrests involve physical restraint, a personal search, and will invariably include moving the suspect to a jail. Such detentions are not brief, and interfere with a suspect's liberty significantly. The need for legal advice is obvious in such circumstances.

The term "without delay" takes on a different meaning in the context of an investigative detention, as distinct from an arrest. It is permissible for "a brief interlude" to pass between the commencement of an investigative detention and the point at which the police advise the accused of his or her right to counsel under s. 10(b). During this brief period, the officer can ask a few exploratory questions in order to make a quick assessment of the situation to decide whether anything more than a brief detention of

---

[97]   *R. v. Mann*, [2004] S.C.J. No. 49, at para. 21 (S.C.C.).

[98]   *R. v. Mann*, [2004] S.C.J. No. 49, at para. 22 (S.C.C.).

[99]   [2007] O.J. No. 317 (Ont. C.A.). *Suberu* was appealed to the Supreme Court of Canada; at the time of writing in May 2009, the Supreme Court of Canada had yet to release its decision in this case.

[100]   *R. v. Suberu*, [2007] O.J. No. 317, at paras. 46-47 (Ont. C.A.).

the individual is warranted. The police conduct during this brief period must be truly exploratory in the sense that the police must be attempting to determine if anything more than a brief detention is necessary. (Justice Doherty acknowledged that an accused could argue in such a case that it would render the trial unfair for the court to admit any incriminating information provided by the accused prior to his being advised of his right to counsel for any purpose other than to explain subsequent police conduct.)[101]

On the other hand, if the officer has effectively made up his or her mind that he or she is going to detain the suspect for more than a brief interval, there is no excuse for not advising the suspect of the right to counsel, Doherty J.A. held. Justice Doherty explained that a delay of more than 30 minutes exceeds the meaning of "without delay".[102]

Thus, in *Suberu*, Doherty J.A. held that it was permissible for the police to tell a man to stop outside a store and to ask him a few questions (some of which resulted in the man providing incriminating answers) in order to see if he was connected to an ongoing fraud being committed by another man inside the store before advising him of his right to counsel.

In reaching this conclusion, Doherty J.A. was concerned in part with what he characterized as the practical realities of the nature, length and purpose of investigative detentions. Since such detentions are supposed to be brief, a person who is advised of his or her right to counsel and then chooses to exercise that right could end up experiencing a longer detention and more intrusion by the state than he might otherwise have endured.[103]

As the following case law illustrates, some lower courts have relied on *Suberu* to hold that brief interludes of about 10 minutes during police encounters with young persons, during which the police try to determine the young person's legal status (such as performing a C.P.I.C. search to see if the young person is in violation of a bail condition) are sufficiently short so that it is not necessary for the police to advise the young persons of their right to retain and instruct counsel without delay.[104]

---

[101]   *R. v. Suberu*, [2007] O.J. No. 317, at para. 61 (Ont. C.A.).
[102]   *R. v. Suberu*, [2007] O.J. No. 317, at para. 54 (Ont. C.A.).
[103]   *R. v. Suberu*, [2007] O.J. No. 317, at paras. 45-46 (Ont. C.A.).
[104]   *R. v. J.D.*, [2007] O.J. No. 1365, at para. 56 (Ont. C.J.).

(iii)   Section 8 — The Right to Be Secure Against Unreasonable Search or Seizure

Like other sections of the *Charter*, the jurisprudence concerning the concept of an unreasonable search is voluminous. The seminal search case of *Hunter v. Southam Inc.*[105] established the basic principles of post-*Charter* search law shortly after the *Charter* came into force in 1982. *Hunter v. Southam Inc.* involved a search under the *Combines Investigation Act.*[106] Its principles have formed the backbone for the discussion of search law in Canada for more than two decades. *R. v. Tessling*[107] provides a contemporary articulation and review of search law concepts by the Supreme Court of Canada.

In *Hunter v. Southam Inc.*, Dickson J. focused on the meaning of a reasonable search in law and recognized the right of every one in Canada to a *reasonable* expectation of privacy. Thus, in every case, an assessment must be made as to whether the public's interest in being left alone by the state must yield to the state interest in intruding into one's privacy in the interests of law enforcement.[108]

Section 8 inquiries generally proceed in two stages: the accused must first establish that he or she has a reasonable expectation of privacy in the circumstances. Only state intrusions into a reasonable expectation of privacy will constitute a search in law.[109] If the state is found to have intruded into a reasonable expectation of privacy, a search has occurred. The court must then proceed to the second stage of the inquiry under s. 8 to determine if the search was conducted reasonably.[110]

In addition to outlining the concept of a reasonable expectation of privacy, *Hunter v. Southam Inc.* establishes other fundamental principles of search law. For example, where feasible, prior authorization in the form of a warrant is a precondition for a valid search.[111] Reasonable and

---

[105]   [1984] S.C.J. No. 36, [1984] 2 S.C.R. 145 (S.C.C.).

[106]   R.S.C. 1970, c. C-23.

[107]   [2004] S.C.J. No. 63, [2004] 3 S.C.R. 432 (S.C.C.).

[108]   [1984] S.C.J. No. 36, at para. 25, [1984] 2 S.C.R. 145 (S.C.C.). A reasonable expectation of privacy is to be assessed based on the overall circumstances. *R. v. Edwards*, [1996] S.C.J. No. 11, [1996] 1 S.C.R. 128 (S.C.C.) identifies a list of factors that should be considered when determining whether the individual has a reasonable expectation of privacy in the circumstances.

[109]   *R. v. Tessling*, [2004] S.C.J. No. 63, [2004] 3 S.C.R. 432 (S.C.C.).

[110]   *R. v. Belnavis*, [1997] S.C.J. No. 81, [1997] 3 S.C.R. 341 (S.C.C.). In order to be reasonable, a search must be authorized by law, the law itself must be reasonable and the search must be conducted in a reasonable manner: *R. v. Collins*, [1987] S.C.J. No. 15, [1987] 1 S.C.R. 265 (S.C.C.).

[111]   *Hunter v. Southam Inc.*, [1984] S.C.J. No. 36, at para. 29, [1984] 2 S.C.R. 145 (S.C.C.).

probable grounds generally constitutes the minimum standard required for authorizing a search.[112] A warrantless search is presumed to be unreasonable but this presumption is rebuttable by the state.[113]

(iv)   Charter Case Studies

a.   Police Questioning

As the courts have noted, average citizens generally do not know their rights when stopped by the police.[114] Young persons are even less likely than adults to know their rights, particularly when they are approached by uniformed police officers on the street who request their I.D.s and start questioning them.

Police questioning during street encounters with young persons, indeed police questioning of citizens generally, is a highly nuanced area of the law. In *R. v. Grafe*,[115] Krever J.A. found that it was permissible for the police to ask citizens walking along the street to identify themselves even though the police had no reason to suspect them of any criminal wrongdoing and were not investigating any particular crime. Although there is no legal duty, there is a moral or social duty on the part of every citizen to answer questions posed by the police and to assist the police in that regard, Krever J.A. held. Implicit in that moral or social duty is the right of a police officer to ask questions even if the officer has no belief that an offence has been committed. "The Charter does not seek to insulate all members of society from all contact with constituted authority, no matter how trivial the contact may be."[116] However, the law in this area is dynamic and evolving; the cases must be examined carefully in relation to the specific facts to determine if the individual felt compelled to answer police questions or was volunteering information freely.

As a general starting point, the Supreme Court of Canada has said that an individual is not obliged to answer questions posed by the police

---

[112] *Hunter v. Southam Inc.*, [1984] S.C.J. No. 36, at para. 43, [1984] 2 S.C.R. 145 (S.C.C.). Justice Dickson qualified this standard at para. 43. But there are exceptions to this general standard. For example, the Supreme Court of Canada held in *R. v. Kang-Brown*, [2008] S.C.J. No. 18, 2008 SCC 18 (S.C.C.) that a sniff of personal belongings by a drug detector dog is a search in law because it is an intrusion into one's privacy but it is reasonable if the police have reasonable suspicion to use the dog.

[113] *Hunter v. Southam Inc.*, [1984] S.C.J. No. 36, at paras. 30 and 36, [1984] 2 S.C.R. 145 (S.C.C.). The standard is a balance of probabilities.

[114] In *R. v. Therens*, [1985] S.C.J. No. 30, at para. 53, [1985] 1 S.C.R. 613 (S.C.C.), Le Dain J. held: "Most citizens are not aware of the precise legal limits of police authority."

[115] [1987] O.J. No. 796 (Ont. C.A.).

[116] *R. v. Grafe*, [1987] O.J. No. 796 (Ont. C.A.).

during an investigative detention.[117] However, the Supreme Court of Canada has also said that not every time the police stop someone for identification or interview amounts to a detention in law.[118] The police can sometimes be involved in a voluntary encounter with a young person on the street during which the young person freely provides information to the police. In other words, in some of these situations, the police officer is merely asking questions and the young person is free to answer, provided the young person realizes that there is generally no legal obligation to do so.[119]

The court often grapples with the nature of police questioning in a given case in order to determine if the individual was effectively detained and indeed whether the questions amounted to a search in law. The next two cases do not involve "young persons" in a strict sense but illustrate the court's analyses of police questioning.

In *R. v. Grant*,[120] a case involving an 18-year-old man, two plainclothes officers on patrol in an unmarked car thought Grant was behaving suspiciously as he walked by them on a Toronto street so they asked a uniformed officer to talk with him. The officer stood on the sidewalk directly in Grant's path, asked him what was going on, and then requested his name and address. Grant produced an OHIP card. When Grant started adjusting his jacket, the officer directed him to keep his hands in front of him. The two plainclothes officers arrived, showed their badges, and stood on the sidewalk behind the uniformed officer. The officers were all taller than Grant and moved every time he moved. Grant was asked if he had ever been arrested. Grant replied that he had gotten into trouble three years earlier. The officer then asked Grant whether he had anything "on him that he shouldn't".[121] Grant initially said no but then admitted to having a small amount of marihuana. After the officer asked "Is that it?" Grant admitted that he also had a firearm, at which point he was arrested and searched, and the police seized the marihuana and the loaded revolver.[122]

---

[117] *R. v. Mann*, [2004] S.C.J. No. 49, at para. 45 (S.C.C.).

[118] *R. v. Mann*, [2004] S.C.J. No. 49, at para. 19 (S.C.C.).

[119] However, in *R. v. Moore*, [1978] S.C.J. No. 82, [1979] 1 S.C.R. 195 (S.C.C.), the court found that the individual was obstructing the officer in the performance of his duties because he refused to identify himself after the police officer observed him committing a summary conviction offence. There are certain situations where an individual may have a legal obligation to answer questions or provide certain information to the police, such as basic motor vehicle information during a routine motor vehicle stop under highway traffic legislation.

[120] [2006] O.J. No. 2179 (Ont. C.A.). A decision from the Supreme Court of Canada in relation to this case was imminent at the time of writing.

[121] *R. v. Grant*, [2006] O.J. No. 2179, at para. 2 (Ont. C.A.).

[122] *R. v. Grant*, [2006] O.J. No. 2179, at para. 19 (Ont. C.A.).

The trial judge in *Grant* found neither a detention nor a search. On appeal, Laskin J.A. found that Grant had been arbitrarily and psychologically detained but that the nature of the questions did not constitute a search in law. Acknowledging that the dividing line between questions that constitute a search in law and questions that do not is not always easy to discern, Laskin J.A. held that a search was not triggered when the police asked Grant if he had anything that he should not.[123] Justice Laskin distinguished the general questions asked in *Grant* from the more specific questions asked in earlier cases such as *R. v. Mellenthin*,[124] where the police had already formed the intention to search when they asked the suspect what was in his open gym bag. In *Mellenthin*, specifically asking the suspect what was in his gym bag amounted to a search of the suspect's gym bag, whereas the more general nature of the police questions in *Grant* did not go that far.[125]

While Laskin J.A. in *Grant* acknowledged that the gun was found because of the officer's improper questioning of Grant during an arbitrary detention, Laskin J.A. concluded that it was not a case of flagrant abuse of police power, and that the officer had not grossly overstepped the bounds of legitimate questioning. These factors reduced the seriousness of the *Charter* breach and the admission of the gun would not bring the administration of justice into disrepute, Laskin J.A. held. The gun was not excluded. Justice Laskin concluded that Grant's sentence of 18 months in jail for various firearms offences, which was reduced to 12 due to the period of pre-trial custody he had already served, was appropriate in the circumstances. This case was appealed to the Supreme Court of Canada.[126]

By contrast to *Grant*, certain police questions in the classic case of *Mellenthin*[127] were found to constitute a search in law. In *Mellenthin*, the accused was pulled over by three R.C.M.P. constables during a motor vehicle check stop program in September 1988 just after midnight. The police had no particular reason to stop Mellenthin. They were simply pulling over motorists at random to check vehicles. After observing that Mellenthin was not wearing his seat belt and requesting Mr. Mellenthin's driver's licence, vehicle registration and insurance, one of the police

---

[123] But see other cases such as *R. v. Simpson*, [1993] O.J. No. 308 (Ont. C.A.) and more recently *R. v. K.W.*, [2004] O.J. No. 5327 (Ont. C.J.), where the courts have held that initial police questioning subject to being stopped by the police can amount to a search in law. The questioning in *R. v. K.W.* was found to have gone beyond a voluntary conversation between a citizen and the police (*R. v. K.W.*, at para. 50).

[124] [1992] S.C.J. No. 100, [1992] 3 S.C.R. 615 (S.C.C.).

[125] *R. v. Grant*, [2006] O.J. No. 2179, at paras. 33-37 (Ont. C.A.).

[126] A decision from the Supreme Court of Canada was imminent at the time of writing on July 6, 2009.

[127] [1992] S.C.J. No. 100, [1992] 3 S.C.R. 615 (S.C.C.).

officers shone a flashlight around the interior of the vehicle to check for drugs and to also ensure the safety of officers involved in the check point. He noticed an open gym bag on the front seat beside Mellenthin and could see a small brown bag with a plastic sandwich bag inside it. The constable asked what was inside the bag and Mellenthin opened the bag and said there was food inside. The officer observed what he thought was glass inside the plastic bag and suspected there were drugs inside. He asked Mellenthin what was inside the brown bag and Mellenthin pulled out the baggie, which contained empty glass vials. Since the officer believed such glass vials were commonly used to store cannabis resin, he believed he had reasonable and probable grounds to believe narcotics were present. The officer asked Mellenthin to exit the vehicle, searched the brown bag and found it contained cannabis resin. Mellenthin was arrested for possession of narcotics. The car was searched and vials of hash oil and some cannabis resin cigarettes were located.

Justice Cory held for the court that the visual inspection of the interior of the vehicle with the flashlight was not a search, but the police questions pertaining to the gym bag constituted an element of a search, and that these questions were conducted without the required reasonable and probable grounds. Thus, these questions amounted to an unreasonable search. Justice Cory concluded that the evidence derived from the search should be excluded.

Following cases such as *R. v. Hufsky*[128] and *R. v. Ladouceur*,[129] Cory J. held in *Mellenthin* that the motorist was arbitrarily detained when the police pulled him over randomly as part of the Alberta Check Stop program but that the detention was justified under s. 1 of the *Charter* in order to address the pressing problem of the dangerous operation of vehicles on the highways. However, the questions about the gym bag went beyond the legitimate questions that could be asked in relation to this traffic stop. When the police questioned Mellenthin, they had no suspicion whatsoever that drugs or alcohol were in the vehicle, nor were there any signs that Mellenthin was impaired. The aim of check stop programs is to check for sobriety, licences, ownership, insurance and mechanical fitness of the vehicle. Random check stops related to highway safety cannot be extended beyond these aims to provide for unfounded general inquisitions or an unreasonable search, the court held.[130]

Police questioning when one is lawfully detained as part of a roadside check stop program and police questioning during a street encounter

---

[128] [1988] S.C.J. No. 30, [1988] 1 S.C.R. 621 (S.C.C.).
[129] [1990] S.C.J. No. 53, [1990] 1 S.C.R. 1257 (S.C.C.).
[130] [1992] S.C.J. No. 100, [1992] 3 S.C.R. 615 (S.C.C.).

are two very different situations requiring distinctly different legal analyses. In the roadside scenario, a driver can be arbitrarily, albeit lawfully, detained, but for a specific and limited purpose: motor vehicle safety. In other words, the police can stop a motorist for general road safety purposes relating to the mechanical fitness of the vehicle, *etc.*, without actually observing the driver commit a driving infraction. In this sense the stop is an arbitrary detention, although the courts have said it is justified in order to address issues of road safety.[131] However, police questions that do not relate to road safety trigger the analysis in relation to whether those questions are a search in law. During street encounters, the nature and substance of the police questioning can assist the court in determining *if* the person is under detention and will also be germane as to whether the questions constitute a search in law.[132]

b.   Street Encounters between Police and Youth: Detention and Search

The first case in this section involves a youthful accused. It illustrates the often ambiguous line between voluntary encounters between police and young persons or young adults, and interactions that can be found by the courts to be detentions in law.

> It needs repeating once again: Stopping and investigating people merely because of some "Spidey Sense" being engaged goes far beyond the standards our society demands and expects of our police. Young people have a right to "just hang out", especially in their neighbourhood, and to move freely without fear of being detained and searched on a mere whim, and without being advised of their rights and without their consent. Mere hunches do not give police the grounds to "surprise" a group of young people, or to "get right on them" for investigative purposes without something further that provides a lawful basis for doing so.[133]

In *R. v. Ferdinand*,[134] which was released just days after the Supreme Court of Canada rendered its significant decision on investigative detention in *R. v. Mann*, the Ontario Superior Court considered whether

---

[131]   *R. v. Hufsky*, [1988] S.C.J. No. 30, [1988] 1 S.C.R. 621 (S.C.C.); *R. v. Ladouceur*, [1990] S.C.J. No. 53, [1990] 1 S.C.R. 1257 (S.C.C.).

[132]   The extent to which *Mellenthin* and similar motor vehicle cases can be used as a basis for analogous arguments in relation to street encounters between citizens and the police is a matter of some judicial debate. For instance in *R. v. Powell*, [2000] O.J. No. 2229, at para. 31 (Ont. C.J.), Lane J. held that "if motorists can be presumed to feel compelled to respond to questions from police, it can reasonably be assumed that pedestrians stopped by the police feel the same compulsion". However, later appellant courts have rejected such analogous arguments and found that the two contexts are so different as to require quite distinct legal analyses. See for example *R. v. H. (C.R.)*, [2003] M.J. No. 90 (Man. C.A.) and *R. v. L.B.*, [2007] O.J. No. 3290 (Ont. C.A.).

[133]   *R. v. Ferdinand*, [2004] O.J. No. 3209, at para. 56 (Ont. S.C.).

[134]   [2004] O.J. No. 3209 (Ont. S.C.).

the conduct of the Toronto police amounted to, *inter alia*, the arbitrary detention of a young black man and thus a violation of his s. 9 rights.

In *Ferdinand*, two Toronto police officers were on foot patrol duty on September 13, 2003. As members of a police section known as the Community Response Unit, they routinely patrolled a certain neighbourhood with the general goal of reducing crime. Among their duties was to converse with local residents and to acquire information about the residents by filling out "208 cards". These are cards upon which the police record information obtained from a person they stop. During their patrols, the police gather information such as the name, alias, date of birth, colour, address and contact location of the individual, as well as the name of his or her associates, plus additional facts such as whether the person associates with gangs, motorcycle clubs, or the drug treatment court. The police eventually input the information into the police computer database.[135]

One of the two constables involved in *Ferdinand* testified that he and his partner completed up to 45 of these cards per shift. Upon approaching an individual, they testified, their normal routine was to ask the person if he or she minded providing the required information. If the person declined to do so, and there were no grounds to detain the person, the officers waved them on. One of the officers testified that if a person refused to answer questions in regard to the 208 cards and simply walked away, that was construed to be all right and the person was free to do so. (However, there was no evidence presented that police officers ever advised people they stopped that they had a right not to answer any questions from this card and that they were free to leave if they wished.)[136]

On the day in question, the two officers were speaking with local youth in a park at around 5 p.m. when they observed a group of youths "just hanging out" behind an apartment building. The officers decided to investigate the group by surprise although they had no reason to suspect they were involved or connected to any criminal activity. Both officers testified that their overall intention in approaching the group was to investigate to see whether any criminal activity was occurring.[137] After walking through the doorway of the apartment building and proceeding to the back of it, one constable immediately engaged in a conversation with a couple of young men by the door while the other walked toward the other members of the group who were about 20 metres away. This other officer observed the accused start to walk away when the police arrived, which

---

[135] *R. v. Ferdinand*, [2004] O.J. No. 3209, at paras. 6-12 (Ont. S.C.).
[136] *R. v. Ferdinand*, [2004] O.J. No. 3209, at para. 16 (Ont. S.C.).
[137] *R. v. Ferdinand*, [2004] O.J. No. 3209, at para. 50 (Ont. S.C.).

engaged his "Spidey sense". The officer reacted by swiftly approaching the accused, at which point he testified that he observed what he perceived to be a marihuana joint. When he ordered the accused to sit down, the accused tried to flee, at which point the officers and the accused struggled and a .45 calibre semi-automatic fully loaded handgun was discovered.

In allowing the application of the accused, excluding the evidence, and entering an acquittal, LaForme J. held that the police were not investigating a specific offence when they approached Ferdinand (although the accused had history in general with the police in as much as he testified that he had been regularly stopped by the police and questioned for the purposes of gathering information for the 208 cards and that they also searched him without his consent). In the case at bar, LaForme J. held, Ferdinand was not a suspect in any investigation and was unknown to the constables at the time. Other than having his "Spidey sense" engaged when Ferdinand began walking away when the police arrived, the officer had no basis for getting physically close to Ferdinand.

Justice LaForme held that the officer walked up to Ferdinand briskly for no apparent reason and demonstrated that he did not plan to allow Ferdinand to leave, and that this police conduct amounted to psychological restraint and was something more than a brief police detention for purposes only of identification and interview. Given Ferdinand's experience of being regularly searched, asked to respond to 208 cards, and having regularly observed other black youth experience the same treatment, it would have been understandable and Ferdinand's lawful right to begin leaving when the officers arrived, LaForme J. held.

The constable had no grounds to detain Ferdinand and did so arbitrarily when he decided to get "right on him", as he put it, once he observed Ferdinand walking away. It was precisely because the accused walked away when he and his partner approached the area that the officers' suspicions were aroused. Ferdinand was therefore detained in law[138] as contemplated by the Supreme Court of Canada in *Mann*. "It is no leap of common sense logic that, in the circumstances as testified to by PC Adams, he had assumed control over Mr. Ferdinand's movements and that for Mr. Ferdinand to continue to leave would have legal consequences to him. In fact, that is precisely what did happen."[139]

It was only after this detention that the constable noticed what he believed to be a marihuana joint and took it from Mr. Ferdinand's hand. In

---

[138]   *R. v. Ferdinand*, [2004] O.J. No. 3209, at para. 43 (Ont. S.C.).
[139]   *R. v. Ferdinand*, [2004] O.J. No. 3209, at para. 44 (Ont. S.C.).

essence, the detention occurred before the police had a reason to justify it, LaForme J. held.

The encounter between the officer and Ferdinand prior to the officer observing the marihuana joint amounted to an investigative detention involving significant psychological restraint, certainly more than required for a brief detention for purposes of identification or interview. Justice LaForme concluded that Ferdinand was subject to an investigative detention without the requisite grounds (reasonable suspicion), and that the subsequent search of his pockets went beyond the parameters of the types of searches that are justified during investigative detentions. In other words, there was no threat of danger to the police or safety issues to justify the search of Ferdinand's pockets. Ferdinand was both arbitrarily detained and unreasonably searched. But for the unlawful detention and search, the evidence would not have been found, LaForme J. held, in excluding the evidence. To admit the evidence in the case would have brought the administration of justice into disrepute.[140]

More recently, in *R. v. J.D.*,[141] the court considered alleged *Charter* violations under ss. 8, 9 and 10 in relation to a street encounter between the police and three young persons (ages 14 and 15) in a high-crime area of Toronto. *R. v. J.D.* is an excellent example of how these three *Charter* issues can arise in one case in the context of what begins as a routine encounter between the police and young persons. The police may view their conduct as proactive policing, while young persons may feel harassed and discriminated against based on age. Justice Jones of the Ontario Court of Justice ultimately excluded all of the evidence against J.D., which included an imitation handgun, due to violations of his rights,

---

[140] See also post-*Mann* cases such as *R. v. S.M.*, [2006] O.J. No. 3775 (Ont. C.J.), where the court found that a 15-year-old was arbitrarily detained by police who were on routine patrol at a public housing complex in Toronto. The area was known to have a high incidence of drug trafficking and the court found that the black youth was detained on the basis that he was found in a known drug trafficking area at 1:30 a.m. and was observed passing a small, unidentified object to another individual and that, as he left the complex, he put his hand into his pocket. Justice Murray held that these facts fell far short of establishing a nexus between the accused and any drug trafficking as required by *R. v. Mann*. Conversely, see earlier cases such as *R. v. H. (C.R.)*, [2003] M.J. No. 90 (Man. C.A.), where Steel J.A. held that there had been no psychological detention in a situation where H. and his friends were asked by the police to approach the cruiser when they were walking after 1 a.m. The youths supplied their names and addresses when asked, which were subsequently entered into the C.P.I.C. system. However, the court held that the police and the youths were merely engaged in a conversation and that there had been no exercise of control by the police over the boys' movements. The police officers did not leave their vehicle and the tone of the conversation was casual. The court found that H. had no reasonable belief that he was under a compulsion to comply with the officers' requests.

[141] [2007] O.J. No. 1365 (Ont. C.J.).

but did not find any violations in relation to W.A. Charges were dismissed against the third young person.

In *R. v. J.D.*, two police officers stopped three teenagers at about 11 p.m. on the night of December 26, 2004, after observing them, dressed in dark clothes, cross a Toronto city street in a high crime area known for purse snatches, break and enters and auto thefts. The officers did not recognize any of the young persons before they stopped them and the officers were not investigating any particular crime. One officer admitted that he found it odd that these three people were out so late on a particularly cold night (a cold warning had been issued), and he asked his partner to intercept them in the marked squad car. When the officers stopped the police car, they called over to the young men saying words to the effect: "Guys, stop for a second, we want to talk to you."[142] Once the three teenagers identified themselves, one officer testified that he planned to run their names on C.P.I.C. If C.P.I.C. did not reveal any information of note, the three would be free to go. Both officers testified that, in their view, the boys were free to refuse to answer police questions; however, both officers acknowledged that the boys were not advised that they had a right to refuse to answer questions and were free to go.[143] One officer indicated that it was part of his duties as a police officer to routinely stop people and run C.P.I.C. checks.[144] Among the reasons he did so was to see if the person was in breach of bail conditions.

Upon stopping the three young persons on this occasion, the youths were told to remove their hoodies and directed to keep their hands visible. Both officers testified that they did not consider the young persons detained at this juncture. However, neither officer advised the boys that they had the right to refuse to answer questions or that they were free to go, Jones J. observed. Once the boys were stopped, Officer Blake recognized having dealt with one of them previously on a robbery charge. He asked all three boys for their names and birth dates and continued to chat with them, questioning them about whether they had any difficulties with the law, while his partner ran their names on C.P.I.C.

The C.P.I.C. search revealed that W.A. was no longer subject to a curfew condition but J.D. was in violation of a bail condition that prohibited him from being in the area where he was stopped. J.D. was arrested for being in breach of an undertaking.

---

[142] *R. v. J.D.*, [2007] O.J. No. 1365, at para. 6 (Ont. C.J.).
[143] *R. v. J.D.*, [2007] O.J. No. 1365, at paras. 10-12 (Ont. C.J.).
[144] *R. v. J.D.*, [2007] O.J. No. 1365, at para. 23 (Ont. C.J.).

The time between the stop and the arrest was about 10 minutes. During a pat-down search incident to the arrest of J.D., Officer Williams discovered a replica handgun hidden in J.D.'s clothing. The other two boys were then searched; their belongings were also searched. Two of them were charged with carrying concealed weapons and all three teenagers were charged with possession of burglary tools. At the time of their arrest, the three youths were advised of the reasons for their detention and arrest and advised of their right to counsel. (As noted earlier, charges against the third young person, J.F., did not proceed.)

J.D. testified during the *Charter voir dire* that he did not believe he was free to leave when the police stopped him, nor did he feel he did not have to answer their questions. He also testified that he had been stopped by the police frequently. They would ask his name and date of birth and let him go if the C.P.I.C. search revealed nothing.[145]

The Crown argued that the police actions that night did not exceed the permissible range of contacts in modern society between the state and its citizens; however, Jones J. of the Ontario Court of Justice saw it differently. Justice Jones held that all three teenagers were psychologically detained[146] from the point the police started directing them to remove their hoodies and to keep their hands where the police could see them. Justice Jones then considered whether the police had grounds to detain them or whether it was arbitrary.

J.D.: Section 9

Regarding J.D., Jones J. held that the detention of the 14-year-old was arbitrary because the brief detention did not satisfy the test set out in *R. v. Mann*, that is to say, the police officer must have reasonable grounds to suspect in all of the circumstances that the individual is connected to a particular crime and that such a detention is necessary.[147] The officers did not have such grounds in this case. There was no crime under investigation; the young persons who were stopped were not implicated in any

---

[145]   These facts are all taken from *R. v. J.D.*, [2007] O.J. No. 1365, paras. 1-22 (Ont. C.J.).

[146]   *R. v. J.D.*, [2007] O.J. No. 1365, at paras. 28-29 (Ont. C.J.).

[147]   *R. v. J.D.*, [2007] O.J. No. 1365, at para. 32 (Ont. C.J.). See other cases, such as *R. v. K.W.*, [2004] O.J. No. 5327 (Ont. C.J.), where the detention and search of a 15-year-old in downtown Toronto was also found to be unconstitutional on the grounds that the police had no grounds to detain the teenager and the search of his person flowed from an arbitrary detention. The police were merely patrolling a high-crime area and stopped the accused, who was standing with a group of males near the men's hostel. The police did not observe any crime, nor were they investigating any recent or ongoing activity (see paras. 38-40).

criminal activity.[148] Justice Jones excluded all of the evidence obtained subsequent to the police stop of J.D. in relation to him.

W.A.: Section 9

Conversely, Jones J. found that the detention of W.A. was not arbitrary and that he was detained for legitimate investigative purposes. When the police stopped the three young persons, Constable Blake immediately recognized W.A. as someone he had previously dealt with on a robbery. The officer knew he had been subject to curfew as one of the conditions of his bail. The officer was justified in detaining him for less than 10 minutes to verify the status of his bail, as there were reasonable grounds to suspect he was in violation of the curfew condition.

The ruling involving W.A. on the detention issue is problematic, however, since the police officer did not recognize W.A. until after the three were stopped and subject to an arbitrary detention. Arguably, the young persons had already been detained without justification before the officer recognized W.A.

J.D.: Section 8

Regarding the searches of J.D., Jones J. found that J.D.'s right to be free from unreasonable search or seizure was violated when he was required to provide his personal identifying information so that the police could conduct a C.P.I.C. search. Justice Jones held that J.D. was arbitrarily detained and then felt compelled to provide to the police the information regarding his name and date of birth, knowing the police were going to check it on C.P.I.C. He felt he could not refuse. Justice Jones found that the police "purposefully" chose not to advise the youth of his right to leave, or his right to refuse to answer their questions. The officers were aware that they were dealing with a young person under 18 but this fact did not inform their discretion to advise him of his rights.[149] It was as a result of the information on C.P.I.C. that the police learned that J.D. was subject to a boundary condition on a release order that was apparently being breached, which provided police with the grounds for his arrest. During the pat-down search incident to his arrest, the imitation weapon was discovered. Justice Jones held that the s. 8 breach was an inevitable consequence of the s. 9 breach and of the computer search.[150] The pat-down search of J.D. was unreasonable and a s. 8 violation.

---

[148]   R. v. J.D., [2007] O.J. No. 1365, at para. 32 (Ont. C.J.).
[149]   R. v. J.D., [2007] O.J. No. 1365, at para. 50 (Ont. C.J.).
[150]   See also R. v. Powell, [2000] O.J. No. 2229 (Ont. C.J.).

W.A.: Section 8

As far as the searches of W.A. are concerned, Jones J. held that W.A. was asked about the status of the charge and whether he was still subject to the curfew but that these questions did not amount to an unreasonable search. Although W.A. advised that the matter had been resolved and he was no longer subject to a curfew, the police did not have to accept his word and were justified in detaining him briefly to do a C.P.I.C. search to confirm his bail status because there were reasonable grounds to suspect that he was in breach of his curfew, Jones J. held. Although the C.P.I.C. check cleared W.A. of any violation, the police had since discovered that J.D. had an imitation pistol when they searched him incident to his arrest. According to Jones J., the officers thus had reasonable grounds to further detain W.A. and to perform a pat-down search on him and to search his backpack due to concerns about officer safety.[151]

J.D.: Section 10(a) and (b)

In relation to J.D.'s right to be informed promptly of the reasons for his detention, Jones J. held that no violation had occurred because case law has held that where the detained person is generally aware of his or her jeopardy, s. 10(a) is complied with, even if the person is not informed of the specific reason for the detention. In this case, Jones J. held it would have been immediately obvious to J.D. that the police were checking all of the youths' names on C.P.I.C.[152] Relying on *R. v. Suberu*,[153] Jones J. also found that, despite the arbitrariness of J.D.'s detention, given the short time frame between the time J.D. was stopped and his initial arrest and the difficulty in determining when the s. 10(b) right arises during a fluid and dynamic encounter with the police, she was not satisfied that his s. 10(b) right was violated.

W.A.: Section 10(a) and (b)

Likewise, Jones J. held that there was no obligation to advise W.A. of his right to counsel during this brief period of investigative detention (less than 10 minutes) during which the police ascertained the status of his bail

---

[151] More discussion of C.P.I.C. searches involving young persons occurs later in this chapter. The courts have held that it is permissible for the police to perform C.P.I.C. checks of young persons in various contexts. For example, in *R. v. C.E.D.*, [2007] S.J. No. 468 (Sask. Prov. Ct.), it was permissible for the police to run the names through C.P.I.C. of all the persons attending a party after the police received a noise complaint about the party and were given permission by one of the occupants to enter the dwelling. The officer requested everyone present to provide I.D., which he then ran through C.P.I.C. As a result, 12 of the persons present raised concerns. The accused youth was among the young persons arrested.

[152] *R. v. J.D.*, [2007] O.J. No. 1365, at para. 60 (Ont. C.J.).

[153] [2007] O.J. No. 317 (Ont. C.A.).

conditions. Again, relying on the Ontario Court of Appeal decision in *R. v. Suberu*,[154] Jones J. held that a brief interlude between the commencement of an investigative detention and the provision of the detained person's right to counsel is consistent with the right of a detained person to be informed of his right to counsel without delay. It would have been obvious to W.A. by the nature of the questions asked to him, *etc.* that the police officer was making inquiries through the computer to verify his compliance with his bail conditions and thus the police were not required to provide more specific information to him at this juncture in order to comply with s. 10(a) of the *Charter*, which obliges police to inform a detained person promptly of the reasons for his or her detention. Likewise, Jones J. was not prepared to find a violation of s. 10(b) due to the difficulty in determining precisely when his s. 10(b) rights arose during the short time frame between the time he was stopped and his initial arrest, at which point he was advised of his rights to counsel.

By contrast, in *R. v. L.B.*,[155] the court held that the young person was not detained when he was questioned by the police about the ownership of a knapsack among other things and, consequently, the trial judge had erred in excluding the gun as evidence. Relying on *Mann* in part Moldaver J.A. held for the court that it has not yet reached the point where the compulsion to reply to police questions will be inferred whenever police officers request information.

Among the facts that distinguish *R. v. L.B.* from *R. v. J.D.*, however, is that the young person in *R. v. L.B.* approached the two plainclothes police officers in an unmarked car without being asked or told to do so, after the police stopped their vehicle and identified themselves because they had observed L.B. and another young person acting suspiciously near a school in downtown Toronto. The police engaged in general, casual conversation with the two youths before asking them to identify themselves. The police had noticed L.B. carrying a black bag, which he left behind when he approached one of the officers. When one of the officers located it and asked who owned it before opening it, L.B. said he didn't know. When the bag was opened, a .22 calibre handgun was found inside, at which point both young persons were arrested.

c.   C.P.I.C. Inquiries

The practice by the police of obtaining identifying personal information from individuals, especially young people, where no crime is being

---

[154] [2007] O.J. No. 317 (Ont. C.A.).
[155] [2007] O.J. No. 3290 (Ont. C.A.).

investigated and there are no reasonable grounds to detain, with the intention of conducting a C.P.I.C. search for the purpose of determining
whether that person is subject to an arrest warrant or is in breach of his
bail, without explaining to that person his right to refuse to provide that
information or the jeopardy he or she faces by providing that information,
amounts, in my opinion, to an abuse of police powers. This is particularly
concerning when one considers that young persons, who are typically the
target of these policing practices, have been granted enhanced procedural
protections (to ensure that young persons are treated fairly and that their
rights, including their right to privacy, are protected) under the *Youth
Criminal Justice Act* because of their age and stage of development: s.
3(1)(b)(iii).[156]

As demonstrated above, the police sometimes stop young persons on
the street when no particular crime is being investigated and without
reasonable suspicion to justify a brief detention, to ascertain their names
and dates of birth, and to run the information on C.P.I.C. to see if this
turns up evidence of wrongful activity, without first explaining to that
young person that he or she does not have to provide the information.[157]
Some members of the judiciary have held that this practice of targeting
youths can constitute an abuse of police powers and is of particular
concern because of the enhanced procedural protections afforded to
youths in the *YCJA* to ensure they are treated fairly.[158] As illustrated
above, the courts have also found in certain instances that the use of
C.P.I.C. can amount to an unreasonable search if it flows from an arbitrary
detention.[159] That said, the C.P.I.C. cases to date are inconsistent and do
not definitively answer the question of if, and when, a C.P.I.C. inquiry
amounts to a s. 8 violation. It is therefore worthwhile to consider more
closely this developing body of law in relation to young persons.

The C.P.I.C. cases raise various issues: Did the young person voluntarily provide the information to the police regarding his or her name and
date of birth, which then allowed the police to do the C.P.I.C. search? Was
the young person detained in law at the time they provided the information for the C.P.I.C. search? Did the police questioning of the young
person in order to get the basic information to do the C.P.I.C. search
amount to a search in law? Does a person have a reasonable expectation
of privacy in the information about them contained on the police database? Assuming a C.P.I.C. search is a search in law, was the C.P.I.C.
search an unreasonable search in the circumstances of the case?

---

[156] *R. v. J.D.*, [2007] O.J. No. 1365, at para. 87 (Ont. C.J.).
[157] *R. v. J.D.*, [2007] O.J. No. 1365, at paras. 82 and 87 (Ont. C.J.) in particular.
[158] *R. v. J.D.*, [2007] O.J. No. 1365, at para. 87 (Ont. C.J.).
[159] *R. v. J.D.*, [2007] O.J. No. 1365, at para. 87 (Ont. C.J.); *R. v. Powell*, [2000] O.J. No. 2229
(Ont. C.J.).

In *R. v. M.E.*,[160] Murray J. of the Ontario Court of Justice addressed the specific question of whether police questioning relating to the identity, date of birth, and whether the individual faces criminal charges, in order to do a C.P.I.C. search, amounts to a search in law. In *R. v. M.E.*, three uniformed police officers entered a Toronto Internet café early one morning and found the accused, who was 17, sleeping in front of a computer station. The police officers advised the accused that he was going to be ticketed for trespassing. The police asked the teenager to identify himself, to provide his date of birth and also whether he was before the court on any charges. The young person was told that if he did not provide the information, he would be arrested.

The information enabled the police to find out through a C.P.I.C. search that the teenager was wanted on a surety warrant, which led to his arrest and search. The search resulted in the discovery of marihuana and ecstasy.

Justice Murray held that in the circumstances of the case the young person likely felt psychologically compelled to submit to the officers' questioning. He further found that the questions went beyond the information that was required to issue a ticket for trespassing and that the police officers' true purpose was to get enough information to run his name on C.P.I.C. and that the young person was actually being subjected to an investigative detention during this questioning absent reasonable suspicion that he was involved in criminal activity. Thus, Murray J. found that the young person was arbitrarily detained and also denied his s. 10(a) right to be advised promptly of the reasons for his detention.

Noting that similar cases had found that such police questioning to elicit information to enable police to run a C.P.I.C. search constitutes a search in law,[161] Murray J. held in *R. v. M.E.* that the courts have recognized an individual's right to informational privacy and that the information the police requested in this case was core biographical information in which the accused had a reasonable expectation of privacy. Thus, the police questions amounted to a search and the search was unreasonable because it occurred during an arbitrary detention. Justice Murray excluded the evidence and acquitted the accused.

Conversely, the use of C.P.I.C. in other contexts has been held to be permissible. In *R. v. H. (C.R.)*,[162] the police stopped their cruiser during routine patrol at about 1:20 a.m. and engaged in casual conversation with

---

[160] [2006] O.J. No. 1657 (Ont. C.J.).
[161] See for example *R. v. Powell*, [2000] O.J. No. 2229 (Ont. C.J.).
[162] [2003] M.J. No. 90 (Man. C.A.).

three young men, who approached the cruiser without a demand or direction. The young men provided their names, dates of births and addresses when asked, although the police had no reason to suspect that they had committed any offences. Upon running their names through C.P.I.C., the police learned that H. was in breach of the curfew provision of his probation order. H. was arrested and charged with breach of probation.

The court found that H. was not detained in these circumstances and further found that the probation order was a matter of public record, as was the criminal record information maintained by the police. The police database is not in an area in which the accused can assert a privacy interest that would exclude the right of access of the police, the court found. Perhaps most germane, the court found that the voluntary supplying of information to the police is distinctly different from situations where a young person feels compelled to answer questions put to him or her by the police, including identifying himself or herself. It is also notable that the three men in this case approached the cruiser without being asked or told to.

d.   Searches of Young Persons in Other Contexts

1.   BEDROOMS

The privacy that a young person has in his or her bedroom or apartment, and thus the circumstances in which the court will find that a search has occurred when the police search those locations, also remains an unsettled area of the law. These cases are highly context-driven. For example, in *R. v. W. (J.P.)*,[163] Howard J. acknowledged the privacy that young persons have in their bedrooms and held that it was not sufficient for the youth's father to give the police permission to search the young person's bedroom. In essence the father could not waive the young person's reasonable expectation of privacy in his bedroom. "Young persons, like adults, are fully entitled to the rights secured by the *Charter* ... What more private place could teenagers have than their bedroom ... The risk that a parent might [lawfully] enter a teenager's bedroom does not destroy the right that a young person has against unlawful and unreasonable intrusion by the agents of the state."[164] Justice Howard excluded the stolen items that the officer located in the young person's bedroom.

---

[163]   [1993] B.C.J. No. 2891 (B.C. Youth Ct.).
[164]   *R. v. W. (J.P.)*, [1993] B.C.J. No. 2891, at paras. 22-25 (B.C. Youth Ct.).

The Alberta Court of Appeal took a different approach six years later in *R. v. D.M.F.*[165] and held in a violent sexual assault case that the two pairs of boxer shorts seized from the room of a 16-year-old youth did not amount to an unreasonable search because the youth's mother permitted the police to enter the youth's bedroom, where the door was closed but not locked. While the police had strong suspicions about the youth, at the time of the seizure the police did not have a search warrant and did not have sufficient evidence to arrest him. In the ruling, Hetherington J.A. conducted the analysis as set out in *R. v. Edwards*[166] and concluded that the young person did not have a reasonable expectation of privacy in his bedroom for various reasons, including the fact that the youth's door could be easily unlocked, his mother routinely entered his room to pick up laundry, and other occupants of the house also went into his room; thus, the youth did not have control over entrance to the room. Consequently, the police entrance into his room did not amount to a search because a search occurs only when there is a state intrusion into a reasonable expectation of privacy.[167] In a more recent case, *R. v. A. (A.)*,[168] the Ontario Court of Justice found that the police had committed an unlawful search when they entered the apartment of four youths after one of the youths consented to let them in. Justice Flaherty excluded the evidence found by the police because the officers had entered the apartment, questioned the youths, searched the apartment and seized evidence without advising the young persons of their rights. Justice Flaherty noted that the youths were unaware of their rights and that the police had made no efforts to contact their parents. "On these facts consent to enter these premises was never sought. In any event, it wasn't given, or acquiesced in."[169]

2. SCHOOLS

School searches have grown increasingly controversial in Canada in recent years, in part because the police, in co-operation with the schools, increasingly brought drug detector dogs into the schools in at least some parts of Canada to sniff the possessions of students as well as their school lockers. The Supreme Court of Canada clarified some years ago that

---

[165] [1999] A.J. No. 1086 (Alta. C.A.).

[166] [1996] S.C.J. No. 11, [1996] 1 S.C.R. 128 (S.C.C.). *R. v. Edwards* is an important case in search law, since it establishes at para. 45 the test for determining if an individual has a reasonable expectation of privacy in a given context.

[167] The consent of a parent was also deemed adequate to permit the police to search the dwelling house and bedroom of a young person in *R. v. F.T.*, [1995] B.C.J. No. 2859 (B.C. Youth Ct.). In *R. v. F.T.* the police found a mini-arsenal of weapons in the accused's bedroom.

[168] [2003] O.J. No. 5137 (Ont. C.J.).

[169] *R. v. A. (A.)*, [2003] O.J. No. 5137, at para. 13 (Ont. C.J.).

young persons have a significantly diminished expectation of privacy in the school context[170] and that school officials can search students based on a more lenient and flexible standard than the standard to which the police must adhere.[171] However the Supreme Court of Canada has now affirmed that young persons retain a privacy interest in their personal belongings while on school premises. The Supreme Court of Canada found in *R. v. A.M.*[172] that the warrantless use of a drug detector dog to sniff a pile of students' knapsacks in the school gymnasium was an unreasonable search because the students had a reasonable expectation of privacy in the concealed contents of their belongings and thus the dog sniff was an intrusion into that privacy and amounted to a search in law. The search was unreasonable because the dog had been permitted to sniff the backpacks absent any grounds to suspect or believe there were drugs in any of the backpacks. Had the police had at least reasonable suspicion that there were drugs in the knapsack, the use of the dog would have been permissible.[173] The decision was driven in part by the high privacy interest that the court found attaches to an item considered highly personal to a student, his or her knapsack, which was likened to a purse, suitcase or briefcase, and characterized as a repository of all that is personal.

Nevertheless, there remain unanswered questions regarding the nature of the privacy interest that a student has in various locales within a school context. The nature of the privacy interest in a school locker is a key example. Justice Cory in *R. v. M.R.M.* suggested that the reasonable expectation of privacy that a young person has in a school locker may be compromised by the degree of control that school authorities have over school lockers.[174] Clearly, it is more difficult to argue that one has a reasonable expectation of privacy in a locker on school premises when the school also has a key to the locker and has indicated that it reserves the right to open the locker at any time. A student's privacy interest can be further challenged if he or she is sharing the locker with one or more students, who can open the locker at any time. Finally, it may make a difference whether the student has concealed the drugs within a personal item in the locker, such as a purse or knapsack, or simply left the drugs clearly visible to anyone who opens the locker. In such cases, applying the classic *R. v. Edwards* test to determine if the young person has a reason-

---

[170] *R. v. M.R.M.*, [1998] S.C.J. No. 83, at para. 33, [1998] 3 S.C.R. 393 (S.C.C.). See also *R. v. J.M.G.*, [1986] O.J. No. 923, 56 O.R. (2d) 705 (Ont. C.A.).

[171] *R. v. M.R.M.*, [1998] S.C.J. No. 83, at para. 47, [1998] 3 S.C.R. 393 (S.C.C.).

[172] [2008] S.C.J. No. 19, 2008 SCC 19 (S.C.C.).

[173] *R. v. A.M.*, [2008] S.C.J. No. 19, 2008 SCC 19 (S.C.C.). See also the companion case of *R. v. Kang-Brown*, [2008] S.C.J. No. 18, 2008 SCC 18 (S.C.C.). These two decisions are complex because the court was so divided in its reasoning in both cases.

[174] *R. v. M.R.M.*, [1998] S.C.J. No. 83, at para. 34, [1998] 3 S.C.R. 393 (S.C.C.).

able expectation of privacy in the circumstances may well result in the conclusion that little to no privacy interest exists in the school locker.[175]

3.   BODILY SAMPLES

The taking of DNA samples from individuals, young persons as well as adults, in various circumstances, clearly engages the privacy interests of individuals. DNA samples can be taken from young persons as well as adults in certain circumstances[176] and the results can be stored in the national DNA databank in accordance with the scheme established in the *Criminal Code*.[177] The DNA warrant scheme and related provisions in the *Criminal Code* have therefore attracted judicial scrutiny in relation to the scheme's compliance with s. 8 of the *Charter*.

The Supreme Court of Canada has upheld the constitutionality of the DNA warrant scheme.[178] Justice Arbour held for the court that the provisions dealing with the issuance of warrants for the purpose of seizing bodily substances for forensic DNA testing for investigative purposes[179] conform with the constitutional requirements of a reasonable search or seizure under s. 8 of the *Charter*.[180] "[I]n general terms, the DNA warrant provisions of the *Criminal Code* strike an appropriate balance between the public interest in effective criminal law enforcement for serious offences, and the rights of individuals to control the release of personal information about themselves, as well as their right to dignity and personal integrity."[181]

However, both statute[182] and common law afford extra protections to young persons to ensure that their privacy rights are respected regarding the taking of DNA samples. Under the *Criminal Code*, a young person against whom a warrant is to be executed, has, in addition to any other rights arising from his or her detention under the warrant, the right to a reasonable opportunity to consult with counsel, and a parent or other adult chosen by the young person. The young person can waive these rights but the waiver must be recorded on audio, video or otherwise, or must be

---

[175]   See for example *R. v. S.M.Z.*, [1998] M.J. No. 587 (Man. C.A.), where a search by a school vice-principal of a student's locker was found to be reasonable in the circumstances.

[176]   *Criminal Code*, s. 487.05.

[177]   *Criminal Code*, ss. 487.04-487.0911. In 1995, Parliament enacted two complementary schemes regulating the collection and use of DNA: DNA warrants and the DNA databank. The scheme was further amended in 2008.

[178]   *R. v. S.A.B.*, [2003] S.C.J. No. 61, [2003] 2 S.C.R. 678 (S.C.C.).

[179]   *Criminal Code*, ss. 487.04-487.0911.

[180]   *R. v. S.A.B.*, [2003] S.C.J. No. 61, at paras. 1 and 62, [2003] 2 S.C.R. 678 (S.C.C.).

[181]   *R. v. S.A.B.*, [2003] S.C.J. No. 61, at para. 52, [2003] 2 S.C.R. 678 (S.C.C.).

[182]   *Criminal Code*, s. 487.07; *YCJA*, ss. 188-189.

made in writing and contain a signed statement in which the young person acknowledges that he or she has been informed of the right being waived.[183] In addition, the *YCJA* establishes shorter time periods for the retention of the DNA samples and the destruction of the records relating to them.[184]

The Supreme Court of Canada has held that it is proper for the principles of the *YCJA* to be considered in relation to whether a DNA sample should be taken from an accused young person found guilty of a primary designated offence.[185] In *R. v. R.C.*,[186] the Supreme Court of Canada reviewed the decision of a Nova Scotia trial judge who had refused to issue an order providing for the taking of a DNA sample from a young person who was 13 at the time of the offence. The young person had been found guilty of assault with a weapon by stabbing his mother in the foot with a pen after she dumped dirty laundry on him as he lay in bed. (The overall facts, which the accused did not dispute, also indicated that he had punched her in the eye and hit her elsewhere about the face during the incident.) At the time, assault with a weapon was among the primary designated offences for which a trial court had to make a DNA order upon a finding of guilt unless the offender established that, were the order to be made, "the impact on the person's or young person's privacy and security of the person would be grossly disproportionate to the public interest in the protection of society and the proper administration of justice".[187]

The central issue before the Supreme Court of Canada in *R. v. R.C.* was whether a youth justice court judge could, when considering whether to make the DNA order, take into account the principles of youth criminal justice legislation.[188] Justice Fish for the majority found that the trial judge, Gass J., had not erred by considering the principles of the *YCJA*, the level of development of an early adolescent and the young person's circumstances. Justice Fish noted that the offence was at the low end of the spectrum of primary designated offences and had involved a dispute between a 13-year-old and his mother that arose from his disinclination to

---

[183]   *Criminal Code*, s. 487.07(4) and (5).

[184]   See ss. 188-189 of the *YCJA*, which are amendments to the *DNA Identification Act*, S.C. 1998, c. 37.

[185]   Primary designated offences are defined under s. 487.04 of the *Criminal Code* and include the most serious and violent offences, such as murder, manslaughter and aggravated sexual assault. As a result of 2008 amendments, s. 487.051(1) now requires a court to make a DNA order upon a guilty finding in relation to category (a) primary designated offences. Previously, the court had discretion as to whether to make the order. *R. v. R.C.*, [2005] S.C.J. No. 62, [2005] 3 S.C.R. 99 (S.C.C.) was decided under the former regime.

[186]   [2005] S.C.J. No. 62, [2005] 3 S.C.R. 99 (S.C.C.).

[187]   *Criminal Code*, s. 487.051(2); *Martin's Annual Criminal Code 2008* (Aurora, Ont.: Canada Law Book Co., 2008).

[188]   See also *R. v. B. (K.)*, [2003] O.J. No. 3553, 179 C.C.C. (3d) 413 (Ont. C.A.).

go to school, and that the assault had been a reflexive response by the young person to the humiliation of having dirty laundry dumped on his bed. R.W.C. was a first-time offender. Justice Gass had correctly weighed the public interest in ordering that a DNA sample be taken and retained in the databank against the impact of such an order on the privacy and security interests of the young person and had properly conducted her assessment in light of the principles and objects of youth criminal justice legislation, the court found.

However, the legislation in this area changed following the ruling in *R. v. R.C.* so that, in relation to certain primary designated offences, s. 487.051 of the *Criminal Code* now states that the DNA order must be made.[189] As a result, the Ontario Court of Justice has ruled that, since these mandatory DNA orders, by their very nature, prohibit a consideration of *YCJA* principles in deciding whether to make the order, s. 487.051(1) is an unreasonable law.[190] Justice Cohen found that the mandatory DNA order amounts to an unreasonable search under s. 8 of the *Charter*. Justice Cohen further found that s. 487.051(2), which is a reverse onus provision that requires a young person to establish (in relation to the less serious primary designated offences) that the impact of the DNA order on the privacy of the young person would be grossly disproportionate to the public interest in the protection of society, places an unconstitutional burden on the young person and is also a s. 8 violation. Both sections were unjustifiable violations of s. 7 as well, the court found.

Justice Cohen's remedy was to order that young persons found guilty of committing mandatory primary designated offences as well as the reverse onus category of primary designated offences be dealt with in terms of process as if these offences were secondary designated offences. In other words, in all cases involving a DNA order against a young person, the judge retains the discretion as to whether to make the order.[191]

The taking of other kinds of bodily samples from young persons is also at issue in the jurisprudence. For example, it is unclear if it is permissible to compel a young person on probation to provide random samples of his or her breath, urine or blood as a condition of his or her

---

[189]   *Martin's Annual Criminal Code 2009* (Aurora, Ont.: Canada Law Book Co., 2009).
[190]   *R. v. C.S.*, [2009] O.J. No. 1115 (Ont. C.J.).
[191]   *R. v. C.S.*, [2009] O.J. No. 1115, at para. 67 (Ont. C.J.), where Cohen J. explains how she sees the procedure working. (This is only an Ontario Court of Justice ruling and has little binding precedential value.) Interestingly, the decision was not referred to in *R. v. D.W.*, [2009] S.J. No. 185, 2009 SKPC 49 (Sask. Prov. Ct.), where the young person was found guilty of unlawful confinement and related charges. Unlawful confinement is a primary designated offence; the mandatory DNA order was made without argument.

probation, in the absence of a statutory scheme. In *R. v. Shoker*,[192] the accused was convicted of breaking and entering a dwelling house with intent to commit sexual assault. In addition to his jail sentence of 20 months, he was placed on two years' probation. One of the conditions was that he abstain from the consumption and possession of alcohol and non-prescription drugs and that he submit to a urine, blood or breathalyzer test upon demand of a peace officer or probation officer to determine compliance with this condition. Any positive reading would constitute a breach of the condition.

Justice Charron held for the majority that the sentencing judge had no authority under s. 732.1 of the *Criminal Code* to authorize a search or seizure of bodily substances as part of a probation order,[193] the impugned condition must be quashed for lack of jurisdiction, and therefore the constitutional question need not be answered. The seizure of bodily samples must be subject to stringent standards and safeguards to meet constitutional requirements and in the case of this probationary condition, Parliament had not provided such a scheme.[194] In the absence of statutory authority to require Shoker to provide bodily samples, the Court of Appeal was correct to delete this aspect of one of the conditions, the Supreme Court of Canada held.

However, the Nova Scotia Court of Appeal later held in *R. v. J.R.L.*[195] that the *Shoker* decision did not apply to probation orders involving young persons. In *J.R.L.*, a young person, who was 16 at the time of the offence, was sentenced to 6 months deferred custody plus 18 months' probation in relation to a violent home invasion. At his sentencing hearing, J.R.L. admitted to using cocaine and marihuana prior to barging into the home as the leader of a gang of at least eight young people. Among the conditions of his deferred custody order as well as his probation order was that he submit to a urinalysis or breath sample upon demand of a peace officer or probation officer to determine if drugs or alcohol were in his system.

Justice Roscoe, writing for the Nova Scotia Court of Appeal, held that the *Shoker* decision, which was an adult sentencing case, did not apply to conditions attached to probation orders and deferred custody orders imposed on young persons under the *YCJA* because the language in the relevant probationary provision under the *YCJA* is virtually identical to the language of one of the conditions that can attach to a conditional

---

[192]   [2006] S.C.J. No. 44, [2006] 2 S.C.R. 399 (S.C.C.).
[193]   *R. v. Shoker*, [2006] S.C.J. No. 44, at para 3, [2006] 2 S.C.R. 399 (S.C.C.).
[194]   *R. v. Shoker*, [2006] S.C.J. No. 44, at para. 25, [2006] 2 S.C.R. 399 (S.C.C.).
[195]   [2007] N.S.J. No. 214 (N.S.C.A.).

sentence order for an adult. Since Charron J. held in *Shoker* that punitive conditions may be imposed as part of a conditional sentence, it follows that punitive conditions can be imposed as part of a deferred custody or probationary order under the *YCJA* because the wording in these *YCJA* provisions mirrors the provision in the conditional sentencing regime for adults.

It remains to be seen how other youth justice courts will respond in light of *Shoker*. Prior to the Supreme Court of Canada ruling in *Shoker*, the Alberta Provincial Court considered the constitutionality of a probation condition requiring a young person to submit to random drug and alcohol tests. In *R. v. S.B.*, Jordan J. held for the court that such a condition offends s. 8 of the *Charter* because there are no legislative or regulatory standards or safeguards for the protection of the appellant's privacy in the enforcement of the condition and the condition is therefore unreasonable. In doing so, the Alberta Provincial Court followed the British Columbia Court of Appeal ruling in *Shoker*, which was, as discussed above, upheld by the Supreme Court of Canada in 2006.[196]

C.   Section 11

(i)   Section 11(b) — Right to Be Tried Within a Reasonable Time

What is a reasonable time, and does this time period differ if the accused is a young person?

In *R. v. M. (G.C.)*,[197] Osborne J.A. held that young persons are not entitled to a special constitutional guarantee to trial within a reasonable time that differs substantially from that of adults. As a general rule, whether the accused is an adult or a young person, the four factors outlined in *R. v. Askov*[198] must be balanced in every case to determine if the accused, whether young or old, has been brought to trial within a reasonable time.[199] Justice Osborne nevertheless held that, as a general proposition, youth justice court proceedings should proceed to a conclusion more quickly than those in the adult criminal justice system. "Delay, which may be reasonable in the adult criminal justice system, may not be reasonable in the youth

---

[196] *R. v. S.B.*, [2006] A.J. No. 1537, at paras. 32 and 33 (Alta. Prov. Ct.).
[197] [1991] O.J. No. 885 (Ont. C.A.).
[198] [1990] S.C.J. No. 106, [1990] 2 S.C.R. 1199 (S.C.C.).
[199] [1990] S.C.J. No. 106, at para. 35, [1990] 2 S.C.R. 1199 (S.C.C.). These four factors are: length of delay, explanation for the delay, waiver and prejudice to the accused.

court."[200] Justice Osborne explained that the reasons for this include the fact that young persons are less able than adults to appreciate the connection between behaviour and consequences.[201] While the constitutional right to trial within a reasonable time remains constant, it differs in its application to young persons because there is a particular element of prejudice that may result if the trial of a young person is unduly delayed.[202] Justice Osborne further found that the trial judge had erred in concluding that *Askov* imposed a systemic delay ceiling or threshold.[203] Thus, there can be no strict rule regarding a maximum period of systemic delay for adults or for young persons, beyond which the *Charter* application must succeed. Yet he held that, in general, youth justice court cases should be brought to trial within five to six months, excluding the initial intake period during which the accused retains counsel, obtains disclosure, *etc.*[204] This is to be interpreted only as an administrative guideline and not a ceiling, threshold or limitation period.[205] Justice Osborne ultimately held that in the case before him, where the total systemic delay was 8.5 months and the accused young person had suffered minimal prejudice, his right to trial within a reasonable time had not been violated.

Fourteen years later, and after the coming into force of the *YCJA*, the Ontario Court of Appeal upheld the reasoning in *R. v. M. (G.C.)*. In *R. v. T.R.*,[206] MacPherson J.A. held for the court that the *YCJA* was merely a codification of the jurisprudence under the *YOA* rather than a new regime and that the leading cases were still good law.[207] Justice MacPherson affirmed that, although delay that may be reasonable in the adult criminal justice system may not be reasonable in the youth justice court, young persons were not entitled to a special constitutional guarantee to trial within a reasonable time. Justice MacPherson expressly rejected the finding of the youth justice court judge that there is an enhanced responsibility on the Crown and on the police to ensure that matters involving young persons are dealt with much more quickly than under the *YOA*.[208]

In the case at bar, which involved a 17-year-old in-custody accused, MacPherson J.A. held that the three-month total time period from arrest to trial for a young person facing serious criminal charges including robbery and possession of proceeds of crime, fell well within the guideline of the

---

[200] *R. v. M. (G.C.)*, [1991] O.J. No. 885, at para. 23 (Ont. C.A.).
[201] *R. v. M. (G.C.)*, [1991] O.J. No. 885, at para. 23 (Ont. C.A.).
[202] *R. v. M. (G.C.)*, [1991] O.J. No. 885, at para. 24 (Ont. C.A.).
[203] *R. v. M. (G.C.)*, [1991] O.J. No. 885, at para. 38 (Ont. C.A.).
[204] *R. v. M. (G.C.)*, [1991] O.J. No. 885, at para. 45 (Ont. C.A.).
[205] *R. v. M. (G.C.)*, [1991] O.J. No. 885, at para. 45 (Ont. C.A.).
[206] [2005] O.J. No. 2150 (Ont. C.A.).
[207] [2005] O.J. No. 2150, at para. 34 (Ont. C.A.).
[208] [2005] O.J. No. 2150, at para. 27 (Ont. C.A.).

five to six months acceptable delay before trial.[209] In fact, MacPherson J.A. stopped short of characterizing the case as a model for timely youth justice court proceedings involving an in-custody youth.[210] While MacPherson J.A. acknowledged that, unlike its predecessor, the Declaration of Principle in the *YCJA* entrenches in s. 3 the importance of matters proceeding promptly in youth justice court "given the young person's perception of time" as well as the need to emphasize timely intervention that reinforces the link between the offending behaviour and its consequences, MacPherson J.A. held that such requirements had also been central to the interpretation of the *YOA*.[211] The British Columbia Court of Appeal came to a similar conclusion in *R. v. R.C.D.*[212]

(ii)   Section 11(d) — Right to Be Presumed Innocent

In *R. v. D.V.*,[213] Cuthbertson J.P. held that the constitutional right to the presumption of innocence includes appearances in bail court, and that bringing a young person into the bail court in handcuffs and leg shackles, pursuant to a blanket police policy that all defendants must be inside the courtroom before restraints can be removed, is not lawful. Justice Cuthbertson took the position that the practice of removing restraints before the young person enters the courtroom is important to the maintenance of the presumption of innocence,[214] that unnecessarily handcuffing and shackling a defendant impedes his or her right to the presumption of

---

[209] [2005] O.J. No. 2150, at para. 42 (Ont. C.A.).
[210] *R. v. T.R.*, [2005] O.J. No. 2150, at para. 46 (Ont. C.A.).
[211] [2005] O.J. No. 2150, at paras. 28 and 29 (Ont. C.A.). See s. 3(1)(b)(v) and (iv), respectively.
[212] [2006] B.C.J. No. 947, 2006 BCCA 211 (B.C.C.A.) in particular at paras. 31 and 32, where the B.C. Court of Appeal agrees with the reasoning in *R. v. T.R.* that the *YCJA* merely codifies the law in this respect as it was under the *YOA* and finds a 10-month delay acceptable. But see *R. v. L.S.*, [2005] O.J. No. 1324, 2005 ONCJ 113 (Ont. C.J.), where the Ontario Court of Justice held that the Declaration of Principle in the *YCJA* changed the paradigm in relation to the meaning of trial within a reasonable time. See also *R. v. M.H.*, [2005] O.J. No. 1585 (Ont. C.A.), where the court upheld the order of a youth court judge who stayed four charges of sexual assault almost two years after the charges were laid. The court observed that even one year was pushing the limits of the definition of trial within a reasonable time for a young person in relation to charges that were not considered complicated. The system was obliged to give this case some priority (at paras. 5 and 6). In the course of the brief ruling the court noted that memories fade over time. In fact, research indicates that the memories of children and youths fade more quickly than those of adults. See Nicholas Bala, "Youth as Victims and Offenders in the Criminal Justice System: A Charter Analysis — Recognizing Vulnerability" in Jamie Cameron and James Stribopoulos, eds., *The Charter and Criminal Justice: Twenty-five Years Later* (Markham, Ont.: LexisNexis, 2008), at 616.
[213] [2007] O.J. No. 3972 (Ont. C.J.).
[214] *R. v. D.V.*, [2007] O.J. No. 3972, at para. 5 (Ont. C.J.).

innocence[215] and that a blanket policy of restraint may bring the administration of justice into disrepute.[216] After a careful consideration of the
relevant case law, Cuthbertson J.P. concluded that the onus rests with the
Crown to apply for restraints to be placed on a defendant, not with a
defendant to have the restraints removed.[217] It is up to the court and not
the police to decide the issue of restraints inside the courtroom, Cuther-
bertson J.P. held.

(iii)   Section 11(i) — Benefit of Lesser Punishment

A novel case arose in the Yukon in 2005 regarding a 36-year-old
man who pled guilty in 2005 to indecent assault in relation to two young
victims, which occurred when he was 12 and 13 and the *JDA* was in
force.[218] The two victims, 8 and 10, were subjected to repeated sexual
acts, aggravated by threats and physical violence, over a one-year period.
The incidents included the accused urinating on the victims.

A central issue before Ruddy J. of the Territorial Court was whether
she could impose jail on the adult at this stage in light of s. 11(i) of the
Charter. Section 11(i) of the *Charter* states: "Any person charged with an
offence has the right ... (i) if found guilty of the offence and if the
punishment for the offence has been varied between the time of commission and the time of sentencing, to the benefit of the lesser punishment."
Since conventional jail was not an option under the *JDA* at the time these
offences were committed, Ruddy J. found that she could not impose jail
now. In her view, the punishment for the offence had effectively changed
between the time of commission and the time of sentencing and the
accused was thus entitled to the benefit of the lesser punishment.

At the heart of Ruddy J.'s conclusion was the finding that an industrial school to which a young person could be sent under the *JDA* is not
equivalent to jail under the *YCJA*, and, in fact, is a lesser punishment.
Justice Ruddy suggested that industrial schools were more appropriately
characterized as treatment facilities designed to rehabilitate young persons
rather than penal institutions. Since jails have replaced industrial schools
as places of confinement for young persons, and it is no longer possible to

---

[215] *R. v. D.V.*, [2007] O.J. No. 3972, at para. 17 (Ont. C.J.).
[216] *R. v. D.V.*, [2007] O.J. No. 3972, at para. 8 (Ont. C.J.).
[217] *R. v. D.V.*, [2007] O.J. No. 3972, at para. 8 (Ont. C.J.).
[218] *R. v. R.S.*, [2005] Y.J. No. 95, 2005 YKTC 72 (Y.T. Terr. Ct.).

send the adult to an industrial school, sending him to jail now would amount to a s. 11(i) violation.[219]

In arriving at this conclusion, Ruddy J. suggested that the aims of open custody facilities today are strikingly similar to the aims of industrial schools. In the case at bar, however, Ruddy J. concluded that she was restricted by s. 89 of the *YCJA*, which indicates that when a young person is 20 years old or older at the time a custodial youth sentence is imposed, the person shall be committed to a provincial correctional facility for adults. Justice Ruddy ultimately concluded that, while she believed jail was the appropriate sentence in the circumstances, she held that she did not have the jurisdiction to impose it.[220] Noting that certain other programs, such as intensive support and supervision programs and attendance orders, were not available for adults, Ruddy J. imposed a probation term of two years with strict conditions.

D.   Section 12 — Right Not to Be Subjected to any Cruel and Unusual Treatment or Punishment

The test for determining whether treatment or punishment by the state is cruel and unusual is whether the punishment is so excessive as to outrage standards of decency. Section 12 is aimed at punishments that are found to be grossly disproportionate.[221]

In the context of young persons, s. 12 cases have often arisen in relation to the quality of the detention facilities in which the young person is being housed. For example, in *R. v. McC. (T.)*,[222] three teenagers were held in cells that were, by their accounts, appalling. Justice King accepted the evidence from the young persons regarding the condition of the cells, which was largely corroborated by the three lawyers: the larger of the two cells was 10 feet by 10 feet and accommodated as many as eight young persons, many of whom had to remain standing or sitting on the floor. Some young persons spent up to seven hours in the holding cells. Both cells were entirely bare, often overcrowded, dirty, hot and poorly-ventilated, with concrete floors and walls, and permeated by a putrid smell. No provisions or diversions of any kind were available, such as reading materials, cards or a radio. Each cell had one bench, which could

---

[219]   *R. v. R.S.*, [2005] Y.J. No. 95, 2005 YKTC 72 (Y.T. Terr. Ct.).

[220]   *R. v. R.S.*, [2005] Y.J. No. 95, at para. 52, 2005 YKTC 72 (Y.T. Terr. Ct.). Justice Ruddy referred to a line of cases to support this conclusion, including *R. v. A.B.M.*, [1993] B.C.J. No. 2642 (B.C. Prov. Ct.) and *R. v. L.C.*, [2001] Y.J. No. 42. (Y.T. Terr. Ct.).

[221]   *R. v. Smith*, [1987] S.C.J. No. 36, [1987] 1 S.C.R. 1045 (S.C.C.).

[222]   [1991] O.J. No. 1382, 4 O.R. (3d) 203 (Ont. Prov. Div.).

accommodate three to four young persons. The remaining young persons had to stand or sit on the concrete floor. The court officers monitored the young persons by observing them through a window.

Although these were merely holding cells, the cells were often home to the youths for the entire day. The young persons were often handcuffed on their way to and from the holding cells. Interviews with counsel had to be conducted in these cells or in an adjoining toilet area. The toilet area had no toilet seat, toilet paper, soap or paper towels.

Justice King concluded that the treatment of the young persons was a "severe outrage to our sense of decency", was humiliating and was grossly disproportionate to what was required in the circumstances and amounted to a s. 12 violation. In the course of his decision, King J. held that the word "treatment" in s. 12 captures more than sentencing and extends to pre-trial detainees and the conditions to which they are subjected in holding cells.

In determining whether the treatment afforded the young persons was a s. 12 violation, King J. considered the following five principles:

- the treatment must not be so excessive as to outrage standards of decency;

- one of the factors in assessing the factor above is whether the treatment is unduly degrading or humiliating;

- treatment must not be grossly disproportionate to what is required in the circumstances;

- one of the factors in assessing disproportionality is whether alternatives could be made available to meet the same end; and

- in assessing the treatment, special considerations must be given to the fact that a young person is involved.

In the case at bar, King J. held that the young persons were degraded, humiliated and treated indecently, and were denied privacy in their interviews with their counsel. Justice King concluded that this treatment was grossly disproportionate to what was required in the circumstances. During his reasoning, King J. also considered principles of international law, such as the *United Nations International Covenant on Civil and Political Rights*, including Article 7, which states, "No one shall be subject to torture or to cruel, inhuman or degrading treatment or punishment", and Article 10, which states that juvenile offenders shall be segregated from adults and be accorded treatment appropriate to their age and understanding. "Contrary to international and Canadian principles, no thought was given to treating youths any differently from adults, other than to separate them."[223]

The court further held that the young persons' right to counsel was also violated since they were unable to instruct counsel in private.

The s. 12 violations were intimately related to the very offences (mischief charges) with which the young persons were charged. Justice King found that a stay of proceedings in relation to the charges (which involved damage to the holding cells) was the only just and appropriate remedy.

More recently, the courts have found s. 12 violations involving young persons in a variety of situations, including where the police have used a taser on a young person without warning and for no justifiable reason. In *R. v. J.W.*,[224] the court found that the 15-year-old young person was tasered after being detained by police in relation to a break and enter and possession of concealed weapons and housebreaking tools. Justice Kvill held that the officer, who acknowledged that tasers inflict excruciating pain,[225] used the taser to punish the young person for breaking and entering a home the day before Christmas and for lying to police about possessing weapons,[226] and that this constituted a shocking abuse of police powers.[227] The court found that the officer attempted to hide the use of the taser by failing to mention it in his notes, by failing to take the young person to the doctor and by failing to file a use of force form.[228] Justice Kvill found *Charter* breaches of both ss. 7 and 12 and granted a stay of prosecution.

Likewise, in *R. v. S.F.*,[229] Katarynych J. stayed robbery charges against two teenage girls after concluding that they were humiliated, degraded and traumatized when they were unnecessarily strip-searched by the police after being detained in relation to charges which involved allegations of robbing another girl in the community.[230] During the course of the ruling, Katarynych J. paid particular attention to the fact that the individuals were both young persons who were subject to the special protections of youth legislation, at that time the *YOA*.[231] During the course

---

[223] *R. v. McC. (T.)*, [1991] O.J. No. 1382, at para. 52, 4 O.R. (3d) 203 (Ont. Prov. Div.).
[224] [2006] A.J. No. 1097 (Alta. Prov. Ct.).
[225] *R. v. J.W.*, [2006] A.J. No. 1097, at para. 27 (Alta. Prov. Ct.).
[226] *R. v. J.W.*, [2006] A.J. No. 1097, at para. 70 (Alta. Prov. Ct.).
[227] *R. v. J.W.*, [2006] A.J. No. 1097, at paras. 105-106 (Alta. Prov. Ct.).
[228] *R. v. J.W.*, [2006] A.J. No. 1097, at paras. 105-110 (Alta. Prov. Ct.).
[229] [2003] O.J. No. 92 (Ont. C.J.).
[230] *R. v. S.F.*, [2003] O.J. No. 92, at para. 126 (Ont. C.J.).
[231] *R. v. S.F.*, [2003] O.J. No. 92, at paras. 63, 137, 144 and 146 (Ont. C.J.).

of the strip searches, the teenagers had to strip completely naked and expose their bodies for inspection to a police matron. As part of the inspections, each girl was required to spread her arms and do deep-knee bends.[232] Their upper bodies were captured on videotape.[233]

Justice Katarynych further found that one of the two girls, who was 15 and visually and cognitively impaired, was subjected to cruel and unusual treatment by being deprived of her eyeglasses, upon which she had been dependent since childhood, effectively blinding her while in custody. She had advised the police she could not see without her glasses.[234]

---

[232] *R. v. S.F.*, [2003] O.J. No. 92, at para. 7, point 26 (Ont. C.J.).

[233] *R. v. S.F.*, [2003] O.J. No. 92, at para. 85 (Ont. C.J.).

[234] *R. v. S.F.*, [2003] O.J. No. 92, at para. 114 (Ont. C.J.).

Chapter 7

YOUNG PERSONS AND ENHANCED PROCEDURAL PROTECTIONS UNDER THE YOUTH CRIMINAL JUSTICE ACT

I. INTRODUCTION

Young persons charged with criminal offences in Canada have the benefit of all of the rights guaranteed by the *Canadian Charter of Rights and Freedoms*[1] and then some. Young persons charged with crimes in Canada not only have the benefit of the rights in the *Charter*, similar to adults, but they are afforded significant additional procedural protection under the *Youth Criminal Justice Act*[2] in recognition of the fact that they are not adults and, hence, are less likely to be aware of their legal rights and are more vulnerable to the powers of the state.[3] These special guarantees,[4] which are found throughout the *YCJA*, operate as an extra layer of insulation against the powers of the state. These additional protections in the *YCJA* can come into play from the first point of contact between the young person and the state actor, such as the police, even if that contact is nothing more than a conversation with a police officer that does not result in a charge. The Supreme Court of Canada has affirmed the enhanced procedural protections afforded young persons in the *YCJA* in cases such as *R. v. C. (R.W.)*[5] and *R. v. L.T.H.*[6]

"In creating a separate criminal justice system for young persons, Parliament has recognized the heightened vulnerability and reduced

---

[1] Part I of the *Constitution Act, 1982*, being Schedule B to the *Canada Act 1982* (U.K.), 1982, c. 11 [hereafter "*Charter*"].
[2] S.C. 2002, c. 1 [hereafter "*YCJA*"].
[3] The enhanced procedural protection afforded young persons is enshrined in s. 3(1)(b)(iii) and (d)(i) of the *YCJA*. The rationale for providing young persons with enhanced protection is discussed in various Supreme Court of Canada rulings, including by Fish J. in *R. v. L.T.H.*, [2008] S.C.J. No. 50, at paras. 1, 3, 18 and 24, 2008 SCC 49 (S.C.C.).
[4] *YCJA*, s. 3(1)(d)(i).
[5] [2005] S.C.J. No. 62, at para. 41, 259 D.L.R. (4th) 1 (S.C.C.).
[6] *R. v. L.T.H.*, [2008] S.C.J. No. 50, at paras. 3 and 18, 2008 SCC 49 (S.C.C.).

maturity of young persons", Fish J. explained in *R. v. C. (R.W.)*.[7] "In keeping with its international obligations, Parliament has sought as well to extend to young offenders enhanced procedural protections ... ."[8]

These enhanced procedural protections enshrined in the *YCJA* afford to young persons in Canada procedural and substantive safeguards that far exceed those provided to adults who are charged with crimes in Canada. These special rules were built into the *YCJA* not only because of the long-standing legal principle that young persons, by virtue of their youth, lesser maturity and greater vulnerability, are presumed to be less morally culpable and thus deserve a greater measure of legal protection[9] but also because of the pervasive belief among Canadian professionals who work in the criminal justice field that young persons are more amenable to rehabilitation than adults,[10] and that all reasonable efforts should be made to support and assist them to reduce the likelihood that they will continue to commit crimes.

The following specific and additional rights and protections in the *YCJA* demonstrate the extent to which the Canadian state has chosen to treat young persons who commit crimes with greater care than adults in large part to foster their rehabilitation.

II.   EXTRAJUDICIAL MEASURES

The expansion of alternatives to prosecution under the *YCJA* through the extrajudicial measures regime (which is a more elaborate regime than the alternative measures that existed for young persons under the *Young Offenders Act*[11] or that exists for adults today under the *Criminal Code*[12]) illustrates the extra protection afforded young persons who are charged with crimes in Canada in contrast to their adult counterparts. The extrajudicial measures regime[13] provides more direction and options than ever before regarding non-court approaches to dealing with young persons who are alleged to have committed criminal offences. No such detailed direction exists in the *Criminal Code* in relation to alternative measures for adults.

---

[7]   [2005] S.C.J. No. 62, 259 D.L.R. (4th) 1 (S.C.C.).

[8]   *R. v. C. (R.W.)*, [2005] S.C.J. No. 62, at para. 41, 259 D.L.R. (4th) 1 (S.C.C.).

[9]   *R. v. D.B.*, [2008] S.C.J. No. 25, at paras. 47, 48 and 59, 2008 SCC 25 (S.C.C.).

[10]   See, for example, the discussion in Nicholas Bala, *Youth Criminal Justice Law* (Toronto: Irwin Law Inc., 2003), at 5.

[11]   R.S.C. 1985, c. Y-1 [hereafter "*YOA*"].

[12]   R.S.C. 1985, c. C-46.

[13]   Extrajudicial measures, Part I of the *YCJA*, ss. 4-12, are discussed in detail in Chapter 5.

The *YCJA* codifies the obligation of the police to actively consider various options, including taking no action against a young person who is alleged to have committed an offence, before deciding to charge the young person. The police have always had discretion as to whether to charge an individual,[14] but, with respect to young persons, this police discretion is now codified in the *YCJA* so that the police are obliged to consider in each case whether it is necessary to charge the young person or whether it would be "sufficient" to resort to other options, such as taking no action, warning or cautioning the young person, or referring him or her to a community program or agency that may assist the young person in not committing offences. This codification operates as an additional protection for young persons. The inclusion of guidelines regarding the use of extrajudicial measures, which provide direction and guidance to the police and Crown counsel and to other criminal justice participants, also illustrate the degree to which young persons are afforded greater protections than adults who are charged with crimes.[15]

In cases where the young person receives an extrajudicial sanction rather than being formally dealt with in the courts, the program administrator must inform a parent of the young person of the sanction,[16] thereby providing notice and warning to at least one parent of the young person that he or she has become involved with the system. Such notice also enables the parents to assist and support the young person in successfully fulfilling the terms of the sanction.

III. NOTICES TO PARENTS

If the young person is detained or charged, the *YCJA* attempts to ensure that parents are made aware.[17] A parent must be notified as soon as possible if his or her child has been arrested and is being detained in custody and the parent must be advised of the reasons for the arrest and where the child is being held.[18] If the whereabouts of a parent are unknown or the parents are unavailable, notice may be given to another adult relative or another adult who is likely to assist the young person.[19] Even if

---

[14] Peter Harris, Brian Weagant & David Cole, "Working 'In the Trenches' with the *YCJA*" (April 2004) Canadian Journal of Criminology and Criminal Justice 367, at 376.
[15] Extrajudicial measures are discussed in Chapter 5.
[16] *YCJA*, s. 11.
[17] A parent is defined in s. 2 of the *YCJA* to include any person who is under a legal duty to provide for the young person, or any person who is, or who has, in law or in fact, the custody or control of the young person but this does not include someone who has that custody or control only because of proceedings under the *YCJA*.
[18] *YCJA*, s. 26(1).
[19] *YCJA*, s. 26(4).

the young person is not being detained in custody, the parents must still be notified if their child has been issued a summons or an appearance notice, or has been released on a promise to appear, an undertaking or a recognizance. These requirements involve the parents at an early stage and enable them to provide assistance, support and supervision. Presumably, by notifying the parents of any upcoming court dates as well as the conditions of the young person's release, it is hoped that the parents will play a key role in ensuring the young person shows up for court as required and complies with any conditions of release.

The notices also remind the parents that the young person has a right to be represented by counsel.[20]

Failure to give notice to parents in a case where the young person has been issued a summons or appearance notice, or has been released on an undertaking or a recognizance, can invalidate the proceedings unless one of the parents attends court with the young person or the judge or justice decides otherwise.[21] On the other hand, the *YCJA* does not specify that failure to notify the parents when a young person has been arrested and is being detained in custody can result in the proceedings relating to the case being rendered invalid.[22] Presumably the rationale for the different potential outcomes in these two scenarios is that it was not considered desirable for proceedings to be rendered invalid in serious cases merely due to a failure to notify the parents.

The requirement to notify parents applies to young persons unless they are 20 by the time of their first appearance before a youth justice court.[23]

IV. ATTENDANCE OF PARENTS

The *YCJA* empowers the youth justice court to order a parent to attend the youth court proceedings involving his or her child if the court considers it necessary or believes it is in the best interests of the young person. A parent who fails to attend court in these circumstances can be found guilty of contempt of court.[24] The court can issue a warrant to compel the attendance of a parent who does not attend when ordered.[25]

---

[20] *YCJA*, s. 26(6)(c).
[21] *YCJA*, s. 26(10).
[22] *YCJA*, s. 26(11).
[23] *YCJA*, s. 26(12).
[24] *YCJA*, s. 27(4).
[25] *YCJA*, s. 27(5).

The attendance of parents at youth justice court proceedings, including at the bail stage, is more important than may be apparent. Judges tend to pay close attention to whether a parent is in court to support the young person and may view the attendance of the parent as an obvious sign that the young person has familial support, which may be perceived as vital to ensuring that the young person will be properly supervised if released. A young person who appears in court with no support may be viewed as less likely to adhere to release conditions. In effect, a young person who is homeless may be more likely to be detained at the pre-trial stage if there is no evidence of familial support. The judge or justice may consider this as part of his or her reasoning in concluding that the young person is unlikely to show up for future court appearances. While a justice or judge cannot detain a young person in custody for reasons of homelessness, poverty or mental health,[26] the young person can be detained indirectly for these reasons because he or she can be detained to ensure his or her attendance in court.[27] A social issue may well be driving the failure to attend court. Young persons who have little to no family support are arguably more vulnerable in terms of their liberty at the bail stage.

In practice, judges are generally aware whether parents are present in the courtroom when a young person is before the court. The Crown or defence counsel routinely draws this fact to the court's attention.

V.   RIGHT TO COUNSEL

Although s. 10(b) of the *Charter* guarantees to everyone the right to retain and instruct counsel without delay upon arrest or detention, and to be informed of that right, the *YCJA* requires that young persons be reminded of that right repeatedly throughout their involvement with the youth criminal justice system. Indeed, from the point of initial detention or arrest, the police are obligated to advise the young person without delay of the right to retain counsel, and the young person must be given an opportunity to obtain counsel.[28] There are no bright lines regarding the precise meaning of critical terms such as "without delay" and "opportunity". These terms have been defined to some degree in the case law; their meaning tends to be viewed within the context and facts of the specific case.

---

[26]   *YCJA*, s. 29(1).
[27]   *Criminal Code*, s. 515(10)(a).
[28]   *YCJA*, s. 25(2).

It is important to recognize at the outset that the young person's right to counsel is a personal right. The young person can exercise this right personally[29] throughout the youth justice court proceedings, even if he or she simply wants advice as to whether to agree to diversion in the form of an extrajudicial sanction. If it appears to the judge or Justice of the Peace (JP) that the interests of the young person are in conflict with the interests of the parents, the judge or JP has an obligation to ensure that the young person is represented by counsel independent of the parent.[30] The expression "counsel independent of the parent" is not defined. Presumably, if the judge or JP has information or concerns that the young person is being represented by his or her parents' lawyer and that the lawyer may be at risk of taking instructions from the parents, who may be paying the legal expenses, the judge or JP can direct that a different lawyer be appointed to act for the young person.

While it may not appear obvious, it is important that a young person seek legal advice even if it appears that the matter is being diverted from the formal court system and the young person will not end up with a finding of guilt against him or her. For example, a young person (and his or her parents) may be eager to agree to diversion from the formal youth justice system because diversion may appear to be the more lenient and expedient response for the young person. However, one of the conditions for the use of the diversionary measure of an extrajudicial sanction is that the young person must accept responsibility for the conduct that forms the basis of the offence that he or she is alleged to have committed. While this is not the same thing as pleading guilty to the offence, the young person is still obliged to accept responsibility for the essential elements of the offence. Since some young persons (with pressure from their parents in some cases) may be inclined to accept responsibility for an offence as a way of making the matter disappear quickly, even if he or she is not, in fact or in law, responsible, it is important that all young persons have the benefit of legal advice before agreeing to an extrajudicial sanction. Counsel would then be in a position to advise the young person that if he or she is not responsible, agreeing to diversion may not be appropriate since it requires the young person to essentially admit that he or she "did" it. In fact, the *YCJA* states

---

[29]   This wording emphasizes the fact that it is the *young person*, and *not* his or her parents, who is providing instructions to the lawyer as to what he or she wishes to do. Practitioners advise that parents do not always understand this fact. Since parents are generally paying the legal bills, the parents sometimes believe that they have the right to advise the lawyer what the young person should do in the circumstances, such as whether the young person should plead guilty to the criminal charge. This section reminds lawyers, young persons and their parents that it is the young person who is the client and is to advise the lawyer, not his or her parents.

[30]   *YCJA*, s. 25(8).

clearly that one of the conditions that must be satisfied before a young person consents to an extrajudicial sanction is that the young person must be advised of his or her right to be represented by counsel and be given a reasonable opportunity to consult counsel.[31]

In addition, while accepting responsibility for the conduct that forms the basis of the offence as a condition for being dealt with by an extrajudicial sanction is not the same thing as pleading guilty, and is inadmissible in evidence against the young person in civil or criminal proceedings,[32] a record of the young person having been dealt with by way of an extrajudicial sanction (as opposed to other extrajudicial measures) can be accessed by various parties for two years from the time that the young person consents to the extrajudicial sanction.[33] A record of the extrajudicial sanction can also be included in a pre-sentence report that the judge will consider in sentencing the young person for a criminal offence in the future provided the record of the sanction is still accessible under the records provisions at the time of the sentencing.[34] Thus, an extrajudicial sanction, which is the most severe form of an extrajudicial measure under the YCJA, can return to haunt a young person in a way that lesser forms of extrajudicial measures cannot.[35] A young person who is considering agreeing to an extrajudicial sanction should therefore be fully aware of the implications. This is why the involvement and advice of legal counsel is important for a young person even if it appears that the matter will be diverted by way of an extrajudicial sanction.

The YCJA obliges criminal justice system participants, such as judges and JPs, to remind young persons of their right to counsel throughout the criminal justice process in situations where the young person is not represented.[36] This obligation arises from the first appearance of the young person before a judge or justice[37] and continues through the bail hearing[38] and the trial,[39] to the sentencing hearing during which a determination may be made that the young person will receive an adult sentence.[40] The judge or justice is also required to issue this advisory before proceedings relating to the possible continuation of custody and conditional supervision and

---

[31]   YCJA, s. 10(2)(d).
[32]   YCJA, s. 10(4).
[33]   YCJA, s. 119(2)(a).
[34]   YCJA, ss. 40(3)(d)(iv) and 119(2)(a).
[35]   As discussed in Chapters 5 and 9, youth records in relation to the less severe forms of extrajudicial measures, such as police warnings, are less accessible.
[36]   YCJA, s. 25(3).
[37]   YCJA, s. 32(1)(b).
[38]   YCJA, s. 25(3)(a).
[39]   YCJA, s. 25 (3)(c).
[40]   YCJA, s. 25(3)(b)

reviews of the decisions relating to those hearings.[41] The young person also has a right to be represented by counsel during a review of a youth justice sentence,[42] as well as at reviews concerning the level of custody. In all instances, the young person must be advised of this right and given a reasonable opportunity to obtain counsel by the judge, justice or review board.

In addition, a written statement that a young person has a right to be represented by counsel must be included in various documents and notices that a young person receives after becoming involved with the criminal justice system, including an appearance notice or summons, an arrest warrant, a promise to appear, and an undertaking or recognizance entered into before an officer in charge.[43]

Procedural issues aside, the scope of the right to counsel for a young person under the *YCJA* also distinguishes it and elevates it above the right to counsel guaranteed to all accused persons under s. 10(b) of the *Charter*. Under the *YCJA*, not only are criminal justice system players obliged to constantly remind a young person of his or her right to counsel from the point of detention or arrest, once the proceedings reach a certain stage,[44] the court must direct that the state provide and pay for a lawyer for a young person who wishes to obtain counsel but cannot obtain counsel through legal aid, and requests representation.[45] If the young person cannot get legal aid but does not request representation, the youth justice court has discretion as to whether to direct that the young person be represented.[46] Upon such direction from the court, the Attorney General must appoint counsel or see that counsel is appointed.[47]

---

[41]   *YCJA*, s. 25(3)(d).

[42]   *YCJA*, s. 25(3)(e).

[43]   *YCJA*, s. 25(9).

[44]   *YCJA*, s. 25(4). In reference to the same section in the *YOA*, the Ontario Court of Appeal found in *R. v. J.H.*, [1999] O.J. No. 3894 (Ont. C.A.) that, before the state pays for counsel, the inability of the young person to obtain counsel must be established and that the question cannot be answered without reference to the parents' finances. In a subsequent case, *R. v. E.R.B.*, [2003] O.J. No. 3738 (Ont. C.J.), the court found it was up to the Legal Aid Plan and not the court to make the inquiries regarding the young person's finances. The Legal Aid Plan is set up to assess financial information and eligibility and that is the proper place for the assessment, the court found.

[45]   *YCJA*, s. 25(4)(b). Young persons have the benefit of this protection unless they have turned 20 by the time they have their first appearance before a youth justice court.

[46]   *YCJA*, s. 25(4)(b).

[47]   *YCJA*, s. 25(4) and (5). In *R. v. R.R.*, [2008] N.L. No. 126 (N.L. Prov. Ct.), Gorman J. ordered that legal counsel be appointed for the 14-year-old accused in relation to an assault charge to avoid further delay in the trial process. The provincial legal aid program had rejected the request for legal aid and the accused has appealed. Justice Gorman found that the young accused was not capable of representing himself. The matter had been ongoing for eight months. During the course of that ruling, Gorman J. noted that the primary cause of

If the young person is appearing before a Justice of the Peace and advises that he or she wishes counsel but is unable to obtain it, the JP can refer the young person to a legal aid program or similar program for the appointment of counsel, but only a judge can actually direct that counsel be appointed in the event that the young person cannot obtain legal aid.[48]

What is particularly noteworthy about s. 25 of the *YCJA* is that it has been held that, in light of the obligation under s. 3 of the *YCJA* that cases involving young persons be dealt with in a timely fashion,[49] the appointment of counsel for a young person may have to be addressed more quickly than if the accused were an adult.[50]

The precise stage in the criminal proceedings at which a young person has a right to state-funded legal representation has been the matter of some litigation since the *YCJA* came into force in 2003. The Ontario Court of Appeal decided the question in *R. v. L.S.*[51] In *R. v. L.S.*, the young person, who was 13 at the time of the alleged offence, was at his first appearance for a charge of uttering a threat to cause bodily harm. He argued that neither he nor his parents had the ability to pay for a lawyer, that he needed counsel to prepare his defence but had been refused legal aid. The Crown was seeking extrajudicial sanctions and a peace bond. The youth justice court judge refused to order publicly funded legal aid, noting that the consequences were minimal for the teenager and requested that duty counsel assist the young person. The accused brought an application for review to the Superior Court, which overturned the lower court and found that the court must direct that counsel be provided where the young person cannot obtain legal aid and directed the youth justice court to refer the matter to legal aid for the funding of counsel.

On further appeal to the Ontario Court of Appeal, McMurtry C.J.O. held that the *YCJA* recognizes the general right of a young person to legal advice, but it is only when the young person has reached a certain stage in the judicial proceedings and is unable to obtain legal aid that the young person may apply for publicly funded counsel. Referring to s. 25(3) and (4), McMurtry C.J.O. concluded: "Parliament has specifically provided that it is only when there is a hearing related to the custody of the young person, including sentencing or when the young person is engaged in a

---

delay in youth proceedings relates to ensuring that young persons are represented by counsel. Justice Gorman also observed in that ruling that all accused are constitutionally entitled to have counsel appointed in certain circumstances, as set out in *R. v. Rowbotham*, [1988] O.J. No. 271, 41 C.C.C. (3d) 1 (Ont. C.A.).

[48]   *YCJA*, s. 25(6).
[49]   *YCJA*, s. 3(1)(b)(iv).
[50]   *R. v. R.R.*, [2008] N.J. No. 126, at paras. 14-23 (N.L. Prov. Ct.).
[51]   [2006] O.J. No. 4808 (Ont. C.A.).

trial that the youth may apply for publicly funded counsel."[52] The young person in *R. v. L.S.* had not yet reached any of the stages in the criminal proceedings referred to in s. 25(3). His custody was not at issue and he had yet to decide whether he wished to go to trial, McMurtry C.J.O. ruled.

In a later decision, Kukurin J. of the Ontario Court of Justice followed the higher court ruling but expressed frustration at its impracticality. In the case at bar, the 16-year-old young person was facing charges of assault and possession of stolen property. The Crown was seeking a non-custodial disposition. By her fourth court appearance, she had been refused legal aid and had applied for state-funded counsel since she argued that she could not pay for a lawyer. Justice Kukurin held that as a general rule, it is preferable that any young person facing charges in youth court be assisted by a lawyer and that, based on experience, the sooner in the process such counsel is retained, the better for the young person, the court and the administration of justice, since young persons have no legal training.[53] It is largely a matter of common sense. Justice Kukurin reluctantly conceded, however, that based on the wording of s. 25(3), it was simply too early in the proceedings for the teenager to apply for state-funded counsel. Section 25(4) indicates that the court can direct that the young person be represented by counsel only *when* a young person is at trial, at a hearing or at a review as defined in s. 25(3).

During the ruling, Kukurin J. engaged in an interesting discussion of the meaning of "at trial", and when the process of being at trial can be said to begin. By interpreting the meaning of "at trial" more broadly, a young person could be said to be "at trial" once the person has been arraigned and entered a plea, Kukurin J. held, but acknowledged that such an interpretation stretches the meaning of the term beyond its intended meaning.[54] Justice Kukurin concluded that it was mandatory to comply with both the legislation and *R. v. L.S.*, which meant, in effect, that the young person would have to wait until she was at trial before the court could direct that she be represented by state-funded counsel.

The frustrating result of this temporal threshold for state-appointed counsel is that it will invariably lead to slowdowns as courts vacate trial dates on the first day of trial so that the young person can begin to instruct freshly-appointed counsel, Kukurin J. held. This critique is well

---

[52]   *R. v. L.S.*, [2006] O.J. No. 4808, at para. 9 (Ont. C.A.).

[53]   *R. v. R.K.S.*, [2007] O.J. No. 1255, at para. 11 (Ont. C.J.).

[54]   *R. v. R.K.S.*, [2007] O.J. No. 1255, at para. 39 (Ont. C.J.). In *R. v. J.F.*, [2004] O.J. No. 1693 (Ont. C.J.), Wright J. found that a s. 810 proceeding qualified as a trial for purposes of s. 25(3)-(4), in terms of being the "hearing of a complaint", and that the court therefore had authority to appoint counsel for the young person in such a proceeding.

taken: by preventing young persons from having a state-funded lawyer early in the process, they will be left to rely, at least initially, on busy duty counsel, who can provide them with only limited assistance. In some jurisdictions, duty counsel do not routinely participate in pre-trials and do not assist young persons at trial.[55] Once the young person is able to retain state-funded counsel, that lawyer will then need time to review the disclosure and prepare, before determining the best course of action. It makes sense both in terms of overall efficiency as well as securing timely legal advice, if young persons who cannot obtain legal aid and want a lawyer can be permitted to have one appointed as early in the process as possible, given their youth and lack of experience and understanding of the criminal justice system.

The courts have also held that the right to counsel of one's choice is not an absolute right for a young person. If the lawyer the young person wishes to retain is not available within a reasonable period of time, the young person will be expected to contact a different lawyer.[56]

The judge, justice or review board can also permit a young person who is unrepresented to be assisted by a "suitable" adult.[57] The term "suitable" is not defined in the YCJA and leaves the judge considerable discretion in terms of deciding whether the proposed adult is suitable.

Under the YCJA, a province or territory can now establish a program to recoup from the young person or the parents the cost of the legal counsel but only after the proceedings and any appeal are finished.[58] This provision is potentially problematic as it may prompt parents to exert pressure on a young person to resolve the matter quickly, even if this is not in the best interests of the young person, if the parents expect that they may eventually have to pay the legal costs.

It is important to bear in mind that most of the protections outlined in s. 25 of the YCJA apply only to a young person who is less than 20 at

---

[55] R. v. R.K.S., [2007] O.J. No. 1255, at paras. 31-35 (Ont. C.J.).

[56] R. v. E.A.D.M., [2007] M.J. No. 471 (Man. C.A.). This is consistent with the rights of adult accused on this point. See for example, R. v. R.R., [2008] N.J. No. 126, at para. 11 (N.L. Prov. Ct.).

[57] YCJA, s. 25(7).

[58] This is a new provision under the YCJA. It is significant that the province cannot try to recoup the costs until after the criminal proceeding and any related appeal are completed. If a province or territory were able to begin trying to recoup the costs while the criminal matter was ongoing, this could conceivably result in the parents of a young person pressuring the young person to plead guilty in a certain case to avoid a costly trial or merely because the parents consider it the right thing to do even if the young person's counsel holds a different view based on his or her assessment of the case.

the time that the young person appears for the first time before the youth justice court in relation to the proceeding.[59]

VI. FIRST APPEARANCE

Section 32 of the *YCJA* imposes particular obligations on the youth justice court judge or, in some cases, the Justice of the Peace, before whom the young person must first appear, to ensure, in part, that an unrepresented young person is treated fairly. If the young person is not represented by counsel at this first appearance, the judge or justice must advise the young person at this juncture of the right to retain and instruct counsel. During this first appearance in court, the judge or JP must also cause the information or the indictment to be read to the young person and also advise the young person in appropriate circumstances that he or she could receive an adult sentence.[60] A young person can waive the requirements of s. 32(1) if he or she has legal counsel and that counsel advises the court that the young person has been informed of the provisions in s. 32(1).

Before accepting a guilty plea from an unrepresented young person, the youth justice court[61] must be satisfied that the young person understands the charge or charges he or she faces. Before accepting a guilty plea, the youth justice court must also advise an unrepresented young person who is charged with an offence that deems them liable to an adult sentence of the possible consequences of that, and the procedures for applying for a youth sentence.[62] The young person must also be advised in these circumstances that he or she can plead guilty or not guilty to the charge and, if the young person has a right to an election regarding the mode of trial, the youth justice court judge must advise the young person of the various options available regarding the mode of trial.[63] If the youth justice court is not satisfied that the unrepresented young person under-

---

[59]   *YCJA*, s. 25(11).

[60]   *YCJA*, s. 32(1).

[61]   It is noteworthy that s. 32(3) refers to a youth justice court rather than to a youth justice court judge or a justice, as is the case in s. 32(1). It is submitted that this means that only a youth justice court judge can accept a guilty plea from a young person under s. 32(3), which is consistent with the express intent of s. 20 of the *YCJA* to limit the powers of JPs in relation to youth matters. Nevertheless, JPs are exercising greater powers in relation to youth justice matters in some regions of Canada based on an interpretation of s. 13(1) of the *YCJA* that appears to suggest that a JP can exercise greater powers over youth matters if he or she is appointed a youth justice court judge.

[62]   Some of the procedures in relation to adult sentences have been altered, in practice, by *R. v. D.B.*, [2008] S.C.J. No. 25, 2008 SCC 25 (S.C.C.), which found the presumption of an adult sentence to be unconstitutional.

[63]   *YCJA*, s. 32(3).

stands these matters, the court must direct that the young person be represented by counsel.[64] Ultimately, if the judge is not satisfied that the young person understands the charges, the judge must enter a plea of not guilty on behalf of the young person and proceed to trial,[65] unless the young person is charged with an offence that requires that the young person be put to his or her election.

Again, these are substantial obligations imposed on state actors to ensure that young persons are treated fairly, and that greater efforts are made to ensure they understand their rights and the jeopardy they face in relation to criminal charges.

VII. BAIL

The *YCJA* also provides greater protections to young persons in contrast to their adult counterparts by reducing the likelihood that they will be placed in custody, even at the bail stage. The *YCJA* provides that young persons cannot be placed in custody at the bail stage simply because they need appropriate child protection, or have mental health issues or require other social measures.[66] Otherwise young persons who come from impoverished backgrounds or severely dysfunctional families, or who are suffering from mental illnesses, could end up in custody simply because they are homeless and there is nowhere in the community for them to go. This provision is designed to ensure that young persons are denied bail for only lawful reasons outlined in statute.[67]

In practice, however, s. 29(1) can be highly problematic. In some parts of the country, such as small, isolated Northern communities, where community resources are sorely lacking, a young person may actually wish to be placed in custody temporarily to get a square meal or to simply have a roof over his or her head during the depths of winter. The Crown, the defence, even the judge, may sometimes all agree that custody is the temporary solution in a situation where the young person has nowhere in the community to go due to lack of community resources. A strict reading of s. 29(1) would prevent this and make it unlawful. A young person cannot be detained for social reasons such as this. This prohibition can place judges and Crowns in a quandary.

---

[64]   *YCJA*, s. 32(5).
[65]   *YCJA*, s. 32(4).
[66]   *YCJA*, s. 29(1).
[67]   *Criminal Code*, s. 515(10). These bail provisions apply to young persons by virtue of s. 28 of the *YCJA* but note additional restrictions under s. 29 of the *YCJA*.

While s. 35 of the *YCJA* is an option for judges in these situations because it permits a judge to refer a young person to a child welfare agency at any stage of the proceedings for an assessment to determine if the young person is in need of child welfare services, s. 35 is of little value in communities that simply do not have adequate social services. A judge or a Crown who is faced with evidence that a young person is at risk of harming himself or herself if released into the community may face a difficult legal, ethical and moral dilemma in the face of s. 29(1) of the *YCJA*. This is among the issues the federal government may wish to consider during future reform of the *YCJA*. There is a reasonable argument to be made for amending the *YCJA* to permit the temporary detention of young persons who would be in danger if released, in situations where there is simply no housing or support for that young person in the community. The criminal justice system cannot be neatly or logically disentangled from social welfare issues in all instances, and must ultimately err on the side of harm reduction.

The Act also establishes a presumption against custody for young persons at the bail stage in certain circumstances. Under the *YCJA*, it is presumed that the young person will not be denied bail for public safety reasons unless he or she could be committed to custody upon a finding of guilt for the offence. This presumption reduces the exposure of a young person to jail.

VIII.   RELEASE TO A RESPONSIBLE PERSON

The *YCJA* further provides that a young person who would otherwise be denied bail can be released into the care of a responsible person provided the person is willing and able to adequately supervise and control the young person and on condition that the young person is willing to be placed in the care of that person.[68] In a situation where the young person would otherwise be detained, the judge or JP must inquire as to whether an appropriate responsible person exists. If such a person exists both parties must sign an undertaking, which includes, among other matters, a commitment from the responsible person to assume responsibility for ensuring the young person attends court as required and complies with the other conditions of his or her release.[69]

---

[68]   *YCJA*, s. 31.
[69]   *YCJA*, s. 31(3).

This provision was the subject of substantial criticism by Nova Scotia's Nunn Commission[70] during its review of the youth justice system. In his 2006 report, Commissioner Nunn recommended amendments to s. 31 of the *YCJA*. In cases where a judge or justice relieves the responsible person of the obligations under s. 31, which the judge or justice can do if satisfied that the young person should not remain under the custody of the person,[71] Nunn noted that s. 31 simultaneously relieves the young person of obligations undertaken at the time of being released into the care of the responsible person. Although the judge is obliged to issue an arrest warrant for the young person when he releases the young person and the responsible person from the terms of the agreement under s. 31, the practical effect is that, until the young person is found and arrested, the young person is no longer bound by the release conditions. Nunn recommended that the province of Nova Scotia lobby the federal government for an amendment to s. 31(5)(a) of the *YCJA* so that, where a responsible person is relieved of his or her obligations under s. 31, the young person's undertaking[72] nevertheless remains in effect.[73] Commissioner Nunn further recommended that the province of Nova Scotia lobby the federal government to also amend s. 31(6) of the *YCJA* to remove the requirement that a new bail hearing be held before placing the young person in detention once the responsible person has been relieved of the undertaking because the young person has already had a bail hearing during which it was decided that he or she should be detained. The young person's release had been permitted in the first place only because there was a responsible person willing to ensure attendance in court and compliance with the conditions of their release.[74] This is another issue that is worthy of further examination by the federal government during any reform exercise.

---

[70]   Nova Scotia Nunn Commission of Inquiry, *Spiralling out of Control: Lessons Learned from a Boy in Trouble: Report of the Nunn Commission of Inquiry* (Halifax, NS: Nunn Commission of Inquiry, 2006). This report is available online at: <http://www.gov.ns.ca/just/nunn _commission/_docs/Report_Nunn_Final.pdf>.

[71]   *YCJA*, s. 31(4)-(5).

[72]   *YCJA*, s. 31(3)(b).

[73]   Nova Scotia Nunn Commission of Inquiry, *Spiralling out of Control: Lessons Learned from a Boy in Trouble: Report of the Nunn Commission of Inquiry* (Halifax, NS: Nunn Commission of Inquiry, 2006), Recommendation 24, at 248. This report is available online at: <http://www.gov.ns.ca/just/nunn_commission/_docs/Report_Nunn_Final.pdf>.

[74]   Nova Scotia Nunn Commission of Inquiry, *Spiralling out of Control: Lessons Learned from a Boy in Trouble: Report of the Nunn Commission of Inquiry* (Halifax, NS: Nunn Commission of Inquiry, 2006), Recommendation 25, and the discussion of rationale for this proposed amendment at 246-48 of the Nunn report.

IX. REVIEW OF BAIL AS DE NOVO HEARING

A young person who is denied bail by a Justice of the Peace can apply at any time to have that decision reviewed by a youth justice court judge as if it were an original application, but the Crown must be given two days' clear notice of the application, in writing.[75] Likewise, the Crown can apply to have a decision by a JP to release a young person reviewed at any time by a youth justice court judge provided the young person has received two days' clear notice. The notice requirements can be waived by either party.[76]

X. SEPARATION OF YOUNG PERSONS FROM ADULTS DURING TEMPORARY DETENTION

In keeping with one of the underlying philosophical themes of the *YCJA*, young persons who are denied bail are generally not to be housed with adults, unless there are safety concerns or no youth detention facility is available within a reasonable distance.[77] Once the young person reaches 18, he or she can be moved to an adult provincial correctional facility; the youth justice court has discretion in this regard.[78] If the young person is at least 20 by the time the temporary detention begins, the young person is to be housed with adults in a provincial correctional facility for adults.[79]

XI. THE ADMISSIBILITY OF YOUNG PERSONS' STATEMENTS — SECTION 146 OF THE YCJA

Section 146 is among the most important additional protections afforded young persons under the *YCJA*. It outlines the procedures in relation to the taking of statements from young persons who are under detention or arrest, or who the police have reasonable grounds to believe have committed criminal offences.[80] Section 146 establishes the conditions that must be

---

[75] *YCJA*, s. 33.
[76] *YCJA*, s. 33(4).
[77] *YCJA*, s. 30(3).
[78] *YCJA*, s. 30(4).
[79] *YCJA*, s. 30(5).
[80] Section 146 does not apply to statements given by young persons who are not suspects or under detention or arrest. In other words, comments given by a young person who is being interviewed as a witness or a complainant are not captured by s. 146 and the police or other person in authority is not required to comply with the requirements in s. 146(2)(b)-(d) before taking statements from such persons. See for example *R. v. J. (J.)*, [1988] O.J. No. 1247, 65 C.R. (3d) 371, at 383 (Ont. C.A.), leave to appeal refused [1989] 1 S.C.R ix, 101 N.R. 231*n*

met before any statement from a young person in these circumstances made to a person in authority (most often a police officer) will be admissible in evidence against the young person. Even prior to the *YOA* and the *YCJA*, the common law recognized that young persons were entitled to special protection before statements made by them would be admissible in evidence against them.[81] This principle was later enshrined in both the *YOA* and the *YCJA*.[82]

Section 146 is almost identical in wording to s. 56 in the *YOA* upon which it is modelled with one notable change that will be discussed later in this chapter. Like its predecessor section in the *YOA*, s. 146 is designed to provide greater protection to young persons based on the belief that young persons are more likely than adults to be susceptible to threats and intimidation from the police and other persons in authority, and are also less likely to appreciate and understand their legal rights.[83]

It is important to appreciate that s. 146 applies *only* to young persons who are under 18 *at the time they give the statement*.[84] A young person who is under 18 at the time of the alleged offence but turns 18 *before* giving a statement is not captured by s. 146 and therefore does not receive the protections provided in this section.

Justice Cory in *R. v. J. (J.T.)*[85] described the intent of s. 56, which applies equally to s. 146 of the *YCJA*:

> ... it must be remembered that the section [s. 56 of the *YOA*] is to protect all young people of 17 years or less. A young person is usually far more

---

(S.C.C.). For a full and contemporary treatment of this point, see *R. v. D.D.T.*, [2008] A.J. No. 731 (Alta. Q.B.).

[81] In *R. v. Yensen*, [1961] O.J. No. 586, [1961] O.R. 703 (Ont. H.C.), McRuer C.J. stated that a child should be accompanied by an adult if a child is being questioned for the purpose of getting a confession. Some critics consider the comments *obiter dicta*. *R. v. Yensen* is referred to in *R. v. L.T.H.*, [2008] S.C.J. No. 50, at para. 25, 2008 SCC 49 (S.C.C.). See also *R. v. R.A.*, [1975] A.J. No. 31, [1975] 5 W.W.R. 425 (Alta. T.D.).

[82] *YOA*, s. 56 and *YCJA*, s. 146.

[83] Academic literature suggests that delinquent young persons, particularly those under 14, are more likely to implicate themselves and waive their due process rights if they are given only the warnings that adults receive. See Sanjeev Anand and James Robb, "The Admissibility of Young People's Statements Under the Proposed *Youth Criminal Justice Act*" (2002) 39 Alta. L. Rev. 771, at para. 2 (QL). See also *R. v. L.T.H.*, [2008] S.C.J. No. 50, at para. 24, 2008 SCC 49 (S.C.C.).

[84] Chief Justice Lamer, as he then was, explained the rationale for this in *R. v. Z. (D.A.)*, [1992] S.C.J. No. 80, [1992] 2 S.C.R. 1025 (S.C.C.), when he indicated that the aim of then s. 56 (now s. 146 of the *YCJA*) is to protect adolescents who, due to their youth and immaturity, are unlikely to fully appreciate their legal rights and the consequences of making a statement to the police. An adult who is arrested years later for a crime committed as a young person does not require all of the protections afforded young persons under the Act by virtue of the fact that he was an adult at the time of the arrest.

[85] [1990] S.C.J. No. 88, at para. 18, [1990] 2 S.C.R. 755 (S.C.C.).

easily impressed and influenced by authoritarian figures. No matter what the bravado and braggadocio that young people may display, it is unlikely that they will appreciate their legal rights in a general sense or the consequences of oral statements made to persons in authority; certainly they would not appreciate the nature of their rights to the same extent as would most adults. Teenagers may also be more susceptible to subtle threats arising from their surroundings and the presence of persons in authority. A young person may be more inclined to make a statement, even though it is false, in order to please an authoritarian figure. It was no doubt in recognition of the additional pressures and problems faced by young people that led Parliament to enact this code of procedure.[86]

Greater procedural safeguards are required to ensure that any incriminating statement that a young person gives to the police is true and given voluntarily,[87] and that the young person fully appreciates his or her legal rights and the implications of giving a statement to the authorities.

Justice Sopinka further explained the purpose of s. 56 of the *YOA*, now s. 146 of the *YCJA*, in *R. v. I. (L.R.) and T. (E.)*:[88]

In my opinion, the purpose of the requirement that the explanation prescribed by s. 56 precede the making of the statement is to ensure that the young person does not relinquish the right to silence except in the exercise of free will in the context of a full understanding and appreciation of his or her rights.[89]

The Ontario Court of Appeal affirmed the rationale for s. 146 in *R. v. S.S.*[90] by noting with approval the purpose as described by the Supreme Court of Canada in both *R. v. J. (J.T.)* and in *R. v. I. (L.R.) and T. (E.)*:

... no matter how well-intentioned the officer, young persons are susceptible to feeling intimidated by the police, whom they consider to be persons of significant authority and power. In addition, young persons may lack the maturity to consider the consequences of unburdening themselves of their misdeeds, particularly when encouraged to do so by an apparently understanding (or, alternatively, formidable) police officer.[91]

In essence, by virtue of the common law and s. 146 of the *YCJA*, before a judge can admit into evidence a statement from a young person during his or her criminal trial, it must be clear to the judge that the statement was voluntarily made and that, prior to giving the statement, the

---

[86]   *R. v. J. (J.T.)*, [1990] S.C.J. No. 88, at para. 18, [1990] 2 S.C.R. 755 (S.C.C.).
[87]   The general rationale for s. 146 of the *YCJA*, which is largely the same as s. 56 of the *YOA* with one notable difference, is explained well in *R. v. J. (J.T.)*, [1990] S.C.J. No. 88, at paras. 18-21, [1990] 2 S.C.R. 755 (S.C.C.). The Supreme Court of Canada reiterated that rationale in *R. v. I. (L.R.) and T. (E.)*, [1993] S.C.J. No. 132, [1993] 4 S.C.R. 504 (S.C.C.).
[88]   [1993] S.C.J. No. 132, [1993] 4 S.C.R. 504 (S.C.C.).
[89]   *R. v. I. (L.R.) and T. (E.)*, [1993] S.C.J. No. 132, at para. 35, [1993] 4 S.C.R. 504 (S.C.C.).
[90]   [2007] O.J. No. 2552 (Ont. C.A.).
[91]   *R. v. S.S.*, [2007] O.J. No. 2552, at para. 30 (Ont. C.A.).

young person was provided with his or her rights under s. 146. In particular, in accordance with s. 146(2)(b) to (d), a young person who is a suspect, or who is under arrest or detention, must be advised prior to giving a written or oral statement to a person in authority that he or she does not have to give a statement, that any such statement given could be used against him or her in a criminal proceeding, that the young person has the right to consult counsel *and* a parent or other person before giving the statement, and that the statement is required to be made in the presence of counsel and any other person consulted unless the young person desires otherwise. The young person must also be given a reasonable opportunity to consult counsel, and a parent or other appropriate adult, before making the statement, and must be given a reasonable opportunity to make the statement in the presence of any person consulted.[92]

Before proceeding with a detailed discussion of s. 146, it is necessary to consider certain seminal concepts in s. 146(2), such as "person in authority" and the common law definition of "voluntary".

A.   Person in Authority

A person in authority is defined in *R. v. Grandinetti*.[93] A person in authority, in law, is generally an individual whom the accused perceives, or knows, to be, a person in authority in the sense of being engaged in the arrest, detention, interrogation or prosecution of the accused *at the time* that the accused makes the statement.[94] It may also be someone perceived by the accused to be involved in the investigation of the matter, an agent of the police or the prosecution authorities, or someone working in collaboration with the police or otherwise allied with the state authorities or acting on behalf of, or in concert with, the police or prosecuting authorities[95] at the time the person gives the statement. The accused person must be aware that the person to whom he or she makes the statement is someone who is capable of controlling or influencing the course of the proceedings at the time the statement is given.[96] Therefore, an undercover police officer to whom an accused confesses is not a person in authority because the accused does not know the undercover officer is a

---

[92]   *YCJA*, s. 146(2)(c) and (d).
[93]   [2005] S.C.J. No. 3, at paras. 35-41, [2005] 1 S.C.R. 27 (S.C.C.). See also *R. v. Hodgson*, [1998] S.C.J. No. 66, 127 C.C.C. (3d) 449 (S.C.C.). *R. v. Young*, [2008] S.J. No. 113 (Sask. Q.B.) also provides a succinct modern summary of the meaning of "person in authority".
[94]   *R. v. Grandinetti*, [2005] S.C.J. No. 3, at para. 37, [2005] 1 S.C.R. 27 (S.C.C.).
[95]   *R. v. Grandinetti*, [2005] S.C.J. No. 3, at para. 43, [2005] 1 S.C.R. 27 (S.C.C.).
[96]   *R. v. Grandinetti*, [2005] S.C.J. No. 3, at para. 39, [2005] 1 S.C.R. 27 (S.C.C.).

police officer at the time he or she confesses to the officer.[97] (Other rules of admissibility apply to statements made by an accused to an undercover officer.)[98]

"The test of who is a 'person in authority' is largely subjective, focusing on the accused's perception of the person to whom he or she is making the statement. The operative question is whether the accused, based on his or her perception of the recipient's ability to influence the prosecution, believed either that refusing to make a statement to the person would result in prejudice, or that making one would result in favourable treatment."[99] The accused's belief that he or she is speaking to a person in authority at the time of giving the statement must also be objectively reasonable.[100]

A person in authority will generally be a police officer. A parent, doctor, teacher, or employer will generally not be found to be a person in authority unless, at the time the accused young person gave the statement, the young person perceived the individual to have some ability to influence the investigation or prosecution of the matter. In order for any of them to be found to be persons in authority, the trial judge must determine at the time the person gave the statement that the accused reasonably believed the receiver of the statement was acting on behalf of the police or prosecuting authorities.[101] Clearly, if a parent or other such person is found to be a person in authority at the time a young person confesses to this person, the statement will usually be ruled inadmissible because the person will not have provided the warnings to the young person that a person in authority must provide under s. 146(2)(b)-(d).

R. v. A.B.[102] provides useful guidance on the meaning of "person in authority". In *R. v. A.B.*, a 13-year-old boy confessed to his mother and stepfather that he had performed sexual acts on his stepsisters after his mother told him about his stepsisters' allegations against him and begged him to tell the truth. She said the family would see that he got help. At the time of the confession, there was no indication that the mother or stepfather intended to call in the authorities and to begin criminal proceedings. At the time that the boy confessed, the boy did not perceive his mother to be collaborating with the police or to have any involvement in the possible institution of criminal proceedings in any way. A.B. made further admissions to the family doctor

[97]   This distinction is explained succinctly in *R. v. Singh*, [2007] S.C.J. No. 48, at para. 40 (S.C.C.).
[98]   *R. v. Hebert*, [1990] S.C.J. No. 64, [1990] 2 S.C.R. 151 (S.C.C.).
[99]   *R. v. Grandinetti*, [2005] S.C.J. No. 3, at para. 38, [2005] 1 S.C.R. 27 (S.C.C.).
[100] *R. v. Grandinetti*, [2005] S.C.J. No. 3, at para. 39, [2005] 1 S.C.R. 27 (S.C.C.).
[101] *R. v. Grandinetti*, [2005] S.C.J. No. 3, at para. 43, [2005] 1 S.C.R. 27 (S.C.C.).
[102] [1986] O.J. No. 91 (Ont. C.A.).

the following week, and made still more admissions to two psychiatrists some time later. There was still no question of any police involvement. A.B. made the admissions on the understanding that his parents were trying to help him. About a year after the boy first confessed to his parents, one of his stepsisters revealed more allegations. The stepfather contacted the police.

Justice Cory held for the Court of Appeal that the statements the boy made to his mother in the presence of his stepfather were admissible in evidence because the mother was not a person in authority at the time he gave the statement. Neither she nor her husband had any intention of contacting the authorities or instituting criminal proceedings at the time A.B. made the incriminating statements. The mother, at that juncture, could not in any way have affected the course of the prosecution because prosecution was not contemplated. In order for a parent to be found to be a person in authority at the time of the giving of the statement, there must be some realistic and close connection between the decision to call the police and the inducement to the child to confess, the court held.[103] Similarly, there was no basis to exclude the statements from the doctors on the grounds that the doctors were persons in authority. Whether the receiver of a statement is a person of authority is a question of fact.[104] These determinations are highly contextual and must be made after a careful and thorough assessment of the facts in a given case.

If the court determines that the accused young person gave a statement to a person whom he or she perceived to be a person in authority at the time the statement was made, under the common law, the court must then determine whether the statement was voluntarily made. Section 146(1) codifies the common law requirement that a statement by an accused person to a person in authority must be voluntary before it will be admissible in evidence against the person. (The voluntariness of the statement is determined by a *voir dire*, which is a trial within a trial to determine through an examination of the facts and circumstances if the statement was voluntarily made and therefore whether it should be admitted into evidence.)

The onus is on the Crown to prove the voluntariness of the statement beyond a reasonable doubt.[105] Given the widespread perception that young persons may be more vulnerable to pressure and intimidation by the police, a judge can be expected to assess the circumstances surrounding the making of the statement with greater care and scrutiny when the maker

---

[103] *R. v. A.B.*, [1986] O.J. No. 91 (Ont. C.A.).
[104] *R. v. A.B.*, [1986] O.J. No. 91 (Ont. C.A.).
[105] *R. v. Oickle*, [2000] S.C.J. No. 38, at para. 30, [2000] 2 S.C.R. 3 (S.C.C.); *R. v. Singh*, [2007] S.C.J. No. 48, at para. 25 (S.C.C.).

of the statement is a young person. In fact, the courts are increasingly encouraging the videotaping of police interrogations and confessions from accused persons generally as a means of providing greater assurance of the voluntariness of the statement. In *R. v. Oickle*,[106] Iacobucci J. observed that police notes of a police interrogation are no match for a videotape of the interrogation, since notes cannot capture the tone of the conversation or the body language. He alluded to research that suggests videotaping is important for four reasons: it enables courts to monitor interrogation practices, it deters police from using interrogation methods that may lead to untrustworthy confessions, it enables courts to make more informed decisions about whether interrogation practices are likely to result in untrustworthy confessions and, finally, the videotaping of interrogation practices is simply sound public policy.[107] "This is not to suggest that non-recorded interrogations are inherently suspect; it is simply to make the obvious point that when a recording is made, it can greatly assist the trier of fact in assessing the confession."[108]

Justice Charron, now a justice of the Supreme Court of Canada, went even further in *R. v. Moore-MacFarlane*[109] by suggesting that the Crown's onus to establish an adequate record of the exchange between the accused and the police is readily satisfied by recording the interaction and that, in fact, a non-recorded interrogation is suspect in situations where a person is in custody, recording facilities are available and the police intentionally interrogate the suspect without turning their minds to the making of a reliable record.[110] "In such cases, it will be a matter for the trial judge on the *voir dire* to determine whether or not a sufficient substitute for an audio or video tape record has been provided to satisfy the heavy onus on the Crown to prove voluntariness beyond a reasonable doubt."[111]

While defence counsel may invariably argue that the videotape did not capture what activities transpired immediately *prior* to the turning on of the video-recorder, a video recording of a statement is preferable to simply the notes of an officer in terms of establishing an accurate record of what transpired. Videotaping statements is particularly appropriate and

---

[106]   [2000] S.C.J. No. 38, at para. 46, [2000] 2 S.C.R. 3 (S.C.C.).

[107]   *R. v. Oickle*, [2000] S.C.J. No. 38, at para. 46, [2000] 2 S.C.R. 3 (S.C.C.).

[108]   *R. v. Oickle*, [2000] S.C.J. No. 38, at para. 46, [2000] 2 S.C.R. 3 (S.C.C.).

[109]   [2001] O.J. No. 4646, 56 O.R. (3d) 737 (Ont. C.A.). See also *R. v. Bunn*, [2001] M.J. No. 31, at para. 13, 153 Man. R. (2d) 264 (Man. C.A.), where the court acknowledges that the law greatly favours the growing practice of recording police interrogations, preferably by videotape.

[110]   *R. v. Moore-MacFarlane*, [2001] O.J. No. 4646, at para. 65, 56 O.R. (3d) 737 (Ont. C.A.).

[111]   *R. v. Moore-MacFarlane*, [2001] O.J. No. 4646, at para. 65, 56 O.R. (3d) 737 (Ont. C.A.).

arguably more important in relation to confessions and statements from young persons, who may be particularly vulnerable to state coercion.[112]

B.   Voluntariness: The Classic Rule

Section 146(2)(a) of the *YCJA* states that, as one of the preconditions to admissibility, the statement from the young person must be voluntary. The classic common law rule for determining whether a statement from an accused person to a person in authority is voluntary is generally traced to the 1914 Privy Council case of *R. v. Ibrahim*.[113] In that case, Ibrahim, a private in the Indian Army stationed on Shameen Island, was charged with murder in relation to the death of an officer in the same regiment. Fifteen minutes following the shooting death of the officer, Ibrahim's commanding officer found Ibrahim in custody and asked: "Why have you done such a senseless act?" He indicated that he said nothing else, that he did not threaten Ibrahim or offer him any inducement in exchange for a confession, nor had anyone else. Ibrahim replied in Hindustani: "Some three or four days he has been abusing me; without a doubt I killed him."[114]

Ibrahim was tried before the Supreme Court of Hong Kong and convicted. Among the grounds of appeal was that his statement was inadmissible because it was not voluntary but rather obtained by pressure of authority and fear of consequences and that it was the answer of a man in custody to a question posed by a person having authority over him as his commanding officer and having custody of him.[115]

In finding that Ibrahim's incriminating statement in this case was not induced by hope or fear, Lord Sumner for the Judicial Committee of the Privy Council affirmed the basic common law confession rule: "It has long been established as a positive rule of English criminal law, that no statement by an accused is admissible in evidence against him unless it is shown by the prosecution to have been a voluntary statement, in the sense that it has not been obtained from him either by fear of prejudice or hope of advantage exercised or held out by a person in authority."[116]

Fear of prejudice generally relates to perceived threats by the police that can lead an accused person to confess. While a confession that is induced by express violence or torture or imminent threats of torture will be

---

[112] Justice Lilles discussed the particular vulnerability of young persons in this regard in *R. v. R. (A.)*, [1990] Y.J. No. 97 (Y.T. Youth Ct.).

[113] [1914] J.C.J. No. 1 (P.C.A. No. 112 of 1914).

[114] *R. v. Ibrahim*, [1914] J.C.J. No. 1, at para. 12 (P.C.A. No. 112 of 1914).

[115] *R. v. Ibrahim*, [1914] J.C.J. No. 1, at para. 13 (P.C.A. No. 112 of 1914).

[116] *R. v. Ibrahim*, [1914] J.C.J. No. 1, at para. 15 (P.C.A. No. 112 of 1914).

found to be involuntary and unreliable and therefore inadmissible,[117] more subtle threats from the police such as "it would be better" to tell can also be found to be inducements and result in the exclusion of the statement.[118] Acknowledging that it is acceptable for the police to try to convince an accused person to confess, the Supreme Court of Canada noted that such conduct becomes improper only when the inducements are strong enough to raise a reasonable doubt as to the voluntariness of the confession.[119] "The most important consideration in all cases is to look for a *quid pro quo* offer by interrogators, regardless of whether it comes in the form of a threat or a promise."[120] Promises of a benefit or a perceived threat can arguably affect a young person to a greater degree than an adult.

Hope of advantage is generally understood to mean a perception by the accused that he or she can expect leniency from the courts in return for a confession, the court held. "It is improper for a person in authority to suggest to a suspect that he or she will take steps to procure a reduced charge or sentence if the suspect confesses."[121] Holding out the possibility of a reduced charge or sentence in exchange for a confession would raise a reasonable doubt as to the voluntariness of any subsequent confession, the court found. An explicit offer from the police to secure lenient treatment in return for a confession is a very strong inducement and will warrant exclusion in all but exceptional circumstances.[122] Offers of psychiatric assistance or counselling, or threats or promises in relation to someone close to the accused, such as a friend or family member, can also be found to be inducements in certain circumstances. The Supreme Court of Canada has warned that cases must be carefully considered with reference to the precise facts to determine whether the accused made the confession in return for some perceived advantage or benefit. The danger, of course, as the Supreme Court of Canada has emphasized, is that the accused will be induced by promises to make a false statement.[123]

In *R. v. Oickle*,[124] the Supreme Court of Canada acknowledged and explained the classic common law confession rule from *R. v. Ibrahim* with reference to modern examples to illustrate its meaning but then expanded the rule by describing additional circumstances that can result in an involuntary statement. In addition to threats or promises, the Supreme

---

[117] *R. v. Oickle*, [2000] S.C.J. No. 38, at para. 53, [2000] 2 S.C.R. 3 (S.C.C.).
[118] *R. v. Oickle*, [2000] S.C.J. No. 38, at para. 53, [2000] 2 S.C.R. 3 (S.C.C.).
[119] *R. v. Oickle*, [2000] S.C.J. No. 38, at para. 57, [2000] 2 S.C.R. 3 (S.C.C.).
[120] *R. v. Oickle*, [2000] S.C.J. No. 38, at para. 57, [2000] 2 S.C.R. 3 (S.C.C.).
[121] *R. v. Oickle*, [2000] S.C.J. No. 38, at para. 49, [2000] 2 S.C.R. 3 (S.C.C.).
[122] *R. v. Oickle*, [2000] S.C.J. No. 38, at para. 49, [2000] 2 S.C.R. 3 (S.C.C.).
[123] *R. v. Oickle*, [2000] S.C.J. No. 38, at para. 51, [2000] 2 S.C.R. 3 (S.C.C.).
[124] [2000] S.C.J. No. 38, [2000] 2 S.C.R. 3 (S.C.C.).

Court of Canada found in *R. v. Oickle* that the creation of a general atmosphere of oppression by the authorities (which, again, may have more of an impact on a young person), can lead to the conclusion that the ultimate confession was involuntary. "Oppression clearly has the potential to produce false confessions. If the police create conditions distasteful enough, it should be no surprise that the suspect would make a stress-compliant confession to escape those conditions. Alternately, oppressive circumstances could overbear the suspect's will to the point that he or she comes to doubt his or her own memory, believes the relentless accusations made by the police, and gives an induced confession. ... Under inhumane conditions, one can hardly be surprised if a suspect confesses purely out of a desire to escape those conditions."[125]

Justice Iacobucci in *R. v. Oickle* cited factors such as depriving the suspect of food, clothing, water, sleep or medical attention, denying access to counsel, the use of false evidence and excessive, aggressive, intimidating questioning over a prolonged period as examples of circumstances that can result in a determination that the confession was not voluntary.[126] Police trickery, or the lack of an operating mind,[127] can also result in findings that the confessions were not voluntary.

A confession can also be excluded if it were preceded by a separate involuntary confession and is found to have been tainted by its relationship to the previous inadmissible statement. Such cases will invariably involve a careful examination of the facts and circumstances to assess the degree of connection between the two statements to determine, in effect, if the second statement was tainted by its relationship to the first.[128]

The Supreme Court of Canada has emphasized that the inquiry in a given case as to whether a confession was voluntary is contextual. In summary, a confession will not be admissible if it is made under circumstances that raise a reasonable doubt as to its voluntariness.[129]

---

[125] *R. v. Oickle*, [2000] S.C.J. No. 38, at paras. 58-60, [2000] 2 S.C.R. 3 (S.C.C.).

[126] *R. v. Oickle*, [2000] S.C.J. No. 38, at paras. 60 and 61, [2000] 2 S.C.R. 3 (S.C.C.).

[127] The classic definition of an operating mind can be found in *R. v. Whittle*, [1994] S.C.J. No. 69, [1994] 2 S.C.R. 914 (S.C.C.). Impairment by drugs or alcohol for example can vitiate the voluntariness of a confession as in *R. v. Clarkson*, [1986] S.C.J. No. 20, [1986] 1 S.C.R. 383 (S.C.C.). See also *R. v. R. (No. 1)*, [1972] O.J. No. 2096, 9 C.C.C. (2d) 274 (Ont. Prov. Ct.).

[128] *R. v. I. (L.R.) and T. (E.)*, [1993] S.C.J. No. 132, at paras. 28 to 35, [1993] 4 S.C.R. 504 (S.C.C.). The concept of taint is also discussed in *R. v. D.D.T.*, [2008] A.J. No. 731 (Alta. Q.B.).

[129] *R. v. I. (L.R.) and T. (E.)*, [1993] S.C.J. No. 132, at para. 71, [1993] S.C.R. 504 (S.C.C.). Justice Iacobucci provides an excellent summary of his views regarding the various circumstances that can lead to a finding that a statement was involuntary at paras. 68-69.

C.   Informational Requirements — Section 146(2)(b) *et al.*

In addition to the common law rule regarding the voluntariness of statements, which the *YCJA* codifies in s. 146(2)(a), the *YCJA* imposes other obligations that must be met before a statement made to a person in authority by a young person who is a suspect or is under detention or arrest will be admissible in evidence against him or her. The *YCJA* establishes a list of requirements with which the police or any other person who is, in law, a person in authority, must comply before statements by young persons will be admissible in evidence against them.

If the court determines that the person to whom the statement is given by an accused young person is a person in authority and the court also determines that the statement was voluntarily given, the statement will only be admissible if that person in authority complied with the additional requirements in s. 146(2)(b) to (d). Principally, the person in authority to whom the statement was made (who will generally be a police officer) must clearly explain to the young person before taking the statement in language appropriate to the young person's age and understanding the following points:[130]

- the young person is not obliged to give a statement;

- any statement made by the young person may be used as evidence in proceedings against him or her;

- the young person has the right to consult counsel, *and* a parent or other adult relative or other appropriate adult; and[131]

- any statement made by the young person is required to be made in the presence of counsel and any other adult person consulted unless the young person decides otherwise.[132]

---

[130]   *YCJA*, s. 146(2)(b).

[131]   *R. v. I. (L.R.) and T. (E.)*, [1993] S.C.J. No. 132, [1993] 4 S.C.R. 504 (S.C.C.); *R. v. K.L.T.*, [2005] O.J. No. 3154, at para. 175 (Ont. C.J.) re the point that a young person is required to have present both a lawyer and a parent or other person consulted during the giving of the statement unless he or she desires otherwise. Pursuant to s. 146(9), in the absence of evidence to the contrary, persons consulted under s. 146(2)(c) are deemed not to be persons in authority.

[132]   *YCJA*, s. 146(2)(b)(iv). In *R. v. S.S.*, [2007] O.J. No. 2552 (Ont. C.A.), the Court of Appeal held that, in order to comply with this subsection, it is not enough for the police to inform a young person that he or she has a *right* to have a lawyer or other specified adult with whom he or she consulted present when giving a statement. Compliance with s. 146(2)(b)(iv) obliges the police to advise the young person that any statement is required to be made in the presence of whoever the young person consulted unless the young person desires otherwise. The actual police form was flawed on that point, the court found. Justice Lang held for the appeal court that telling young persons about the requirement that anyone consulted must be present when they give a statement unless they decide otherwise alerts young

If the young person indicates that he or she wishes to consult with counsel, and with a parent or other adult, the young person must be given a reasonable opportunity to do so before making the statement. If the young person consults with counsel and/or with a parent or other adult, the young person must also be given a reasonable opportunity to make the statement in the presence of that person or persons.[133]

In 2008, in *R. v. L.T.H.*,[134] the Supreme Court of Canada clarified the scope and breadth of the informational requirements in s. 146(2)(b)(i) to (iv), as well as the requirements on the Crown under s. 146(4) in relation to the waiver of the consultative rights under s. 146(2)(c) and (d).

In *R. v. L.T.H.*, a 15-year-old young person was arrested after a police chase in the early morning of August 8, 2004 and charged with various offences including dangerous driving causing bodily harm. He was taken into custody and asked several times if he wished to contact a lawyer, an offer he consistently declined. About 12 hours after his arrest, a constable interviewed him. The police constable first reviewed a young offender statement form with him. When asked if he understood his rights, L.T.H. said yes. He also said he did not wish to call a lawyer or to talk with a lawyer in private. Likewise he answered no when asked if he wished to consult privately with a parent or another appropriate adult or to have them present while giving a statement or while being questioned. *L.T.H.* eventually signed a waiver of rights form. The officer then questioned him. L.T.H. provided an inculpatory statement that formed the basis of the Crown's case. The interview with L.T.H. was videotaped. When asked, at the end of the interview, if he wished to contact his mother, L.T.H. declined.

His mother later gave evidence at the *voir dire*. She testified that her son had a learning disorder, and that she told this to a police officer at the Dartmouth police station before L.T.H. was taken to the Halifax police station and questioned. She also testified that at other times when she had been with her son during police questioning, he would rely on her to explain the question.

The trial judge ruled that while she found L.T.H.'s statement to be voluntary, it was inadmissible because she was not convinced beyond a

---

persons to the significance of any statement provided and young persons will then be in a better position to make an informed decision about whether to consult a lawyer or an adult. This liberal interpretation of s. 146(2)(b)(iv) is in keeping with the overall intent of s. 146 to provide enhanced procedural protection to young persons, Lang J.A. held.

[133] *YCJA*, s. 146(2)(c) and (d).
[134] [2008] S.C.J. No. 50, 2008 SCC 49 (S.C.C.).

reasonable doubt that L.T.H. understood his rights and the consequences of waiving them.

On appeal, the Court of Appeal overturned the trial judge, set aside the verdict of acquittal and ordered a new trial. Justice Oland held for the Court of Appeal that, while the Crown must prove beyond a reasonable doubt that the young person was given a clear and appropriate explanation of his or her rights and options in s. 142(2)(b), the Crown does not have to prove that the young person understood those rights. Based on a plain reading of the legislation, the legal test outlined in the legislation concerns the clarity of the explanation, not an inquiry into whether the young person clearly understood his or her rights,[135] Oland J.A. held. The youth justice court judge erred in law by obliging the Crown to prove that the young person actually understood the explanation, and by requiring that the police officer ask the young person to recite back what he understood his rights to mean, the court held. The Court of Appeal further held that the Crown must prove waiver under s. 146(4) on a balance of probabilities rather than beyond a reasonable doubt.

On further appeal, the Supreme Court of Canada agreed with the trial judge that the young person's statement should not be admitted, and restored the acquittal. In the course of his decision, Fish J., writing for the 4-3 majority (Rothstein J. wrote partially concurring reasons but agreed with Fish J. that the acquittal should be restored), provided considerable guidance regarding the obligations on the police and the Crown, largely in relation to the informational component of s. 146(2)(b), as well as the meaning of a valid waiver of a young person's right to consult counsel and a parent, adult relative or other appropriate adult under s. 146(4).

Regarding the informational component under s. 146(2)(b), Fish J. held that the person in authority, generally the police officer, must make reasonable efforts to ensure that the particular young person is capable of understanding the explanation of the rights given. This will require the police officer to make some inquiries about the particular young person, to ascertain educational level, language and vocabulary skills, faculties of understanding, level of sophistication, and emotional state at the time, as well as any previous experience with the criminal justice system. "Without some knowledge of the young person's level of understanding, the officer will be unable to demonstrate that the explanation was tailored to the capabilities of the young person concerned."[136]

---

[135]   *R. v. L.T.H.*, [2006] N.S.J. No. 409, at para. 25 (N.S.C.A.).
[136]   *R. v. L.T.H.*, [2008] S.C.J. No. 50, at para. 22, 2008 SCC 49 (S.C.C.).

Interestingly, Fish J. suggests that the police officer who is interviewing the young person must make a reasonable effort to become aware of significant factors, such as any learning disabilities, in determining the appropriate language to use in explaining a young person's rights.[137] In effect, the police officer will have to demonstrate that he or she had a reasonable basis for his or her opinion as to the age and understanding of the particular young person, the court held.[138] While the mere reading of a standardized form will generally not suffice[139] (in *R. v. L.T.H.*, the trial judge had found that the police officer read the form rapidly in a monotone voice and that its completion appeared a mere formality), the police are not required to go so far as to ask the young person to recite back or explain back their rights[140] although this may tend to show that the rights waived were understood. Nor is the Crown required to prove that the young person understood the rights and options explained pursuant to s. 146(2)(b).[141] In the end, if the trial judge is satisfied beyond a reasonable doubt that the rights and options were clearly explained, it can be presumed that the young person understood those rights and the effect of waiving them.[142] In other words, Fish J. held that where compliance with the informational component is established beyond a reasonable doubt, the trial judge can infer, in the absence of evidence to the contrary, that the young person understood his or her rights under s. 146 and the effect of waiving them.[143]

A significant aspect of *R. v. L.T.H.* is that it clarifies the onus as well as the standard of proof in s. 146 regarding both the informational component as well as the waiver of the right to consult with counsel and a parent or other adult and to have them present during the taking of the statement. The onus (or burden) of proof is on the Crown in relation to both components.[144] The standard of proof throughout s. 146 is beyond a reasonable doubt rather than the lower standard of a balance of

---

[137] *R. v. L.T.H.*, [2008] S.C.J. No. 50, at para. 30, 2008 SCC 49 (S.C.C.). This obligation may take on enhanced meaning and importance as the prevalence of cognitive impairment caused by conditions such as Fetal Alcohol Spectrum Disorder becomes increasingly well known and well documented in our society.

[138] *R. v. L.T.H.*, [2008] S.C.J. No. 50, at para. 23, 2008 SCC 49 (S.C.C.).

[139] *R. v. L.T.H.*, [2008] S.C.J. No. 50, at para. 27, 2008 SCC 49 (S.C.C.).

[140] *R. v. L.T.H.*, [2008] S.C.J. No. 50, at para. 26, 2008 SCC 49 (S.C.C.).

[141] *R. v. L.T.H.*, [2008] S.C.J. No. 50, at para. 21, 2008 SCC 49 (S.C.C.).

[142] *R. v. L.T.H.*, [2008] S.C.J. No. 50, at para. 48, 2008 SCC 49 (S.C.C.).

[143] *R. v. L.T.H.*, [2008] S.C.J. No. 50, at paras. 8 and 48, 2008 SCC 49 (S.C.C.).

[144] The fact that the onus or burden is on the Crown in relation to both the informational requirement as well as proof of waiver is implicit throughout this decision. The focus of the disagreement between Fish J. and Rothstein J. relates to the nature of the standard of proof on the Crown. Justice Fish takes the position that the Crown must prove all components in s. 146 beyond a reasonable doubt, whereas Rothstein J. takes the position that the Crown need only establish the two components at issue on a balance of probabilities.

probabilities.[145] Thus, the Crown must prove beyond a reasonable doubt that the statutory requirements in s. 146(2)(b) have been met.[146] The Crown must also establish beyond a reasonable doubt that the waiver of the right to consult counsel and a parent or other adult and to have anyone consulted present while giving a statement to the police. A waiver will be valid only if the judge is satisfied that it is premised on a true understanding of the rights involved and the consequences of relinquishing them.[147] The young person must understand what he or she is giving up.

Prior to the Supreme Court of Canada ruling in *R. v. L.T.H.*, the nature of the standard of proof in relation to both the informational component (s. 146(2)(b)) as well as waiver under s. 146(4) was unsettled. Indeed, in his partially concurring reasons in *R. v. L.T.H.*, Rothstein J. held that the standard of proof for whether there was compliance by the person in authority with the informational and waiver requirements of s. 146 is proof on a balance of probabilities.[148] Nevertheless, the majority in *R. v. L.T.H.* has clarified that there is a single standard of proof throughout s. 146, and it is beyond a reasonable doubt.

R. v. L.T.H., to some degree, appears to circumscribe the obligations on the police that were suggested or implied in the earlier jurisprudence. Rather than placing an obligation on the police to ensure that the young person understands the rights explained under s. 146(2)(b), *L.T.H.* requires the police only to take steps to verify the capacity of the young person to understand. In *R. v. B.S.M.*,[149] the court held that young people require more than the offering of information in relation to their rights and the waiver of their rights. "They require not just explanations, but clear explanations that they are able to understand."[150] In that case, the police read the young person a waiver of rights form that was designed to comply with the rights in s. 56(2) and (4), which are now s. 146(2) and (4). The form advised the young person of his rights and provided a place for him to sign the waiver of those rights but the court held that the police officer did not go far enough in explaining to B.M. what those rights

---

[145] *R. v. L.T.H.*, [2008] S.C.J. No. 50, at paras. 32 and 47, 2008 SCC 49 (S.C.C.).

[146] *R. v. L.T.H.*, [2008] S.C.J. No. 50, at para. 38, 2008 SCC 49 (S.C.C.).

[147] *R. v. L.T.H.*, [2008] S.C.J. No. 50, at paras. 40 and 41, 2008 SCC 49 (S.C.C.).

[148] *R. v. L.T.H.*, [2008] S.C.J. No. 50, at para. 68, 2008 SCC 49 (S.C.C.).

[149] [1995] M.J. No. 85 (Man. C.A.). Similarly, see *R. v. M.A.M.*, [1986] B.C.J. No. 1262, 32 C.C.C. (3d) 566 (B.C.C.A.), where the court held that simply reading a form to a young person in which available options are set out that were available to him prior to giving a statement was not sufficient to meet the requirements in the *YOA* that an explanation be given to a young person in language appropriate to the young person's age and understanding.

[150] *R. v. B.S.M.*, [1995] M.J. No. 85, at para. 9 (Man. C.A.).

meant.[151] The court noted that the young person must be able to understand those explanations, thus implying the taking of steps to ascertain such understanding.

In *R. v. T.W.*, the court found that the statement of a young person was inadmissible because s. 146 had not been complied with. In order to comply with s. 146, the court found, the written waiver form must accurately set out all of the factors contained in s. 146. It is not enough for the police to read them verbatim or skim over them with the young person. "Rather, the officer must take the time to ensure that the young person properly understands what his or her rights are. They must be given to the young person in a manner that the young person truly understands and can thus effectively recite back to the officer."[152]

The Ontario Court of Justice reached a similar conclusion in *R. v. K.L.T.*,[153] after conducting a particularly detailed examination of the conduct of various police officers following the detention of K.L.T. in relation to a stolen vehicle and vehicle chase. In ruling on the admissibility of two statements made by the young person, MacLean J. held that, *inter alia*, the officers should have explained to the young person in age appropriate language his rights on a waiver form that advised him that he did not have to say anything but that anything he did say could be used against him, and that the police should have had K.L.T. articulate his understanding of those rights.[154] At the very least, the uniformed officers should have had K.L.T. articulate his understanding of his rights to determine if further clarification was necessary. Had they done this, K.L.T.'s cognitive limitations may have become apparent.[155] Justice MacLean concluded in this case, after a detailed assessment of the facts and circumstances, that the videotaped statement was inadmissible because the police had failed to comply fully with the requirements of s. 146. The young person was not properly informed that he could have his foster mother and a lawyer present when making a statement to the police and also because K.L.T. did not understand what a duty counsel was.

Courts have also found that the forms used by police forces to advise young persons of their rights have not always complied fully and accurately with the requirements in s. 146.[156] Justice MacLean actually held in

---

[151] *R. v. B.S.M.*, [1995] M.J. No. 85, at para. 10 (Man. C.A.).

[152] *R. v. T.W.*, [2005] O.J. No. 2785, at para. 36 (Ont. C.J.).

[153] [2005] O.J. No. 3154 (Ont. C.J.).

[154] *R. v. K.L.T.*, [2005] O.J. No. 3154, at paras. 119 and 133 (Ont. C.J.).

[155] *R. v. K.L.T.*, [2005] O.J. No. 3154, at para. 224, point 4 (Ont. C.J.). Medical reports filed as evidence showed that K.L.T. had a low level of cognitive intelligence.

[156] See *R. v. K.L.T.*, [2005] O.J. No. 3154, at para. 127 (Ont. C.J.).

K.L.T. that, when dealing with a written document, it is essential that the police ascertain if the young person is literate.[157]

Nevertheless, *R. v. L.T.H.* is now the law across the country in relation to seminal aspects of s. 146. As a result of *R. v. L.T.H.*, the courts can now be expected to rigorously assess the conduct and actions of the police to determine if the police took adequate steps to ensure that the young persons before them were capable of understanding the information they were given before taking statements from them.

D.   Waiver of Rights

Young persons can waive their s. 146 rights to be given a reasonable opportunity to consult with counsel and/or with a parent or other adult, and to be given a reasonable opportunity to make the statement in the presence of that person but any such waiver must either be recorded or in writing.[158] In order for any such waiver to be valid, it must be established by clear and unequivocal evidence that the person is waiving the procedural safeguard with full knowledge of the rights the procedure was designed to protect and the effect that waiver will have on those rights.[159] As a result of *R. v. L.T.H.*, the Crown is now required to prove beyond a reasonable doubt the validity of the waiver. The judge must be satisfied that the waiver is based "on a true understanding of the rights involved and the consequences of giving them up".[160]

A youth justice court can find that a waiver is valid even if it is not made in strict accordance with the requirements in s. 146(4) owing to a technical irregularity, provided the judge is satisfied that the young person was informed of his or her rights and voluntarily waived them.[161]

E.   Technical Irregularities

While s. 146 is almost identical to s. 56 of the *YOA*, there is one significant difference. Section 146 permits the admission into evidence of a statement from a young person even if there has been a "technical irregularity" in complying with the requirements under s. 146(2)(b) to (d),

---

[157]   *R. v. K.L.T.*, [2005] O.J. No. 3154, at para. 164 (Ont. C.J.).

[158]   *YCJA*, s. 146(4).

[159]   *R. v. L.T.H.*, [2008] S.C.J. No. 50, at paras. 7, 26 and 40, 2008 SCC 49 (S.C.C.). See also *R. v. B.C.W.*, [1986] M.J. No. 264, 27 C.C.C. (3d) 481 (Man. C.A.) and more recently see *R. v. I. (L.R.) and T. (E.)*, [1993] S.C.J. No. 132, at para. 27, [1993] 4 S.C.R. 504 (S.C.C.).

[160]   *R. v. L.T.H.*, [2008] S.C.J. No. 50, at paras. 39-40, 2008 SCC 49 (S.C.C.).

[161]   *YCJA*, s. 146(5).

provided the admission of the statement would not bring into disrepute the principle that young persons are entitled to enhanced procedural protection.[162] The term "technical irregularity" is not defined in the *YCJA*, but such wording can be expected to capture only minor and superficial breaches of s. 146(2)(b) to (d) rather than significant violations, such as a failure to advise a young person of a substantial informational component of s. 146(2)(b) to (d). A technical irregularity would have to be in the nature of a minor defect or deficiency that is not a matter of substance[163] and does not compromise or bring into disrepute the principle of enhanced procedural protection. "Technical" in this context must be understood to mean "immaterial" in the sense of not affecting substantial rights.[164] A technical irregularity, as noted in *R. v. K.L.T.*, could include a failure to have the young person initial all of the pages of a written waiver, provided the court is satisfied that the waiver was voluntary and fully informed.[165] The courts have also found that the use of the wrong forms or the omission of words from forms used to create arrest warrants or informations amount to technical irregularities provided they do not result in the exclusion of information of substance.[166]

Depriving young persons of information that can be considered substantial or fundamental to the understanding and exercising of their rights cannot be considered a technical irregularity. In *R. v. S.S.*[167] the Court of Appeal held that the police breached s. 146(2)(b)(iv) of the *YCJA* when they failed to advise a 17-year-old young person facing robbery charges that he was required to have any person with whom he consulted present during the giving of a statement unless he desired otherwise. In the case at bar, the young person was contacted by the police and told that he had been named as a suspect in a robbery. The young person agreed to an interview at the police station the next day. The police picked him up the next day and drove him to the police station. He was told he was not under arrest. Prior to taking his statement, the police officer reviewed a police form specifically designed to give to a young person prior to taking a statement from him or her. The young person was advised that he did not have to give a statement, that any statement could be used against him and that he could consult with a lawyer and a parent or other adult. The young person said he did not wish to consult with a lawyer, a parent or other adult. However, the waiver form that was read to the young person

---

[162] *YCJA*, s. 146(6).
[163] *R. v. K.L.T.*, [2005] O.J. No. 3154, at paras. 218-223 (Ont. C.J.).
[164] *R. v. Y.N.*, [2005] O.J. No. 6329 (Ont. C.J.).
[165] *R. v. K.L.T.*, [2005] O.J. No. 3154, at para. 220 (Ont. C.J.).
[166] *R. v. Pigeau*, [1990] N.S.J. No. 162, 96 N.S.R. (2d) 412 (N.S.C.A.) and *Re Lanteigne*, [1981] N.B.J. No. 367, 43 N.B.R. (2d) 440 (N.B.Q.B.).
[167] [2007] O.J. No. 2552 (Ont. C.A.).

indicated that a young person has a *right* to have anyone consulted present during the taking of the statement unless he decides otherwise rather than saying that it is a requirement that anyone he consults be present during the taking of a statement unless he desires otherwise. The form was, to that degree, not in strict compliance with the wording of s. 146(2)(b)(iv). The young person subsequently gave a statement to the police at the end of an hour-long interview, at which point he was charged and arrested.

The Ontario Court of Appeal held that the failure of the police to characterize s. 146(2)(b)(iv) as a requirement deprived the young person of a substantial informational component of s. 146(2)(b)(iv) and could not be considered merely a technical irregularity of the kind that would permit the admission of the statement. Had the young person been informed that it was a requirement to have anyone consulted present during the taking of the statement unless the young person desired otherwise, the young person would have been alerted to the significance of any statement that he might provide and would be in a better position to make an informed decision about whether to consult a lawyer or an adult, Lang J.A. said. The Ontario Court of Appeal concluded that the breach was more than a technical irregularity and, therefore, the statement could not be admitted under s. 146(6).

F.   Spontaneous Statements

The *YCJA* also provides that the requirements in s. 146(2)(b) to (d) do not apply if the young person makes oral statements spontaneously before the peace officer or other person in authority has had a reasonable opportunity to comply with those requirements.[168] The rationale for this exception in s. 146 relates to the general belief that spontaneous utterances are more likely to be reliable because the maker of the statement is under no pressure or compulsion to make the statement. Such statements are endowed with an inherent reliability or trustworthiness by virtue of the circumstances surrounding the making of them. However, since this exception robs the young person of other protections in s. 146, the onus on the Crown to establish an absence of influence is high.[169] In the case of a truly spontaneous statement, the probative value of a statement that is so reliable and free of external influences from authority takes precedence over the protections afforded a young person in s. 146.[170] Whether a statement from a young person is held to be spontaneous and therefore not

---

[168]   *YCJA*, s. 146(3).
[169]   *R. v. V.G.*, [2007] A.J. No. 390, at para. 15 (Alta. Prov. Ct.).
[170]   *R. v. V.G.*, [2007] A.J. No. 390, at para. 14 (Alta. Prov. Ct.).

subject to the requirements in s. 146(2)(b) to (d) before it can be admitted, will depend very much on a careful examination of the facts, context and circumstances in which it was made.

The Ontario Court of Appeal defined the concept of spontaneous in *R. v. J.W.*[171] by referring to its dictionary definition: "Arising, proceeding, or acting entirely from natural impulse, without any external stimulus or constraint."[172] An external stimulus need not take the form of a police question or demand from a person in authority. The mere presence of a person in authority in some cases could be viewed as enough of a stimulus to provoke a spontaneous utterance but the presence of a person in authority in and of itself will not automatically defeat a claim of spontaneous utterance.[173]

Since the section of the *YCJA* concerning spontaneous statements is virtually identical (one word is different) to its predecessor section under the *YOA*, the courts today often rely on this definition and focus on the nature of any potential external stimulus in determining whether a statement from a young person was spontaneously made.

A spontaneous statement is likely to be found when a young person blurts out something without any prompting from the authorities. In *R. v. K.L.T.*,[174] MacLean J. found that a young person who was arrested and placed in the back of a police cruiser in relation to a stolen vehicle and vehicle chase made a spontaneous statement while in the cruiser. The constable, who was in the driver's seat while K.L.T. sat in the back, read him his rights but did not ask any questions. On the way back to the police station, the two did not speak except for the reading of the accused's rights and his responses. As they waited to enter the police station, the constable testified that the accused said: "I did not know the car was stolen and the only thing I know was the guys I was with had a beef with someone in the van. I don't know what the big deal was. It was not a real gun, it's a pellet gun."[175] The constable asked the young person a question following his initial statement. After reviewing the law in this area,[176] MacLean J. held that there was no evidence of an oppressive atmosphere in the cruiser and nothing else had occurred to cause the statement to have been made involuntarily. The statement came after he had been advised in clear language that he did not have to make any statement unless he

---

[171] [1996] O.J. No. 3003 (Ont. C.A.).
[172] *R. v. J.W.*, [1996] O.J. No. 3003, at para. 7 (Ont. C.A.).
[173] *R. v. J.W.*, [1996] O.J. No. 3003, at para. 8 (Ont. C.A.).
[174] [2005] O.J. No. 3154 (Ont. C.J.).
[175] *R. v. K.L.T.*, [2005] O.J. No. 3154, at para. 70 (Ont. C.J.).
[176] *R. v. K.L.T.*, [2005] O.J. No. 3154 (Ont. C.J.) is a useful case because it provides a contemporary summary of the law in this area in relation to young persons.

wanted to. Although he had requested to speak with his foster mother and with a lawyer, the officers had not yet had a reasonable opportunity to comply with those requests. Justice MacLean concluded that K.L.T. acted entirely from natural impulse without any external stimulus or constraint when he made the statement and that the statement was a spontaneous utterance within the meaning of s. 146 of the *YCJA*.[177]

In *R. v. O.K.*,[178] the court also found a statement from the young person to be admissible as a spontaneous utterance. The young person had been read his rights and warnings and was then being transported to the detachment by another officer. As they walked toward the vehicle, without the constable saying anything, the young person said: "I didn't hit him, seriously I didn't."[179] Similarly, the court ruled admissible as a spontaneous statement a comment from a 17-year-old young person that he made within minutes of the police arriving at the door of his home and telling him he was being arrested for use of a stolen credit card and was being investigated for a home invasion. The young person responded that he used the credit card but did not do the home invasion. Justice Kastner held that the statement had not been made in response to a direct question from the police or due to any other overt conduct by the police designed to provoke, elicit or stimulate a response[180] but had been made just after the arrest before the police had time to advise the young person of his rights.[181]

Conversely, a statement that comes in response to police questioning, a police allegation or where the young person is clearly a suspect is unlikely to be held to be spontaneous.[182]

Any ambiguity or doubt as to whether the statement is spontaneous should be resolved in favour of the young person.[183] In *R. v. V.G.*,[184] an admission from a 16-year-old girl that she, and not her boyfriend, was entirely responsible for the murder was ruled inadmissible because the judge doubted its spontaneity in all of the circumstances. She and her

---

[177] *R. v. K.L.T.*, [2005] O.J. No. 3154, at para. 86 (Ont. C.J.).

[178] [2004] B.C.J. No. 1458 (B.C. Prov. Ct.).

[179] *R. v. O.K.*, [2004] B.C.J. No. 1458, at para. 72 (B.C. Prov. Ct.).

[180] *R. v. Y.N.*, [2005] O.J. No. 6329 (Ont. C.J.).

[181] *R. v. Y.N.*, [2005] O.J. No. 6329, at para. 41 (Ont. C.J.).

[182] See *R. v. J. (J.T.)*, [1990] S.C.J. No. 59, at paras. 27-34, [1990] 2 S.C.R. 3 (S.C.C.), where the young person made the statement after being questioned over a period of four hours. After being confronted with the allegation that he was lying, he made an inculpatory statement. While the young person had been advised of some of his rights upon detention, the Supreme Court of Canada held that the police should have complied with all of the requirements of s. 56(2) of the *YOA*.

[183] *R. v. J.W.*, [1996] O.J. No. 3003 (Ont. C.A.).

[184] [2007] A.J. No. 390 (Alta. Prov. Ct.).

boyfriend, a young adult, had been arrested at gun point. Her statement was made when she was in the police vehicle, having been arrested for first degree murder and given her rights. The uniformed police officer made no note of the statement or the circumstances surrounding the making of it so that the precise words and actions that may have precipitated it are unclear. Justice Anderson was concerned that the advice of the police officer that the young person could have an adult present may have stimulated her to make the comment. She was also in custody at the time. The circumstances surrounding it were not free of influence, angst or external stimuli, Anderson J. held, in expressing concerns about its reliability.

G. Mistake as to Age

A judge can rule admissible a statement or waiver under s. 146 if the young person held himself or herself out to be 18 or older at the time of the making of the statement and the person to whom the statement or waiver was made conducted reasonable inquiries into the age of the young person and had reasonable grounds to believe the young person was 18 or older and the statement or waiver would otherwise be admissible.[185]

H. Statements Made Under Duress

A youth justice court judge can rule inadmissible a statement from a young person upon being satisfied by the young person that the statement was made under duress[186] imposed by any person who is not, in law, a person in authority. Duress is not defined in the *YCJA* for purposes of s. 146. The jurisprudence relating to the common law defence of duress in relation to the commission of an offence as outlined in s. 17 of the *Criminal Code* may be of some guidance and assistance. In *R. v. Ruzic*,[187] the common law defence of duress is defined as a real threat to the personal integrity of a person during which the individual is deprived of

---

185   *YCJA*, s. 146(8).
186   See some explanation of the meaning of duress in *R. v. G.F.D.*, [2006] B.C.J. No. 1271 (B.C. Prov. Ct.), particularly at para. 26. A young person may be able to successfully argue that he or she made a statement to a parent under duress as a result of extreme pressure exerted by the parents. However, the standard for establishing the existence of duress is high. In relation to s. 17 of the *Criminal Code*, the common law defence of duress has been defined in cases such as *R. v. Ruzic*, [2001] S.C.J. No. 25, [2001] 1 S.C.R. 687 (S.C.C.) and *R. v. Hibbert*, [1995] S.C.J. No. 63, [1995] 2 S.C.R. 973 (S.C.C.) and will be of some guidance in relation to its meaning and application to s. 146 of the *YCJA*.
187   [2001] S.C.J. No. 25, [2001] 1 S.C.R. 687 (S.C.C.).

any safe avenue of escape in the eyes of a reasonable person.[188] It involves intentional threats of physical harm or death.[189] Some have characterized duress in this context as meaning the loss of free will.[190] If the facts support a contention by the young person that he or she felt compelled or forced by violence or threats of violence to make a statement against his or her will, the court may find duress.

---

[188] *R. v. Ruzic*, [2001] S.C.J. No. 25, at para. 62, [2001] 1 S.C.R. 687 (S.C.C.).

[189] *R. v. Ruzic*, [2001] S.C.J. No. 25, at para. 57, [2001] 1 S.C.R. 687 (S.C.C.).

[190] Sanjeev Anand and James Robb, "The Admissibility of Young People's Statements Under the Proposed *Youth Criminal Justice Act*" (2002) 39 Alta. L. Rev. 771, at para. 22 (QL).

Chapter 8

SENTENCING UNDER THE YOUTH CRIMINAL JUSTICE ACT

Whoever reads, with a philosophic eye, the history of nations, and their laws, will generally find, that the ideas of virtue and vice, of a good or bad citizen, change with the revolution of ages ...[1]

Punishment can therefore be a kind of social barometer that gauges the structure and moral standards of an era with remarkable precision.[2]

I.   INTRODUCTION

Our concept of reasonable punishment has changed markedly with the ages. Even in the 1800s, a 13-year-old boy was hanged for stealing a cow and a young girl jailed for stealing a gooseberry from a garden.[3] Will there come a time when modern sentencing philosophy in Canada will be viewed with some equal measure of shock and disbelief, or scorned for its lack of enlightenment?

The sentencing regime under the *Youth Criminal Justice Act*[4] is among the most significant and controversial aspects[5] of the new Act. It is significant because it provides judges with more guidance and direction than ever before

---

[1] Cesare Beccaria, *Of Crimes and Punishments*, Second American Edition (Philadelphia (No. 175, Chestnut St.)) (Published by Philip H. Nicklin: A. Walker, printer, 24, Arch St., 1819), c. 6. This classic treatise is available online at: <http://www.constitution.org/cb/crim_pun.htm>.

[2] John A. Winterdyk, *Issues and Perspectives on Young Offenders in Canada*, 2d ed. (Toronto: Harcourt Canada, 2000), at 1.

[3] As referred to in Chapter 1, at notes 63 and 64.

[4] S.C. 2002, c. 1, Part 4 [hereafter "*YCJA*"].

[5] The federal Conservative party publicly acknowledged its belief in the value of toughening sentences for young persons in its election platform, *Stand Up for Canada*, before winning the January 2006 election. In the autumn of 2007, the federal government introduced Bill C-25, which, among other things, incorporates the adult sentencing principles of deterrence and denunciation into the *YCJA*. This bill died on the Order Paper in the fall of 2008, when the election was called. When the Conservative government was re-elected with a stronger minority, economic concerns dominated the agenda.

regarding the sentencing of young persons who commit crimes in Canada. It is controversial because some Canadians perceive the youth sentences available under the *YCJA* as too lenient,[6] and believe that the imposition of stiffer sentences on young offenders will deter youth crime.[7]

When the *YCJA* came into force on April 1, 2003, it created a detailed sentencing code for young persons in Canada for the first time in history. While previous youth justice legislation contained principles that applied to the sentencing of young persons, the *YCJA* is more expansive in this regard: it contains a sentencing purpose statement, specific sentencing principles and factors that the judge must consider when sentencing a young person to a youth sentence, as well as new and more stringent guidelines describing when custody can be imposed. The sentencing principles and sentences under the *Criminal Code* that apply to adults[8] do not apply to young persons unless it is determined that the young person should receive an adult sentence.[9]

---

[6]   Comments by federal Justice Minister Rob Nicholson during his introduction to the Second Reading debate on Bill C-25, *House of Commons Debates* (21 November 2007), at 1535. Justice Rothstein also discusses the prevailing public perception that young persons are treated too leniently in his partial dissent in *R. v. D.B.*, [2008] S.C.J. No. 25, at para. 13, [2008] SCC 25 (S.C.C.).

[7]   Youth justice experts in Canada generally contend that increasing the severity of youth sentences has no impact on youth crime, in part because young persons have less foresight and judgement than adults. Young persons are generally not considering the possibility of getting caught or the consequences of offending, while they are offending. See Nicholas Bala, *Youth Criminal Justice Law* (Toronto: Irwin Law Inc., 2003), at 4 and 408. See also his testimony before the Nunn Commission of Inquiry, Transcript of Hearing, Vol. 16, February 16, 2006, at 2877 and 2878; and the Nova Scotia Nunn Commission of Inquiry *Spiralling out of Control: Lessons Learned from a Boy in Trouble: Report of the Nunn Commission of Inquiry* (Halifax, NS: Nunn Commission of Inquiry, 2006). This report is available online at <http://www.gov.ns.ca/just/nunn_commission/_docs/Report_Nunn_Final.pdf>.

See also a good discussion of this point in Anthony Doob and Carla Cesaroni, "Conclusion: How Do We Best Approach the Problem of Youth Crime?" in *Responding to Youth Crime in Canada* (Toronto: University of Toronto Press, 2004), in particular at 250, where the point is made that increasing policing and increasing the chance that a young offender will be apprehended almost certainly has a greater deterrent effect on youthful criminality than increasing sentences.

See also the majority ruling of Abella J. in *R. v. D.B.*, [2008] S.C.J. No. 25, at para. 41, 2008 SCC 25 (S.C.C.), where she held that young persons have heightened vulnerability, less maturity and a reduced capacity for moral judgement: Anthony Doob and Cheryl Webster, "Sentencing Severity and Crime: Accepting the Null Hypothesis" in Michael Tonry, ed., *A Review of Research*, Crime and Justice, vol. 30 (Chicago: University of Chicago Press, 2003), at 143-95, and P. Gendreau and D.A. Andrews, "Tertiary Prevention: What the Meta-analyses of the Offender Treatment Literature Tell Us About 'What Works'" (January 1990) 32 Can. J. Crim. 173.

[8]   These sentencing principles are found in Part XXIII of the *Criminal Code*, R.S.C. 1985, c. C-46, generally in s. 718.

[9]   *YCJA*, s. 50. See also *R. v. B.W.P.*; *R. v. B.V.N.*, [2006] S.C.J. No. 27, [2006] 1 S.C.R. 941 (S.C.C.).

Canadian experts in youth justice and sentencing law describe this new sentencing regime for young persons as the "most systemic attempt in Canadian history to structure judicial discretion regarding the sentencing of juveniles [and] an ambitious attempt to change sentencing practices in the youth justice system".[10] They also characterize it as more detailed and directive than similar youth justice reforms recently introduced in other common law jurisdictions.[11] The Supreme Court of Canada has held that the *YCJA* sentencing regime is so distinctly different from that of the *Young Offenders Act*[12] that there is little to gain by examining the *YOA* provisions and jurisprudence in an attempt to gain insight into the new *YCJA* sentencing regime.[13] In essence, the sentencing rules for young persons in Canada have been so fundamentally altered that the *YOA* and its jurisprudence are of little assistance.

The inclusion of more detailed sentencing guidelines in the *YCJA* was largely a response to research in the 1990s, which revealed that Canada was incarcerating young persons at a much higher rate than many other western nations, including the U.S., Australia and New Zealand,[14] and that Canada's youth incarceration rate was four times higher than the adult incarceration rate in Canada.[15] Youth incarceration rates were also found to vary widely among the provinces. The rates were three to four times higher in some provinces than in others but without comparable

---

[10]   Julian V. Roberts and Nicholas Bala, "Understanding Sentencing Under the *Youth Criminal Justice Act*" (2003) 41 Alta. L. Rev. 395, at paras. 3 and 4 (QL).

[11]   Julian V. Roberts and Nicholas Bala, "Understanding Sentencing Under the *Youth Criminal Justice Act*" (2003) 41 Alta. L. Rev. 395, at para. 4 (QL).

[12]   R.S.C. 1985, c. Y-1 [hereafter "*YOA*"].

[13]   *R. v. B.W.P.; R. v. B.V.N.*, [2006] S.C.J. No. 27, at para. 21, [2006] 1 S.C.R. 941 (S.C.C.).

[14]   See Department of Justice, *A Strategy for the Renewal of Youth Justice* (Ottawa: Ministry of Supply and Services, 1998) (section on Concerns about the Current Youth Justice System). This document was the federal government's response to *Renewing Youth Justice: Thirteenth Report of the Standing Committee on Justice and Legal Affairs*, released in April 1997. At the time of writing, *A Strategy for the Renewal of Youth Justice* could be accessed through the Department of Justice website at: <http://www.justice.gc.ca/eng/pi/yj-jj/about-apropos/toc-tdm.html>. In this document, the federal government reviews the shortcomings of the *YOA* and outlines its rationale for introducing the *YCJA*. This document is the evidentiary and philosophical foundation for the *YCJA*; it is the policy paper.

      In *R. v. L.E.K.*, [1999] Y.J. No. 119, at para. 60 (Y.T. Youth Ct.), Lilles J. referred to federal government statistics which revealed that the youth incarceration rate in Canada was also considerably higher than that of Scotland, England and Wales.

      See Anthony Doob and Jane Sprott, "Sentencing under the *Youth Criminal Justice Act*: An Historical Perspective" in Kathryn Campbell, ed., *Understanding Youth Justice in Canada* (Toronto: Pearson Education Canada Inc., 2005), at 229.

[15]   Department of Justice, *A Strategy for the Renewal of Youth Justice* (Ottawa: Ministry of Supply and Services, 1998) (section on Children, Youth and Youth Crime), on the Department of Justice website at: <http://www.justice.gc.ca/eng/pi/yj-jj/about-apropos/toc-tdm.html>.

variations in crime rates.[16] In addition, Canada was also often incarcerating young persons for non-violent crimes, including offences that some would characterize in certain circumstances as minor, such as failing to appear in court as required or breaching a probation condition.[17]

In reviewing Canada's history regarding the sentencing of young persons, Bastarache J. of the Supreme Court of Canada observed in *R. v. C.D.; R. v. C.D.K.*[18] that the *YOA* had created a discretionary sentencing regime, which, when compared to the *Juvenile Delinquents Act*,[19] led to a substantial increase in custodial sentences for young persons. Between 1986 and 1994, the average daily population of young offenders in custody in Canada increased by 24 per cent (although, on average, the actual length of sentences under the *YOA* was shorter than the length of sentences (to training schools) under the *JDA*).[20]

As Bastarache J. observes in his historical review, the federal government began taking legislative steps as early as 1986 to reduce the youth incarceration rate. It first amended s. 24(1) of the *YOA* to prevent the overuse of custody by prohibiting a judge from committing a young person to custody unless it was considered necessary for the protection of society, due to both the seriousness of the crime and the circumstances in which it was committed, and having regard to the needs and circumstances of the young person. According to Bastarache J., the amendment appeared to have little effect. Parliament amended the *YOA* again in 1995 to impose still greater restrictions on custody and to provide more direction for judges regarding its imposition. Nevertheless, the provisions continued to allow for the exercise of significant judicial discretion by youth court judges and had little effect on sentencing patterns.[21] Indeed, in 1999, Lilles J. of the Yukon Territorial Youth Court described the incarceration rate of young persons in Canada as a "national disgrace".[22]

Among the foremost goals of the *YCJA*, therefore, was to reduce the youth incarceration rate in Canada, and to ensure that jail was generally a

---

[16] Department of Justice, *A Strategy for the Renewal of Youth Justice* (Ottawa: Ministry of Supply and Services, 1998) (section on Concerns about the Current Youth Justice System).

[17] Department of Justice, *A Strategy for the Renewal of Youth Justice* (Ottawa: Ministry of Supply and Services, 1998) (section on Legislative and Supporting Program Components). In the late 1990s, research demonstrated that more than 50 per cent of young persons were being jailed for property and process offences. Justice Lilles notes this in *R. v. L.E.K.*, [1999] Y.J. No. 119, at para. 60 (Y.T. Youth Ct.), citing Statistics Canada, Canadian Centre for Justice Statistics, "Youth Court Statistics 1997-98 Highlights" (1999) 19:2 Juristat 1, at 7.

[18] [2005] S.C.J. No. 79, at para. 45 (S.C.C.).

[19] S.C. 1908, c. 40 [hereafter "*JDA*"].

[20] *R. v. C.D.; R. v. C.D.K.*, [2005] S.C.J. No. 79, at para. 45 (S.C.C.).

[21] *R. v. C.D.; R. v. C.D.K.*, [2005] S.C.J. No. 79, at paras. 46-49 (S.C.C.).

[22] *R. v. J.K.E.*, [1999] Y.J. No. 119, at para. 61 (Y.T. Youth Ct.).

last resort for all but the most serious youthful offenders. The intent of the federal government, as outlined in the documentary record, was that clear and specific sentencing principles would result in fewer custodial sentences and in more uniform and principled sentencing of young persons across Canada. Under the *YCJA*, it was expected to be far more likely that two young persons sentenced for similar crimes in similar circumstances in Canada would receive similar sentences.

When she discussed the new *YCJA* in the House of Commons on February 14, 2001, Liberal Justice Minister Anne McLellan was clear that one of the central aims of the new legislation was to reduce the youth incarceration rate:

> ... the existing *YOA* has resulted in the highest youth incarceration rate in the western world, including our neighbours to the south, the United States. Young persons in Canada often receive harsher custodial sentences than adults receive for the same type of offence. Almost 80% of custodial sentences are for non-violent offences. Many non-violent first offenders found guilty of less serious offences such as minor theft are sentenced to custody.
>
> The proposed youth criminal justice act is intended to reduce the unacceptably high level of youth incarceration that has occurred under the Young Offenders Act. The preamble to the new legislation states clearly that the youth justice system should reserve its most serious interventions for the most serious crimes and thereby reduce its over-reliance on incarceration.
>
> In contrast to the *YOA*, the new legislation provides that custody is to be reserved primarily for violent offenders and serious repeat offenders. The new youth justice legislation recognizes that non-custodial sentences can often provide more meaningful consequences and be more effective in rehabilitating young persons. We also believe that the Young Offenders Act has resulted in the overuse of the court for minor cases that can be better dealt with outside the court.[23]

It is noteworthy that the maximum length of youth sentences under the *YCJA* has not changed from the latter days of the *YOA*. What is different is that there are now:

- detailed sentencing principles and factors to guide judges in the imposition of a youth sentence;

- tighter restrictions on the imposition of custody;

- an expanded range of sentencing options (provided, in some cases, that the province or territory has implemented the new sentencing option); and

---

[23]   *House of Commons Debates* (14 February 2001), at 1530.

- a new test to determine in certain cases whether the young person should receive an adult sentence under the *Criminal Code*.

The balance of this chapter explores these significant changes.

II. SENTENCING PRINCIPLES UNDER THE YCJA

A.   Purpose and Principles — Section 38

Purpose

38. (1) The purpose of sentencing under section 42 (youth sentences) is to hold a young person accountable for an offence through the imposition of just sanctions that have meaningful consequences for the young person and that promote his or her rehabilitation and reintegration into society, thereby contributing to the long-term protection of the public.

Sentencing principles

(2) A youth justice court that imposes a youth sentence on a young person shall determine the sentence in accordance with the principles set out in section 3 and the following principles:

(a)   the sentence must not result in a punishment that is greater than the punishment that would be appropriate for an adult who has been convicted of the same offence committed in similar circumstances;

(b)   the sentence must be similar to the sentences imposed in the region on similar young persons found guilty of the same offence committed in similar circumstances;

(c)   the sentence must be proportionate to the seriousness of the offence and the degree of responsibility of the young person for that offence;

(d)   all available sanctions other than custody that are reasonable in the circumstances should be considered for all young persons, with particular attention to the circumstances of aboriginal young persons; and

(e)   subject to paragraph (c), the sentence must

(i)   be the least restrictive sentence that is capable of achieving the purpose set out in subsection (1),

> (ii) be the one that is most likely to rehabilitate the young per-
> son and reintegrate him or her into society, and
>
> (iii) promote a sense of responsibility in the young person, and
> an acknowledgement of the harm done to victims and the
> community.
>
> *Factors to be considered*
>
> *(3) In determining a youth sentence, the youth justice court shall
> take into account*
>
> (a) the degree of participation by the young person in the commis-
> sion of the offence;
>
> (b) the harm done to victims and whether it was intentional or rea-
> sonably foreseeable;
>
> (c) any reparation made by the young person to the victim or the
> community;
>
> (d) the time spent in detention by the young person as a result of
> the offence;
>
> (e) the previous findings of guilt of the young person; and
>
> (f) any other aggravating and mitigating circumstances related to
> the young person or the offence that are relevant to the purpose
> and principles set out in this section.

B.   The Purpose of a Youth Sentence

Section 50 of the *YCJA* indicates that Part XXIII of the *Criminal
Code*, which is the sentencing regime for adults, does not apply to young
persons who receive youth sentences under s. 42 of the *YCJA*.[24] A young
person is subject to the adult sentencing principles contained in the
Criminal Code only in certain limited circumstances. Otherwise the
sentencing principles under the *YCJA* govern the sentencing.

While some of the principles in s. 3 of the *YCJA* are particularly
relevant to youth sentences, ss. 38 and 39 of the *YCJA* are of greater

---

[24]   Justice Charron affirmed this in *R. v. B.W.P.; R. v. B.V.N.*, [2006] S.C.J. No. 27, at para. 22,
[2006] 1 S.C.R. 941 (S.C.C.).

significance regarding youth sentences because these sections are aimed solely and specifically at the sentencing stage of the process.[25]

Section 38 of the *YCJA* is intended to explain the purpose of youth sentences under s. 42 of the *YCJA*. Similar to most clauses in the Preamble, however, this purpose statement is replete with undefined concepts and phrases such as "meaningful consequences" and "just sanctions", and is of limited practical assistance to the sentencing judge. What is meaningful? What is just? The sentencing purpose statement in the *Criminal Code* also contains nebulous and subjective concepts such as "just sanctions", but it is clearer and more directive overall because it indicates that an adult sentence must have one or more of a series of objectives that are clearly identified. The adult sentencing regime also identifies proportionality as the fundamental sentencing principle.[26] By contrast, the *YCJA* does not identify any principle as the fundamental sentencing principle. The purpose statement in the *YCJA* is too general to be of much assistance to judges. The specific sentencing principles and factors in s. 38(2) are more helpful.

III. SENTENCING PRINCIPLES IN RELATION TO YOUTH SENTENCES — SECTION 38(2)

Section 38(2) reminds the judiciary that, when imposing a youth sentence, a youth justice court judge *shall* consider the principles in s. 3 of the *YCJA*,[27] as well as the specific sentencing principles in s. 38(2). The use of the imperative word "shall" in the introductory clause to s. 38(2) is noteworthy. The judge *must* consider both the principles in s. 3 and those in s. 38(2).

Certain principles in s. 3 of the *YCJA* are of particular relevance at the sentencing stage, such as the direction in s. 3 that the youth criminal justice system is intended to rehabilitate young persons and to reintegrate them into society, and that, in order to promote the long-term protection of the public, the youth justice system must emphasize rehabilitation and reintegration, the fair and proportionate accountability of young persons that is consistent with their greater dependency and reduced maturity, and their enhanced

---

[25] This is in keeping with the basic paramountcy rule of statutory interpretation expressed by the Latin maxim *specialia generalibus non derogant*, which stands for the proposition that in the event of a conflict between a specific provision concerning a particular matter and a more general provision dealing with the specific matter as well as other matters, the specific provision prevails. On this point, see Ruth Sullivan, *Statutory Interpretation* (Concord: Irwin Law, 1997), at 226.

[26] *Criminal Code*, s. 718.1.

[27] Section 3 of the *YCJA*, the Declaration of Principle, is discussed in detail in Chapter 3.

procedural protection, and, finally, that "special considerations" apply in proceedings against young persons, and that young persons have special guarantees of their rights and freedoms.

In addition to these basic sentencing principles, the 2008 decision in *R. v. D.B.*[28] can be expected to have a significant impact on the sentencing of young persons. While it may be years before the implications of the decision for the youth justice system are fully clear, the ruling recognizes a legal presumption of the diminished moral blameworthiness of young persons in criminal law because of their heightened vulnerability, lesser maturity and reduced capacity for moral judgement.[29] Significantly, the Supreme Court of Canada has affirmed that this presumption of diminished moral culpability of young persons is not only a long-standing legal principle[30] but a principle of fundamental justice,[31] and that this concept is recognized in international conventions ratified by Canada, such as the *U.N. Convention on the Rights of the Child.*[32]

The court split 5-4 regarding the constitutionality of the provisions in the *YCJA* that presume a young person will receive an adult sentence in certain circumstances unless the young person can persuade the court otherwise, but was nevertheless unanimous in holding that young persons charged with crimes have the benefit of a presumption of reduced moral culpability, and that this presumption (although rebuttable) is a principle of fundamental justice.[33] Indeed, Abella J. held for the majority in *R. v. D.B.* that the *YCJA* reflects a "statutory preoccupation with ensuring that sentencing reflects the reduced maturity and moral sophistication of young persons".[34] Noting that the Supreme Court of Canada had earlier held in *R. v. C.D.; R. v. C.D.K.*[35] that the *YCJA* was designed in part to reduce the over-reliance on custodial sentences, Abella J. stated in *R. v. D.B.* that "the approach to the sentencing of young persons is animated by the principle that there is a *presumption* of diminished moral culpability to which they are entitled".[36]

While Abella J. stated in *R. v. D.B.* that young persons are entitled to a presumption of diminished moral culpability throughout *any* proceedings

28 [2008] S.C.J. No. 25, 2008 SCC 25 (S.C.C.).
29 *R. v. D.B.*, [2008] S.C.J. No. 25, at para. 41, 2008 SCC 25 (S.C.C.).
30 *R. v. D.B.*, [2008] S.C.J. No. 25, at para. 59, 2008 SCC 25 (S.C.C.).
31 *R. v. D.B.*, [2008] S.C.J. No. 25, at para. 70, 2008 SCC 25 (S.C.C.).
32 *R. v. D.B.*, [2008] S.C.J. No. 25, at para. 60, 2008 SCC 25 (S.C.C.).
33 *R. v. D.B.*, [2008] S.C.J. No. 25, 2008 SCC 25 (S.C.C.). See Rothstein J. (Bastarache, Deschamps and Charron JJ. concurring), writing for the minority, dissenting in part, at para. 106.
34 *R. v. D.B.*, [2008] S.C.J. No. 25, at para. 44, 2008 SCC 25 (S.C.C.).
35 [2005] S.C.J. No. 79 (S.C.C.).
36 *R. v. D.B.*, [2008] S.C.J. No. 25, at para. 45, 2008 SCC 25 (S.C.C.).

against them, including during sentencing,[37] *R. v. D.B.* is likely to have particular resonance at the sentencing stage, in part because the sentencing judge must consider the meaning of fair and proportionate accountability in s. 3(1)(b)(ii) of the *YCJA*, as well as the meaning of proportionality in s. 38(2)(c) of the *YCJA*. In light of *R. v. D.B.*, the degree of responsibility of the young accused person in relation to a particular offence is likely to receive greater attention.

A.   Parity — Section 38(2)(a) and (b)

Section 38(2)(a) and (b) of the *YCJA* addresses the principle of sentencing parity in youth sentences in two ways: parity in youth sentencing is to be sought both in relation to the sentencing of a young person *vis-à-vis* an adult who commits a similar crime in similar circumstances, as well as in relation to another young person who commits a similar crime in similar circumstances.

(i)   Section 38(2)(a)

Section 38(2)(a) provides clear direction to the judiciary that a youth sentence cannot be greater than the sentence that would be appropriate for an adult who is convicted of the same offence committed in similar circumstances. This principle was included to address the federal government's concern that young persons were sometimes being sentenced more harshly for certain offences than adults in similar circumstances.[38]

Some scholars suggest that this principle is problematic for two reasons: (1) youth court judges may not always know the sentence an adult would receive in similar circumstances unless they routinely sentence adults;[39]and (2) the evidence to support the proposition that young persons have traditionally received more severe punishments than adults for similar offences committed in similar circumstances is not overwhelmingly strong. A Statistics Canada sentencing study of nine common offences, published in 2000, found that incarceration rates were significantly higher for adults, but, for those young persons who received custodial sentences, the sentence

---

[37]   *R. v. D.B.*, [2008] S.C.J. No. 25, at para. 69, 2008 SCC 25 (S.C.C.).

[38]   Julian V. Roberts and Nicholas Bala, "Understanding Sentencing Under the *Youth Criminal Justice Act*" (2003) 41 Alta. L. Rev. 395, at para. 28 (QL).

[39]   This is a valid point; however, judges can readily acquire the information they need. In addition, counsel can, and do, make relevant submissions to assist the judiciary. See, for example, *R. v. M.A.J.*, [2005] O.J. No. 829, at paras. 29 and 30 (Ont. S.C.), and *R. v. T.M.*, [2003] S.J. No. 722, at para. 18 (Sask. Prov. Ct.).

lengths were sometimes longer than for adults convicted of the same offence.[40] The federal government was presumably concerned that there appeared to be a risk that young persons were being sentenced more severely than adults for similar crimes, at least some of the time, and it sought to take legislative steps to curtail this. The *YOA* contained a provision similar to that now contained in s. 38(2)(a)[41] of the *YCJA*, with one significant difference: the *YOA* provision states that a young person's disposition (which is now referred to as a sentence under the *YCJA*) cannot be greater than the *maximum* punishment that an adult could get for the same offence. The reality is, however, that adults seldom receive the maximum sentence for the offence.[42] The similar provision in the *YCJA* is more meaningful because it refers to the sentence that the adult is likely to get, rather than to the maximum.

Interestingly, while the *YCJA* says that as a general rule, a young person cannot receive a sentence that is greater than what an adult would receive for the same crime committed in similar circumstances, the *YCJA* does not expressly say that a young person should receive a lesser sentence than an adult for a similar crime committed in similar circumstances on account of age. An argument can be made that s. 3(1)(b)(ii) of the *YCJA* implies that there should be a "discount" on account of youth because it says that the youth criminal justice system must emphasize fair and proportionate accountability that is consistent with the reduced level of maturity of young persons. This principle arguably suggests that a young person should generally receive a lesser sentence than an adult for the same crime committed in similar circumstances because he or she was a young person at the time of the crime and the courts must take into account the reduced maturity of the young person. Justice Saunders of the British Columbia Court of Appeal essentially reached that conclusion in the 2007 case of *R. v. Pratt*[43] when he held, in reducing the sentence of a 16-year-old, on appeal, that the fact of youth creates a discount from the adult tariff of sanctions.[44]

In its 2008 decision in *R. v. D.B.*, the Supreme Court of Canada did not go that far. While Abella J., speaking for the majority, was clear that young persons are entitled to a presumption of diminished moral

---

[40]   Julian V. Roberts and Nicholas Bala, "Understanding Sentencing Under the *Youth Criminal Justice Act*" (2003) 41 Alta. L. Rev. 395, at para. 29 (QL). See also n. 43 to that paragraph.

[41]   *YOA*, s. 20(7).

[42]   Anthony Doob and Jane Sprott, "Sentencing under the *Youth Criminal Justice Act*: An Historical Perspective" in Kathryn Campbell, ed., *Understanding Youth Justice in Canada* (Toronto: Pearson Education Canada Inc., 2005), at 233.

[43]   [2007] B.C.J. No. 670 (B.C.C.A.).

[44]   *R. v. Pratt*, [2007] B.C.J. No. 670, at para. 57 (B.C.C.A.).

blameworthiness based on age, she was equally clear that this presumption is rebuttable.[45] In fact, Abella J. stated, in *obiter*, early in her ruling that, in some cases, it may even be that a young person should receive the *same* sentence as an adult.[46] That said, logic dictates that a young person should receive a lesser sentence than an adult for the same crime committed in identical circumstances due to his or her being under 18 at the time of the offence, bearing in mind that the likelihood of all other variables being equal is virtually impossible. A young person and an adult being sentenced for the same crime can always be differentiated on the basis of age, despite the similarity of all other factors.

(ii)   Section 38(2)(b) — Regional Parity

This principle is similar to the provision for adults in the *Criminal Code*,[47] but with one significant difference. Unlike s. 718.2(b) of the *Criminal Code*, s. 38(2)(b) qualifies the principle by reference to geography. The principle indicates that sentences that young persons receive must be similar to sentences imposed *in the region* on similar young persons found guilty of the same offence committed in similar circumstances. The term "region" is not defined. Had Parliament intended the word "region" to mean the province, presumably it would have used the more clear and specific term. One can only presume that Parliament intended the term to mean smaller regions within the province or territory,[48] since identifying regions beyond provincial borders makes less sense. (Conceivably, Parliament could have intended the term to refer to regions larger than the province, such as the Maritime provinces, the Atlantic Region or the Western provinces, which share common characteristics related to geography.) Youth justice experts reasonably suggest the term was likely intended to refer to local regions within a province since programming can vary among regions and municipalities within a province[49] but two young persons in the same municipality can generally expect to have access to the same programs and facilities.

The inclusion of the phrase "in the region" has prompted academic discussion because it appears to fly in the face of one of the underlying

---

[45]   [2008] S.C.J. No. 25, at paras. 45 and 93, 2008 SCC 25 (S.C.C.).

[46]   *R. v. D.B.*, [2008] S.C.J. No. 25, at para. 5, 2008 SCC 25 (S.C.C.).

[47]   *Criminal Code*, s. 718.2(b).

[48]   Nicholas Bala suggests in his book *Youth Criminal Justice Law* (Toronto: Irwin Law Inc., 2003), at 406, that region is intended to mean the local region, based on the assumption that all young persons that come before the court in a certain region have access to the same types of programs and resources. Similar sentences can be crafted based on available programming in that region.

[49]   Nicholas Bala, *Youth Criminal Justice Law* (Toronto: Irwin Law Inc., 2003), at 406.

goals of the new *YCJA* sentencing regime: to reduce disparity in sentencing across Canada. One of the key aims of the new sentencing regime is to increase the likelihood that young persons across Canada who commit similar offences in similar circumstances will receive similar sentences.[50] Yet the phrase, in the region, could well lead to increased disparity in youth sentencing, not only among provinces and territories, but within them.[51] This phraseology suggests that the sentence need only be similar to other sentences imposed in that particular region, and need not be similar to other sentences elsewhere in the province or territory or in other provinces or territories. Further, this section assumes that the sentencing judge has knowledge of local sentencing patterns, which is not always the case, particularly if the judge has come from another area to hear the matter.

Provincial courts have tended to simply *de facto* decide that the region means the province largely because they are bound by higher level rulings in their provinces and territories anyway, to the extent that such decisions cannot be distinguished.[52] In one of the earliest cases decided under the *YCJA*, *R. v. D.L.C.*,[53] Gorman J. queried the intent of this section and concluded that "region" must connote "the province". Youth court judges are bound to follow the sentencing precedents established by their respective Courts of Appeal in any event, Gorman J. held.[54]

The issue of parity in sentencing is further complicated by Charron J.'s holding in *R. v. B.W.P.; R. v. B.V.N.* that the approach to sentencing under the *YCJA* is highly individualized and offender-centric.[55] On the one hand, the youth sentence must be similar to youth sentences imposed on similar young persons in the region found guilty of the same offence committed in similar circumstances. On the other hand, the sentence must be carefully crafted to fit the circumstances and rehabilitative needs of the particular young person before the court. These two principles can, and do, conflict, and are not always reconcilable.

The appellate courts have acknowledged that determining the role of parity in sentencing is a delicate and difficult exercise.[56] The Nova Scotia

---

[50]   Julian V. Roberts and Nicholas Bala, "Understanding Sentencing Under the *Youth Criminal Justice Act*" (2003) 41 Alta. L. Rev. 395, at para. 33 (QL).

[51]   Julian V. Roberts and Nicholas Bala, "Understanding Sentencing Under the *Youth Criminal Justice Act*" (2003) 41 Alta. L. Rev. 395, at para. 33 (QL).

[52]   There are many examples of this. See, for example, the brief discussion of this in *R. v. T.M.*, [2003] S.J. No. 722, at para. 20 (Sask. Prov. Ct.).

[53]   [2003] N.J. No. 94, at paras. 35-46 (N.L. Prov. Ct.).

[54]   See also *R. v. M.A.J.*, [2005] O.J. No. 829, at para. 32 (Ont. C.J.); *R. v. T.M.*, [2003] S.J. No. 722, at paras. 20-36 (Sask. Prov. Ct.) and *R. v. D.P.*, [2004] B.C.J. No. 352, at paras. 22-24 (B.C. Prov. Ct.).

[55]   [2006] S.C.J. No. 27, at paras. 31-33, [2006] 1 S.C.R. 941 (S.C.C.).

[56]   *R. v. G. (S.N.)*, [2007] N.S.J. No. 297, at para. 30, 224 C.C.C. (3d) 563 (N.S.C.A.).

Court of Appeal held in a violent home invasion case[57] that parity should be considered at sentencing, but it is not the overriding factor. In that case, the Crown had argued that the leniency shown toward one accused offended the principle of parity because his co-accused received harsher sentences. Their sentences ranged from six years' incarceration for an adult to a conditional sentence for a young woman who had only minimal involvement in the incident, whereas J.R.L. had received only six months' deferred custody plus 18 months' probation. J.R.L. was the 16-year-old gang leader of at least eight young people who burst into a home and kicked, beat and struck the residents with a baseball bat and unloaded shotguns. The Crown was particularly concerned that J.R.L. received a much more lenient sentence than one co-accused, C.C., who had a far lesser role in the incident. C.C. was similar in age to J.R.L., he had no prior record compared with J.R.L.'s one prior offence, he was minimally involved as a follower compared to J.R.L.'s leadership role, and he pled guilty several months before J.R.L., yet he received 18 months' custody and 12 months' probation.

The Court of Appeal nevertheless concluded that the principle of parity is only one of the principles that the sentencing judge must consider. In concluding that the sentencing judge did not err in principle, Roscoe J.A. held that the sentencing judge was satisfied, based on J.RL.'s supportive parents and his adherence to most of the conditions of his release over a period of 10 months, that J.R.L. did not need the same measure of control to effect rehabilitation and reintegration as did C.C. J.R.L.'s sentence was upheld on appeal.

Reconciling the principles of parity and proportionality can be equally challenging. *R. v. J.R.L.* also illustrates this point. On the face of it, this ruling offends the principle of proportionality in s. 38 of the *YCJA*. It appears to suggest that a longer sentence than is proportional to the degree of responsibility of the offender can be imposed to permit rehabilitation. As discussed in the next section, the principle of proportionality is designed to prevent that very reasoning.[58]

B.   Section 38(2)(c) and (e) — Proportionality

The principle of proportionality is a key sentencing principle in relation to youth sentences, as it is for adults under the *Criminal Code*. However, the concept must be interpreted differently in the context of a youth

---

[57]   *R. v. J.R.L.*, [2007] N.S.J. No. 214 (N.S.C.A.).
[58]   See also *R. v. C.J.A.*, [2005] S.J. No. 64, at para. 59 (Sask. Prov. Ct.).

sentence under the *YCJA*. In the *Criminal Code*, the principle of proportion-ality, which instructs the sentencing judge to ensure that the sentence achieves proportionality between the gravity of the offence and the degree of responsibility of the adult offender, is identified as a fundamental principle of sentencing.[59] The principle of proportionality has not been given an equal measure of prominence *vis-à-vis* a youth sentence under the *YCJA*. Nevertheless, proportionality has an elevated status in contrast to certain other sentencing principles in s. 38, specifically those identified in s. 38(2)(e). A youth sentence must be the least restrictive sentence that is capable of achieving the purpose of sentencing in s. 38(1), the one most likely to rehabilitate the young person and reintegrate him or her into society and the one that promotes a sense of responsibility in the young person and an acknowledgement of the harm done to victims and the community, *provided* that it meets the sentencing principle of proportional-ity. The considerations in s. 38(2)(e) can be taken into account only to the extent that the sentence meets the requirement of proportionality. The principles in s. 38(2)(e) are subservient to the principle of proportionality. In the context of a youth sentence, therefore, proportionality is not necessarily to be given the same weight as it is to be given in the sentencing of an adult, since it is not identified as a fundamental principle of youth sentencing, but it is to be given greater weight than certain other sentencing principles that are identified in s. 38(2)(e).

Secondly, as suggested earlier in this chapter, the concept of propor-tionality, which concerns the relationship between the seriousness of the offence and *the degree of responsibility of the individual*, should generally be interpreted differently when the offender is a young person because of the long-standing principle of the diminished responsibility of young persons.[60] Although the Supreme Court of Canada has now operational-ized this principle as a rebuttable presumption of diminished moral culpability,[61] and stated that a young person can sometimes receive the same sentence as an adult,[62] the degree of responsibility of a young person, arguably, will always be less than that of an adult who commits the same crime in similar circumstances by virtue of the fact that the accused was a young person at the time of the commission of the offence and is less accountable due to their reduced age. It is submitted that the sentencing principle of proportionality, when applied to a young person,

---

[59] *Criminal Code*, s. 718.1.
[60] In *R. v. D.B.*, [2008] S.C.J. No. 25, 2008 SCC 25 (S.C.C.), Abella J. begins discussing this long-standing principle of diminished responsibility of young persons at para. 48. The ori-gins of this concept in the common law, as well as in statute law, are discussed in Chapter 1 of this text.
[61] *R. v. D.B.*, [2008] S.C.J. No. 25, at para. 45, 2008 SCC 25 (S.C.C.).
[62] *R. v. D.B.*, [2008] S.C.J. No. 25, at para. 5, 2008 SCC 25 (S.C.C.).

can never be identical to its meaning and impact on an adult accused. The degree of responsibility of a young person will always be less.

As alluded to earlier, in reference to the sentencing of a young person as an adult, the B.C. Court of Appeal held that the fact of youth effectively creates a "discount" from the adult tariff of sanctions.[63] In the case of an adult sentence, Saunders J.A. held that the sentence will not necessarily be identical to the sentence that would be imposed upon an adult in circumstances that are identical except for the offender's age. "[I]t may generally be expected that the fact of youth, considered within the terms of the *Act*, will moderate a sentence, particularly for those who are some time away from the upper limit of the definition of a young person."[64]

The *YCJA* has been criticized for not expressly including age as a mitigating factor in sentencing: "After all, the degree of mitigation accorded young offenders is generally held to vary inversely with their age: young persons near the lower limit of criminal responsibility of twelve years of age should receive a far steeper 'discount' from the adult tariff than a 17-year-old. This correlation between age and severity of punishment is the one feature common to all Western juvenile justice systems."[65]

Proportionality under the *YCJA* can be understood as a legislative response to the controversial 1993 Supreme Court of Canada decision in *R. v. M. (J.J.).*[66] This case concerned a series of property offences committed by J.J.M., who had a record for property offences at the time of his sentencing. His home life was highly dysfunctional and characterized by parental alcohol abuse and violence between the parents, as well as violence by the parents toward the children. Of the nine children, eight of them were subject to probation orders at the time of J.J.M.'s sentencing. J.J.M. and his siblings had been apprehended on several occasions by child protection services and placed in foster homes. The sentencing judge paid careful attention to J.J.M.'s record and family history, and sentenced him to open custody for two years. The Manitoba Court of Appeal upheld the sentence, but Helper J.A., in dissent, expressed concern that the sentence attempted to provide welfare assistance rather than determining the appropriate sentence. At the Supreme Court of Canada, Cory J. upheld the lower courts. In his decision, which was decided under the *YOA*, Cory J. held that proportionality has greater significance for adult offenders

---

[63]   *R. v. Pratt*, [2007] B.C.J. No. 670, at para. 57 (B.C.C.A.).

[64]   *R. v. Pratt*, [2007] B.C.J. No. 670, at para. 57 (B.C.C.A.).

[65]   Julian V. Roberts and Nicholas Bala, "Understanding Sentencing Under the *Youth Criminal Justice Act*" (2003) 41 Alta. L. Rev. 395, at para. 53 (QL).

[66]   [1993] S.C.J. No. 14, [1993] 2 S.C.R. 421 (S.C.C.).

than for young persons. In sentencing young persons, the court must consider not only the seriousness of the crime but other relevant factors as well.[67] Abysmal home conditions justified the two-year open custody sentence in order to provide the young person with the necessary guidance and assistance that he was not receiving at home. In essence, Cory J. concluded that the custodial sentence was necessary to achieve J.J.M.'s rehabilitation.

Academics and youth justice experts widely criticized the majority reasoning in *R. v. M. (J.J.)* for imposing a disproportionate sentence in order to achieve rehabilitation. The federal government appeared to be listening. Various provisions, including the inclusion of the paramountcy of proportionality in s. 38(2), were included in the *YCJA*,[68] and seek to ensure that, in future, a young person will not receive a sentence that is more severe than the principle of proportionality will permit, to address social welfare needs or to achieve rehabilitation.[69] The sentence cannot be longer (or arguably shorter) than proportionality demands to achieve rehabilitation. The sentence must be the one most likely to rehabilitate the young person and reintegrate him or her into society, provided it is proportionate in terms of the seriousness of the offence and the degree of responsibility of the offender. In fact, the Ontario Court of Appeal has held that proportionality under s. 38(2)(c) must be seen as providing an upper limit on the sentence that can be imposed on the offender. "... even if a long sentence were deemed necessary to rehabilitate the offender and hold him or her accountable, the sentence still must not be longer than what would be proportionate to the seriousness of the offence and the offender's degree of responsibility."[70]

That said, the relationship between rehabilitation and proportionality in the *YCJA* remains unclear. Given the wording of s. 38(2)(e) and the early jurisprudence, rehabilitation and reintegration are secondary to proportionality when a young person is being sentenced under the *YCJA*. Yet s. 38(2) also states that a sentencing judge must determine a youth sentence in accordance with the principles in s. 38 *and* the principles in

---

[67]   *R. v. M. (J.J.)*, [1993] S.C.J. No. 14, at para. 23, [1993] 2 S.C.R. 421 (S.C.C.).

[68]   For example, s. 39(5) states that a prison sentence cannot be imposed as a substitute for child protection, mental health or other social purposes. As Bala and Roberts suggest, this appears to prohibit a custody sentence for rehabilitative purposes if doing so would represent a disproportionately intrusive response to the offence: see Julian V. Roberts and Nicholas Bala, "Understanding Sentencing Under the *Youth Criminal Justice Act*" (2003) 41 Alta. L. Rev. 395, at paras. 3 and 4 (QL).

[69]   See some discussion of this in Richard Barnhorst, "The *Youth Criminal Justice Act*: New Directions and Implementation Issues" (April 2004) 46 Can. J. Crim. and Crim. J. 231, at 234.

[70]   *R. v. A.O.*, [2007] O.J. No. 800, at para. 44, 84 O.R. (3d) 561 (Ont. C.A.).

s. 3. Section 3 imposes an express duty on the youth criminal justice system (of which the judiciary is a key component) to emphasize rehabilitation and reintegration.[71] The importance of rehabilitation and reintegration is evident elsewhere in the Act and is also recognized in the binding jurisprudence, such as Charron J.'s holding in *R. v. B.W.P.; R. v. B.V.N.*[72] Justice Charron states clearly in that decision that sentencing under the *YCJA* is intended to be an individualized process that focuses on underlying causes, rehabilitation, reintegration and meaningful consequences for the offender.[73] Nevertheless, the Supreme Court of Canada has yet to directly consider the nature of the relationship between proportionality and rehabilitation in youth sentences.[74] Meanwhile, a combined reading of s. 38(2)(c) and (e) clearly suggests that a youth sentence cannot be disproportionate in terms of being overly severe to provide for rehabilitation, nor can it be less severe than proportionality requires to achieve rehabilitation. While some scholars reasonably contend that rehabilitation is to be given greater weight in the sentencing of young persons as compared to adults by virtue of the prominence of the concept throughout the *YCJA* and also because proportionality is not characterized as a fundamental sentencing principle in the *YCJA* as it is in the *Criminal Code*,[75] the concept of rehabilitation is subordinate to proportionality in s. 38 of the *YCJA*, which is the specific section of the *YCJA* aimed at sentencing.[76] This has led some scholars to query if rehabilitation can ever prevail over proportionality in the sentencing of young persons.[77] Short of definitive jurisprudential or statutory guidance, it appears at this juncture that whatever rehabilitative youth sentence is crafted, it must be fashioned within the confines of proportionality.[78]

---

[71]   *YCJA*, s. 3(1)(b)(i).

[72]   [2006] S.C.J. No. 27, [2006] 1 S.C.R. 941 (S.C.C.).

[73]   *R. v. B.W.P.; R. v. B.V.N.*, [2006] S.C.J. No. 27, at para. 31, [2006] 1 S.C.R. 941 (S.C.C.).

[74]   In *Reference re: Bill C-7 respecting the criminal justice system for young persons*, [2003] Q.J. No. 2850, at paras. 145-147 and 241 (Que. C.A.), the Quebec Court of Appeal takes the position that the proportionality principle is not a preponderant principle in the sentencing regime but only one of the key principles in the Act that must guide the court.

[75]   Julian V. Roberts and Nicholas Bala, "Understanding Sentencing Under the *Youth Criminal Justice Act*" (2003) 41 Alta. L. Rev. 395, at para. 39 (QL).

[76]   See a discussion of the relationship between proportionality and rehabilitation in Richard Barnhorst, "The *Youth Criminal Justice Act*: New Directions and Implementation Issues" (2004) 46 Can. J. Crim. and Crim. J. 231, at 244.

[77]   Richard Barnhorst, "The *Youth Criminal Justice Act*: New Directions and Implementation Issues" (2004) 46 Can. J. Crim. and Crim. J. 231, at para. 40.

[78]   The relationship between proportionality and rehabilitation remains the subject of ongoing debate. A discussion of this can be found in S. Anand, "Crafting Youth Sentences: The Roles of Rehabilitation, Proportionality, Restraint, Restorative Justice, and Race under the *Youth Criminal Justice Act*" (2003) 40 Alta. L. Rev. 943.

C.   Section 38(2)(d)

> (d)   all available sanctions other than custody that are reasonable in
> the circumstances should be considered for all young persons, with
> particular attention to the circumstances of aboriginal young
> persons

The principle of restraint in the use of custody for young persons, which is captured by s. 38(2)(d) of the *YCJA*, mirrors the principle of restraint in the sentencing of adults in s. 718.2(e) of the *Criminal Code*. Section 38(2)(d) is a general proviso that all available sanctions other than custody that are reasonable in the circumstances should be considered for all young persons, with particular attention to the circumstances of aboriginal young persons. To emphasize the point, the similar principle in s. 718.2(e) of the *Criminal Code* is expressly imported into the youth sentencing regime by virtue of s. 50 of the *YCJA*. Section 718.2(e) of the *Criminal Code* states: "A court that imposes a sentence shall also take into consideration the following principles: ... (e) all available sanctions other than imprisonment that are reasonable in the circumstances should be considered for all offenders, with particular attention to the circumstances of aboriginal offenders." The permissive nature of both of these clauses is noteworthy. The clause in both statutes instructs the judiciary that all available alternatives to custody *should* be considered in the circumstances. It does not use the imperative term *must*.

It is a significant provision, nevertheless, which was added to the *Criminal Code* as part of a major sentencing reform initiative that came into force in 1996.[79] The principle was replicated in the *YCJA* when it came into force in April 2003. Section 38(2)(d) of the *YCJA* is further buttressed by s. 3(1)(c)(iv) of the *YCJA*, which states that, within the limits of fair and proportionate accountability, the measures taken against young persons who commit offences should respect gender, ethnic, cultural and linguistic differences and respond to the needs of aboriginal young persons and of young persons with special requirements.[80]

Such provisions reflect in part the federal government's concern prior to the implementation of the *YCJA* regarding the overrepresentation of aboriginal people in the justice system generally, including the overrepresentation of aboriginal youth in correctional facilities throughout the country. Studies have consistently found that aboriginal youth are

---

[79]   The history of the 1996 sentencing reform initiative that culminated in a new Part XXIII of the *Criminal Code* is discussed in *R. v. Gladue*, [1999] S.C.J. No. 19, [1999] 1 S.C.R. 688 (S.C.C.).

[80]   See further discussion of the meaning of s. 3(1)(c)(iv) in Chapter 3.

overrepresented at every stage of the criminal justice process, including arrests, convictions and imprisonment.[81] Statistics Canada reported in 2001 that aboriginal youth represented about 7 per cent of the juvenile population in select provinces and territories but comprised 25 per cent of admissions to custodial facilities in 1998/99 in those same provinces and territories.[82] (A February 2004 study by the Research and Statistics Division of the federal Department of Justice entitled "A One-Day Snapshot of Aboriginal Youth in Custody Across Canada — Phase II" noted substantial reductions in the number of aboriginal youth in custody since 2000. Nevertheless, the snapshot found that aboriginal youth continued to experience significantly higher incarceration rates than non-aboriginal young persons — aboriginal youth were almost eight times more likely to be in custody compared to their non-aboriginal counterparts. While aboriginal youth comprised about 5 per cent of the Canadian population at the time of the study, 33 per cent of youth in custody were aboriginal.)[83]

The first version of the *YCJA*, Bill C-68, did not include specific references to aboriginal young persons. These references were added following the testimony of various witnesses at the committee stage. The National Criminal Justice Section of the Canadian Bar Association recommended the inclusion of s. 38(2)(d).[84]

The Supreme Court of Canada has provided considerable guidance on the meaning of s. 718(2)(e) of the *Criminal Code*. This jurisprudence, although developed in relation to an adult accused, is relevant to the sentencing of aboriginal young persons by virtue of s. 50 of the *YCJA*. Indeed, the courts have found that the principles enunciated in *Gladue*, as discussed below, apply with even greater force to the sentencing of young persons.[85]

---

[81] See the discussion in M. Denov, "Children's Rights, Juvenile Justice, and the U.N. *Convention on the Rights of the Child*: Implications for Canada" in Kathryn Campbell, ed., *Understanding Youth Justice in Canada* (Toronto: Pearson Education Inc., 2005), 65 at 76.

[82] J. Latimer and L. Casey, "A One-Day Snapshot of Aboriginal Youth in Custody Across Canada: Phase II", Research and Statistics Division, Department of Justice Canada, Youth Justice Policy, February 2004, at 1.

[83] J. Latimer and L. Casey, "A One-Day Snapshot of Aboriginal Youth in Custody Across Canada: Phase II", Research and Statistics Division, Department of Justice Canada, Youth Justice Policy, February 2004, at iii and 3.

[84] Canadian Bar Association, Submission on Bill C-3 (Ottawa: Canadian Bar Association, 2000), at 17. Julian V. Roberts and Nicholas Bala, "Understanding Sentencing Under the *Youth Criminal Justice Act*" (2003) 41 Alta. L. Rev. 395, at para. 48 (QL).

[85] *R. v. L.E.K.*, [1999] Y.J. No. 119, at para. 60 (Y.T. Youth Ct.).

In *R. v. Gladue*,[86] Cory and Iacobucci JJ. reviewed the parliamentary record, the legislative history of the new *Criminal Code* sentencing regime as well as the evidence concerning Canada's historical use of incarceration. They observed that Canada had the second or third highest incarceration rate generally, and that "the serious problem of aboriginal overrepresentation in Canadian prisons" is well documented.[87] Justices Cory and Iacobucci held that s. 718.2(e) was designed to respond to the problem of "overincarceration" in Canada generally and, in particular, to address the more acute problem of the disproportionate incarceration of aboriginal peoples.[88]

The court referred to comments by then Justice Minister Allan Rock, who had stated that the specific reference to aboriginal persons in s. 718.2(e) was an attempt to encourage courts to consider alternatives to custody because of the overrepresentation of aboriginal persons in the prison population, where it is consistent with protection of the public. By 1997, aboriginal people comprised about 3 per cent of the population but amounted to 12 per cent of all federal inmates.[89] The situation was significantly worse in some provinces, such as Manitoba and Saskatchewan, where, by the mid-1990s, aboriginal persons made up 55 per cent and 72 per cent of admissions to provincial correctional facilities respectively, the court noted.[90]

Justices Cory and Iacobucci interpreted s. 718.2(e) as Parliament's direction to the judiciary to attempt to address this social problem by inquiring into its causes and doing whatever they could within their mandate to alleviate it through the sentencing process.[91] Although the court recognized that the disproportionate incarceration of aboriginal persons stems from various factors including poverty and substance abuse, and that sentencing judges have a limited role in solving the problem, it nevertheless noted that sentencing judges determine most directly whether an aboriginal person will go to jail or whether other sentencing options may be more useful in repairing the harm done and in preventing future crime.[92]

---

[86] [1999] S.C.J. No. 19, [1999] 1 S.C.R. 688 (S.C.C.). See also *R. v. Wells*, [2000] S.C.J. No. 11, [2000] 1 S.C.R. 207 (S.C.C.) and *R. v. Kakekagamick*, [2006] O.J. No. 3346, at para. 39, 211 C.C.C. (3d) 289 (Ont. C.A.).

[87] *R. v. Gladue*, [1999] S.C.J. No. 19, at paras. 52 and 59, [1999] 1 S.C.R. 688 (S.C.C.).

[88] *R. v. Gladue*, [1999] S.C.J. No. 19, at para. 50, [1999] 1 S.C.R. 688 (S.C.C.).

[89] *R. v. Gladue*, [1999] S.C.J. No. 19, at para. 58, [1999] 1 S.C.R. 688 (S.C.C.).

[90] *R. v. Gladue*, [1999] S.C.J. No. 19, at para. 58, [1999] 1 S.C.R. 688 (S.C.C.).

[91] *R. v. Gladue*, [1999] S.C.J. No. 19, at para. 64, [1999] 1 S.C.R. 688 (S.C.C.).

[92] *R. v. Gladue*, [1999] S.C.J. No. 19, at para. 65, [1999] 1 S.C.R. 688 (S.C.C.).

The court ultimately held that the effect of s. 718.2(e) is to alter the method of analysis that judges use in determining a fit sentence for aboriginal offenders. The section directs sentencing judges to pay particular attention to the circumstances of aboriginal offenders because those circumstances are unique and different from those of non-aboriginal offenders. In particular, the section requires the judge to consider the unique systemic or background factors which may have played a role in bringing the aboriginal person before the court, such as the impact of dislocation, in the form of poverty, substance abuse and poor social and economic conditions, as well as systemic and direct discrimination. Judges must also consider the types of sentencing procedures and sanctions that may be appropriate in light of the aboriginal person's heritage, the court found. Aboriginal people generally have different conceptions of appropriate sentencing procedures and sanctions, it noted. The traditional sentencing ideals of deterrence, separation and denunciation are often out of sync with the understanding of sentencing held by offenders and their community, said the court. Most traditional aboriginal conceptions of sentencing place a primary emphasis on the principles of restorative justice, the court held. Community-based sanctions coincide with the aboriginal concept of sentencing and the needs of aboriginal people and communities.[93]

By applying this different method of analysis, the *Gladue* court concluded that the jail term for an aboriginal offender may, in some circumstances, be less than the sentence of a non-aboriginal person for the same offence. But the more violent the crime, the more likely that the length of the jail sentence will be the same for similar offences and offenders, whether or not the offender is aboriginal.[94]

In practice, this means that all judges must take judicial notice of the systemic or background factors and the approach to sentencing that is relevant to aboriginal offenders. In individual cases it may mean that some evidence will be required to assist the judge in determining the sentence. If a particular offender does not want such evidence to be adduced, the right to have particular attention paid to his or her circumstances can be waived.[95]

Several years later, in *R. v. Wells*,[96] the Supreme Court of Canada clarified that while s. 718.2(e) requires a different methodology for

---

[93]   *R. v. Gladue*, [1999] S.C.J. No. 19, at paras. 66-75, [1999] 1 S.C.R. 688 (S.C.C.), in particular in relation to the comments in this paragraph.

[94]   *R. v. Gladue*, [1999] S.C.J. No. 19, at para. 37, [1999] 1 S.C.R. 688 (S.C.C.).

[95]   *R. v. Gladue*, [1999] S.C.J. No. 19, at para. 83, [1999] 1 S.C.R. 688 (S.C.C.).

[96]   [2000] S.C.J. No. 11, [2000] 1 S.C.R. 207 (S.C.C.).

determining a fit sentence for an aboriginal offender, is does not necessarily mandate a different result.[97] Section 718.2(e) does not alter the fundamental duty of the sentencing judge to impose a fit sentence,[98] nor does the application of s. 718.2(e) mean that aboriginal offenders must be sentenced so that the principle of restorative justice always trumps other sentencing principles such as deterrence, denunciation and separation.[99]

Section 38(2)(d) should be considered in the context of *Gladue* and its progeny, and, predictably, it has been the subject of considerable academic discourse and debate.[100] Some critics suggest that the section, when read within the larger context of the Act, is a specific direction to youth justice court judges to use non-custodial sentences for aboriginal young persons unless there appears to be too great a risk that the young person will not comply with a community-based sentence or poses too great a risk to public safety. They further suggest that the provision, because it has not been made subject to proportionality, permits a judge to impose a disproportionately lenient sentence on a young aboriginal person.[101] During the parliamentary debates, most political parties did not refute this interpretation.

Federal Justice Minister Martin Cauchon explained at the time: "It is disturbing to see such a large number of young aboriginals in detention centres . . . The amendment proposed by the Senate (adding s. 38(2)(d) to the *YCJA*) and the new act will provide a framework that will promote a fairer justice system that will be better suited to young aboriginals' needs."[102] Canadian Alliance MP Chuck Cadman criticized the new section for singling out young aboriginal offenders as worthy of less punitive sanctions by virtue of race alone.[103] The academic literature of the day documented the controversy, noting that critics charged that

---

[97] *R. v. Wells*, [2000] S.C.J. No. 11, at para. 44, [2000] 1 S.C.R. 207 (S.C.C.).

[98] *R. v. Wells*, [2000] S.C.J. No. 11, at para. 44, [2000] 1 S.C.R. 207 (S.C.C.).

[99] *R. v. Wells*, [2000] S.C.J. No. 11, at para. 44, [2000] 1 S.C.R. 207 (S.C.C.).

[100] See for example S. Anand, "Crafting Youth Sentences: The Roles of Rehabilitation, Proportionality, Restraint, Restorative Justice, and Race Under the *Youth Criminal Justice Act*" (2003) 40 Alta. L. Rev. 943, at paras. 40-41 (QL); P. Stenning and J.V. Roberts, "Empty Promises: Parliament, The Supreme Court, and the Sentencing of Aboriginal Offenders" (2001) 64 Sask. L. Rev. 137 and J. Rudin and K. Roach, "Broken Promises: A Response to Stenning and Roberts' 'Empty Promises'" (2002) 65 Sask. L. Rev. 3.

[101] S. Anand, "Crafting Youth Sentences: The Roles of Rehabilitation, Proportionality, Restraint, Restorative Justice, and Race Under the *Youth Criminal Justice Act*" (2003) 40 Alta. L. Rev. 943, at paras. 40-41 (QL).

[102] *House of Commons Debates* (30 January 2002), at 8491, 8492.

[103] *House of Commons Debates* (30 January 2002), at 8505, and as discussed in S. Anand, "Crafting Youth Sentences: The Roles of Rehabilitation, Proportionality, Restraint, Restorative Justice, and Race Under the *Youth Criminal Justice Act*" (2003) 40 Alta. L. Rev. 943.

aboriginal status in particular, rather than a disadvantaged background in general, was being permitted to determine the sentence.[104]

Despite the suggestion that s. 38(2)(d) is not subservient to the principle of proportionality whereas certain other sentencing principles in s. 38(2) are, a plain reading of s. 38(2)(c) suggests that *all* youth sentences must be proportionate. In effect, the result of the interplay of these two provisions is that, when considering reasonable alternatives to custody under s. 38(2)(d), the youth justice court judge is obliged to pay particular attention to the circumstances of an aboriginal young person. An examination of the circumstances of a young aboriginal person before the court may well result in the judge defining proportionality differently in a given case as a result of his or her assessment of the degree of responsibility of the young aboriginal person.

Some scholars have predicted that the practical effect of the new section, as discussed in *Gladue*, will result in aboriginal offenders being less likely to receive custodial sentences than non-aboriginal persons. When they do receive a custodial sentence, it can be expected to be a shorter sentence than that received by a non-aboriginal offender in similar circumstances.[105] That said, the Supreme Court of Canada unquestionably clarified the scope of s. 718.2(e) (and by logical extension s. 38(2)(d)) when it held in *R. v. Wells* that, despite the obligation of a sentencing judge to pay particular attention to the circumstances of aboriginal offenders, the fundamental duty of a sentencing judge is to impose a fit sentence.[106]

D.   The Absence of Deterrence and Denunciation

The sentencing principles in s. 38(2) of the *YCJA*, which are designed to assist judges in imposing youth sentences, are notable, in part, for what is missing from them. A number of the key sentencing principles in the *Criminal Code* that apply to adults are not sentencing principles for young persons who receive youth sentences under the *YCJA*. The principles of general and specific deterrence, as well as the principle of denunciation, all of which are sentencing principles for those sentenced as adults under the *Criminal Code*, are not included among the sentencing principles in s. 38(2)

---

[104]   Julian V. Roberts and Nicholas Bala, "Understanding Sentencing Under the *Youth Criminal Justice Act*" (2003) 41 Alta. L. Rev. 395, at para. 48 (QL).

[105]   P. Stenning and J.V. Roberts, "Empty Promises: Parliament, The Supreme Court, and the Sentencing of Aboriginal Offenders" (2001) 64 Sask. L. Rev. 137, at 162.

[106]   For an excellent illustration of the application of the *Gladue* factors (s. 718.2(e)) in a case involving a young aboriginal person, see *R. v. T.D.P.*, [2004] S.J. No. 254 (Sask. Prov. Ct.). See also *R. v. Bird*, [2008] A.J. No. 609, at paras. 65-68 (Alta. Q.B.).

of the *YCJA*. It is well documented and widely acknowledged that Parliament deliberately excluded deterrence (both specific and general) as a sentencing principle for young persons who are being sentenced to youth sentences under the *YCJA*.[107] By virtue of s. 50 of the *YCJA*, the only adult sentencing principle that is a consideration in sentencing a young person to a youth sentence under the *YCJA* is s. 718.2(e), which concerns the principle of restraint in the use of custody, as previously discussed. As Charron J. of the Supreme Court of Canada held for the majority in *R . v. B.W.P.; R. v. B.V.N.*, the sentencing principle of deterrence in the *Criminal Code* was not imported into the *YCJA*. "Since Parliament has expressly included other provisions, in particular one of the adult sentencing principles — s. 718.2(e) with respect to aboriginal offenders — one can only conclude that the omission is deliberate. Parliament chose not to incorporate the adult sentencing principle of deterrence into the new youth sentencing regime."[108] Had Parliament intended to make deterrence part of the youth sentencing regime, one would reasonably expect that it would have expressly included the principle, Charron J. held.[109] The record of the Parliamentary Standing Committee on Justice and Human Rights, which examined the provisions of the *YCJA*, reveals that the possible exclusion of deterrence as a sentencing principle in the *YCJA* was a live issue, which further supports the conclusion that the drafters' omission of it was deliberate,[110] Charron J. concluded.

The 2006 decision in *R. v. B.W.P.; R. v. B.V.N.* settled a significant sentencing issue that had divided the lower courts across Canada since the *YCJA* came into force in 2003. Under the *YOA*, the Supreme Court of Canada had recognized deterrence as a sentencing principle for young persons but one of lesser import in the sentencing of young persons than for adults.[111]

Canadian youth justice experts suggest that the principle of general deterrence was excluded as a sentencing principle for young persons who receive youth sentences under the *YCJA* because it was believed that a young person should not be punished more severely for a particular crime in order to deter other young persons from committing similar crimes. This position is consistent with research that indicates that increasing the severity

---

[107] Justice Charron reaches this conclusion in *R. v B.W.P.; R. v. B.V.N.*, [2006] S.C.J. No. 27, at paras. 22-23, [2006] 1 S.C.R. 941 (S.C.C.).

[108] *R. v B.W.P.; R. v. B.V.N.*, [2006] S.C.J. No. 27, at para. 23, [2006] 1 S.C.R. 941 (S.C.C.). Justice Charron held that the concept of deterrence could not be read into the *YCJA* based on the wording of the Act.

[109] *R. v. B.W.P.; R. v B.V.N.*, [2006] S.C.J. No. 27, at para. 24, [2006] 1 S.C.R. 941 (S.C.C.).

[110] *R. v. B.W.P.; R. v B.V.N.*, [2006] S.C.J. No. 27, at para. 37, [2006] 1 S.C.R. 941 (S.C.C.).

[111] *R. v. M. (J.J.)*, [1993] S.C.J. No. 14, [1993] 2 S.C.R. 421 (S.C.C.).

of punishment, such as through the imposition of more severe jail sentences, will not deter youthful offending, whereas increasing the perceived certainty of apprehension can have a deterrent effect.[112] "The reality is that young people who are committing these offences are simply not thinking about the consequences of getting caught."[113] That said, there are documented cases where young persons have admitted planning and committing crimes at least in part because they believed that they would not get caught, or that the punishment would be so minimal as to be irrelevant. The U.S. case of *Roper v. Simmons* is a case in point.[114] At the age of 17, Christopher Simmons planned and committed a murder, which involved breaking into a home with his 15-year-old accomplice, where they bound the woman inside, drove her to a state park, walked her to a railroad trestle spanning a river, hog-tied her with electrical cable, bound her face completely with duct tape and pushed her, still alive, from the trestle. She drowned in the waters below. Prior to the murder, the evidence indicates that Simmons encouraged his friends to participate and indicated that they could get away with it

---

[112] Nicholas Bala, *Youth Criminal Justice Law* (Toronto: Irwin Law Inc., 2003), at 408. See also the testimony of Bala before the Nunn Commission of Inquiry, Transcript of Hearing, Vol. 16, February 16, 2006, at 2876; and the Nova Scotia Nunn Commission of Inquiry, *Spiralling out of Control: Lessons Learned from a Boy in Trouble: Report of the Nunn Commission of Inquiry* (Halifax, NS: Nunn Commission of Inquiry, 2006). This report is available online at: <http://www.gov.ns.ca/just/nunn_commission/_docs/Report_Nunn_Final.pdf>.

See also A.N. Doob, V. Marinos and K.N. Varma, *Youth Crime and the Youth Justice System in Canada* (Toronto: University of Toronto, Centre of Criminology, 1995), at 69. In his classic treatise, *Of Crimes and Punishments*, published in 1764, Cesare Beccaria made this same fundamental point — that it is not the severity of punishment but the certainty of detection — that can deter criminals. Further, as the Supreme Court of Canada observes in *R. v. Gladue*, [1999] S.C.J. No. 19, at para. 60, [1999] 1 S.C.R. 688 (S.C.C.), study after study in Canada since 1914 has repeatedly concluded that prison is not effective in reducing crime.

The issue of deterrence came to the fore in the House of Commons in the fall of 2007 when Opposition parties challenged the Conservative government by suggesting that there is no evidence that stiffer sentences will deter young persons from offending and therefore no logical reason to include deterrence as a principle of sentencing under the *YCJA*. See, for example, *House of Commons Debates* (22 November 2007), at 1155 (Lib) and 1330 (BQ) and *House of Commons Debates* (26 November 2007), at 1715 (NDP) and 1745 (BQ).

The controversial issue of whether deterrence "works" is a large question beyond the scope of this book; it has its own sizeable body of research. It is not the goal of this book to consider or answer that question. However, some interesting recent work that has considered the general relationship between stiffer jail sentences and crime rates include F. Zimring, *The Great American Crime Decline* (Oxford: Oxford University Press, 2007) and James Austin *et al.*, *Unlocking America* (Washington, D.C.: The JFA Institute, 2007). Both pieces of research find little empirical support for the contention that stiffer penalties act as a general deterrent.

[113] Testimony of Nicholas Bala before the Nunn Commission of Inquiry, Transcript of Hearing, Vol. 16, February 16, 2006, at 2877; see also the Nova Scotia Nunn Commission of Inquiry, *Spiralling out of Control: Lessons Learned from a Boy in Trouble: Report of the Nunn Commission of Inquiry* (Halifax, NS: Nunn Commission of Inquiry, 2006). This report is available online at: <http://www.gov.ns.ca/just/nunn_commission/_docs/Report_Nunn_Final.pdf>.

[114] *Roper v. Simmons*, 543 U.S. 551 (2005).

because they were minors. While it is unclear what Simmons meant by believing they could "get away with it" because they were minors, he appears to have meant that the penalty would not be significant because they were minors. The fact that they were minors at the time of the commission of the crime only becomes relevant if they were caught. Simmons therefore appears to have turned his mind to the severity of the punishment, perhaps in addition to considering the likelihood of getting caught, prior to the commission of the crime.

This distinction between a young person's perception of the certainty of detection and his or her knowledge of the severity of the punishment, if caught and punished, is, to some degree, illusory. The two concepts are linked. A young person is less likely to be deterred from committing a crime even if the perceived likelihood of getting caught is high if the penalty is perceived to be so minor that it is virtually non-existent.[115]

The principle of denunciation, which is also absent from the sentencing principles regarding youth sentences under the *YCJA*, has been the subject of less jurisprudential attention. The Supreme Court of Canada has defined the concept as the "communication of society's condemnation of the offender's conduct ... a symbolic, collective statement that the offender's conduct should be punished for encroaching on our society's basic code of values".[116] Similar to the principle of deterrence, the principle of denunciation was also excluded as a sentencing principle under the *YCJA* by virtue of s. 50 of the *YCJA*.[117] Justice Hamilton of the Manitoba Court of Appeal reasoned that a sentence premised on the principle of denunciation is intended to communicate a symbolic statement to the public, which is at odds with the focus of the sentence being on the young person.[118] Nevertheless, Hamilton J.A. distinguished between the effect of finding a young person guilty (which is in effect denunciation of the young person's conduct) and the *specific application* of the principle of denunciation when sentencing a young person under the *YCJA*.[119]

In summary, what the youth justice court judge cannot do is to increase the severity of a youth sentence to address the principles of either

---

[115] A great deal has been written on this subject by experts in the field. It is not a subject that can be properly examined within the confines of this book.

[116] The words of Lamer C.J.C. are referred to in *R. v. C.T.*, [2005] M.J. No. 515, at para. 24 (Man. C.A.).

[117] On this point, see cases such as *R. v. A.O.*, [2007] O.J. No. 800, 218 C.C.C. (3d) 409 (Ont. C.A.) and *R. v. C.T.*, [2005] M.J. No. 515, at para. 25 (Man. C.A.).

[118] *R. v. C.T.*, [2005] M.J. No. 515, at para. 29 (Man. C.A.).

[119] *R. v. C.T.*, [2005] M.J. No. 515, at para. 28 (Man. C.A.).

denunciation or deterrence, since neither principle is a sentencing principle in relation to the imposition of youth sentences under the *YCJA*.

Nevertheless, the distinction between the related concepts of deterrence and denunciation remains somewhat amorphous. The distinction can perhaps be best understood by adopting a purposive approach. While the application of the denunciation principle means imposing a sentence that sends a message of societal condemnation for certain criminal conduct, often in relation to particularly offensive or egregious crimes, the application of the deterrence principle means imposing a sentence for the express purpose of deterring future crimes similar in nature. That said, both general deterrence and denunciation are dependent in part on the publicizing of the sentencing. Neither principle can be given its full effect if the sentence is not publicized to the larger society.

The federal Conservative government introduced a bill in November 2007 that would, among other things, have incorporated deterrence and denunciation into the *YCJA* as sentencing principles for young persons who receive youth sentences under the *YCJA*. The proposed reform said that, subject to proportionality, the sentence *may* have the following objectives: to denounce unlawful conduct, and to deter the young person and other young persons from committing offences.[120] These particular reforms could have resulted in more severe penalties for young persons at a time when the value and efficacy of jail as a punishment remains a live issue among researchers, academics, politicians and the public at large.[121] In fact, as the Supreme Court of Canada has noted, study after study in Canada since 1914 has found that incarceration has failed to reduce the crime rate, is not a strong deterrent, and is not effective in rehabilitating the individuals who are imprisoned.[122] There has been at least one commission or inquiry in Canada concerning the effectiveness of prison in each decade of the 20th century since 1914, all of which have reached the conclusion noted above.[123]

While most young persons who receive prison sentences will eventually be released back into the community, temporary incapacitation — keeping a particular young person off the streets even for a period of time — may be enough of an achievement for some Canadians. It provides certainty that a particular young person will not pose a threat to

---

[120] Bill C-25, *An Act to amend the Youth Criminal Justice Act*, 2d Sess., 39th Parl., 2007 (1st reading 19 November 2007).

[121] Bill C-25 died on the Order Paper in the fall of 2008.

[122] *R. v. Gladue*, [1999] S.C.J. No. 19, at paras. 54 to 57, [1999] 1 S.C.R. 688 (S.C.C.).

[123] Justice Vancise made this observation in his dissent in *R. v. McDonald*, [1997] S.J. No. 117, 113 C.C.C. (3d) 418 (Sask. C.A.).

public safety during the period of imprisonment. But, in view of the preponderance of research that has concluded that stiffer sentences do not reduce crime, Canadians may risk their own public safety if they believe that more and stiffer jail sentences are the panacea, and if they fail to press their governments for ongoing research regarding what measures and programs are most effective in reducing youth crime. Why, for example, is Quebec the only province in which youth crime rates are not increasing?[124] It appears that no targeted Canadian government research has been undertaken to explore this interesting question, which could yield useful insights and lessons for crime prevention and future policy making.

E. Relationship Between Sentencing Principles in the *YCJA* and Other Federal Acts

In addition to the sentencing principles in the *Criminal Code*, the *Controlled Drugs and Substances Act*[125] contains additional sentencing principles, and aggravating factors that pertain to most drug offences. The relationship between these *CDSA* sentencing principles and aggravating factors and the sentencing principles and factors in the *YCJA* is not explicitly addressed in the *YCJA*. Nor is the relationship between the sentencing principles and penalties in other federal Acts and those in the *YCJA* directly addressed (except for the *Criminal Code*). For example, which penalties prevail when a young person is to receive a youth sentence in relation to an offence under the *Excise Act, 2001*,[126] which contains a system of fines different (and greater) than those available for youth sentences under the *YCJA*? While s. 50 of the *YCJA* indicates that most of the sentencing principles in the *Criminal Code* do not apply to young persons who receive youth sentences under the *YCJA*, s. 50 is silent regarding the relationship between the sentencing principles and penalties in other federal Acts and those in the *YCJA* when a young person is to receive a youth sentence.

Both the existence of the specific sentencing scheme in the *YCJA* as well as the wording of ss. 38 and 42 of the *YCJA* indicate that the sentencing principles and penalties in the *YCJA* prevail when a youth sentence is being imposed on a young person.[127] The Supreme Court of Canada has

---

[124] According to Statistics Canada, all provinces except Quebec reported an annual increase in their police-reported youth crime rate in 2006. Andrea Taylor-Butts and Angela Bressan, Youth Crime in Canada, 2006 Statistics Canada — Catalogue no. 85-002-XIE, Vol. 28, no. 3.

[125] S.C. 1996, c. 19 [hereafter "*CDSA*"].

[126] S.C. 2002, c. 22.

[127] The implied exception rule of statutory interpretation, otherwise known as *generalia specialibus non derogant*, also suggests that the specific provisions in the *YCJA* regarding

affirmed that, pursuant to s. 50 of the *YCJA*, the sentencing principles in the *YCJA* govern the sentencing of a young person who is to receive a youth sentence.[128] That said, the Supreme Court of Canada has not directly considered the relationship between the *CDSA* sentencing principles and aggravating factors and those of the *YCJA* in cases where a young person has been found guilty of a drug offence. Nor has it considered the question in relation to a conflict between a penalty available under another federal Act and the penalties available under the *YCJA* for a young person who is to receive a youth sentence.

The answer to the question may seem obvious in the case of youth sentences imposed on young persons in relation to offences under most federal Acts. But the answer may be more nuanced in relation to sentences for drug offences under the *CDSA*. Section 38(2) of the *YCJA* indicates that a youth justice court that imposes a youth sentence shall determine the sentence in accordance with the principles set out in s. 3 and s. 38(2) of the *YCJA*. Nevertheless, neither s. 3 nor s. 38 expressly excludes the sentencing principles or aggravating factors identified in other federal Acts, such as those in the *CDSA*. In fact, s. 38(3)(f) of the *YCJA* permits the court to consider any other aggravating circumstances related to the young person or the offence but does not specifically identify them. In a relevant drug case involving a young person, it is reasonable for the Crown to draw to the court's attention a particular aggravating factor in s. 10(2) of the *CDSA* that is relevant.

Defence counsel could conceivably argue that these aggravating factors in s. 10(2) of the *CDSA* were not intended to apply to young persons because s. 10(2) of the *CDSA* refers to a person *convicted* of a designated substance offence whereas young persons are generally not *convicted* of offences, they are found guilty. The term conviction is not used in relation to a young person found guilty of an offence under the *YCJA* unless that young person receives an adult sentence for the offence,[129] or the young person is convicted of committing an offence as an adult while access to his or her youth record is open, in which case the youth record is considered a conviction for purposes of the *Criminal Records Act*.[130]

---

the sentencing of young persons trump more general sentencing and penalty provisions in other federal statutes, although this argument may be less persuasive in relation to the sentencing principles and aggravating factors in the *CDSA*, which deal specifically with drug offences. For a discussion of this rule, see Ruth Sullivan, *Sullivan on the Construction of Statutes*, 5th ed. (LexisNexis Canada Inc., 2008), at 343.

[128]   *R. v. B.W.P.; R. v. B.V.N.*, [2006] S.C.J. No. 27, [2006] 1 S.C.R. 941 (S.C.C.).

[129]   *YCJA*, s. 117.

[130]   *YCJA*, s. 119(9)(b) and (c).

The general practice of the trial courts is to sentence young persons for drug offences in accordance with the sentencing principles and factors in the *YCJA* that govern youth sentences[131] unless the young person has been found to be eligible for an adult sentence, in which case the sentencing principles in the *Criminal Code* apply.

Section 14 of the *YCJA* is arguably a complete answer to the question. As discussed in Chapter 2, s. 14 of the *YCJA* assigns to the youth justice court exclusive jurisdiction in respect of any offence alleged to have been committed by a young person and states that the young person shall be dealt with as provided in the *YCJA despite any other Act of Parliament* (subject to only the *National Defence Act* and the *Contraventions Act*). Thus, unless the offence is dealt with under the *Contraventions Act* or the *National Defence Act*, or the young person is determined to be eligible for an adult sentence, in which case the sentencing principles in the *Criminal Code* apply, the *YCJA* sentencing principles apply to a young person who is to be sentenced.

IV. FACTORS TO BE CONSIDERED — SECTION 38(3)

> *(3) In determining a youth sentence, the youth justice court shall take into account*
>
> *(a) the degree of participation by the young person in the commission of the offence;*
>
> *(b) the harm done to victims and whether it was intentional or reasonably foreseeable;*
>
> *(c) any reparation made by the young person to the victim or the community;*
>
> *(d) the time spent in detention by the young person as a result of the offence;*
>
> *(e) the previous findings of guilt of the young person; and*
>
> *(f) any other aggravating and mitigating circumstances related to the young person or the offence that are relevant to the purpose and principles set out in this section.*

In addition to the sentencing principles in s. 3 and s. 38(2) of the *YCJA*, the sentencing judge is obliged to consider the above-mentioned

---

[131] By way of random example, see *R. v. T.M.*, [2003] S.J. No. 722 (Sask. Prov. Ct.); *R. v. L.P.*, [2004] O.J. No. 1484 (Ont. C.J.) and *R. v. J.F.*, [2004] O.J. No. 3357 (Ont. C.J.).

factors in s. 38(3) in determining the appropriate youth sentence in a given case. Most of these factors are straightforward, and their relevance as aggravating or mitigating factors will be determined based on the facts of the specific case. However, because s. 38 of the *YCJA* does not rank the sentencing principles and factors in order of importance beyond suggesting that the principles in s. 38(2)(e) are subservient to the principle of proportionality, it is unclear how the factors in s. 38(3) relate to the principles in s. 3 and in s. 38(2) in the event of a conflict.

The focus of academic critique of the s. 38(3) factors is sometimes on those that are excluded. Scholars have registered surprise that the mitigating factor of age is not among the factors cited, since, they argue, correlation between age and severity of punishment is common to all Western juvenile justice systems. In other words, the younger the person, the more significant the factor of age as a mitigating factor on sentence: the 12-year-old will be treated more leniently than the 17-year-old.[132] Parliament may have reasoned that age, as a factor, was already addressed in s. 3(1)(b)(ii), which recognizes the relevance of the reduced level of maturity of young persons.[133]

A.   Section 38(3)(a) — The Degree of Participation in the Offence

The role of the young person in the commission of the offence is a highly relevant sentencing factor. The courts are likely to sentence a young person more harshly if he or she were the gang leader or the instigator of the crime rather than merely a party to it, or an aider or abetter. Likewise the courts will look more harshly on a crime that involves planning as opposed to a crime that is spontaneous, such as a violent reaction to a lifetime of parental abuse. In *R. v. E.B.C.*,[134] the 17-year-old accused broke into the victim's home with four others and beat him with a baseball bat following a confrontation earlier in the day between the victim and the accused's sister. The beating affected the victim's short-term memory, caused him to suffer seizures and prevented him from working for 14 months. The other four individuals were never arrested, consequently, the Crown could not clarify the accused's role in the assault since the victim did not know who struck the blows. The trial judge concluded that the assault was prompted by an altercation between

---

[132]   Julian V. Roberts and Nicholas Bala, "Understanding Sentencing Under the *Youth Criminal Justice Act*" (2003) 41 Alta. L. Rev. 395, at para. 53 (QL).

[133]   *YCJA*, s. 3(1)(b)(ii).

[134]   [2005] A.J. No. 120 (Alta. C.A.).

the victim and the sister of the accused, which suggested that the accused was the instigator. He further found that because the accused had acted as part of a gang, he must accept the highest degree of responsibility. The Alberta Appeal Court upheld the trial judge in finding the accused fully responsible for the assault, having found nothing to indicate that the accused was anything other than a full and active participant in the offence. The gang nature of the activity was significant. "When a person acts in concert with members of a group or gang to victimize a single victim, that person must accept the consequences that flow from the group action."[135]

B.   Section 38(3)(b) and (c) — Harm Done to the Victim

Section 38(3)(b) and (c) requires the judge to assess the harm done to the victim and whether it was intentional or reasonably foreseeable, as well as any reparation made by the offender to the victim or to the community. This assessment will be based on facts and evidence that are before the court.

C.   Section 38(3)(d) — Credit for Time Served

Section 38(3)(d) requires the judge to "take into account" any time the young person has already spent in detention prior to trial in determining the length of the youth sentence. This section is modelled on the general practice in the adult system of giving adults credit for time already served in custody prior to sentence, although the wording in the two sections is notably different. Section 719(3)[136] of the *Criminal Code* says that any time spent in custody *may* be taken into account in determining the sentence, whereas s. 38(3)(d) of the *YCJA* says that the court *shall* take into account the time spent in detention.[137] In practice, this mandatory obligation on the youth justice court judge to take into account any time spent in custody by the young person in determining his or her sentence led, at least initially, to some inconsistent decisions across jurisdictions because judges tended to give wide-ranging interpretations to the meaning of the term "take into account". While the law on this point is nuanced and actively evolving, the jurisprudential trend at the appellate level is that courts are finding that the expression "take into account" does not necessarily mean that the young person will receive a reduction in the

---

[135] *R. v. E.B.C.*, [2005] A.J. No. 120, at para. 9 (Alta. C.A.). See also *R. v. N. (H.T.)*, [2006] B.C.J. No. 974, 209 C.C.C. (3d) 318 (B.C.C.A.).

[136] At the time of writing, a bill (Bill C-25) to amend the *Criminal Code* to limit the credit a judge may allow for any time spent in pre-sentencing custody was before Parliament.

[137] *R. v. B. (T.)*, [2006] O.J. No. 584, at para. 24, 206 C.C.C. (3d) 405 (Ont. C.A.).

length of the custodial sentence to account for time already served; it simply means that the court must consider the time already spent in custody in determining the sentence. In other words, the judge is obliged to consider or acknowledge the time the young person spent in pre-trial custody without necessarily giving him or her credit for it by reducing the sentence. Credit may be given in other ways.

In *R. v. N.W.P.*,[138] the Manitoba Court of Appeal held that the trial judge did not err when he declined to grant a young person any credit in terms of sentence reduction for the 238 days spent in custody prior to his plea and sentencing. The sentencing judge was required to consider the time the young person spent in detention before the trial in determining an appropriate sentence and he did so, but he was not bound, especially in cases where the maximum sentence or near maximum is imposed, to reduce the sentence to be served to reflect the time spent in detention, the court held. The Manitoba Court of Appeal upheld the 10-year sentence that the young person received following his guilty plea for first degree murder, the maximum sentence under the *YCJA*. During the course of his decision, Monnin J.A. conducted a detailed review of the relevant jurisprudence. Justice Monnin relied in part on the ruling of the Supreme Court of Canada in *R. v. D.B.*,[139] observing that the high court appeared to accept that a youth justice court judge may impose the maximum sentence even when the offender has already spent significant time in pre-sentence custody.

Likewise, the Ontario Court of Appeal held in *R. v. D.W.*[140] that it was proper to sentence a young person to the maximum sentence available for second degree murder under the *YCJA* despite the 2.5 years he had already spent in pre-trial custody. Although the sentencing judge was required to take pre-trial custody into account, the term "taking into account" does not mean the sentencing judge must directly deduct the time spent in pre-trial custody. Rather, the sentencing judge has a broad discretion to take pre-trial custody into account as a consideration in deciding whether D.W. would serve a youth or an adult sentence. The Ontario appeal court imposed the maximum youth sentence for a guilty finding for second degree murder. (Having reasoned that he was required to give the young person full credit for the 2.5 years already spent in pre-trial custody, the trial judge had concluded that a further 18 months in custody available under the *YCJA* would not be enough to hold the young persons sufficiently accountable; thus, he concluded that he had to impose an adult sentence.)[141]

---

[138]   [2008] M.J. No. 304 (Man. C.A.).
[139]   [2008] S.C.J. No. 25, at para. 14, 2008 SCC 25 (S.C.C.).
[140]   [2008] O.J. No. 1356 (Ont. C.A.).
[141]   *R. v. D.W.*, [2008] O.J. No. 1356, at paras. 1-6 (Ont. C.A.).

More recently, in *R. v. S. (D.)*,[142] the Ontario Court of Appeal explained that the credit to be given for pre-sentence custody is a discretionary matter; it is not a mechanical calculation. "There are a number of ways in which pre-sentence detention can be 'taken into account', including in the decision to reduce the type or severity of the sentence."[143] However, the court also appeared to affirm the principle that only in exceptional cases should the youth justice court exercise its discretion to reduce the credit given below 1:1.[144]

The Ontario Court of Appeal had initially appeared more emphatic in suggesting that s. 38(3)(d) generally requires the judge to deduct time served from the sentence of a young person. The sentencing judge has a residuary discretion, however, within a certain range, to assess the amount of credit to be given.[145] While credit of 1.5:1 may be a starting point in relation to the sentencing of young persons, the amount of credit awarded will depend on various factors, including the conditions of pre-trial detention, the reasons for detention, the length of detention, the reasons for any delay in the trial or sentencing, as well as the young person's need for further custody or community service.[146]

In *R. v. B. (T.)*, the Ontario appeal court upheld the decision of the trial judge to award the young person credit based on a 1:1 ratio. In determining the credit amount, the trial judge had considered the circumstances of the offence and the offender, the offender's record and his prospects for rehabilitation, as well as the impact of the offences on the victim and the compressed duration of the maximum sentence available.[147] However, the court noted even then, that a sentencing judge can decline to give even 1:1 credit for pre-sentence custody if to do so would exhaust the custodial term available and result in a sentence contrary to the purposes of the *YCJA*.[148]

---

[142] [2008] O.J. No. 4231, 93 O.R. (3d) 211 (Ont. C.A.).

[143] *R. v. S. (D.)*, [2008] O.J. No. 4231, at para. 26, 93 O.R. (3d) 211 (Ont. C.A.).

[144] *R. v. S. (D.)*, [2008] O.J. No. 4231, at paras. 25 and 27-29, 93 O.R. (3d) 211 (Ont. C.A.).

[145] *R. v. B. (T.)*, [2006] O.J. No. 584, at paras. 25 and 34, 206 C.C.C. (3d) 405 (Ont. C.A.).

[146] *R. v. B. (T.)*, [2006] O.J. No. 584, at para. 42, 206 C.C.C. (3d) 405 (Ont. C.A.).

[147] *R. v. B. (T.)*, [2006] O.J. No. 584, at paras. 43-44, 206 C.C.C. (3d) 405 (Ont. C.A.).

[148] *R. v. B. (T.)*, [2006] O.J. No. 584, at para. 35, 206 C.C.C. (3d) 405 (Ont. C.A.). See also *R. v. E.L.*, [2004] O.J. No. 1517 (Ont. C.A.), where the Ontario appeal court held that it is only in exceptional cases that the amount of credit should be reduced below a 1:1 ratio. In *R. v. E.L.*, the young person, who was 17 at the time of the offence, pled guilty to first degree murder in the killing of his mother and the use of a firearm in the commission of an indictable offence. He received a six-year intensive rehabilitative (closed) custody sentence and two years' community supervision, and an additional 14 months' closed custody and seven months' community supervision for the accompanying charge of use of a firearm. He was credited with three months for time spent in pre-trial custody but not given any credit for a further 16 months served in pre-sentence custody. In light of the joint submission in the case

In *R. v. A.O.*,[149] the Ontario Court of Appeal upheld the sentencing judge's decision to award only three years' credit for 2.5 years in pre-trial custody (which is a 1.2:1 ratio) because the conditions in the youth court facility were not as harsh as in many adult facilities and also because the young persons had access to excellent treatment, counselling, educational and vocational programs and had availed themselves of these. In that same decision, the Ontario Court of Appeal clarified that credit could be denied in some circumstances but that credit for pre-sentence custody should not be denied without good reason.[150]

Ontario's initial position that fairness requires that credit generally not be denied without good reason (although it was up to the judge to decide how much)[151] is in accordance with the early cases from the Manitoba Court of Appeal, which also took the position that, in relation to a custodial sentence, the judge must first decide on an appropriate sentence and then reduce the sentence by taking into account time spent in pre-trial custody. "A consideration of time in custody will mitigate and reduce what would have been the higher quantum imposed on the day of sentencing."[152] Some lower courts have followed the early reasoning of the Ontario and Manitoba appellate level courts. The Newfoundland and Labrador Provincial Court has held that some credit is mandatory because of the use of the word "shall" in s. 38(3)(d), but that the amount of credit awarded will depend on the circumstances of the case. No specific formula or ratio need be applied.[153]

Conversely, in Nova Scotia and Saskatchewan, the jurisprudence is in line with the more recent jurisprudence from Ontario and Manitoba. In *R. v. J.R.L.*, the Nova Scotia Court of Appeal held in a violent home invasion case that a court can take into account the time spent in pre-trial custody without giving specific credit for time served by deducting the number of days or some part of that number from the number of days of a custodial sentence. In that case, the young person was given the maximum six-month deferred custody and supervision order, which was not reduced to reflect the 16 days the young person had already spent in custody. However, it may well have been *because* the young person had already spent some time in custody that the judge saw fit to impose a deferred custody and supervision order. "When the sentence imposed is not a custodial sentence to be served in an institution, taking the remand time into account does not necessarily have to result in a deduction in the

and the extensive negotiations concerning the rehabilitative needs of the accused, the Ontario appeal court concluded that the youth court justice made no error and that the sentence was fit.

[149] [2007] O.J. No. 800, 218 C.C.C. (3d) 409 (Ont. C.A.).
[150] *R. v. A.O.*, [2007] O.J. No. 800, at para. 76, 218 C.C.C. (3d) 409 (Ont. C.A.).
[151] *R. v. A.O.*, [2007] O.J. No. 800, at para. 76, 218 C.C.C. (3d) 409 (Ont. C.A.).
[152] *R. v. G.A.T.*, [2007] M.J. No. 210, at para. 19 (Man. C.A.).
[153] *R. v. I.C.*, [2007] N.J. No. 280, at para. 35 (N.L. Prov. Ct.).

length of sentence. It can be taken into account by reducing the type or severity of the sentence."[154]

The Saskatchewan Court of Appeal made a similar ruling.[155] Both courts were of the view that so long as the sentencing judge has considered the fact that the young person has already spent some time in custody, the young person need not receive a specific deduction for it. In both cases, it was implied that the young person might not have received the deferred custody sentence had they not already spent some time in custody. Arguably, the young person did, in fact, receive a benefit or credit for the time already spent in custody.[156]

On its face, the wording of s. 38(3)(d) says only that the judge is obliged to take into account any time spent in pre-sentence custody in determining a youth sentence. The phrase "take into account" appears to mean only that the judge is obliged to consider any time spent in pre-sentence custody in determining the sentence. There is no express obligation on the judge to actually reduce a jail sentence because of it although this may well be the usual practice in many cases.

V. SECTION 39 — RESTRICTIONS ON CUSTODY

> *Committal to custody*
>
> **39. (1)** *A youth justice court shall not commit a young person to custody under section 42 (youth sentences) unless*
>
> *(a) the young person has committed a violent offence;*
>
> *(b) the young person has failed to comply with non-custodial sentences;*
>
> *(c) the young person has committed an indictable offence for which an adult would be liable to imprisonment for a term of more than two years and has a history that indicates a pattern of findings of guilt under this Act or the Young Offenders Act, chapter Y-1 of the Revised Statutes of Canada, 1985; or*

---

[154] *R. v. J.R.L.*, [2007] N.S.J. No. 214, at para. 47 (N.S.C.A.).

[155] *R. v. C.J.A.*, [2005] S.J. No. 410, 200 C.C.C. (3d) 233 (Sask. C.A.) also involved the imposition of a six-month deferred custody and supervision order on a young person who had already spent 10 weeks on remand.

[156] *R. v. J.R.L.*, [2007] N.S.J. No. 214, at paras. 46-47 (N.S.C.A.). See also *R. v. C.J.A.*, [2005] S.J. No. 410, at paras. 41 and 42, 200 C.C.C. (3d) 233 (Sask. C.A.). However, clearly judges are sometimes giving credit to young persons for time served in pre-trial detention in some cases. See for example *R. v. M.N.*, [2005] Nu.J. No. 4 (Nu. C.J.), where credit was granted on a 1:1 basis.

> (d) in exceptional cases where the young person has committed an indictable offence, the aggravating circumstances of the offence are such that the imposition of a non-custodial sentence would be inconsistent with the purpose and principles set out in section 38.

Alternatives to custody

> (2) If any of paragraphs (1)(a) to (c) apply, a youth justice court shall not impose a custodial sentence under section 42 (youth sentences) unless the court has considered all alternatives to custody raised at the sentencing hearing that are reasonable in the circumstances, and determined that there is not a reasonable alternative, or combination of alternatives, that is in accordance with the purpose and principles set out in section 38.

Factors to be considered

> (3) In determining whether there is a reasonable alternative to custody, a youth justice court shall consider submissions relating to
>
> (a) the alternatives to custody that are available;
>
> (b) the likelihood that the young person will comply with a non-custodial sentence, taking into account his or her compliance with previous non-custodial sentences; and
>
> (c) the alternatives to custody that have been used in respect of young persons for similar offences committed in similar circumstances.

Imposition of same sentence

> (4) The previous imposition of a particular non-custodial sentence on a young person does not preclude a youth justice court from imposing the same or any other non-custodial sentence for another offence.

Custody as social measure prohibited

> (5) A youth justice court shall not use custody as a substitute for appropriate child protection, mental health or other social measures.

Pre-sentence report

> (6) Before imposing a custodial sentence under section 42 (youth sentences), a youth justice court shall consider a pre-sentence report and any sentencing proposal made by the young person or his or her counsel.

Report dispensed with

(7) A youth justice court may, with the consent of the prosecutor and the young person or his or her counsel, dispense with a pre-sentence report if the court is satisfied that the report is not necessary.

Length of custody

(8) In determining the length of a youth sentence that includes a custodial portion, a youth justice court shall be guided by the purpose and principles set out in section 38, and shall not take into consideration the fact that the supervision portion of the sentence may not be served in custody and that the sentence may be reviewed by the court under section 94.

Reasons

(9) If a youth justice court imposes a youth sentence that includes a custodial portion, the court shall state the reasons why it has determined that a non-custodial sentence is not adequate to achieve the purpose set out in subsection 38(1), including, if applicable, the reasons why the case is an exceptional case under paragraph (1)(d).

The general principle of restraint in the use of custody in the Canadian criminal law can be traced to the United States in the 1960s, when the American Law Institute proposed in its Model Penal Code of 1962 that the courts should impose custody on an offender only if certain conditions were met. Canada's Ouimet Committee endorsed this recommendation in its 1969 report.[157] This principle has since been affirmed by a litany of Canadian commissions and reports, including the Law Reform Commission of Canada, *The Criminal Law in Canadian Society* (which is a 1982 federal government publication outlining the rationale and underlying principles of the Canadian criminal law) and the report of the Canadian Sentencing Commission in 1986.[158]

The principle of restraint in the use of custody was codified in the *Criminal Code* in 1996 when s. 718.2(e) came into force. The Supreme Court of Canada has since opined that its inclusion must be understood as a reaction to the overuse of prison as a sanction in Canada.[159]

---

[157] Canada, Canadian Committee on Corrections, *Toward Unity: Criminal Justice and Corrections* (Ottawa: Queen's Printer, 1969), at 191.
[158] P. Stenning and J.V. Roberts, "Empty Promises: Parliament, The Supreme Court, and the Sentencing of Aboriginal Offenders" (2001) 64 Sask. L. Rev. 137, at para. 11, and n. 17 (QL).
[159] *R. v. Gladue*, [1999] S.C.J. No. 19, at para. 57, [1999] 1 S.C.R. 688 (S.C.C.).

The principle of restraint in the use of incarceration has long been a principle in relation to young persons as well. All evidence suggested that Canada was too quick to imprison its young persons, that it imprisoned too many of them and often for non-violent offences, and that high incarceration rates were ineffective in reducing crime. Thus, from the early days of the *YOA*, the federal government took legislative steps to limit the circumstances in which prison could be imposed, to no avail.[160] The incarceration rate of young persons in Canada remained unacceptably high throughout the 1990s, the highest in the western world.[161]

Unlike the *YOA*, which permitted judges considerable discretion in deciding whether a young person should be jailed,[162] the *YCJA* seeks to significantly curtail judicial discretion at the sentencing stage by establishing clear, explicit and more detailed preconditions that must be met before a young person can be imprisoned in Canada. From its Preamble onwards, the *YCJA* clarifies that one of its main goals is to restrict the use of custody for non-violent young persons, and for young persons who have not committed serious crimes. The *Criminal Code* includes no similar detailed restrictions on the imposition of custody regarding the sentencing of adults. The Supreme Court of Canada acknowledged in one of its first decisions concerning the principles of the *YCJA* that the Act is aimed at restricting the use of custody for young persons.[163]

Under the *YCJA*, a young person can receive a custodial sentence only if the young person (1) has committed a violent offence, (2) has failed to comply with non-custodial sentences, (3) has committed an indictable offence for which an adult would be liable to imprisonment for a term of more than two years *and* has a history that indicates a pattern of findings of guilt under the *YCJA* or the *YOA* or, (4) in exceptional cases, where the young person has committed an indictable offence, the aggravating circumstances of the offence are such that the imposition of a non-custodial sentence would be inconsistent with the purpose and principles set out in s. 38.

---

[160] A review of this legislative history can be found in *R. v. C.D.; R. v. C.D.K.*, [2005] S.C.J. No. 79, at paras. 44-49 (S.C.C.).

[161] Canada, *House of Commons Debates* (14 February, 2001), at 704, as referred to in *R. v. C.D.; R. v. C.D.K.*, [2005] S.C.J. No. 79 (S.C.C.).

[162] Under s. 24(1) of the *YOA*, in deciding whether the young person should receive a custodial sentence, the judge was required to consider whether a jail sentence was necessary for the protection of society having regard to the seriousness of the offence and the circumstances in which it was committed and having regard to the needs and circumstances of the young person. The judge was required to consider all available and reasonable alternatives to custody and also to remain mindful that a young person who committed an offence that did not involve serious personal injury was to be held accountable through a non-custodial disposition "whenever appropriate".

[163] *R. v. C.D.; R. v. C.D.K.*, [2005] S.C.J. No. 79, at paras. 38, 41 and 50 (S.C.C.).

A.   Section 39(1)(a) — What Is a Violent Offence?

A young person can be sentenced to custody as part of a youth sentence if he or she commits a *violent* offence. During the early days of the *YCJA*, the courts grappled with the meaning of a "violent offence" because the term is not defined in the *YCJA*. The term "serious violent offence", which appears elsewhere in the Act, is defined in the Act.[164] Consequently, there was a logical tendency to define a violent offence by comparing it to the definition of a serious violent offence. Some of the courts initially reasoned that, since a serious violent offence means an offence in the commission of which a young person causes or attempts to cause serious bodily harm, a violent offence must logically mean an offence in the commission of which a young person causes or attempts to cause bodily harm.[165]

The Supreme Court of Canada clarified the meaning of a violent offence in 2005 when it decided *R. v. C.D.; R. v. C.D.K.*[166] The Supreme Court of Canada held that a violent offence, for purposes of s. 39(1)(a), means an offence in the commission of which a young person causes, attempts to cause or threatens to cause bodily harm.[167]

In reaching its decision, the Supreme Court of Canada considered two Alberta cases. In one case, C.D. pled guilty to possession of a weapon for a purpose dangerous to the public peace, arson to property and breach of a recognizance. C.D. and an adult offender had set fire to a truck on an isolated street late at night with the use of gasoline and propane. In a separate proceeding, C.D.K. pled guilty to dangerous driving (which involved a high-speed police chase through city streets), possession of stolen property and theft under $5,000. Both young persons were sentenced to six months of deferred custody[168] followed by probation. The Court of Appeal upheld both sentences, holding that the sentencing judges did not err in determining that C.D.'s arson to property and C.D.K.'s dangerous driving were violent offences. In its

---

[164]   *YCJA*, s. 2.

[165]   See, for example, *R. v. D. (T.M.)*, [2003] N.S.J. No. 488, 181 C.C.C. (3d) 518 (N.S.C.A.) and *R. v. C. (J.J.)*, [2003] P.E.I.J. No. 99, 180 C.C.C. (3d) 137 (P.E.I.C.A.).

[166]   [2005] S.C.J. No. 79 (S.C.C.).

[167]   *R. v. C.D.; R. v. C.D.K.*, [2005] S.C.J. No. 79, at para. 17 (S.C.C.). Bodily harm is not defined in the *YCJA* but it is defined in s. 2 of the *Criminal Code* to mean any hurt or injury to a person that interferes with the health or comfort of the person and that is more than merely transient or trifling in nature. Section 2(2) of the *YCJA* indicates that, unless otherwise provided, words and expressions used in the *YCJA* have the same meaning as in the *Criminal Code*. In *R. v. McCraw*, [1991] S.C.J. No. 69, [1991] 3 S.C.R. 72 (S.C.C.), the court held that bodily harm includes both physical and psychological harm.

[168]   *YCJA*, s. 42(2)(p).

decision in C.D.,[169] the Appeal Court held that an act is violent if it causes bodily harm, is intended to cause bodily harm, or if it is reasonably foreseeable that the action may cause bodily harm. In the arson case, the appeal court was mindful of the risk to anyone using the street that night, including those charged with controlling the fire. It held that a reasonable person would have foreseen a risk of bodily harm. Likewise, in its decision in *R. v. C.D.K.*,[170] the court concluded that an offence is violent for purposes of s. 39(1)(a) if it is reasonably foreseeable that criminal conduct may result in bodily harm that is more than merely trifling or transitory. In the case of the dangerous driving offence, the potential for harm was obvious, the court ruled, because high-speed chases are very dangerous and can easily result in serious injury or death.[171] Both accused persons appealed, which gave the Supreme Court of Canada an early opportunity to define the meaning of a violent offence within the context of s. 39(1)(a) of the *YCJA*.

Justice Bastarache, writing for the Supreme Court of Canada (Le-Bel J. issued separate reasons but agreed in the result), held that the Alberta Court of Appeal had defined a violent offence too broadly. He quashed the custodial sentences, and remitted the matters back to the youth court. The object, scheme and intention of the *YCJA* indicate that the *YCJA* is designed in part to reduce the over-reliance on custodial sentences for young offenders and therefore a narrow interpretation of the term "violent offence" is preferable since the paragraph is one of the gateways to custody, Bastarache J. held.[172]

A violent offence can be best understood by focusing on the concept of harm, Bastarache J. explained. A harm-based definition of "violent offence" includes offences in which bodily harm is threatened as well as caused or attempted, which accords with the commonly held view that a threat to cause harm is an act of violence.[173] The meaning of violent offence should not be interpreted so broadly as to include situations where bodily harm is merely intended. Something more than a guilty mind is required before criminal punishment is imposed, nor should the definition of a violent offence be extended to include offences where bodily harm is merely reasonably foreseeable, which again, would be inconsistent with a narrow interpretation of a violent offence, Bastarache J. held. Too many *Criminal Code* offences would be captured based on a standard of

---

[169]   [2004] A.J. No. 237, 346 A.R. 289 (Alta. C.A.).

[170]   [2004] A.J. No. 237, 346 A.R. 289 (Alta. C.A.).

[171]   *R. v. C.D.K.*, [2004] A.J. No. 237, at para. 7, 346 A.R. 289 (Alta. C.A.).

[172]   *R. v. C.D.; R. v. C.D.K.*, [2005] S.C.J. No. 79, at para. 50 (S.C.C.).

[173]   *R. v. C.D.; R. v. C.D.K.*, [2005] S.C.J. No. 79, at paras. 26, 81-86 (S.C.C.). This of course relates to the psychological impact of the threat on the victim.

reasonable foreseeability. The *Criminal Code* recognizes a distinction between violent and dangerous offences, and so too should the *YCJA*.[174] C.D. did not cause, attempt to cause, or threaten to cause, bodily harm in relation to the arson offence, nor did C.D.K. cause, attempt to cause, or threaten to cause bodily harm in the commission of the dangerous driving offences.

It follows from this narrow interpretation that pure property crimes are not violent offences, otherwise the gate-keeping effect of s. 39(1)(a) would be severely diminished, Bastarache J. stated. A jail sentence should be an option in relation to a property offence only if the offence meets the criteria and qualifies as an exceptional case under s. 39(1)(d).[175] (However, if the Crown could prove that the accused caused, attempted to cause, or threatened to cause bodily harm in the course of a property crime such as arson, the Crown may be successful in demonstrating that the property offence in that instance is a violent offence under s. 39(1)(a), such as, for example, in the case of arson where the fire is set in an area where people are present or expected to be present shortly, and the accused had knowledge of this, and there is thus evidence that the accused caused or attempted to cause bodily harm.)

Justice Bastarache further held that it was inappropriate to interpret the term "violent offence" solely by reference to the definition of a serious violent offence. While the meaning of a violent offence must logically be connected to the statutory definition of a serious violent offence, Parliament chose not to define a violent offence in s. 39 and that decision must be given meaning and respected.[176]

This focus on bodily harm,[177] or on attempts or threats[178] to cause it, has been criticized as too narrow a definition of "violent offence" since it excludes dangerous conduct by young persons from being categorized as violent[179] and therefore prevents a young person from being jailed for conduct that endangers the public, unless the circumstances of the offence bring it within any of the other gateways to custody in s. 39.

---

[174] *R. v. C.D.; R. v. C.D.K.*, [2005] S.C.J. No. 79, at paras. 74-80 (S.C.C.).

[175] *R. v. C.D.; R. v. C.D.K.*, [2005] S.C.J. No. 79, at para. 51 (S.C.C.).

[176] *R. v. C.D.; R. v. C.D.K.*, [2005] S.C.J. No. 79, at paras. 20, 23-26 and 86 (S.C.C.).

[177] The Supreme Court of Canada determined in *R. v. McCraw*, [1991] S.C.J. No. 69, [1991] 3 S.C.R. 72 (S.C.C.) that bodily harm includes both physical and psychological harm.

[178] Based on Bastarache J.'s discussion at paras. 81-87 of *R. v. C.D.; R. v. C.D.K.*, [2005] S.C.J. No. 79 (S.C.C.), the meaning of the term "threatens to cause bodily harm" appears to be limited to explicit verbal threats to cause such harm.

[179] This matter is dealt with in detail in Chapter 4, which considers the bail provisions. Section 39 is also relevant at the judicial interim release stage.

In fact, among its recommendations, the Nunn Commission of Inquiry in Nova Scotia recommended that the Nova Scotia government lobby the federal government to amend the definition of "violent offence" in s. 39(1)(a) to include conduct that endangers or is likely to endanger the life or safety of another person.[180] The Manitoba government has also complained about young persons using stolen vehicles as weapons and the need to take steps to address this, such as the classification of auto theft as an indictable violent offence.[181]

Since the December 2005 decision in *R. v. C.D.; R. v. C.D.K.*, the Ontario Court of Appeal has refined the definition of a violent offence by defining it as "an offence in the commission of which a young person causes, attempts to cause or threatens to cause physical or psychological harm or injury to a person that is more than transient or trifling in nature".[182] In that case, *R. v. S. (J.)*, the Ontario Court of Appeal held that a home invasion involving armed accused persons who broke into the victims' home brandishing a machete and a shotgun is a violent offence.[183] In the course of the judgment, Blair J.A. noted the degree to which the victims were traumatized by the incident, during which one intruder pointed a shotgun at one of the victims and pulled the trigger. The weapon did not discharge. The ruling centres on the violation of the family's sense of sanctity and security in their home and their exposure to the threat of physical and psychological harm.[184] Justice Blair reduced the length of the sentence slightly on appeal and sentenced the young person (who was 16 at the time, living with friends because his family was in the shelter system, had no criminal or youth record but was the one armed with the machete) to a total of 13 months' custody and five months' community supervision.[185]

Robbery has also been held to be a violent offence,[186] as has being a party to a robbery.[187] In *R. v. N. (H.T.)*, the British Columbia Court of Appeal upheld its lower court in finding that a young person whose conduct makes them a *party* to a violent offence is captured by the

---

[180] See the Nova Scotia Nunn Commission of Inquiry, *Spiralling out of Control: Lessons Learned from a Boy in Trouble: Report of the Nunn Commission of Inquiry* (Halifax, NS: Nunn Commission of Inquiry 2006), Recommendation 21, at 289. This report is available online at: <http://www.gov.ns.ca/just/nunn_commission/_docs/Report_Nunn_Final.pdf>.

[181] *House of Commons Debates* (4 February 2008) at 1525.

[182] *R. v. S. (J.)*, [2006] O.J. No. 2654, at para. 23, 81 O.R. (3d) 511 (Ont. C.A.).

[183] *R. v. S. (J.)*, [2006] O.J. No. 2654, at para. 23, 81 O.R. (3d) 511 (Ont. C.A.).

[184] *R. v. S. (J.)*, [2006] O.J. No. 2654, at para. 30, 81 O.R. (3d) 511 (Ont. C.A.).

[185] *R. v. S. (J.)*, [2006] O.J. No. 2654, at para. 57, 81 O.R. (3d) 511 (Ont. C.A.).

[186] *R. v. C.D.; R. v. C.D.K.*, [2005] S.C.J. No. 79, at para. 32 (S.C.C.).

[187] *R. v. N. (H.T.)*, [2006] B.C.J. No. 974, 209 C.C.C. (3d) 318 (B.C.C.A.). See also *R. v. T.N.*, [2006] B.C.J. No. 788 (B.C. Prov. Ct.).

definition of violent offence in s. 39(1)(a).[188] In that case, the young person was convicted of robbery. He argued that he did not cause, attempt to cause, or threaten to cause bodily harm. His involvement in the robberies included being present during the planning of the robbery, remaining in the co-accused's car with the two adults who executed the robberies while the victims were lured to the scene, making telephone calls to the two adults during the robbery to warn them that someone was watching, and arranging to pick them up after the robberies were finished. The two adults were armed with a gun and a knife. One of the victims was shot in the back and paralyzed for several months; another victim was beaten.

The trial judge had found that his limited role in the robberies was relevant in considering his degree of participation under s. 38(3)(a) as part of the determination of his sentence, but his conduct in aiding and abetting the robberies nevertheless meant that he committed a violent offence because s. 21 of the *Criminal Code* eliminates the legal distinction between aiding and abetting and personally committing the offence. Whether the person aids or abets or actually personally commits the offence, he is guilty of the offence, the court concluded. Although s. 140 of the *YCJA* states that the provisions of the *Criminal Code* apply to offences alleged to have been committed by young persons only to the extent that they are not inconsistent with or excluded by the *YCJA*, a clearer expression of legislative intent would be required before it could be held that s. 21 of the *Criminal Code* is inconsistent with the *YCJA*, the court held.

In *R. v. K.K.*,[189] another ruling following the Supreme Court of Canada decision in *R. v. C.D.; R. v. C.D.K.*, the court held that a 15-year-old young person who stole a car and prompted a police chase that included his driving directly at a police cruiser three times committed a violent offence. Justice Feldman distinguished the case from the dangerous driving offence considered by the Supreme Court of Canada in *R. v. C.D.; R. v. C.D.K.* not only because the young person in *R. v. K.K.* drove directly at a police cruiser but also because there was evidence that one of the officers suffered psychological harm.[190] Conversely, a young person who pled guilty to charges of flight from the police, dangerous driving and possession of stolen property was found not to have committed a violent offence. Justice McIlhargey of the Alberta Provincial Court suggested that, while bodily harm may have been reasonably foreseeable

---

[188] *R. v. N. (H.T.)*, [2006] B.C.J. No. 974, 209 C.C.C. (3d) 318 (B.C.C.A.).

[189] [2006] O.J. No. 933 (Ont. C.J.).

[190] *R. v. K.K.*, [2006] O.J. No. 933, at para. 24 (Ont. C.J.).

on the facts of the case, it did not meet the definition in *R. v. C.D.; R. v. C.D.K.* that a violent offence is one where bodily harm is caused or attempted.[191]

(i)   Are Sexual Offences Violent Offences?

Among the important legal questions that have arisen in the wake of *R. v. C.D.; R. v. C.D.K.* is whether sexual offences, no matter how "minor", are, by their very nature, violent offences for purposes of s. 39(1)(a). The Supreme Court of Canada did not directly address this question and the common law is unsettled across jurisdictions. Prior to the 2005 Supreme Court of Canada ruling, it had been successfully argued that a sexual offence involving the touching of a child constituted a violent offence even if there were no physical violence, apart from the obvious violation of the victim's physical integrity.[192] Justice Abella, writing for the majority of the Court of Appeal in *R. v. Stuckless*, held that: "Sexual abuse is an act of violence. When committed against children, the violence is both physical and profoundly psychological."[193] (In that case, while there was no physical violence inflicted, there was ample evidence of the psychological harm caused by the sexual assaults.) In the course of that ruling, Abella J.A. referred to an unreported 1992 ruling from the Ontario General Division, *R. v. McF.*, in which Moldaver J. held that crimes of incest and sexual assault are inherently violent.[194]

---

[191]   *R. v. Z.J.L.*, [2007] A.J. No. 15 (Alta. Prov. Ct.).

[192]   *R. v. Stuckless*, [1998] O.J. No. 3177, at paras. 34 and 43, 127 C.C.C. (3d) 225 (Ont. C.A.).

[193]   *R. v. Stuckless*, [1998] O.J. No. 3177, at para. 44, 127 C.C.C. (3d) 225 (Ont. C.A.).

[194]   *R. v. McF.*, unreported, April 27, 1992 (Ont. Gen. Div.). See also *R. v. A. (E.S.)*, [2003] A.J. No. 571 (Alta. Prov. Ct.), where Lipton J. held at para. 30 that sexual touching and sexual assaults are inherently violent offences. This case is also noteworthy because it supports the position that there need not be evidence on the record that the sexual offence at bar caused harm to the victim in order for the court to conclude that the sexual offence is violent for purposes of the *YCJA*. Although the judge did not have evidence of harm to the victim, he found that he was still able to conclude that the sexual contact (sexual touching) between the 17-year-old male and the 12-year-old girl was a violent offence. Re sexual assault being a violent offence, see also *R. v. A.A.B.*, [2004] M.J. No. 506, 194 Man. R. (2d) 143 (Man. Prov. Ct.), which involved the sexual assault of a young girl between age four and six, over a three-year period, during which the court again concluded that sexual offences against children are violent offences within the meaning of s. 39(1)(a) of the *YCJA*. See also *R. v. A.A.*, [2004] O.J. No. 2820, at para. 57, 62 W.C.B. (2d) 405 (Ont. C.J.), where Cole J. held that while not every unlawful touching by a youthful offender amounts to a violent offence, where the touching is of a sexual nature and particularly where there is digital penetration, the offence amounts to a violent offence. In fact, in *R. v. P.H.*, [2004] O.J. No. 4509, 193 C.C.C. (3d) 424 (Ont. C.J.), the defence conceded that sexual assault under s. 271 is a violent offence for purposes of s. 39(1)(a). (That case concerned whether the sexual assault by the 14-year-old on the five-year-old was a serious violent offence.) Justice Clark held that the sexual assault was inherently violent, but the court was not convinced that serious

More recently, in *R. v. J.G.*,[195] a 2004 decision of the Nova Scotia Provincial Court, Williams J. held that the offence of sexual interference, s. 151 of the *Criminal Code*, concerns the interference with the bodily integrity of a person and is a form of assault because it requires an inappropriate touching; it requires touching for a sexual purpose. Justice Williams further found that the violation of a person's bodily integrity under s. 151 is both physical and psychological, that offences of sexual touching constitute sexual abuse and that, as per Abella J.A.'s decision in *Stuckless*, sexual abuse is thus an act of violence. Thus, sexual interference is a violent offence for purposes of s. 39(1)(a) of the *YCJA*, Williams J. found,[196] without requiring the Crown to prove that the victim suffered bodily harm.

In the wake of *R. v. C.D.; R. v. C.D.K.*, however, the judiciary has questioned whether the more narrow formulation of the definition of a violent offence in *R. v. C.D.; R. v. C.D.K.* continues to permit a sexual offence to be categorized as a violent offence without the Crown proving actual physical or psychological harm to the victim.[197] In *R. v. N.P.*,[198] which was released just four days after *R. v. C.D.; R. v. C.D.K.*, Gorman J. opined that it is well known that the harm caused to children who are victims of sexual abuse may not be known until many years later. However, he observed that *R. v. C.D.; R. v. C.D.K.* does not indicate whether the harm caused to the victim must be established at the time of sentencing. While Gorman J. took the position that based on the facts of the case at bar, it was difficult to see how the case met the definition of a violent offence as set out in *R. v. C.D.; R. v. C.D.K.*, he noted that he did not have to decide the point, since the court could impose custody under s. 39(1)(c) and (d). In *R. v. N.P.*, the 15-year-old accused was caught attempting anal intercourse with an eight-year-old, which the child later describes as having hurt him.

What complicates the matter is that *R. v. C.D.; R. v. C.D.K.* does not directly consider whether sexual offences can be found to be violent offences absent proof of actual harm or proof that the accused attempted

---

bodily harm had occurred. There was no actual sexual touching in the case. The accused had masturbated in front of the five-year-old while the two were in the same bed. See also *R. v. V.I.C.*, [2005] S.J. No. 469 (Sask. C.A.), where the court held that the sexual assaults amounted to rape as the child (aged five and six) did not consent, and the offence was by its nature a violent offence. There was also evidence that the child has suffered psychological trauma.

[195] [2004] N.S.J. No. 160, 226 N.S.R. (2d) 374 (N.S. Prov. Ct.).

[196] [2004] N.S.J. No. 160, at paras. 16-18, 226 N.S.R. (2d) 374 (N.S. Prov. Ct.).

[197] It is noteworthy that in *R. v. McDonnell*, [1997] S.C.J. No. 42, [1997] 1 S.C.R. 948 (S.C.C.), which was decided a year before *Stuckless*, the court held that psychological harm cannot be presumed in cases of sexual assault. If the Crown wishes to rely on it, the Crown must prove it.

[198] [2005] N.J. No. 395, at paras. 32 and 33, 68 W.C.B. (2d) 146 (N.L. Prov. Ct.).

or threatened to cause harm to the victim. Are sexual offences, by their very nature, violent, in as much as the act of sexual touching of a child by an adult is always a form of sexual abuse and thus always causes physical harm (that can be physical or psychological)? Justice Bastarache held that his definition of violent offence can be expected to exclude only relatively minor assaults. If one takes the position that the sexual assault of a young person can never be categorized as a minor assault because it is always a form of sexual abuse and involves an unwanted interference with the bodily integrity of a young person, one can conclude that sexual offences always cause bodily harm. This is certainly the approach to analysis that some judges have adopted post-*R. v. C.D.; R. v. C.D.K.*

In *R. v. D.W.*,[199] the question of whether sexual interference is a violent offence under s. 39(1)(a) arose in relation to a bail matter. The specific question the Saskatchewan Queen's Bench was considering was whether *R. v. J.G.*,[200] which found that sexual interference is a violent offence for purposes of s. 39(1)(a), could still be taken to be correct in light of the narrow definition of a violent offence outlined in *R. v. C.D.; R. v. C.D.K.* In *R. v. D.W.*, the 17-year-old accused was alleged to have accosted the 13-year-old girl in a back alley. Justice Wilkinson held that the Supreme Court of Canada's reasoning in *R. v. C.D.; R. v. C.D.K.* is entirely compatible with a conclusion that sexual interference with a person under the age of 14 is a violent offence for purposes of the *YCJA*.[201]

> It is self-evident that the harm that results from threats must be of psychological origin, and that psychological and emotional harm amount to bodily harm even where no physical force is involved. ... The psychological harm engendered by the sexual touching of children is implicit and requires little in the way of enunciation or explanation. Although a simple touching of an individual without their consent is a technical assault, and could fall into the category of a "minor" assault that is not a "violent offence" under the *R. v. C.D.* definition, the sexual touching of a child under 14, cannot be considered as minor, and free of any connotations of violence. It is exactly why we teach children about good and bad touching. I find that the offence of sexual interference with a child under the age of fourteen is a "violent offence" for purposes of the *YCJA*.[202]

Justice Wilkinson did not require the Crown to prove, in this post-*R. v. C.D.; R. v. C.D.K.* case, that the victim experienced bodily harm in order to determine that the sexual offence was a violent offence for

---

[199]   [2006] S.J. No. 683, 287 Sask. R. 237 (Sask. Q.B.).
[200]   [2004] N.S.J. No. 160, 226 N.S.R. (2d) 374 (N.S. Prov. Ct.).
[201]   *R. v. D.W.*, [2006] S.J. No. 683, at para. 10, 287 Sask. R. 237 (Sask. Q.B.).
[202]   *R. v. D.W.*, [2006] S.J. No. 683, at para. 19, 287 Sask. R. 237 (Sask. Q.B.).

purposes of s. 39(1)(a). Likewise, in *R. v. T.C.*[203] Schuler J. found that the actions of a teenager in forcing his younger cousins to perform oral sex and masturbation on him amounted to violent offences without requiring the Crown to prove that the victims had suffered bodily harm, either physical or psychological. However, Schuler J. had observed in his ruling, prior to the consideration of whether the offences were violent offences for purposes of s. 39, that both victims had suffered emotionally because of the assaults.[204]

Conversely, in the 2008 case of *R. v. T.F.*, a 15-year-old boy pled guilty to sexual assault, which involved two incidents in which he forced sexual intercourse with a 13-year-old victim. He was 14 at the time of the incidents.[205] Justice Gorin rejected the Crown's arguments that all cases of sexual assault are violent offences for purposes of s. 39(1)(a).[206] In determining the sentence, based on the definition of a violent offence, Gorin J. reasoned that, before he could conclude that the sexual assault in this case constituted a violent offence, he first had to determine that bodily harm (physical or psychological) was caused, threatened or attempted. The evidence before him had to establish this. Relying on *R. v. McDonnell*,[207] Gorin J. held that the Crown is required to prove the bodily harm alleged beyond a reasonable doubt. If the Crown wished to rely on psychological harm, it must prove beyond a reasonable doubt that psychological harm occurred and that it was more than merely transitory or trifling in nature.[208] Both physical and psychological harm can be established without expert evidence. Justice Gorin ultimately held in the case at bar that the Crown had established beyond a reasonable doubt that the victim had suffered psychological harm that was more than merely trifling and therefore that the sexual assault was a violent offence for purposes of s. 39(1)(a).[209]

---

203 [2006] N.W.T.J. No. 21 (N.W.T.S.C.).

204 *R. v. T.C.*, [2006] N.W.T.J. No. 21, at paras. 16-18 (N.W.T.S.C.).

205 [2008] N.W.T.J. No. 66, 2008 NWTTC 11 (N.W.T. Terr. Ct.).

206 *R. v. T.F.*, [2008] N.W.T.J. No. 66, at para. 14, 2008 NWTTC 11 (N.W.T. Terr. Ct.).

207 [1997] S.C.J. No. 42, [1997] 1 S.C.R. 948 (S.C.C.).

208 *R. v. T.F.*, [2008] N.W.T.J. No. 66, at para. 13, 2008 NWTTC 11 (N.W.T. Terr. Ct.).

209 But see *R. v. R.A.A.*, [2003] B.C.J. No. 1386, BCPC 212 (B.C. Youth Ct.), which was decided just days after the *YCJA* came into force and prior to *R. v. C.D.; R. v. C.D.K.* This was an incest case, in which Gove J. held for the B.C. Youth Court that the 15-year-old male, who had sex with his sister for a three-year period, had not committed a violent offence for purposes of the *YCJA*, even though the accused had forced intercourse with his sister and the Crown had contended that he caused her psychological harm. The Crown did not supply expert evidence of that psychological harm. At the time of this ruling, Gove J. stated that he was aware of only one case having been decided re the definition of a violent offence under the *YCJA*. Justice Gove distinguished between the offence of incest and offences such as sexual assault or rape, and appears to imply at para. 23 that those offences, unlike incest, by the very nature of the charge, are violent offences. Incest, by contrast, is a

There is a compelling argument to be made that sexual offences are, by their very nature, violent for purposes of s. 39(1)(a) of the *YCJA* because they are offences of unwanted sexual touching, and are, thus, harmful, at least psychologically. There is considerable support for this argument in the case law. Nevertheless, at this juncture, it remains unclear and unsettled under the common law whether the Crown must prove bodily harm in order for the court to find that a sexual offence is a violent offence for purposes of s. 39(1)(a).

(ii)   Are Drug Offences Violent Offences?

Even prior to the Supreme Court of Canada ruling in *R. v. C.D.; R. v. C.D.K.*, the lower courts were giving a fairly restrictive definition to the meaning of a violent offence in s. 39(1)(a) of the *YCJA* in relation to drug offences. For example, trafficking in a serious drug such as ecstasy, without additional aggravating facts, such as the use of guns or violence, was held not to be a violent offence.[210] Drug offences that, by their nature, entail the mere possibility of harm, such as the fact that someone could become ill or worse after ingesting the drug, are generally not enough to bring the offence within the definition of a violent offence.[211]

Based on the Supreme Court of Canada's definition of a violent offence as an offence in the commission of which a young person causes, attempts to cause or threatens to cause bodily harm, prosecutors face challenges in successfully arguing that drug offences are violent offences, unless a weapon or violence is present or used during the commission of the offence.[212] That said, there is no definitive or binding common law on this point. Reasonable arguments can be made, based on the Supreme Court of Canada definition of a violent offence in *R. v. C.D.; R. v. C.D.K.*,[213] that, in certain circumstances, depending on the facts, a young person who traffics in addictive and life-destroying drugs such as heroin or the notorious crystal methamphetamine has

---

status offence, Gove J. held. Justice Gove also noted that the defence had disputed that the victim had suffered psychological harm, and that the Crown had failed to prove the facts in dispute by providing evidence of the harm. Justice Gove held that he could not conclude that this offence, involving years of incest, was a violent offence.

[210]   *R. v. N.S.O.*, [2003] O.J. No. 2251 (Ont. C.J.).

[211]   *R. v. N.S.O.*, [2003] O.J. No. 2251 (Ont. C.J.).

[212]   In *R. v. N.S.O.*, [2003] O.J. No. 2251 (Ont. C.J.), King J. held that a broad definition of violent offence would cast too wide a net. "Every act in life and every offence may at some point lead to harm." (*R. v. N.S.O.*, at para. 13.) In another case, *R. v. L.P.*, [2004] O.J. No. 1484 (Ont. C.J.), the judge rejected arguments that a case involving a young person found guilty of importing three kilos of cocaine constituted a violent offence.

[213]   [2005] S.C.J. No. 79 (S.C.C.).

attempted to cause bodily harm (which, as previously discussed, captures psychological harm as well). The destructive impact of crystal methamphetamine has been widely publicized and documented, and is increasingly well known. A young person of 16 or 17 who is trafficking could be expected to be well aware of its risks and effects. Depending on the evidence called, it is reasonable that a judge could find that a young person who is found guilty of trafficking "crystal meth" has committed a violent offence, based on Bastarache J.'s definition. Evidence concerning the offender's knowledge of the drug and its side effects, as well as the impact of the drug on a particular user, or on users generally, could be called.[214]

Nevertheless, the direction of the jurisprudence suggests that the Crown may have more success arguing that certain drug crimes qualify as exceptional cases under s. 39(1)(d) due to the aggravating facts in particular cases (such as trafficking in serious drugs such as heroin).[215] As part of the legal analysis in relation to s. 39(1)(d), the courts are considering the damage that certain illicit drugs can do to society at large, as well as to the individuals who become addicted to them.[216] Arguably, many of the same arguments could be considered under s. 39(1)(a).

(iii) Is Violence to an Animal a Violent Offence?

Another active legal question regarding the definition of a violent offence in s. 39(1)(a) is whether violence to an animal falls within the definition. Despite several relevant rulings prior to *R. v. C.D.; R. v. C.D.K.* that violence to an animal can constitute a serious violent offence[217] (which under Bastarache J.'s definition would also make such

---

[214] Methamphetamine, also known as crystal meth, is a highly destructive synthetic stimulant drug that is made from a combination of chemical ingredients, which can include drain cleaner, battery acid, antifreeze and hydrochloric acid. It is a white, odourless powder that can be snorted, smoked, injected and eaten. It is a highly psychologically addictive substance. Side effects include the loss of short-term memory, mood swings, periods of rage, suicidal tendencies, malnutrition, delusions, nausea and depression. Users can experience violent behaviour at higher doses and chronic use can lead to "meth mouth", where the user experiences severe tooth decay and tooth loss. The federal government increased the maximum penalty for production and distribution of methamphetamine in 2005 from 10 years to life in prison.

[215] *R. v. P.T.B.*, [2006] O.J. No. 2327 (Ont. C.J.). This case law is considered later in this chapter during the discussion of s. 39(1)(d).

[216] *R. v. P.T.B.*, [2006] O.J. No. 2327, at para. 21 (Ont. C.J.).

[217] In *R. v. L.M.F.*, [2003] A.J. No. 1171 (Alta. Prov. Ct.), three 17-year-old persons committed a number of offences including killing three horses and wounding another. Justice Pahl noted that, *inter alia*, the killing and wounding of the horses caused deep upset to those who owned and loved them, and the entire series of events, mischief and property damage in

offences violent offences),[218] it appears that violence to an animal is not captured by Bastarache J.'s definition of a violent offence in s. 39(1)(a). Bodily harm is defined in the *Criminal Code* as injury *to a person*. Since the *YCJA* imports *Criminal Code* definitions in cases where the terms are not defined in the *YCJA*,[219] the *Criminal Code* definition applies, thus excluding injury to an animal. Justice Bastarache alludes to this issue in *R. v. C.D.; R. v. C.D.K.* but he does not analyze or discuss the issue, and his one-sentence comment can be considered *obiter dicta*. "If it seems incongruous to some that a general act involving the destruction of property or cruelty to animals is excluded simply because no person was physically harmed, I believe it is for Parliament to amend the *YCJA* if it deems it is required."[220] Although the Supreme Court of Canada had not been asked to address the question of whether a violent offence in s. 39(1)(a) captures violence to an animal, based on its definition of a violent offence, the court can be taken to have answered it. Nevertheless, Parliament may not have intended to exclude violence to animals from the s. 39 definition of a violent offence. Parliament may simply not have turned its mind to this question.

The wording of s. 39(1)(a), when read in combination with the definition of "serious violent offence" in the *YCJA* and the definition of "bodily harm" in s. 2 of the *Criminal Code*, suggests that the concept of "violent" in s. 39(1)(a) was meant to capture only violence directed toward a person, and that violence to animals was intended to be captured by other legislation, including other provisions of the *Criminal Code*.[221] That said, an argument can be made that violence to a household pet (such

---

which the young persons engaged had terrorized the community over nine days. Without engaging in a legal analysis in relation to s. 39(1)(a), or discussing the definition of a serious violent offence in s. 2 of the *YCJA*, Pahl J. characterized the offences as serious and violent in the extreme (para. 19), and offences that included significant violence and psychological and economic harm. The three young persons received 20 to 30 days of custody followed by short periods of community supervision and 18 months' probation.

See also *R. v. C.J.* (June 20, 2007), an apparently unreported Manitoba Provincial Court case, where a young person who stabbed and drowned the pet cat and left it in the bathtub in a plastic bag for his parents to discover while high on drugs was found to have committed a serious violent offence. Justice Stewart imposed the serious violent offence designation without discussing *R. v. C.D.; R. v. C.D.K.*, nor did he engage in a detailed analysis or consideration of the definition of a serious violent offence. The Crown had argued that the definition of serious violent offence in the *YCJA* does not indicate that the serious bodily harm must be to a person. The defence did not take issue with the serious violent offence designation. The young person, who was 18 at the time of sentencing, received two years' probation.

[218] In *R. v. C.D.; R. v. C.D.K.*, [2005] S.C.J. No. 79 (S.C.C.), Bastarache J. suggests at para. 23 that any serious violent offence must also be a violent offence.

[219] *YCJA*, s. 2(2).

[220] *R. v. C.D.; R. v. C.D.K.*, [2005] S.C.J. No. 79, at para. 51 (S.C.C.).

[221] A young person can be charged with cruelty to animals under s. 446 of the *Criminal Code*.

as fatally stabbing the family cat, microwaving to death a pet cat,[222] killing a cat by placing it in the washing machine, or stabbing a puppy in the eye) constitutes bodily harm to a person by virtue of the trauma and psychological harm suffered by the pet owners, since the definition of bodily harm in law includes psychological harm. Certainly, some of the case law would support this interpretation.

B.   Section 39(1)(b)

A young person can also receive a youth custodial sentence under s. 42 if he or she has failed to comply with non-custodial sentences. To engage this section, there must be evidence that the young person has failed to comply with at least two non-custodial sentences. The section does not require that the young person be found guilty of failing to comply with two non-custodial sentences to meet the definition of failing to comply; all that is required is evidence that the young person has failed to comply with two separate non-custodial sentences. A guilty finding for a breach of probation is only one way of demonstrating a failure to comply.[223] Multiple breaches of a single sentence are not enough to engage the section; what is required are breaches of at least two sentences, such as breaches of two separate probation orders,[224] at least two failures to comply with two separate non-custodial sentences,[225] but breaches of release orders will not bring one within the paragraph.[226]

Some courts have held that the sentence for which the young person is currently before the court can "count" as one of the two non-custodial sentences referred to in s. 39(1)(b), but there is no unanimity on this point.[227] In *R. v. M.S.*, the Newfoundland and Labrador Provincial Court held that s. 39(1)(b) provides that the young person may be committed to custody if he or she has failed to comply with one breach prior to the one for which the accused is being sentenced.[228] It is the number of breaches

---

[222] S. Montgomery, "Activists protest at court over cat killing" *The Globe and Mail* (8 February 2008), A6.

[223] *R. v. J.E.C.*, [2004] B.C.J. No. 2244 (B.C.S.C.). See also *R. v. P.G.*, [2006] N.W.T.J. No. 70, at para. 14 (N.W.T. Terr. Ct.).

[224] *R. v. I.C.*, [2007] N.J. No. 280 (N.L. Prov. Ct.); *R. v. G.M.S.*, [2004] N.J. No. 468 (N.L.T.D.) and *R. v. A.M.*, [2007] N.J. No. 76, at para. 29 (N.L. Prov. Ct.).

[225] *R. v. G.M.S.*, [2004] N.J. No. 468, at para. 30 (N.L.T.D.).

[226] *R. v. J.S.*, [2004] O.J. No. 754 (Ont. C.J.).

[227] *R. v. P.G.*, [2006] N.W.T.J. No. 70 (N.W.T. Terr. Ct.) provides a good overview of the jurisprudence on this point.

[228] *R. v. M.S.*, [2005] N.J. No. 199 (N.L. Prov. Ct.). See also *R. v. P.G.*, [2006] N.W.T.J. No. 70, at paras. 18 and 21 (N.W.T. Terr. Ct.).

of non-custodial sentences as of the time of sentencing[229] that is relevant to the determination as to whether the young person falls within s. 39(1)(b).

The courts have further found that the term "non-custodial sentences" captures both non-custodial dispositions under the *YOA* as well as non-custodial sentences under the *YCJA*.[230] The courts have rejected arguments that s. 33(2) of the *Interpretation Act*,[231] which states that words in the singular include the plural and words in the plural include the singular, enables one to conclude that non-compliance with only one non-custodial sentence is sufficient to make a young person eligible for a custodial sentence under s. 39(1)(b).[232]

C.   Section 39(1)(c)

Under the *YCJA*, a young person can be sentenced to custody under s. 39(1)(c) if he or she has committed an indictable offence for which an adult would be liable to imprisonment for a term of more than two years *and* has a *history* that indicates a *pattern* of findings of guilt under the *YCJA* or the *YOA*. Neither the term "history" nor "pattern" is defined in the *YCJA*. Both terms have been the subject of considerable judicial consideration. The law across the country regarding the meaning of s. 39(1)(c) was inconsistent on various points, which were not clarified until the Supreme Court of Canada released its 2008 decision in *R. v. S.A.C.*[233]

In *R. v. S.A.C.*, the young person had a significant record and was being sentenced for 15 additional offences, which consisted mainly of auto theft and break and enter into a dwelling house. In concluding that there was a history that indicated a pattern of findings of guilt, the trial judge considered not only the young person's record but the 15 offences for which he was being sentenced on that day. One of the issues on appeal was whether the judge was correct to consider the offences before the court in determining whether there is a *history that indicates a pattern of findings of guilt*. Justice Bateman of the Nova Scotia Court of Appeal held that the trial judge had not erred in considering the offences for which the

---

[229] *R. v. A.M.*, [2007] N.J. No. 76, at para. 33 (N.L. Prov. Ct.). But see *R. v. J.H.*, [2004] O.J. No. 5151 (Ont. C.J.).

[230] *R. v. E.B.*, [2004] O.J. No. 205 (Ont. C.J.). See also *R. v. R.P.B.*, [2003] A.J. No. 925 (Alta. Prov. Ct.) and *R. v. A. (E.)*, [2006] O.J. No. 3329, 66 O.R. (3d) 265 (Ont. C.J.).

[231] R.S.C. 1985, c. I-21.

[232] *R. v. A. (E.S.)*, [2003] A.J. No. 571 (Alta. Prov. Ct.).

[233] [2008] S.C.J. No. 48, 2008 SCC 47 (S.C.C.).

young person was being sentenced. The Supreme Court of Canada would later disagree with this reasoning.

Justice Bateman for the Nova Scotia Court of Appeal had relied in part on *R. v. C.D.J.*,[234] where a *pattern* of findings of guilt was held to mean that there must be at least two, and likely more, findings of guilt before a pattern can be identified. All findings of guilt — both prior findings of guilt, as well as current findings of guilt for which the young person is being sentenced,[235] were held to be relevant. Justice Bateman agreed with Franklin J. in *R. v. A.E.A.*[236] that history means the time period prior to the date of sentencing.[237] All that is required before the judge can consider the finding of guilt as part of the history of the accused is that the finding was made prior to the consideration of whether to impose a custodial sentence under s. 39(1)(c). In reaching that conclusion, various judges had observed that if a sentencing judge were able to consider at sentencing only the findings of guilt that had actually been entered prior to the sentencing date, this would encourage young persons to delay dealing with their charges individually in order to deal with them all at once at a final hearing, permitting them to argue at the time of sentencing that they had no history.[238]

The lower courts had also considered if the term "history" could include guilty findings for offences committed subsequent to the offence for which the young person was being sentenced. The trend of the appellate courts has been to permit consideration of all findings of guilt that are before the court as part of the record at the time of sentencing,[239] regardless of whether the offences to which they relate occurred before or after the offence for which the young person is being sentenced. This approach is consistent with a plain reading of the section, and also makes sense in

---

[234] [2005] A.J. No. 1190 (Alta. C.A.).

[235] *R. v. S.A.C.*, [2007] N.S.J. No. 191, at para. 16 (N.S.C.A.).

[236] [2007] A.J. No. 360 (Alta. Prov. Ct.).

[237] *R. v. S.A.C.*, [2007] N.S.J. No. 191, at para. 17 (N.S.C.A.).

[238] As Franklin J. notes in *R. v. A.E.A.*, [2007] A.J. No. 360, at para. 22 (Alta. Prov. Ct.), counsel sometimes gather all outstanding charges together in one place and at one time for sentence. This practice was identified by the Nova Scotia Nunn Commission of Inquiry, *Spiralling out of Control: Lessons Learned from a Boy in Trouble: Report of the Nunn Commission of Inquiry* (Halifax, NS: Nunn Commission of Inquiry, 2006), at 239. This report is available online at: <http://www.gov.ns.ca/just/nunn_commission/_docs/Report_Nunn_Final.pdf>. The practice has enabled defence counsel to sometimes successfully argue that the young person has no history of findings of guilt at the time of sentencing and therefore is ineligible for a custodial sentence under s. 39(1)(c). Later case law appeared to circumscribe that practice. See comments from Chartier J.A. in *R. v. D.J.M.*, [2007] M.J. No. 345, at para. 32 (Man. C.A.), and Bateman J.A. in *R. v. S.A.C.*, [2007] N.S.J. No. 191, at para. 16 (N.S.C.A.).

[239] *R. v. D.J.M.*, [2007] M.J. No. 345 (Man. C.A.) and *R. v. S.A.C.*, [2007] N.S.J. No. 191 (N.S.C.A.).

ensuring that the sentencing judge has all relevant information and background about the young person at the time of sentencing.

The Manitoba Court of Appeal adopted this approach in *R. v. D.J.M.*[240] The Crown had sought a custody sentence pursuant to s. 39(1)(c) for one of seven offences that were before the court for sentencing. In determining sentence, the trial judge considered guilty findings for offences committed subsequent to the offence (but of which he was aware at the time of sentencing) and found that there was a history indicating a pattern of findings of guilt. After engaging in fairly detailed statutory interpretation and a review of the relevant jurisprudence, Chartier J.A. held for the Manitoba Court of Appeal that the court is to consider all present and existing findings of guilt *at the time of sentencing*, regardless of whether some of the offences occurred after the offence for which the young person is being sentenced. Relying in part on *R. v. B.W.P.; R. v. B.V.N.*,[241] where the court held that all relevant factors about the offence and the offender form part of the sentencing process, Chartier J.A. held that it is important for the court to have all relevant information about the young person at the time of sentencing. "Part of this relevant background must surely include not only the findings of guilt at the time of the offence for which the young person is being sentenced, but also all other findings of guilt that are before the court that day for sentencing. To not consider all findings of guilt is to artificially sever potentially relevant information that can and ought to be used in customizing the most appropriate disposition for the young person."[242]

According to *R. v. D.J.M.*, the sentencing judge can, and should, consider all findings of guilt that are before him or her as of that point, as part of the history, in order to consider the totality of the young person's criminal past.[243] The succinct reasoning of Franklin J. in *R. v. A.E.A.*[244] makes the point clearly: "What is meant by the 'history'? The provisions dealing with the sentencing of an accused speak to the Court's deliberation *at the time the sentence is to be imposed*, not the date of the offence, the date the guilty plea was entered or any other date. It is the date that sentence is imposed that is the operative date."[245] The judge can look backward in time to consider the young person's history of findings of

---

[240] *R. v. D.J.M.*, [2007] M.J. No. 345 (Man. C.A.) and *R. v. S.A.C.*, [2007] N.S.J. No. 191 (N.S.C.A.).

[241] [2006] S.C.J. No. 27, [2006] 1 S.C.R. 941 (S.C.C.).

[242] *R. v. D.J.M.*, [2007] M.J. No. 345, at paras. 37-38 (Man. C.A.).

[243] See *R. v. D.R.U.*, [2004] B.C.J. No. 1639 (B.C. Youth Ct.) and *R. v. J.L.M.*, [2005] S.J. No. 362, 265 Sask. R. 84 (Sask. Prov. Ct.).

[244] [2007] A.J. No. 360 (Alta. Prov. Ct.).

[245] *R. v. A.E.A.*, [2007] A.J. No. 360, at paras. 20-21 and 30, 42-43 (Alta. Prov. Ct.).

guilt as of that juncture. Justice Franklin's decision was cited with approval by the Nova Scotia Court of Appeal in *R. v. S.A.C.*[246] However, the Supreme Court of Canada would later refute that reasoning.

Regarding the definition of a pattern, the courts initially interpreted a pattern to mean *either* a pattern of like offences (by comparing the nature of the offences themselves and the behaviour of the young person), or simply a pattern of criminal conduct that could be measured by the number of findings of guilt over a period of time.[247] Some appellate level courts later took the position that the offences must be at least broadly similar in order to constitute a pattern. The Nova Scotia Court of Appeal in *R. v. S.A.C.* accepted the reasoning of the Alberta Court of Appeal in *R. v. C.D.J.*[248] that the term "pattern" requires some recognizable regularity, consistency or similarity to the offences.[249] It means more than just a prior history of findings of guilt.

In *R. v. S.A.C.*, the trial judge considered all of the offences committed by S.A.C. between May and September 2005, which included the three break and enters and the nine car thefts that were currently before the court, as well as other break and enters for which he had been sentenced earlier. A stolen vehicle was sometimes used to carry out the break and enters and most of the vehicles were stolen from places of residence within a period of three months. The trial judge concluded that the number of offences, the similarity of circumstances of the offences, as well as the similarity of the offences themselves, established a *pattern* of behaviour and a pattern of findings of guilt. Considering the offences as a whole, Bateman J.A. upheld the lower court in finding that the activity unquestionably demonstrated the regularity, repetition and similarity sufficient to form a pattern.[250] By contrast, in *R. v. C.D.J.*, which involved a dial-a-doper operation, as discussed below, the accused had a history of six findings of guilt that included attempted robbery, shoplifting, and trafficking in 1.5 grams of cocaine, as well as various failures to comply. The court held that his record did not involve even broadly similar offences, nor did it form a recognizably consistent pattern of behaviour. The most serious offences — the

[246] [2007] N.S.J. No. 191 (N.S.C.A.).
[247] See a good discussion of this point in *R. v. D.R.U.*, [2004] B.C.J. No. 1639 (B.C. Youth Ct.), and, in particular, the conclusion on the point at para. 41.
[248] [2005] A.J. No. 1190 (Alta. C.A.).
[249] *R. v. S.A.C.*, [2007] N.S.J. No. 191, at para. 16 (N.S.C.A.). See also an excellent discussion of the meaning of a pattern in *R. v. A.E.A.*, [2007] A.J. No. 360 (Alta. Prov. Ct.), during which Franklin J. accepted the reasoning of the appellate courts.
[250] *R. v. S.A.C.*, [2007] N.S.J. No. 191, at para. 24 (N.S.C.A.).

attempted robbery and the trafficking offence — were also separated by a large span of time.[251]

The jurisprudence in relation to s. 39(1)(c) clearly required clarification regarding its meaning and intent. Some argued that excessive circumscribing of the term "pattern" was inconsistent with the intention of the provision. The provision refers to only a pattern of findings of guilt, indicating that all that is required to meet this aspect of the test is a repetition of guilty findings. On the other hand, if the provision were intended to mean only a repetition of guilty findings with no similarity among the offences, the word "pattern" was arguably superfluous. The phrase "history of guilty findings" is adequate to demonstrate repetitive criminal conduct. The word "pattern" was necessary as part of the definition only if drafters intended to suggest more than a pattern of criminal behaviour, for example, if drafters intended to suggest a pattern in relation to the nature of the offences themselves. The inclusion of the word "pattern" suggested that Parliament intended the word to connote something more than simply a consideration of the number of guilty findings, and that Parliament intended the judiciary to seek a pattern and similarity in relation to the nature and type of criminal offences committed.

The number of findings of guilt required to constitute a pattern has also been the subject of significant jurisprudential discussion. While some courts have logically argued that a pattern cannot be established until there are at least three examples of the conduct[252] (otherwise there is no necessity for the inclusion of the word "pattern" since the term "findings of guilt" connotes at least two findings),[253] other courts permitted more wiggle room. The Alberta Court of Appeal held in *R. v. C.D.J.* that there must be at least two, and likely more, findings of guilt before a pattern can be found.[254]

The Supreme Court of Canada expediently settled the main questions concerning the meaning and intent of s. 39(1)(c), when it decided *R.*

---

[251] *R. v. C.D.J.*, [2005] A.J. No. 1190, at para. 28 (Alta. C.A.). But see *R. v. B.K.B.*, [2005] A.J. No. 1379 (Alta. C.A.), where the court found an escalating pattern of criminal conduct and non-compliance with court orders. While one could argue that this case also involved an array of charges that did not demonstrate a similarity of offences, the court focused on B.K.B.'s track record of non-compliance with his prior deferred custody order and other dispositions rather than on examining the similarity of the substantive criminal offences, for example, the theft and trafficking in cocaine charges.

[252] *R. v. D.R.U.*, [2004] B.C.J. No. 1639 (B.C. Youth Ct.). Justice Galati concluded that in most cases a pattern will require more than two findings of guilt.

[253] *R. v. D.N.*, [2003] O.J. No. 3736 (Ont. C.J.).

[254] *R. v. C.D.J.*, [2005] A.J. No. 1190, at para. 23 (Alta. C.A.). See also a discussion of the meaning of a pattern in *R. v. C.S.T.*, [2008] O.J. No. 1309 (Ont. C.J.), where the court found that a pattern of findings of guilt had not been established in this drug case in part because possession of marihuana was not in kind or in any way related to the offence of trafficking in crack cocaine.

v. S.A.C. in July 2008. The top court refuted the reasoning of the appellate courts. In a unanimous decision, Deschamps J., who compared the wording of the French and English versions of the section, concluded that the only findings of guilt to be considered for the purposes of the provision are ones that were entered prior to the commission of the offence for which the young person is being sentenced. In addition, to demonstrate a pattern of findings of guilt, the Crown must generally adduce evidence of at least three prior guilty findings. The prior guilty findings need not relate to similar or to indictable offences.[255]

As alluded to earlier, S.A.C. was facing a slew of offences, and had pled guilty to most of them. The offences had generally been committed between January and May of 2006 and included nine counts of auto theft and three counts of breaking and entering and theft. His sentencing hearing for all of the charges had been adjourned to one date. At the time of sentencing, S.A.C. had several prior convictions for offences under the *Criminal Code*, including motor vehicle theft, as well as several guilty findings under the *YCJA*.

In her analysis, Deschamps J. noted that three key issues had to be addressed regarding the interpretation of s. 39(1)(c): (1) the date by which the prior findings of guilt must have been entered; (2) the number of findings of guilt required to conclude that a pattern existed; and (3) the nature of the offences on which the findings of guilt were based.

Applying the rules of statutory interpretation regarding the interpretation of bilingual statutes, Deschamps J. was able to expeditiously decide the first two issues: Based on the wording of the French version of s. 39(1)(c), which was narrower and permitted only one interpretation, Deschamps J. concluded that the only findings of guilt to be considered for the purpose of determining whether the young person may be committed to custody are those made before the commission of the offence for which the person is being sentenced, thus excluding any guilty findings that post-dated the commission of the offence.[256] Justice Deschamps held that the word "pattern" relates to prior findings of guilt, not to the guilty finding in respect of which the young person is being sentenced. In addition, unless the sentencing court finds that the offences are so similar that a pattern of findings of guilt can be found in only two prior convictions, the threshold for demonstrating a pattern of findings of guilt is at least three prior convictions.[257]

---

[255] *R. v. S.A.C.*, [2008] S.C.J. No. 48, at para. 1, 2008 SCC 47 (S.C.C.).
[256] *R. v. S.A.C.*, [2008] S.C.J. No. 48, at para. 19, 2008 SCC 47 (S.C.C.).
[257] *R. v. S.A.C.*, [2008] S.C.J. No. 48, at para. 22, 2008 SCC 47 (S.C.C.).

Justice Deschamps refuted the argument that findings of guilt must concern only indictable offences. "Although similarity can be relevant to the determination whether a pattern exists, the threshold is a pattern of findings of guilt, not a pattern of findings of guilt for the same type of offence as the one for which the young person is being sentenced."[258] This narrower interpretation of s. 39(1)(c) was held to be consistent with Parliament's express intent to reduce the youth incarceration rate because the court's analysis required that custody be limited to cases where the findings of guilt were made prior to the commission of the offence for which the young person is being sentenced and where the prior convictions indicate a pattern of findings of guilt.[259] Clearly, if a pattern of findings of guilt were interpreted so as to include the guilty findings for which the young person was being sentenced on that day, the threshold for custody would be reached much sooner.

Justice Deschamps noted that her interpretation was consistent with the principle of statutory interpretation that generally prevails in relation to penal statutes: "Where the interpretation of penal provisions is concerned, courts must generally ensure that any ambiguity is resolved in favour of the liberty of the accused whose liberty is at stake."[260]

The Supreme Court of Canada decision did not change the outcome for the accused in *R. v. S.A.C.*, since, even when the offences that were before the court for sentencing were excluded, his record still contained five offences for which he had already been found guilty and sentenced, three of which were related to motor vehicles. Given S.A.C.'s history, which still indicated a pattern of findings of guilt based on the analysis of the Supreme Court of Canada, the youth justice court had properly imposed a custodial sentence. The Supreme Court of Canada dismissed the appeal.

D.   39(1)(d) — Exceptional Cases

This residual clause permits a custody sentence in *exceptional cases* where the young person has committed an indictable offence, the aggravating circumstances of which are such that a non-custodial sentence would be inconsistent with the purpose and principles of sentencing in s. 38 of the *YCJA*. The term "exceptional cases" is not defined in the *YCJA*[261] but

---

[258] *R. v. S.A.C.*, [2008] S.C.J. No. 48, at para. 24, 2008 SCC 47 (S.C.C.).

[259] *R. v. S.A.C.*, [2008] S.C.J. No. 48, at para. 29, 2008 SCC 47 (S.C.C.).

[260] *R. v. S.A.C.*, [2008] S.C.J. No. 48, at para. 30, 2008 SCC 47 (S.C.C.).

[261] In the early days of the *YCJA*, it was held to apply in cases such as *R. v. K.G.B.*, [2005] N.B.J. No. 433 (N.B.C.A.), which concerned the premeditated rape of a 15-year-old girl,

Rosenberg J.A. for the Ontario Court of Appeal defined it in 2006 in the macabre case of *R. v. R.E.W.*[262] Within the context of that case, Rosenberg J.A. defined exceptional cases so narrowly that very few cases can be expected to meet the test unless they can be distinguished from *R. v. R.E.W.* Based on his definition, s. 39(1)(d) is applicable only in those very rare (non-violent) cases where the circumstances of the crime are so extreme that anything less than custody would fail to reflect societal values.[263] One example of an exceptional case is where the circumstances of the offence are so shocking as to threaten widely shared community values.[264] Exceptional cases are limited to the clearest of cases where a custodial disposition is the only one that can be justified.[265] The focus of the inquiry in s. 39(1)(d) is therefore on the circumstances of the offence.[266]

R. v. R.E.W. concerned the sentence appeal of a 14-year-old boy who was initially sentenced to four months in custody, two months community supervision, and two years probation after being found guilty of being an accessory after the fact to murder. The boy had befriended a man in his 30s, who became a father figure to him. He ended up helping his older accomplice, a violent criminal who had a conviction for homicide, dispose of the bodies of two men that the older man had murdered. The boy watched Douglas Moore cut up the bodies with an electric saw and helped him dispose of the body parts.

The main issue on appeal was the interpretation of s. 39(1)(d), and whether the circumstances of the case permitted the court to sentence R.E.W. to custody on the basis that this was an exceptional case and the aggravating facts were such that a non-custodial sentence would be inconsistent with the purpose and principles of s. 38 of the *YCJA*.

Justice Rosenberg, writing for the court, upheld the custodial sentence imposed by the trial judge, finding that it was one of the clearest cases for which a custodial disposition was the only reasonable response and that any other disposition would undermine public confidence in the youth criminal justice system. Accessory after the fact to murder is one of the most serious offences in the *Criminal Code* that is not caught by the definition of a violent offence in s. 39(1)(a), Rosenberg J.A. held. The young person's role in the case was substantial: he disposed of the saw

---

who, at the time of the incident, was found to be incapacitated and defenceless due to alcohol (at paras. 55-56).

[262] [2006] O.J. No. 265, 79 O.R. (3d) 1 (Ont. C.A.).
[263] *R. v. R.E.W.*, [2006] O.J. No. 265, at paras. 43-44, 79 O.R. (3d) 1 (Ont. C.A.).
[264] *R. v. R.E.W.*, [2006] O.J. No. 265, at para. 44, 79 O.R. (3d) 1 (Ont. C.A.).
[265] *R. v. R.E.W.*, [2006] O.J. No. 265, at paras. 4 and 44, 79 O.R. (3d) 1 (Ont. C.A.), but see summary of his conclusions at para. 44.
[266] *R. v. R.E.W.*, [2006] O.J. No. 265, at para. 44, 79 O.R. (3d) 1 (Ont. C.A.).

blade used to cut up the bodies on his own initiative. He had known Moore planned to take violent action against the two men but did nothing to stop him even though he knew Moore wrongly suspected them of stealing money and drugs that the boy himself had taken. The gruesome murders had a profound effect on the community in which they occurred, Rosenberg J.A. held.

In concluding that s. 39(1)(d) should be given a narrow interpretation, Rosenberg J.A. reviewed the legislative history of the wording of the section and noted that the wording had been broader in two earlier versions of the youth justice bill and that it had clearly been the intention of Parliament that s. 39(1) should be interpreted narrowly. This was commensurate with Parliament's intent to retreat from the broad discretionary regime under the *YOA* to require instead that specific conditions be met before custody can be imposed under the *YCJA*.[267] Justice Rosenberg reasoned that paragraphs (a) to (c) of s. 39(1) capture most of the circumstances where custody can be expected to be imposed and that s. 39(1)(d) is a residual category focused solely on the circumstances of the offence. "The circumstances of the offence must be so aggravating that nothing less than custody will vindicate the purpose and principles set out in s. 38."[268]

Although *R. v. R.E.W.* is binding only on lower courts in Ontario, this decision from an experienced Ontario appeal court judge can be expected to be persuasive across the country to the extent that it cannot be distinguished, and, if applied widely, could curtail the number of young persons found eligible for custody under s. 39(1)(d). Justice Rosenberg has set the bar very high. However, the early indications are that drug offences involving serious drugs and weapons offences, as well as cases involving a long string of serious property offences over a relatively short span of time, are meeting the definition of an exceptional case, and that the judiciary, mindful of the unique context at issue in *R.E.W.*, is distinguishing that ruling on its facts.

(i)   Drug Offences

Prior to the January 2006 ruling in *R. v. R.E.W.*, cases involving young persons found guilty of importing large amounts of the most lethal drugs such as cocaine,[269] or trafficking in cocaine,[270] or crack cocaine,[271]

---

[267] *R. v. R.E.W.*, [2006] O.J. No. 265, at paras. 36-37, 79 O.R. (3d) 1 (Ont. C.A.).

[268] *R. v. R.E.W.*, [2006] O.J. No. 265, at para. 40, 79 O.R. (3d) 1 (Ont. C.A.).

[269] In *R. v. L.P.*, [2004] O.J. No. 1484 (Ont. C.J.), the young person was found with 3 kilos of cocaine on her person with a street value of $460,000.

ecstasy,[272] or heroin,[273] were found to meet the definition of an exceptional case under s. 39(1)(d), and the young persons were therefore found to be eligible for custodial sentences. Conversely, the circumstances of a young person found in possession of 70 grams of marihuana[274] did not meet the exceptional case test in s. 39(1)(d), nor did the case of a 15-year-old girl who trafficked in a single marihuana cigarette by selling it to another youth near a school.[275]

In the wake of *R. v. R.E.W.*, it may be too early to assess if drug cases involving trafficking or importing in relation to drugs such as heroin, cocaine or "crystal meth" will routinely meet the exceptional case test and thereby deem the young person eligible for a jail sentence. However, in *R. v. P.T.B.*,[276] which was decided just a few months after *R. v. R.E.W.*, in the Toronto youth justice court, Scully J. held that trafficking in half an ounce of heroin is an exceptional case as defined under s. 39(1)(d). "There is no question that the offence in this case is a very serious one. Heroin is a deadly drug. It is, on occasion, lethal to individuals who become addicted to it. It can be lethal on a first intake. Even when not lethal, it imposes on those who use it a life of misery and depravation. ... Indeed, trafficking in heroin, because of the consequences to the community and to the society at large and the misery inflicted upon those that become addicted to it and, indeed, the lethal nature of the drug, is such that I find that trafficking in heroin does amount to a case that must come under the exception category in Section 39(1)(d). It would indeed shock societal values, truly shock societal values, for an individual who traffics in half an ounce of heroin not to be considered for a custodial sentence."[277]

Justice Scully ultimately imposed a deferred custody sentence of five months to be followed by 12 months' probation to reflect the seriousness of the crime and to also allow the accused to continue with his

---

[270] In *R. v. T. (A.)*, [2004] A.J. No. 572 (Alta. Prov. Ct.), the court held that there were sufficient aggravating circumstances to bring the case within the ambit of s. 39(1)(d). In this case, the 17-year-old young person was a major player in a dial-a-doper operation that involved trafficking in cocaine. He distributed cocaine at the street level to homeless people. The operation involved a large stash of illegal drugs. The young person earned about $12,000 over a 51-day period.

[271] *R. v. O.G.*, [2003] O.J. No. 4323 (Ont. C.J.).

[272] *R. v. N.S.O.*, [2003] O.J. No. 2551 (Ont. C.J.).

[273] *R. v. J.B.*, [2003] O.J. No. 2339 (Ont. C.J.) re trafficking in heroin by a 17-year-old sophisticated mid-level trafficker who trafficked near a school, shopping mall and library purely for financial gain.

[274] *R. v. T.M.*, [2003] S.J. No. 722 (Sask. Prov. Ct.).

[275] *R. v. F.A.G.*, [2003] Y.J. No. 130 (Y.T. Youth Ct.).

[276] [2006] O.J. No. 2327 (Ont. C.J.).

[277] *R. v. P.T.B.*, [2006] O.J. No. 2327, at paras. 9, 21 and 22 (Ont. C.J.).

studies and to avail himself of rehabilitative programs. More recently, in *R. v. L.B.*[278] the court held that the circumstances in which a young person who was part of a dial-a-dope operation in Sechelt, B.C., was found guilty of possession of cocaine for the purpose of trafficking (he was found with 11 spitballs of crack cocaine and one of soft cocaine worth a total street value of $480) brought that case within the definition of an exceptional case. It is noteworthy that the Crown filed a report, detailing the impact of cocaine on the Sunshine Coast area of B.C. Justice Rounthwaite noted, in the course of the decision, the serious impact of cocaine trafficking on the community.

Conversely, in the 2008 Ontario case of *R. v. C.S.T.*,[279] Campbell J. concluded that a 16-year-old who was found guilty of possession of crack cocaine (about 111 grams) for the purpose of trafficking was involved in only routine trafficking and that the circumstances were not such so as to bring the matter within the definition of an exceptional case. In the course of the ruling, Campbell J. distinguished the case from *R. v. T. (A.)*,[280] in which the young person was a major player in the dial-a-dope operation, and from *R. v. L.P.*,[281] which involved the importation of 3 kilos of cocaine, to hold that there was nothing to place the case at bar within the category of an exceptional case. Justice Campbell also noted that the test for an exceptional case in *R. v. R.E.W.* was established against the backdrop of a horrifying case. By contrast, the facts of *R. v. C.S.T.* did not bring it within the definition of an exceptional case, despite the serious-ness of the drug being trafficked.

(ii)   Weapons Cases

Regarding possession of firearms by young persons, the decisions vary as to whether the circumstances of these offences bring the cases within the definition of an exceptional case under s. 39(1)(d). Justice Bloomenfeld of the Ontario Court of Justice stressed in the 2007 case of *R. v. C.W.*[282] that the variance in results emphasizes the individualized nature of youth sentencing. After reviewing the jurisprudence in her jurisdiction, Bloomenfeld J. held in *R. v. C.W.* that the facts of that case brought it within the definition of an exceptional case: The police had found a loaded Walther P38 semi-automatic handgun with three live

---

[278]   [2007] B.C.J. No. 2921 (B.C. Prov. Ct.).
[279]   [2008] O.J. No. 1308 (Ont. C.J.).
[280]   [2004] A.J. No. 572 (Alta. Prov. Ct.).
[281]   [2004] O.J. No. 1484 (Ont. C.J.).
[282]   [2007] O.J. No. 4929 (Ont. C.J.).

rounds in the magazine in a vehicle in which C.W. was the sole occupant. Justice Bloomenfeld considered the case against the backdrop of gun crime in Toronto, including the fact that the possession of guns by young men is at the forefront of public safety concerns in Toronto. On the facts of C.W., the accused was in possession of a loaded restricted handgun that he had no right to possess and he appeared to be transporting it somewhere for purposes that were neither innocent nor benign.[283]

Justice Tuck-Jackson, also of the Ontario Court of Justice, has held in another weapons case, R. v. A.R.,[284] that the circumstances of that case also met the definition of an exceptional case. That case involved a break-in and possession of firearms by a 15-year-old and two other young persons. In her ruling, Tuck-Jackson J. relied on the analytical framework in R. v. R.E.W. to conclude that A.R. was an exceptional case: "... in my respectful view the community would find it shocking that a 15-year-old would participate in the theft of firearms and the conversion of one of them into a prohibited weapon, together with the planning of those activities".[285]

(iii) Property Offences and Distinguishing R. v. R.E.W.[286]

Some courts are distinguishing R. v. R.E.W. because of its unique facts, particularly in cases involving chronic property offences committed over a relatively short span of time, where the impact on the community is considered highly relevant. In R. v. D.B.,[287] Hyslop J. concluded that R. v. R.E.W. was not a good comparator for the case at bar. The case before Hyslop J. concerned a low-level assault resulting in no injury, as well as six school break-ins, two of which involved arson and property damage, totalling $38,000. Justice Hyslop relied on another property damage case involving a break-in to a school, resulting in property damage of about $30,000.[288] Justice Hyslop concluded that the case before him qualified as

---

[283] R. v. C.W., [2007] O.J. No. 4929, at paras. 14 and 15 (Ont. C.J.).

[284] [2007] O.J. No. 1202 (Ont. C.J.).

[285] R. v. A.R., [2007] O.J. No. 1202, at para. 26 (Ont. C.J.). Weapons offences have fallen within the definition of an exceptional case in other cases such as R. v. M.J., [2007] O.J. No. 2696 (Ont. C.J.) and R. v. G.S.M.P., [2007] O.J. No. 2385 (Ont. C.J.). But see R. v. N.G., [2007] O.J. No. 1199 (Ont. C.J.), which involved one of the parties to the same offences as A.R. where Gage J. relied on his observation that possession of a prohibited firearm by a youth in Toronto youth court is not an unusual or unique event and in the end concluded that it was not an exceptional case.

[286] [2006] O.J. No. 265, 79 O.R. (3d) 1 (Ont. C.A.).

[287] [2007] N.J. No. 423 (N.L. Prov. Ct.).

[288] R. v. W. (A.B.), [2003] B.C.J. No. 3013 (B.C. Prov. Ct.). In concluding that this case was exceptional, the judge considered the degree of calculation, the $30,000 in damage, and the number of persons affected (the staff was upset, the community was shocked and the children were traumatized), as well as the fact that the elementary school had to be closed for four days for clean-up. The accused was 17. R. v. W. (A.B.), [2003] B.C.J. No. 3013, at paras. 16 and 17 (B.C. Prov. Ct.).

an exceptional case under s. 39(1)(d) because the accused and two other young persons broke into six schools in the space of a few hours and conducted a "sustained, deliberate, concerted, and repeated attack on schools which form the heart of the community. This was [a] deliberate course of criminal conduct conducted under the cover of darkness which could only be considered a rampage. Such attacks shock the community as schools are a valued community asset. They are institutions set apart for the special purpose of learning ... An attack against a school is an attack against learning and against civilization. ... Hence they attack the community as a whole".[289] In addition, in at least two of the break-ins, the entire school could have been lost due to fire, Hyslop J. added. The facts surrounding these particular school break-ins were so "unique, so fraught with danger to so many, and so base, as to shock the conscience of the community and imperil its sense of safety",[290] Hyslop J. found. Conversely, the judge who sentenced the sister regarding the same events (she was the central figure in relation to the arson charges) did not find that the facts brought the case within the definition of an exceptional case.[291]

Given the frequency of break-ins, vandalism and related conduct by young persons, the concept of an exceptional case may not have been intended to capture offences such as those outlined in *R. v. D.B.* which, at their core, are nuisance and property offences involving relatively insignificant damages of $38,000. In a more recent decision from the same court, Gorman J. held that the circumstances involving a 16-year-old who pled guilty to 26 offences, including breach of undertakings, break and enter, theft, possession of stolen goods and illegal possession of alcohol in relation to incidents over a period of about six months, did not qualify as an exceptional case.[292] Overall, the circumstances lacked the required aggravating factors.

However, in an interesting 2009 decision from the Nunavut Court of Justice, Kilpatrick J. held that Nunavut's isolated communities would not be protected by the *YCJA* if the court adopted the very narrow interpretation of the exceptional case advanced in *R. v. R.E.W.* "Ontario has the non-custodial alternatives that are necessary to implement the philosophy of the YCJA. Nunavut does not."[293] Justice Kilpatrick found that the facts in *R. v. K.G.S.* (a string of property offences over a short span of time) brought that case within the definition of an exceptional case: the troubled 16-year-old had persistently committed break-ins over a nine-month

---

[289]   [2007] N.J. No. 423, at para. 17 (N.L. Prov. Ct.).

[290]   *R. v. D.B.*, [2007] N.J. No. 423, at para. 19 (N.L. Prov. Ct.).

[291]   The contrary decision of Spracklin J. appears to be unreported.

[292]   *R. v. J.B.*, [2008] N.J. No. 326 (N.L. Prov. Ct.).

[293]   *R. v. K.G.S.*, [2009] Nu.J. No. 10, at paras. 30 and 31 (Nu. C.J.).

period and was considered to be out of control. Fifteen of the offences were indictable crimes involving homes, and were described by the judge as having had a significant impact on the community of Rankin Inlet. Finding that there were no practical alternatives to custody, the judge sentenced the young person to a term of 11 months, 7.5 of which would be served in actual custody.

Perjury by a young person in relation to a first degree murder allegation has also been found to meet the exceptional case test,[294] as have two escapes from lawful custody.[295]

R. v. R.E.W. is binding on lower courts only in Ontario to the extent that it cannot be distinguished, although it may be persuasive in other jurisdictions. In addition, the evolving jurisprudence suggests that whether a case falls within the definition of an exceptional case may depend, at least in part, on perceived community values and concerns, which can vary across jurisdictions and, indeed, even within a jurisdiction. An incident could well be perceived to be an exceptional case in rural Newfoundland but would not be found to fall within the definition of an exceptional case in an urban environment, such as Toronto. It is premature to predict how extensively the test for an exceptional case established by the Ontario Court of Appeal in *R. v. R.E.W.* will be relied on outside of Ontario, particularly in light of the unusual and serious facts that inspired it.

(iv) *Alternatives to Custody Must Still Be Canvassed*

Even if the circumstances in any of paragraphs (a) to (c) in s. 39(1) are found to apply in a given case (note that s. 39(1)(d) is not mentioned here), this does not mean that the young person will receive custody. It means only that custody is an available option for the young person in the circumstances and the judge is not prohibited from imposing it. If the judge determines that one of the three options above apply, he or she must first consider all alternatives to custody raised at the sentencing hearing that are reasonable in the circumstances and determine that there is not a reasonable alternative or combination of alternatives to custody that is in accordance with the purpose and principles in s. 38 before imposing custody under the relevant section.[296] If the judge imposes a sentence that includes a custodial portion, the judge is obliged to provide reasons why a

---

[294] *R. v. S.L.*, [2006] O.J. No. 3609 (Ont. C.J.).

[295] *R. v. D.J.B.*, [2007] N.J. No. 87 (N.L. Prov. Ct.).

[296] *YCJA*, s. 39(2). On this point, see *R. v. S.L.*, [2003] B.C.J. No. 2397, 179 C.C.C. (3d) 97 (B.C.C.A.).

non-custodial sentence was not considered adequate, including why the judge determined that the case was an exceptional case.[297] In addition, the judge is required to state his or her reasons for the youth sentence in the record of the case and is required, upon request, to provide a copy of the sentence and the reasons to various parties, including the young person and his or her parents and counsel.[298]

The *YCJA* prohibits a youth justice court judge from imposing custody as a substitute for appropriate child protection, mental health or other social measures.[299] This provision has long been perceived as a legislative response to the 1993 decision of *R. v. M. (J.J.)*,[300] in which Cory J. upheld what many youth justice experts considered to be a disproportionately severe custodial sentence in order to address welfare concerns. Some critics viewed the decision in *R. v. M. (J.J.)* as punishing the young person for having suffered a difficult childhood and disadvantaged background.[301] As discussed earlier in this chapter, Cory J. concluded that a two-year open custody sentence was justified in order to provide the young person with the necessary guidance and assistance that he was not receiving at home. In essence, Cory J. held that the custodial sentence was necessary to achieve J.J.M.'s rehabilitation. By including s. 39(5) in the *YCJA*, Parliament took legislative steps to ensure that young persons could not be jailed unless a custody sentence was warranted due to the nature of the offence and other relevant circumstances. The section sends a strong message to the judiciary that young persons are not to be jailed as a means of child protection or to address other social welfare concerns. A young person is not to be punished through jail because he or she comes from a dysfunctional home.

VI. PRE-SENTENCE REPORT

Pre-sentence reports are a critical element of the sentencing process for young persons, and can play a major role in determining an appropriate sentence. A thorough pre-sentence report is a great aid to the sentencing judge. A pre-sentence report is required before a judge can impose a custodial youth sentence under s. 42, unless the prosecutor and the young person or his or her counsel agree that it is not necessary and the judge

---

[297]   *YCJA*, s. 39(9). *R. v. S.L.*, [2003] B.C.J. No. 2397, 179 C.C.C. (3d) 97 (B.C.C.A.).

[298]   *YCJA*, s. 48.

[299]   *YCJA*, s. 39(5). The *YOA* contained a similar prohibition in s. 24(1.1)(a).

[300]   [1993] S.C.J. No. 14, [1993] 2 S.C.R. 421 (S.C.C.).

[301]   A good discussion of the implications of *R. v. M. (J.J.)* can be found in Nicholas Bala, *Youth Criminal Justice Law* (Toronto: Irwin Law Inc., 2003), at 452.

agrees.[302] The judge is free to order a pre-sentence report in any circumstances if he or she considers it advisable.[303] A well-prepared report is of great assistance to the sentencing judge, and is usually advantageous to the young person because it is an opportunity for the young person to demonstrate to the judge that he or she has made positive changes since the incident. In practice, the judge often adjourns the matter following a guilty finding to allow time for the preparation of a pre-sentence report. Statements made by young persons during the course of the preparation of pre-sentence reports are inadmissible in criminal or civil proceedings involving the young persons except for their sentencing under s. 42, reviews of non-custodial sentences, hearings under s. 72 where the court is considering whether to impose an adult sentence, or reviews or other proceedings relating to custodial sentences.[304]

The value of a pre-sentence report should not be underestimated. A good one should give the judge a comprehensive and accurate history of the young person who is appearing for sentencing. The report usually contains an abundance of information about the young person's history and background, and how they have fared and responded since the incident. It contains information about their family life, school performance, and their criminal past,[305] if relevant, and should identify any and all emotional, psychological and other problems, issues and challenges they may be facing. It is a chance for a young person to ensure that all of the facts and circumstances that may have contributed to that young person finding himself or herself before the court come to the attention of the judge.[306] Any recommendations from a conference held in accordance with s. 41, as discussed below, are among the pieces of information that are to be included in the pre-sentence report. A pre-sentence report can also contain information from the victim.

If the young person or the young person's counsel, or the prosecutor, takes issue with any statements made in the pre-sentence report, they can,

---

[302] YCJA, s. 39(6) and (7).

[303] YCJA, s. 40(1)(b).

[304] YCJA, s. 40(10).

[305] The YCJA does not provide for inclusion in the pre-sentence report information relating to extrajudicial measures taken against the young person except for extrajudicial sanctions. Further, information relating to the previous criminal conduct of the young person can be included only if the record is still accessible under s. 119(2) of the YCJA. Extrajudicial sanctions are the only type of extrajudicial measures that are accessible to various parties under s. 119. Records of other types of extrajudicial measures are accessible to a narrower group of people under s. 119(4).

[306] YCJA, s. 40(2) outlines in detail the nature of the information generally contained in a pre-sentence report.

on application, cross-examine the person who prepared the report,[307] who is usually a probation officer or a youth worker.

VII. CONFERENCES UNDER SECTION 41[308]

When a youth justice court finds a young person guilty of an offence, the court may convene or cause to be convened a conference under s. 19 to seek recommendations to the court on an appropriate sentence. While it is unclear how widely judges across the country are availing themselves of their power to convene judicial conferences under s. 41, some judges are clearly exercising their powers under this section to establish s. 19 conferences to bring together various parties to receive advice on a youth sentence prior to imposing the sentence.[309] Judges are not obliged to follow the recommendations and advice received but if a consensus is reached among various parties, including the victim and the community regarding an appropriate sentence, the judge can be expected to give it careful consideration. Conferences can take many forms and tend to vary in format across jurisdictions; a sentencing circle falls within the parameters of a conference.

Section 19 of the *YCJA* concerns conferences generally and is broader than s. 41. While s. 41 provides specific authority to a judge, upon finding a young person guilty, to call a conference to solicit advice on sentencing, if he or she desires, s. 19 is a broader provision under the *YCJA* that permits various parties, in addition to a judge, such as a police officer, a prosecutor or a youth worker, to convene or cause to be convened a conference in order to assist in making a decision under the Act. A conference can be organized under s. 19 to seek advice on various matters in addition to sentencing, such as extrajudicial measures, bail conditions, sentence reviews and re-integration plans, but the mandate of a s. 19 conference is not limited to those subject matters.

---

[307] *YCJA*, s. 40(6).

[308] Conferences are discussed in Chapter 5 on diversion.

[309] *R. v. T.D.P.*, [2004] S.J. No. 254, 250 Sask. R. 3 (Sask. Prov. Ct.). See also Charmaine Panko, "R v. T.D.P.: A Young Offender, His Sentencing Circle, and the YCJA" (2005) 68 Sask. L. Rev. 455. See also *R. v. T.C.*, [2006] N.S.J. No. 531 (N.S. Prov. Ct.). That said, the anecdotal evidence suggests that at least some judges are reluctant to convene s. 41 conferences because the Act provides no guidelines regarding these conferences.

VIII.   YOUTH SENTENCES — SECTION 42

A.   Section 42(2) — Types of Sentences

Under the *YCJA*, Canadian judges have a wider range of potential youth sentences than most other common law jurisdictions.[310] The sentences cover a broad spectrum, from a stern judicial scolding known as a reprimand to various forms of restitution, compensation, community or personal service work orders and supervision in the community, to custodial and conditional supervision orders for the most serious crimes of up to 10 years for first degree murder.

Under the new regime, custodial sentences must always include a period of supervision in the community to assist the young person in reintegrating into the community. A custodial youth sentence cannot be imposed under any of paragraphs (a) to (c) in s. 39(1) if there is a reasonable alternative or combination of alternatives to custody that is in keeping with the sentencing principles in s. 38 of the *YCJA*.[311]

Prior to imposing a youth sentence, the judge is obliged to consider any recommendations that arise from a s. 41 conference, any pre-sentence report, as well as any representations made by or on behalf of the parties, including from the parents of the young person.[312] A victim impact statement can also be read during the sentencing hearing and considered in determining the sentence.[313]

The judge can impose any one of the sanctions in s. 42(2) or any combination of them that are not inconsistent with each other except that, if the young person is found guilty of first or second degree murder, the court must impose the sanctions specified in paragraph (q) or sub-paragraph (r)(ii) or (iii) in s. 42(2) and may also impose any other sanction in s. 42(2) that the judge considers appropriate.

With the exception of murder, the maximum duration of one youth sentence (which may have multiple sanctions) is two years, unless an

---

[310] Julian V. Roberts and Nicholas Bala, "Understanding Sentencing Under the *Youth Criminal Justice Act*" (2003) 41 Alta. L. Rev. 395, at para. 66 (QL).

[311] *YCJA*, s. 39(2).

[312] *YCJA*, s. 42(1).

[313] Similar to the *YOA*, victim impact statements can be considered under the *YCJA* by a youth justice court judge for the purpose of determining a youth sentence. Section 50 of the *YCJA* incorporates s. 722 of the *Criminal Code* into the *YCJA*, which provides for victim impact statements. A victim is now entitled to read his or her statement to the court, describing the harm done to, or the loss suffered by, the victim, arising from the commission of the offence. In the event that the victim is deceased or otherwise incapable of making a statement, a spouse or common-law partner or any relative of the victim can provide a statement.

adult could receive life for the offence, in which case a young person can receive a maximum of three years.[314] A single youth sentence in the case of attempt to commit murder, manslaughter or aggravated sexual assault cannot exceed three years.[315] As mentioned above, the maximum sentence for first degree murder is 10 years, and the maximum sentence for second degree murder is seven years.[316] Prohibition, seizure or forfeiture orders can continue in effect for more than two years.[317]

Unless a second youth sentence is imposed before the completion of one or more other youth sentences, the continuous combined duration of more than one youth sentence imposed in relation to different offences cannot exceed three years, unless one of the offences is murder, in which case the continuous combined duration of those youth sentences shall not exceed 10 years in the case of first degree murder or seven years in the case of second degree murder.[318]

Seven of the sentencing options under the *YCJA* are new; three of these are available only if the province has established a program providing for them. The seven new sentencing options are: judicial reprimands, a custody and supervision order (CASO), a deferred custody and community supervision order (DCSO), a sentence of intermittent custody, an intensive support and supervision program (ISSP), an attendance order, and an intensive rehabilitative custody and supervision order (IRCS). The latter three options are available provided the province or territory has implemented them.[319]

B.   Reprimands[320]

A judicial reprimand, which has been described as a "stern judicial warning"[321] is a new sentencing option under the *YCJA*. This is the most lenient youth sentence available. Some judges suggest that the reprimand is not a sanction or sentence at all but merely a warning to the young

---

[314] *YCJA*, s. 42(2)(n) and (14).

[315] *YCJA*, s. 42(2)(o), (q) and (r).

[316] *YCJA*, s. 42(2)(q).

[317] *YCJA*, s. 51(2), s. 42(2)(j) and s. 42(14).

[318] *YCJA*, s. 42(15). This section is analyzed in *R. v. S. (D.)*, [2008] O.J. No. 4231 (Ont. C.A.). Duration and merger of sentences is discussed further in ss. 42, 43 and related sections.

[319] In *R. v. K.G.S.*, [2009] Nu.J. No. 10, at paras. 19 and 20 (Nu. C.J.), Kilpatrick J. commented on the "sad reality" that, in Nunavut, many of the alternatives to custody contemplated by the *YCJA* do not exist. He noted that, six years after the *YCJA* came into force, there were no attendance programs or Intensive Support and Supervision Programs in Nunavut.

[320] *YCJA*, s. 42(2)(a).

[321] *R. v. D.J.M.*, [2007] M.J. No. 450, at para. 28 (Man. Q.B).

person not to reoffend.[322] Reprimands were intended to be used in relation to relatively minor first offences, and to include a discussion between the judge and the young person.[323] In practice, it is believed by some that judges sometimes impose reprimands to send a message to the Crown that the matter should not have proceeded through the formal system,[324] and that an extrajudicial measure may have been more appropriate. The perceived leniency of this "sentence" is buttressed by the fact that a record of the reprimand can be accessed for only two months from the date of the guilty finding, similar to a situation under the Act where the charge has been dismissed or withdrawn.

To some degree, the perceived leniency of a reprimand is in the eyes of the beholder. Some young persons, particularly those who have never before come into conflict with the criminal law, may be profoundly influenced by the judicial reprimand. The fact is that the reprimand *is* a formal court sanction, which requires the young person to experience the court process: they appear in court and are found guilty by a judge. This process is likely to have an impact on at least some first time youthful offenders. For many first-time offenders, a judicial reprimand may be comparable in its impact to receiving a stern lecture from a police officer who stops the teenager for speeding along a busy highway on his way to the ski hill with his baby sister in the seat beside him. A law-abiding teenager who has had no involvement with the law up until that point could well be shaken up by such an interaction. Some young persons would learn from such experiences.

In addition, while a judicial reprimand is arguably the most lenient youth sentence that can be imposed under the *YCJA*, it is not a particularly lenient criminal justice system response because a guilty finding has been entered against the young person. He or she has been exposed to the court process and the judicial system, and thus must endure the stigma and repercussions attached to that. A record of the reprimand remains accessible for two months from the time the guilty finding is entered.[325]

---

[322] *R. v. D.J.M.*, [2007] M.J. No. 450, at para. 18 (Man. Q.B).

[323] Nicholas Bala, *Youth Criminal Justice Law* (Toronto: Irwin Law Inc., 2003), at 431.

[324] Nicholas Bala, *Youth Criminal Justice Law* (Toronto: Irwin Law Inc., 2003), at 432 and Julian V. Roberts and Nicholas Bala, "Understanding Sentencing Under the *Youth Criminal Justice Act*" (2003) 41 Alta. L. Rev. 395, at n. 109. This purpose for a reprimand is also discussed in the federal government website materials on the *YCJA* in YCJA Explained, in the Explanatory Text on Youth Sentencing, which can be accessed at the Department of Justice's website at: <http://www.justice.gc.ca/eng/pi/yj-jj/ycja-lsjpa/ycja-lsjpa.html>. One can also infer this from *R. v. K.D.*, [2003] N.S.J. No. 165 (N.S.S.C.), where Lynch J. appeared to consider the case largely a matter for the health and social service authorities rather than for the criminal justice system. The 15-year-old young person was very troubled.

[325] *YCJA*, s. 119(2)(c).

Two recent Manitoba appeal cases decided by the same judge and issued on the same day in December 2007 illustrate how the reprimand is being used, or not, as the case may be, as a sentencing option. In both cases, the appeal court rejected the sentencing judge's decision to issue reprimands in cases related to serious charges. In one case, Joyal J. suggested that sentencing judges appear to be using the reprimand in cases involving a period of pre-sentence custody when they do not wish to impose any additional custody or other available disposition under the *YCJA*.[326]

In *R. v. D.J.M.*, the young person had threatened to assault and shoot his teacher in the head, and spent 43 days in custody for the offence of uttering threats. Since he had already spent 43 days in custody, the judge noted seven days of time in custody and issued a reprimand as the official sentence when sentencing the 14-year-old.[327] On appeal, Joyal J. noted that the sentence did not satisfy the sentencing principles of parity or proportionality under s. 38 of the *YCJA*. Justice Joyal found that pre-sentence custody is not part of the sentence. Although it must be taken into account and may be noted, the sentence is the disposition imposed on the day of sentencing.[328] Justice Joyal set aside the reprimand and substituted one day of custody.

In a sister decision, *R. v. M.A.P.*,[329] Joyal J. overturned the reprimand imposed by the sentencing judge regarding a young person who had breached his probation in relation to serious offences by failing to report, defying his curfew and failing to co-operate to the point of getting expelled from his job-training program. (The young person had been placed on one year's probation in relation to guilty findings for dangerous operation of a motor vehicle, possession of property obtained by crime under $5,000 (the motor vehicle) and assault with a weapon.) At the time of the breaches, the young person already had guilty findings for seven prior criminal offences including another theft of a motor vehicle. By his sentencing date for the breaches, the young person had spent 15 days in pre-trial custody. The sentencing judge took that into account and rejected the Crown's submission that he receive an additional 12 months of probation.

Justice Joyal of the Manitoba Queen's Bench held that a reprimand was not a fit sentence in the circumstances, that it was not in accordance with either the principle of regional parity or proportionality because the young person violated his probation for a number of serious offences in a

---

[326] *R. v. D.J.M.*, [2007] M.J. No. 450 (Man. Q.B.).
[327] *R. v. D.J.M.*, [2007] M.J. No. 450, at para. 11 (Man. Q.B.).
[328] *R. v. D.J.M.*, [2007] M.J. No. 450, at para. 31 (Man. Q.B.).
[329] [2007] M.J. No. 452 (Man. Q.B.).

prolonged and serious way in relation to serious offences.[330] In overturning the sentence and replacing it with a one-year probationary term, the appeal court judge also considered that a record of the reprimand would have been accessible for only two months.[331]

It is also noteworthy that once the finding of guilt is entered in relation to the reprimand, with certain exceptions, the sentence is deemed to have been effectively "served" or completed. This means that the youth sentence (the reprimand) has ceased to have effect as of that point and that, pursuant to s. 82 of the *YCJA*, the young person is deemed as of that juncture not to have been found guilty or convicted of an offence. While the record concerning the reprimand remains available for two months from the date of the guilty finding, the fact of the reprimand cannot generally prejudice the young person in terms of their future work prospects. For example, as of the date of the guilty finding in relation to the reprimand, no application in relation to employment in the federal government or with the Canadian Forces can require the young person as an applicant to disclose that he or she has been charged with or found guilty of an offence for which he or she has completed the youth sentence. This same principle applies to absolute discharges, as discussed immediately below.[332]

C.   Absolute Discharge[333]

An absolute discharge is similar to a reprimand because neither sanction once imposed, requires anything further of the young person. Similar to a reprimand, an absolute discharge is imposed after a finding of guilt.[334] An absolute discharge can be imposed if the court considers it in the best interests of the young person and not contrary to the public interest.[335] One significant distinction between the two sanctions is that access to the record of a young person who has been granted an absolute discharge lasts for one year from the date of the guilty finding, compared to two months for a reprimand,[336] which suggests that a reprimand is the more lenient sanction.

---

[330] *R. v. M.A.P.*, [2007] M.J. No. 452, at paras. 22-27 (Man. Q.B.).

[331] *R. v. M.A.P.*, [2007] M.J. No. 452, at para. 32 (Man. Q.B.).

[332] *YCJA*, s. 82 and s. 82(3) in particular.

[333] *YCJA*, s. 42(2)(b).

[334] *YCJA*, s. 42(2).

[335] *YCJA*, s. 42(2)(b).

[336] *YCJA*, s. 119(2)(c).

Again, similar to a reprimand, the imposition of an absolute discharge is significant in as much as the young person is generally[337] deemed not to have been found guilty or convicted of the offence from the date of the absolute discharge in order to reduce any prejudice or stigma the young person may suffer in relation to involvement in the youth justice system. For example, after receiving an absolute discharge, the young person cannot be required to disclose the fact of the absolute discharge on an application form relating to employment in any federal government department or enrolment with the Canadian Forces.[338]

D.   Conditional Discharge[339]

The young person can also be discharged on any conditions the court considers appropriate, which may include requiring the young person to report to a probation officer. At least some of the conditions of a conditional discharge are apt to be the same as those imposed as part of a probation order.[340] A youth court record in relation to a conditional discharge can be accessed for a period of three years from the date of the guilty finding.[341] A sentence of a conditional discharge cannot be combined with probation, an intensive support and supervision program (ISSP) or an attendance program,[342] presumably because such sentences contain similar supervisory elements and are inconsistent with each other.

If the young person fulfils the conditions of the discharge, he or she will be considered discharged. If he or she does not obey the conditions of the discharge, the young person can be charged with failure to comply with the sentence.[343]

The record of the conditional discharge remains accessible for a three-year period from the date of the guilty finding so that if the young person commits another offence during that period, the conditional discharge can be considered in relation to the sentencing for that subsequent offence.

---

[337] There are exceptions to this, which are spelled out in s. 82 of the *YCJA*.

[338] *YCJA*, s. 82(3)(a).

[339] *YCJA*, s. 42(2)(c). *R. v. P.J.S.*, [2008] N.S.J. No. 538 (N.S.C.A.) provides a contemporary discussion of a conditional discharge and compares it to other sentences under the *YCJA*, such as an absolute discharge and probation.

[340] The conditions that can be included in a probation order are contained in s. 55.

[341] *YCJA*, s. 119(2)(f).

[342] *YCJA*, s. 42(11).

[343] *YCJA*, s. 137.

E.   Fines[344]

A young person can also receive a fine of up to $1,000. For various reasons, fining a young person is not always a desirable sentence. Firstly, fines are punitive with little rehabilitative value.[345] In addition, a young person may not be in a position to pay a fine. While the judge is obliged to inquire into the young person's present and future ability to pay the fine,[346] even if the judge is satisfied that the young person can pay the fine, the judge has no way of knowing if in fact the young person actually pays the fine, or whether the parents end up footing the bill. It is quite likely that in many instances the parents pay the fine. This outcome teaches a young person little about responsibility. Fines can also expose an obvious inequity between young persons whose parents can pay the fine for them and those whose parents cannot. The latter young person is more likely to soon find herself or himself back before the courts for non-payment of the fine.

F.   Compensation and Restitution[347]

The *YCJA* also provides for the young person to make various forms of compensation or restitution for the offence to various persons for various purposes including for personal injury, loss of, or damage to, property, and loss of income or support. Similar to a fine, if a judge orders the young person to make compensation or restitution under s. 42(2)(e) or (h), respectively, the judge must consider the young person's present and future means to pay.[348] The judge cannot order a young person to compensate a person in kind or by way of personal service under s. 42(2)(h) for loss, damage or injury in relation to the offence until the youth justice court has first obtained the consent of the person (*i.e.*, the victim) to be compensated.[349] Some victims, understandably, may not want to have any involvement or contact with the young person.

---

[344] *YCJA*, s. 42(2)(d).

[345] Nicholas Bala, *Youth Criminal Justice Law* (Toronto: Irwin Law Inc., 2003), at 433.

[346] *YCJA*, s. 54(1).

[347] *YCJA*, s. 42(2)(e)-(h).

[348] *YCJA*, s. 54(1).

[349] *YCJA*, s. 54(6).

G.   Community Service[350]

A young person can also be ordered to perform community service, but whether ordered to perform a personal service or a community service, the service cannot exceed 240 hours and must be performed within a year of the order.[351] In addition, the judge cannot impose either personal or community service unless satisfied that the young person is a suitable candidate for the service and that the performance of the work does not interfere with the normal hours of work or education of the young person.[352] The term "suitable candidate" is not defined but presumably a judge must be satisfied that the young person is capable of performing the work in a reasonable and responsible fashion. A sentence of community service is often favoured by the judiciary as it enables the young person to repay the community for the harm caused and is in accord with principles of restorative justice that encourage reparation of the harm done to the victim and/or the community. Such orders give meaning to restorative justice principles of the *YCJA*, such as s. 3(1)(c)(ii) of the Declaration of Principle, which says that, within the limits of fair and proportionate accountability, the measures taken against young persons who commit offences should encourage the repair of harm done to victims and the community.

H.   Orders of Prohibition, Seizure or Forfeiture

A youth justice court judge can also make any order of prohibition, seizure or forfeiture[353] that can be made in relation to any Act of Parliament.[354] The court must make an order of at least two years[355] in relation to the prohibition of possession of any firearms and other dangerous weapons if the young person is found guilty of any of the offences listed in s. 109 of the *Criminal Code*, such as offences against a person in which violence was used, attempted or threatened and for which the young

---

[350]   *YCJA*, s. 42(2)(i).

[351]   *YCJA*, s. 54(8).

[352]   *YCJA*, s. 54(7). This condition also applies to attendance orders under s. 42(2)(m), which are discussed later in this chapter.

[353]   *YCJA*, s. 42(2)(j).

[354]   Common prohibition orders can include prohibitions on driving and the possession of weapons. Prohibition orders can also be made in relation to owning an animal if the young person has been found guilty of cruelty to an animal under s. 446(1)(a) of the *Criminal Code*.

[355]   *YCJA*, s. 51. This mandatory prohibition is in addition to any other sentence imposed under s. 42. Section 113 of the *Criminal Code* provides for an exception to the mandatory prohibition if the young person requires the weapon for hunting or trapping purposes or in relation to employment.

person could be sentenced to prison for 10 years or more, weapons offences, and serious drug offences under the *CDSA* such as trafficking, producing and importing. A firearms prohibition can be imposed as a term of probation. However, an order cannot be made against a young person under s. 161 of the *Criminal Code*, which is the section that is aimed at sexual offenders and prohibits their attendance at locations where young persons under the age of 14 can reasonably be expected to be, such as school grounds, public parks or community centres. The rationale for this is that a young accused person will invariably be around other young persons in the course of his or her daily life so that such a prohibition is considered inappropriate.

I.   Probation[356]

A young person may also be placed on probation for up to two years.[357] Historically, breach of probationary conditions has often resulted in young persons being sentenced to custody in Canada, which became a concern for the federal government. The federal government has indicated that under the *YOA*, 20 per cent of custody sentences resulted from a young person found guilty of a breach of a condition of probation. About 50 per cent of young persons found guilty of a breach were being sentenced to custody.[358]

In its background materials on the *YCJA*, the federal government suggests that probation conditions must be carefully assessed to determine if there is a clear relationship between the young person's criminal behaviour and the condition. The materials also advise that consideration should be given to the likelihood of the young person being able to comply with the condition. In the event of a breach of a probation condition, the federal government further indicates that a charge of breach of probation does not have to be laid. A review of the probation order can occur instead, which provides an opportunity to alter the conditions if necessary. The federal government further advocates that if a probation condition is actually an attempt to address child welfare concerns, it

---

[356]   *YCJA*, s. 42(2)(k).

[357]   Section 55 of the *YCJA* lists mandatory and optional conditions of probation.

[358]   These statistics are contained in Department of Justice materials concerning the *YCJA*, which are available on the Department of Justice website under YCJA Explained — Youth Sentencing: Explanatory Text. At the time of writing, these materials could be accessed at: <http://www.justice.gc.ca/eng/pi/yj-jj/ycja-lsjpa/ycja-lsjpa.html>.

should not be imposed, and a referral to a child welfare agency under s. 35 should be made instead.[359]

J.   Intensive Support and Supervision Program (ISSP)[360]

This is a new non-custodial sentencing option under the *YCJA*. It is available only if the province or territory has established a program.[361] It is designed to do largely what its name suggests: provide intensive supervision and support to young persons in the community. It has been described as "super probation" and is designed to provide a greater degree of support and supervision than probation. This new sentence was envisioned to provide more intensive monitoring, supervision and support to young persons (than probation) in addressing behavioural issues. It is also expected to be particularly appropriate for offenders who would have received custody under the *YOA* and is, in effect, intended to be an alternative to custody.[362] The same conditions that must be imposed in relation to a probation order must be made in relation to an intensive support and supervision order.[363] Likewise, the optional conditions that can be imposed as terms of a probation order can be imposed as conditions of an intensive support and supervision order. Therefore, similar concerns regarding the appropriateness of probationary conditions arise in relation to intensive support and supervision orders. An intensive support and supervision order cannot exceed two years.[364]

---

[359] Department of Justice materials concerning the *YCJA*, which are available on the Department of Justice website under YCJA Explained — Youth Sentencing: Explanatory Text. At the time of writing, these materials could be accessed at: <http://www.justice.gc.ca/eng/pi/yj-jj/ycja-lsjpa/ycja-lsjpa.html>.

[360] *YCJA*, s. 42(2)(l).

[361] See comments from Kilpatrick J. of the Nunavut Court of Justice on the lack of this program in Nunavut, as discussed at note 319, above. At the time of writing in 2008, this program was not uniformly available across Canada. In Ontario, for example, it existed only by way of a pilot project in certain areas of the province. It was operating as a kind of "super probation" in certain parts of Ontario. It is actually part of the probation order. In the provinces and territories where this program exists, it tends to vary widely in how it operates. Manitoba, for example, also has an ISSP program but it is not administered as a sentence under s. 42 but rather it is a program developed by provincial corrections to which young persons are referred as needed.

[362] YCJA Explained: Youth Sentencing: Explanatory Text, accessible online at the Department of Justice's website at: <http://www.justice.gc.ca/eng/pi/yj-jj/ycja-lsjpa/ycja-lsjpa.html>. See also Nicholas Bala, *Youth Criminal Justice Law* (Toronto: Irwin Law Inc., 2003), at 437.

[363] *YCJA*, s. 55(1).

[364] *YCJA*, s. 55(2).

K.   Attendance at Non-residential Centres[365]

This is another new community sentence under the *YCJA* that is contingent on the province or territory establishing a program authorizing the sentence and establishing attendance centres.[366] It provides for the attendance of a young person at a non-residential centre for up to 240 hours over a maximum six-month period, where the young person can receive support and assistance. It is designed to focus on the particular needs and circumstances of the young person and can be crafted to require the young person to attend at specific times and days when the young person would otherwise be unsupervised and has tended to violate the law.[367] For instance, the young person may be required to attend at a centre after school or on weekends to participate in a counselling program related to anger management or substance abuse. Similar to orders to perform personal or community service, an attendance order can be imposed only if the judge is satisfied that the young person is a suitable candidate for the program and that his or her participation will not interfere with his education or employment.[368] While not all provinces and territories had established attendance centres even six years after the implementation of the Act, the evidence suggests that some judges are reluctant to use this sentencing option even in the jurisdictions that have approved the program, due to the time limits on the program. They have opted to impose probation instead.[369] A senior B.C. government official testified before the Nunn Commission of Inquiry in Nova Scotia that he approved of the value of attendance centres but characterized the time limitation as "madness". Alan Markwart, Assistant Deputy Minister of Children and Family Services for the province, testified that it was impossible to turn around a difficult young person in so short a period of time.[370] The Nunn Commission subsequently recommended that the

---

[365] *YCJA*, s. 42(2)(m).

[366] At the time of writing in March 2008, programs providing for attendance centres were not in existence across the country. For example, in Ontario, such programs existed as a pilot project.

[367] YCJA Explained: Youth Sentencing: Explanatory Text, accessible online at the Department of Justice's website at: <http://www.justice.gc.ca/eng/pi/yj-jj/ycja-lsjpa/ycja-lsjpa.html>.

[368] *YCJA*, s. 54(7).

[369] Nova Scotia Nunn Commission of Inquiry, *Spiralling out of Control: Lessons Learned from a Boy in Trouble: Report of the Nunn Commission of Inquiry* (Halifax, NS: Nunn Commission of Inquiry, 2006), at 207. This report is available online at: <http://www.gov.ns.ca/just/nunn_commission/_docs/Report_Nunn_Final.pdf>.

[370] Nova Scotia Nunn Commission of Inquiry, *Spiralling out of Control: Lessons Learned from a Boy in Trouble: Report of the Nunn Commission of Inquiry* (Halifax, NS: Nunn Commission of Inquiry, 2006), at 207. This report is available online at: <http://www.gov.ns.ca/just/nunn_commission/_docs/Report_Nunn_Final.pdf>.

province of Nova Scotia advocate for an amendment to s. 42(2)(m) of the YCJA to remove both time limits in the paragraph.[371]

While both ISSPs and attendance orders can include counselling and therapy, the YCJA indicates that a young person cannot be compelled to undergo treatment, such as to take drugs in relation to his or her mental health.[372]

Obviously a judge can only impose ISSPs and attendance orders if such programs exist in the province or territory. Prosecutors and defence counsel need to keep current as to whether such programs exist in their provinces and territories in order to advise the judge in this regard.

IX. CUSTODIAL SENTENCES

Part 5 of the YCJA sets out the general principles that relate to youth custody and supervision orders.[373] Under the YCJA, YOA custodial sentences have been replaced by the concept of a single order of custody and supervision. In other words, there is a general and fundamental expectation that a portion of all custodial youth sentences will be served in the community.[374] Any time a custodial youth sentence is imposed, a youth worker is immediately designated to work with the young person to develop a plan for his or her reintegration into the community. This is linked to the underlying assumption that most young persons sentenced to custody will eventually be released into the community and that, consequently, well developed reintegration plans must be devised to support them and to reduce the likelihood of their reoffending.[375]

This important philosophical shift was instituted to address a perceived weakness in the YOA. Under the former Act, young persons were often released into the community after a period of custody with little to no period of community supervision to assist them during the transition

---

[371] Nova Scotia Nunn Commission of Inquiry, *Spiralling out of Control: Lessons Learned from a Boy in Trouble: Report of the Nunn Commission of Inquiry* (Halifax, NS: Nunn Commission of Inquiry, 2006), Recommendation 11, as discussed at 208. This report is available online at: <http://www.gov.ns.ca/just/nunn_commission/_docs/Report_Nunn_Final.pdf>.

[372] YCJA, s. 42(8).

[373] See s. 83 in particular.

[374] There are exceptions to this general rule. See for example s. 98 of the YCJA, which provides that the young person can be detained in custody for his or her entire sentence if the youth justice court judge is satisfied that there are reasonable grounds to believe that the young person is likely to commit a serious violent offence before the expiry of his or her sentence and the conditions of his or her release would not be adequate to prevent the offence. See also s. 104 of the YCJA.

[375] YCJA, s. 90.

period. This lack of community supervision or after-care following a period of custody caused concern because the period immediately following custody was considered to be a time when the young person was at high risk to reoffend.[376]

This new sentencing approach in Canadian youth justice law coincides with research demonstrating that supervising prisoners in the community prior to the expiry of their sentence reduces recidivism and promotes the individual's rehabilitation and reintegration into society.[377] Since the maximum sentences under the *YCJA* are the same as those under the *YOA*, this change in the nature and quality of custodial sentences under the *YCJA* means that, in fact, the time served by young persons in custody will generally be reduced because a portion of the sentence will now routinely be spent under community supervision.

A.   Regular Custody and (Community) Supervision Orders[378]

Under the *YCJA* regime, all offences except the most serious ones — murder, attempt to commit murder, manslaughter and aggravated sexual assault — are generally designed to consist of two-thirds custody and one-third community supervision.[379] For these sentences, the court must state the actual number of days or months to be spent in custody and the corresponding period of time to be spent in the community subject to conditions.[380] The maximum total length of a custody and supervision order for these offences is two years, or three years if the sentence is one for which an adult could receive a life sentence under the *Criminal Code* or any other Act of Parliament.[381] The *YCJA* provides for the review of youth sentences, which could result in the early release of the young person or in his or her detention in custody for the remainder of the sentence.[382]

The *YCJA* contains a list of mandatory conditions that apply to young persons who are released under supervision into the community in

---

[376] Julian V. Roberts and Nicholas Bala, "Understanding Sentencing Under the *Youth Criminal Justice Act*" (2003) 41 Alta. L. Rev. 395, at para. 68 (QL).

[377] Julian V. Roberts and Nicholas Bala, "Understanding Sentencing Under the *Youth Criminal Justice Act*" (2003) 41 Alta. L. Rev. 395, at para. 69 (QL).

[378] *YCJA*, s. 42(2)(n). See also ss. 97 and 98 of the *YCJA* concerning conditions and the continuation of custody respectively.

[379] *YCJA*, s. 42(2)(n). *R. v. R.I.R.M.-M. (YCJA)*, [2008] B.C.J. No. 1235, 2008 BCCA 273 (B.C.C.A.) contains a recent discussion of s. 42(2)(n).

[380] *YCJA*, s. 42(4). See the particular wording here.

[381] *YCJA*, s. 42(2)(n).

[382] *YCJA*, ss. 94-98.

relation to these sentences.[383] Additional conditions which are aimed at addressing the particular needs of the young person, the promotion of his or her reintegration into the community and protection of the public can be imposed. (The provincial director, and not the youth justice court, has the power to set conditions regarding the community supervision portion of these regular custody and community supervision orders, whereas, in relation to conditional supervision orders concerning the more serious offences, the youth justice court sets the conditions.)

In relation to regular custody and community supervision orders, if the provincial director has reasonable grounds to believe that a young person has breached a condition while under supervision in the community, the matter can be reviewed, but such a review is not mandatory.[384] This review can result in a change in the conditions or in the detention of the young person in custody to serve the remainder of the sentence.

It is possible that the young person may never actually serve any portion of the community supervision aspect of the custodial sentence. Prior to his or her release into the community, the court can order the young person to remain in custody if the court is satisfied that there are reasonable grounds to believe that the young person is likely to commit a serious violent offence before the expiry of the youth sentence he or she is serving.[385]

B.   Custody and Conditional Supervision Orders for Attempt to Commit Murder, Manslaughter or Aggravated Sexual Assault[386]

The maximum length of a custody and supervision order for the offences of attempt to commit murder, manslaughter and aggravated sexual assault is three years. These are *maximum* sentences. These custody and supervision orders cannot exceed three years but there is no restriction on what portion of that sentence must be spent in custody.[387]

Unlike sentences imposed under s. 42(2)(n) (where the offender must spend two-thirds in custody and one-third under community supervision), in the case of sentences under s. 42(2)(o), the court determines what portion of the sentence will be spent in custody and what

---

[383] *YCJA*, s. 97(1).
[384] *YCJA*, ss. 102, 107-109.
[385] *YCJA*, s. 98.
[386] *YCJA*, s. 42(2)(o).
[387] *R. v. B.W.P.; R. v. B.V.N.*, [2006] S.C.J. No. 27, at para. 43, 2006 SCC 27 (S.C.C.).

portion will be served in the community under conditional supervision. This provides the court with greater flexibility to tailor sentences in relation to these more serious offences.[388] If a young person breaches a condition of his or her release, he or she can be returned to custody.

The court is not required to impose a custodial sentence for these offences. The court can impose other sentences under s. 42(2).

C.   Deferred Custody and Supervision Order (DCSO)[389]

This is another new sentencing option under the *YCJA*. This sentence is similar to the conditional sentence under the *Criminal Code* for adults, except that it can be for a maximum of only six months, whereas a conditional sentence under s. 742.1 of the *Criminal Code* can be for up to two years less a day. Similar to a conditional sentence for an adult, if a young person does not comply with the conditions of the deferred custody and supervision order,[390] the young person can be required to serve the remainder of the sentence as if it were a custody and supervision order under s. 42(2)(n).[391]

In the event of a breach of a condition of his or her release into the community, the young person can end up serving the remainder of the deferred custody and supervision order in custody.[392] For all intents and purposes, a DCSO should be considered similar in nature to a conditional sentence in as much as it is a custodial sentence that the young person is being permitted to serve in the community on conditions.[393]

This characterization of DCSOs is illustrated by the common practice in the courts of finding that a young person is eligible for a custodial sentence under s. 39 and then opting to impose a deferred custody and supervision order. A deferred custody and supervision order is unavailable if the offence for which the young person is sentenced is a serious violent

---

[388]   YCJA Explained: Youth Sentencing: Explanatory Text, accessible online at the Department of Justice's website at: <http://www.justice.gc.ca/eng/pi/yj-jj/ycja-lsjpa/ycja-lsjpa.html>.

[389]   *YCJA*, s. 42(2)(p).

[390]   These conditions are set out in s. 105(2) and (3).

[391]   *YCJA*, s. 42(6) and, in particular, s. 109(2)(c) and (3).

[392]   *YCJA*, s. 103(2)(b).

[393]   The mandatory conditions are the same as those set out in s. 105(2). The court may also impose optional conditions under s. 105(3).

offence.[394] The DCSO must also be consistent with the purpose and principles of sentencing in s. 38 and the restrictions on custody in s. 39.[395]

D.   Custody and Supervision Order for Murder[396]

In the case of first and second degree murder, the court must impose the sanctions set out in paragraph (q) or (r)(ii) or (iii) of s. 42(2), and may impose any other sanctions in s. 42(2) that the court considers appropriate, unless it is determined that the young person is eligible for an adult sentence. For first degree murder, this means that a young person can receive a maximum youth custodial sentence of 10 years under s. 42(2)(q) comprised of a maximum sentence of six years in custody[397] and a further period under conditional supervision in the community.

A young person found guilty of second degree murder is liable to a maximum youth custodial sentence of seven years, a maximum four years of which is to be served in custody and a further period to be served in the community under conditional supervision. These are maximum periods. Theoretically, a sentence for first or second degree murder could be comprised of only one day in custody and one day under conditional supervision in the community since there is no minimum sentence that must be imposed for either first or second degree murder under the *YCJA*. By contrast, an adult convicted of first degree or second degree murder must serve a minimum sentence of life imprisonment. The life sentence is a minimum punishment.[398]

Similar to the offences of attempt to commit murder, manslaughter and aggravated sexual assault, in the case of first or second degree

---

[394]   In *R. v. C.O.*, [2008] O.J. No. 2844 (Ont. C.A.), the Ontario Court of Appeal held that the reference to a serious violent offence in s. 42(5) means an offence for which a s. 42(9) application has been brought and a judicial determination made. Absent a s. 42(9) determination, a deferred custody and supervision order can be made by a sentencing judge whether or not the sentencing judge views the offence as meeting the definition of a serious violent offence in s. 2 of the *YCJA*. The designation is required in order to bar the DCSO. See also *R. v. C.J.A.*, [2005] S.J. No. 410, 200 C.C.C. (3d) 233 (Sask. C.A.). *Contra*, *R. v. D.A.K.*, [2006] A.J. No. 1386, 2006 ABPC 247 (Alta. Prov. Ct.), where the designation was not required in order for the accused to be barred from a DCSO because the sentencing judge determined that the offence was serious and violent. See also *R. v. A.D.*, [2008] N.S.J. No. 345 (N.S.C.A.) and *R. v. D.W.*, [2009] S.J. No. 185, 2009 SKPC 49 (Sask. Prov. Ct.).

[395]   *YCJA*, s. 42(5)(b). The definition of a serious violent offence can be found in s. 2 of the *YCJA* and is discussed later in this chapter.

[396]   *YCJA*, s. 42(2)(q).

[397]   It is possible that the young person will spend the entire period in custody, including the community portion of it. Section 104 provides for the continuation of custody in certain circumstances.

[398]   *Criminal Code*, s. 235.

murder, the court determines the date of release and sets the conditions of conditional supervision one month prior to the release of the young person.[399] In either case, the young person could end up serving the entire sentence in custody either because he or she is perceived to pose a risk of causing death or serious harm to another person if released,[400] or because he or she has breached conditions of release into the community.[401]

E.   Intensive Rehabilitative Custody and Supervision Orders (IRCSs)[402]

Intensive Rehabilitative Custody and Supervision Orders (known colloquially as IRCSs)[403] can be imposed only on young persons who have committed the most serious crimes of murder, attempt to commit murder, manslaughter, aggravated sexual assault, or who have been found guilty of a serious violent offence[404] for which an adult could receive a jail term of more than two years and who have previously been found guilty of at least two serious violent offences. The young person must also be suffering from a mental illness or disorder, a psychological disorder or an emotional disturbance, an effective plan of treatment and intensive supervision must have been developed for the young person and there must also be reasonable grounds to believe the treatment plan might reduce the risk of the young person repeating the offence or committing a serious violent offence. The provincial director must also determine that the program is available and that the young person's participation is appropriate.[405] The length of an IRCS order can range from two years, to 10 years for first degree murder.

Media reports indicate that only about 30 young people across Canada had received this sentence during the first four years of the *YCJA*.[406] The federally-funded sentence is estimated to cost $100,000 a year largely because it involves intensive therapy.[407]

This new sentence gained public attention in November 2007 when J.R., the Medicine Hat 14-year-old who was found guilty of first degree

---

[399] *YCJA*, s. 105.
[400] *YCJA*, s. 104.
[401] *YCJA*, s. 109.
[402] *YCJA*, s. 42(2)(r).
[403] *YCJA*, s. 42(2)(r).
[404] The concept of a serious violent offence is discussed later in this chapter.
[405] *YCJA*, s. 42(7).
[406] Dawn Walton, "Courts: Canada's Youngest Triple Murderer" *The Globe and Mail* (9 November 2007), A8.
[407] "Unusual sentence strives for rehabilitation" *The Calgary Herald* (9 November 2007), A4.

murder in the stabbing deaths of her parents and brother, was the subject of an IRCS order as part of her 10-year youth sentence for their murders.[408] J.R. was 12 at the time of the April 2006 murders.

F.   Intermittent Custodial Sentence

A judge can also order that a young person sentenced to less than 90 days of custody under s. 42(2)(n) serve the custodial portion of that sentence intermittently provided this is consistent with the purpose and principles of sentencing set out in s. 38.[409] The judge must first be apprised of the availability of a youth custody facility in the province or territory that would permit the enforcement of such a sentence.

X.   OTHER REASONABLE AND ANCILLARY CONDITIONS[410]

The court can also impose any other reasonable and ancillary conditions that the court considers advisable and in the best interests of this young person and the public.[411]

XI. A YOUNG PERSON CANNOT BE FORCED TO TAKE TREATMENT

None of these sentences permits the provision of treatment regarding the mental or physical health of the young person without his or her consent.[412]

XII. SERIOUS VIOLENT OFFENCES

The legal concept of a serious violent offence, and the implications of such a designation for a young person, is another new feature of the *YCJA*. The notion is relevant to both youth sentences and adult sentences.

---

[408] Her much older accomplice, Jeremy Steinke, 25, was found guilty of three counts of first degree murder in December 2008 and received life in prison.
[409] *YCJA*, s. 47(2) and (3).
[410] *YCJA*, s. 42(2)(s).
[411] Such conditions could include an array of conditions, such as requiring the young person to research and prepare a speech for his or her class on the damage that can be caused by the use of methamphetamine.
[412] *YCJA*, s. 42(8).

The concept is discussed here in the context of youth sentences. It will be discussed later in relation to adult sentences.[413]

The designation is relevant to youth sentences in two significant ways: if an offence is found to be a serious violent offence, the young person cannot receive a deferred custody and supervision order.[414] Three serious violent offence determinations also deem a young person eligible for an IRCS,[415] provided other conditions are satisfied.

What is a serious violent offence for purposes of the *YCJA*? A serious violent offence is defined in s. 2(1) of the *YCJA* as an offence in the commission of which a young person causes or attempts to cause serious bodily harm. However, neither bodily harm nor serious bodily harm is defined in the *YCJA*. Bodily harm is defined in the *Criminal Code* as "any hurt or injury to a person that interferes with the health or comfort of the person and that is more than merely transient or trifling in nature".[416] Justice Bastarache clarified the definition of a serious violent offence in *R. v. C.D.; R. v. C.D.K.*[417] by first noting that the *YCJA* imports *Criminal Code* definitions in cases where the words are not defined in the *YCJA*.[418] Justice Bastarache then held that the Supreme Court of Canada's definition of serious bodily harm in *R. v. McCraw*[419] (which was based on the definition of bodily harm in the *Criminal Code*) could also be used for purposes of the *YCJA*. As a result, for purposes of the definition of a serious violent offence in the *YCJA*, serious bodily harm means "any hurt or injury, whether physical or psychological, that interferes in a substantial way with the physical or psychological integrity, health or well-being of the complainant".[420]

Various appellate courts have since held that a serious violent offence designation can be made where the offender causes serious bodily harm or where the offender merely attempts to cause serious bodily harm.[421] The cases dealing with attempts focus on the intention of the offender.[422] The Crown does not necessarily have to prove that serious bodily harm actually occurred. The Crown will not always be required to

---

[413] The concept of a serious violent offence and the case law to date were discussed at length in *R. v. E.F.*, [2007] O.J. No. 1000 (Ont. C.J.).

[414] *YCJA*, s. 42(5)(a).

[415] *YCJA*, s. 42(7)(a)(ii).

[416] *Criminal Code*, s. 2.

[417] [2005] S.C.J. No. 79, at para. 20 (S.C.C.).

[418] *YCJA*, s. 2(2).

[419] [1991] S.C.J. No. 69, [1991] 3 S.C.R. 72 (S.C.C.).

[420] *R. v. C.D.; R. v. C.D.K.*, [2005] S.C.J. No. 79, at para. 20 (S.C.C.).

[421] *R. v. V.J.T.*, [2007] M.J. No. 122, at para. 29, 2007 MBCA 45 (Man. C.A.). See also *R. v. G.B.*, [2008] A.J. No. 454, at para. 7 (Alta. C.A.).

[422] *R. v. V.J.T.*, [2007] M.J. No. 122, 2007 MBCA 45 (Man. C.A.).

call medical evidence to prove the injuries.[423] The attempt itself must still be proven beyond a reasonable doubt.

The courts are also distinguishing between a finding that serious bodily harm was caused and the making of a serious violent offence designation. In other words, a court can find that an offence caused serious bodily harm without designating the offence as a serious violent offence. A designation that an offence is a serious violent offence requires both the commission of the offence and the causing or attempting to cause serious bodily harm by the young person.

As Bloomenfeld J. explained in *R. v. M.E.*, "... the inquiry extends beyond the legal elements of the offence committed to the precise nature of the young person's role in causing or attempting to cause serious bodily harm in perpetrating the offence."[424] Essentially, Bloomenfeld J. concluded that the specific role played by the young person must be considered, and that his or her role in the offence is highly relevant to whether the designation should issue. The sentencing court retains a residual discretion on an application for a serious violent offence designation.[425]

In terms of the designation process itself, after a young person has been found guilty of an offence, the Attorney General can apply to have the offence designated a serious violent offence.[426] The youth justice court can make such a determination after giving both parties an opportunity to be heard. The information or indictment can then be endorsed accordingly. According to the Supreme Court of Canada, an offence is not a serious violent offence until the court declares it so under s. 42(9).[427]

---

[423] In *R. v. V.J.T.*, a beating was found to be a serious violent offence even though no medical evidence was tendered and no victim impact statement was filed. An attempt to cause serious bodily harm was inferred from the conduct of the accused (which could be viewed on a videotape) and the surrounding circumstances rather than the actual injuries.

[424] *R. v. M.E.*, [2008] O.J. No. 919, at para. 12 (Ont. C.J.).

[425] *R. v. G.B.*, [2008] A.J. No. 454, at para. 10 (Alta. C.A.). See also *R. v. M.E.*, [2008] O.J. No. 919 (Ont. C.J.), where Bloomenfeld J. provides a detailed analysis at paras. 11-13 and 19 to support the proposition that a finding that an offence caused serious bodily harm does not automatically result in a serious violent offence designation.

[426] *YCJA*, s. 42(9). *R. v. K.G.B.*, [2005] N.B.J. No. 433 (N.B.C.A.) is an early illustration of applying the definition of a serious violent offence to the facts; in that case the appeal court overturned its youth justice court to find that a rape is a serious violent offence.

[427] *R. v. C.D.; R. v. C.D.K.*, [2005] S.C.J. No. 79, at para. 21 (S.C.C.). However, the Supreme Court of Canada did not directly consider the relationship between s. 42(9) and s. 42(5) of the *YCJA*. Specifically, the Supreme Court of Canada did not address whether a determination must be made under s. 42(9) in order for the offence to be considered a serious violent offence for purposes of s. 42(5) although this is arguably implicit in its reasoning. In *R. v. C.O.*, [2008] O.J. No. 2844 (Ont. C.A.), the Ontario Court of Appeal held that the reference to a serious violent offence in s. 42(5) means an offence for which a s. 42(9) application has been brought and a judicial determination made. Absent a s. 42(9) determination, a deferred

During the determination hearing, the onus is on the Crown, and the standard of proof is beyond a reasonable doubt[428] that the offence meets the definition of a serious violent offence in the *YCJA*.[429] The burden of establishing the necessary facts beyond a reasonable doubt and proving any disputed facts lies on the Crown.[430] The sentencing judge must find beyond a reasonable doubt that the young person has, in the commission of the offence, caused or attempted to cause serious bodily harm. The courts have held that the determination can be made on the basis of an agreed statement of fact[431] and that a victim impact statement that goes unchallenged can also be relied upon to support the designation.[432]

The hearing at which the serious violent offence determination is made is part of the sentencing process.[433] Justice Sharpe reasoned for the Ontario Court of Appeal that this makes sense because the provisions are found in Part 4 of the *YCJA*, which is the sentencing section. In addition, the operation and outcome of the provisions pertaining to serious violent offences implicate sentencing and, procedurally, the designation is made following a guilty finding. The courts have generally treated the serious violent offence designation as part of the sentencing, as have the academics.[434]

For purposes of an appeal, as well, a judicial determination that an offence is a serious violent offence is considered part of the sentence.[435]

XIII. NOTICE OF GREATER PUNISHMENT

The provision in the *Criminal Code* which permits the Crown to seek a greater punishment in cases where the accused is convicted of an offence for which a greater punishment can be imposed by reason of previous convictions has been restricted in relation to guilty findings under the *YCJA* but not to the extent that it was restricted under the *YOA*. Under the *YOA*, s. 36(5) stated that a finding of guilt under the *YOA* is not

---

custody and supervision order can be made by a sentencing judge whether or not the sentencing judge views the offence as meeting the definition of a serious violent offence in s. 2 of the *YCJA*, the court found.

[428]   *R. v. V.J.T.*, [2007] M.J. No. 122, at para. 20, 2007 MBCA 45 (Man. C.A.). See also *R. v. E.F.*, [2007] O.J. No. 1000 (Ont. C.J.).

[429]   See *R. v. K.G.B.*, [2005] N.B.J. No. 433, at para. 29 (N.B.C.A.). See also *R. v. D.P.*, [2006] B.C.J. No. 2113 (B.C.C.A.).

[430]   *R. v. M.E.*, [2008] O.J. No. 919, at para. 20 (Ont. C.J.).

[431]   *R. v. K.G.B.*, [2005] N.B.J. No. 433, at para. 29 (N.B.C.A.).

[432]   *R. v. D.P.*, [2006] B.C.J. No. 2113, at paras. 35-37 (B.C.C.A.).

[433]   *R. v. V.W.*, [2008] O.J. No. 234, at para. 17 (Ont. C.A.).

[434]   *R. v. V.W.*, [2008] O.J. No. 234, at paras. 17-19 (Ont. C.A.).

[435]   *YCJA*, s. 42(10).

a previous conviction for the purposes of any offence under any Act of Parliament for which a greater punishment is prescribed by reason of previous convictions. Under the *YCJA*,[436] this wording has been changed so that a guilty finding is not a previous conviction for the purposes of any offence under any Act of Parliament for which a greater punishment is prescribed by reason of previous convictions, except for the purpose of establishing that an offence is a third serious violent offence or for the purpose of determining the adult sentence to be imposed.[437]

XIV.   REVIEW OF YOUTH SENTENCES

The *YCJA* provides for the review of both custodial and non-custodial sentences.

A review of a non-custodial sentence can occur six months from the date of the sentence or earlier with leave of the youth justice court.[438] Such a review can be initiated by various parties, on application, including the young person, the Crown or the provincial director, on various grounds, but the youth justice court judge must first be satisfied that there are grounds for the review. These grounds can include a material change in the circumstances that led to the youth sentence, an inability or serious difficulty on the part of the young person to comply with the youth sentence, contravention of conditions of a probation order or an intensive support and supervision program order without reasonable excuse, or on the grounds that the terms of the sentence are adversely affecting the young person's opportunities to obtain services, education or employment.

As a result of a review hearing, the youth justice court can: confirm the sentence; terminate the sentence and discharge the young person; or vary the youth sentence or impose a new non-custodial sentence. The new sentence cannot be longer than the remainder of the earlier sentence nor can it be more onerous (without the consent of the young person). The youth justice court can also extend by up to 12 months the amount of time the young person has been allotted to comply with certain youth sentences (fines, compensation, restitution, personal service orders and community service orders).[439]

---

[436]   *YCJA*, s. 82(4).
[437]   Under the *YOA*, see Priscilla Platt, *Young Offenders Law in Canada*, 2d ed. (Markham, Ont.: Butterworths Canada Inc., 1995), at 489. See also *R. v. W. (J.) (No. 2)*, unreported, March 25, 1992 (Y.T. Terr. Ct.).
[438]   *YCJA*, s. 59.
[439]   *YCJA*, s. 59(9).

When a young person receives a youth custodial sentence of more than one year, the young person must have an annual review of that sentence (a year from the date of sentence).[440] Likewise, if a young person receives youth sentences relating to more than one offence that total more than one year in custody, an annual review is also mandatory and must occur one year from the date of the earliest youth sentence.[441] (A deferred custody and supervision order is not classified as a custodial sentence for these purposes.) In addition to the annual review, custodial sentences exceeding one year can be reviewed on request after six months from the date of the most recent youth sentence in relation to the offence.[442] There are also provisions for review of youth custodial sentences of less than one year.[443] The youth justice court judge may grant leave for a review of a custodial sentence at any other time.[444]

Despite the mandatory wording in s. 94(1) and (2) that young persons who receive one youth sentence or several youth sentences in relation to more than one offence shall have their sentences reviewed annually, the wording of s. 94(5) states that the youth justice court shall review the sentence if the youth court judge is satisfied that there are grounds for review. These grounds include: that the young person has made sufficient progress to justify a change in the sentence, that the circumstances that led to the youth sentence have changed materially, that new services and programs are available that were not available at the time of sentence or that opportunities for rehabilitation are now greater in the community.[445] The youth justice court judge can also review the sentence on any other ground that the judge considers appropriate.

While the wording of s. 94(5) implies that the court must be first satisfied that there are grounds for review prior to reviewing any custodial sentence, it is submitted that s. 94(5) applies to only optional reviews under s. 94(3) and that the youth justice court is obliged to conduct annual reviews under s. 94(1) and (2) without first considering whether there are grounds for the review. This position flows logically from the clear, express and mandatory wording of s. 94(1) and (2). In addition, the optional review subsection (s. 94(3)) states that the optional review can be based on any of the grounds set out in s. 94(6), whereas the two mandatory review sections do not refer to the need to rely on any grounds. This analysis is consistent with the practice under the *YOA* and with the

---

[440] *YCJA*, s. 94(1).
[441] *YCJA*, s. 94(2).
[442] *YCJA*, s. 94(3)(b).
[443] *YCJA*, s. 94(3)(a).
[444] *YCJA*, s. 94(4).
[445] *YCJA*, s. 94(6).

jurisprudence under the *YCJA*.[446] While the wording of s. 94 in this regard is not as clear as it was in the predecessor section of the *YOA* (s. 28), the intent is arguably clear when the relevant subsections of s. 94 are read in their entirety. Thus, the need to establish any of the grounds in s. 94(6) applies to only optional reviews, not to the mandatory reviews that must be conducted under s. 94(1) and (2).[447]

As a result of reviews under s. 94, the court has various options: the judge can confirm the sentence, release the youth on conditional supervision for a period not exceeding the remainder of the youth sentence or, if the provincial director recommends, convert an intensive rehabilitative custody and supervision order to a custody and conditional supervision order under s. 42(2)(q) if the offence was murder or to a custody and supervision order under s. 42(2)(n) or (o) as the case may be if the offence was an offence other than murder.

Notice is required to be given in relation to these reviews.[448]

Reviews of youth sentences are not appealable.[449]

XV. PLACEMENT OF YOUNG PERSONS WHO RECEIVE YOUTH SENTENCES

As a general rule, a young person who is committed to custody is to be held separate and apart from any adult who is detained or held in custody.[450] There are exceptions to this rule; the youth court judge or justice or the provincial director, as the case may be, often has discretion regarding where the individual is temporarily detained or where he or she will serve the sentence.[451] Whether the offender serves his or her youth sentence, or a portion of it, in a youth or adult facility relates largely to the age of the individual.

The general rules for placement upon receiving a youth sentence are set out below.

---

[446] See for example *R. v. C.K.*, [2008] O.J. No. 1951, at para. 13 (Ont. C.J.) and *R. v. D.H.*, [2008] O.J. No. 779, at paras. 13-15 (Ont. C.J.).

[447] This interpretation is also consistent with the commentary and interpretation in Rochelle Direnfeld *et al.*, *Annotated Youth Criminal Justice Act Service*, looseleaf (LexisNexis Canada Inc., 2003), at 5400.

[448] *YCJA*, s. 94(13)-(18).

[449] *YCJA*, s. 37(11).

[450] *YCJA*, s. 84.

[451] At the temporary detention stage, see s. 30(3). Place of detention upon receiving a youth sentence is discussed in this portion of the chapter. Placement upon receiving an adult sentence is discussed later in this chapter.

When a young person receives a youth custodial sentence, they are to be placed in a youth custody facility.[452] The provincial director determines the level of custody.[453]

Once the young person reaches 18, the youth justice court may, on application of the provincial director,[454] authorize the young person to serve the remainder of the sentence in a correctional facility for adults, provided the court considers it to be in the best interests of the young person or in the public interest.[455] The young person can also be directed to serve the remainder of the sentence in a penitentiary in certain circumstances.[456] The youth justice court judge has discretion in this regard.

A young person who is serving his or her youth sentence in a youth custody facility is to be transferred to a provincial correctional facility for adults upon turning 20 to serve the remainder of the sentence, unless the provincial director orders the sentence to be served in a youth custody facility.[457] The provincial director can exercise discretion in this regard. The youth justice court also has the discretion to further authorize the transfer of a young person in a provincial correctional facility to a penitentiary to serve the remainder of the sentence if the court considers it to be in the best interests of the young person or in the public interest and if two years or more are remaining in the sentence at the time of the application.[458]

If the young person is 20 years old or older at the time the youth custodial sentence is imposed, however, it is mandatory that the young person be placed in an adult provincial correctional facility to serve the youth sentence. The youth justice court judge can also later authorize, on application of the provincial director at any time after the young person begins to serve a portion of the sentence in the provincial correctional facility for adults, the young person to serve the remainder of the youth sentence in a penitentiary if there are more than two years remaining in the sentence at the time of the application and if the court considers it in the best interests of the young person or in the public interest.[459]

---

[452] See s. 85(3). The level of custody within the youth custody facility is determined in accordance with s. 85.

[453] *YCJA*, s. 85(3).

[454] The term "provincial director" often means, in practice, a probation officer or a youth worker. The term is defined in s. 2. A provincial director can delegate his or her power by virtue of s. 22 of the *YCJA*.

[455] *YCJA*, s. 92.

[456] *YCJA*, s. 92(2).

[457] *YCJA*, s. 93(1).

[458] *YCJA*, s. 93(2).

[459] *YCJA*, s. 89(2).

Similar provisions exist in relation to places of temporary detention at the pre-trial and pre-sentencing stage.[460] While the general principle that a young person is to be held separate and apart from adults applies at the pre-trial and pre-sentencing stage as well, this is not mandatory. The *YCJA* provides for the detention of young persons in adult facilities at the pre-trial stage if a justice or youth court justice is satisfied that it is necessary in relation to the safety of the young person or the safety of others, or no place of detention for young persons is available within a reasonable distance.[461] Other provisions provide for the placement of young persons in adult correctional facilities at the pre-trial stage after they turn 18. If the young person is 20 or older at the time his temporary detention begins, it is mandatory that the young person be detained at this stage in an adult provincial correctional facility.[462]

XVI. ADULT SENTENCES

'No, no!' said the Queen. 'Sentence first — verdict afterwards.'

'Stuff and nonsense!' said Alice loudly. 'The idea of having the sentence first.!'[463]

…..

'What sorts of things do *you* remember best?' Alice ventured to ask.

'Oh, things that happened the week after next,' the Queen replied in a careless tone. 'For instance, now,' she went on, sticking a large piece of plaster [band-aid] on her finger as she spoke, 'there's the King's Messenger. He's in prison now, being punished: and the trial doesn't even begin till next Wednesday: and of course the crime comes last of all.'

'Suppose he never commits the crime?' said Alice.

'That would be all the better, wouldn't it?' the Queen said, as she bound the plaster round her finger with a bit of ribbon.

Alice felt there was no denying *that*. 'Of course it would be all the better,' she said: 'but it wouldn't be all the better his being punished.'

'You're wrong *there*, at any rate,' said the Queen: 'were YOU ever punished?'

'Only for faults,' said Alice.

'And you were all the better for it, I know!' the Queen said triumphantly.

---

[460] *YCJA*, s. 30.
[461] *YCJA*, s. 30(3).
[462] *YCJA*, s. 30(4) and (5).
[463] Lewis Carroll, *Alice's Adventures in Wonderland* (New York: Random House, 1992), c. 12, at 146.

'Yes, but then I *had* done the things I was punished for,' said Alice: 'that makes all the difference.'[464]

The Canadian youth criminal justice system has always permitted young persons to receive adult sentences in certain circumstances. What has changed significantly under the *YCJA* (and also as a result of the common law)[465] is the procedure for imposing adult sentences on young persons. The youth criminal justice law has evolved markedly in relation to the imposition of adult sentences largely to ensure that the process for imposing adult sentences is procedurally fair for young persons.

Under both the *JDA* and the *YOA*, a young person who was at least 14 at the time of the alleged offence could be transferred to adult court for trial if he or she were alleged to have committed certain serious crimes. For example, Steven Truscott was transferred to adult court for trial in 1959 for the alleged murder of 12-year-old schoolmate Lynne Harper.[466]

There are two main procedural differences regarding the imposition of adult sentences under the *YCJA*, as compared to the two former Acts. First, a young person under the former Acts could be ordered transferred to ordinary adult court *for trial*, as a result of a transfer hearing, which was often lengthy and complex, whereas, under the *YCJA*, the pre-trial transfer hearing has been eliminated. The young person under the *YCJA* will always be tried in youth justice court. It is only after a finding of guilt that the court will consider in certain circumstances whether the young person should receive an adult sentence under the *Criminal Code* rather than one of the youth sentences under the *YCJA*. This change resolved long-standing legal, ethical and constitutional concerns about the transfer hearing, where the judge was essentially considering facts and circumstances surrounding the event that had not been proven at trial (and might never be proven or even admissible at trial) in order to decide which justice system, the youth or the adult system, should deal with the young person. The *YOA* judge was obliged to consider, and in essence, determine, the seriousness and circumstances of the alleged offence and the young person's role in it, before trial, before hearing all of the evidence, and without knowing whether the

---

[464] Lewis Carroll, *Through the Looking Glass* (New York: Random House, 1992), c. 5, at 234-35.

[465] *R. v. D.B.*, [2008] S.C.J. No. 25, 2008 SCC 25 (S.C.C.) changed significantly the procedures in this regard, since it essentially eliminated the concept of presumptive offences. As a result of *D.B.*, there are no criminal offences that automatically result in an adult sentence for a young person upon a guilty finding unless the young person can convince the court otherwise. Now, in every case where the Crown is seeking an adult sentence for a young person, the Crown must satisfy the court that an adult sentence is appropriate.

[466] *Re S.M.T.*, [1959] O.J. No. 737, 125 C.C.C. 100 (Ont. S.C.). The Ontario Court of Appeal acquitted him of that crime in 2007 following his application for a review of his case pursuant to s. 696.1 of the *Criminal Code*. Truscott was awarded $6.5 million in compensation the following year.

evidence that was heard during the transfer hearing (during which more relaxed rules of evidence applied) would end up being admitted into evidence at trial.[467] The judiciary was routinely compelled to pre-judge the matter, which, some argued, was inconsistent with the most fundamental principle of criminal law: the presumption of innocence.

Since the identity of the young person could be published by the press once a transfer order to adult court was made,[468] the decision by the judge to transfer a young person to adult court for trial sent a clear message to the public that this matter was very serious, and, thus, essentially stigmatized and imposed a societal "verdict" on the young person prior to trial. The young person was labelled by the transfer hearing process although he or she might never be found guilty of the offence or might be found guilty of a lesser offence. After trial, even if the young person were found guilty of a less serious offence, they were now in the adult system and eligible for an adult sentence. In addition, under the *YOA*, the trial in adult court following the transfer hearing invariably attracted increased publicity because attention had been drawn to the case by virtue of the transfer hearing. The young person's identity became widely known even if they were not ultimately found guilty of the offence.

The *YOA* transfer process inspired literary allusions to *Alice's Adventures in Wonderland* and *Through the Looking Glass* because the transfer to adult court for trial (which, as previously mentioned, was often based on broad and incomplete evidence, including hearsay and opinion evidence)[469] was perceived by some as the imposition of punishment prior to a determination of guilt. Judges and academics harkened back to comments by the Queen of Hearts in *Alice's Adventures in Wonderland* or similar remarks by the White Queen in *Through the Looking Glass*.[470] The Alberta Court of Appeal opined: "Such an inquiry — one commencing with sentence to be followed by judgment — is no longer the private precinct of Alice and the Queen of Hearts."[471]

In terms of procedural fairness, the approach under the *YCJA* is preferable. Under the *YCJA*, as mentioned, a young person will always be tried in youth justice court (or in a court that is deemed to be sitting as a

---

[467] *YOA*, s. 16(2)(a). See Nicholas Bala, *Youth Criminal Justice Law* (Toronto: Irwin Law Inc., 2003), at 502-505 re a succinct discussion of issues in relation to transfer hearings under the *YOA*. See also R. Bromwich, "Compassion, Human Rights and Adult Sentencing Under the Y.C.J.A.: Guidance for Interpretation of the Adult Sentencing Provisions of Canada's New Youth Justice Law" (November 2002) 14 W.R.L.S.I. 71.

[468] *YOA*, s. 38(1)(a).

[469] Nicholas Bala, *Youth Criminal Justice Law* (Toronto: Irwin Law Inc., 2003) at 502-506.

[470] *R. v. M. (G.J.)*, [1993] A.J. No. 109, 135 A.R. 204 (Alta. C.A.).

[471] *R. v. M. (G.J.)*, [1993] A.J. No. 109, 135 A.R. 204 (Alta. C.A.).

youth justice court for purposes of the proceeding).[472] It is only if the young person has been found guilty of the offence that the court determines in certain circumstances whether an adult sentence will be imposed. Unless the application for an adult sentence is unopposed, a separate hearing is held *following the guilty finding* to determine if the young person should receive an adult sentence. This procedural change ensures that the young person has the benefit of the enhanced procedural protections afforded young persons under the *YCJA* during the trial, including the protection of his or her identity.

Under the *YCJA* regime, the Crown can apply to the youth justice court for an order deeming the young person liable to an adult sentence after the young person has been found guilty of an indictable offence in youth justice court for which an adult could be sentenced to prison for more than two years. The young person must also have been at least 14 years of age at the time of the alleged offence.

In addition, until May 16, 2008, under the *YCJA*, if a young person were charged with one of the most serious offences — murder, attempt to commit murder, manslaughter, aggravated sexual assault or a third serious violent offence,[473] and was at least 14 at the time of the alleged offence, there was a presumption that the young person would receive an adult sentence unless the young person could convince the court that a youth sentence should be imposed instead. In the case of these presumptive offences, the onus was on the young person to satisfy the court that a youth sentence would be of sufficient length to hold him or her accountable. However, the Supreme Court of Canada held in *R. v. D.B.*[474] that it was an unjustifiable violation of s. 7 of the *Charter* and therefore unconstitutional to place the onus on the young person in relation to these presumptive offences to justify why he or she should receive a youth sentence. Rather the burden should be on the Crown to justify why a more severe adult sentence is appropriate in the circumstances.[475] The reverse onus also contravenes another principle of fundamental justice, Abella J. held, that the Crown is obliged to prove beyond a reasonable doubt any aggravating factors in sentencing on which it relies. "Putting the onus on the young person to prove the *absence* of aggravating factors in order to justify a youth sentence, rather than on the Crown to prove the aggravating factors that justify a lengthier adult sentence, reverses the onus."[476]

---

[472] *YCJA*, s. 13(2) and (3).

[473] A serious violent offence is defined in s. 2(1) of the *YCJA*.

[474] [2008] S.C.J. No. 25, 2008 SCC 25 (S.C.C.).

[475] *R. v. D.B.*, [2008] S.C.J. No. 25, 2008 SCC 25 (S.C.C.), which was a 5-4 split decision, is discussed in greater detail in Chapter 6.

[476] *R. v. D.B.*, [2008] S.C.J. No. 25, at para. 78, 2008 SCC 25 (S.C.C.).

Thus, the onus is now always on the Crown to satisfy the court that an adult sentence should be imposed.

As a result of *R. v. D.B.*, in cases where the Crown wishes to seek an adult sentence, assuming, of course, that the young person meets the basic threshold criteria for an adult sentence, it now appears that the Crown should give notice to the young person prior to a plea being entered or, with leave of the court, before the beginning of the trial, that it intends to seek an adult sentence.[477] Under the former (pre-*R. v. D.B.*) regime, the Crown was not required to give notice when it was seeking an adult sentence in relation to the presumptive offences of murder, attempt to commit murder, manslaughter and aggravated sexual assault. The Crown was always required to give notice in cases where it wished to seek an adult sentence in relation to a third serious violent offence.[478] Provided the court is satisfied that the young person was given notice, the Crown can make the application for an adult sentence.[479]

A.   Adult Sentencing Hearing

Upon a guilty finding for the offence, a Crown application for an adult sentence will be heard at a special hearing, at the start of the sentencing hearing. While the Crown and defence counsel, as well as the parents of the young person, can make submissions[480] during this eligibility hearing, the onus[481] is now on the Crown in all cases to persuade the court that an adult sentence is appropriate in the circumstances. The youth justice court must impose an adult sentence without a hearing if the young person gives notice to the youth justice court that he or she does not oppose the application for an adult sentence and the young person is found

---

[477] *YCJA*, s. 64(2).

[478] *YCJA*, s. 64(4).

[479] *YCJA*, s. 68(2) (read in light of *R. v. D.B.*).

[480] *YCJA*, s. 71.

[481] Section 72 does not indicate the nature of the standard of proof required but merely says that the judge must impose an adult sentence if he or she is *of the opinion* that a youth sentence would not be of sufficient length to hold the young person accountable. Prior to *D.B.*, the Ontario Court of Appeal in *R. v. A.O.*, [2007] O.J. No. 800, 218 C.C.C. (3d) 409 (Ont. C.A.) relied on Supreme Court of Canada decisions such as *R. v. M. (S.H.)*, [1989] S.C.J. No. 93, [1989] 2 S.C.R. 446 (S.C.C.) to hold that the judge is required to weigh and balance the enumerated factors in deciding whether a youth sentence is long enough to hold the young person accountable but that the judge was not required to be satisfied beyond a reasonable doubt. See also the pre-*R. v. D.B.* case of *R. v. Bird*, [2008] A.J. No. 609, at para. 9 (Alta. Q.B.), regarding the point that the onus does not require proof beyond a reasonable doubt. However, Abella J. in *D.B.* indicated at para. 78 that the Crown is required to prove the aggravating factors that justify an adult sentence beyond a reasonable doubt.

guilty of an offence for which an adult could receive two years.[482] The power to decide whether to impose a youth sentence or an adult sentence in cases where this matter is contested, which will generally be the case, rests with the judge.[483] Crown and defence counsel can make all the submissions they wish but the judge makes the decision, based on a specific test.[484]

The substance of this test is the second major change in the adult sentencing process under the *YCJA*. The test for determining whether to impose an adult sentence under the *YCJA* is very different than that under the former Acts and, arguably, far more focused on the principle of accountability. The nature and focus of the test under the *YCJA* can be expected to increase the number of adult sentences in Canada.

Under the *JDA*, the court could transfer a young person of at least 14, such as Steven Truscott, to adult court for trial for an indictable offence if the court was of the opinion that "the good of the child and the interest of the community demand it".[485] This test was broad and ambiguous and left ample room for the exercise of discretion. In the Truscott case, for example, during the hearing of a leave application to the Ontario High Court to appeal the order to transfer Truscott to adult court, Schatz J. held that it would be for the good of the child to have the matter determined in open court by a jury, notwithstanding the publicity and strain of a public trial, rather than having the matter determined by a single judge in *in camera* proceedings. "I think it is also in the interests of the community that the public be assured that in a matter of this kind where public sentiment may have been aroused, the trial and disposition of the matter shall be in the ordinary course and free from any criticism."[486]

Under the *YOA*, in deciding whether to transfer a young person to adult court for trial, the judge was obliged to consider the interest of society, which were defined to include the objectives of protection to the public as well as the rehabilitation of the young person. If the judge found that these objectives could be reconciled within the youth justice system, the young person was not to be ordered transferred to the adult system. If the objectives could not be reconciled, the court was directed that protection of the public was to be paramount and the young person was to be transferred to the adult system. During the determination hearing, the *YOA*

---

[482] *YCJA*, s. 64(5).
[483] *YCJA*, s. 71.
[484] *YCJA*, s. 72. *R. v. Bird*, [2008] A.J. No. 609 (Alta. Q.B.) is a good example of a consideration and application of the test.
[485] *JDA*, s. 9.
[486] *Re S.M.T.*, [1959] O.J. No. 737, 125 C.C.C. 100 (Ont. S.C.).

judge was obliged to consider, among other factors, the availability of treatment programs and other resources in each system as well as the adequacy of the *YOA* and the *Criminal Code* in relation to the circumstances of the case. This assessment could include a consideration of the effect of the adult correctional system on a young person, as well as the availability of treatment programs in both systems. The judge was also required to consider a number of the same factors that the youth justice court judge must consider under the *YCJA*, such as the seriousness of the offence and the circumstances in which it was committed, as well as the age, maturity, character and background of the young person and any criminal history. The inquiry under the *YOA* also appeared to have a greater focus on the rehabilitation of the young person.

By contrast, the modern test under the *YCJA* for determining whether a young person should receive an adult sentence under the *Criminal Code* is focused on the principle of accountability, and whether a youth sentence would be of *sufficient length* to hold the young person accountable. In making its decision as to whether to impose a youth or adult sentence under the *YCJA*, the youth justice court is obliged to consider the seriousness and the circumstances of the offence, as well as the age, maturity, character, background and previous record of the particular young person and any other factors that the court considers relevant, *and*, if the youth justice court judge concludes that a youth sentence imposed in accordance with s. 3(1)(b)(ii) and s. 38 of the *YCJA* is of *sufficient length* to hold the young person accountable, the judge must impose a youth sentence. If the judge concludes, however, that a youth sentence imposed in accordance with s. 3(1)(b)(ii) and s. 38 of the *YCJA* would not be of *sufficient length* to hold the youth accountable, an adult sentence must be imposed.

Under the *YCJA*, rehabilitation is no longer mentioned as a factor in the test that the judge must consider in determining whether an adult sentence should be imposed, although the concept of rehabilitation is indirectly included because the *YCJA* judge is obliged to consider the sentencing principles in s. 38 of the *YCJA* when determining if a youth sentence would be of sufficient length to hold the young person accountable. Under s. 38, a youth sentence is intended to promote the young person's rehabilitation and reintegration into society and, subject to proportionality, must be the sentence that is most likely to rehabilitate the young person and reintegrate him or her into society.[487] Regardless, the concept of rehabilitation is not given the same measure of attention under the modern test for the imposition of an adult sentence and can be expected

---

[487]   *YCJA*, s. 38(1) and (2)(e)(ii).

to be perceived by the judiciary as less important than the listed factors.[488] In fact, some scholars describe the new test as punitive in tone.[489]

That said, the new test directs the judge to be mindful of the broad and general youth justice principle of proportionate accountability (or diminished responsibility) that is commensurate with the greater dependency and lesser maturity of young persons generally, and the judge must also consider characteristics of the particular young person, such as the particular age, maturity, character and criminal history, if any. (Under both the *YOA* and the *YCJA*, the judge is permitted to consider any other factors that the court considers relevant.) Under the *YCJA*, however, the judge is considering these factors only to assist in determining if the sentence imposed in accordance with s. 3(1)(b)(ii) and s. 38 of the *YCJA* is long enough to satisfy the principle of accountability. The focus of the *YCJA* test is on holding the young person accountable. Some academics have predicted that comparisons of the maximum lengths of sentences under the adult and youth sentencing regimes will become a central factor in adult sentencing determinations.[490]

The Ontario Court of Appeal considered and applied the new *YCJA* test under s. 72 to determine whether a young person should be eligible for an adult sentence. *R. v. A.O.*[491] involved a series of six armed robberies of convenience stores committed by two 16-year-old teenagers, A.O. and J.M., which the Appeal Court described as "well-planned, violent and terrifying".[492] It involved robberies of store clerks working alone late at night while the accused brandished knives or an imitation gun. Four of the clerks sustained knife wounds, one was severely beaten and stabbed, and all six clerks were traumatized.[493]

The Crown successfully argued that both accused should receive adult sentences. The two accused appealed the decision on various grounds, including the imposition of adult sentences. The Appeal Court upheld the sentencing judge, finding that there had been no error in

---

[488] See the discussion of this in R. Bromwich, "Compassion, Human Rights and Adult Sentencing Under the Y.C.J.A.: Guidance for Interpretation of the Adult Sentencing Provisions of Canada's New Youth Justice Law" (November 2002) 14 W.R.L.S.I. 71, at Part III, s. B.d.

[489] R. Bromwich, "Compassion, Human Rights and Adult Sentencing Under the Y.C.J.A.: Guidance for Interpretation of the Adult Sentencing Provisions of Canada's New Youth Justice Law" (November 2002) 14 W.R.L.S.I. 71, at Part III, s. B.d.

[490] R. Bromwich, "Compassion, Human Rights and Adult Sentencing Under the Y.C.J.A.: Guidance for Interpretation of the Adult Sentencing Provisions of Canada's New Youth Justice Law" (November 2002) 14 W.R.L.S.I. 71, at Part III, s. B.d.

[491] [2007] O.J. No. 800, 218 C.C.C. (3d) 409 (Ont. C.A.).

[492] *R. v. A.O.*, [2007] O.J. No. 800, at paras. 8 and 9, 218 C.C.C. (3d) 409 (Ont. C.A.).

[493] *R. v. A.O.*, [2007] O.J. No. 800, at para. 9, 218 C.C.C. (3d) 409 (Ont. C.A.).

sentencing each young person to a total of eight years in prison, which was reduced to five years each, in light of the 2.5 years they had already spent in custody.

The Ontario Court of Appeal held that the new test to determine whether an adult sentence should be imposed specifically directs the sentencing judge to ss. 3(1)(b)(ii) and 38, but that the combined effect of ss. 72, 3 and 38 of the *YCJA* is to identify accountability as the purpose that the youth justice court judge must consider when deciding whether to impose an adult sentence under the *YCJA*. The judge must weigh and balance the list of factors, such as the seriousness and circumstances of the offence as well as the age, maturity, character and background, and previous record of the young person, in order to decide if a youth record is of sufficient length to hold the young person accountable. The court rejected arguments that the Crown must prove on an adult sentencing application that the young person cannot be rehabilitated by a youth sentence. Assessing the young person's prospects of rehabilitation in terms of determining whether a youth sentence would be sufficient to hold the young person accountable is only one of the important factors that are integral to the accountability inquiry mandated by s. 72, the court held.[494] Rather, the Crown's burden is to satisfy the youth court, on consideration of all relevant factors, that a youth sentence would be of insufficient length to meet the base requirements of accountability that drives the entire youth sentencing regime.[495]

"The purpose of accountability in this context would seem to ex-clude accountability to society in any large sense or any notion of deterrence", which is consistent with the *"offender-centric nature"* of youth sentencing identified by the Supreme Court of Canada in *R. v. B.W.P.; R. v. B.V.N.*, the court found.[496]

The Appeal Court equated the concept of accountability to the adult sentencing principle of retribution, as defined by Lamer C.J.C. in the 1996 Supreme Court of Canada case *R. v. C.A.M.*[497] The court cited Lamer C.J.C.'s definition that retribution is "an objective, reasoned and measured determination of an appropriate punishment which properly reflects the moral culpability of the offender, having regard to the intentional risk-taking of the offender, the consequential harm caused by the offender and the normative character of the offender's conduct".[498] Unlike vengeance,

---

[494]   *R. v. A.O.*, [2007] O.J. No. 800, at para. 57, 218 C.C.C. (3d) 409 (Ont. C.A.).

[495]   *R. v. A.O.*, [2007] O.J. No. 800, at para. 59, 218 C.C.C. (3d) 409 (Ont. C.A.).

[496]   *R. v. A.O.*, [2007] O.J. No. 800, at paras. 42-43, 218 C.C.C. (3d) 409 (Ont. C.A.).

[497]   [1996] S.C.J. No. 28, 105 C.C.C. (3d) 327 (S.C.C.).

[498]   *R. v. A.O.*, [2007] O.J. No. 800, at para. 46, 218 C.C.C. (3d) 409 (Ont. C.A.).

Lamer C.J.C. explained, retribution incorporates the principle of restraint. It requires the imposition of a just and appropriate punishment, nothing more.[499]

After considering Lamer C.J.C.'s definition of retribution, the Ontario Court of Appeal concluded in *R. v. A.O.* that this was the only rational way to measure accountability.[500] While the Court of Appeal held that the need to consider the normative character of an offender's behaviour requires the court to consider societal values, it concluded that this is not the same thing as imposing on a youth sentence an element of general deterrence or denunciation.[501] In other words, in holding a young person accountable, the court is free to consider how society perceives the crime in terms of the severity of sentence required to reflect its seriousness.[502]

Several months later, the Ontario Court of Justice in *R. v. M.J.*[503] sought to more clearly define the meaning of the normative character of the offender's conduct. The term "normative", Wong J. held, refers to society's values and acceptable standards regarding a particular offence. For example, "the basic code of values our society holds is that handguns are unacceptable".[504]

If it is determined that a young person should receive an adult sentence, the sentencing principles under the *Criminal Code* apply.[505] However, the British Columbia Court of Appeal has held that the principles in s. 3 of the *YCJA* are relevant when a young person receives an adult sentence because s. 3 states that the s. 3 principles apply in the *YCJA*. Justice Saunders, who wrote for the court, considered it largely a question of statutory interpretation: since s. 74, which is the section of the *YCJA* that incorporates the sentencing principles in the *Criminal Code* in cases where a young person is to receive an adult sentence, is a section *in* the *YCJA*, it logically follows that the s. 3 principles in the *YCJA* are relevant to an adult sentence.[506] Section 74 does not expressly exclude the s. 3 principles in the sentencing of a young person as an adult, and, barring any inconsistency, between s. 3 and Part XXIII of the *Criminal Code*, Saunders J.A. could see no reason to conclude that s. 3 of the *YCJA* had no application to an adult sentence. Rather, the effect of s. 74 is to

---

[499] *R. v. C.A.M.*, [1996] S.C.J. No. 28, at paras. 80 and 81, 105 C.C.C. (3d) 327 (S.C.C.).

[500] [2007] O.J. No. 800, at para. 47, 218 C.C.C. (3d) 409 (Ont. C.A.).

[501] *R. v. A.O.*, [2007] O.J. No. 800, at para. 48, 218 C.C.C. (3d) 409 (Ont. C.A.).

[502] *R. v. A.O.*, [2007] O.J. No. 800, at para. 52, 218 C.C.C. (3d) 409 (Ont. C.A.).

[503] [2007] O.J. No. 2696 (Ont. C.J.).

[504] *R. v. M.J.*, [2007] O.J. No. 2696, at para. 62 (Ont. C.J.).

[505] *YCJA*, s. 74.

[506] *R. v. Pratt*, [2007] B.C.J. No. 670 (B.C.C.A.).

incorporate the sentencing principles under the *Criminal Code* while not excluding the general principles under s. 3.

"To hold that s. 3 has no bearing upon an adult sentence of a young person, is to move away from that long-held appreciation of the limitations of the not-yet-matured mind. I see no evidence in the Act that Parliament intended such a result."[507]

Section 3 of the *YCJA* simply heightens the consideration a court must give to the age of a young person by directing an approach to adult sentencing which expressly recognizes the greater dependency of young persons and their reduced level of maturity.[508]

In essence, the court held that a young person should receive a "discount" from the adult sanctions by virtue of being a young person; the fact of youth should operate to moderate the adult sentence. Judges are therefore required to consider the s. 3 principles in the *YCJA* when imposing an adult sentence, which means that the principle of rehabilitation is enhanced in the adult sentencing of a young person. It also means that the principle of accountability must recognize the diminished responsibility of the young person as may be revealed by the evidence.[509]

In *Pratt*, the Court of Appeal ultimately held that the sentencing judge erred in principle by not adequately considering the s. 3 principles in the case at bar. Justice Saunders noted that the sentencing judge's reasons suggest that s. 3 had no bearing at all on the adult sentence. After considering the s. 3 principles, Saunders J.A. reduced the sentence in the case from nine years to seven in relation to a guilty plea for manslaughter.

It is arguable that it was not the intention of Parliament that these s. 3 *YCJA* principles, which are highly relevant when a young person receives a youth sentence under the *YCJA*, were to be considered during an adult sentencing, particularly when age has always been a mitigating factor in sentencing under the common law in any event. It is contended that an adult sentence was not to be construed as a sentence under the *YCJA* but, rather, was envisioned to operate by largely removing the young person from the ambit of the *YCJA*. The *Pratt* decision, when read in the context of the entire *YCJA*, does not appear consistent with the overall intent and scheme of the *YCJA*, namely, that, once it is determined that a young person is liable to an adult sentence, the young person is subject to the adult regime. That said, s. 74 of the *YCJA* does not expressly exclude the s. 3 principles. Section 74 of the *YCJA* says only that Part XXIII of the *Criminal Code* (which is the part concerning sentencing) applies.

---

[507] *R. v. Pratt*, [2007] B.C.J. No. 670, at para. 54 (B.C.C.A.).

[508] *R. v. Pratt*, [2007] B.C.J. No. 670, at para. 53 (B.C.C.A.).

[509] *R. v. Pratt*, [2007] B.C.J. No. 670, at para. 58 (B.C.C.A.).

B.   Placement of Young Persons Who Receive Adult Sentences

> ... if it were the wish and aim of Magistrates to effect the destruction present and future of young delinquents, they could not devise a more effectual method, than to confine them so long in our prisons, those seats and seminaries (as they have been very properly called) of idleness and every vice.[510]

If a young person receives an adult sentence, the youth justice court can generally decide whether to place the young person in a youth custody facility or an adult facility based on various considerations, including the age of the young person at the time of the sentencing, as well as the best interests of the young person and the safety of others.[511] The youth justice court is expected to be guided by the basic presumption that a young person who is under 18 at the time of sentencing will be placed in a youth custody facility, and a young person who is 18 or older at the time of sentencing will serve the sentence in an adult correctional facility, or in the penitentiary if he or she has received a sentence of more than two years, unless it is satisfied that it would not be in the best interests of the young person or would jeopardize the safety of others.[512]

Academics, advocates, government watchdog agencies, and even the judiciary have raised significant concerns over the years about placing young persons in adult correctional facilities, where they face particularly damaging, destructive and violent environments.[513] In one example, Brooke J.A. of the Ontario Court of Appeal refused to transfer teenagers to ordinary court in 1989 in relation to the sexual assault of a 14-year-old teenager over three days, citing the risks of placing young persons in the adult system: "One cannot determine to impose a penitentiary sentence without having regard to the nature of the imprisonment and its most probable effect on the individual. The punishment in a penitentiary is much harsher than in an institution in which it is intended that youthful offenders would be incarcerated. A witness from Corrections Canada made this very clear, particularly its effect on youthful or young sex offenders. This included the fact that there was a real

---

[510] John Howard, *The State of the Prisons in England and Wales* (Warrington 1777), at 15-16, 21 (editor's lib.), as cited in *Juvenile Offenders for a Thousand Years, Selected Readings from Anglo-Saxon Times to 1900*, Wiley B. Sanders, ed. (Chapel Hill: University of North Carolina Press, 1970), at 63. Prison conditions in Britain in the later 1700s are described well in Thomas Keneally, *A Commonwealth of Thieves: The Improbable Birth of Australia* (New York: Anchor Books, 2007), at 10-11.

[511] *YCJA*, ss. 76, 79 and 80.

[512] *YCJA*, s. 76. A good practical discussion of s. 76 can be found in *R. v. A.O.*, [2007] O.J. No. 800, at paras. 83-120, 218 C.C.C. (3d) 409 (Ont. C.A.). See also *R. v. M.B.W.*, [2008] A.J. No. 40 (Ont. Prov. Ct.) re s. 76(2)(b).

[513] Nicholas Bala, *Youth Criminal Justice Law* (Toronto: Irwin Law Inc., 2003), at 528.

risk of physical danger, a risk of becoming involved in involuntary homo-
sexual activities and the likelihood of the young person having to accept or
adopt the codes of behaviour in living in such a place."[514]

More recently, Canada's Office of the Correctional Investigator has
criticized the housing of young persons in federal penitentiaries in any
circumstances and has taken the position that this should never be done.[515]
Judges and other professionals who work in the criminal justice system have
made similar comments, pointing to the increased risk of exposure to
violence, drugs and alcohol in Canada's adult correctional system,[516] as well
as greater negative influences generally if the young person is placed in the
adult system.[517] American research supports these observations: a 2007 U.S.
study found that juveniles placed in adult prisons are at heightened risk of
physical and sexual assault by older, more mature prisoners. Among its conclusions, the Equal Justice Initiative found that children are five times more
likely to be sexually assaulted in adult prisons than in juvenile facilities.[518]

---

[514]   *R. v. S. (W.)*, [1989] O.J. No. 65, 69 C.R. (3d) 168 (Ont. C.A.).

[515]   In its 2002-2003 Annual Report, the Office of the Correctional Investigator said that it
continued to be of the view that, in line with international law, minors should be legisla-
tively barred from placement in penitentiaries. It took the position in that report, in the
section called Young and Elderly Offenders, that penitentiaries are an inappropriate environment for minors, and indeed for young adults, especially those who are 20 or younger,
and it called for legislative amendments in this regard. This report is accessible online at:
<http://www.oci-bec.gc.ca/rpt/annrpt/annrpt20022003-eng.aspx#IVP>.

[516]   *R. v. L. (R.A.)*, [1995] B.C.J. No. 2459 (B.C.C.A.). During this transfer hearing, Wood J.A.
pointed to evidence from Crown witnesses who testified that placing the appellant in the
federal corrections system would expose him to an adult population, which might have a
negative effect on his rehabilitative efforts. Justice Wood further noted that witnesses acknowledged the increased risk of exposure to drugs, alcohol and physical abuse in the federal system (para. 10).

[517]   *R. v. A.O.*, [2007] O.J. No. 800, at para. 103, 218 C.C.C. (3d) 409 (Ont. C.A.). Various John
Howard Societies, as well as the Canadian Association of Elizabeth Fry Societies, have
expressed similar concerns over the years about the risks of young persons being victimized
and exploited by older, more experienced offenders, which reinforces offending behaviour,
if they are placed in the adult system. The Standing Committee on Justice and Legal Affairs
noted these comments when it issued its 1997 report on the youth justice system in Canada,
House of Commons, *Renewing Youth Justice: Thirteenth Report of the Standing Committee
on Justice and Legal Affairs*, released in April 1997 (Discussion to Recommendation 11).

[518]   *Cruel and Unusual: Sentencing 13 and 14-Year-Old Children to Die in Prison*, Equal
Justice Initiative, November 2007, at 14. The Equal Justice Initiative of Alabama is a
private, non-profit organization that provides legal representation to indigent defendants and
prisoners who have been denied fair and just treatment in the legal system. The organization
litigates on behalf of condemned prisoners, juvenile offenders, people wrongly convicted or
charged with violent crimes, poor people denied effective representation, and others whose
trials are marked by racial bias or prosecutorial misconduct. The Equal Justice Initiative also
prepares reports, newsletters and manuals to assist advocates and policymakers in the
critically important work of reforming the administration of criminal justice.

Placing young persons in adult prisons also conflicts with basic tenets of international law.[519]

This study also concluded that transferring young persons to adult court does not have a deterrent effect on violent juvenile crime.[520] American studies have found that young persons transferred to the adult system are more likely to reoffend and to reoffend more quickly and more often than young persons who remain in the juvenile system.[521]

There is an argument to be made that young persons should remain within youth justice facilities until *at least* the age of 18 and even along into their 20s to avoid exposure to older career criminals. If there is clear evidence that the young person poses safety risks to fellow inmates in the youth facility, efforts can be made to house the young person more securely within the youth custodial system. This is an important issue the federal government should consider as part of any reform initiative.

XVII. SENTENCE APPEALS AND STANDARD OF REVIEW

Section 37 of the *YCJA* governs sentence appeals. Similar to the *YOA*, young persons under the *YCJA* generally have the same rights of appeal in criminal proceedings as adults. The standard of review regarding the appeal of a youth sentence is the same standard of review that applies to the appeal of a sentence in criminal matters generally, *i.e.*, in relation to

---

[519] Article 37(c) of the *U.N. Convention on the Rights of the Child* states that every child deprived of liberty shall be separated from adults unless it is considered in the child's best interests not to do so. Canada has made a reservation to Article 37 in this regard. The Convention also states that children, defined as those under 18, by reason of their physical and mental immaturity, need special safeguards and care. In addition, Article 10 of the *U.N. International Covenant on Civil and Political Rights*, to which Canada is also a signatory, states that accused juvenile persons shall be separated from adults and brought as speedily as possible for adjudication and that the penitentiary system shall comprise treatment of prisoners, the essential aim of which shall be their reformation and social rehabilitation. It further states that juvenile offenders shall be segregated from adults and be accorded treatment appropriate to their age and legal status. (Canada's Office of the Correctional Investigator criticized the Correctional Service in its 2005-2006 Annual Report for failing to provide special housing, programming or other services for younger offenders.) The U.N. Covenant can be accessed at: <http://www.hrweb.org/legal/cpr.html>.

[520] Benjamin Steiner, Craig Hemmens and Valerie Bell, "Legislative Waiver Re-considered: General Deterrent Effects of Statutory Exclusion Laws Enacted Post-1979" (March 2006) 23(1) Justice Quarterly 34.

[521] D.M. Bishop and C. Frazier, "Consequences of Transfer" in J. Fagan and F.E. Zimring, eds., *The Changing Borders of Juvenile Justice: Transfer of Adolescents to the Criminal Court* (Chicago: Chicago University Press, 2000), at 227-76.

a sentence meted out in adult (ordinary) court.[522] This same standard of review applies to an appeal of a serious violent offence designation since the designation is part of the sentence, for appeal purposes.[523]

An order that a young person is subject to a youth sentence or an adult sentence as the case may be under s. 72 and an order regarding the placement of a young person who has received an adult sentence are both appealable as part of the sentence.[524]

In summary matters, or in matters involving hybrid offences where the Crown has not elected, the appeal is to the superior court and then to the provincial Court of Appeal. In indictable matters, the appeal goes directly to the appeal court. Youth justice matters involving indictable matters can be appealed to the Supreme Court of Canada with leave of that court.[525] In considering the predecessor section in the *YOA* to s. 37(10) of the *YCJA*, the Supreme Court of Canada has explained that Parliament did not extend appeals in youth matters to the Supreme Court of Canada as of right largely because youth justice policy favours the early resolution of youth matters to facilitate rehabilitation.[526] Nevertheless the Supreme Court of Canada will grant leave in cases involving important legal issues that have implications for youthful offenders generally.

XVIII. CONCLUSION

The sentencing of young persons is among the most controversial issues in Canada in relation to the youth criminal justice system. The law in this area reveals a fundamental contradiction in the youth criminal justice system: an obvious disconnect between youth justice philosophy and practice.

Canada has enshrined in legislation a statutory commitment to a criminal justice system for young persons, which is separate from that of adults.[527] In practice, however, the Canadian state has a separate youth justice system only for *most* young persons *most* of the time. Canada blurs

---

[522] *R. v. V.J.T.*, [2007] M.J. No. 122, 2007 MBCA 45 (Man. C.A.). Re the general standard of review for sentence appeals in criminal matters, see *R. v. Shropshire*, [1995] S.C.J. No. 52, [1995] 4 S.C.R. 227 (S.C.C.).

[523] *R. v. V.J.T.*, [2007] M.J. No. 122, at para. 15, 2007 MBCA 45 (Man. C.A.). See also *YCJA*, ss. 42(10) and 37(4).

[524] *YCJA*, ss. 37(4) and 72(5).

[525] *YCJA*, s. 37(10). Section 41 of the *Supreme Court Act*, R.S.C. 1985, c. S-26, governs appeals to the Supreme Court of Canada in summary conviction matters. See also *R. v. C. (T.L.)*, [1994] S.C.J. No. 70, [1994] 2 S.C.R. 1012 (S.C.C.).

[526] *R. v. C. (T.L.)*, [1994] S.C.J. No. 70, [1994] 2 S.C.R. 1012 (S.C.C.).

[527] *YCJA*, s. 3(1)(b).

the boundaries between the adult and the youth criminal justice systems significantly by permitting young persons to be subject to the same penalties as adults for certain crimes[528] in certain circumstances, and by also sanctioning the loss of other legal protections for young persons who receive adult sentences. For example, the name of a young person can be published if he or she receives an adult sentence. The young person can also be housed in an adult correctional facility or in a penitentiary in certain circumstances.[529]

This is not new. The Canadian state has permitted some blending of the youth and adult criminal justice systems ever since the formal youth criminal justice system was established a century ago. Canada has never had a purely "separate" youth justice system. The "separate" youth justice system has always allowed for the sentencing of young persons as adults in certain circumstances. In effect, young persons in Canada have traditionally been perceived to be less accountable by virtue of their age and lesser maturity — unless they commit the most serious crimes. In such cases, the state has traditionally reserved the right to subject them to the same penalties adults could receive for the same crimes. But, as critics argue, their age and level of maturity has not changed. They remain young persons. It is simply that, when young persons commit the most serious crimes, the nature of the crime (rather than the fact of youth) becomes the paramount factor in determining the regime.[530] The wisdom and logic of this approach is questionable if one accepts the basic premise that young persons by virtue of their status as young persons must be seen to be less morally culpable and thus less accountable for criminal conduct, regardless of the crime.

The practice of permitting young persons to receive adult sentences in certain circumstances raises fundamental questions about the nature and quality of the Canadian youth criminal justice system. Simply because Canada has traditionally permitted the sentencing of young persons as adults in certain circumstances and has also traditionally allowed some young persons to be imprisoned in adult penitentiaries is not a rationale to

---

[528] A recent American study found that young persons who are transferred to adult court recidivate at much higher rates than those youths who are kept in the youth system. See Benjamin Steiner, Craig Hemmens and Valerie Bell, "Legislative Waiver Re-considered: General Deterrent Effects of Statutory Exclusion Laws Enacted Post-1979" (March 2006) 23(1) Justice Quarterly 34.

[529] *YCJA*, s. 76. Figures were not available regarding the number of young persons under 18, if any, who are in federal correctional facilities or penitentiaries in Canada; the figure is believed to be extremely low.

[530] Anthony Doob and Carla Cesaroni engage in an interesting discussion on this subject in "Transfers to Adult Court: Treating Children as Adults" in *Responding to Youth Crime in Canada* (Toronto: University of Toronto Press, 2004), at 171.

continue either practice. The health of a modern democracy lies, in part, in its ongoing questioning of convention and tradition.

> It is revolting to have no better reason for a rule of law than that so it was laid down in the time of Henry IV. It is still more revolting if the grounds upon which it was laid down have vanished long since and the rule simply persists from blind imitation of the past.[531]

This unexpected hiatus in youth justice reform enables the Canadian state to re-examine these practices and pose critical questions, including: What are the advantages and disadvantages of housing young persons in adult correctional facilities and penitentiaries? What is the recidivism rate for young persons housed in adult institutions versus those housed in youth facilities? What are the benefits of subjecting certain young persons to adult sentences? Could the same goals be achieved by dispensing with the concept of adult sentences and simply increasing the sentences for the most serious crimes within the *YCJA*? To what degree does the current practice of sentencing and housing some young persons as if they were adults conflict with basic principles of international law, such as the *U.N. Convention on the Rights of the Child*, which Canada ratified in 1992?[532] Does Canada require additional research to address these questions?

The asymmetry between Canadian youth justice philosophy and practice has been accentuated in recent years, in part, as a result of the evolution of international law. Permitting adult sentences for young persons in *any* circumstances is, in the eyes of some, a fundamental digression from the principles of the *United Nations Convention on the Rights of the Child*,[533] and the principles of the *U.N. International Covenant on Civil and Political Rights*. The Committee on the Rights of the Child, which monitors state compliance with the *U.N. Convention on*

---

[531] Justice Oliver Wendell Holmes Jr., The Path of the Law, An Address delivered by Mr. Justice Holmes, then of the Supreme Court of Massachusetts, on January 8, 1897, as reprinted in *The World of Law, II, The Law as Literature*, Ephraim London, ed. (New York, Simon and Schuster, 1960), 614 at 626.

[532] Article 3 of the Convention states that, in all actions concerning children, including those undertaken by courts of law, the best interests of the child shall be a primary consideration. Further, Article 37(c) says that: "State parties shall ensure that: ... every child deprived of liberty shall be separated from adults unless it is considered in the child's best interest not to do so ..."

[533] Sandra J. Bell, *Young Offenders and Juvenile Justice: A Century After the Fact*, 2d ed. (Scarborough: Nelson, a division of Thomson Canada Ltd., 2003), at 340. While Canada made a reservation to Article 37(c) of the U.N. Convention, academics argue that provisions for adult sentencing breach the spirit, if not the letter, of international obligations under the U.N. Convention. See also R. Bromwich, "Compassion, Human Rights and Adult Sentencing Under the Y.C.J.A.: Guidance for Interpretation of the Adult Sentencing Provisions of Canada's New Youth Justice Law" (November 2002) 14 W.R.L.S.I. 71, at Part III, s. B.d. In addition, Canada expressly states in the Preamble to the *YCJA* that it is a party to the *U.N. Convention on the Rights of the Child*.

the Rights of the Child, recently criticized the *YCJA* in various respects, including the continuing legality of mixing juveniles and adults in detention facilities.[534]

It remains for Parliament and the Supreme Court of Canada to give texture and precise definition to the meaning and the boundaries of a separate youth criminal justice system within a modern and enlightened Canadian state.

---

[534] M. Denov, "Children's Rights, Juvenile Justice, and the U.N. *Convention on the Rights of the Child*: Implications for Canada" in Kathryn Campbell, ed., *Understanding Youth Justice in Canada* (Toronto: Pearson Education Inc., 2005), 65 at 81-82.

Chapter 9

YOUNG PERSONS, PRIVACY, THE PUBLIC AND THE PRESS: A COLLISION OF LAW AND VALUES

At some point, in some cases, under some circumstances, we think the right for society to know exceeds the right for an individual — even a young person with so many years ahead of him — to be protected from further vilification ... The 18th-century philosopher, Jeremy Bentham, once said of the right to a free press: "Where there is no publicity, there is no justice." We assert that justice, in this case, also means justice, full awareness and safety for our community. There must be publicity.[1]

Scholars agree that "[p]ublication increases a youth's self-perception as an offender, disrupts the family's abilities to provide support, and negatively affects interaction with peers, teachers, and the surrounding community" ... .[2]

Stigmatization or premature "labelling" of a young offender still in his or her formative years is well understood as a problem in the juvenile justice system. A young person once stigmatized as a lawbreaker may, unless given help and redirection, render the stigma a self-fulfilling prophecy.[3]

I. INTRODUCTION

With the exception of the sentencing code for young persons in the *Youth Criminal Justice Act*,[4] the privacy regime in Part 6 of the *YCJA* is the most contentious illustration of the extent to which the Canadian state sanctions the differential treatment of young persons under the criminal law.

---

[1] Kirk LaPointe, Editorial, *The Hamilton Spectator* (4 November 1999).
[2] *R. v. D.B.*, [2008] S.C.J. No. 25, at para. 84, 2008 SCC 25 (S.C.C.).
[3] *Re F.N.*, [2000] S.C.J. No. 34, at para. 14, [2000] 1 S.C.R. 880 (S.C.C.).
[4] S.C. 2002, c. 1 [hereafter "*YCJA*"].

When an adult is charged with a crime, generally, his or her name becomes a matter of public record. However, the Canadian state has entrenched in law for more than a century the protection (in most cases) of the identities of young persons who are charged and found guilty of crimes.

This routine protection raises the ire of many Canadians, including parents, members of victims' rights groups, and the media, who believe the public has a right to know the identities of young persons who commit crimes, especially chronic and violent youthful offenders who show no promise of rehabilitation.[5] Not only is publishing the identities of youthful suspects and offenders linked to fundamental principles of openness and transparency within the criminal justice system but it also addresses accountability and should be the norm, at least for young persons found guilty of the most violent crimes, they argue. Others view it as an issue of press freedom.[6]

By contrast, the predominant view among Canadian criminologists and youth criminal justice experts (which has been largely accepted by pre-eminent Canadian jurists) is that youthful offenders' chances of rehabilitation are most sedulously fostered if they are not stigmatized by society through publication of their identities, and thus, the long-term protection of society is more likely to be assured.[7] In fact, in *R. v. D.B.*,[8] Abella J., speaking for the majority of the Supreme Court of Canada, acknowledges that Canadian youth justice experts, as well as the Canadian common law and international instruments, have recognized the negative impact of media attention on young persons. Justice Abella noted, in particular, that the publication of the identities of young persons can make them vulnerable to greater psychological and social stress.[9]

---

[5]   In 1999, *The Hamilton Spectator* challenged the privacy laws under the *Young Offenders Act*, R.S.C. 1985, c. Y-1 [hereafter "*YOA*"], which have not changed substantially under the *YCJA*, in a series of articles that it published November 4-9, 1999.

[6]   The competing views and values triggered by this issue were acknowledged in Department of Justice, *A Strategy for the Renewal of Youth Justice* (Ottawa: Ministry of Supply and Services, 1998), in the section on Legislative and Supporting Program Components. This document is the federal government's foundation policy document for the *YCJA*. It was the federal government's response to *Renewing Youth Justice: Thirteenth Report of the Standing Committee on Justice and Legal Affairs*, released in April 1997. At the time of writing, this 1998 Strategy document was accessible through the Department of Justice website at: <http://www.justice.gc.ca/eng/pi/yj-jj/about-apropos/toc-tdm.html>.

[7]   Various experts outlined their views in this regard in *R. v. Southam Inc.*, [1984] O.J. No. 3398, 16 C.C.C. (3d) 262 (Ont. H.C.), affd [1986] O.J. No. 2349, 25 C.C.C. (3d) 119 (Ont. C.A.), leave to appeal refused [1986] 1 S.C.R. xiv (S.C.C.), which is still good law. This general view that publication of the identities of young persons impedes their rehabilitation was reiterated by Binnie J. in *Re F.N.*, [2000] S.C.J. No. 34, [2000] 1 S.C.R. 880 (S.C.C.) and more recently acknowledged in *R. v. D.B.*, [2005] S.C.J. No. 25, 2008 SCC 25 (S.C.C.).

[8]   [2005] S.C.J. No. 25, 2008 SCC 25 (S.C.C.).

[9]   *R. v. D.B.*, [2008] S.C.J. No. 25, at paras. 84-87, 2008 SCC 25 (S.C.C.).

These conflicting perspectives are captured by two fundamental and competing legal principles: the right to privacy of young persons facing criminal charges or found guilty of criminal offences, versus the public's historic right to know who stands accused in the criminal courtrooms of the nation. The *YCJA* clarifies that a young person's right to privacy is to be emphasized; in addition, the Canadian common law and international law also recognize the right to privacy of young persons.[10] On the other hand, Iacobucci and Arbour JJ. of the Supreme Court of Canada affirmed in *Re Vancouver Sun* that "[t]he open court principle has long been recognized as a cornerstone of the common law ... Public access to the courts guarantees the integrity of judicial processes by demonstrating 'that justice is administered in a non-arbitrary manner, according to the rule of law'".[11] The open court principle is also inextricably linked to freedom of expression as guaranteed by s. 2(b) of the *Canadian Charter of Rights and Freedoms*.[12]

Despite the sanctity of the open court principle and the breadth of interests protected by it, as well as the entrenchment of freedom of the press in the *Charter* in 1982, Canadian courts have generally held that protecting young persons in conflict with the criminal law from the harmful effects of publicity is a social value of such "superordinate importance" that it justifies the abrogation of these competing principles.[13]

What the youth justice law requires, in practice today, in order for the privacy of young persons to be protected in these circumstances may not be entirely understood. As this chapter explains, despite contemporary legal restrictions on the publication of information about young persons who have been dealt with under the *YCJA*, members of the public in Canada are generally free[14] to attend the trials of young persons charged with crimes. Youth justice court trials are open and public in that sense. What distinguishes Canadian youth justice court trials from adult trials

---

[10] *R. v. D.B.*, [2008] S.C.J. No. 25, at paras. 84-87, 2008 SCC 25 (S.C.C.), *per* Abella J.

[11] *Re Vancouver Sun*, [2004] S.C.J. No. 41, at paras. 24 and 25, [2004] 2 S.C.R. 332 (S.C.C.). Other seminal Canadian cases concerning the open court principle include *Nova Scotia (Attorney General) v. MacIntyre*, [1982] S.C.J. No. 1, 40 N.R. 181 (S.C.C.) and *Vickery v. Nova Scotia Supreme Court (Prothonotary)*, [1991] S.C.J. No. 23, 64 C.C.C. (3d) 65 (S.C.C.). In *R. v. T.C.*, [2006] N.S.J. No. 531 (N.S. Youth J. Ct.), Williams J. described the open court principle as a hallmark of a democratic society, which applies to all judicial proceedings (*R. v. T.C.*, at para. 14).

[12] Part I of the *Constitution Act, 1982*, being Schedule B to the *Canada Act 1982* (U.K.), 1982, c. 11 [hereafter "*Charter*"].

[13] On these points, see in particular *R. v. Southam Inc.*, [1984] O.J. No. 3398, 16 C.C.C. (3d) 262 (Ont. H.C.), affd [1986] O.J. No. 2349, 25 C.C.C. (3d) 119 (Ont. C.A.), leave to appeal refused [1986] 1 S.C.R. xiv (S.C.C.). See more recently *Re F.N.*, [2000] S.C.J. No. 34, at para. 10, [2000] 1 S.C.R. 880 (S.C.C.), where the Supreme Court of Canada affirms that the privacy of youthful offenders is one example where the public interest in confidentiality outweighs the public interest in openness.

[14] But see *YCJA*, s. 132.

regarding the privacy of the accused is that the *YCJA* generally prohibits publication of any information that could serve to identify the young accused person or the young offender to the general public.[15] The identities of young persons who are victims or witnesses in youth justice court matters are also generally protected.

On a practical level, it works like this: as a general rule, when an adult (a person who is 18 or more at the time of the alleged offence) is charged with an offence, the media can publish or broadcast the name of the accused and the fact that he or she has been charged with a criminal offence. The journalist can go to the local courthouse and request to see the information or the indictment, which identifies the accused and indicates the charges that have been laid, the dates of the alleged offences, and other basic information about the incident. Once the charge is laid, this is a matter of public record. Generally, the media can publish these basic facts. Likewise, when a journalist is covering the trial of an adult accused, the journalist is generally free to report on the identity of the accused as well as the information that is revealed during the trial, subject to any publication bans or other restrictions that are imposed, such as publication bans in relation to the identity of a sexual assault complainant. However, as noted above, the media are significantly circumscribed when reporting on criminal matters involving young persons who are being dealt with under the *YCJA,* including alleged victims and witnesses.

II.   THE PUBLIC TRIAL, PUBLICITY AND THE PRESS

The notion of the open court and a public trial is firmly rooted in legal history. In the ancient world, the public trial was the norm: in fifth-century Athens, assemblies of up to 1,001 would judge a case.[16] In arguably the most celebrated ancient trial of them all, the prosecution of Socrates in 399 B.C., 501 male citizens sat on wooden benches in the People's Court, located in the agora, the civic centre of Athens, and voted on the fate of the most well-known philosopher in the Western world. Given Socrates' fame, even then, many spectators were believed to have attended.[17] In Ancient Rome too, trials were often popular events. During the heyday of Roman orator, Cicero, who was born in 106 B.C., Romans thronged to the Forum, which was the major venue for public trials. Trials

---

[15]   *YCJA,* s. 110.
[16]   Sadakat Kadri, *The Trial: A History, from Socrates to O.J. Simpson* (New York: Random House, 2005), at 8.
[17]   Sadakat Kadri, *The Trial: A History, from Socrates to O.J. Simpson* (New York: Random House, 2005), at 11 and 12.

were held in the open air, where hordes congregated to listen and to cheer the greatest advocates of the day.[18]

Under the common law, to which the Canadian legal system is most indebted, the inception of the public trial can be traced to Pope Innocent III's decision to abandon trial by ordeal in 1215. Some method of determining guilt had to replace these barbarous methods. Although a link between 12 triers and criminal justice can be identified as far back as King Alfred the Great in 879 A.D., a trial in 1220 marks the origin of the jury trial,[19] which, based on practices of the day, also meant a public trial. In that 13th century Westminster trial, 12 property-owning neighbours were amassed to swear to the characters of five accused men. "The need to assemble jurors made it impossible to exclude the public, and although sheriffs and jailers would extort admission fees until the 1700s, large crowds invariably entered in their wake."[20] While Henry VIII found this novel approach convenient for public condemnations of public figures such as Thomas More and Anne Boleyn, it was during the Elizabethan era that vast crowds were encouraged to attend trials, in large part so the state could demonstrate to the throngs where power resided.[21] In the mid to late 1500s, rudimentary reports of trials began to appear. Such reports soon became common. "By the 1670s, suitably salacious and brutal trials were being reported within days of a verdict."[22] Indeed, it wasn't terribly long in relative terms before courtrooms started getting crowded. During the following century, court attendance became an integral aspect of any respectable person's education.[23] (This was, of course, notably unlike the secret manner in which trials were conducted on the continent. In France, under the inquisitorial system, trials did not become public until after the French revolution, in the 1790s).[24] Within decades, liberal thinkers on the Continent were extolling the virtues of England's transparent criminal justice system. "In England, no trial is secret," French philosopher

---

[18]   Anthony Everitt, *Cicero: The Life and Times of Rome's Greatest Politician* (New York: Random House Trade Paperbacks, 2003), at 29-30.

[19]   Sadakat Kadri, *The Trial: A History, from Socrates to O.J. Simpson* (New York: Random House, 2005), at 70.

[20]   Sadakat Kadri, *The Trial: A History, from Socrates to O.J. Simpson* (New York: Random House, 2005), at 74.

[21]   Sadakat Kadri, *The Trial: A History, from Socrates to O.J. Simpson* (New York: Random House, 2005), at 76-77.

[22]   Sadakat Kadri, *The Trial: A History, from Socrates to O.J. Simpson* (New York: Random House, 2005), at 95.

[23]   Sadakat Kadri, *The Trial: A History, from Socrates to O.J. Simpson* (New York: Random House, 2005), at 93-94.

[24]   Sadakat Kadri, *The Trial: A History, from Socrates to O.J. Simpson* (New York: Random House, 2005), at 68.

Voltaire declared publicly in 1762. "Witnesses testify in open court and any trial of interest is reported in the newspapers."[25]

Since Canada inherited the British common law system, public trials are an integral aspect of our legal culture. However, when the new nation of Canada began contemplating its first piece of comprehensive national legislation to deal with youthful accused in the early 1900s, the state veered from the established practice of the public trial. Public condemnation and scrutiny were considered appropriate and fitting for adult criminals but not for youthful offenders. For decades, the trials of young persons under the *Juvenile Delinquents Act*[26] were held *in camera*. This approach would change by the 1980s so that members of the public, including the media, were able to attend youth court trials but the media remained restricted, as it does today, in its capacity to identify young persons charged with crimes in its media coverage.

A.   Publicity and the *JDA*

In the years preceding the enactment of the *JDA* in 1908, youth justice advocates who were lobbying for a separate and comprehensive youth justice system argued that young persons charged with crimes should be shielded from publicity in a way that adults were not. They were very much aware of the 1891 Commission of Inquiry into the Prison and Reformatory System of Ontario,[27] which made a number of recommendations relating to the privacy of young persons who were brought before the criminal justice system. Commissioners recommended, for example, that no child be arrested and taken through public streets if it could be avoided, that if the matter were trivial, a summons be issued to the parents instead to produce the child in court, and that no child under 14 be tried in public on any charge but rather that the child be tried in private with only a few key individuals in attendance, such as the officers of the court, the necessary witnesses, the probation officer and the parents or guardians.[28]

Toronto journalist J.J. Kelso was paying close attention to the Commission's work. With the help of others, he lobbied federal Justice Minister Sir John Thompson to act on the Commission's recommendations and to

---

[25]   Francois Marie Arouet de Voltaire, *Histoire d'Elisabeth Canning et de Calas* (London, 1762), at 3, as quoted in Sadakat Kadri, *The Trial: A History, from Socrates to O.J. Simpson* (New York: Random House, 2005), at 101.

[26]   S.C. 1908, c. 40 [hereafter "*JDA*"].

[27]   *Report of the Commissioners Appointed to Enquire into the Reformatory System of Ontario* (Toronto: Warwick, 1891).

[28]   Jeffrey S. Leon, "The Development of Canadian Juvenile Justice: A Background for Reform" (1977) Vol. 15, No. 1, Osgoode Hall L.J. 71, at 85.

pass legislation so that the first Canadian *Criminal Code* of 1892 provided that, where expedient and practicable, trials of persons under 16 should be held *in camera* and separate and apart from those of adult offenders and without publicity.[29] Kelso soon noticed, however, that the judges virtually never found it expedient and practicable to grant separate trials so he pushed for legislation that would make it compulsory for juveniles to be tried separately from other accused and without publicity.[30] In 1894, Parliament responded by passing *An Act Respecting Arrest, Trial, and Imprisonment of Youthful Offenders*, which achieved Kelso's goal of providing for *in camera* and mandatory separate trials for young persons under 16.

> The 1894 act encompassed many of the changes that reformers had sought since at least the early part of the century. Children would now be kept away from the contaminating influence of adult criminals, afforded more privacy, and processed separately by the courts. The essence of the legislation was that delinquents would be treated not as criminals in need of punishment but as young people requiring help and understanding.[31]

During debate in the House of Commons in 1894, Justice Minister Thompson explained that compassion was the driving force behind the differential treatment of youthful offenders: "A great many magistrates from motives of humanity" were trying young persons separately, he conceded.[32] Liberal MP William Mulock, who was later to become the Chief Justice of Ontario, voiced similar comments, although he warned that trials without publicity "raise a danger of justice being interfered with".[33]

The *JDA* of 1908, which Kelso assisted Secretary of State W.L. Scott in drafting, codified in s. 12 the principle of ensuring privacy for young persons charged with crimes. Section 12(1) of the *JDA* stated: "The trials of children shall take place without publicity and separately and apart from the trials of other accused persons ... ."[34] Parliament arguably intended s. 12(1) to mean that the trials of young persons were to be held in private, that young persons alleged to be delinquents under the *JDA* and

---

[29] D. Owen Carrigan, *Juvenile Delinquency in Canada: A History* (Toronto: Irwin Publishing, 1998), at 67. See also Sanjeev Anand, "Catalyst for Change: The History of Canadian Juvenile Justice Reform" (Spring 1999) Vol. 24, No. 2, Queen's L.J. 515, at 531.

[30] Jeffrey S. Leon, "The Development of Canadian Juvenile Justice: A Background for Reform" (1977) Vol. 15, No. 1, Osgoode Hall L.J. 71, at 88. See also D. Owen Carrigan, *Juvenile Delinquency in Canada: A History* (Toronto: Irwin Publishing, 1998), at 66-67.

[31] D. Owen Carrigan, *Juvenile Delinquency in Canada: A History* (Toronto: Irwin Publishing, 1998), at 68.

[32] Jeffrey S. Leon, "The Development of Canadian Juvenile Justice: A Background for Reform" (1977) Vol. 15, No. 1, Osgoode Hall L.J. 71, at 89.

[33] Jeffrey S. Leon, "The Development of Canadian Juvenile Justice: A Background for Reform" (1977) Vol. 15, No. 1, Osgoode Hall L.J. 71, at 89.

[34] *JDA*, s. 12.

tried under that legislation were to be shielded from the glare of publicity. Such intent was in keeping with the welfare-oriented, paternal nature of the *JDA*, which is aptly illustrated by s. 31 of the original *JDA*: "the care and custody and discipline of a juvenile delinquent shall approximate as nearly as may be that which should be given by its parents, and that as far as practicable every juvenile delinquent shall be treated, not as a criminal, but as a misdirected and misguided child, and one needing aid, encouragement, help and assistance".[35]

For many decades, the *JDA* appeared to have achieved its objective. From 1908 until its dying days in the early 1980s, the public knew little about criminal cases involving young persons because the media was not permitted to be present in juvenile court under the *JDA*.[36] Not until the *Charter* was imminent, with its guarantees of both freedom of the press and the right to a public trial[37] did the media begin to vociferously challenge the secrecy of juvenile court proceedings. It would not be long before the doors of youth justice courtrooms swung open across the country — at least a good part of the way. The media would eventually win the right to be present in the courtroom as a result of constitutional challenges.[38] But not even the *Charter* could alter the state's persistent and historical inclination to protect the privacy of young persons charged with crimes. The media would never win the right to routinely publish the names of young persons charged with criminal offences in Canada. Protecting the privacy of young persons who come into contact with the criminal law remains a fundamental principle under the *YCJA* today.[39]

B. The Meaning of Privacy for Young Persons in the *Charter* Era

Under the *JDA*, youth court proceedings were held without the public in attendance and without publicity.[40] Just a few years before the *YOA* came into force in April 1982, however, two Winnipeg radio stations

---

[35] *JDA*, s. 31.

[36] See, in general, Susan A. Reid, "Youth Crime and the Media" in Kathryn Campbell, ed., *Understanding Youth Justice in Canada* (Toronto: Pearson Education Canada Inc., 2005), 135 at 137. See also *R. v. C.B.*, [1981] S.C.J. No. 94, [1981] 2 S.C.R. 480 (S.C.C.).

[37] *Charter*, ss. 2(b) and 11(d), respectively.

[38] *R. v. Southam Inc. (No. 1)*, [1983] O.J. No. 2962, 41 O.R. (2d) 113 (Ont. C.A.). See also *R. v. Southam Inc.*, [1984] O.J. No. 3398, 16 C.C.C. (3d) 262 (Ont. H.C.), affd [1986] O.J. No. 2349, 25 C.C.C. (3d) 119 (Ont. C.A.), leave to appeal refused [1986] 1 S.C.R. xiv (S.C.C.).

[39] In addition to Part 6 of the *YCJA*, which concerns Publication, Records and Information, see also s. 3(1)(b)(iii) of the *YCJA*.

[40] See, in general, Susan A. Reid, "Youth Crime and the Media" in Kathryn Campbell, ed., *Understanding Youth Justice in Canada* (Toronto: Education Canada Inc., 2005), 135 at 137.

applied to be present in the juvenile court to hear and report on the proceedings involving the juvenile C.B. The radio station was requesting permission only to be present in the courtroom and to report on the proceedings without identifying the juvenile. The radio stations were granted permission by the Manitoba Court of Appeal to be present in the courtroom to report on the proceedings, subject to restrictions regarding identification. The appellant appealed the matter to the Supreme Court of Canada; it was heard in June of 1981.

At the time, s. 12 read as follows:

> 12. (1) The trials of children shall take place without publicity and separately and apart from the trials of other accused persons, and at suitable times to be designated and appointed for that purpose.
>
> (2) Such trials may be held in the private office of the judge or in some other private room in the court house or municipal building, or in the detention home, or if no such room or place is available, then in the ordinary court room, but when held in the ordinary court room an interval of half an hour shall be allowed to elapse between the close of the trial or examination of any adult and the beginning of the trial of a child.
>
> (3) No report of a delinquency committed, or said to have been committed, by a child, or of the trial or other disposition of a charge against a child, or of a charge against an adult brought in the juvenile court under section 33 or under section 35, in which the name of the child or of the child's parent or guardian or of any school or institution that the child is alleged to have been attending or of which the child is alleged to have been an inmate is disclosed, or in which the identity of the child is otherwise indicated, shall without the special leave of the court, be published in any newspaper or other publication.
>
> (4) Subsection (3) applies to all newspapers and other publications published anywhere in Canada, whether or not this Act is otherwise in force in the place of publication.[41]

In deciding *R. v. C.B.*, Chouinard J. of the Supreme Court of Canada considered the meaning of the phrase "without publicity" in s. 12. During his ruling, he observed that, throughout most of the history of the *JDA*, the meaning of the term had never been considered. He was aware of only one appellate level ruling directly on point where the court held that a judge had the discretion to permit members of the public to attend the trial of a child charged with a delinquency. Otherwise, the courts appear to have generally assumed that "without publicity" in s. 12(1) meant *in camera*.[42]

---

[41]   *JDA*, s. 12.

[42]   *R. v. C.B.*, [1981] S.C.J. No. 94, [1981] 2 S.C.R. 480 (S.C.C.). Justice Chouinard cited as an example the Truscott case in 1959, where Schatz J. of the Ontario High Court, in ordering 14-year-old Steven Truscott to be proceeded against in ordinary court on a murder charge,

In a succinct decision, Chouinard J. held that "without publicity", when read within the context of the entire s. 12, meant *in camera*, *i.e.*, in private rather than in open court. The words "without publicity" mean the opposite of "in open court", that is, *in camera*.[43] In Chouinard J.'s view, his conclusion was bolstered by s. 12(2), which states that the trials of young persons are to be held in a private office or a private room or at a place where there is no public access. In the event that the trial of a child must be held in the ordinary court because no private room is available, the fact that s. 12(2) requires 30 minutes to elapse between the end of an adult trial and the beginning of the child's trial is further evidence that the intent is for the room to be empty so that the child will not come into contact with adult accused or other persons who might have a bad influence upon them. Justice Chouinard held that his interpretation was reinforced by other provisions of the *JDA*, which specifically state that other parties have the right, or the obligation, to attend the proceeding, such as the parents or guardians, members of the juvenile court committee, and the probation officer. "If the trial of a child were to be open to the public at large there would be no need for such provisions ... ."[44] While mindful of the fundamental principle of the law that all criminal and civil trials are to be held in open court, Chouinard J. acknowledged that there were known exceptions to that rule and that s. 12 of the *JDA* constituted one such exception. The press were not to be present in the courtroom.[45]

When the *Charter* came into force in 1982, the media launched constitutional challenges, first to s. 12 of the *JDA* and later to similar provisions of the *YOA*, based on the newly enshrined principle of freedom of the press under s. 2(b) of the *Charter*.[46] The media not only launched constitutional challenges, but they won, thus fundamentally altering the daily practices of media outlets across the country. As a result of various court decisions in the 1980s, the Canadian media were finally allowed inside youth justice courtrooms, although they were prohibited from including in their reports any information that would enable members of the public to identify the young person who was the subject of the criminal proceeding.

---

assumed that a trial in juvenile court meant *in camera* before a single judge, whereas a trial in adult court meant in open court before the public (*R. v. C.B.*, at 486 (S.C.R.)). The appellate level case to which Chouinard J. is referring, where the court held that the media could be present in the courtroom is *R. v. N.*, [1979] B.C.J. No. 633 (B.C.C.A.).

[43] *R. v. C.B.*, [1981] S.C.J. No. 94, [1981] 2 S.C.R. 480, at 492 (S.C.C.).

[44] *R. v. C.B.*, [1981] S.C.J. No. 94, [1981] 2 S.C.R. 480, at 490 (S.C.C.).

[45] *R. v. C.B.*, [1981] S.C.J. No. 94, [1981] 2 S.C.R. 480, at 487 and 492 (S.C.C.).

[46] The *Canadian Bill of Rights* also recognizes freedom of the press in Part I, s. 1(f). See *Canadian Bill of Rights*, S.C. 1960, c. 44.

R. v. Southam Inc. (No. 1)[47] was among a number of groundbreaking cases in the early 1980s. It was decided just a year after the *Charter* came into force. In this case, the Ontario Court of Appeal held that s. 12(1) of the *JDA*, which requires that the trial of all juveniles be held *in camera*, was unconstitutional in light of the freedom of the press guaranteed by s. 2(b) of the *Charter*. Associate Chief Justice MacKinnon, writing for the court, concluded that access to the courts was integral to, and implicit in, the freedom of the press guarantee in s. 2(b), and that an absolute ban on such public access was not a reasonable limit on it.[48] The Ontario Court of Appeal was presumably aware that its decision was, to a large degree, academic, since an entirely new Act, the *YOA*, had already been enacted and the court acknowledged that it was soon to be proclaimed in force.

C. Privacy Under the *YOA*

Under the *YOA*, ss. 38 and 39 concerned the privacy of young persons and generally prohibited the media from publishing any information that would identify a young person who was charged with, or found guilty of an offence under the *YOA*, or from publishing any information that would identify the victims or witnesses in relation to the offence. There were exceptions to this general rule. In addition, s. 39 of the *YOA* permitted the judge to exclude members of the public from the youth court proceedings in certain circumstances. The court retained a discretion to exclude any or all members of the public from the courtroom if it considered it in the interest of public morals, the maintenance of order or the proper administration of justice.[49]

The sections read as follows:

> 38. (1) No person shall publish by any means any report
>
> (a) of an offence committed or alleged to have been committed by a young person, unless an order has been made under section 16 with respect thereto, or
>
> (b) of a hearing, adjudication, disposition or appeal concerning a young person who committed or is alleged to have committed an offence
>
> in which the name of the young person, a child or a young person aggrieved by the offence or a child or a young person who appeared as a witness in connection with the offence, or in which any information serving to identify such young person or child, is disclosed.

---

[47] [1983] O.J. No. 2962, 41 O.R. (2d) 113 (Ont. C.A.).
[48] *R. v. Southam Inc. (No. 1)*, [1983] O.J. No. 2962, 41 O.R. (2d) 113 (Ont. C.A.).
[49] *YOA*, as enacted by S.C. 1980-81-82-83, c. 110.

. . . . .

39. (1) Subject to subsection (2), where a court or justice before whom proceedings are carried out under this Act is of the opinion

(a) that any evidence or information presented to the court or justice would be seriously injurious or seriously prejudicial to

(i) the young person who is being dealt with in the proceedings,

(ii) a child or young person who is a witness in the proceedings,

(iii) a child or young person who is aggrieved by or the victim of the offence charged in the proceedings, or

(b) that it would be in the interest of public morals, the maintenance of order or the proper administration of justice to exclude any or all members of the public from the court room,

the court or justice may exclude any person from all or part of the proceedings if the court or justice deems that person's presence to be unnecessary to the conduct of the proceedings.

These new provisions were soon challenged. The courts responded by reiterating the limits of press freedom and the open court principle in these circumstances: the press and the public could generally be present in the courtroom, but the press could not report or broadcast the names or any information that would enable members of the public to identify the young person charged or found guilty in the youth court proceeding, nor could the press report any information that would serve to identify a victim or witness in relation to a youth court proceeding.

In the seminal case of *R. v. Southam Inc.*,[50] Southam Inc., as owner and publisher of *The Ottawa Citizen*, challenged the constitutionality of ss. 38(1) and 39(1)(a) on the grounds that these new sections of the *YOA* were an unreasonable limit on freedom of the press under s. 2(b) of the *Charter*. During the hearing, the Attorney General of Canada conceded that the sections infringed freedom of the press under s. 2(b). The issue for litigation was whether the sections amounted to a reasonable limit prescribed by law, under s. 1 of the *Charter*, as can be demonstrably justified in a free and democratic society. As Holland J. put it, the case involved balancing two competing interests: freedom of expression,

---

[50]   [1984] O.J. No. 3398, 16 C.C.C. (3d) 262 (Ont. H.C.), affd [1986] O.J. No. 2349, 25 C.C.C. (3d) 119 (Ont. C.A.), leave to appeal refused [1986] 1 S.C.R. xiv (S.C.C.). Eventually, in *Re F.N.*, [2000] S.C.J. No. 34, [2000] 1 S.C.R. 880 (S.C.C.), the Supreme Court of Canada would affirm that the privacy of youthful offenders is one example where the public interest in confidentiality outweighs the public interest in openness.

including freedom of the press, and society's interest in the manner in which young persons in conflict with the law are treated.

During the proceeding, the Attorney General of Canada called five witnesses in an attempt to justify the limit imposed on freedom of the press by virtue of ss. 38 and 39. Justice Holland accepted the evidence of the expert witnesses, whose expertise ranged from criminology, to child psychiatry, to psychology. All five were firmly of the view that allowing information about young persons who come into conflict with the criminal law to be published or broadcast in the media would impede their rehabilitation, and that the retention of ss. 38(1) and 39(1)(a) were in the best interests of young persons involved in the criminal justice system and society as a whole.[51] Their reasoning was grounded in general concerns about the damaging impact of publicity on the young person's rehabilitation due to the harm that the young person could suffer as a result of being labelled or stigmatized at a young age. Merely being labelled or identified as a child or youthful offender could escalate or perpetuate antisocial behaviour, they suggested. The experts also expressed concerns about the effect of stress and shame on the family as a result of publicity about the case, as well as the negative effect of publicity on the young person's peer relationships, on his or her reputation generally and on the young person's treatment within the family or community. The experts raised similar concerns in relation to the identification of victims and witnesses in these youth cases.[52]

Justice Holland concluded that the protection and rehabilitation of young people involved in the criminal justice system were social values of "superordinate importance", which justifiy the abrogation of fundamental freedom of expression, including freedom of the press, to the extent effected by s. 38(1) and that, as a result, s. 38(1) is a reasonable limit on that freedom. Likewise, s. 39(1)(a) permits the youth court to exclude any member of the public, but it is not an absolute ban, as was the case under s. 12(1). Again, Holland J. held that the protection and rehabilitation of young people involved in youth court proceedings was of such superordinate importance that it justified the judicial discretion under s. 39(1)(a) and was a reasonable limit on freedom of the press under s. 2(b) of the *Charter*. The Ontario Court of Appeal affirmed the lower court decision; leave to appeal to the Supreme Court of Canada was refused.

---

[51]   *R. v. Southam Inc.*, [1984] O.J. No. 3398, at paras. 26-46, 16 C.C.C. (3d) 262 (Ont. H.C.).

[52]   See, for example, paras. 27-39 in *R. v. Southam Inc.*, [1984] O.J. No. 3398, 16 C.C.C. (3d) 262 (Ont. H.C.). See also *R. v. T.R. (No. 1)*, [1984] A.J. No. 601, 10 C.C.C. (3d) 481 (Alta. Q.B.), where the court recognized the harmful and stigmatizing effect of publicity during a consideration of s. 12(3) of the *JDA*.

As a result of decisions such as *Southam* and its progeny, by the mid-1980s, Canadian journalists were routinely observing youth court proceedings, but they had a legal obligation to ensure that their articles or broadcast items did not provide so much information about the case that it enabled the public to identify the youthful accused, or victims or witnesses involved in the case. In other words, journalists could sit in the courtroom and observe the proceedings, and they could write the "story" for their newspapers but they had to tell the story in such a way so as to avoid reporting any facts or details in the news story that would enable members of the public to identify the young accused or any victims and witnesses.

The new privacy regime for youthful accused soon attracted its share of critics. Academics, the media, victims' rights advocates, sometimes even the judiciary, and certainly many average Canadians, complained, sometimes bitterly, about the protection and the privacy being afforded to some very violent young people.

Youth justice expert Priscilla Platt, author of *Young Offenders Law in Canada*, was strongly critical of the privacy regime established under the *YOA*. She described the *YOA* privacy regime as a process "shrouded in secrecy".[53] Platt contended that the regime was excessive in its scope. In addition to forbidding the media from identifying young persons in the press, the *YOA* prevented journalists from accessing or seeing many of the court documents unless they got a judge's order. Platt suggested that not every victim of crime, such as a youth who had his or her bike stolen, required such "dramatic" protection. "To require state authorization in these circumstances is the essence of censorship. ... clearly, as noted above, the non-publication provision over-reaches in that it assumes that every young person and child involved in a youth court proceeding is in need of such protection and is in need of it in perpetuity."[54]

In 1999, *The Hamilton Spectator* launched a bold challenge to s. 38 of the *YOA*, the precursor to ss. 110 and 111 of the *YCJA*.[55] With full knowledge of the law, *The Hamilton Spectator* deliberately revealed that a 19-year-old male in the community, whom they identified by name, had a youth court record, despite the fact that s. 38 of the *YOA* prohibited the newspaper from revealing this fact.

---

[53]   Priscilla Platt, *Young Offenders Law in Canada*, 2d ed. (Markham, Ont.: Butterworths Canada Ltd., 1995), at 523.

[54]   Priscilla Platt, *Young Offenders Law in Canada*, 2d ed. (Markham, Ont.: Butterworths Canada Ltd., 1995), at 523-25.

[55]   Four articles ran in *The Hamilton Spectator* on November 4-9, 1999.

The teenager was at large and considered dangerous at the time they ran the articles. The newspaper argued that it had a duty to inform the community of his long youth court record as a matter of public safety, since his adult record alone did not provide a true picture of his extensive criminal past. In essence, the newspaper asserted that the public's right to know superseded the young man's right to privacy. The privacy provisions of the *YOA* were designed to give youths a second chance, to give them a break for the mistakes of their past, the newspaper argued. But this particular offender had amply demonstrated that he had not been rehabilitated and that he was not worthy of the protection. In other words, the youth in question had effectively forfeited his right to privacy by his continued criminal conduct and had no reputation to protect, the newspaper alleged. The newspaper also made the point that the *YOA* provided no mechanism whereby the media could get court approval to reveal this information.

Kirk LaPointe, who was editor-in-chief and associate publisher at the time, was charged with violating s. 38 of the *YOA*. He eventually pled guilty on February 21, 2001 before Zabel J. of the Ontario Court of Justice and was granted an absolute discharge.[56] Mr. LaPointe's counsel indicated at his sentencing that Mr. LaPointe had intended to challenge the constitutionality of the law, but later resolved that such a challenge would absorb a lot of valuable court time.

Victims' rights advocates also tackled this issue. When the federal government was reviewing the *YOA* and the Canadian youth justice system in 1996, Ottawa grandmother Theresa McCuaig was among those who pressed for changes to the Act so that the names of young persons charged with violent crimes could be published. McCuaig's 17-year-old grandson, Sylvain Leduc, had been murdered in 1995 in a gang-related torture and killing. Leduc was beaten to death and his cousin was sexually assaulted with a hot curling iron. Leduc had been caught in the snare of a local street gang, Ace Crew. He was abducted, blindfolded and killed during a crime that the media described as so well planned that gang members had prepared the apartment in advance by taping garbage bags over the windows so the blood could be easily cleaned up. Five young persons and three adults were eventually convicted of a range of offences, including murder, manslaughter, forcible confinement, and aggravated sexual assault. The adults received life sentences, while the young persons received sentences ranging from 18 months to three years.[57] When the young persons were

---

[56] *R. v. Kirk LaPointe*, unreported, February 21, 2001, Hamilton, Ontario, Zabel J. (Ont. C.J.).

[57] Christie Blatchford, "Beating survivor takes a step for fledgling alliance" *The National Post* (12 January 2000).

charged, their identities were protected in accordance with the provisions of the *YOA*. McCuaig later implored the federal government to amend the youth justice legislation so that the names of young offenders, at least the most violent ones, could be made public. "The names of young offenders *should* be made public so that we can protect ourselves from them."[58]

"If a young offender is charged, let's say, with manslaughter or murder, put his name in the paper so the neighbour knows. ... Just make the public aware. Protect them. We don't know right now who's coming at us."[59]

Even some judges broke their customary silence and dared to speak publicly about the issue. Madam Justice Southin of the British Columbia Court of Appeal referred to s. 38 of the *YOA* as "one of the law's sillier provisions, at least in cases of serious crime. ... What we have are laws that keep the citizenry in ignorance and, thus, contribute to the ruination of the child who is embarking on a life of crime".[60]

Despite challenges and pressures from stakeholders across the criminal justice system, the principle and practice of protecting the privacy of young persons remained firmly entrenched in youth justice law. Chief Justice Lamer, in *Dagenais v. Canadian Broadcasting Corp.*,[61] observed that non-publication is designed to "maximize the chances of rehabilitation for young offenders".[62]

The Supreme Court of Canada affirmed the legitimacy of the privacy and records regime of the *YOA* in *Re F.N.*[63] Justice Binnie, writing for the court, recognized the non-disclosure provisions of the *YOA* as an exception to the general constitutional rule of open courts whereby the public interest in confidentiality outweighs the public interest in openness. Justice Binnie acknowledged that confidentiality assists the rehabilitation of young persons, and that stigmatization or premature labelling of a young offender is well understood as a problem in the juvenile justice system: "A young person once stigmatized as a lawbreaker may, unless

---

[58]   House of Commons of Canada, 35th Parliament, 2d Session, Evidence, Standing Committee on Justice and Legal Affairs, Chair: Shaughnessy Cohen, Meeting No. 3, Tuesday, April 16, 1996, at 1010.

[59]   House of Commons of Canada, 35th Parliament, 2d Session, Evidence, Standing Committee on Justice and Legal Affairs, Chair: Shaughnessy Cohen, Meeting No. 3, Tuesday, April 16, 1996, at 1040.

[60]   Mary F. Southin, "On the Prevention of Criminals" (1994) Vol. 52, Pt. 6, The Advocate 871, at 871.

[61]   [1994] S.C.J. No. 104, [1994] 3 S.C.R. 835 (S.C.C.).

[62]   *Dagenais v. Canadian Broadcasting Corp.*, [1994] S.C.J. No. 104, at para. 83, [1994] 3 S.C.R. 835 (S.C.C.).

[63]   [2000] S.C.J. No. 34, [2000] 1 S.C.R. 880 (S.C.C.).

given help and redirection, render the stigma a self-fulfilling prophecy."[64] Justice Binnie further observed, as other Supreme Court of Canada judges later would, that a young person's right to privacy and the risk of labelling have also been recognized internationally.[65] While Canadian youth justice experts suggest that there is little Canadian research to support the argument that publicizing information about young offenders hinders their rehabilitation, Binnie J. noted that Canadian experts cite American research on point.[66]

(*Re F.N.* concerned the disclosure of information in a youth court docket to a Newfoundland school board. The court found that a court docket fell within the definition of a youth record under the *YOA* records regime, but the case is also clear recognition by Canada's highest court that the protection of a young person's privacy is a predominant value within the Canadian youth justice system, and that safeguarding that privacy is inextricably linked to a young person's rehabilitation.)

By the time *Re F.N.* was released in 2000, however, the privacy and records regime of the *YOA* was nearing obsolescence. The *YCJA* had already been drafted and re-drafted. Within three years (after a third draft and a total of 160 amendments),[67] the comprehensive privacy and records regime of the *YCJA* would be the law.

D.   The *YCJA* and the Privacy of Young Persons

The privacy of young persons who come into conflict with the criminal law remains a cornerstone of youth justice in Canada under the *YCJA*. In its 1998 background document, *A Strategy for the Renewal of Youth Justice*, which is the evidentiary and policy basis for the *YCJA*, the federal government acknowledges that it is aware of public concerns about the long-standing practice of protecting the identities of young persons but that, nevertheless, in most cases, shielding the identities of young persons from the public is the proper course.[68]

---

[64]   *Re F.N.*, [2000] S.C.J. No. 34, at para. 14, [2000] 1 S.C.R. 880 (S.C.C.).

[65]   *Re F.N.*, [2000] S.C.J. No. 34, at para. 16, [2000] 1 S.C.R. 880 (S.C.C.). Justice Binnie was referring to the *U.N. Standard Minimum Rules for the Administration of Juvenile Justice* (Beijing Rules), Rules 8.1 and 8.2.

[66]   *Re F.N.*, [2000] S.C.J. No. 34, at para. 15, [2000] 1 S.C.R. 880 (S.C.C.).

[67]   Sandra J. Bell, *Young Offenders and Juvenile Justice: A Century After the Fact*, 2d ed. (Scarborough: Nelson, a division of Thomson Canada Ltd., 2003), at 59.

[68]   Department of Justice, *A Strategy for the Renewal of Youth Justice* (Ottawa: Ministry of Supply and Services, 1998) (section on Legislative and Supporting Program Components). At the time of writing, this 1998 document was accessible through the Department of Justice website at: <http://www.justice.gc.ca/eng/pi/yj-jj/about-apropos/toc-tdm.html>.

The *YCJA* emphasizes the importance of protecting the privacy of young persons more than the *YOA* did, by codifying an express right to privacy. The *YCJA* states explicitly that the criminal justice system for young persons must emphasize enhanced procedural protection, including their right to privacy.[69] The recognition of a young person's right to privacy can also be read into the Preamble of the *YCJA*, which states that Canada is a party to the *United Nations Convention on the Rights of the Child*.[70] Most importantly, Part 6 of the *YCJA* establishes the most comprehensive legislative regime to date to protect the privacy of young persons who are dealt with under the criminal law, as well as those who are victims and witnesses in youth justice court proceedings In addition, key terms relating to the privacy of young persons, which have never before been defined in federal youth justice law in Canada, are defined in the *YCJA*, and include the meaning of publication and disclosure, as well as the meaning of youth record.

(i)   Two Distinct but Mutually Reinforcing Regimes[71]

Part 6 of the *YCJA* contains two distinct but related regimes that regulate information about a young person who comes into conflict with the criminal law: the first regime (ss. 110-112) concerns restrictions on the publication of information about young persons who are dealt with under the *YCJA*, as well as those who are alleged victims and witnesses in relation to youth justice court proceedings. The second regime (ss. 113-129) concerns the use, retention and destruction of youth records. It strictly regulates and controls what entities can keep youth records and for what purpose, who can access these records and the terms and conditions of that access, as well as rules regarding the destruction of youth records.

As discussed in this chapter, the restrictions on publication do not apply in cases where the young person receives an adult sentence.[72] Likewise, the records regime does not apply to the youth record in cases where the young person continues to commit offences as an adult while

---

[69]   *YCJA*, s. 3(1)(b)(iii).

[70]   Article 40 2. (b)(vii): Every child accused of infringing the criminal law is entitled to a guarantee "[to] have his or her privacy fully respected at all stages of the proceedings".

[71]   Justice Binnie used this phrase in *Re F.N.*, [2000] S.C.J. No. 34, at para. 18, [2000] 1 S.C.R. 880 (S.C.C.) to describe the distinct publication and records aspects of the privacy regime under the *YOA*. The phrase is equally apt in describing Part 6 of the *YCJA*, which consists of distinct provisions relating to prohibitions on publishing information about young persons dealt with under the *YCJA* and certain other provisions that relate specifically to youth records.

[72]   *YCJA*, s. 110(2)(a).

the access period to the youth record is open.[73] Nor does the records regime apply to the offence in cases where the young person receives an adult sentence for it, provided the adult sentence is upheld on appeal.[74] In both of these cases, the youth record shall be treated like an adult record, and the guilty finding is deemed a conviction for purposes of the *Criminal Records Act*.[75]

(ii) Distinction Between Publication and Disclosure

In its interpretation section, the *YCJA* distinguishes between publication and disclosure. Publication is defined as "the communication of information by making it known or accessible to the general public through any means, including print, radio, or television broadcast, telecommunications or electronic means".[76] Disclosure, by contrast, means the communication of information other than by way of publication.[77] The meaning of disclosure is relevant to the records provisions of the *YCJA*, which shall be discussed later in this chapter; it relates to the access to, and disclosure of, youth records under the *YCJA*. A record is also defined in the *YCJA*; this definition will be discussed in section III. Records, later in this chapter.

(iii) Section 110

Section 110 of the *YCJA* generally prohibits the publication of the name of a young person and any information that would serve to identify the young person as a young person *dealt with* under the *YCJA*, subject to certain exceptions. The same basic rule of non-publication existed under

---

[73] *YCJA*, s. 119(9)(b).

[74] *YCJA*, s. 117.

[75] *YCJA*, ss. 119(9)(b) and (c) and 117. See *R. v. A.A.B.*, [2006] N.S.J. No. 226 (N.S. Prov. Ct.).

[76] *YCJA*, s. 2(1). In *R. v. Scott*, [1984] O.J. No. 3470, 16 C.C.C. (3d) 17 (Ont. Co. Ct.), McDermid Co. Ct. J. held that Parliament cannot have intended the meaning of publication in s. 38 to be interpreted so as to prevent an accused person the right to cross-examine a 13-year-old complainant regarding his record as a juvenile delinquent or young offender. The right of the accused to cross-examine a young person on his youth record trumps the right of the witness to have his identity withheld in the interest of a fair trial. Likewise, in *R. v. Strain*, [1994] O.J. No. 1513 (Ont. Gen. Div.), Weekes J. held that an accused should be able to have access to a young person's record, even if the access period to the record has passed, in order to engage in legitimate cross-examination, which would show that, at least during a part of his or her life, the young person demonstrated behaviour that is relevant to the trier of fact for purposes of assessing the credibility of the person, as a witness.

[77] *YCJA*, s. 2(1).

the *YOA*. The media cannot publish the names of these young persons, or any information that would enable a member of the public to identify them merely by reading the facts in the story. If a member of the public is able to discern the identity of the young person because the journalist has included too many identifying facts or characteristics, the journalist and/or newspaper could be charged under s. 138 of the *YCJA*. Large mainstream newspapers in Canada generally have legal counsel available to assist by reading the article prior to publication to ensure the journalist has not gone too far or included too much information in the news story.

However, the breadth of s. 110(1) is unclear. In order for the publication ban under this section to apply, the young person must be *dealt with* under the *YCJA*. Parliament has left it to the courts to define the concept of being "dealt with".

Presumably, a young person will be dealt with under the *YCJA* when there is *any* interaction between the young person and a state actor, such as a police officer, a prosecutor or a judge, where any of the provisions of the *YCJA* come into play. Therefore, a young person will be *dealt with* under the *YCJA* not only in clear cases, such as when they are charged, found guilty or acquitted of an offence, but also when the young person is under investigation, or is dealt with by way of an informal, extrajudicial measure, such as when the police take any of the actions they are authorized to take under s. 6 of the *YCJA*. This clearly includes a young person who is detained by the police, however briefly, and then released without charge. Such young persons have still been dealt with. (As discussed in Chapter 5, taking no action is one of the measures a police officer is required to consider under s. 6(1) of the *YCJA* in cases where he or she is interacting with a young person and believes the young person has committed an offence.)

Section 6(1) of the *YCJA* states: "A police officer shall, before starting judicial proceedings or taking any other measures under this Act against a young person alleged to have committed an offence, consider whether it would be sufficient, having regard to the principles set out in section 4, to take no further action, warn the young person, administer a caution, if a program has been established under section 7, or, with the consent of the young person, refer the young person to a program or agency in the community that may assist the young person not to commit offences."

Information that a young person has been given a Crown caution under s. 8 of the *YCJA*, or information that a young person has been dealt with by way of any other extrajudicial measure, including a sanction, is also information that a young person had been dealt with under the *YCJA* and, thus, also information that cannot be published.

Although non-publication is the general rule, there are several exceptions to s. 110(1). The identity of the young person and the details relating to the incident can be published if:

* the young person receives an adult sentence;[78]

* the Crown seeks an adult sentence but the young person receives a youth sentence for a presumptive offence, which includes murder, attempt to commit murder, manslaughter, aggravated sexual assault or a third serious violence offence;[79]

* the publication of the information is made in the course of the administration of justice and it is not the purpose of the publication to make the information known in the community;[80]

* the young person decides to go public after reaching the age of 18 and is not in custody pursuant to either the *YOA* or the *YCJA* at the time of publication;[81]

* the young person is under 18 and successfully applies to the youth justice court for permission to publish information that would identify him or her as having been dealt with under either the *YOA* or the *YCJA*;[82]

---

[78]   *YCJA*, s. 110(2)(a).

[79]   *YCJA*, s. 110(2)(b) and s. 75(1). *R. v. D.B.*, [2008] S.C.J. No. 25, 2008 SCC 25 (S.C.C.) has significantly modified these provisions in practice by striking down the reverse onus aspect of them. In other words, as a result of *R. v. D.B.*, the onus is now on the Crown under these sections to convince the court that the publication ban should be lifted rather than on the young person to satisfy the court as to why the publication ban should remain.

[80]   *YCJA*, s. 110(2)(c). The meaning of this exception is not clear in law. Litigation continues in this area. A similar provision existed in the *YOA*. Its meaning hinges on the meaning of the term "administration of justice" and, to a lesser degree, on the meaning of publication in s. 2 of the *YCJA*, which appears to be qualified by this paragraph. In *Re F.N.*, [2000] S.C.J. No. 34, at para. 43, [2000] 1 S.C.R. 880 (S.C.C.), Binnie J. held that the term "in the course of the administration of justice" under the *YOA* in s. 38(1.1) could be interpreted to include the disclosure of information to persons engaged in the administration of justice, including court officials, witnesses and young people involved with the law. However, Binnie J. appeared to suggest at para. 34 that the disclosure in such situations should be limited to those officials involved in the administration of the particular youth case. By contrast, in *Manitoba Housing Authority v. Everett*, [2006] M.J. No. 386 (Man. C.A.), Scott C.J.M. held that information released during a Residential Tenancies Commission hearing that revealed that one of the tenant's sons, a young person, had been named and identified as being charged with a criminal offence, was a publication made in the course of the administration of justice. It was relevant to, and made in the course of, the proceedings before the Commission. It is noteworthy that the *YCJA* chose to distinguish between the concept of publication on the one hand and the disclosure of youth records on the other, by defining the terms and by separating these aspects in Part 6. It should be borne in mind that publication is defined in s. 2 as *making it known or accessible to the general public.*

[81]   *YCJA*, s. 110(3).

[82]   *YCJA*, s. 110(6).

- the police can apply *ex parte* to a youth justice court judge for an order permitting any person to publish the name of a young person who has committed or allegedly committed an indictable offence if the judge is satisfied that: the young person is a danger to others or publication is necessary to assist in the apprehension of the young person. The order lasts for five days.[83]

Nevertheless, there is a significant gap in the general publication ban under s. 110 of the *YCJA*. When newspapers take different approaches while covering or reporting on the same event or trial, the young accused person can inadvertently be identified. The coverage of the murder trial of a 13-year-old Medicine Hat teenager illustrates the point. The teenager was tried and found guilty in July 2007 of first degree murder in the stabbing deaths of her entire family. Although her identity was undoubtedly well known in the small south-eastern Alberta community of 57,000 and the public is generally free to attend the trials of young persons, the cumulative effect of the differing media approaches to the trial coverage resulted in the girl being identified to anyone who chose to read several Canadian newspapers a day. Some newspapers identified the slain family by name, even ran a photograph of the couple, but did not identify the girl by name or indicate that she was the daughter of the slain couple.[84] Other media outlets did not report the family name but reported that the young accused was the daughter of the slain couple and the sister of the eight-year-old boy who was also murdered. Consequently, members of the public who read, heard, or watched various media accounts of the trial could put the information together and easily deduce the last name of the 13-year-old girl and the fact that she is the daughter in the family. In fact, the only detail they would not know is the first name of the young girl (unless they read or heard the very first news reports of the incident in which the girl was temporarily named before she became a suspect). J.R. was identified by name in the first reports because she was not yet considered a suspect in the case, only the missing member of the family. As soon as it became clear to police that she was a suspect, and someone who was being "dealt with" under the *YCJA*, the publication ban under s. 110 of the *YCJA* became relevant. While each newspaper, technically and individually, did not violate the publication ban, the end result of their

---

[83]   *YCJA*, s. 110(4) and (5). These provisions essentially enable a police force to send out a press release, identifying by name a young person who is at large and dangerous. The provisions also enable the media to publish this information for the brief period.

[84]   See for example "Alberta girl, 13, guilty of murders" in *The National Post* (10 July 2007), A1-A8.

differing approaches to covering the trial resulted in the young girl being identified to the public at large.[85]

It is an offence under s. 138 of the *YCJA* to publish information that would result in the identification of a young person in these circumstances, but no one single newspaper committed the elements of the offence. It is only the combined effect of their coverage that resulted in the breach. One way to avoid such an outcome is if the media voluntarily agreed upon a common approach to compliance with s. 110, which is highly unlikely in this competitive field. Alternatively, the state could be more proscriptive about codifying precisely what details the news media could report about an accused young person so that all news outlets would be obliged to report the same facts about the accused.

In the case at issue, the identification of J.R. appeared to have gone unnoticed, perhaps largely because only those with particular expertise would be aware of the violation. More to the point, J.R. is not a sympathetic figure in the eyes of most Canadians; few would be inclined to lead the campaign to protect her rights.

Another emerging issue in relation to the general publication ban under s. 110 of the *YCJA* is that individuals have begun to post the names of young persons charged with offences on the popular social networking website known as Facebook. Those doing so may be unaware that they may be violating s. 110 of the *YCJA*, or they do not care. Given the novelty of Facebook, the courts have not yet definitively determined whether putting such information on a Facebook page constitutes publication for purposes of the *YCJA*.

The police in Camrose, Alberta had to shut down certain Facebook pages in early January 2008 after the names of four teenage boys accused of killing a cat in a microwave were posted. The media reported that the names were accompanied by violent threats, including a message from one person who wrote: "I think people like that should be shot. I would say these monsters should be tortured, let society at them."[86] A similar

---

[85]   *The Globe and Mail* did not identify her by name but indicated that she was alleged to have killed her mother, her father and her eight-year-old brother. See Christie Blatchford, "I just wanted him to go to sleep" *The Globe and Mail* (5 July 2007), A1-A8. However, *The Ottawa Citizen* reported the names of the three family members who were killed, but did not identify the girl by name or indicate that she is the other member of that family. See Sherri Zickefoose, "'I'm too young to die,' boy told accused" *The Ottawa Citizen* (4 July 2007), A3. Readers of both newspapers would therefore know the name of the family members and know also that the girl was the other member. The only missing point was her first name; she was identified as J.R. in *The Globe and Mail* story.

[86]   "Accused teen cat killers named on Facebook" *The Ottawa Citizen* (7 January 2008), A3. Two Alberta teenagers were sentenced in September 2008 to 100 hours of community service for killing the family cat by placing it in a microwave and turning on the microwave.

incident occurred in Toronto early in 2008 when the names of two teenagers charged with fatally stabbing a 14-year-old girl were also reported on Facebook.[87]

The definition of "publication" in s. 2 of the *YCJA* means the communication of information by making it known or accessible to the "general public" through any means, including print, radio, or television broadcast, telecommunication or electronic means. What is meant by the term "general public"? Posting information on a Facebook page may not be synonymous with making it known to the general public. This will depend to some degree on the extent to which access to the page is controlled. In some instances, publishing information on Facebook may not be equivalent to making it known or accessible to the general public. It will depend on the facts of the case. This can be expected to be a prime area of litigation in the years ahead.

Finally, while s. 110 indicates that the publication ban does not apply if the young person receives an adult sentence, the *YCJA* fails to clarify the status of a publication ban under s. 110 in the event that the young person appeals his adult sentence. Section 117 of the *YCJA* is clear that the young person loses the benefits of the records protections under the *YCJA* as a consequence of receiving an adult sentence unless the adult sentence is overturned on appeal,[88] but there is no similar wording in relation to the loss of the publication ban under s. 110 as a result of receiving an adult sentence. Unlike s. 117, s. 110(2)(a) does not say that the loss of a publication ban upon receiving an adult sentence is subject to the adult sentence being upheld on appeal.

This issue was considered by the Nova Scotia Court of Appeal in *R. v. G.D.S.*[89] G.D.S. had received an adult sentence of life imprisonment without parole eligibility for seven years after pleading guilty to second degree murder in relation to the stabbing death of a taxi driver. He appealed the sentence and applied for a publication ban pending the outcome of the appeal. Justice Fichaud of the Nova Scotia Court of Appeal first held that he had jurisdiction to hear the matter and to issue a publication ban.[90] He granted an interim publication ban pending the release of his decision on the application for the final publication ban. In

---

The two were also banned from owning animals for at least two years. The two pled guilty to causing unnecessary pain and suffering to the cat.

[87] Betsy Powell and Bob Mitchell, "Gag orders in a Facebook age" *The Toronto Star* (4 January 2008), online at: <http://www.thestar.com/News/GTA/article/290941>.

[88] *YCJA*, s. 117.

[89] [2007] N.S.J. No. 390 (N.S.C.A.).

[90] *R. v. G.D.S.*, [2007] N.S.J. No. 390, at paras. 26-27 (N.S.C.A.).

his decision on the main publication ban, he observed that Parliament had not addressed the status of a publication ban under s. 110(2)(a) in the event that a young person appealed the adult sentence but that this policy choice by Parliament did not prevent a young person who received an adult sentence from applying to a court for a publication ban pending the result of the appeal. However, after considering the *Dagenais/Mentuck*[91] test as well as particular youth cases that had considered the appropriate balance between a young person's privacy and the open court principle, Fichaud J.A. held that G.D.S. had failed to satisfy the court that the publication of his identity would hamper his rehabilitation. Justice Fichaud concluded that there was no basis for a publication ban of identity pending the outcome of the appeal.[92] What is clear from *R. v. G.D.S.* and from more recent cases, as well, is that, even if a young person receives an adult sentence and is subject to the loss of the publication ban pursuant to s. 110(2)(a), the courts remain willing to consider imposing a publication ban under the common law.

(iv) Section 111 — Victims and Witnesses

The *YCJA* also generally prevents the publication of information that would identify a child or a young person as a victim or witness in relation to an offence committed or alleged to have been committed by a young person. Again, this general prohibition is subject to the following exceptions:

- the child or young person can permit such information to be published once he or she reaches 18 or before that age with his or

---

[91] This refers to the principles identified by the Supreme Court of Canada in *Dagenais v. Canadian Broadcasting Corp.*, [1994] S.C.J. No. 104, [1994] 3 S.C.R. 835 (S.C.C.) and *R. v. Mentuck*, [2001] S.C.J. No. 73, [2001] 3 S.C.R. 442 (S.C.C.) that govern applications for common law discretionary publication bans in criminal proceedings.

[92] An application for leave to appeal in this case was dismissed without costs June 12, 2008 (*R. v. G.D.S.*, [2007] S.C.C.A. No. 582 (S.C.C.)). More recently, in *R. v. Bird*, [2008] A.J. No. 609 (Alta. Q.B.), Ross J., also relying on the *Dagenais/Mentuck* test, considered imposing both a temporary and a permanent publication ban in a case where the young person received an adult sentence and was immediately subject to the loss of the ban under s. 110(2)(a). Justice Ross concluded that the young person had not satisfied him that a real and tangible benefit would flow from the requested ban, that he had identified deleterious effects that would result from the proposed ban to the *Charter* right to freedom of expression, the open court principle and the principle of general deterrence, and that the balancing of the various interests had satisfied him that the request for a publication ban, both temporary and permanent, should be denied.

her parents' consent, and the parents can permit publication if the child or young person is deceased;[93]

- the youth justice court can also allow publication of information that identifies the child or young person as a victim or witness in relation to an offence committed or alleged to have been committed by a young person on the application of the child or young person if the court is satisfied that the publication would not be contrary to his or her best interests or the public interest.

Once the information about the child or young person is lawfully published, in accordance with the exceptions outlined in s. 110 or 111, the information has entered the public domain and the publication ban in these sections no longer applies in relation to that information.[94]

It is noteworthy that s. 111 permits publication of the name of a young victim or witness in relation to youth cases if the victim or witness is deceased and the parents consent to the publication of the name. A recent illustration of this exception occurred in Toronto in early January 2008 when the parents of 14-year-old Stefanie Rengel, who was fatally stabbed, consented to the release of her name.[95] There is no comparable provision in s. 110 of the *YCJA* to permit the publication of the name of a deceased accused young person or a youthful offender. Given that the point was specifically addressed in s. 111 of the *YCJA*, it appears to have been Parliament's intention to provide greater protection to a deceased young person who was dealt with under the *YCJA* than to a deceased victim or witness who was involved in the youth court proceedings. One possible explanation for this distinction is that protecting the identity of the young person who has come into contact with the criminal law, even after death, not only protects his or her reputation in perpetuity but also protects the reputation of his or her family. In the case of victims and witnesses who are not offenders in any event, there is less reason or need for the ban to survive their deaths because the risk of stigmatization is much less. The identities of victims and witnesses are protected in part during their lives to make it easier for them to testify and so that they can live their lives freely without the public knowing that they have been victims of offences, or witnesses to offences. Upon their death, the protection is arguably no longer required.

---

[93]   *YCJA*, s. 111(2)(a) and (b). "Parent" is defined in s. 2(1) of the *YCJA* to include any person who is under a legal duty to provide for the young person or any person who has, in law or in fact, the custody or control of the young person but does not include a person who has custody or control by virtue only of proceedings under the *YCJA*.

[94]   *YCJA*, s. 112.

[95]   Betsy Powell and Bob Mitchell, "Gag orders in a Facebook age" *The Toronto Star* (4 January 2008), online at: <http://www.thestar.com/News/GTA/article/290941>.

In contrast, the family of a young person who has come into contact with the criminal law can continue to suffer significant stigma from his or her crime even after the young person is deceased if the privacy shield that attaches to the young person's identity dies with the young person. Arguably, since the privacy protections are designed largely to reduce the stigmatization that a young person faces as a result of having been involved in the youth justice court system, in order to improve his or her chances of rehabilitation, it would make sense that the privacy protections under s. 110 are extinguished upon the death of the young person because rehabilitation is no longer an issue.

To date there does not appear to be a case directly on point under the *YCJA* that has considered whether the publication ban on the identity of a young accused person under s. 110 of the *YCJA* is intended to be extinguished upon his or her death, or whether the ban is intended to continue in perpetuity. A number of cases under the *YOA* are of some assistance. Section 38 of the *YOA*, the precursor to ss. 110 and 111 of the *YCJA*, generally prohibited the publication of the identity of a young accused person as well as that of a child or a young person aggrieved by the offence or a child or a young person who appeared as a witness in connection with the offence. In the 1986 Quebec Court of Appeal case of *R. v. Publications Photo-Police Inc.*,[96] Tyndale J.A. held that the identity of a victim could be published after her death because there was no longer any need to protect her privacy. "A dead young person has no life, private or otherwise, to be protected."[97] Although the decision was rendered in relation to a deceased young victim, the wording of Tyndale J.A.'s brief decision suggests that he intended his rationale to capture deceased accused young persons as well. "I agree that the main object of s. 38 is to protect young persons in their immaturity from the stigma that tends to mark any one involved in penal offences, so that their development and future success will not be jeopardized. Obviously, a deceased person is not in contemplation,"[98] Tyndale J.A. ruled. Arguably, a deceased accused young person is not a young person for purposes of s. 38 of the *YOA* any more than a deceased victim or witness is. The same arguments can be made in relation to ss. 110 and 111 of the *YCJA*.

The Northwest Territories Court of Appeal accepted this line of reasoning years later in *R. v. Canadian Broadcasting Corp.*[99] That decision upheld the Northwest Territories Supreme Court ruling of Vertes J. that,

---

[96]   (1986), 31 C.C.C. (3d) 93 (Que. C.A.).
[97]   *R. v. Publications Photo-Police Inc.* (1986), 31 C.C.C. (3d) 93 (Que. C.A.).
[98]   *R. v. Publications Photo-Police Inc.* (1986), 31 C.C.C. (3d) 93 (Que. C.A.).
[99]   [1998] N.W.T.J. No. 156 (N.W.T.C.A.), affg [1997] N.W.T.J. No. 83 (N.W.T.S.C.).

when considering whether to report the crime, "[a] dead complainant may have no privacy interest, but a live victim ... may have a concern over her dignity and reputation whether during life or after death".[100]

This issue has also arisen in relation to the youth court records of deceased young persons. In a Manitoba Provincial Court decision, *R. v. Coutu*,[101] an accused young person was seeking the youth record of the young person he was accused of murdering. Similar to the publication ban in s. 110 of the *YCJA*, s. 45.1 of the *YOA* was silent in relation to the records of deceased young persons. Justice Kimelman held that death does not destroy the confidentiality and that the rights of the family still exist. The privacy right of the deceased youth in his youth court record was not extinguished upon death and extended to the estate of the youth.

In the Ontario Provincial Court case of *Re G. (C.G.)*,[102] however, which also involved an application for the youth records of a deceased young person, the records were ordered released. The information in the records was expected to assist an inquest jury in making recommendations to prevent further deaths similar to that of the young person. While Vogelsang J. accepted Kimelman J.'s view as correct, he found on the facts of the case before him that there was a valid and substantial interest in the record and that releasing the information contained in them could help the inquest craft recommendations to prevent further deaths in similar circumstances. This ambiguity in s. 110 regarding the life of a publication ban should be clarified.

Section 132 of the *YCJA* provides related powers in relation to youth justice court proceedings which enable the judge to exclude parties from the youth justice court in certain circumstances. Section 132, which contains wording similar to s. 39 of the *YOA*, permits a court or justice before whom proceedings are carried out under the *YCJA* to exclude persons, *i.e.*, witnesses or members of the public, from all or part of the proceedings if: the court or justice considers that the person's presence is unnecessary to the conduct of the proceedings and the court or justice finds that any evidence or information presented to the court or justice would be seriously injurious or seriously prejudicial to the young person, or a child or young person who is a witness or a child or young person who is aggrieved by or a victim of the offence charged in the proceedings, *or* that it would be in the interest of public morals, the maintenance of order or the proper administration of justice to exclude any or all members of the public from the court room. For example, a judge may choose to

---

[100]   [1998] N.W.T.J. No. 156, at para. 7 (N.W.T.C.A.).
[101]   [1990] M.J. No. 536 (Man. Prov. Ct.)
[102]   [1992] O.J. No. 4056, 7 O.R. (3d) 678 (Ont. Prov. Div.).

exclude members of the public in cases where a very young witness is testifying to ensure the witness does not feel intimidated by the presence of strangers in the courtroom. Or a judge may ask a witness in a case to leave the courtroom while other witnesses are testifying to ensure that the potential witness is not influenced by the testimony of others.

In a recent Nova Scotia case, a judge relied on s. 132 to exclude the public and the media from a pre-sentence conference to prevent a serious risk to the administration of justice. Justice Williams was concerned that if the media were permitted to attend, the various professionals scheduled to participate at the conference would not do so due to legal and ethical obligations relating to confidentiality. Justice Williams held that the evidence had demonstrated that confidentiality concerns would prevent many of them from participating in the conference in a meaningful way or bowing out altogether if the media were present at the conference.[103]

Publication bans are possible in adult court proceedings to protect the privacy of young victims and witnesses under 18 but such publication bans are generally imposed in adult proceedings only upon application and the judge generally has discretion in this regard[104] unless the young person is the alleged victim or witness in a case involving a sexual offence.[105] In sexual offence cases, the ban is automatic upon application by the Crown, the complainant or the witness.[106] Youth justice experts, such as University of Toronto criminologist Anthony Doob, characterize this differential treatment of young persons who are victims or witnesses as "bizarre".[107] Why should a young person who is a victim or witness in an adult proceeding not have the same measure of protection regarding his or her privacy as a young person who is a victim or witness in a youth court proceeding?

III. RECORDS

A.   Overview and Definition of a Record

Sections 113-129 of Part 6 of the *YCJA* comprise the records regime of the *YCJA*; it is contended that these sections also apply to records kept

---

[103]   *R. v. T.C.*, [2006] N.S.J. No. 531, at paras. 64 and 65 (N.S. Youth J. Ct.).
[104]   See s. 486.5 of the *Criminal Code*, R.S.C. 1985, c. C-46.
[105]   *Criminal Code*, s. 486.4.
[106]   *Criminal Code*, s. 486.4(2).
[107]   Betsy Powell and Bob Mitchell, "Gag orders in a Facebook age" *The Toronto Star* (4 January 2008), online at: <http://www.thestar.com/News/GTA/article/290941>.

under the *JDA* and under the *YOA*.[108] These records provisions, when read in combination with s. 2 of the *YCJA*, seek to clarify the meaning of a youth record. They identify the type of youth records that are regulated under the *YCJA* and the parties that can keep these records, and also list the parties who can have access to youth records, for what purpose, and for how long. Finally, these provisions establish guidelines, rules and obligations regarding the destruction of youth records.

Part 6 is the most intricate and complicated network of provisions in the *YCJA*; it must be read carefully and in its entirety, as a complete, interconnected scheme. Unfortunately, this complex code is beset with ambiguity, lack of procedural clarity, and occasional absurdities. The judiciary, as well as practitioners, are grappling with the scheme. The decisions to date are primarily at the lower court level. The judiciary has not hesitated to comment on the vagueness, the complexity, and at times, the illogicality of the regime. Such observations are considered and examined in this section.

Despite some significant shortcomings, the records regime illustrates Parliament's intention to maintain strict control over the access, use and retention of youth records. The Ontario Court of Appeal has held that the *YCJA* has exclusive jurisdiction regarding decisions about access to youth records.[109]

Among its strengths, the *YCJA* records regime defines a youth record. Similar to the term "publication", the term "record" was not defined under the *YOA*. For purposes of the *YOA*, Binnie J. provided a practical working definition of a record in *Re F.N.*[110] Justice Binnie concluded that a record within the meaning of the *YOA* contained two characteristics: it identified the young person to whom it related as a young person dealt with under the Act and, secondly, it recorded information kept by a youth court or review

---

[108] *YCJA*, s. 163. This section is clear and specific that the *YCJA* records regime applies to records kept under the *JDA* and the *YOA* as well; however, the case law is conflicting on this point. Some courts are interpreting s. 159(1) of the *YCJA* to mean that if proceedings are commenced under the *YOA*, the records regime under the *YOA*, and not under the *YCJA*, applies. It is submitted that s. 163 is an express exception to the general rule outlined in s. 159. See *Y.A.Y. v. Canada (Minister of Citizenship and Immigration)*, [2008] F.C.J. No. 1174 (F.C.), but see *R. v. P.A.D.*, [2008] O.J. No. 567 (Ont. C.J.).

[109] *L. (S.) v. B. (N.)*, [2005] O.J. No. 1411, 195 C.C.C. (3d) 481 (Ont. C.A.). Justice Doherty cited in particular the wording of s. 118(1) of the *YCJA* for the proposition that access to youth records is the exclusive domain of the *YCJA*. Justice Doherty relied on an earlier decision under the *YOA* which reached the same conclusion: *B.G. v. British Columbia*, [2002] B.C.J. No. 168 (B.C.C.A.). See more recently *Ontario (Human Rights Commission) v. Toronto Police Services Board*, [2008] O.J. No. 4546 (Ont. C.J.) and *R. v. Laycock*, [2008] O.J. No. 366, 2008 ONCJ 29 (Ont. C.J.), both of which affirm the jurisdiction of the youth court over youth records.

[110] [2000] S.C.J. No. 34, [2000] 1 S.C.R. 880 (S.C.C.).

board, or kept by the police or a government agency for purposes related to the juvenile justice system or kept by another organization or person involved in alternative measures or other disposition under the Act.[111] In essence, the fundamental identifying characteristic of a youth record under the *YOA* was that it contained information demonstrating a link or a connection between a particular young person and the *YOA*. Information constitutes a youth record if it links or connects a young person to proceedings under the *YOA*: "... the nub of the statutory non-disclosure provisions taken as a whole is the avoidance of unauthorized disclosure of a document that links the identity of the young person with a charge, proceeding or disposition under the Act." In determining if the information in question constitutes a record, therefore, the focus should be on the nature of the information, Binnie J. suggested.[112]

Justice Binnie's definition of a youth record is a useful starting point for analysis and provides helpful guidance since many of the records provisions of the *YOA* are similar and sometimes identical to those of the *YCJA*, both in content and purpose. However, Parliament sought to remedy any confusion or ambiguity about the meaning of a record by defining it in the *YCJA* and ascribing to it a distinct meaning: in s. 2(1) of the *YCJA* a record "includes any thing containing information, regardless of its physical form or characteristics, including microform, sound recording, videotape, machine-readable record, and any copy of any of those things, *that is created or kept for the purposes of this Act or for the investigation of an offence that is or could be prosecuted under this Act*".[113] Fingerprints or photographs taken of the young person upon arrest comprise a record under this definition, as do video-recorded statements taken by the police and exhibits filed in court.[114]

Akin to Binnie J.'s definition of a record under the *YOA* in *Re F.N.*, various sections of the *YCJA* suggest that a youth record includes any information that would identify the young person to whom it relates as a young person dealt with under this Act. Any information that links a young person to any action taken in accordance with the *YCJA* arguably meets the definition of a record. When one is determining if a piece of information constitutes a youth record, the material must both identify the individual by name and indicate that he or she is a young person who is being, or has been, dealt with under the *YCJA*. A police accident report

---

[111]   *Re F.N.*, [2000] S.C.J. No. 34, at para. 27, [2000] 1 S.C.R. 880 (S.C.C.).

[112]   *Re F.N.*, [2000] S.C.J. No. 34, at paras. 26 and 27, [2000] 1 S.C.R. 880 (S.C.C.).

[113]   *YCJA*, at s. 2(1).

[114]   Re exhibits as records, see *R. v. A.A.B.*, [2006] N.S.J. No. 226 (N.S. Prov. Ct.).

that does not reveal that the young person was dealt with under the *YCJA* is not captured by the meaning of a record under the *YCJA*.

In other cases, the *source* of disclosure could reveal or suggest that the young person has a youth record. The production of a copy of a driver's licence from a youth court registry arguably suggests that the young person has been involved in some way in criminal proceedings.[115] Likewise, the provision of information about a young person from a jail or similar custodial institution suggests that the young person has been incarcerated there.

There remain elements of ambiguity in the definition of a youth record in s. 2 of the *YCJA*. For example, information inadvertently collected by the police through the use of a wiretap in relation to an adult suspect could reveal that a young person in that household has a youth record. The information itself revealed in the wiretap about the young person is arguably not a youth record under the *YCJA* definition of a record in s. 2 because the record was not created or kept for purposes of the *YCJA* or for the investigation of an offence that is or could be prosecuted under this Act. It was created in relation to an investigation of an adult accused. This would appear to suggest that this information, in this form, is not regulated or caught by the records provisions in the *YCJA*; in other words, the *YCJA* records provisions would not control or regulate access to this information although other statutory laws may apply. (Bear in mind, also, that the issue of access to records under the *YCJA* is separate and distinct from the issue of the admissibility of such information during a trial.)

Likewise, what about police records, such as police notes, based on conversations between police and young persons during voluntary street encounters? If these encounters were simply attempts at intelligence gathering and the notes were not taken or kept for the purposes of the *YCJA* or for the investigation of an offence that is, or could be prosecuted under the *YCJA*, these notes may not constitute a youth record.

That said, the definition of a record in s. 2 must also be read in combination with other *YCJA* sections that bear on the definition of particular kinds of records, such as the definition of a police record in s. 115.

Under the *YCJA*, there is no binding jurisprudence to date at the national level concerning the meaning of a youth record. There is only *Re F.N.*, which was decided under the *YOA*. It is therefore unclear to what

---

[115] See the wording in s. 118(1) for example. See also the discussion of Categories of Records by accessing the section on Publication and Records: Explanatory Text in YCJA Explained on the Justice Canada website at: <http://www.justice.gc.ca/eng/pi/yj-jj/ycja-lsjpa/ycja-lsjpa.html>.

extent the definition of a record in s. 2 of the *YCJA* alters the meaning of a youth record as defined by Binnie J. in *Re F.N.*

The lower court decisions under the *YCJA* are of some assistance. In the Ontario Court of Justice decision, *Reodica v. Ontario (Attorney General)*,[116] Scully J. considered the meaning of a record in s. 2 of the *YCJA*. The parents of a young person who died after being shot during the course of his arrest by the Toronto Police Services sought access under s. 123 of the *YCJA* to the investigation records of the Toronto Police Services and the Special Investigation Unit, an arm's length agency of the Attorney General of Ontario. Justice Jones of the Ontario Court of Justice had earlier ordered that the notes, reports and statements of the Toronto Police Services regarding the arrest and investigation of the applicant's son be provided to the parents. In *Reodica v. Ontario (Attorney General)*, however, Scully J. concluded that the notes, reports and statements prepared by the SIU in the course of its investigation did not constitute a record as defined by the *YCJA*. The SIU investigation pertained to the conduct of police officers for the purposes of determining whether the officers should be prosecuted under the *Criminal Code*. Based on his reading of the definition of a record in s. 2 of the *YCJA*, Scully J. concluded that the SIU records were neither created nor kept for the purposes of the *YCJA*, or for the investigation of an offence that is or could be prosecuted under the *YCJA*. Justice Scully concluded that he had no jurisdiction under the *YCJA* to direct what access, if any, ought to be granted to the records collected by the SIU in the course of investigating the police conduct as it pertained to the circumstances relating to the death of the young person.

The term "report" is also used in various sections throughout the *YCJA*; it is used, for example, in relation to medical, psychological or psychiatric reports pursuant to s. 34, and in relation to pre-sentence reports under s. 40. The term is not defined. Such reports are obviously youth records, in as much as they clearly contain information that is created or kept for the purposes of the *YCJA*. In the absence of a definition of report in the *YCJA*, again, *Re F.N.* provides some guidance. Justice Binnie considered the meaning of a report as distinguished from a record, and concluded that one can label the information as one chooses, but for the purpose of determining if it is a record, the focus should be on the nature of the information. The document in question will constitute a youth record if it links the identity of the young person to a charge, proceeding or disposition under the *YOA*.[117] Medical, psychiatric and

---

[116] [2006] O.J. No. 531 (Ont. C.J.).
[117] *Re F.N.*, [2000] S.C.J. No. 34, at para. 26, [2000] 1 S.C.R. 880 (S.C.C.).

psychological reports would constitute records under the *YCJA*[118] but s. 34 also circumscribes to whom the report can be given, as well as certain instances when all or part of the report can be withheld.[119] Its disclosure may be more restricted than other records. A pre-sentence report is also a youth record[120] but its disclosure is also regulated under that section.[121] When a youth justice court withholds access to all or part of a report under s. 34 or s. 40, the person cannot gain access under s. 119(1), which is the general access provision. The restrictions on disclosure in each of these sections prevail over the general access provisions in s. 119.[122]

B.   Record-Keepers Under the *YCJA*

The *YCJA* regulates access to youth records kept by five entities identified in the *YCJA*:

- review boards;[123]

- a youth justice court or any court dealing with matters arising out of *YCJA* proceedings;

- the police;

- a department or agency of any government in Canada (including the Crown); or

- a person or organization as a result of extrajudicial measures used to deal with the young person or for the purpose of administering or participating in the administration of a youth sentence.[124]

The key entities, of course, who can keep youth records are the courts, the police, and government departments or agencies (which include the Crown prosecutor).

Section 114 deals with records kept by the youth justice court, a review board or any court addressing matters arising out of *YCJA* proceedings.

Section 115 concerns youth records kept by the police. Police records include records kept by the investigating police force, as well as records kept by the R.C.M.P. on the Canadian Police Information Centre

---

[118]   *YCJA*, s. 34(12). *R. v. D.B.M.*, [2003] B.C.J. No. 2646 (B.C. Prov. Ct.) is an early decision on this point.

[119]   *YCJA*, s. 34(9), (10) and (11).

[120]   *YCJA*, s. 40(4).

[121]   *YCJA*, s. 40.

[122]   *YCJA*, s. 119(5).

[123]   *YCJA*, s. 2 makes clear that this is a review board as defined in s. 87(2) of the *YCJA*.

[124]   *YCJA*, ss. 114-116.

(C.P.I.C.). Under s. 115(1), a local police force responsible for, or participating in, the investigation of an offence alleged to have been committed by a young person, has discretion as to whether to keep a record of the matter, including any fingerprints or photographs of the young person. If a young person is charged with any offence for which an adult could be processed under the *Identification of Criminals Act* (which generally means an indictable offence), the local force *may provide* that record to the R.C.M.P. However, if the young person is found guilty of such an offence, the local police force *must provide* the record to the R.C.M.P.[125] In both cases, the R.C.M.P. is obliged to keep these records in its central repository, *i.e.*, C.P.I.C.

One troubling aspect of this police records regime is that young persons may be treated differently across Canada depending on local police practices and policies regarding records. The content of the R.C.M.P. youth records database will depend, to some degree, on local police practices. Some local police forces may routinely provide to the R.C.M.P. records of all young persons who have been charged with offences as described in s. 115(2), while other police forces may exercise their discretion not to provide these records unless the young person has been found guilty of the offence. Consequently, the R.C.M.P. may have information on C.P.I.C. about one young person who was charged with an offence whereas they will not have similar information about another young person charged with the same offence in another part of the country. This difference in practice could affect how these two young persons with similar backgrounds are treated in future encounters with the police since the police will have more information about one young person than the other.

Section 116 concerns government records, which means that a department or an agency of any government in Canada may keep records. This section appears to capture a department or agency of the federal or provincial government, but excludes a department or agency of a municipal government.[126] Such government departments or agencies, which include provincial and federal Attorneys General, may keep youth records containing information obtained by the department or agency for the purposes of:

---

[125] *YCJA*, s. 115(2).

[126] Section 118 of the *Criminal Code* defines "government" as either the Government of Canada or the government of a province. The *YCJA* indicates in s. 2 that when a term is not defined in the *YCJA* but is defined in the *Criminal Code*, the *Criminal Code* definition applies. This arguably suggests that municipal government records are not subject to the records regime of the *YCJA* (unless they are found to fall within the definition of the government of a province). But see Priscilla Platt, *Young Offenders Law in Canada*, 2d ed. (Markham, Ont.: Butterworths Canada Ltd., 1995), at 546 regarding the point that municipal corporations may, for certain purposes, be agents of government.

- the investigation of an offence alleged to have been committed by a young person;

- proceedings against a young person under the *YCJA*;

- administering a youth sentence or an order of the youth justice court;

- considering whether to use extrajudicial measures to deal with a young person or as the result of the use of extrajudicial measures to deal with a young person.[127]

A person or organization may also keep records containing information obtained by the person or organization as a result of the use of extrajudicial measures to deal with a young person or for the purpose of administering or participating in the administration of a youth sentence.[128] This section captures non-governmental organizations that run programs for young persons to which the young person can be referred for extrajudicial measures or in which the young person may participate as part of his or her youth sentence.

C.   Who Can Have Access to Youth Records

Section 119(1) of the *YCJA* describes the persons who can access youth records as defined under the *YCJA*, upon request. Section 119 does not specify to whom the request should be made or the procedure for access, such as whether the request must be in writing. While it makes sense that the request should be directed to the record-keeper, practices vary.

Upon request, the court *must* provide a court record, under s. 114, provided the person requesting the record fits within one of the categories identified in s. 119(1). By contrast, if the person is requesting a police record or a government record, the record-keeper has discretion as to whether to provide access to the record, since s. 119(1) says that the person *may* be given access to s. 115 and s. 116 records, upon request. This permissive wording suggests that, with respect to police and government youth records, the record-keeper must turn his or her mind to the matter and actively consider whether the record should be provided and decide whether to grant access to the record.[129] (If the person requesting access to the record is not included in the list of people and entities who can be given access to the record under s. 119(1), the person can apply to a judge for access under s. 119(1)(s).)

---

[127]   *YCJA*, s. 116(1).

[128]   *YCJA*, s. 116(2).

[129]   Justice Senniw makes this point in *R. v. B.J.O.*, [2005] B.C.J. No. 1112, at para. 13 (B.C. Prov. Ct.).

Generally speaking, the persons who can have access to youth records, upon request, include:

- the young person to whom the record relates;

- the young person's counsel or a representative;

- the Attorney General, *i.e.*, the prosecutor;

- the victim of the offence or alleged offence to which the record relates;

- the parents of the young person for limited periods;

- any adult assisting an unrepresented young person during the course of proceedings relating to the offence or alleged offence to which the record relates or during the term of any youth sentence in relation to the offence;

- any peace officer for law enforcement purposes, or any purpose relating to the administration of the case to which the record relates, during the course of proceedings against the young person or the term of the youth sentence;

- a judge, court or review board for any purpose relating to the proceedings against the young person or proceedings against the person after he or she becomes an adult, in relation to offences committed or alleged to have been committed by that person;

- the provincial director, or the director of the provincial correctional facility for adults or the penitentiary at which the young person is serving a sentence;

- a person participating in a conference or in the administration of extrajudicial measures, if required for the administration of the case to which the record relates;

- a member of a department or agency of a government in Canada who is acting in the exercise of his or her duties under the Act;

- a person for the purposes of carrying out a criminal record check required by the Government of Canada or the government of a province or a municipality for purposes of employment or the performance of services, with or without remuneration;

- an accused or his or her counsel[130] who swears an affidavit to the effect that access to the record is necessary to make full answer and defence;

---

[130] The term "counsel" is not defined in the *YCJA*; however, the *YCJA* indicates that unless otherwise provided, words and expressions in the *YCJA* have the same meaning as in the

•   any person or member of a class of persons that a youth justice court judge considers has a valid interest in the record, to the extent directed by the judge, if the judge is satisfied that access to the record is desirable in the public interest for research or statistical purposes or desirable in the interest of the proper administration of justice.[131]

If the party seeking access to the record is not listed under s. 119(1) as one of the entities who can have access to it, the party can apply to a judge for access by virtue of s. 119(1)(s). Once the court determines the issue, the record-keeper must disclose the information as directed by the court.[132]

Section 119(1) restricts access to a police or government record concerning any extrajudicial measure except extrajudicial sanctions.[133] It also restricts access to s. 34 medical and psychological reports, as well as the results of DNA tests in relation to DNA samples taken from young persons pursuant to DNA warrants.[134]

It is noteworthy that the media are not recognized among the entities that are expressly mentioned in s. 119 as parties who can have access to youth records. The media can access a youth record only by applying under s. 119(1)(s). Given the revered status of the open court principle in the common law, as well as the constitutional right to freedom of the press in the *Charter*, there is a reasonable argument to be made that the media should be among the recognized categories of persons who may be granted access to records, upon request, under s. 119.

D.   The Period of Access to Youth Records

Under s. 119(2) of the *YCJA*, the period of access to a youth record is generally determined by the seriousness of the sentence and whether there is subsequent offending. As a general rule, the more severe the offence and the sentence, the longer the period of access to the record for the parties listed in s. 119(1). For example, if the young person receives an

---

Criminal Code. "Counsel" in s. 2 of the *Criminal Code* is defined as a barrister or solicitor. This suggests that only a defence counsel (as opposed to his or her student-at-law) can have access to the record under this section.

[131]   See s. 119(1) for the complete list.

[132]   See, for example, *Saskatchewan West School Division No. 42 v. J.A.*, [1997] S.J. No. 620 (Sask. Q.B.).

[133]   Pursuant to s. 119(4) only the following persons can have access to a police record or a government record relating to an extrajudicial measure (except for a sanction under s. 10) used in relation to a young person: a peace officer or the Attorney General *i.e.*, the Crown prosecutor, or a person participating in a conference.

[134]   *YCJA*, s. 119(4)-(6).

extrajudicial sanction, the record can be accessed for two years from the time the person agrees to participate in the sanction. If the young person is found guilty of a summary conviction offence, the record can be accessed for three years from the time the young person completes the sentence. If the young person is found guilty of an indictable offence, the record can be accessed for five years from the time the young person completes the sentence.

In the event of a subsequent finding of guilt while access to the youth record is open under either s. 119(2)(g) or (h), the access period will be re-calculated. The length of the new access period will depend on whether the first offence was summary or indictable and on whether the subsequent offence was summary or indictable.[135] For example, if the young person is found guilty of a summary offence, the access period to the record will remain open for three years from the time the young person completes the sentence. If the young person is then found guilty of an indictable offence while the access period is still open for the summary offence, the access period will last for five years after the young person completes his or her sentence in relation to the indictable offence.[136]

A highly significant element of the *YCJA* records regime is that if a person continues to commit offences as an adult, their youth record is no longer shielded. If a person is convicted of an offence as an adult while the access period to his or her youth record is open, Part 6 of the *YCJA* no longer applies to the youth record. The young person will no longer have the benefit of the special protections in the *YCJA* in relation to his or her youth record and his record will be treated like the criminal record of an adult.[137] In addition, any findings of guilt that are part of the youth record are deemed to be convictions for the purposes of the *Criminal Records Act*.[138] The young person will also lose the benefit of s. 82 of the *YCJA*. Under s. 82, in the normal course, once the young person receives an

---

[135] *YCJA*, s. 119(2)(i) and (j).

[136] *YCJA*, s. 119(2)(g) and (j).

[137] *YCJA*, s. 119(9). This section was considered in the case of *R. v. J.K.E.*, [2005] Y.J. No. 21 (Y.T. Terr. Ct.). The CBC and the general public were entitled to access J.K.E.'s youth court file as if it were an adult file because J.K.E. received an adult criminal conviction during the access period defined in s. 119(2). However, Lilles C.J. prohibited publication of the contents of the youth court record, including J.K.E.'s identity, until the preliminary hearing in the matter that was currently before the court was completed and J.K.E. was either discharged or committed to trial and the trial had ended. The judge was concerned that J.K.E.'s right to a fair trial would be negatively affected if the contents of her 1999 youth record regarding a conviction for criminal negligence causing bodily harm were published before then. Justice Lilles noted that all counsel were cognizant of the dangers of tainting the jury pool in small communities such as Dawson City, Yukon. This case also emphasizes the distinction between access to a record and publication.

[138] R.S.C. 1985, c. C-47. See *YCJA*, s. 119(9)(b) and (c).

absolute discharge or completes his or her disposition or youth sentence under the *YOA* or the *YCJA*, he or she is deemed not to have been found guilty or convicted of the offence (although the guilty finding can still be considered in relation to applications for bail, sentencing, parole or pardons).[139]

What is particularly interesting about the wording of s. 119(9)(b) is that, in the event that the person is convicted of an offence committed when he or she is an adult while access to his or her youth record is open under s. 119, this paragraph states that Part 6 of the *YCJA* no longer applies to his or her youth record. Since Part 6 includes the prohibitions on publication as well, this paragraph indicates that the person loses the publication protections in these circumstances. Thus, if a person is convicted of an offence committed as an adult while access to his or her youth record under s. 119(g) to (j) is open, the fact that he or she committed offences as a young person can be published. In these circumstances, the individual has forfeited the protections under Part 6 of the *YCJA*.

E.   Access to R.C.M.P. Records

The *YCJA* provides for longer access periods to R.C.M.P. records in relation to the most serious offences by certain people, including the Attorney General (the prosecutor) and the police, in certain circumstances. The *YCJA* contains a schedule of offences at the end of the Act, which includes the most serious offences with which a young person can be charged, including murder, manslaughter, attempt to commit murder, assault with a weapon or causing bodily harm, aggravated assault, aggravated sexual assault, as well as the *Controlled Drugs and Substances Act* offences of trafficking, importing, exporting, and production. Section 120(1) of the *YCJA* permits extended access to R.C.M.P. records in relation to offences in the schedule for a small group of people in certain situations. The prosecutor and the police can access these records for a longer period of time when the young person is, or has been, charged with another offence in the schedule or the same offence more than once, for the purpose of investigating any offence that the young person is suspected of having committed, or in respect of which the young person has been arrested or charged, whether as a young person or as an adult.

If the offence is an indictable offence, other than a presumptive offence, the period of access in these circumstances is extended for an additional five years, starting from the end of the access period identified

---

[139]   *YCJA*, s. 82.

in s. 119(2)(h) to (j). However, if the offence is a presumptive offence as defined in paragraph (a) of the definition "presumptive offence" in s. 2(1), or an offence as defined in paragraph (b) of that definition for which the Attorney General has given notice (this captures the most serious offences, including murder, attempt to commit murder, and manslaughter), the period of access starts at the end of the applicable period set out in s. 119(2)(h) to (j) and continues indefinitely.

If the young person is convicted of an additional offence set out in the schedule, committed as an adult, during the period of extended access to the R.C.M.P. record under s. 120(3), Part 6 no longer applies to the R.C.M.P. record and the record shall be dealt with as the record of an adult and can be included on C.P.I.C.[140] Again, the use of the term "Part 6" suggests that the publication provisions also cease to apply in these circumstances, since the publication provisions are also contained in Part 6.

In summary, if young persons with youth records continue to commit offences as adults while access to their youth records remains open, they generally forfeit the special privacy protections regarding their criminal pasts that are granted under the *YCJA*.

F.   Access to Records Once the Access Period Has Expired

After the end of the access period identified in s. 119(2), a person can apply to a youth justice court judge under s. 123 for access to youth records kept by the various entities referred to in ss. 114 to 116. The youth justice court judge can grant access to all or part of any of the records kept under ss. 114 to 116 if the youth justice court judge is satisfied that the person has a valid and substantial interest in the record or part, it is necessary for access to be given to the record or part in the interest of the proper administration of justice, and disclosure of the record or part of the information in it is not prohibited under any other Act of Parliament or the legislation of a province (or territory).[141] It is generally required that five days' written notice be given to the young person and to the keeper of the record.[142] A youth justice court judge can also grant access to a youth record in the public interest for research and statistical purposes.[143]

---

[140]   *YCJA*, s. 120(6).
[141]   *YCJA*, s. 123(1)(a).
[142]   *YCJA*, s. 123(3) and (4).
[143]   *YCJA*, s. 123(1)(b).

When a youth justice court judge grants access to a youth record under s. 123, he or she must identify the purposes for which the record may be used.[144]

Section 123 is a stricter test for accessing records than the test that judges apply under s. 119(1)(s) when the access period is still open. Section 119(1)(s) states that any person or member of a class of persons that a youth justice judge considers has a valid interest in the record shall be given access to a court record and may be given access to a police or government record to the extent directed by the judge, if the judge is satisfied that access to the record is desirable in the public interest for research or statistical purposes or is desirable in the interest of the proper administration of justice.

Once the access period has closed, it is more difficult to access the record. Section 123 also imposes more conditions, such as notice requirements that allow the young person and the keeper of the record to be heard, and an obligation on the youth justice court judge to clearly set out the purposes for which the record can be used in cases where he or she decides to grant access.

Section 123(2) is ambiguous in its wording and could be read so as to significantly restrict access to records under s. 123(1), but the courts have tended not to adopt this restrictive interpretation in order to grant access to records in a variety of circumstances under s. 123(1).[145]

---

[144] *YCJA*, s. 123(5). The wording of s. 123(2) is ambiguous; it is unclear to what degree s. 123(2) restricts or qualifies s. 123(1)(a). The courts have tended to ignore s. 123(2) in terms of its possible restriction of s. 123(1).

[145] See *R. v. J.B.*, [2008] O.J. No. 1720 (Ont. C.J.) and *R. v. J.B.*, [2008] O.J. No. 1719 (Ont. C.J.). These decisions relate to defence access to police records regarding Crown witnesses.

In *R. v. H.M.L.S.*, [2005] B.C.J. No. 1360 (B.C. Prov. Ct.), a Vancouver police officer and Crown witness was granted access to records under s. 123(1) in order to testify at trial in relation to the accused, H.M.L.S. Justice Romilly held that, had the accused applied for access to the records after the end of the applicable period in order to make full answer and defence, a youth court justice would in all likelihood have granted such access "in the interest of the proper administration of justice". Thus, to allow an accused access to records to make full answer and defence but to deny the prosecution access to records in similar circumstances would be granting the accused an advantage. Justice Romilly held that access to the police records was necessary for the police officer to be able to give proper and relevant testimony to the court and to assist the court in its quest for truth "in the interest of the proper administration of justice". Justice Romilly also found that the police officer had a valid and substantial interest in the record. The court did not consider s. 123(2) during its analysis.

Likewise, in *R. v. C.F.*, [2005] O.J. No. 3708 (Ont. C.J.), Feldman J. granted the Crown access to the youth record of an adult accused under s. 123(1) after the access period to the record had expired under s. 119 after balancing the privacy interests of the young person versus the public interest in law enforcement. The Crown had argued that two letters seized from Mr. C.F.'s residence appeared to provide cogent evidence of the accused's connection

G.   Disclosure of Information in a Record — Sections 125-127

During the access period outlined in s. 119, a peace officer may disclose to any person any information contained in a court record or police record that it is necessary to disclose in the conduct of the investigation of an offence.[146] Likewise the Attorney General may disclose, in the course of proceedings under the *YCJA* or under any other federal Act, any information in a s. 114 court record or a s. 115 police record, to a person who is a co-accused with the young person in respect of the offence for which the record is kept. The Attorney General may also disclose, in the course of a proceeding under the *YCJA* or any other federal Act, to an accused in a proceeding, information in court or police youth records that identifies a witness in the proceeding as a young person who has been dealt with under the *YCJA*.

It is somewhat unclear, however, how the obligations of the Attorney General in relation to records of witnesses under s. 125(2)(b) interact with the Crown's broad common law disclosure obligations.[147] Section 125(2)(b) says that the Crown may disclose to an accused in a proceeding under the *YCJA* or under any other federal Act (such as the *Criminal Code*), information in a court or police record that identifies the witness as a young person who has been dealt with under the *YCJA*. However, if the record is relevant, the Crown will generally be obliged to disclose it in any event, subject to privilege, as well as any other relevant information about the witness, in order to comply with its *Stinchcombe* obligations.

If the defence is not satisfied with the information received about a witness under s. 125(2)(b), the defence can apply under s. 119(1)(q) for access to the witness's youth record, arguing that the record is needed in order for the accused to make a full answer and defence. Since the duty of disclosure is a component of the constitutional right to make full answer

---

to a subset of a criminal organization while he was a younger person. The letters appeared to permit the inference that he had been involved in a criminal organization for some time. The Crown was seeking access to the youth record in further support of that inference. Justice Feldman held that while disclosure of Mr. C.F.'s youth record could impact both his liberty interests and testimonial credibility, at the same time, criminal organization charges are serious allegations that, if true, serve to undermine in a pervasive and near-impenetrable way the peace and stability of this community. Justice Feldman held that Mr. C.F.'s youth record had potential relevance at trial in relation to the criminal organization charges and that there was an overriding community interest in disclosure of the youth record.

The judiciary took a similar approach under s. 45.1 of the *YOA*, which contained wording identical to that in s. 123(1)(a). See, for example, *R. v. E.H.B.M.*, [1996] B.C.J. No. 1019, 106 C.C.C. (3d) 535 (B.C.C.A.).

[146] *YCJA*, s. 125. An offence is defined in s. 2 of the *YCJA* and means an offence under a federal Act.

[147] *R. v. Stinchcombe*, [1991] S.C.J. No. 83, [1991] 3 S.C.R. 326 (S.C.C.).

and defence, the records provisions of the *YCJA* must arguably be read through this constitutional prism.[148]

There are other entities to whom the police, the Attorney General or other professionals can disclose youth records under s. 125 for various purposes, such as to ensure the safety of staff, students or other persons, or to foster the rehabilitation of the young person. Information under s. 125 can only be disclosed during the access periods permitted under s. 119(2).

The youth justice court can also make an order on the application of certain parties permitting the applicant to disclose to specified persons during the s. 119 access period any information about a young person if the court is satisfied that the disclosure is necessary because the young person has been found guilty of a serious personal injury offence, the young person poses a risk of serious harm to persons and the disclosure of the information is relevant to avoid the risk.[149]

H.   Effect of the End of the Access Period/Destruction of Records

Subject to ss. 123, 124 and 126,[150] no court record, police record or government record can be used for any purpose that would identify the young person as a person dealt with under the Act after the end of the applicable access periods set out in s. 119 or 120.

(i)   Destruction of Youth Records

There may be some misunderstanding within the general public re-garding how the state handles the youth records of young persons. Some Canadians may believe that the youth records of all young persons are destroyed after a certain period of time. This is not the case. Some youth

---

[148] Priscilla Platt made this point in her book *Young Offenders Law in Canada*, 2d ed. (Mark-ham, Ont.: Butterworths Canada Ltd., 1995), at 541-43 in relation to the *YOA* records provi-sions. The general principle remains apposite in relation to the *YCJA*.

[149] *YCJA*, s. 127. See also s. 110(4), which provides for the publication of the identity of a dangerous young person who is at large, and the publication is believed necessary to assist in the apprehension of the young person.

[150] Under s. 126 of the *YCJA*, the Librarian and Archivist of Canada or any provincial archivist can further disclose information in the record for research and statistical purposes in certain circumstances. But see *Dann v. New Brunswick (Minister of Supply and Services)*, [2007] N.B.J. No. 476, 328 N.B.R. (2d) 128 (N.B.Q.B.) re the interplay between ss. 126 and 124 of the *YCJA*.

records, such as certain R.C.M.P. records in relation to the most serious crimes, can be kept indefinitely. They are never destroyed.[151]

In fact, generally speaking, there is no obligation to destroy court records, police records or government records in relation to young persons, unless it is an R.C.M.P. record kept pursuant to s. 115(3) in the central repository (C.P.I.C.), or a record disclosed to a professional or other person engaged in the supervision or care of a young person under s. 125(6). Other record-keepers may destroy records at any time before or after the end of the access period outlined in s. 119,[152] but they have discretion in this regard, a fact that some members of the judiciary have described as absurd.[153]

In the case of R.C.M.P. records, these records must be destroyed, or if the Librarian or Archivist of Canada requires it, transmitted to them, at the end of the applicable periods set out in s. 119 or 120.[154] What this means, in practice, is that records in relation to presumptive offences (the most serious offences) are never destroyed because the access period never ends.[155] This also means that the R.C.M.P. must remove a record from the automated criminal conviction records retrieval system at the end of the applicable period set out in s. 119.[156]

In the case of disclosure to a professional under s. 125(6), the person to whom the record is disclosed is obligated to destroy his or her copy of the record when the information is no longer required for the purpose for which it was disclosed.[157]

The YCJA defines "destroy" as shredding, burning or otherwise physically destroying the record when the record is in other than electronic form. If it is an electronic record, "destroy" means to delete, write over, or otherwise render the record inaccessible.[158]

An individual who has a youth record would be well advised to ensure that his or her record is being handled in accordance with the YCJA, and that any such record is destroyed as required under the Act. This may mean contacting the local police force involved or the R.C.M.P. to verify

---

[151] YCJA, ss. 120(3)(b) and 128(3).
[152] YCJA, s. 128(2).
[153] R. v. J.S., [2005] O.J. No. 5044 (Ont. C.J.).
[154] According to R. v. T.S.R., [2005] A.J. No. 1053 (Alta. C.A.), when a young person's youth record is destroyed, so is his DNA.
[155] YCJA, s. 120(3)(b) and s. 128(3). But note the limited number of persons and purposes for which access to the records is permitted under s. 120(1).
[156] YCJA, s. 128(4), but note exception for prohibition orders.
[157] YCJA, s. 125(7)(c).
[158] YCJA, s. 128(7).

the status of the record and to ensure that it has been destroyed, if this is required under the Act, or to request that it be destroyed if the record-keeper has discretion in this regard. It is also important for young persons to realize that certain youth records, such as those in relation to the most serious offences, can be retained indefinitely in a special records reposi-tory, and that records of serious offences listed in the schedule of the *YCJA* can be retained longer than other records.[159]

It is an offence under s. 138 of the *YCJA* to wrongly provide access to a record,[160] to fail to properly dispose of an R.C.M.P. youth record,[161] or to disclose information to which one has been given access under the *YCJA* to any other person unless the disclosure is authorized under the *YCJA*.[162]

(ii)   Contentious Records Issues

There are numerous unresolved legal issues in relation to the records provisions of the *YCJA*; various sections are the subject of ongoing litigation. For example, ss. 114, 115 and 116 identify the entities that can keep youth records under the *YCJA* — mainly the court, the police and the government. However, these three sections generally indicate that these entities *may* keep such records;[163] the permissive wording suggests that they are not *required* to keep these records. In addition, s. 128(2) permits most record-keepers identified under ss. 114, 115 and 116 the discretion to destroy a youth record at any time, *before* or after, the access periods in s. 119.[164] This is inconsistent in light of s. 119 and other sections, which are based on the premise that these records will be kept so that they will be accessible for certain time periods. In fact, s. 123 provides that they can be accessed even after the end of the access periods in s. 119 in certain circumstances. To resolve this conflict, Little J. found in *R. v. J.S.*[165] that the use of the word "may" in sections such as s. 114 does not make the retention of records optional. "If the retention of records was optional

---

[159] *YCJA*, s. 120(3).
[160] *YCJA*, s. 118.
[161] *YCJA*, s. 128(3).
[162] *YCJA*, s. 129.
[163] The exception is s. 115(3). In addition, local police forces must effectively keep records of cases in which young persons were found guilty of indictable offences at least until they have provided the record to the R.C.M.P. as they are obliged to do under s. 115(2) in these cases.
[164] The exceptions are s. 115(3) records and s. 125(7)(c) records, which must be destroyed in accordance with established time frames.
[165] [2005] O.J. No. 5044 (Ont. C.J.).

rather than authorized, many other provisions of Part 6 ... would be meaningless."[166]

What is the point of specifying in the *YCJA* that access to records is permissible for certain specified periods of time if the courts, most police forces and government departments are not obliged to keep the records?

In relation to s. 128(2), Little J. stated:

> Section 128(2) is on its face inconsistent with the obligation of the court to maintain records in the interest of accused young persons and in the public interest to safeguard the administration of justice. When records can be destroyed or transferred in the discretion of record keeping persons or bodies across the province, there is no publicly accountable standard for the retention of records. ... I believe the public would be surprised to learn there is no real obligation on the part of courts administration to keep YCJA records, especially when the YCJA provides the exclusive means for access to such records.[167]

Section 119 also lacks procedural clarity, another shortcoming of Part 6. Section 119 indicates that, subject to certain exceptions, various parties *shall* have access to court records, and *may* have access to police and government records, *upon request*, but the Act provides no guidance regarding the procedure for accessing the records. What form should such a request take? Must the request be in writing, or can it be made informally? To whom should the request be made? Can it be made electronically? If the request for a police record or a government record is made electronically, presumably some checks and balances must be in place before the requester is provided access in order for the police and government record-keepers to exercise their discretion as to whether to provide the record to the requester under s. 119(1). It has been left to practitioners, including the judiciary, to resolve these matters, which has led to variation in practices across the country.

Justice Doherty of the Ontario Court of Appeal provided some guidance on the procedure for making an access request in *L. (S.) v. B. (N.)*.[168] Neither formal motion to the court nor notice to any individuals is required, Doherty J.A. held. In the case of a court record, a request under s. 119 merely means making a simple request to the court office, presumably directed to the court administrator. Provided the person is among the parties who is identified as being eligible to request access to a court record under s. 114, and the application is made within the access period, subject to certain exceptions outlined in s. 119, the court administrator

---

[166] *R. v. J.S.*, [2005] O.J. No. 5044, at para. 10 (Ont. C.J.).

[167] *R. v. J.S.*, [2005] O.J. No. 5044, at paras. 20 and 21 (Ont. C.J.).

[168] [2005] O.J. No. 1411, 195 C.C.C. (3d) 481 (Ont. C.A.).

would be obliged to provide access to the record.[169] The procedure would be the same if the person, a victim, for example, were requesting government records from the Crown Attorney under s. 116. The victim would merely make an informal request to the Crown Attorney. No notice is required to other parties. In the event that the Crown Attorney declined to exercise its jurisdiction to provide the record, the victim could bring a motion before a youth justice court judge under s. 119(1)(s) for an order granting access.[170]

The fact that the police and the government have discretion as to whether to provide access to the records they keep has led to some absurd and, arguably, unintended results. For example, the Act is unclear as to whether a police officer would have to formally request access to a record kept by his own force or, likewise, whether a Crown Attorney would have to request access to records kept within his or her own office. There have been inconsistent decisions on this point.[171]

---

[169] *L. (S.) v. B. (N.),* [2005] O.J. No. 1411, at para. 47, 195 C.C.C. (3d) 481 (Ont. C.A.). See exceptions outlined in s. 119(4) to (6).

[170] *L. (S.) v. B. (N.),* [2005] O.J. No. 1411, at paras. 49-51, 195 C.C.C. (3d) 481 (Ont. C.A.). See also s. 119(1)(q). This section does not specify to whom the affidavit should be provided, to whom the access request should be made, or whom it is contemplated should provide access to the records. Justice Werier observed and commented upon these shortcomings in *R. v. D.B.M.,* [2003] B.C.J. No. 2646 (B.C. Prov. Ct.). *R. v. D.B.M.* and *R. v. Keith,* [2003] O.J. No. 2256 (Ont. C.J.) are examples of cases where the court appears to take the position that the court is the appropriate body to whom to make the record request, even if the records are not court records, *i.e.,* even if the court is not the record-keeper. In *R. v. Keith,* the records at issue were police records under s. 115.

[171] In *R. v. Corall,* [1993] A.J. No. 856 (Alta. Prov. Ct.), a police officer with the identification branch of the Calgary Police Force used a computer program to match fingerprints found at a crime scene with fingerprints known to police. When the computer returned a match, the police officer pulled the fingerprints of the accused, which had been taken when he was a young offender. There was no evidence that she made any request of anyone before doing so nor was there any evidence that the Calgary Police Service had a system in place whereby requests could be made and considered. Justice Fradsham held that Constable Lee ought to have requested the record and been granted permission to access it before pulling the fingerprints and examining them. Conversely, in *R. v. S.A.S.,* [1994] A.J. No. 167 (Alta. Prov. Ct.), which had facts identical to *Corall,* Jordan J. held that it made no sense to require the police to request the record of the fingerprint after the computer had already inspected the record through the use of technology. If such a line of reasoning were accepted, the police would never be able to use fingerprint evidence to link prints taken at a crime scene with a young offender whose prints are on file because they would never be able to do a blanket computer search to obtain the young person's name and then request permission to inspect the prints. If Fradsham J.'s interpretation were accepted, Jordan J. argued, it would effectively tie the hands of police in investigating offences where young persons are suspected on the basis of fingerprint evidence alone, which would represent a significant departure from the well-established use of fingerprints in the criminal justice system in Canada. While these two cases can be confined to their facts, they raise the question of whether drafters intended that individual police officers or government employees are expected to make a request for a record that is being kept by their own institution.

Further, as mentioned, s. 119(1) indicates that, unlike court records (to which a person shall generally be given access upon request provided he or she is among the parties allowed access under s. 119(1)), the police, the government, and persons or organizations in certain circumstances are not obliged to provide youth records upon request. They have discretion in that regard. Yet the Act provides no guidelines or criteria to assist these record-keepers in exercising their discretion. Thus, record-keepers under ss. 115 and 116 may need to develop policies, if they have not already done so, to assist in the proper exercise of discretion in this important area.

There are numerous other unsettled legal questions regarding the records regime. Section 119(1)(q) and (s), and related sections, illustrate the point. Section 119(1)(q) and (s) can be construed, at least ostensibly, to conflict with the Crown's disclosure obligations under *R. v. Stinchcombe*.[172]

Section 119(1)(q) specifies that an accused or his or her counsel *shall* be given access to a youth court record, but *may* be given access to a police or government youth record, upon swearing an affidavit that the record is necessary to make a full answer and defence. This discretionary wording in relation to access to police or government youth records under s. 119(1)(q) raises questions in light of *Stinchcombe*. It is well established in *Stinchcombe* that the Crown has a general duty to disclose to the defence all relevant information that it proposes to use at trial, including all evidence that may assist the accused, even if the Crown does not propose to adduce it, subject to privilege. The discretion of the Crown in this regard is reviewable by the trial judge, who should be guided by the general principle that information ought not to be withheld if there is a reasonable possibility that the withholding of information will impair the right of the accused to make full answer and defence, unless the non-disclosure is justified by the law of privilege.[173] Yet the use of the permissive term "may" in the introduction to s. 119(1) arguably permits the Crown and the police, as the record-keepers, the discretion to refuse the request from the defence in relation to police and government records even if it is established that the information is relevant to make full answer and defence.

This discretionary wording at the outset of s. 119(1) may perhaps be best understood as intending to capture situations where the record is relevant but subject to privilege, such as in the case of a confidential police informer. The Crown is obligated to protect the identity of a

---

[172] [1991] S.C.J. No. 83, [1991] 3 S.C.R. 326 (S.C.C.).
[173] *R. v. Stinchcombe*, [1991] S.C.J. No. 83, at paras. 19-22, [1991] 3 S.C.R. 326 (S.C.C.).

confidential police informer.[174] Informer privilege is subject to only one exception: a case where the information is required to establish the innocence of the accused, commonly known as the "innocence at stake" exception.[175]

Section 119(1)(s) raises further questions concerning the relationship between the records provisions and the Crown disclosure obligation. If the defence requests the youth record from the Crown under s. 119(1)(q), and the Crown declines to provide it, the defence can apply to a judge for the record under s. 119(1)(s). But such an application imposes on the defence the burden of satisfying the judge that the applicant has a valid interest in the record and that the record is desirable in the interest of the proper administration of justice. This time-consuming and burdensome application process under s. 119(1)(s) appears onerous for the defence and questionable in light of the procedures established in *Stinchcombe*. Alternatively, the defence could request the s. 116 government (Crown) record from the court in the first instance under s. 119(1)(q), since there is no express stipulation in the Act that the request must be made to the record-keeper (although some would argue that this is implicit).

In addition, s. 125(2)(b) appears to limit the information about a witness contained in a court record or a police record that the Crown can disclose to an accused in a proceeding, despite the Crown's disclosure obligation mandated by *Stinchcombe*.[176] Under *Stinchcombe*, if the Crown has information about a witness that is relevant to the proceeding, the Crown has a general duty to disclose that information to the defence, subject to certain exceptions, such as privilege. Indeed, Sopinka J. noted in *Stinchcombe* that the Royal Commission on the Donald Marshall Jr. prosecution outlined an extensive regime of disclosure including the recommendation that an accused, without request, is entitled before electing mode of trial or entering a plea, to information including a copy of the criminal record of any proposed witness.[177] Yet, s. 125(2)(b) appears to suggest that the Crown is obliged to indicate only that the witness *has* a youth record.

The intent of s. 125(2)(b) may be to put the accused on notice that the court or police record exists so that the accused can then apply to the

---

[174]   *R. v. Scott*, [1990] S.C.J. No. 132, 61 C.C.C. (3d) 300 (S.C.C.).

[175]   *R. v. Leipert*, [1997] S.C.J. No. 14, 112 C.C.C. (3d) 385 (S.C.C.).

[176]   Priscilla Platt discussed this concern in her book *Young Offenders Law in Canada*, 2d ed. (Markham, Ont.: Butterworths Canada Ltd., 1995), at 541-43. Although the *YCJA* arguably remedies the concerns raised by Platt by including s. 119(1)(q), the interplay of some of these *YCJA* records sections remains unclear both in relation to the disclosure principles in *Stinchcombe* and from a procedural point of view.

[177]   *R. v. Stinchcombe*, [1991] S.C.J. No. 83, at para. 17, [1991] 3 S.C.R. 326 (S.C.C.).

appropriate record-keeper for the record. However, if the record is relevant and in the possession of the Crown, and not subject to privilege, arguably, under *Stinchcombe*, the Crown should provide the entire record to the defence as part of the disclosure package rather than merely advising the accused of its existence.

The lower courts have considered these sections to some degree in relation to the Crown's obligations in *Stinchcombe*. The jurisprudence suggests that there is often uncertainty about the proper procedure for addressing the matter. In *R. v. K.H.*,[178] Lipton J. reviewed the relevant decisions while considering an application to the court from the accused under ss. 119(1)(q) and 125(2)(b), in which the accused requested that the Crown disclose the complainant's government record under s. 116. The accused brought the application after the Crown declined to provide the record unless the accused made a formal application to the court. (The Crown had advised the accused that there was no youth court record but that the Crown did not wish to release any information concerning any previous investigation or participation in any extrajudicial sanctions by the victim.) As per s. 119(1)(q), the accused filed an affidavit in which she alleged that the complainant intimidated people and had resorted to violent behaviour in the past. The accused's counsel argued that the record would enable her to make full answer and defence to the s. 266 assault charge under the *Criminal Code*. The accused sought disclosure of all records within the Crown's possession, including any police records sent to the Crown.

The Crown argued, *inter alia*, that *Stinchcombe* did not apply to the application because the record being requested would normally not be found in the Crown's possession in relation to the s. 266 charge against the accused, and that the complainant's record bore no relation to the accused's s. 266 charge.[179] Due to restrictions in the *YCJA*, including the penalties under s. 138 for wrongly disclosing information, the Crown took the position that it could not comply with the accused's request. The

---

[178] [2007] A.J. No. 16 (Alta. Prov. Ct.).

[179] In the case of *R. v. C.S.M.*, [2005] B.C.J. No. 2879 (B.C. Youth Ct.), which involved a similar request under s. 119(1)(q) for the youth record of the victim in relation to an assault charge, the Crown agreed that the victim's criminal record, if it related to past assaults by the victim, may be relevant to C.S.M.'s defence to the assault charge, that it had the records in its possession and that the record could form part of what is necessary disclosure outlined in *Stinchcombe*. However, the Crown argued that it did not have the authority to release the record unless there was a formal application to the court and the court granted access after the victim had been given an opportunity to be heard. Justice Meyers held that there was a reasonable likelihood that the record was relevant and ordered the Crown to provide the youth record to the defence despite the restriction on revealing information in records relating to young persons under s. 125(2)(b).

Crown argued that the accused's only option was to make a request under s. 119(1)(q).

The court concluded that *Stinchcombe* did not apply in this case because the complainant's record was not included in the Crown's file in relation to the s. 266 charge. Had it been, Lipton J. held that he would have reached a different conclusion. Justice Lipton reasoned that s. 119(1)(q) is ambiguous because it does not explain how a party is to gain access to a s. 116 government record, such as a record kept by the Crown Attorney, when the Crown exercises its discretion under this section not to comply with the request: "Is the Crown's decision appealable, and if so, to whom? Should the Crown be the final authority on whether an affidavit is or isn't deficient? Who should provide access? Is providing access different than the obligation to disclose?"[180] In the end, he noted that as a fundamental principle of law, an accused should be provided with all relevant information necessary to defend the case and that, if a court concludes that the record is relevant in order for the accused to make full answer and defence, the judge should exercise his or her discretion and order its release.

In *R. v. K.H.*, Lipton J. concluded that the accused had not established the relevance of the record and that he was therefore obliged to conclude that the affidavit was defective. Justice Lipton further held that the Crown had acted properly in requiring the accused to make an application to the court for access to the record by virtue of the penalty provisions in s. 138 of the *YCJA* regarding improper disclosure of records. The Crown was also correct in refusing to disclose the complainant's record because it was not in the Crown's file in relation to the assault charge.[181] "Unless the record is part of the Crown's file with respect to the specific case before the Court and therefore required to be disclosed because of *Stinchcombe*, an accused is obligated to make a section 119(1)(q) application to Court on notice to the young person whose record is being sought. If the record is on the Crown file with request to the specific case before the Court, a section 119(1)(q) application is not necessary."[182] The reality is, however, that the disclosure package provided to the Crown in the first instance by the police will not always contain all information relevant to the prosecution.

---

[180]   *R. v. K.H.*, [2007] A.J. No. 16, at para. 64 (Alta. Prov. Ct.).
[181]   *R. v. S.E.T.*, [2005] B.C.J. No. 813 (B.C. Prov. Ct.) and *R. v. B.J.O.*, [2005] B.C.J. No. 1112 (B.C. Prov. Ct.) arrived at similar conclusions regarding the defence obligation to establish a nexus between the incident that gave rise to the charges and the youth records that the defence were requesting, but see *R. v. C.S.M.*, [2005] B.C.J. No. 2879 (B.C. Youth Ct.).
[182]   *R. v. K.H.*, [2007] A.J. No. 16, at para. 97 (Alta. Prov. Ct.).

In *R. v. D.B.M.*,[183] which was decided early in the life of the *YCJA*, Werier J. observed that the *YCJA* specifies in s. 125 the limited disclosure that the Crown may make with regard to the record of its intended witnesses but concluded that access to records provided for in s. 119 was meant to override the general protection to privacy provisions set out elsewhere in the *YCJA*. Justice Werier further held that although s. 119 does not specify who is obligated to provide the defence with access to the record in order for the accused to make full answer and defence, it made sense that, in the case at bar, the court should provide the record because the records at issue were those which the court was authorized to maintain and also because the court is best placed to review and consider the sufficiency of the affidavit when determining if access is justified in order to make full answer and defence. The records were in the hands of the Crown only in light of their own entitlement to access to them under s. 119, Werier J. held. Justice Werier observed that the Act does not appear to contemplate that it should be the Crown who provides access to the records under s. 119(1)(q). There was no discussion of whether the records were relevant to the Crown's case.

Other courts have considered s. 119(1)(q) and related *YCJA* provisions in light of the *Stinchcombe* principles, but these cases are also generally at the lower court levels. While they take different approaches, adopt different analyses, and sometimes reach different conclusions, none of them is definitive.[184] Greater clarity and procedural direction may be required regarding the interplay of these records sections in light of *Stinchcombe*.

Another important records issue within the *YCJA* records regime relates to situations where a young person has an interaction with the police and is delayed or detained but is later released without any charges laid or other police action taken. Section 119 does not provide for access to

---

[183]   [2003] B.C.J. No. 2646 (B.C. Prov. Ct.).

[184]   See for example earlier decisions under the *YOA*, such as *R. v. D.K.*, [2003] O.J. No. 641 (Ont. C.J.), and *R. v. T.S.*, [2002] O.J. No. 3968 (Ont. C.J.), where Pringle J. held that it is unnecessary for the Crown to obtain an order to release normal *Stinchcombe* disclosure just because the accused is a young person. In the case of *R. v. D.K.*, the accused was seeking the disclosure of a videotaped statement in relation to a complainant concerning sexual assault and related charges, and in the case of *R. v. T.S.*, the accused was seeking various items such as the criminal records of the other young persons involved in a confrontation in the park. In both causes, Pringle J. relied on the reasoning in *R. v. D.I.T.*, [1997] O.J. No. 3682 (Ont. Gen. Div.), which was a case decided under the *YOA*, to hold that documents properly in the hands of the Crown do not require an order under the *YOA*. Justice Pringle noted in *R. v. T.S.* at para. 12 that Kennedy J. in *R. v. D.I.T.* rejected the notion that the *YOA* created a forum for privilege for youth court records and held that where documents relating to young persons were properly in the hands of the Crown, disclosure was mandated by the principles in *Stinchcombe*.

records of these incidents. (If an extrajudicial sanction was used, there is access to the record.[185] If any other extrajudicial measure is used, only the police, the Attorney General or a person participating in a conference has access to the police or Crown record.[186])

This lack of access to the record of the incident where no action was taken can create obstacles in civil proceedings or in the case of human rights complaints where young persons allege that they were detained and mistreated by the police and require the record of the incident. While a young person or his or her counsel can access the young person's record at any time under s. 124 of the *YCJA*, other parties generally cannot access the record in these situations. On a plain reading of s. 124 in combination with s. 129, the young person is prohibited from further sharing the record with other parties who might require the record for purposes of investigating the matter, such as a human rights commission, even if the young person does not object.[187]

Section 123 of the *YCJA* does not solve the quandary because one can apply for access to a record under s. 123 only in situations where the s. 119 access period has expired. Since there is no "access period" *per se* in s. 119 for most parties in relation to records where no charges were laid, or other actions taken (except in the case of an extrajudicial sanction), there appears to be no access to these records under s. 123 either.

The courts are addressing this lacuna in various ways: in *K.F. v. Peel (Regional Municipality) Police Services Board*,[188] both K.F., the young person, and the Ontario Human Rights Commission sought access to the young person's police record. The young person had been arrested by the police in relation to the theft of $5 worth of chips and pop from a school cafeteria. The young person alleged that he was later strip-searched at the police station. He was eventually released without charge, having been dealt with by an extrajudicial measure, and later complained to the Ontario Human Rights Commission about his treatment by the Peel Regional Police Department and other parties. The police were of the view that s. 119(4) of the *YCJA* applied and prevented them from releasing the police record because the section indicates that a police or government record of an extrajudicial measure, excluding an extrajudicial sanction, can be released to only a certain number of specified parties.

---

[185] *YCJA*, s. 119(2)(a).
[186] *YCJA*, s. 119(4).
[187] *YCJA*, s. 129.
[188] [2008] O.J. No. 3178 (Ont. C.J.).

Justice Blacklock of the Ontario Court of Justice had concerns in part over this analysis because he could conceive of situations where young persons would have difficulty in subsequent civil proceedings against the police in cases involving alleged police abuse if police resolved the matter by way of an extrajudicial measure. In other words, when police resolve a matter through an extrajudicial measure other than a sanction, only a limited number of parties can have access to that record. This could prevent parties, such as a Human Rights Commission, from accessing such a record. Justice Blacklock concluded that this would effectively result in the *YCJA* records provisions, which are designed to act as a privacy shield for young persons, functioning as a sword against them.[189]

Justice Blacklock resolved the matter by giving a broad interpretation to s. 124 and concluding that the section provides sufficient authority to order that the young person and his counsel could have access to his record, and that the young person could further share that record with third parties who required access to the record to ensure an appropriate and fair resolution of the complaint before the human rights authorities.[190]

The Ontario Court of Justice came to the opposite conclusion in *Ontario (Human Rights Commission) v. Toronto Police Services Board*[191] in which Weagant J. gave a more restrictive interpretation to s. 124. In this case, the young person was arrested and handcuffed outside of his school, detained, questioned, and his locker and backpack searched by police, in relation to the alleged possession of a stolen car. He was eventually released and not charged with any offence. S.M., who is black, later filed a complaint with the Human Rights Commission against the Toronto Police Services and related parties, alleging racial profiling.

All parties in the case agreed that the records were required in relation to the human rights complaint. Justice Weagant held, however, that the youth record in question was an extrajudicial measure and that access

---

[189] *K.F. v. Peel (Regional Municipality) Police Services Board*, [2008] O.J. No. 3178, at para. 15 (Ont. C.J.).

[190] This interesting records question was a live issue at the time of writing. During his ruling, Blacklock J. considered both *R. v. R.L.*, [2008] O.J. No. 366 (Ont. C.J.) and *R. v. R.L.*, [2007] O.J. No. 5293 (Ont. S.C.). See also the related case of *R. v. R.L.*, [2008] O.J. No. 861 (Ont. S.C.).

In *Dann v. New Brunswick (Minister of Supply and Services)*, [2007] N.B.J. No. 476, [2007] 328 N.B.R. (2d) 128 (N.B.Q.B.), Clendening J. also adopted a broad interpretation of s. 124, similar to that of Blacklock J., to allow a former young offender access to his youth records under s. 124 in order to negotiate a settlement with the Attorney General regarding harm he alleged he suffered at a youth training centre. In order to settle the matter, the young person would clearly have to share the records further, despite the wording of s. 124, which, on its face, limits access to only the young person and his or her counsel.

[191] [2008] O.J. No. 4546 (Ont. C.J.).

was restricted under s. 119(4). The record could be given to only the parties outlined in s. 119(4). In addition, while the young person and his counsel could have access to the record under s. 124, they could not share the record further.

While Weagant J. held that he could not permit access to the youth record to all of the parties who requested it for the purposes sought, under s. 124, he noted that the Act placed insurmountable barriers to accessing the records and that it was probable that Parliament had not contemplated this scenario. Justice Weagant observed that the parties were not precluded from challenging the constitutionality of the access provisions under both ss. 7 and 15 of the *Charter*.[192]

These cases raise fundamental questions about access to youth records in cases that involve interactions between young persons and the police that do not result in charges or where means other than an extrajudicial sanction are used. The Act does not generally provide for access to youth records in these circumstances to parties who may have a legitimate purpose for seeking access. This result cannot have been what Parliament intended, is not in keeping with the overall intention of the *YCJA* to afford enhanced protections to young persons, and is perhaps simply a scenario that was not contemplated.

Another records issue concerns whether a finding of guilt under the *YCJA* is a "conviction" for purposes of s. 12 of the *Canada Evidence Act*.[193] This is important because s. 12 of the *CEA* permits a witness to be questioned as to whether the witness has ever been *convicted* of an offence. At this juncture, however, in light of the interaction of various provisions of the *YCJA*, the arguments are nuanced and circuitous, and the answer unclear.

Under the *YCJA*, as under the *YOA*, a young person is not *convicted* of an offence; he or she is found guilty[194] (subject to certain exceptions, such as receiving an adult sentence or being convicted of an offence as an adult while access to the youth record is open, in which case the guilty finding is deemed to be a conviction).[195] The question becomes whether a young person who has received a guilty finding under the *YCJA* must disclose that fact if he or she takes the stand pursuant to s. 12 of the *CEA*, since he or she has not technically been convicted of an offence. The matter is further complicated by the fact that s. 82 of the *YCJA*, which is

---

[192] This case was ongoing at the time of writing.

[193] R.S.C. 1985, c. C-5 [hereafter "*CEA*"].

[194] See the wording of s. 36 or of s. 42(2) of the *YCJA*, for example. The word "conviction" is not used. A young person is *found guilty* of an offence under the *YCJA*.

[195] *YCJA*, ss. 117, 74(2) and 119(9).

largely identical to s. 36 of the *YOA*, indicates that a young person who receives an absolute discharge, or completes a disposition under the *YOA* or a sentence under the *YCJA*, is generally deemed not to have been found guilty or convicted of an offence.[196] That said, s. 82 of the *YCJA* expressly stipulates that s. 82 is subject to s. 12 of the *CEA*, suggesting that it was clearly intended that a finding of guilt under the *YCJA* should be considered a conviction for purposes of the questioning of a witness under s. 12[197] of the *CEA*. While the phrase "subject to section 12 [examination as to previous convictions] of the *Canada Evidence Act*" strongly supports this interpretation,[198] it remains arguable in law that a young person who has been found guilty of an offence under the *YCJA*, even if he or she has not completed the sentence, has not been convicted of an offence and could accurately answer no when asked on the stand if they have ever been convicted of an offence. The jurisprudence is not definitive.

In *R. v. Morris*,[199] the Supreme Court of Canada held that, for the purposes of s. 12 of the *CEA*, a finding of delinquency under the *JDA* is equivalent to a conviction and that such a finding of guilt could be construed as a conviction. A few years later, however, the Ontario Court of Appeal held in *R. v. Danson*[200] that s. 12 of the *CEA* does not permit

---

[196] Except that the defence of *autrefois convict* would remain open to the young person, and the finding of guilt could be considered when a youth justice court is considering a bail application or a sentencing in relation to the young person or when a national or provincial parole board is considering an application for conditional release or for a pardon.

[197] Considering the wording of s. 36(1) of the *YOA* (which is almost identical to that of s. 82 of the *YCJA*), Priscilla Platt, *Young Offenders Law in Canada*, 2d ed. (Markham, Ont.: Butterworths Canada Ltd., 1995), at 563, writing about the *YOA*, concluded that the accused young person may be questioned as a witness about his or her prior youth court record, pursuant to s. 12 of the *CEA*.

[198] Priscilla Platt, *Young Offenders Law in Canada*, 2d ed. (Markham, Ont.: Butterworths Canada Ltd., 1995), at 379-82, adopts this interpretation based on the similar wording of s. 36 of the *YOA*. It is also the view of this author that this is the correct interpretation.

[199] [1979] S.C.J. No. 93, [1979] 1 S.C.R. 405 (S.C.C.). See also *R. v. Scott*, [1984] O.J. No. 3470, 16 C.C.C. (3d) 17 (Ont. Co. Ct.), where McDermid J. held for the Ontario County Court that Parliament cannot have intended the meaning of "publication" in s. 38 to be interpreted so as to prevent an accused person the right to cross-examine a 13-year-old complainant regarding his record as a juvenile delinquent or young offender. The right of the accused to cross-examine a young person on his youth record trumps the right of the witness to have his identity withheld in the interest of a fair trial. Likewise, in *R. v. Strain*, [1994] O.J. No. 1513 (Ont. Gen. Div.), Weekes J. held that an accused should be able to have access to a young person's record, even if the access period to the record has passed, in order to engage in legitimate cross-examination, which would show that, at least during a part of his or her life, the young person demonstrated behaviour that is relevant to the trier of fact for purposes of assessing the credibility of the person, as a witness.

[200] [1982] O.J. No. 3182, 66 C.C.C. (2d) 369 (Ont. C.A.). But in *R. v. Corbett*, [1988] S.C.J. No. 40, 41 C.C.C. (3d) 385 (S.C.C.), Dickson C.J.C. held that the Crown cannot advance evidence against an accused of prior convictions unless the accused takes the stand, and further that an accused may be cross-examined only as to convictions strictly construed and

cross-examination of the accused regarding offences for which an accused has been found guilty and granted a discharge because a guilty finding followed by a discharge is not a conviction within s. 12 of the *CEA*. Since a person granted a discharge is deemed not to have been convicted, it is clear that an adjudication of guilt followed by the granting of a discharge is not a conviction within s. 12 of the *CEA*, Martin J.A. held for the court.[201] In *R. v. Clark*,[202] decided in relation to the *YOA*, Howden J. held that *R. v. Morris* is still good law and that the meaning of a conviction in the *CEA* includes a finding of guilt under the *YOA*. Justice Howden distinguished between cases where the person was granted a discharge, such as in *Danson*, cited with approval by the Supreme Court of Canada in *Corbett*, and cases where there was a finding of guilt but no discharge by the court.

Notably, in *R. v. Smith*,[203] Trafford J. of the Ontario Superior Court relied on *Morris*, in part, to support his finding that differential treatment of young persons charged with crimes does not spill over into s. 12 of the *CEA*. In other words, a young person can be cross-examined in relation to offences under the *YCJA* even though these offences are not technically convictions but rather guilty findings. In *Smith*, defence counsel was attempting to prohibit the cross-examination of his client on his youth record on other grounds and had not specifically argued that s. 12 did not permit it when read in conjunction with various provisions of the *YCJA*.

In *R. v. Sheik-Qasim*,[204] Molloy J. held that cross-examination of a Crown witness on his youth record was not permissible, but for different reasons. The defence had not applied for the record and knew of it only because defence had asked the witness about it during the preliminary without objection from the Crown. The witness then disclosed the nature and extent of it. The defence did not have the record in his possession. The defence had sought to challenge the credibility of the witness at the trial by cross-examining him on his youth record, but Molloy J. ruled this was impermissible. After Molloy J.'s oral ruling, defence applied to a youth court judge for production but was refused. In written reasons, Molloy J. held that only a youth justice *court* judge has jurisdiction to order production of youth records under the *YCJA*, that since the records in question were not subject to production under the Act, the information contained in the records cannot be used either, and that s. 82 does not

---

that there can be no cross-examination where the accused was found guilty and granted a conditional discharge, conditions subsequently having been fulfilled.

[201] *R. v. Danson*, [1982] O.J. No. 3182, at paras. 11 and 12, 66 C.C.C. (2d) 369 (Ont. C.A.).
[202] [1998] O.J. No. 5580 (Ont. Gen. Div.).
[203] [2007] O.J. No. 2585 (Ont. S.C.).
[204] [2007] O.J. No. 4799 (Ont. S.C.).

extend the access period to records outlined in s. 119(2).[205] The access period to the record had expired in this case. Justice Molloy further held that none of the exceptions in the *YCJA* that provide for access to a record after the end of the access period in s. 119 applied to the record in this case.

Again relying on *R. v. Morris*,[206] the Nova Scotia Supreme Court[207] rejected Molloy J.'s reasoning, based largely on the argument that the long-standing practice of cross-examination of witnesses is an essential component of the right to make full answer and defence.[208] According to Beveridge J., it makes no difference if the witness is being cross-examined in relation to a conviction or guilty finding under the *YOA* or the *YCJA* — the fundamental legal principle remains.[209]

> With all due respect to Molloy J., the plain ordinary meaning of s. 82 of the *Y.C.J.A.* is that the deeming provision for young persons not to have been found guilty or convicted of an offence is specifically made subject to s. 12 of the *Canada Evidence Act*. To adopt his proposed interpretation is to render meaningless the phrase "Subject to section 12 (examination as to previous convictions) of the *Canada Evidence Act*". It therefore appears that at least with respect to an ordinary witness, he or she can be cross-examined with respect to any adjudication of guilt, whether or not it resulted in a discharge or a conviction.[210]

The express wording of s. 82 of the *YCJA* certainly suggests that it was intended that witnesses could be questioned about their youth records pursuant to s. 12 of the *CEA* and that the youth record could be considered a conviction for purposes of s. 12 even though the individual could not otherwise be prejudiced or impacted if he or she had received an absolute discharge, a reprimand, or otherwise completed the sentence.

Even if one takes the position that s. 12 permits a witness who has a youth record to be asked about it, in the event that the individual denies the youth record, s. 12(2) indicates that the opposite party can then prove the record. This suggests that a counsel seeking to cross-examine an individual on his or her youth record under s. 12 must have the youth record in his or her possession at the time of cross-examination, which is what *R. v. Sheik-Qasim* stands for, in part. It appears therefore that counsel must be in a position to gain lawful access

---

[205] *R. v. Sheik-Qasim*, [2007] O.J. No. 4799, at para. 18 (Ont. S.C.).

[206] [1979] S.C.J. No. 93, [1979] 1 S.C.R. 405 (S.C.C.).

[207] *R. v. Upton*, [2008] N.S.J. No. 505 (N.S.S.C.). See also *R. v. Frater*, [2008] O.J. No. 5329, at para. 26 (Ont. S.C.).

[208] *R. v. Upton*, [2008] N.S.J. No. 505, at paras. 14, 15 and 16 (N.S.S.C.).

[209] *R. v. Upton*, [2008] N.S.J. No. 505, at para. 23 (N.S.S.C.).

[210] *R. v. Upton*, [2008] N.S.J. No. 505, at para. 32 (N.S.S.C.).

to the record under the *YCJA* provisions before being able to make effective use of s. 12 of the *CEA*.

Considering the unsettled state of the jurisprudence on this point, any person who anticipates being asked about his or her youth record pursuant to s. 12 of the *CEA* during a criminal proceeding should seek legal advice before taking the stand.

What is clear is this: If a young person has received an adult sentence for an offence, he or she is deemed to have been convicted of the offence (as opposed to having been found guilty).[211] Also, if during the period of access to a record under s. 119 the young person is convicted of an offence committed as an adult, Part 6 and s. 82 no longer apply to the record. The record is to be treated as the record of an adult and the finding of guilt is deemed to be a conviction for purposes of the *Criminal Records Act*.[212] Likewise, if during the period of access to a record under s. 120, the young person is convicted of an additional offence set out in the schedule as an adult, Part 6 no longer applies to the record and it shall be treated like an adult criminal record and considered a conviction for purposes of the *Criminal Records Act*.[213]

Young persons should also be mindful of the fact that even though a young person is deemed not to have been found guilty or convicted of an offence once he or she receives an absolute discharge or a reprimand, or completes his or her sentence under s. 82, there is still a record of the incident. The record can remain accessible long after the young person has been deemed not to have been found guilty or convicted of the offence. The youth record (for even an absolute discharge) remains accessible under s. 119 or s. 120 to certain parties for the periods set out in those sections. An extrajudicial sanction, for example, that is successfully completed does not result in a guilty finding, but is nevertheless a youth record under the *YCJA*; the record of this sanction is accessible for two years under s. 119(2)(a) from the time that the young person agrees to be subject to the sanction.[214] While one could argue that upon the completion of the youth sentence as per s. 82 of the *YCJA*, there is no longer any youth record in existence, *ergo*, it cannot be accessed, there is, of course, a compelling counter-argument that a plain reading of the Act as a whole, and of s. 119 in particular, strongly suggests the intent of the Act is otherwise.

---

[211] *YCJA*, s. 117.

[212] *YCJA*, s. 119(9).

[213] *YCJA*, s. 120(6).

[214] See some discussion of this point in *R. v. K.H.*, [2005] A.J. No. 16, at para. 53 (Alta. Prov. Ct.).

Another issue that may be unclear to federal government department officials is the extent to which one federal government department can share a youth record with another federal government department. For example, if one government department or agency correctly receives a youth record, it may assume that it can further disclose that record to another federal government entity. It is important to bear in mind that the Act generally prohibits such further disclosure.[215] Generally, in each case, the government department that wants the youth record must request access to the record through the access provisions.

IV. FINGERPRINTING AND PHOTOGRAPHS

A young person can be fingerprinted and photographed by the police in the same circumstances that allow for the fingerprinting and the photographing of adults under the *Identification of Criminals Act*.[216] In essence, a young person can be fingerprinted if he or she is charged with an indictable offence, which includes hybrid offences.[217] Fingerprints and photographs of young persons, which are created or kept for the purposes of the *YCJA*, or for the investigation of an offence that is, or could be, prosecuted under the *YCJA*, are youth records. The original or a copy of any fingerprints or photographs of the young person that are part of the record may be kept by any police force responsible for or participating in the investigation of the offence.[218] When a young person is charged with an indictable offence, the police force responsible for the investigation of the offence has discretion as to whether to provide the record relating to it to the R.C.M.P. If the young person is found guilty of the indictable offence, the police force must provide the record to the R.C.M.P., where it shall be kept in the central repository.[219] The fingerprints and photographs are part of that record.

The fingerprints and photographs are thus subject to the records provisions of the *YCJA* relating to accessibility under ss. 119 and 120 in the same way that other records are. If a police force has exercised its discretion and provided the fingerprints and photograph of the young person in a case where the young person is only charged and the young person is subsequently found not guilty, for example, the C.P.I.C. record must be destroyed three months after all proceedings in relation to any

---

[215] *YCJA*, s. 129.
[216] *YCJA*, s. 113.
[217] *Identification of Criminals Act*, R.S.C. 1985, c. I-1.
[218] *YCJA*, s. 115(1).
[219] *YCJA*, s. 115(2) and (3).

appeal of the matter are complete, or two months after the expiry of the time allowed for the taking of an appeal.[220]

V.   PRIVACY AND INTERNATIONAL LAW/ INFORMATION SHARING

A.   International Law

The Canadian practice of protecting the privacy of young persons is in keeping with international norms, although some scholars suggest Canada is not entirely measuring up to international standards in this area and has not gone far enough to protect the privacy of young persons.

Article 40 2(b)(vii) of the *U.N. Convention on the Rights of the Child* indicates that every child accused of infringing the criminal law is entitled to a guarantee "to have his or her privacy fully respected at all stages of the proceedings".[221] In addition, Article 16 states that "[n]o child shall be subjected to arbitrary or unlawful interference with his or her privacy ...".[222]

Other international instruments also establish rules and guidelines regarding the privacy of young persons but, unlike the Convention, they are not treaties, and, consequently, are non-coercive written instruments.[223] The Beijing Rules are among these instruments.[224] Rule 8 of the Beijing Rules states:

> 8.1 The juvenile's right to privacy shall be respected at all stages in order to avoid harm being caused to her or him by undue publicity or by the process of labelling.

---

[220] *YCJA*, s. 128(3) and s. 119(2)(b).

[221] The Convention defines a child as a human being under 18. Canada has ratified this treaty, which came into force on September 2, 1990. Other international instruments are also germane. For a good discussion of the relevant international instruments on this point and an analysis of the extent to which the *YCJA* is in compliance with them, see M.S. Denov, "Children's Rights, Juvenile Justice, and the UN Convention on the Rights of the Child", c. 4 in Kathryn M. Campbell, ed., *Understanding Youth Justice in Canada* (Toronto: Pearson Education Canada Inc., 2005), 65 at 77-84.

[222] The Convention can be found on the website of the Office of the High Commissioner for Human Rights at: <http://www.unhchr.ch/html/menu3/b/k2crc.htm>.

[223] As discussed in *Reference re: Bill C-7 respecting the criminal justice system for young persons*, [2003] Q.J. No. 2850, at paras. 87-192 (Que. C.A.).

[224] This discussion comes from *Reference re: Bill C-7 respecting the criminal justice system for young persons*, [2003] Q.J. No. 2850, at paras. 87-192 (Que. C.A.).

8.2 In principle, no information that may lead to the identification of a juvenile offender shall be published.[225]

Some scholars suggest that the *YCJA* falls short in permitting the publication of the names of young persons who receive adult sentences.[226] These critics also assert that the *YCJA* allows potentially harmful disclosure of information to victims and other individuals whom the court considers acceptable, and that the court is not required to consider the young person's best interests before disclosing such information. Such practices may lead to harmful stigmatization and are not in compliance with Article 16 of the Convention, some suggest.[227]

In addition, the Committee on the Rights of the Child, which is a monitoring body that attempts to ensure state compliance with the Convention, has expressed concerns about the *YCJA*'s level of compliance with the Convention. Among other things, it criticized Canada for permitting access to youth records and public identification (in some instances).[228]

B. Information Sharing with Foreign States

The Attorney General or a peace officer can disclose to the Minister of Justice of Canada information in a youth court record or a youth police record in order to deal with requests to, or by, foreign states under the *Mutual Legal Assistance in Criminal Matters Act* or for the purposes of an extradition matter under the *Extradition Act*. The Minister of Justice of

---

[225] The text of both international instruments can be accessed online through the Office of the High Commissioner for Human Rights at: <http://www2.ohchr.org/english/law/index.htm#core>.

[226] M.S. Denov, "Children's Rights, Juvenile Justice, and the UN Convention on the Rights of the Child", c. 4 in Kathryn M. Campbell, ed., *Understanding Youth Justice in Canada* (Toronto: Pearson Education Canada Inc., 2005), at 82. Nicholas Bala also raises this point in his book *Youth Criminal Justice Law* (Toronto: Irwin Law, 2003), at 134. He refers, in particular, to some of the exceptions to the publication ban in s. 110 of the *YCJA*.

[227] M.S. Denov, "Children's Rights, Juvenile Justice, and the UN Convention on the Rights of the Child", c. 4 in Kathryn M. Campbell, ed., *Understanding Youth Justice in Canada* (Toronto: Pearson Education Canada Inc., 2005), at 80.

[228] As discussed in M.S. Denov, "Children's Rights, Juvenile Justice, and the UN Convention on the Rights of the Child", c. 4 in Kathryn M. Campbell, ed., *Understanding Youth Justice in Canada* (Toronto: Pearson Education Canada Inc., 2005), at 82. Interestingly, in the Reference case on Bill C-7, the Quebec Court of Appeal considered various provisions of the *YCJA*, including s. 110(2)(b), which permits the publication of the name of a young person who receives a youth sentence, in certain circumstances. The court held that, since s. 110(2)(b) is an exception to the general rule and basic standard of confidentiality under the *YCJA*, and the rule established by the international treaties does not formally exclude exceptions, there is no incompatibility between s. 110(2)(b) and the two treaties — the *Convention on the Rights of the Child* and the *International Covenant on Civil and Political Rights*.

Canada, in turn, can disclose the information to the foreign state in respect of which the request was made or to which the extradition matters relates.[229]

Other provisions of the *YCJA* may also apply to permit the sharing of youth records with foreign states. Presumably, in a case where Canada declined to provide the record under s. 125(3), a foreign state could apply for access to a Canadian youth record under s. 119(1)(s), which would allow a Canadian youth justice court judge to consider the request and exercise his or her discretion in that regard. Section 119(1)(s) indicates that *any person* or member of a class of persons can have access if the youth justice court judge determines that he or she has a valid interest in the record if the judge is satisfied that access is desirable in the interest of the proper administration of justice. In cases where the access period under s. 119 has expired, presumably the foreign state actor could apply under s. 123.

What is less clear, however, is what happens to Canadian youth records that are properly shared with a foreign state in accordance with the *YCJA* after they pass into the hands of the foreign state and into its information data banks. What control, if any, does Canada have over youth records that have found their way into U.S. data banks, properly or otherwise? The *YCJA* does not address this. Despite a detailed regime in Canada that tightly regulates the use that can be made of youth records and also contains provisions regarding the destruction of these records by Canadian entities, it is unclear what happens to the information that ends up beyond Canadian borders.

If an adult Canadian becomes aware, for example, while trying to cross the Canada-U.S. border, that the U.S. has information on its system that the adult was sentenced as a young person in relation to possession of marihuana in Canada, what power, if any, does the adult have to try to get that record expunged from the U.S. data bank, if in fact the record has already been legally destroyed in Canada in accordance with the *YCJA*? Certainly, Canada can attach conditions and caveats to information that it discloses or is considering disclosing to a foreign country, including conditions that the foreign entity comply with the provisions of the *YCJA*, but ensuring that these conditions are honoured over time is a more challenging undertaking and, in fact, perhaps practically impossible. Once the record finds its way into a U.S. data bank, it may be impossible for Canadian authorities to control access to, and further use and dissemination of, that information.

---

[229] *YCJA*, s. 125(3).

Should a Canadian become aware that a record of a crime he or she committed as a young person (which was subsequently destroyed in Canada in accordance with the *YCJA*) remains in the information management system of a foreign country, the individual could, at the very least, take steps to ascertain the terms under which the information was shared with the foreign entity to ensure that the information was properly shared. If conditions limiting the subsequent use of that information were attached to its disclosure, such as an undertaking that the information be destroyed or access to the record be sealed in accordance with the provisions of the *YCJA*, the individuals could raise these matters with the appropriate authorities in an effort to get the administration to comply with its undertakings.

VI. CONCLUSION

The Canadian state has achieved an uneasy compromise in this difficult area: On the one hand, the state recognizes that preventing the publication of the identities of young persons in most circumstances, and strictly controlling access to, and the use of, their youth records, may be the best way to foster their rehabilitation. Yet the state supports the publication of their identities in certain circumstances, such as when they commit the most serious offences and receive adult sentences, or if they continue to commit offences as adults. Likewise, the *YCJA* records regime ceases to have effect if young persons continue to commit offences as adults while access to their youth records remains open.

The Canadian law unquestionably protects the privacy of young persons much more than it does that of adults, but it is not a blanket protection. The *YCJA* does not protect the identities of all young persons or their youth records all of the time. The *YCJA* is largely designed to prevent most young persons who have made mistakes in their youth from being forever stigmatized, provided they have learned from their mistakes and do not continue to commit crimes.

The privacy regime under Part 6 of the *YCJA* is less forgiving of chronic and violent young persons.

Chapter 10

THE YOUTH CRIMINAL JUSTICE SYSTEM IN CANADA — A TIME OF UNCERTAINTY

It is revolting to have no better reason for a rule of law than that so it was laid down in the time of Henry IV. It is still more revolting if the grounds upon which it was laid down have vanished long since and the rule simply persists from blind imitation of the past.[1]

I. INTRODUCTION

One hundred years after the establishment of a separate youth criminal justice system in Canada, the direction of that system is uncertain. Political circumstances in 2008 created an unexpected but perhaps fortuitous hiatus in plans to reform the system, providing an opportunity for politicians and youth justice experts, as well as average Canadians, to reflect upon the nature and effectiveness of Canada's youth criminal justice system and to consider carefully its future path.

Overhauling Canada's *Youth Criminal Justice Act*[2] has been a priority for this federal government since even before it came to power in 2006. During 2008, however, the political importance of youth criminal justice reform in Canada dwindled, in almost direct inverse proportion to growing concerns about the economy and uncharacteristic political uncertainty in Canada. In the summer of 2008, Prime Minister Stephen Harper described Canada's youth justice system as an "unmitigated failure", and

---

[1]   Justice Oliver Wendell Holmes Jr., "The Path of the Law", in (1897) 10 Harv. L. Rev. 457. This essay was delivered by Mr. Justice Holmes, then of the Supreme Court of Massachusetts, on January 8, 1897. It is reprinted in *The World of Law, II, The Law as Literature*, Ephraim London, ed. (New York: Simon and Schuster, 1960), 614 at 626.

[2]   S.C. 2002, c. 1 [hereafter "*YCJA*"].

repeated promises to reform the *YCJA*.[3] By the fall, his proposed reforms were effectively stalled when the federal election was called. When his government was re-elected with only a stronger minority on October 14, 2008, youth criminal justice reform was no longer a priority. The Conservative government focused instead on fostering co-operation among the political parties to address the perceived economic crisis facing the country.[4] (The Liberals, the NDP and the Bloc Québécois all publicly denounced the Conservative government's proposed reforms to the *YCJA* prior to, and during, the fall election of 2008.[5])

Following the release of the federal government's economic update in late November 2008, the Liberals and the NDP, with the support of the Bloc Québécois, formed a coalition to defeat the minority Conservative government. The government avoided defeat by proroguing Parliament. When the federal government introduced its economic budget in late January 2009, the Liberal-led coalition chose not to defeat it.[6]

This unexpected pause regarding youth criminal justice reform enables the federal government, youth justice experts, scholars, practitioners and average Canadians to take stock of Canada's youth criminal justice system at a critical juncture in our legal history, and to pose fundamental questions about the direction of reform.

What role, if any, can reform to the *YCJA* play in reducing youth crime? What can we reasonably expect legislation to achieve? What do we want it to achieve? What does the research reveal about the best means to reduce youth crime? Is the Canadian state acting in accordance with the advice and knowledge of the experts in the field? What lessons can we learn from Quebec, which has the lowest youth crime rate in Canada?[7] What can we learn from the approaches of other nations? Public discourse

---

[3]   Speech by Prime Minister Stephen Harper, on June 6, 2008, to the 6th Annual Gala and Fundraiser for the Canadian Crime Victims Foundation, online at: <http://pm.gc.ca/eng/media.asp?id=2145>.

[4]   Janice Tibbets and David Aki, "Tories back off law-and-order plan" *The Ottawa Citizen* (18 November, 2008), A5.

[5]   Their criticisms are documented later in this chapter.

[6]   This remained the situation as of August 2009.

[7]   Andrea Taylor-Butts and Angela Bressan, Youth Crime in Canada, 2006, Statistics Canada-Catalogue no. 85-002-XIE, Vol. 28, no. 3. Quebec has the lowest crime rate in the country according to the Statistics Canada study cited above. As various Canadian scholars have observed, Quebec has the lowest charge rate for young persons in Canada and also brings youths to court at a much lower rate than any other region. This observation is worthy of further study. See Nicholas Bala, Peter Carrington and Julian Roberts, "The *Youth Criminal Justice Act* After Five Years — A Qualified Success", which was an unpublished article at the time of writing. The final version can be found in Bala, Carrington & Roberts, "Evaluating the *Youth Criminal Justice Act* After Five Years — A Qualified Success" (2009) 51(2) Can. J. Crim. & Crim. J. 131.

generally, as well as legal reform in particular, must be based on reliable data and research. Has Canada done adequate homework? In addition, has the state taken steps to ensure that this information makes its way into the mainstream press so that Canadians are better informed, in order to elevate the level of public debate?

Canadians, and their elected officials and policymakers, share a responsibility to think critically and objectively about the future direction of the youth criminal justice system in Canada.

II. THE ROAD TO REFORM

The federal Conservative government vowed to reform the *YCJA*, which was introduced and passed by the predecessor Liberal government, from the time it assumed power in February 2006; indeed, promises to reform the Act were part of its election platform.[8] Among the Conservative party's consistently stated aims, which were routinely repeated once it formed the federal minority government, were plans to toughen up the Act by expanding the sentencing principles under the *YCJA* to include the adult sentencing principles of deterrence and denunciation, and to also ensure that anyone 14 years old or older who is charged with serious violent or repeat offences is automatically subject to adult sentences.

Former federal Justice Minister Vic Toews stated in the early days of the new federal government in 2006 that "accountability and responsibility for serious crimes needs to be enforced in our youth justice system", and that the *YCJA* is a "very badly drafted act", that needs to be reviewed.[9] That October, Toews indicated that a new law implementing harsher treatment of young offenders was to be introduced in a few months.[10] His comments followed an incident in the north end of Winnipeg, where two boys, aged eight and nine, apparently encouraged by two 12-year-old girls, locked a disabled 14-year-old in a shed in a public housing complex and set it afire. One of the boys told a reporter they had tried to extinguish the fire, but could not. A stranger came running and rescued the teenager.[11] The boys were under 12 and could not be charged.

---

[8] *Stand Up for Canada*, 2006 Federal Election Platform of the Conservative Party, at 25. Justice Minister Rob Nicholson repeated this commitment when he appeared before the Standing Committee on Justice and Human Rights on April 24, 2007, Number 063, 1st Sess., 39th Parl., April 24, 2007, at 0930.

[9] Kirk Makin, "Youth jail terms less common after 2003 law, study says" *The Globe and Mail* (24 June 2006), A8.

[10] "Toews backs off prosecuting 10-year-olds" *The Ottawa Citizen* (18 October 2006), A8.

[11] Joe Friesen, "Do it, push him in there or I'll beat you up" *The Globe and Mail* (21 October 2006), A1 and A6.

However, no youth justice legislation was introduced during Minister Toews's tenure.

Shortly after Robert Nicholson was sworn in as federal Justice Minister in January 2007 as a result of a pre-election cabinet shuffle, he appeared before the Standing Committee on Justice and Human Rights[12] and again indicated that youth justice reform was a priority. Nicholson told the committee that the *YCJA* was often raised with him by provincial Justice Ministers, that it should be improved, and that the federal government planned to introduce legislation to that end. He also reminded the committee that the Conservative party had been saying since the election that deterrence and denunciation should be included among the sentencing principles for young persons under the *YCJA*, and that the federal government also planned to review the penalty sections for young persons who commit serious or violent or repeat offences. Minister Nicholson also launched a comprehensive review of the pre-trial detention and release provisions under the *YCJA*, which included the public release of a detailed consultation paper on that topic on June 1, 2007.[13] The release of that consultation document was a clear signal that the federal government was considering reforms to the bail provisions of the *YCJA*. A national review of the *YCJA*, during which Nicholson travelled to the provinces and territories, also occurred in 2008.

Much of the political pressure to reform the *YCJA* came from "the East". The Nova Scotia government led the crusade for change following the release of the Nunn Commission report in December 2006.[14] From the time of the report's release, the Nova Scotia government routinely made public statements that were widely reported in the press, in which it stated that the *YCJA* was not adequately protecting the public from young persons who were chronic, and often dangerous, repeat offenders. A series of attacks in the Halifax area during the summer of 2007 in which teenagers were generally the suspects prompted the Nova Scotia premier and the provincial Justice Minister to repeat calls for measures to toughen the *YCJA*. Interestingly, statistics from the Halifax Regional Police

---

12   Standing Committee on Justice and Human Rights, Number 063, 1st Sess., 39th Parl., April 24, 2007, at 0930 and 1015.
13   At the time of writing in November 2008, this paper was still available online at: <http://www.justice.gc.ca/eng/pi/yj-jj/latest-derni/latest-derni.html>.
14   Nova Scotia Nunn Commission of Inquiry, *Spiralling out of Control: Lessons Learned from a Boy in Trouble: Report of the Nunn Commission of Inquiry* (Halifax, NS: Nunn Commission of Inquiry, 2006), available online at: <http://www.gov.ns.ca/just/nunn_commission/_docs/Report_Nunn_Final.pdf>.

released at the time revealed a nearly 8 per cent drop in violent crime during the first half of 2007.[15]

The Nova Scotia government announced in January 2007 that it had accepted all 34 Nunn Commission recommendations. It also widely publicized the fact that its Justice Minister, Murray Scott, had visited Ottawa three times by June of 2007 in an effort to push the federal government to act on the recommendations flowing from the Nunn Commission. In its June 2007 update on the implementation of the recommendations, the Nova Scotia government expressed frustration that the federal government had not yet taken concrete steps to implement any of the reforms to the *YCJA* advocated by the Nunn Commission:

> Nova Scotia has been calling for changes to the federal Youth Criminal Justice Act (YCJA) since 2005. The required changes have been repeatedly outlined by Nova Scotia, other provinces, youth criminal justice experts, the public through the Minister's Task Force, and Commissioner Nunn's recommendations. Justice Minister Murray Scott traveled to Ottawa three times in 2007 alone and pressed the Federal Justice Minister for implementation of Commissioner Nunn's recommendations relating to the YCJA. Although disappointed with the lack of progress by the federal government, Nova Scotia will continue to advocate for changes that will better protect the public and serve young people in conflict with the law.[16]

The Nunn Commission was established by the provincial government in June 2005 following the death of 52-year-old Theresa McEvoy on October 14, 2004. Its goal was to inquire into, and make recommendations, in relation to the release from custody of a 16-year-old young person who, two days later, went through a red light at a Halifax intersection at very high speed while joyriding in a stolen car and crashed into Ms. McEvoy's vehicle, killing her instantly.[17] On the day of his release, the young person pled guilty to operating a motor vehicle in a manner dangerous to the public and two counts of theft of motor vehicles.[18] He had no prior convictions but was facing 38 outstanding criminal charges at the time of his release, generally relating to car theft and joyriding.[19] He had accumulated these charges between January and October 12, 2004.[20] The province of Nova Scotia called a public inquiry

---

[15] Alison Auld, "Statistics rebut Halifax crime-wave claims, experts say" *The Globe and Mail* (31 August 2007), A6.

[16] Government's Response to Nunn Commission, Update June 2007.

[17] Government's Response to Nunn Commission, Update June 2007.

[18] Government's Response to Nunn Commission, Update June 2007.

[19] Government's Response to Nunn Commission, Update June 2007.

[20] Government's Response to Nunn Commission, Update June 2007.

to consider the handling of his charges and other matters relating to why he was released.[21]

Retired Nova Scotia Supreme Court Justice D. Merlin Nunn, who presided over the commission, identified the *YCJA* as the "real culprit" when he submitted his report in December 2006 to the Nova Scotia government because it failed to deal adequately with the young person whose conduct resulted in the death of Ms. McEvoy.[22]

While many of the Nunn Commission recommendations apply to only the youth justice system in Nova Scotia, the Nunn Commission specifically recommended that the Nova Scotia government advocate that the federal government amend the *YCJA* in a number of specific ways, including adding a clause to the Declaration of Principle in s. 3 to indicate that protection of the public is one of the primary goals of the *YCJA* and making it easier to deny bail to young persons who pose a danger to the life or safety of others if released.[23]

Scott hand-delivered a copy of the Nunn Commission report to then federal Justice Minister Vic Toews within days of receiving it. Following his December 11, 2006 meeting with Toews, Scott indicated that Toews had advised him that the federal government was working on draft legislation that took into consideration Commissioner Nunn's recommendations.[24]

While the Nova Scotia government was the most vocal of the provinces in its campaign for changes to the *YCJA*, several other provinces supported the Nova Scotia government when federal, provincial and

---

[21]   Nova Scotia Nunn Commission of Inquiry, *Spiralling out of Control: Lessons Learned from a Boy in Trouble: Report of the Nunn Commission of Inquiry* (Halifax, NS: Nunn Commission of Inquiry, 2006), available online at: <http://www.gov.ns.ca/just/nunn_commission/_docs/Report_Nunn_Final.pdf>. See the cover page of the report, as well as the Introduction, at 9-11. See also Chapters 4 and 5 of the report, which detail the teenager's descent into crime in 2004.

[22]   Nova Scotia Nunn Commission of Inquiry, *Spiralling out of Control: Lessons Learned from a Boy in Trouble: Report of the Nunn Commission of Inquiry* (Halifax, NS: Nunn Commission of Inquiry, 2006), available online at: <http://www.gov.ns.ca/just/nunn_commission/_docs/Report_Nunn_Final.pdf>. See Chapter 10 of the report, "Advocacy for Changes to the *Youth Criminal Justice Act*".

[23]   Nova Scotia Nunn Commission of Inquiry, *Spiralling out of Control: Lessons Learned from a Boy in Trouble: Report of the Nunn Commission of Inquiry* (Halifax, NS: Nunn Commission of Inquiry, 2006), available online at: <http://www.gov.ns.ca/just/nunn_commission/_docs/Report_Nunn_Final.pdf>. The recommendations in relation to the *YCJA* are discussed in Chapter 10, and all of the recommendations are consolidated in Chapter 12.

[24]   "Minister Meets with Federal Counterpart on Nunn Recommendations", Nova Scotia Department of Justice, Press Release, December 11, 2006.

territorial Justice Ministers gathered in October 2006 in Newfoundland and Labrador.[25] That support grew over the next year.

By the fall of 2007, a number of provinces were publicly pressing the federal government for changes to the youth criminal justice regime. Foremost on the long list of provincial grievances was a widespread concern that it was too difficult to detain repeat and potentially dangerous young persons under the *YCJA*. Newspaper editorialists had taken to facetiously reminding the public that the *YCJA* actually stands for: "You can't jail anyone."[26] Even leading youth justice experts in Canada, such as Queen's University law professor Nicholas Bala, expressed public support for the fundamental assessment that it could often be too difficult to detain young persons under the *YCJA* even if there were evidence that a particular young person posed a risk to public safety if released.[27]

Other provinces, including Manitoba and British Columbia, were also calling publicly for reforms to the *YCJA*, to address problems such as youth gangs and young car thieves.[28] In an interview with the Vancouver *Province*, which was published in September 2007, B.C.'s Attorney General, Wally Oppal, described youth gangs in B.C. as a "serious problem".[29] Oppal indicated that the penalties are generally adequate to address the problem and that it is already "fairly easy" to elevate young offenders to adult court under the *YCJA*, but agreed that general deterrence should be a factor in the youth justice system.[30] Oppal said he was most concerned about repeat offenders and those who cannot be rehabilitated.[31]

Manitoba called on the federal government to make auto theft a stand-alone offence in the *YCJA* so that judges would be more likely to

---

[25] "Minister Receives Federal Commitment to Improve Youth Justice", Press Release, Nova Scotia Department of Justice, October 13, 2006.

[26] "Youth Criminal Justice Act" *The Globe and Mail* (11 October 2007), A26.

[27] Regarding Bala's views concerning the detention of young persons under the *YCJA*, see his testimony before the Nunn Commission of Inquiry, Transcript of Hearing, Vol. 16, February 16, 2006, at 2909.

[28] Kathleen Harris, "Tougher Laws Coming" *The Winnipeg Sun* (21 September 2007), 5; Mary Agnes Welch, "Manitoba posse hits Ottawa, Demands toughening of crime laws", *Winnipeg Free Press* (21 September 2007), A9, and Lena Sin, "B.C. ignored all the warning signs of growing youth gangs" *The Province* (21 September 2007), A14.

[29] Lena Sin, "B.C. ignored all the warning signs of growing youth gangs" *The Province* (21 September 2007), A14.

[30] Lena Sin, "B.C. ignored all the warning signs of growing youth gangs" *The Province* (21 September 2007), A14.

[31] Lena Sin, "B.C. ignored all the warning signs of growing youth gangs" *The Province* (21 September 2007), A14.

deny bail and impose jail time, and to create tougher penalties in the *YCJA*, especially for repeat offenders and car thieves.[32]

Nicholson responded by stating again publicly that he was "on-side with them in terms of their concerns", and that he intended to move forward with "improvements" to the *YCJA*, although he did not provide a timetable.[33]

It was no surprise, therefore, when Nicholson announced reforms to the *YCJA* on October 9, 2007,[34] along the lines of what the Nunn Commission had recommended. Fittingly, Nicholson made the announcement in Halifax, Nova Scotia, following a meeting with Nova Scotia Justice Minister Murray Scott.

> Youth in our country can often times make bad decisions that can draw them into a lifestyle that is marked by drugs and violence. This can lead to crimes that are so heinous that they shock entire communities out of their complacency and require the government to continuously examine the legislation that we have enacted.
>
> We believe that the youth criminal justice system must effectively hold young offenders accountable for serious crimes with meaningful consequences, instil within them a sense of responsibility for their behaviour and give them better opportunity for rehabilitation so they do not reoffend.[35]

The most contentious reforms Nicholson announced in October 2007, however, did not reflect the Nunn Commission recommendations but were rather a manifestation of the Conservative government's preoccupation: plans to include deterrence and denunciation as sentencing principles for young persons who are sentenced under the *YCJA*.

The federal government introduced Bill C-25 on November 19, 2007. It provided that deterrence (both specific and general) and denunciation would become principles of sentencing for young persons who receive youth sentences under the *YCJA*, as they are for adults. By attempting to incorporate deterrence and denunciation as sentencing principles for young persons under the *YCJA*, the federal government was fulfilling an election promise, and responding to public concerns about youth crime.

---

[32]   Mary Agnes Welch, "Manitoba posse hits Ottawa, Demands toughening of crime laws" *The Winnipeg Free Press* (21 September 2007), A9.

[33]   Kathleen Harris, "Tougher Laws Coming" *The Winnipeg Sun* (21 September 2007), 5.

[34]   Keith Doucette, "Conservative Party: Tories vow to toughen young offender sentences" *The Globe and Mail* (10 October 2007), A4.

[35]   Amy Smith, "Changes to youth law promised" *The Chronicle-Herald* (10 October 2007), A1.

The bill also included amendments to the youth bail regime to simplify it, as the Nunn Commission had recommended, and to also make it easier to detain young persons at the pre-trial stage if they posed a risk to public safety. Specifically, Bill C-25 sought to broaden the circumstances in which a young person could be detained at the pre-trial stage for the protection of the public to include cases where the young person was charged with an offence that endangered the public by creating a substantial likelihood of serious bodily harm to another person or the young person had failed to comply with conditions of release. The amendments also included a residual clause that provided for the detention of a young person at the pre-trial stage if the court were satisfied that there was a substantial likelihood, having regard to all of the relevant factors, including any pending charges against the young person, that the young person would, if released from custody, commit a violent offence or an offence that otherwise endangered the public by creating a substantial likelihood of serious bodily harm to another person. Thus, Bill C-25 responded, in part, to the concerns of the Nunn Commission.

Early in 2008, the federal government also launched its nationwide consultations on the *YCJA*. This was the first federal government review of Canada's youth criminal justice system since 1996, when the Standing Committee on Justice and Legal Affairs conducted a major review at the behest of then Liberal Justice Minister Allan Rock. That benchmark Committee report, *Renewing Youth Justice*,[36] was released in April 1997. Its 14 recommendations are discussed in Chapter 1. The federal government responded to that 1997 report a year later when it released *A Strategy for the Renewal of Youth Justice*,[37] which is the document that forms the philosophical foundation for the *YCJA*.

The 2008 review was nowhere near the magnitude of these earlier reviews. Nevertheless, Nicholson travelled the country, participating in roundtables from coast to coast, during which various groups and individuals expressed their views on the youth criminal justice system generally, as well as the *YCJA* in particular. Nicholson said only that Canadians could expect further reform to the youth justice system, which would include stiffer sentences for young persons. But he had made that promise even before his cross-Canada tour was complete: "Canadians are fed up with sentences that fail to reflect the seriousness of the crime," Minister Nicholson said in July 2008 when he toured the William E. Hay

---

[36] Canada, House of Commons, *Renewing Youth Justice: Thirteenth Report of the Standing Committee on Justice and Legal Affairs*, April 1997.

[37] At the time of writing, *A Strategy for the Renewal of Youth Justice* could be accessed through the Department of Justice website at: <http://www.justice.gc.ca/eng/pi/yj-jj/about-apropos/toc-tdm.html>.

Centre in Ottawa, a residential facility for youth in secure detention. "Our Government is responding to serious youth crime by strengthening the *YCJA* and using fair and appropriate measures to hold young people accountable when they break the law."[38] Nicholson repeated this get tough theme during roundtables throughout the country: "Our goal is to strengthen the *YCJA*, reduce crime and keep our communities safe."[39]

Bolstering these proposed reforms were figures from Statistics Canada, revealing that youth crime was increasing, including violent youth crime. In May 2008, while Bill C-25 was still before Parliament, Statistics Canada released its most recent report on youth crime in Canada, which showed that youth crime had increased 3 per cent in 2006 over 2005. The statistics also revealed that violent youth crime had increased 12 per cent over the previous decade. However, the 2008 study indicated that youth crime in Canada was still 6 per cent lower in 2006 than it was a decade previously and 25 per cent lower than the 1991 peak.[40]

Then came the election call of September 2008. Bill C-25 died on the Order Paper. During the election campaign, the Conservative Party not only promised to resurrect its proposed youth justice reforms but vowed to go further by making it easier to sentence persons as young as 14 to life in prison. (Although the general public may not be widely aware of the fact, this can already be done under the *YCJA* if the young person is found eligible for an adult sentence following a guilty finding in youth justice court for certain crimes and was at least 14 at the time of the offence. Even if the young person receives an adult sentence of life in prison, however, he or she is eligible for parole sooner than an adult.[41])

In fact, in his election platform, *The True North Strong and Free*, Harper appeared to suggest the possibility of introducing a completely new piece of youth justice legislation. He promised to replace Canada's young offenders' law with new, balanced legislation that focused on deterrence and responsibility. He indicated that the new law would make the primary goal of the legislation to protect society and the primary goal of sentencing to discourage others from committing crimes. The new law would also ensure that young offenders found guilty of very serious and

---

[38]   Department of Justice Canada, "Minister of Justice Meets Young Offenders Face to Face" (29 July 2008), online at: <http://www.justice.gc.ca/eng/news-nouv/nr-cp/2008/doc_32275.html>.

[39]   Department of Justice Canada, "Government of Canada Reviewing the *Youth Criminal Justice Act*" (11 August 2008), online at: <http://www.justice.gc.ca/eng/news-nouv/nr-cp/2008/doc_32287.html>.

[40]   Andrea Taylor-Butts and Angela Bressan, Youth Crime in Canada, 2006, Statistics Canada-Catalogue no. 85-002-XIE, Vol. 28, no. 3.

[41]   *Criminal Code*, R.S.C. 1985, c. C-46, s. 745.1.

violent crimes would face appropriate sentences and that, upon being found guilty, they would be identified. However, he indicated that provinces (and territories) would be able to determine the age at which the sentencing provisions kicked in.[42]

In a September 22, 2008 statement,[43] Harper provided greater detail about his reform plan. He said the new legislation would provide for maximum enhanced youth sentences of up to 14 years for violent offences, and maximum enhanced youth sentences of life in prison for first or second degree murder for young persons, 14 and older. These stiffer sentences would ensure that youth sentences were proportionate to the severity of the crime and the level of responsibility of the offender. The new law would also expressly state that deterring and denouncing unlawful conduct is a primary goal of sentencing. Upon conviction, the names of persons 14 and older who committed the most serious crimes would be made public. The new law would also make it easier for prosecutors to apply for pre-trial detention of youths charged with violent crimes, in order to protect the public.

Despite public criticism that the Conservative Party's position on youth crime was among the key reasons it lost support in the province of Quebec and failed to win a majority upon re-election in October 2008,[44] the new Conservative government initially vowed to press ahead with its youth justice reform agenda, threatening to make its reforms confidence motions.[45] Within weeks, however, the federal government retreated from this position, and indicated that it no longer planned to make its justice reforms matters of confidence and would focus instead on the economy and on working co-operatively with the other parties.[46] The striking absence of justice reforms in its Speech from the Throne in November 2008 was further evidence that, at least in the short term, the federal government would seek to avoid controversy and rancour in the House of Commons by avoiding controversial justice initiatives. In one paragraph of its speech, the newly elected federal government said only that legal provisions in relation to youth justice would be strengthened:

---

[42] *The True North Strong and Free* (7 October 2008), online at: <http://www.conservative.ca/media/20081007-Platform-e.pdf>.

[43] "Balancing Rehabilitation and Responsibility" (22 September 2008), online at: <http://www.conservative.ca/EN/1091/106115>.

[44] Don Butler, "Canadians fear young criminals but don't want them jailed, survey suggests" *The Ottawa Citizen* (13 November 2008).

[45] Gloria Galloway, "Won't back crime bills, MPs say" *The Globe and Mail* (5 November 2008), A4.

[46] Janice Tibbets and David Aki, "Tories back off law-and-order plan" *The Ottawa Citizen* (18 November, 2008), A5.

Canadians look to governments to ensure that the justice system is working effectively and that Canadians are safe. Our Government will take tough action against crime and work with partners to improve the administration of justice. Serious offences will be met with serious penalties. Legal provisions will be strengthened in key areas, such as youth crime, organized crime and gang violence. Gun laws will be focused on ending smuggling and stronger penalties for gun crimes, not at criminalizing law-abiding firearms owners. More broadly, Canada's criminal justice system will be made more efficient. Citizens need to know that justice is served, and that it is served swiftly.[47]

The federal government's retrenchment from its planned reforms was likely inspired in part by the widespread political opposition to Bill C-25, which had served as a telling litmus test for the degree of opposition it would have encountered had it tried to move ahead with its proposed reforms. At a time when the minority federal government was seeking greater co-operation in the House of Commons to address challenging economic issues, controversial youth justice reforms were not what the federal government needed.

Bill C-25 was debated for three days in the House of Commons in November 2007 and again in early February 2008 before being read the second time and referred to the Standing Committee on Justice and Human Rights on February 5, 2008.

In introducing the second reading debate on Bill C-25[48] on November 21, 2007, Nicholson explained that the bill was being introduced to respond to the concerns of Canadians, who, he said, believe that changes to sentences can be helpful and who want to stem the reported recent increase in violent youth crime.[49] Although Nicholson spoke of the widespread support of the provinces across the country, the other federal parties expressed opposition to the bill.

Liberal MP Marlene Jennings said the bill did not go far enough in responding to the recommendations in the Nunn Commission report, such as including protection of the public as one of the primary goals of the Act.[50] Members of the Bloc Québécois said the party could not support the bill for various reasons, including the fact that the principles of deterrence and denunciation were to be included as sentencing principles while principles such as rehabilitation and the overall philosophy of intervention

---

[47]   Speech from the Throne: Protecting Canada's Future, online at: <http://pm.gc.ca/eng/media. asp?id=2312>.

[48]   Bill C-25, *An Act to amend the Youth Criminal Justice Act*, 2d Sess., 39th Parl., 2007 (2d reading 21 November 2007).

[49]   *House of Commons Debates* (21 November 2007), at 1540.

[50]   *House of Commons Debates* (21 November 2007), at 1115 to 1620.

that Quebec has adopted would be relegated to secondary importance.[51] BQ member Réal Ménard expressed concern that adding the principle of deterrence to the youth sentencing regime would lead to greater incarceration of youths.[52] Members of the Bloc vowed to do everything possible to block the passage of the bill.[53] The NDP, likewise, indicated that it would try to change the bill at the committee stage, since including the principle of deterrence in the *YCJA* would achieve nothing.[54]

The debate in the House of Commons foreshadowed a confrontation at the committee stage as to whether there was any empirical evidence to support the Conservative government's decision to include deterrence as a sentencing principle under the *YCJA*. Opposition parties suggested in the House that there was no evidence that deterrence works, in other words, there was no evidence that increasing the severity of sentences for young persons would reduce youth crime.[55]

Beyond the hallowed halls of Parliament, the reaction to the federal government's bill across the country was immediate and divided. Some provinces, such as Nova Scotia's Conservative government, voiced immediate support for it.[56] Others, such as the deputy chief of police in Halifax, were critical. Deputy Chief Chris McNeil attacked the bill for not going far enough by failing to implement all of the recommendations of the Nunn Commission, including the one that recommends the *YCJA* be amended so that it states that public safety is a primary purpose of the legislation. He described the bill as containing only minor amendments that are carefully crafted to do nothing.[57]

Youth justice experts lambasted the proposed reforms for being out of step with the direction of expert thinking on crime prevention. Barbara Benoliel, a restorative justice coach and Terance Brouse, director of community relations with the PACT Youth Crime Reduction Program, wrote in *The Toronto Star* that the federal government was moving toward

---

[51] *House of Commons Debates* (21 November 2007), at 1630-1640.

[52] *House of Commons Debates* (21 November 2007), at 1645.

[53] *House of Commons Debates* (21 November 2007), at 1640.

[54] *House of Commons Debates* (21 November 2007), at 1710.

[55] See, for example, *House of Commons Debates* (22 November 2007), at 1330 (BQ); *House of Commons Debates* (26 November 2007), at 1715 (NDP) and 1745 (BQ). See also Professor Nicholas Bala's testimony before the Nunn Commission of Inquiry, Transcript of Hearing, Vol. 16, February 16, 2006, at 2877, 2937 and 2938; and Nova Scotia Nunn Commission of Inquiry, *Spiralling out of Control: Lessons Learned from a Boy in Trouble: Report of the Nunn Commission of Inquiry* (Halifax, NS: Nunn Commission of Inquiry, 2006), available online at: <http://www.gov.ns.ca/just/nunn_commission/_docs/Report_Nunn_Final.pdf>

[56] "Justice Minister Welcomes Youth Criminal Justice Act Amendments", Department of Justice press release (20 November 2007).

[57] Michael Tutton, The Canadian Press, "Youth Crime bill fixes 'do nothing'" in *The Chronicle Herald* (4 December 2007).

tougher sentences for young persons as part of its law-and-order agenda at a time when the most recent research being released in the United States indicated that tougher sentences in the U.S. had not led to a reduction in crime rates in that country. The premise, that stiffer jail sentences would deter others from committing similar offences represents a shift backward in thinking and is contrary to the major evidence about youth in conflict with the law and their behaviour, they said.[58]

> The concept of deterrence, which proposes that youth will understand and be deterred by the potential consequence of a stiff sentence, is beyond the capability of many youth, and therefore useless as a strategy for community security. Current research on youth brain development shows delays long past adolescence in the area of the brain that understands consequences.[59]

The comments of Benoliel and Brouse have been echoed by other knowledgeable and respected youth justice experts in Canada, such as Nicholas Bala and University of Toronto criminologist Anthony Doob.[60]

> The unfortunate reality is that those youths who commit the most serious and senseless crimes are precisely those who lack foresight and judgment, and who will not likely be deterred by adult sentences. ... A reduction in serious violent offending cannot be achieved by a "legislative quick fix", but rather requires a resource-intensive combination of preventative, enforcement and rehabilitative services.[61]

---

[58]   Barbara Benoliel and Terance Brouse, "'Tough-on-Crime' policies actually make us less safe" *The Toronto Star* (6 December 2007), AA08. The writers were referring in particular to a November 2007 report, *Unlocking America: Why and How to Reduce America's Prison Population* (Washington, DC: JFA Institute, 2007), available online at: <http://www.jfa-associates.com/publications/srs/UnlockingAmerica.pdf>.

[59]   Barbara Benoliel and Terance Brouse, "'Tough-on-Crime' policies actually make us less safe" *The Toronto Star* (6 December 2007), AA08.

[60]   Leading youth justice experts in Canada generally contend that increasing the severity of youth sentences will not deter youthful offending, in part because young persons have less foresight and judgement than adults and they are not considering the consequences of offending while they are offending. See Nicholas Bala, *Youth Criminal Justice Law* (Toronto: Irwin Law Inc., 2003), at 4 and 408. See also his testimony before the Nunn Commission of Inquiry, Transcript of Hearing, Vol. 16, February 16, 2006, at 2877 and 2878; and Nova Scotia Nunn Commission of Inquiry, *Spiralling out of Control: Lessons Learned from a Boy in Trouble: Report of the Nunn Commission of Inquiry* (Halifax, NS: Nunn Commission of Inquiry, 2006), available online at: <http://www.gov.ns.ca/just/nunn_commission/_docs/Report_Nunn_Final.pdf>.

    See also Anthony Doob and Cheryl Webster, "Sentencing Severity and Crime: Accepting the Null Hypothesis" in Michael Tonry, ed., *A Review of Research*, Crime and Justice, vol. 30 (Chicago: University of Chicago Press, 2003), at 143-95 [Volume 6, Number 2, December 2003, Item 1] and P. Gendreau and D.A. Andrews, "Tertiary Prevention: What the Meta-analyses of the Offender Treatment Literature Tell Us About 'What Works'", Can. J. Crim., January 1990.

[61]   Nicholas Bala, "Youth as Victims and Offenders in the Criminal Justice System: A Charter Analysis — Recognizing Vulnerability" in Jamie Cameron and James Stribopoulos, eds.,

In fact, in a 2009 academic paper, Bala and two other youth justice experts contend that, while there is a need to imprison some young persons, the inappropriate use of custody is expensive, ineffective and inhumane and that imprisonment may contribute to a cycle of juvenile reoffending. Bala, Peter Carrington and Julian Roberts point to research suggesting that the more exposure the young person has to the youth justice system, the less likely he or she is to desist from further offending. They cite research indicating that jail deprives young persons of the social milieu on which they depend for moral and psychological development and that this developmental disruption results in a higher likelihood of school failure, which is a well-established contributor to juvenile delinquency.[62]

III. THE WAY AHEAD

Since Canadians of all political stripes presumably share the common goal of wanting to see a reduction in youth crime, the most logical direction for the federal government is to focus on what works, to consider the reliable empirical evidence, to undertake whatever further research may assist, and to focus on the evidence-based policies that appear to be the most effective in reducing youth crime.

When youth justice expert Nicholas Bala testified before the Nunn Commission of Inquiry in Nova Scotia in 2006, he suggested that the answer to reducing youth crime can be found in the substance and quality of our social, education and mental health policies, and in our culture and values, much more than in our youth legal regime. He noted, for example, that the United States sentences young persons much more severely than Canada (including the imposition of adult sentences at a much higher rate) yet their youth crime rate remains a much more serious problem.[63] He questioned why Newfoundland's youth crime rate is relatively low

---

The Charter and Criminal Justice: Twenty-five Years Later (Markham, Ont., LexisNexis, 2008), 595 at 607.

[62] See Nicholas Bala, Peter Carrington and Julian Roberts, "The *Youth Criminal Justice Act* After Five Years — A Qualified Success", which was an unpublished article at the time of writing but was to be published in a 2009 issue of the Canadian Journal of Criminology and Criminal Justice. The final version can be found in Bala, Carrington & Roberts, "Evaluating the *Youth Criminal Justice Act* After Five Years — A Qualified Success" (2009) 51(2) Can. J. of Crim. & Crim. J. 131.

[63] Nicholas Bala testimony before the Nunn Commission of Inquiry, Transcript of Hearing, Vol. 16, February 16, 2006, at 2938-2939; and Nova Scotia Nunn Commission of Inquiry, *Spiralling out of Control: Lessons Learned from a Boy in Trouble: Report of the Nunn Commission of Inquiry* (Halifax, NS: Nunn Commission of Inquiry, 2006), available online at: <http://www.gov.ns.ca/just/nunn_commission/_docs/Report_Nunn_Final.pdf>.

compared to other provinces despite a fairly high level of poverty.[64] Quebec politicians have made similar observations about the decreasing youth crime rate in Quebec; they have urged federal politicians to consider carefully why Quebec's youth crime rate is decreasing and to learn from Quebec.[65] The Quebec government attributes Quebec's success to its focus on rehabilitation and its strong tendency to keep young persons out of the correctional system.[66]

Examining successful Canadian youth justice models makes sense; undertaking targeted research that explores why certain jurisdictions in this country have lower youth crime rates than others would be useful and instructive. It is worth investigating, for example, why Quebec has the lowest youth crime rate in the country, and why it was the only province that experienced a decline in its youth crime rate in 2006.

If the Canadian government should choose to engage in further study and research before proceeding with youth criminal justice reforms, the following are among the additional questions and issues worth exploring:

*   Should the federal government establish in s. 3 of the Declaration of Principle and in s. 38 regarding sentencing a hierarchy of principles? In other words, should the federal government rank the principles in order of importance to provide greater clarity and guidance to decision-makers?

*   Should s. 3 of the Declaration of Principle in the *YCJA* be amended, as suggested by the Nunn Commission, to add a clause indicating that protection of the public is one of the primary goals of the Act?

*   Should deterrence and denunciation be sentencing principles for young persons who are receiving youth sentences under the *YCJA*?

---

[64]   Nicholas Bala testimony before the Nunn Commission of Inquiry, Transcript of Hearing, Vol. 16, February 16, 2006, at 2938-2939; and Nova Scotia Nunn Commission of Inquiry, *Spiralling out of Control: Lessons Learned from a Boy in Trouble: Report of the Nunn Commission of Inquiry* (Halifax, NS: Nunn Commission of Inquiry, 2006), available online at: <http://www.gov.ns.ca/just/nunn_commission/_docs/Report_Nunn_Final.pdf>.

[65]   *House of Commons Debates* (21 November 2007), at 1705 (NDP MP Joe Comartin); see also comments from Serge Menard, BQ MP, in *House of Commons Debates* (22 November 2007), at 1213-15. See also comments in relation to looking to Quebec as a successful model from NDP member Olivia Chow in *House of Commons Debates* (22 November 2007), at 1224.

[66]   *House of Commons Debates* (21 November 2007), at 1705 (NDP MP Joe Comartin); see also comments from Serge Menard, BQ MP, in *House of Commons Debates* (22 November 2007), at 1213-15. See also comments in relation to looking to Quebec as a successful model from NDP member Olivia Chow in *House of Commons Debates* (22 November 2007), at 1224.

- Should the federal government clarify in the *YCJA* the breadth of the jurisdiction of the youth justice court over federal offences involving young persons, given the unsettled nature of the jurisprudence?

- Should the *YCJA* bail provisions be reformed to simplify the process by creating a stand-alone bail regime in the *YCJA* and to also ensure that young persons can be more easily detained if they pose a safety risk to themselves or others if released?

- Rather than permitting the imposition of adult sentences for young persons in certain circumstances, should the federal government consider increasing the maximum youth sentences for young persons under the *YCJA* in relation to the most serious crimes, which largely achieves the same objective but ensures that all penalties are part of the separate youth criminal justice regime?

- Should the federal government consider whether it is ever appropriate to place a young person under 18 in an adult correctional facility or institution and undertake whatever research may be required to properly answer this question?

- Should the Canadian state reconsider the age of criminal responsibility in Canada?

- Has Canada conducted adequate research regarding what programs in Canada have proven most effective at preventing and reducing offending among young persons?

- What lessons can Canada learn from other countries in relation to reducing youth crime?

- What features and elements of youth justice regimes in other countries are worth incorporating into Canada's youth justice system?

INDEX